The Institute of Chartered Accountants in England and Wales

FINANCIAL ACCOUNTING AND REPORTING

For exams in 2016

Study Manual

www.icaew.com

Financial Accounting and Reporting
The Institute of Chartered Accountants in England and Wales

ISBN: 978-1-78363-214-5
Previous ISBN: 978-0-85760-994-6

First edition 2013
Fourth edition 2015

The content of this publication is intended to prepare students for the ICAEW
examinations, and should not be used as professional advice.

British Library Cataloguing-in-Publication Data
A catalogue record for this book is available from the British Library

Originally printed in the United Kingdom by Polestar Wheatons on paper
obtained from traceable, sustainable sources.

Polestar Wheatons
Hennock Road
Marsh Barton
Exeter
EX2 8RP

Welcome to ICAEW

I am delighted that you have chosen ICAEW to progress your journey towards joining the chartered accountancy profession. It is one of the best decisions I also made.

The role of the accountancy profession in the world's economies has never been more important. People making financial decisions need knowledge and guidance based on the highest technical and ethical standards. ICAEW Chartered Accountants provide this better than anyone. They challenge people and organisations to think and act differently, to provide clarity and rigour, and so help create and sustain prosperity all over the world.

As a world leader of the accountancy and finance profession, we are proud to promote, develop and support over 144,000 chartered accountants worldwide. Our members have the knowledge, skills and commitment to maintain the highest professional standards and integrity. They are part of something special, and now, so are you. It's with our support and dedication that our members and hopefully yourself, will realise career ambitions, maintain a professional edge and contribute to the profession.

You are now on your journey towards joining the accountancy profession, and a highly rewarding career with endless opportunities. By choosing to study for our world-leading chartered accountancy qualification, the ACA, you too have made the first of many great decisions in your career.

You are in good company, with a network of over 26,000 students around the world made up of like-minded people, you are all supported by ICAEW. We are here to support you as you progress through your studies and career: we will be with you every step of the way, visit page x to review the key resources available as you study.

I wish you the best of luck with your studies and look forward to welcoming you to the profession in the future.

Michael Izza
Chief Executive
ICAEW

Contents

1 Introduction

ACA qualification

The ICAEW chartered accountancy qualification, the ACA, is a world-leading professional qualification in accountancy, finance and business.

The ACA has integrated components that give you an in-depth understanding across accountancy, finance and business. Combined, they help build the technical knowledge, professional skills and practical experience needed to become an ICAEW Chartered Accountant.

Each component is designed to complement each other, which means that you can put theory into practice and you can understand and apply what you learn to your day-to-day work. Progression through all the elements of the ACA simultaneously will enable you to be more successful in the workplace and exams.

The components are:

- Professional development
- Ethics and professional scepticism
- 3-5 years practical work experience
- 15 accountancy, finance and business modules

To find out more on the components of the ACA and what is involved in training, visit your dashboard at icaew.com/dashboard.

2 Financial Accounting and Reporting

The full syllabus and technical knowledge grids can be found within the module study guide. Visit icaew.com/dashboard for this and more resources.

2.1 Module aim

To enable candidates to prepare complete single entity and consolidated financial statements, and extracts from those financial statements, covering a wide range of International Financial Reporting Standards (IFRS).

Candidates will also be required to explain accounting and reporting concepts and ethical issues, and the application of IFRS to specified single entity or group scenarios.

On completion of this module, students will be able to:

- Explain the contribution and inherent limitations of financial statements, apply the International Accounting Standards Board's (IASB) conceptual framework for financial reporting and identify and explain key ethical issues

- Prepare and present financial statements from accounting data for single entities, whether organised in corporate or in other forms, in conformity with IFRS and explain the application of IFRS to specified single entity scenarios

- Identify the circumstances in which entities are required to present consolidated financial statements, prepare and present them in conformity with IFRS and explain the application of IFRS to specified group scenarios.

2.2 Method of assessment

The Financial Accounting and Reporting module will be 3 hours long containing four written test questions. Candidates may use the IASB's IFRS open book text.

The module will include questions on:

(a) Preparation of single entity financial statements (excluding statement of cash flows) from trial balance or draft financial statements;

(b) Preparation of consolidated financial statements (excluding consolidated statement of cash flows) from individual financial statements or draft consolidated financial statements; and

(c) Explanation of the application of IFRS to specified scenarios.

Other question types could include:

(a) Preparation of consolidated statement of cash flow, or extracts therefrom, from consolidated financial statements or draft consolidated statement of cash flow; and

(b) Mixed or single topic questions requiring extracts from single entity or consolidated financial statements (including from statement of cash flows) and/or explanation of accounting treatment with supporting calculations.

Concepts and ethics will be tested in any of the written test questions.

2.3 Specification grid

This grid shows the relative weightings of subjects within this module and should guide the relative study time spent on each. Over time the marks available in the assessment will equate to the weightings below, while slight variations may occur in individual assessments to enable suitably rigorous questions to be set.

Syllabus area	Weighting (%)
1 Accounting and reporting concepts and ethics	10
2 Single entity financial statements	60
3 Consolidated financial statements	30
	100

3 Permitted Texts

At the Professional and Advanced Levels there are specific texts that you are permitted to take into your exams with you. All information for these texts, the editions that are recommended for your examinations and where to order them from, is available on www.icaew.com/permittedtexts.

Professional Level Examinations	Permitted Text
Audit and Assurance	✓
Financial Accounting and Reporting	✓
Tax Compliance	✓
Business Strategy	✗
Financial Management	✗
Business Planning: Banking/Insurance/Taxation	No restrictions

Advanced Level Examinations	
Corporate Reporting	No restrictions
Strategic Business Management	No restrictions
Case Study	No restrictions

Business Planning: Banking/Insurance/Taxation and the Advanced Level exams have no restrictions so you may take any hard copy materials in to these exams that you wish, subject to practical space restrictions.

Although the examiners use the specific editions listed to set the assessment, you **may** use a different edition of the text at your own risk. If you use a different edition within your exams, you should note this inside your answer booklet, at the beginning of the question.

This information, as well as what to expect and what is and is not permitted in your exams is available in the Instructions to Candidates. You will be sent this with your exam admission details and it is also available on our website; www.icaew.com/exams.

4 Key Resources

Student support team

Our student support team are here to help you as much as possible, providing full support throughout your studies.

T +44 (0)1908 248 250
F +44 (0)1908 248 069
E studentsupport@icaew.com

Student website

The student area of our website provides the latest information, guidance and exclusive resources to help you progress through the ACA. Find everything you need (from sample papers to errata sheets) at icaew.com/dashboard.

Online student community

The online student community provides support and practical advice – wherever you are, whenever you need it. With regular blogs covering a range of work, life and study topics as well as a forum where you can post your questions and share your own tips. Join the conversation at icaew.com/studentcommunity.

Tuition

The ICAEW Partner in Learning scheme recognises tuition providers who comply with our core principles of quality course delivery. If you are receiving structured tuition with an ICAEW Partner in Learning, make sure you know how and when you can contact your tutors for extra help. If you are not receiving structured tuition and are interested in classroom, online or residential learning, take a look at our recognised Partner in Learning tuition providers in your area, on our website icaew.com/dashboard.

Faculties and Special Interest Groups

Faculties and special interest groups support and develop members and students in areas of work and industry sectors that are of particular interest.

Our seven faculties provide knowledge, events and essential technical resources. Register to receive a complimentary e-magazine from one faculty of your choice each year throughout your studies.

Our 12 special interest groups provide practical support, information and representation within a range of industry sectors. Register to receive free provisional membership of one group each year throughout your studies.

Find out more about faculties and special interest groups at icaew.com/facultiesandsigs.

The Library & Information Service

The Library & Information Service is ICAEW's world-leading accountancy and business library.

The library provides access to thousands of resources online and a document delivery service, you'll be sure to find a useful eBook, relevant article or industry guide to help you. Find out more at icaew.com/library.

CHAPTER 1

Reporting framework and ethics

Introduction
Examination context
Topic List

Introduction

Learning objectives

- Explain the nature of financial reporting and objectives of financial statements ☐

- Explain the standard-setting process used by national and international bodies (IASB) and the authority of the national and international standards, using appropriate examples as an illustration ☐

- Explain, in non-technical language and with appropriate examples, the current work to achieve convergence between UK GAAP and international reporting standards ☐

- Apply the principles of the IASB *Conceptual Framework*, including the qualitative characteristics of financial information, the elements of financial statements, recognition and measurement of the elements ☐

- Explain and demonstrate the differences between financial statements produced using the accrual basis, cash accounting and the break-up basis ☐

- Discuss the concepts of 'fair presentation' and 'true and fair view' and the circumstances in which these concepts may override the detailed provisions of legislation or of accounting standards ☐

- Explain the regulatory framework affecting not-for-profit entities ☐

- Recognise the ethical and professional issues for a professional accountant undertaking work in and giving advice on accounting and financial reporting: explain the relevance and importance of these issues and evaluate the relative merits of different standpoints taken in debate ☐

Specific syllabus references for this chapter are: 1a, 1b, 1c, 1d, 1e, 1f, 1g, 1i, 2g.

Syllabus links

The issues covered by this chapter and particularly the principles introduced by the IASB *Conceptual Framework* are a fundamental part of the Financial Accounting and Reporting syllabus.

This chapter takes your knowledge of current issues and particularly the progress of the convergence process which aims to produce a set of global accounting standards much further. These are areas which are also likely to be highly relevant at the Advanced Stage. The ethical considerations at the end of the chapter are dealt with specifically here but will be pervasive across all areas of the syllabus.

Examination context

Accounting and reporting concepts constitute 10% of the syllabus. In the examination, candidates may be required to:

- Discuss the purpose of accounting regulations and standards for both profit-making and not-for-profit entities

- Explain, with examples, the objectives and limitations of financial statements

- Explain the qualitative characteristics of financial information and the constraints on such information

- Describe the financial effects of the application of the definitions of the IASB *Conceptual Framework*

- Perform simple calculations to demonstrate the difference between the accrual basis, cash accounting and the break-up basis

- Discuss and comment on the convergence process, including recent developments

- Identify and explain the ethical and professional issues for a professional accountant

1 Financial statements

Section overview

- In the UK all companies must comply with the provisions of the Companies Act.
- In the UK financial statements must be prepared in accordance with either UK GAAP or IFRS. They must also give a true and fair view.

1.1 What is financial reporting?

Financial reporting is the process of identifying, measuring and communicating economic information to others so that they may make decisions on the basis of that information and assess the stewardship of the entity's management.

Financial reporting involves:

- Recording transactions undertaken by a business entity.
- Grouping similar transactions together which are appropriate to the business.
- Presenting periodic results.

The Financial Accounting and Reporting syllabus focuses on the preparation of published financial information. Typically, this information is made available annually or half-yearly (sometimes quarterly) and is presented in formats laid down or approved by governments in each national jurisdiction. (The Advanced syllabus deals with more complex reporting issues and analysis and interpretation.)

By contrast, **management accounting** or reporting is **internal reporting** for the use of the management of a business itself. Internal management information can be tailored to management's own needs and provided in whatever detail and at whatever frequency (eg continuous real-time information) management decides is best suited to the needs of their business.

General principles relating to financial reporting are set out in the IASB *Conceptual Framework for Financial Reporting (Conceptual Framework)*, which is explained further below.

1.2 Entity

Most accounting requirements are written with a view to use by any type of accounting entity, including companies and other forms of organisation, such as a partnership. In this text, the term 'company' is usually used, because the main focus of the Financial Accounting and Reporting syllabus is on the accounts of companies and groups of companies.

1.3 Financial statements

The principal means of providing financial information to external users is the annual financial statements. Financial statements provide a summary of the performance of an entity over a particular period and of its position at the end of that period.

A complete set of financial statements prepared under IFRS comprises:

- The statement of financial position.

- The statement of profit or loss and other comprehensive income or two separate statements being the statement of profit or loss and the statement of other comprehensive income (statements of financial performance).

- The statement of changes in equity (another statement of financial performance).

- The statement of cash flows.

- Notes to the financial statements.

The notes to the financial statements include:

- Accounting policies, ie the specific principles, conventions, rules and practices applied in order to reflect the effects of transactions and other events in the financial statements.

- Detailed financial and narrative information supporting the information in the primary financial statements.

- Other information not reflected in the financial statements, but which is important to users in making their assessments.

The individual elements that are included in the financial statements are covered in detail later in this chapter.

1.4 Requirement to produce financial statements

Limited liability companies are **required by law** to prepare and publish financial statements annually. The form and content may be regulated primarily by national legislation, and in most cases must also comply with Financial Reporting Standards.

In the UK, **all companies** must comply with the provisions of the **Companies Act 2006 (CA 2006)**. The key impact of this is as follows:

- Every UK registered company is required to prepare **financial statements** for each financial year which give a **true and fair view.**

- The individual (and some group) financial statements may be prepared:

  - In accordance with the **CA 2006** (as regards **format** and **additional information** provided by way of notes), **or**

  - In accordance with international accounting standards.

1.5 Filing deadlines

Legal regulations concerning the financial statements of an entity are of course specific to the country of incorporation. UK companies come under the **Companies Act 2006**.

The Companies Act establishes deadlines for the filing of financial statements:

Private companies: nine months after the financial year end

Public companies: six months after the financial year end

Listed companies are required by the Financial Conduct Authority to file their financial statements within four months of the financial year end.

1.6 Financial reporting standards

Company financial statements must also comply with relevant Financial Reporting Standards and other professional guidance. In the UK these are as follows.

- **Accounting Standards**

  The new UK accounting standards are:

  FRS 102 *The Financial Reporting Standard Applicable in the UK and Republic of Ireland*

  FRS 101 *Reduced Disclosure Framework*

  These are explained more fully later in this chapter.

- **Financial Reporting Standard for Smaller Entities (FRSSE)**

  This brings together **all the accounting guidance** which UK **small companies** are required to follow in drawing up their financial statements.

- **International Financial Reporting Standards (IFRS)**

  These are issued by the **International Accounting Standards Board (IASB)**. UK companies **whose securities are traded** in a regulated public market, eg the London Stock Exchange, must prepare their **group accounts** in accordance with IFRS.

These learning materials assume the preparation of financial statements in accordance with IFRS.

Unincorporated entities are exempt from the above requirements but may need to follow other regulation, eg charities must comply with the Charities Act. Incorporated charities **must** prepare their financial statements **in accordance with the CA 2006** (ie the IFRS option is not open to them).

Point to note

The term UK **Generally Accepted Accounting Practice (GAAP)** refers to all the rules, from whatever source, which govern UK accounting. In the UK this is seen primarily as a combination of:

- **Company law** (mainly CA 2006 – see Section 1.4)
- **Accounting Standards**
- **Stock Exchange requirements** (These are not examinable in the syllabus)

In the UK, GAAP has **no statutory or regulatory authority or definition** (unlike some other countries such as the United States) although the use of the term is increasingly common in practice.

1.7 Fair presentation

IAS 1 *Presentation of Financial Statements* requires financial statements to 'present fairly' the financial position and performance of an entity.

'Present fairly' is explained as representing faithfully the effects of transactions. In general terms this will be the case if IFRS are adhered to. IAS 1 states that **departures** from international standards are only allowed:

- In extremely rare cases.

- Where compliance with IFRS would be so misleading as to conflict with the objectives of financial statements as set out in the *Conceptual Framework*, that is to provide information about financial position, performance and changes in financial position that is useful to a wide range of users.

1.8 True and fair view

In the UK there is an **overriding Companies Act requirement** that financial statements should present **'a true and fair view'**. This term is not defined in the Companies Act or Accounting Standards.

Truth is usually seen as an objective concept reflecting factual accuracy within the bounds of materiality.

Fairness is usually seen as meaning that the view given is objective and unbiased.

True and fair is usually defined in terms of GAAP. This means:

- **Compliance with Accounting Standards** (which can be overridden on true and fair grounds only very rarely)

- **Adherence to the requirements of the Companies Act 2006**, including its true and fair override (see below)

- In the absence of more specific requirements, **application of general accounting principles and fundamental concepts** and, where appropriate, adherence to accepted industry practices

Points to note

- The CA 2006 uses the term '**a** true and fair view' rather than '**the** true and fair view' because it is possible for there to be more than one true and fair view. For example, financial statements based on historical cost can be true and fair, as can financial statements which incorporate revaluations.

- What constitutes a true and fair view can then be restricted by stating that where a choice of treatments or methods is permitted, the one selected should be the most appropriate to the company's circumstances. This restriction is likely to ensure compliance with the spirit and underlying intentions of requirements, not just with the letter of them.

- A further restriction is that financial statements should reflect the economic position of the company, thereby reflecting the **substance of transactions** (ie commercial reality), not merely their legal form. In most cases this will be achieved by adhering to GAAP.

1.9 The statutory 'true and fair override'

The CA 2006 requires that where compliance with its accounting rules would not lead to a true and fair view, **those rules should be departed from** to the extent necessary to give a true and fair view.

Where the override of the statutory accounting requirements is invoked, eg to comply with an accounting standard, **the Act requires disclosure** of the particulars of the departure, the reason for it, and the financial effect.

The CA 2006 also states that where compliance with its disclosure requirements is insufficient to give a true and fair view, **additional information should be disclosed** such that a true and fair view is provided.

1.10 Comparison of UK GAAP and IFRS

As 'fair presentation' is explained as representing faithfully the effects of transactions, there is unlikely to be any substantial difference in practical terms between it and the true and fair concept.

Because international standards are designed to operate in all legal environments, they cannot provide for departures from the legal requirements in any particular country. IAS 1 indicates that there are few, if any, circumstances where compliance with IFRS will be fundamentally misleading. In effect, UK companies applying IFRS cannot take advantage of the true and fair override.

Companies reporting under FRS 101 or FRS 102 are however reporting under the Companies Act, so the true and fair override is still available to them.

1.11 Judgements and financial statements

Although IFRS narrow down the range of acceptable alternative accounting treatments, there are still many areas which are left to the discretion of the directors of the company. On the whole, the concept of faithful representation should result in transactions being 'presented fairly'. However, commercial and financial considerations may result in pressure being brought to bear to account for and report transactions in accordance with their strict legal form. This can raise ethical questions for a professional accountant.

2 Purpose and use of financial statements

Section overview

- Financial statements are used to make economic decisions by a wide range of users.

- All users require information regarding:

  - Financial position
  - Financial performance
  - Changes in financial position

2.1 Users and their information needs

The form and content of financial statements must be influenced by the use to which they are put. The IASB *Conceptual Framework* emphasises that financial statements are used to make economic decisions, such as:

- To decide when to **buy, hold or sell an equity investment**
- To assess the **stewardship or accountability of management**
- To assess an entity's ability to pay and **provide other benefits to employees**
- To assess **security** for amounts lent to the entity
- To determine **taxation policies**
- To determine **distributable profits and dividends**
- To prepare and use **national income statistics**
- To **regulate** the activities of entities

Much of the information needed for these different decisions is in fact common to them all. Financial statements aimed at meeting these common needs of a wide range of users are known as '**general purpose**' financial statements.

We can identify the following **users** of financial statements and their specific **information needs**.

Users	Need information to

Present and potential investors	• Make investment decisions, therefore need information on:
	  – Risk and return on investment
	  – Ability of entity to pay dividends

Employees	• Assess their employer's stability and profitability • Assess their employer's ability to provide remuneration, employment opportunities and retirement and other benefits
Lenders	• Assess whether loans can be repaid, and related interest can be paid, when due
Suppliers and other trade payables	• Assess the likelihood of being paid when due
Customers	• Assess whether the entity will continue in existence – important where customers have a long-term involvement with, or are dependent on, the entity, eg where there are product warranties or where specialist parts may be needed
Governments and their agencies	• Assess allocation of resources and, therefore, activities of entities • Assist in regulating activities • Assess taxation • Provide a basis for national statistics
The public	• Assess trends and recent developments in the entity's prosperity and its activities – important where the entity makes a substantial contribution to a local economy, eg by providing local employment and using local suppliers

In most cases the users will need to analyse the financial statements in order to obtain the information they need. This might include the calculation of accounting ratios. (The calculation of accounting ratios and the analysis of those ratios is covered in the Advanced syllabus.)

2.2 Objective of financial statements

The objective of financial statements is to provide information about the reporting entity's **financial position and financial performance that is useful to a wide range of users in making economic decisions**.

This objective can usually be met by focusing exclusively on the information needs of present and potential investors. This is because much of the financial information that is relevant to investors will also be relevant to other users.

In the UK equivalent of the IASB *Conceptual Framework* – the ASB's *Statement of Principles* – investors and potential investors are described as 'the defining class of user'.

2.3 Accountability of management

Management also has a **stewardship role**, in that it is accountable for the safe-keeping of the entity's resources and for their proper, efficient and profitable use. Providers of risk capital are interested in information that helps them to assess how effectively management has fulfilled this role, but again this assessment is made only as the basis for economic decisions, such as those about investments and the reappointment/replacement of management.

It is also the case that in a smaller entity the owner and manager can be the same individual.

Financial reporting helps management to meet its need to be accountable to shareholders, and also to other stakeholders (eg employees or lenders), by providing information that is useful to the users in making **economic decisions**.

However, financial statements cannot provide the complete set of information required for assessing the stewardship of management (see Section 7 'Inherent limitations of financial statements' later in this chapter).

2.4 Financial position, performance and changes in financial position

All economic decisions are based on an evaluation of an entity's ability to generate cash and of the timing and certainty of its generation. Information about the entity's financial position, performance and changes in financial position provides the foundation on which to base such decisions.

2.4.1 Financial position

An entity's financial position covers:

- The **economic resources** it controls
- Its **financial structure** (ie debt and share finance)
- Its **liquidity and solvency** and
- Its **capacity to adapt to changes** in the environment in which it operates

Investors require information on financial position because it helps in assessing:

- The entity's ability to **generate cash in the future**.

- How **future cash flows will be distributed** among those with an interest in, or claims on, the entity.

- Requirements for **future finance** and ability to raise that finance.

- The ability to meet **financial commitments** as they fall due.

Information about financial position is primarily provided in a **statement of financial position**.

2.4.2 Financial performance

The profit earned in a period is used as the measure of financial performance, where profit is calculated as income less expenses. Information about performance and variability of performance is useful in:

- Assessing **potential changes in the entity's economic resources** in the future
- **Predicting the entity's capacity to generate cash** from its existing resource base, and
- **Forming judgements** about the effectiveness with which additional resources might be employed.

Information on financial performance is provided by:

- The **statement of profit or loss and other comprehensive income** and/or **statement of profit or loss**.

- The **statement of changes in equity**.

2.4.3 Changes in financial position

Changes in financial position can be analysed under the headings of **investing, financing** and **operating activities** and are presented in a **statement of cash flows**.

Cash flow information is largely free from the more **judgemental allocation and measurement issues** (ie in which period to include things and at what amount) that arise when items are included in the statement of financial position or performance statements. For example, depreciation of non-current assets involves judgement and estimation as to the period over which to charge depreciation. Cash flow information excludes non-cash items such as depreciation.

Cash flow information is therefore seen as being **factual in nature**, and hence more reliable than other sources of information.

Information on the generation and use of cash is useful in evaluating the entity's ability to generate cash and its need to use what is generated.

2.4.4 Notes and supplementary schedules

Notes and schedules attached to financial statements can provide **additional information** relevant to users, for example the non-current assets note (see Chapter 2).

3 Bases of accounting

Section overview

- There are three bases of accounting which you need to be familiar with:
    - Accrual basis
    - Cash basis
    - Break-up basis

- The going concern basis is referred to by the IASB's *Conceptual Framework* as the 'underlying assumption'.

3.1 Accrual basis

Under this basis of accounting, **transactions are recognised when they occur**, not when the related cash flows into or out of the entity. You will be familiar with this basis from your Accounting studies. Examples of the importance of this basis are as follows:

- Sales are recorded in the period in which the **risks and rewards of ownership pass from seller to buyer**, not when the seller receives full payment. While this basis has no effect on the timing of the recognition of cash sales, it does mean that credit sales are recorded earlier than if the cash basis of accounting was used. When credit sales are recognised, a receivable is set up in the entity's books.

- Expenses are recognised **in the period when the goods or services are consumed**, not when they are paid for. An amount payable will be set up in the entity's books for credit purchases, again leading to earlier recognition than if the cash basis was used.

- The consumption of non-current assets, such as plant and machinery, is recognised **over the period during which they are used by the entity** (ie the asset is depreciated), not in the year of purchase as they would be under the cash basis of accounting.

Financial statements prepared on this basis provide information both about past transactions involving cash and about future resources flowing into the entity (when customers pay up) and flowing out of it (when suppliers are paid). They are therefore more useful for the making of economic decisions than those produced on the cash basis.

The IASB's *Conceptual Framework* makes it clear that information in an entity's financial statements should be prepared on the accrual basis.

3.2 Going concern basis

The accrual basis of accounting assumes that an entity is a going concern. Under this basis, financial statements are prepared on the assumption that the entity will **continue in operation for the foreseeable future**, in that management has neither the intention nor the need to liquidate the entity by selling all its assets, paying off all its liabilities and distributing any surplus to the owners. Examples of the importance of this basis are as follows:

- The measurement of receivables from trade customers is made on the basis that there is **no time limit over which management will chase slow payers**. If the entity were to cease operation in, say, three months, a number of balances might have to be regarded as bad (irrecoverable) debts.

- The measurement of non-current assets is made on the basis that **they can be utilised throughout their planned life**. Otherwise, they would have to be valued at what they could immediately be sold for, which might not be very much, in the case of assets used in markets where there is excess capacity.

Going concern is referred to by the IASB's *Conceptual Framework* as the '**underlying assumption**'.

3.3 Cash basis

The cash basis of accounting is not used in the preparation of a company statement of financial position and performance statements as it is not allowed by IFRS or UK GAAP, although the cash effect of transactions is presented in the form of a statement of cash flows. (We will look at the statement of cash flows in Chapter 2.) The cash basis may be used, however, for small unincorporated entities, for example clubs and societies.

In many ways the cash basis of accounting is very simple. Only the **cash impact of a transaction is recorded**. Examples of the impact of this are as follows:

- Sales are recorded in the period in which the seller receives full payment. For credit sales this will delay the recognition of the transaction.

- Purchases are recorded in the period in which goods are paid for rather than the period in which the goods are purchased. For credit purchases this will delay the recognition of the purchase.

- The purchase of a capital asset is treated as a cash outflow at the point that the cash consideration is paid. No subsequent adjustment is made for depreciation as this has no impact on the cash balance of the business.

Worked example: Comparison of accrual basis and cash basis

Joe Co buys 100 T-shirts in January at £3.50 each. The purchase is made for cash. During January 30 T-shirts are sold for cash at £7.00 each.

Using accrual based accounting the results for January would be as follows:

	£	£
Revenue (30 × £7)		210
Cost of sales		
Purchases (100 × £3.50)	350	
Closing inventory (70 × £3.50)	(245)	
		(105)
Profit		105

Using cash accounting the results for January would be as follows:

	£
Revenue (30 × £7)	210
Cost of sales (100 × £3.50)	(350)
Loss	(140)

Notice that there is an overall loss of £140 using cash accounting even though there is a profit for the month of £105 using the accrual basis. The difference of £245 is the value of the closing inventories which is carried forward as an asset under the accruals basis.

3.4 Break-up basis

As we saw in Section 3.1 one of the key assumptions made under the accruals basis is that the business will continue as a going concern. However, this will not necessarily always be the case. There may be an intention or need to sell off the assets of the business. Such a sale typically arises where the business is in **financial difficulties** and needs the cash to pay its creditors. Where this is the case an alternative method of accounting must be used (in accordance with IAS 1 *Presentation of Financial Statements*). In these circumstances the financial statements will be prepared on a basis other than going concern, which is commonly referred to as the 'break-up' basis. The break-up basis values assets and liabilities today as if the entity was about to cease trading and had to dispose of all its assets and liabilities.

The effect of this is seen primarily in the statement of financial position as follows:

- **Classification of assets**

  All assets and liabilities would be classified as **current** rather than non-current.

- **Valuation of assets**

  Assets would be valued on the basis of the recoverable amount on sale. This is likely to be substantially lower than the carrying amount of assets held under historical cost accounting.

4 The IASB *Conceptual Framework*

Section overview

The IASB *Framework for the Preparation and Presentation of Financial Statements* was the conceptual framework upon which all IASs and IFRSs were based up to 2010. It is gradually being replaced by the *Conceptual Framework for Financial Reporting*. The extant framework determines:

- How financial statements are prepared
- The information they contain

4.1 Conceptual Framework

The IASB *Framework for the Preparation and Presentation of Financial Statements* was produced in 1989 and has been gradually replaced by the new *Conceptual Framework for Financial Reporting*. This was the result of an IASB/FASB joint project to be carried out in phases. The first phase, comprising Chapters 1 and 3, was published in September 2010. Chapter 2 entitled 'The reporting entity' has not yet been published. The current version of the *Conceptual Framework* includes the remaining chapters of the 1989 Framework as Chapter 4.

The *Conceptual Framework for Financial Reporting* is currently as follows:

Chapter 1: The objective of general purpose financial reporting

Chapter 2: The reporting entity (to be issued)

Chapter 3: Qualitative characteristics of useful financial information

Chapter 4: Remaining text of the 1989 Framework:

- Underlying assumption
- The elements of financial statements
- Recognition of the elements of financial statements
- Measurement of the elements of financial statements
- Concepts of capital and capital maintenance

In this chapter we have already introduced some of the concepts dealt with by the *Conceptual Framework*.

We will now look specifically at each section in turn.

4.2 Introduction to the Conceptual Framework

The Introduction provides a list of the purposes of the *Conceptual Framework*:

(a) To assist the Board in the **development of future IFRSs** and in its review of existing IFRSs.

(b) To assist the Board in **promoting harmonisation** of regulations, accounting standards and procedures relating to the presentation of financial statements by providing a basis for reducing the number of alternative accounting treatments permitted by IFRSs.

(c) To assist **national standard-setting bodies** in developing national standards.

(d) To assist **preparers of financial statements** in applying IFRSs and in dealing with topics that have yet to form the subject of an IFRS.

(e) To assist **auditors** in forming an opinion as to whether financial statements comply with IFRSs.

(f) To assist **users of financial statements** in interpreting the information contained in financial statements prepared in compliance with IFRSs.

(g) To provide those who are interested in the work of the IASB with **information** about its approach to the formulation of IFRSs.

The *Conceptual Framework* is not an IFRS and so does not overrule any individual IFRS. In the (rare) case of conflict between an IFRS and the *Conceptual Framework*, the **IFRS will prevail**.

4.3   Chapter 1: The objective of general purpose financial reporting

The *Conceptual Framework* states that:

'The objective of general purpose financial reporting is to provide information about the reporting entity that is useful to existing and potential investors, lenders and other creditors in making decisions about providing resources to the entity.'

These users need information about:

*   The **economic resources of the entity**;
*   The **claims against the entity**; and
*   Changes in the entity's **economic resources and claims**

Information about the entity's **economic resources and the claims against it** helps users to assess the entity's liquidity and solvency and its likely needs for additional financing.

Information about a reporting entity's financial performance (the **changes in its economic resources and claims**) helps users to understand the return that the entity has produced on its economic resources. This is an indicator of how efficiently and effectively management has used the resources of the entity and is helpful in predicting future returns.

The *Conceptual Framework* makes it clear that this information should be prepared on an **accruals basis**.

Information about a reporting entity's cash flows during a period also helps users assess the entity's ability to generate future net cash inflows and gives users a better understanding of its operations.

4.4   Chapter 3: Qualitative characteristics of useful financial information

4.4.1 Overview

Qualitative characteristics are the attributes that make the information provided in financial statements useful to users.

The two **fundamental qualitative characteristics** are **relevance** and **faithful representation**.

There are then four **enhancing qualitative characteristics** which enhance the usefulness of information that is relevant and faithfully represented. These are: **comparability**, **verifiability**, **timeliness** and **understandability**.

The key issues can be summarised as follows:

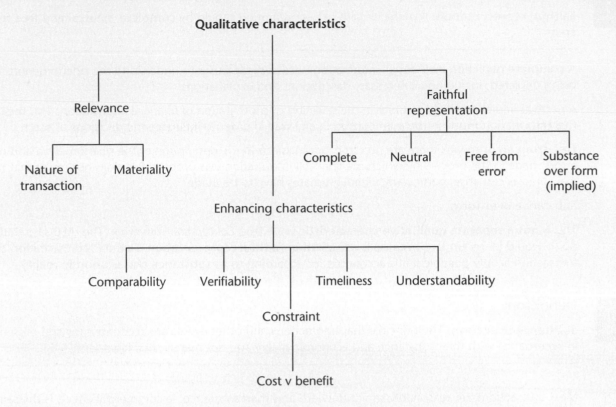

Qualitative characteristics
- Relevance
  - Nature of transaction
  - Materiality
- Faithful representation
  - Complete
  - Neutral
  - Free from error
  - Substance over form (implied)
- Enhancing characteristics
  - Comparability
  - Verifiability
  - Timeliness
  - Understandability
- Constraint
  - Cost v benefit

4.4.2 Relevance

Relevant financial information can be of **predictive value, confirmatory value** or both. These roles are interrelated.

Definition

Relevance: Relevant financial information is capable of making a difference in the decisions made by users.

Information on financial position and performance is often used to predict future position and performance and other things of interest to the user, eg likely dividend, wage rises. The **manner of presentation** will enhance the ability to make predictions, eg by highlighting unusual items.

The relevance of information is affected by **its nature and its materiality**.

Definition

Materiality: Information is material if omitting it or misstating it could influence decisions that users make on the basis of financial information about a specific reporting entity.

Information may be judged relevant simply because of its nature (eg remuneration of management). In other cases, both the nature and materiality of the information are important. Materiality is not a qualitative characteristic itself (like relevance or faithful representation), because it is merely a threshold or cut-off point.

4.4.3 Faithful representation

Financial reports represent **economic phenomena** in words and numbers. To be useful, financial information must not only represent relevant phenomena but must faithfully represent the phenomena that it purports to represent. The user must be able to depend on it being a **faithful representation**.

Definition

Faithful representation: A perfectly faithful representation should be **complete**, **neutral** and **free from error**.

A **complete** depiction includes all information necessary for a user to understand the phenomenon being depicted, including all necessary descriptions and explanations.

A **neutral** depiction is without bias in the selection or presentation of financial information. This means that information must not be manipulated in any way in order to influence the decisions of users.

Free from error means there are no errors or omissions in the description of the phenomenon and no errors made in the process by which the financial information was produced. It does not mean that no inaccuracies can arise, particularly where estimates have to be made.

Substance over form

This is **not a separate qualitative characteristic** under the *Conceptual Framework*. The IASB says that to do so would be redundant because it is **implied in faithful representation**. Faithful representation of a transaction is only possible if it is accounted for according to its **substance and economic reality**.

Definition

Substance over form: The principle that transactions and other events are accounted for and presented in accordance with their substance and economic reality and not merely their legal form.

Most transactions are reasonably straightforward and their substance, ie commercial effect, is the same as their strict legal form. However, in some instances this is not the case as can be seen in the following worked example.

Worked example: Sale and repurchase agreement

A Ltd sells goods to B Ltd for £10,000, but undertakes to repurchase the goods from B Ltd in 12 months' time for £11,000.

The legal form of the transaction is that A has sold goods to B as it has transferred legal title. To reflect the legal form, A Ltd would record a sale and show the resulting profit, if any, in profit or loss for the period. In 12 months' time when legal title is regained, A Ltd would record a purchase. There would be no liability to B Ltd in A Ltd's statement of financial position until the goods are repurchased.

The above treatment does not provide a faithful representation because it does not reflect the economic substance of the transaction. After all, A Ltd is under an obligation from the outset to repurchase the goods and A Ltd bears the risk that those goods will be obsolete and unsaleable in a year's time.

The substance is that B Ltd has made a secured loan to A Ltd of £10,000 plus interest of £1,000. To reflect substance, A Ltd should continue to show the goods as an asset in inventories (at cost or net realisable value, if lower) and should include a liability to B Ltd of £10,000 in payables. A Ltd should accrue for the interest over the duration of the loan.

When A Ltd pays £11,000 to regain legal title, this should be treated as a repayment of the loan plus accrued interest.

Other examples of accounting for substance:

* **Leases**

    Accounting for finance leases under IAS 17 *Leases* (which is covered in Chapter 7) is an example of the application of substance as the lessee includes the asset in its statement of financial position even though the legal form of a lease is that of renting the asset, not buying it.

- **Group financial statements**

  Group financial statements are covered in detail in Chapters 10 to 15. The central principle underlying group accounts is that a group of companies is treated as though it were a single entity, even though each company within the group is itself a separate legal entity.

4.4.4 Enhancing qualitative characteristics

Comparability

Comparability is the qualitative characteristic that enables users to identify and understand similarities in, and differences among, items. Information about a reporting entity is more useful if it can be compared with similar information about other entities and with similar information about the same entity for another period or another date.

Consistency, although related to comparability, **is not the same**. It refers to the use of the same methods for the same items (ie consistency of treatment) either from period to period within a reporting entity or in a single period across entities.

The **disclosure of accounting policies** is particularly important here. Users must be able to distinguish between different accounting policies in order to be able to make a valid comparison of similar items in the accounts of different entities.

Comparability is **not the same as uniformity**. Entities should change accounting policies if those policies become inappropriate.

Corresponding information for preceding periods should be shown to enable comparison over time.

Verifiability

Verifiability helps assure users that information faithfully represents the economic phenomena it purports to represent. It means that different knowledgeable and independent observers could reach consensus that a particular depiction is a faithful representation.

Timeliness

Information may become less useful if there is a delay in reporting it. There is a **balance between timeliness and the provision of reliable information**.

If information is reported on a timely basis when not all aspects of the transaction are known, it may not be complete or free from error.

Conversely, if every detail of a transaction is known, it may be too late to publish the information because it has become irrelevant. The overriding consideration is how best to satisfy the economic decision-making needs of the users.

Understandability

Financial reports are prepared for users who have a **reasonable knowledge of business and economic activities** and who review and analyse the information diligently. Some phenomena are inherently complex and cannot be made easy to understand. Excluding information on those phenomena might make the information easier to understand, but without it those reports would be incomplete and therefore misleading. Therefore matters should not be left out of financial statements simply due to their difficulty as even well-informed and diligent users may sometimes need the aid of an advisor to understand information about complex economic phenomena.

4.4.5 The cost constraint on useful financial reporting

This is a pervasive constraint, not a qualitative characteristic. When information is provided, its benefits must exceed the costs of obtaining and presenting it. This is a **subjective area** and there are other difficulties: others, not the intended users, may gain a benefit; also the cost may be paid by someone other than the users. It is therefore difficult to apply a cost-benefit analysis, but preparers and users should be aware of the constraint.

4.5 Chapter 4: The elements of financial statements

4.5.1 Overview

Transactions and other events are grouped together in broad **classes** and in this way their financial effects are shown in the financial statements. These broad classes are the elements of financial statements.

The *Conceptual Framework* lays out these elements as follows.

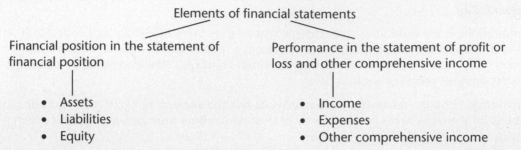

Contributions from equity participants and distributions to them are shown in the statement of changes in equity.

4.5.2 Definitions of elements

Element	Definition	Comment
Asset	A resource controlled by an entity as a result of past events and from which future economic benefits are expected to flow to the entity.	Technically, the asset is the access to future economic benefits (eg cash generation) not the underlying item of property itself (eg a machine).
Liability	A present obligation of the entity arising from past events, the settlement of which is expected to lead to the outflow from the entity of resources embodying economic benefits.	An obligation implies that the entity is not free to avoid the outflow of resources.
Equity	The residual amount found by deducting all of the entity's liabilities from all of the entity's assets.	Equity = ownership interest = net assets. For a company, this usually comprises shareholders' funds (ie capital and reserves).
Income	Increases in economic benefits in the form of asset increases/liability decreases not resulting from contributions from equity participants.	Income comprises revenue and gains, including all recognised gains on non-revenue items (eg revaluations of non-current assets).
Expenses	Decreases in economic benefits in the form of asset decreases/liability increases not resulting from distributions to equity participants.	Expenses includes losses, including all recognised losses on non-revenue items (such as write-downs of non-current assets).

Note the way that the changes in economic benefits resulting from asset and liability increases and decreases are used to define:

- Income
- Expenses

This arises from the '**balance sheet approach**' adopted by the *Conceptual Framework* which treats performance statements, such as the statement of profit or loss, as a means of reconciling changes in the financial position amounts shown in the statement of financial position.

These key definitions of 'asset' and 'liability' will be referred to again and again in these learning materials, because they form the foundation on which so many accounting standards are based. It is very important that you can reproduce these definitions accurately and quickly.

4.5.3 Assets

We can look in more detail at the components of the definitions given above.

Assets must give rise to **future economic benefits**, either alone or in conjunction with other items.

Definition

Future economic benefit: The potential to contribute, directly or indirectly, to the flow of cash and cash equivalents to the entity. The potential may be a productive one that is part of the operating activities of the entity. It may also take the form of convertibility into cash or cash equivalents or a capability to reduce cash outflows, such as when an alternative manufacturing process lowers the cost of production.

In simple terms, an item is an asset if:

- It is **cash** or the **right to cash** in future, eg a receivable, or a **right to services** that may be used to generate cash, eg a prepayment.

or

- It can be used to **generate cash** or **meet liabilities**, eg a tangible or intangible non-current asset.

The **existence** of an asset, particularly in terms of **control**, is **not reliant** on:

- **Physical form** (hence intangible assets such as patents and copyrights may meet the definition of an asset and appear in the statement of financial position – even though they have no physical substance).

- **Legal ownership** (hence some leased assets, even though not legally owned by the company, may be included as assets in the statement of financial position. (See Chapter 7.)

Transactions or events in the **past** give rise to assets. Those expected to occur in future do not in themselves give rise to assets.

4.5.4 Liabilities

Again we look more closely at some aspects of the definition.

An essential feature of a liability is that the entity has a **present obligation**.

Definition

Obligation: A duty or responsibility to act or perform in a certain way. Obligations may be legally enforceable as a consequence of a binding contract or statutory requirement. Obligations also arise, however, from normal business practice, custom and a desire to maintain good business relations or act in an equitable manner.

As seen above, obligations may be:

- **Legally enforceable** as a consequence of a binding contract or statutory requirement. This is normally the case with amounts payable for goods and services received.

- The result of **business practice**. For example, even though a company has no legal obligation to do so, it may have a policy of rectifying faults in its products even after the warranty period has expired.

A **management decision** (to acquire an asset, for example) **does not in itself create an obligation**, because it can be reversed. But a management decision implemented in a way which creates expectations in the minds of customers, suppliers or employees, becomes an obligation. This is sometimes described as a **constructive obligation**. This issue is covered more fully in Chapter 9 in the context of the recognition of provisions.

Liabilities must arise from **past transactions or events**. For example, the sale of goods is the past transaction which allows the recognition of repair warranty provisions.

Settlement of a present obligation will involve the entity **giving up resources** embodying economic benefits in order to satisfy the claim of the other party. In practice, most liabilities will be met in **cash** but this is not essential.

Interactive question 1: Asset or liability? [Difficulty level: Easy]

Question	Fill in your answer
(a) Oak plc has purchased a patent for £40,000. The patent gives the company sole use of a particular manufacturing process which will save £6,000 a year for the next five years.	
(b) Elm plc paid John Brown £20,000 to set up a car repair shop, on condition that priority treatment is given to cars from the company's fleet.	
(c) Sycamore plc provides a warranty with every washing machine sold.	

See **Answer** at the end of this chapter.

4.5.5 Equity

Equity is the **residual of assets less liabilities**, so the amount at which it is shown is dependent on the measurement of assets and liabilities. It has nothing to do with the market value of the entity's shares.

Equity may be **sub-classified** in the statement of financial position providing information which is relevant to the decision-making needs of the users. This will indicate legal or other restrictions on the ability of the entity to distribute or otherwise apply its equity.

In practical terms, the important distinction between liabilities and equity is that creditors have the **right** to insist that the transfer of economic resources is made to them regardless of the entity's financial position, but owners do not. All decisions about payments to owners (such as dividends or share capital buy-back) are at the discretion of management.

4.5.6 Performance

Profit is used as a **measure of performance**, or as a basis for other measures (eg earnings per share (EPS)). It depends directly on the measurement of **income and expenses**, which in turn depend (in part) on the concepts of capital and capital maintenance adopted.

Income and expenses can be **presented in different ways** in profit or loss and in other comprehensive income, to provide information relevant for economic decision-making. For example, a statement of profit or loss could distinguish between income and expenses which relate to continuing operations and those which do not.

Items of income and expense can be **distinguished** from each other or **combined** with each other.

Income

Both **revenue** and **gains** are included in the definition of income. **Revenue** arises in the course of ordinary activities of an entity. (We will look at revenue in more detail in Chapter 6.)

Definition

Gains: Increases in economic benefits. As such they are no different in nature from revenue.

Gains include those arising on the disposal of non-current assets. The definition of income also includes **unrealised gains**, eg on **revaluation** of non-current assets.

A **revaluation** gives rise to an increase or decrease in equity.

These increases and decreases appear in other comprehensive income.

(Gains on revaluation, which are recognised in a revaluation surplus are covered in Chapter 4.)

Expenses

As with income, the definition of expenses includes **losses** as well as those expenses that arise in the course of ordinary activities of an entity.

Definition

Losses: Decreases in economic benefits. As such they are no different in nature from other expenses.

Losses will include those arising on the disposal of non-current assets. The definition of expenses will also include **unrealised losses**.

4.6 Chapter 4: Recognition of the elements of financial statements

4.6.1 Meaning of recognised

An item is recognised when it is included in the statement of financial position, statement of profit or loss or statement of other comprehensive income.

Definition

Recognition: The process of incorporating in the statement of financial position, statement of profit or loss or statement of other comprehensive income an item that meets the definition of an element and satisfies the following criteria for recognition:

- It is probable that any future economic benefit associated with the item will flow to or from the entity, and

- The item has a cost or value that can be measured with reliability.

Points to note

(1) Regard must be given to materiality (see Section 4.4.3 above).

(2) An item which fails to meet these criteria at one time may meet it subsequently.

(3) An item which fails to meet the criteria may merit disclosure in the notes to the financial statements. (This is dealt with in more detail by IAS 37 *Provisions, Contingent Liabilities and Contingent Assets* which is covered in Chapter 9.)

4.6.2 Probability of future economic benefits

Probability here refers to the **degree of uncertainty** that the future economic benefits associated with an item will flow to or from the entity. This must be judged on the basis of the **characteristics of the entity's environment** and the **evidence available** when the financial statements are prepared.

The *Conceptual Framework* does not give a definition of 'probable'. A working definition is 'more likely than not'.

4.6.3 Reliability of measurement

The cost or value of an item in many cases must be **estimated**. The use of reasonable estimates is an essential part of the preparation of financial statements and **does not undermine their reliability**. Where no reasonable estimate can be made, the item should not be recognised (although its existence should be disclosed in the notes).

4.6.4 Recognition of items

We can summarise the recognition criteria for assets, liabilities, income and expenses, based on the definition of recognition given above.

Item	Recognised in	When
Asset	The statement of financial position	It is probable that the future economic benefits will flow to the entity and the asset has a cost or value that can be measured reliably.
Liability	The statement of financial position	It is probable that an outflow of resources embodying economic benefits will result from the settlement of a present obligation and the amount at which the settlement will take place can be measured reliably.
Income	The statement of profit or loss and other comprehensive income	An increase in future economic benefits related to an increase in an asset or a decrease of a liability has arisen that can be measured reliably.
Expenses	The statement of profit or loss and other comprehensive income	A decrease in future economic benefits related to a decrease in an asset or an increase of a liability has arisen that can be measured reliably.

Points to note

(1) There is a **direct association** between expenses being recognised in profit or loss for the period and the generation of income. This is commonly referred to as the accruals basis or matching concept. However, the application of the accruals basis **does not permit recognition of assets or liabilities** in the statement of financial position which do not meet the appropriate definition.

(2) Expenses should be **recognised immediately** in profit or loss for the period when expenditure is not expected to result in the generation of future economic benefits.

(3) An expense should also be **recognised immediately** when a liability is incurred **without the corresponding recognition of an asset**.

4.7 Chapter 4: Measurement of the elements of financial statements

For an item or transaction to be recognised in an entity's financial statements it needs to be **measured as a monetary amount**. IFRS uses **several different measurement bases** but the *Conceptual Framework* refers to just four.

The **four** measurement bases referred to in the *Conceptual Framework* are:

- **Historical cost**. Assets are recorded at the amount of cash or cash equivalents paid or the fair value of the consideration given to acquire them at the time of their acquisition. Liabilities are recorded at the amount of proceeds received in exchange for the obligation, or in some circumstances (for example, income taxes), at the amounts of cash or cash equivalents expected to be paid to satisfy the liability in the normal course of business.

- **Current cost**. Assets are carried at the amount of cash or cash equivalents that would have to be paid if the same or an equivalent asset was acquired currently.

  Liabilities are carried at the undiscounted amount of cash or cash equivalents that would be required to settle the obligation currently.

- **Realisable (settlement) value**.

  - **Realisable value**. The amount of cash or cash equivalents that could currently be obtained by selling an asset in an orderly disposal.

  - **Settlement value**. The undiscounted amounts of cash or cash equivalents expected to be paid to satisfy the liabilities in the normal course of business.

- **Present value**. A current estimate of the present discounted value of the future net cash flows in the normal course of business.

Historical cost is the most commonly adopted measurement basis, but this is usually combined with other bases, eg an historical cost basis may be modified by the revaluation of land and buildings.

4.8 Chapter 4: Concepts of capital and capital maintenance

The final section of the *Conceptual Framework* is devoted to a brief discussion of the different concepts of capital and capital maintenance, pointing out that:

- The choice between them should be made on the basis of the needs of users of financial statements.

- The IASB has no present intention of prescribing a particular model.

4.8.1 Financial capital and capital maintenance

Definition

Financial capital maintenance: Under a financial concept of capital maintenance, such as invested money or invested purchasing power, capital is synonymous with the net assets or equity of the entity.

The financial concept of capital is adopted by most entities.

This concept measures capital as the **equity in the statement of financial position**. Profit is only earned in an accounting period **if the equity at the end of the period is greater than it was at the start**, having excluded the effects of distributions to or contributions from the owners during the period.

Monetary measure of capital

Financial capital is usually measured in **monetary terms**, eg the £ sterling or the euro. This is the concept applied in historical cost accounting. This measure can be quite stable over short periods of years, but is debased by even quite low rates of general inflation over longer periods, such as 20 years. So comparisons between capital now and capital 20 years ago are invalid, because the measurement instrument is not constant.

Constant purchasing power

A variant on the monetary measure of financial capital is the constant purchasing power measure. On this basis, **the opening capital (ie equity) is uprated by the change in a broadly based price index**, often a retail prices index, over the year. Also, the transactions during the year are uprated by the change in the same index. A profit is only earned if **the capital at the end of the year exceeds these uprated values**. (The value of the uprating is taken to equity, but is not regarded as a profit, merely a 'capital maintenance' adjustment.) So this capital maintenance adjustment can be thought of as an additional expense. Comparisons over a 20-year period will be more valid if the capital 20 years ago is uprated for general inflation over that 20-year period.

However, there is no reason why inflation measured by a retail prices index should be at all close to the inflation experienced by an individual company. The physical capital maintenance concept (see below) seeks to address this.

4.8.2 Physical capital and capital maintenance

Definition

Physical capital maintenance: Under a physical concept of capital, such as operating capability, capital is regarded as the productive capacity of the entity based on, for example, units of output per day.

This concept looks behind monetary values, to the underlying **physical productive capacity of the entity**. It is based on the approach that an entity is nothing other than a means of producing saleable outputs, so a profit is earned only after that productive capacity has been maintained by a 'capital maintenance' adjustment. (Again, the capital maintenance adjustment is taken to equity and is treated as an additional expense in the statement of profit or loss.) Comparisons over 20 years should be more valid than under a monetary approach to capital maintenance.

The difficulties in this approach lie in making the capital maintenance adjustment. It is basically a current cost approach, normal practice being to use industry-specific indices of movements in non-current assets, rather than go to the expense of annual revaluations by professional valuers. The difficulties lie in finding indices appropriate to the productive capacity of a particular entity.

Worked example: Capital maintenance concepts

Meercat plc purchased 20,000 electrical components on 1 January 20X7 for £10 each. They were all sold on 31 December 20X7 for £250,000. On that date the replacement cost of an electrical component was £11.50. The general rate of inflation as measured by the general price index was 12% during the year.

Profit could be calculated as follows:

	Financial capital maintenance (monetary terms) £	Financial capital maintenance (constant purchasing power) £	Physical capital maintenance £
Revenue	250,000	250,000	250,000
Cost of sales			
20,000 × 10	(200,000)		
20,000 × 11.2		(224,000)	
20,000 × 11.5			(230,000)
Profit	50,000	26,000	20,000

5 The regulatory framework

Section overview

- Financial reporting is the provision of financial information to those outside the entity.

- The organisation responsible for setting IFRSs comprises the International Financial Reporting Standards Foundation (IFRS Foundation), the Monitoring Board, the International Accounting Standards Board (IASB), the IFRS Advisory Council (Advisory Council) and the IFRS Interpretations Committee (Interpretations Committee).

- The process of setting IFRSs is an open dialogue involving co-operation between national and international standard setters.

5.1 The IFRS Foundation

IASCF was formed in March 2001 as a not-for-profit corporation and was the parent entity of the **IASB**. In 2010 it was renamed as the **IFRS Foundation**. The IFRS Foundation is an independent organisation and its trustees **exercise oversight** and raise necessary **funding** for the IASB to carry out its role as standard setter. It also oversees the work of the IFRS Interpretations Committee (formerly called the **International Financial Reporting Interpretations Committee** (IFRIC)) and the IFRS Advisory Council (formerly called the **Standards Advisory Council** (SAC)). These are organised as follows:

```
┌─────────────────────────────────────────────┐
│ IFRS Foundation is responsible for:           │
│ • Funding                                      │
│ • Appointment of members of IASB, IFRS         │
│   Advisory Council and IFRS Interpretations    │
│   Committee                                    │
└─────────────────────────────────────────────┘
```

```
┌────────────────────────────────────┐        ┌────────────────────────────────────────┐
│ IASB is responsible for:            │        │ IFRS Advisory Council is responsible for:│
│ • All technical matters in general  │········│ • Input on IASB's agenda                 │
│ • In particular, the preparation and│        │ • Input on IASB's project timetable and  │
│   issue of International Financial   │        │   priorities                             │
│   Reporting Standards               │        │ • Advise on standard-setting projects    │
└────────────────────────────────────┘        │ • Supporting IASB in promotion/adoption  │
                                               │   of IFRS throughout the world           │
    ┌────────────────────────────────────┐     └────────────────────────────────────────┘
    │ IFRS Interpretations Committee is   │
    │ responsible for:                    │
    │ • Interpretation and application of │
    │   International Financial Reporting  │
    │   Standards                         │
    └────────────────────────────────────┘
```

5.2 Membership

Membership of the IFRS Foundation has been designed so that it represents an international group of preparers and users, who become IFRS Foundation trustees. The selection process of the **22 trustees** takes into account geographical factors and professional background. IFRS Foundation trustees **appoint the IASB members**.

5.3 The IASB

The IASB is responsible for setting accounting standards. It is made up of 15 full-time members and has no particular geographical dominance. Members have a variety of backgrounds and include:

- Auditors
- Preparers of financial statements
- Users of financial statements
- Academics

5.4 Objectives of the IASB

The *Preface to IFRSs* states that the objectives of the IASB are as follows:

- To develop, in the public interest, **a single set of high-quality, understandable, enforceable and globally accepted financial reporting standards** based on clearly articulated principles. These standards should require high quality, transparent and comparable information in financial statements and other financial reporting to help investors, other participants in the various capital markets of the world and other users of the information to make economic decisions;

- To promote the **use and rigorous application** of those standards;

- In fulfilling the above objectives to take account of, as appropriate, the needs of a range of sizes and types of entities in diverse economic settings; and

- To promote and facilitate the adoption of IFRSs through the **convergence** of national accounting standards and IFRSs.

5.5 The purpose of accounting standards

The overall purpose of accounting standards is to identify **proper accounting practices** for the preparation of financial statements.

Accounting standards create a **common understanding** between users and preparers on how particular items, for example the valuation of property, are treated. Financial statements should therefore comply with all applicable accounting standards.

5.6 Application of IFRS

Within each individual country **local regulations govern**, to a greater or lesser degree, the issue of financial statements. These local regulations include accounting standards issued by the national regulatory bodies or professional accountancy bodies in the country concerned.

Over the last 25 years however, the **influence of IFRS on national accounting requirements and practices has been growing**. For example:

- Since accounting periods commencing on or after 1 January 2005, all EU companies whose securities are traded on a regulated public market such as the London Stock Exchange, **must prepare their consolidated accounts in accordance with IFRS**. (Note that although **group** financial statements must follow IFRS the **individual** financial statements do not need to.)

- In the UK **unquoted companies are permitted** (but not required) to adopt IFRS.

5.7 Setting of IFRS

The overall agenda of the IASB is initially set by discussion with the IFRS Advisory Council. The process for developing an individual standard involves the following steps.

Step 1
During the early stages of a project, IASB may establish an **Advisory Committee or working group** to give advice on issues arising in the project. Consultation with the Advisory Committee and the Advisory Council occurs throughout the project.

Step 2
IASB may develop and publish a **Discussion Paper** for public comment.

Step 3
Following the receipt and review of comments, IASB would develop and publish an **Exposure Draft** for public comment.

Step 4
Following the receipt and review of comments, the IASB would issue a final **International Financial Reporting Standard**.

The period of exposure for public comment is normally 120 days. However, in some circumstances, proposals may be issued with a comment period of not less than 30 days. Draft IFRS Interpretations are exposed for a 60-day comment period.

5.8 Scope and authority of IFRS

The *Preface to IFRSs* makes the following points:

- IFRS apply to **all general purpose financial statements** ie those directed towards the common information needs of a wide range of users.

- The IASB's objective is to **require like transactions and events to be accounted for and reported in a like way. The IASB intends not to permit choices in accounting treatment.** The IASB is reconsidering those transactions and events for which IFRSs permit a choice of accounting treatment with the objective of reducing the number of those choices.

- Standards include paragraphs in bold and plain type. **Bold type paragraphs** indicate the **main principles**, but **both types have equal authority.**

- Any limitation of the applicability of a specific IFRS is made clear in that standard.

5.9 UK regulatory framework

5.9.1 UK standard-setting process

From 1 August 1990 to 2 July 2012 all UK accounting standards were issued by the Accounting Standards Board (ASB). From 2 July 2012 responsibility for issuing accounting standards was assumed by the Board of the Financial Reporting Council (FRC).

UK accounting standards are known as Financial Reporting Standards (FRSs). They include the Financial Reporting Standard for Smaller Entities (FRSSE). Prior to the formation of the ASB, standards were issued known as Statements of Standard Accounting Practice (SSAPs). Most of these have been replaced by FRSs, but some are still in force today.

FRSs are first issued as exposure drafts for consultation that are known as Financial Reporting Exposure Drafts (FREDs). FREDs are then amended or not according to the results of the consultation and issued as FRSs.

5.9.2 Abbreviated accounts and micro-entities

In the UK small companies are allowed to file abbreviated accounts. The thresholds for a small company are:

- Turnover below £6.5 million
- Balance sheet total below £3.26 million
- Fewer than 50 employees

Companies meeting two of these requirements can file an abbreviated profit and loss account. They must still file a balance sheet and an audit report.

The advantage of this to small companies is that abbreviated accounts cost less to prepare and give away less information to competitors. A possible downside is that they may give insufficient information for potential lenders.

In November 2013 the UK Government approved regulations that introduced simpler reporting for **micro-entities** – a newly-defined sub-category of small company. The qualifying conditions are:

- Turnover below £632,000
- Balance sheet total below £316,000
- Fewer than 10 employees

Certain types of organisation, including charities, LLPs, investment companies and insurance companies, are excluded from being treated as micro-entities.

The micro-entity regulations set out a simplified profit and loss account and balance sheet which can be filed by qualifying entities

5.9.3 UK financial reporting

UK companies must produce their financial statements in line with the requirements of:

- The Companies Act 2006
- Accounting standards, whether IFRS or the UK Financial Reporting Standards

Companies whose shares or debt are traded on a regulated securities exchange have been required to prepare their consolidated financial statements in accordance with IFRS from 2005. (This requirement does not apply to the separate financial statements of the parent company or the separate financial statements of any subsidiaries, although it is permissible to use IFRS for these as well.) From 2007 onwards this regulation also applies to companies whose share capital or debt is traded on the London Alternative Investment Market (AIM).

All other companies can choose whether to prepare both consolidated and separate financial statements in accordance with UK GAAP or IFRS. However, when a company chooses to change the basis of preparation to IFRS, it cannot subsequently change back to using UK GAAP.

To date few companies have made a voluntary transition to IFRS. They have preferred to remain with UK GAAP.

In 2012 and 2013 the FRC revised UK financial reporting standards. This revision replaced all extant standards with three new Financial Reporting Standards:

- FRS 100 *Application of Financial Reporting Requirements*
- FRS 101 *Reduced Disclosure Framework*
- FRS 102 *The Financial Reporting Standard Applicable in the UK and Republic of Ireland*

FRS 100 sets out the financial reporting requirements for UK and Republic of Ireland entities. These are as follows:

(a) An entity eligible to apply the FRSSE may continue to do so.

(b) Other entities should apply FRS 102 or, in the case of the individual financial statements of a qualifying entity, FRS 101.

A qualifying entity for the purposes of FRS 101 is a member of a group whose consolidated financial statements are prepared under IFRS. FRS 101 allows group members in their **individual** financial statements to take advantage of exemption from a number of disclosures required by full IFRS.

The IFRSs to which disclosure exemptions apply are: IAS 1, IAS 7, IAS 8, IAS 24, IAS 36, IFRS 2, IFRS 3, IFRS 5, IFRS 7 and IFRS 13. These exemptions are explained more fully in the relevant chapters of this manual for those standards which are included in the FAR syllabus.

Chapter 16 of this manual is dedicated to FRS 102, highlighting the accounting treatment under UK GAAP. A comparison with IFRS is summarised at the end of Chapter 16 and forms part of the examinable FAR syllabus.

6 Convergence process

Section overview

- There has been a drive in recent years towards increased harmonisation of accounting standards.

- Groups whose shares or debt are traded on a supervised securities exchange in EU countries must now prepare their consolidated financial statements under IFRS.

- The IASB Convergence programme includes collaboration with the US Financial Accounting Standards Board (FASB) in order to create a set of global reporting standards.

- In the UK the ASB has worked closely with the IASB in order to converge UK accounting standards with IFRS. This has resulted in new standards FRS 100, FRS 101 and FRS 102.

6.1 National and international financial reporting

Companies are required to prepare their financial statements according to the accounting requirements of the country in which the company is registered. In the UK this now means compliance with:

- Companies Act 2006
- FRSs 100, 101 and 102

The issue of these new UK standards is the result of UK/IFRS convergence. However, convergence with US GAAP may be some way off.

Many multi-national groups have their shares traded on stock exchanges in different countries around the world and have often been required to prepare financial statements in line with the reporting standards in each country; they have then needed to make adjustments prior to consolidating them in their home country under that country's reporting standards.

US-based entities are required to prepare their financial statements in accordance with the financial reporting standards issued by the US FASB. Non-US entities which prepared their financial statements under different standards, such as IFRS, and whose shares are traded on a US stock exchange used to be required to prepare reconciliations of the profit and equity amounts measured under these different standards and the equivalent amounts under US GAAP. These restatements often required a substantial amount of work.

For some decades there has been increased pressure for the adoption of a single set of global accounting standards. This drive towards worldwide harmonisation of financial reporting has two main causes:

- Increased globalisation of trade and of capital markets, with the result that:

    - Management wants all group entities to produce financial statements on the same basis.

    - Investors and lenders are now adopting an international approach to their activities and want to be spared the trouble of having to understand a number of different bases for the preparation of financial statements.

- It is also the case that the increasing pace of information technology development now provides companies with the communications to take advantage of such harmonisation.

The benefits from the convergence of global financial reporting include:

- Reducing the cost of capital as investors/lenders understand all financial statements better
- Encouraging investment growth
- Improving the quality of financial reporting
- Reducing the time and cost of preparing financial statements

There are some who would also argue that there are costs of global convergence, in particular:

- The cost of changing accounting practices and systems to suit IFRS

- A perceived dilution of national sovereignty

- A concern that the desire to converge with US requirements (see below) will lead to standards which are really only appropriate for the very largest, international companies, which regularly raise finance on the capital markets. Such standards are just too complex, and compliance with them too expensive, for companies operating only in their domestic markets and raising the finance they need from their local banks

It should also be pointed out that convergence has appeared to lose momentum in recent years. This is perhaps due to renewed confidence in US GAAP within the US itself. Also, many US investors tend to see IFRS as a predominantly European project. The euro crisis has not helped persuade investors that accounting rules are in safe hands under IFRS. Nevertheless, convergence remains an ongoing objective.

6.2 The European Union

For many years the European Union (EU) has had an overall objective of creating a properly functioning internal market. It has therefore set a specific objective in the financial arena of developing an integrated and efficiently operating capital market. The adoption of internationally accepted accounting standards with few measurement options, leading to a single set of global accounting standards, is a major contribution to the achievement of this objective.

In 2000, as part of this process, the International Organisation of Securities Commissions (IOSCO) adopted a core set of IFRS for use by multi-national entities. IOSCO represents the regulators of securities markets and keeps a watching brief over the major regulatory issues associated with international securities in general and with multi-national disclosure and accounting in particular.

In June 2002 the European Commission issued a Regulation requiring the **adoption of IFRS** for the preparation of consolidated financial statements for financial periods starting on or after 1 January 2005 for entities incorporated in a member state and whose securities, debt or equity, are traded on a regulated market in the EU. The consolidated financial statements of many of Europe's top multinationals are now prepared in conformity with national requirements, EC directives and IFRS. Member states currently have the discretion to extend the implementation of IFRS to include non-listed companies.

To maintain some political control over standards and prevent them being solely under the control of unelected accountants, the European Commission set up an endorsement mechanism whereby the European Parliament and the Council of the EU must adopt new international accounting standards before companies are required to comply with them. In deciding whether to adopt a standard they take advice from two committees:

- The Accounting Regulatory Committee (ARC) which is made up of representatives of member states and works at a political level.

- The European Financial Reporting Advisory Group (EFRAG) which is made up of technical experts such as national standard setters, national regulators and preparers and users of financial statements. This group provides advice to the Commission on all issues relating to the application of IFRS in the EU. It is expected to identify early in the development of an IFRS whether the IASB proposals are going to cause significant problems within the EU.

In 2006 the European Commission established a Standards Advice Review Group (SARG) whose task is to assess whether the endorsement advice given by EFRAG is well-balanced and objective.

Although the IASB issues IFRS, it has no legal authority to require compliance with them, so the use of IFRS requires specific legislation in each country or on the part of the EU. Within the EU enforcement is delegated to the regulatory authorities in member states, but must be carried out in line with the enforcement principles set out by the European Securities and Markets Authority (ESMA). These principles can be summarised as follows:

- The purpose of enforcement is to protect investors and promote securities market confidence.

- Enforcement shall take the form of a review to see whether IFRS have been properly complied with.

- Enforcement shall be 'ex-post', in that there shall be reviews of financial statements only after they have been published.

- The selection of financial statements to be reviewed should combine a risk-based approach together with a sampling and/or rotation approach.

- Total reliance on a risk-based approach may be acceptable, but total reliance on a rotation approach is not.

- A purely reactive approach (conducting a review only when someone complains) is not acceptable.

- Restatements of financial statements should be demanded where appropriate.

In 2010 regulatory authorities within the EU performed full reviews of c1,000 (2009: 1,200) companies' accounts covering 15% of listed entities and partial reviews of 700 (2009: 900) accounts covering 10% of listed entities. In 22 cases (2009: 19) revised financial statements had to be issued and in 220 cases (2009: 160) corrective notes had to be issued. Impairment of assets, financial and other, was the most problematic area.

In early 2014 the European Parliament issued a draft **Directive on Statutory Audit**. The proposed legislation requires EU auditors to publish audit reports according to ISAs and introduces a new 'mandatory rotation' rule. Public-interest entities will be obliged to put their audit out to tender every 10 years. EU auditors will no longer be allowed to provide certain non-audit services to their clients and the rules establish a cap on fees generated for non-audit services to public-interest entities.

In the UK there are three main bodies which regulate financial statements:

- The Financial Conduct Authority (FCA) which is the UK regulator of financial services. The FCA supervises the provision of information to the investing public when an entity wishes to make a public offering of its securities

- The Prudential Regulation Authority which regulates banks, building societies and insurance companies

- The Financial Reporting Review Panel (FRRP)

The FRRP is independent of the ASB but is, like it, answerable to the Financial Reporting Council. It was set up to enquire into financial statements and directors' reports which appear not to comply with the requirements laid down in the UK. In line with the ESMA principles it adopts a proactive approach to the review of all financial information within its remit. If the FRRP considers that inappropriate accounting has been adopted, its aim is to reach agreement with the directors for the voluntary restatement of financial statements. Failing voluntary correction, the FRRP does have the power to restate the financial statements through a court order.

Unlisted companies in the UK now report under FRS 102 *The Financial Reporting Standard Applicable in the UK and Republic of Ireland*, which is based on the IFRS for SMEs (see Chapter 16). FRS 102 is effective from January 2015 and applies to entities not applying EU-adopted IFRS, FRS 101 *Reduced Disclosure Framework*, or the FRSSE (see further in section 6.6 below).

6.3   IASB and US regulators

IFRS are leading the way as the generally accepted accounting standards for capital market reporting outside of the US. However, an overwhelming volume of financial capital is traded through US markets, and any attempts at global convergence must incorporate the US at its core.

After a joint meeting in September 2002, the US FASB and the IASB issued their Norwalk Agreement. In this agreement they each:

* Acknowledged their commitment to the development of high quality, compatible accounting standards that could be used for both domestic and cross-border financial reporting,

* Pledged to use their best efforts to make their existing financial reporting standards fully compatible as soon as is practicable, and

* Pledged to co-ordinate their future work programmes to ensure that once achieved, compatibility is maintained.

This is known as the **IASB Convergence Project** and IFRS 5 *Non-Current Assets Held for Sale and Discontinued Operations* was the first standard to be issued as a result of this agreement.

6.4   Progress in general convergence

In October 2004 and subsequent to the Norwalk Agreement there was an agreement between IASB and FASB to develop a common conceptual framework. The intention was to divide the project into two phases:

* The initial focus being on particular aspects of the framework such as objectives, qualitative characteristics, elements, recognition and measurement.

* In the later stage to apply these aspects to other aspects (see below).

In February 2006 'A Roadmap for convergence between IFRSs and US GAAP 2006–2008 Memorandum of Understanding between the FASB and IASB' (known as the **Memorandum of Understanding** (MoU)) was issued. Progress on convergence was such that in November 2007 the Securities and Exchange Commission (SEC), the regulator of US securities markets removed the requirement referred to above for non-US companies listed in the US and reporting under IFRS to prepare the reconciliations of profit and equity under IFRS to the amounts under US GAAP.

In November 2008 the SEC produced for comment its proposals for a 'Roadmap for the Potential Use of Financial Statements Prepared in Accordance with International Financial Reporting Standards by US Issuers'. The proposals were revised in 2010 and now set out six headings on which progress needs to be made. These headings include:

* Further improvements to IFRS

* Changes to the accountability and funding arrangements for the IFRS Foundation, to demonstrate beyond doubt its independence

* Investor understanding and education regarding IFRS

If these proposals are adopted and assuming that the SEC judges that sufficient progress has been made under the six headings, then the use of IFRS, as opposed to US financial reporting standards, would become **compulsory** for all US entities, starting in approximately 2015 or 2016. This would be a major step along the road to a single set of global reporting standards.

As well as the work on convergence between IFRS and US standards, the IASB has also been working closely on projects with the national accounting standard setters of Canada, Japan and China, all of which countries are committed to adopting or converging their national financial reporting standards with IFRS.

6.5 Conceptual framework

An essential part of harmonising US GAAP and IFRS was to create a common conceptual framework. An agreement on the underpinning concepts is seen as vital to international convergence.

The IASB and the US FASB have done some work towards developing a **common conceptual framework** (that is a single converged framework) which is:

- Complete and internally consistent.

- An improvement on the existing frameworks of both boards.

- Capable of providing a sound foundation for developing future accounting standards.

- Essential to fulfilling the boards' goal of **developing standards** that:
    - Are principles-based
    - Are internally consistent
    - Are internationally converged, and
    - Lead to financial reporting that provides the information needed for investment, credit and similar decisions.

The boards were conducting the project in eight phases.

Phase	Topic
A	Objectives and qualitative characteristics
B	Definitions of elements, recognition and derecognition
C	Measurement
D	Reporting entity concept
E	Boundaries of financial reporting and presentation and disclosure
F	Purpose and status of the framework
G	Application to not-for-profit entities
H	Remaining issues, if any

Phase A was completed and implemented (see Section 4 above) and an exposure draft in respect of Phase D was published in March 2010. Work had started in relation to Phases B and C also. However, during late 2010, the IASB effectively deferred further work on the joint project until after more urgent convergence projects were finalised. The project was then reactivated in September 2012 as an **IASB only** project. In July 2013 the IASB issued a Discussion Paper as a first step towards issuing a revised *Conceptual Framework*.

6.6 Convergence of UK standards and IFRS

The convergence process between UK GAAP and IFRS began in 2003 but was subsequently paused. During that time, UK standards did not keep pace with business changes and with evolving types of transaction, particularly with regard to financial instruments. The FRC undertook a consultation process over a number of years. During this process Deloitte remarked that most trainees were now being trained on IFRS, making UK GAAP 'a dying language' and ICAEW commented that 'UK GAAP is now outdated and in places lacks coherence, and action to rectify the situation is long overdue'.

The FRC took the view that the optimum solution was a transition to an IFRS-based framework and over the course of 2012 and 2013 issued three new standards.

- FRS 100 *Application of Financial Reporting Requirements* – issued November 2012

- FRS 101 *Reduced Disclosure Framework* – issued November 2012

- FRS 102 *The Financial Reporting Standard Applicable in the UK and Republic of Ireland* – issued March 2013

FRS 100 provides rules and guidance on how to select the appropriate accounting framework for a particular entity or group.

FRS 101 provides a reduced disclosure framework for qualifying entities, such as subsidiaries of groups reporting under IFRS.

FRS 102 replaces the majority of UK accounting standards, adopts an IFRS-based framework and improves accounting for financial instruments. It is based on the IFRS for SMEs, amended to ensure compliance with company law. It is intended for all UK entities other than those applying the FRSSE, or listed companies preparing group financial statements, who are already required to report under IFRS. Such companies will still be allowed to apply FRS 101 or FRS 102 in preparing their individual entity financial statements.

UK companies currently reporting under IFRS will be allowed to move to FRS 102 if they are reporting under IFRS on a voluntary basis. If they are required to report under IFRS (consolidated financial statements of a listed company) they will continue to do so.

The objectives and intended effects of the new standards are stated by the FRC to be 'to enable users of accounts to receive high-quality understandable financial reporting proportionate to the size and complexity of the entity and users' information needs'.

FRS 102 has 35 chapters based mainly on the IFRS for SMEs with some cross-reference to full IFRS. The disclosure requirements are less than for full IFRS. Some of the changes that will impact UK companies on moving to FRS 102 are:

* New requirements for financial instruments, bringing all derivatives on balance sheet at fair value

* More intangible assets to be recognised separately from goodwill when there is a business combination

* Useful life of goodwill and intangible assets not to exceed five years when no reliable estimate can be made

* Merger accounting only permitted in limited cases

The new standards are mandatory for accounting periods beginning on or after 1 January 2015.

UK companies should benefit in a number of ways from the transition to FRS 102:

* For private companies that are looking for venture capital, private equity or to make the transition to a public market, moving to IFRS-based reporting will be an advantage to potential investors in terms of making it easier to compare financial performance

* Improved transparency against international companies

* Assistance to overseas trade development with international partners

7 Inherent limitations of financial statements

Section overview

There are limitations inherent in financial statements, including the fact that they are:
* A conventionalised representation, involving classification, aggregation and the allocation of items to particular accounting periods
* Historical (backward-looking), and
* Based almost exclusively on financial data

Integrated reporting attempts to deal with some of these limitations.

7.1 Conventionalised representation

Financial statements are **highly standardised** in terms of their overall format and presentation although businesses are very diverse in their nature. This may limit the usefulness of the information.

Financial statements are **highly aggregated** in that information on a great many transactions and balances is combined into a few figures in the accounts, which can often make it difficult for the reader to evaluate the components of the business.

Allocation issues include, for example, the application of the accrual concept and depreciation of non-current assets, where management's judgements and estimates affect the period in which expenses or income are recognised.

7.2 Backward-looking

Financial statements are **backward-looking** whereas most users of financial information base their decisions on expectations about the future. Financial statements contribute towards this by helping to identify trends and by confirming the accuracy of previous expectations, but cannot realistically provide the complete information set required for all economic decisions by all users.

7.3 Omission of non-financial information

By their nature, financial statements contain financial information. They do not generally include non-financial data such as:

- **Narrative description** of the major operations
- Discussion of **business risks and opportunities**
- Narrative **analysis** of the entity's **performance and prospects**
- **Management policies** and how the business is **governed and controlled**

Financial statements include the elements as defined in the IASB *Conceptual Framework*. This means that items which do not meet those definitions are not included. For example, the value of the entity's internally generated goodwill ie through its reputation, loyalty and expertise of its management and employees, or its client portfolio. While some companies do experiment with different types of disclosure for such items, these disclosures are considered unsuitable for inclusion in the financial statements (precisely because such items do not fall within its definition of assets).

7.4 Other sources of information

Some of the limitations of financial statements are addressed in the **other information** which is often provided along with the financial statements, especially by large companies, such as operating and financial reviews and the Chairman's statement.

There are also many other sources of information available to at least some users of financial statements, for example:

- In owner-managed businesses, the owners have access to internal management information because they are the management. This information is, potentially, available on a continuous real-time basis and may include:
    - Future plans for the business
    - Budgets or forecasts
    - Management accounts, including, for example, divisional analysis

- Banks will often obtain additional access to entity information under the terms of loan agreements

- Potential investors (eg if they are planning to take a major stake or even a controlling interest) will often negotiate additional access to corporate information

- Publicly available information, such as entity brochures and publicity material (eg press releases)

- Brokers' reports on major companies

- Press reports and other media coverage (eg television or internet)

7.5 Integrated reporting

Integrated reporting (IR) presents an organisation's strategy, governance and performance in terms of its wider social, environmental and economic context. By reinforcing these connections it is thought that IR can help an organisation to take more sustainable decisions and enable stakeholders to understand how the organisation is really performing.

The International Integrated Reporting Council (IIRC) was set up in 2010 comprising a cross-section of leaders from corporate investment, accounting, regulatory and standard-setting bodies and the Integrated Reporting Framework was released in December 2013.

The Framework reflects the IIRC's view that corporate reporting must evolve to communicate the full range of factors that affect an organisation's ability to create value over time.

The FRC has now issued guidance stating that annual reports should include information about a company's human rights approach, gender representation and greenhouse gas emissions. This will form part of a new **strategic report** which will include strategy, business model and principal risks and challenges.

8 Not-for-profit entities

Section overview

- Not-for-profit entities include charities, clubs, and public sector organisations.
- Reporting requirements will vary depending on the nature of the entity.

8.1 Not-for-profit entities

The objective of most company directors is to manage the shareholders' investment. In a majority of cases this will mean creating a profit. However, this is not always the case. For some entities their primary purpose is to **provide a service** rather than to make a profit.

Interactive question 2: Not-for-profit entities   **[Difficulty level: Easy]**

List as many types of not-for-profit organisations as you can.

See **Answer** at the end of this chapter.

As this exercise has demonstrated not-for-profit entities include a broad range of organisations involved in very different activities. Not-for-profit entities also vary considerably in size from the local rugby club to an internationally renowned charity.

8.2 Reporting requirements

Many of the organisations mentioned above may be **companies**. In this case they will need to prepare financial statements and have them audited in accordance with **local legislation and accounting regulation**. In the UK this would include compliance with the Companies Act and UK accounting standards.

For unincorporated entities the reporting requirements are normally less onerous, although best practice would be to follow local **GAAP** (see Section 1.5).

In addition, many not-for-profit organisations will need to comply with regulations specific to their sector. For example in the UK, charities are required to comply with the **Charities Act 1993**, as updated by the **Charities Act 2006**, and the **Statement of Recommended Practice: Accounting and Reporting by Charities**.

8.3 International public sector accounting standards

International Public Sector Accounting Standards (IPSAS) are issued by the International Public Sector Accounting Standards Board (IPSASB). The objective of IPSASB is to:

- Develop **high quality** public sector financial reporting standards.
- **Facilitate convergence** of international and national standards.
- Enhance the **quality and uniformity** of financial reporting.

Currently there is **no general requirement** for IPSAS to be adopted and in jurisdictions where national standards already exist it is the local regulation which will be applied. The IPSASB however, envisage an increasing role for IPSAS in future, particularly in the following areas:

- **Assisting national standard-setters** in the development of new standards and the revision of existing standards.

- Being applied in jurisdictions **where there is no national legislation**.

9 Ethical and professional issues

Section overview

- The ICAEW has issued a Code of Ethics which is principles-based and centres around five fundamental principles.

- A professional accountant is responsible for recognising and assessing the potential threats to these fundamental principles.

- A professional accountant must then implement safeguards to eliminate these threats or reduce them to an acceptable level.

9.1 ICAEW Code of Ethics

Chartered Accountants are expected to demonstrate the highest standards of professional conduct and to take into consideration the public interest. Ethical behaviour by Chartered Accountants plays a vital role in ensuring public trust in financial reporting and business practices and upholding the reputation of the accountancy profession.

The ICAEW's Code of Ethics (the Code) applies to all its members and is based upon the International Federation of Accountants (IFAC) Code of Ethics.

The Code is **principles-based** and members are responsible for:

- Identifying threats to compliance with the fundamental principles.
- Evaluating the significance of these threats.
- Implementing safeguards to eliminate them or reduce them to an acceptable level.

The guidance in the Code is given in the form of:

- Fundamental principles
- Illustrations as to how they are to be applied in specific situations

The Code applies to all members, students, affiliates, employees of member firms and, where applicable, member firms, in all of their professional and business activities, whether remunerated or voluntary. The ICAEW is committed to enforcing the Code through disciplining members who do not meet reasonable ethical and professional expectations of the public and other members.

A copy of the Code is included in the Member's Handbook and is available at www.icaew.com.

Members (or students) who are in doubt as to their ethical position may seek advice from the following ICAEW sources:

- The ethics advisory helpline within Technical Advisory Services. The advisor is exempt from the normal duty to report misconduct, hence details of the ethical problem will not be divulged to third parties, including other departments of the ICAEW.

- The Support Members Scheme. This is wider in scope than the Technical Advisory Services. The Scheme is run by volunteer members of the ICAEW from a wide range of backgrounds. It is a confidential, free service exempt from the duty to report misconduct and provides advice and help to **members** in difficulties.

- Money laundering helpline. This helpline offers advice on all aspects of complying with the money laundering legislation. The advisors can answer calls on both general issues concerning the regulations and reporting suspected illegal activity, and specific issues, which can be discussed anonymously.

9.2   Fundamental principles

Professional accountants are expected to follow the guidance contained in the fundamental principles in all of their professional and business activities. The professional accountant should also follow the requirements in the illustrations. However, he/she should be guided not just by the terms but also by **the spirit of the Code**.

The Code sets out five fundamental principles, the spirit of which must always be complied with:

1 Integrity

A professional accountant should be straightforward and honest in all professional and business relationships.

A professional accountant should not be associated with reports, returns, communications or other information where they believe that the information:

- Contains a materially false or misleading statement.

- Contains statements or information furnished recklessly.

- Omits or obscures information required to be included where such omission or obscurity would be misleading.

2 Objectivity

A professional accountant should not allow bias, conflict of interest or undue influence of others to override professional or business judgements.

3 Professional competence and due care

A professional accountant has an obligation to:

- Maintain professional knowledge and skill at the level required to ensure that a client/employer receives competent professional services based upon current developments in practice, legislation and techniques.

- Act diligently and in accordance with applicable technical and professional standards.

Professional competence may be divided into two separate phases:

- Attainment of professional competence – initial professional development
- Maintenance of professional competence – continuing professional development (CPD)

Diligence encompasses the responsibility to act in accordance with the requirements of an assignment, carefully, thoroughly and on a timely basis.

4 Confidentiality

A professional accountant should:

- Respect the confidentiality of information acquired as a result of professional and business relationships.

- Not disclose any such information to third parties without proper and specific authority (unless there is a legal or professional duty to disclose).

- Not use such information for the personal advantage of himself or third parties.

The professional accountant must maintain confidentiality even in a social environment and even after employment with the client/employer has ended.

A professional accountant may be required to disclose confidential information:

- Where disclosure is permitted by law and is authorised by the client or employer.
- Where disclosure is required by law, for example

    - Production of documents or other provision of evidence in the course of legal proceedings
    - Disclosure to the appropriate public authorities of infringements of the law that come to light

5 Professional behaviour

A professional accountant should comply with relevant laws and regulations and should avoid any action that discredits the profession.

In marketing and promoting themselves professional accountants should not bring the profession into disrepute. That is, they should not make:

- Exaggerated claims for the services they are able to offer, the qualifications they possess or experience they have gained.

- Disparaging references or unsubstantiated comparisons to the work of others.

Two sets of legislation which may have a particular impact on the work of a professional accountant are:

- Money laundering regulations

    Money laundering is the process by which money from illegal sources is made to appear legally derived and it is a criminal offence for a person knowingly to help another person launder the proceeds of criminal activity.

    In addition, there is a **duty to report**. Where a person discovers in the course of his/her work information which makes him/her believe or suspect, or where a person has reasonable grounds for being suspicious, that money laundering is occurring, this must be reported to the National Crime Agency. It is a criminal offence not to make such a report. Making such a report does not breach any duty of confidentiality owed by a professional accountant.

- Bribery Act 2010

    For individuals it is a criminal offence to:

    - Offer, promise or give a financial or other advantage to another person where the advantage is intended to induce improper performance of an activity or a function or as a reward for the improper performance of an activity or a function.

    - Request, agree to receive or accept a financial or other advantage intending that, in consequence (or as reward for), a relevant function or activity be performed improperly (even if performance is by another person).

    - Offer, promise or give a financial or other advantage to a foreign public official in order to obtain or retain business or retain or gain an advantage in the conduct of business.

    The definition of function or activity is wide and includes any activity connected with a business.

    A commercial organisation is guilty of a criminal offence if an employee, agent or subsidiary of the organisation bribes another person to obtain/retain business.

    It should be noted that the Act includes offences committed outside of the UK by UK citizens.

9.3 Threats

Compliance with these fundamental principles may potentially be threatened by a broad range of circumstances. Many of these threats fall into five categories:

A **Self-interest threat** the threat that a financial or other interest of a professional accountant or of an immediate or close family member will inappropriately influence the professional accountant's judgment or behaviour.

Examples of circumstances that may create such threats include:

- Financial interests, loans or guarantees
- Incentive compensation arrangements

- Inappropriate personal use of corporate assets
- Concern over employment security
- Commercial pressure from outside the employing organisation

B **Self-review threat** the threat that a professional accountant will not appropriately evaluate the results of a previous judgement made by the professional accountant.

C **Advocacy threat** the threat that a professional accountant will promote a client's or employer's position to the point that the professional accountant's objectivity is compromised.

D **Familiarity threat** the threat that due to a long or close relationship with a client or employer, a professional accountant will be too sympathetic to their interests or too accepting of their work.

Examples of circumstances that may create such threats include:

- A professional accountant in business, who is in a position to influence financial or non-financial reporting or business decisions, where an immediate or close family member would benefit from that influence.

- Long association with business contacts influencing business decisions.

- Acceptance of a gift or preferential treatment, unless the value is clearly insignificant.

E **Intimidation threat** the threat that a professional accountant will be deterred from acting objectively by threats, either actual or perceived.

Examples of circumstances that may create such threats include:

- Threat of dismissal or replacement in business, of yourself, or of a close or immediate family member, over a disagreement about the application of an accounting principle or the way in which financial information is to be reported.

- A dominant personality attempting to influence the decision making process, for example, with regard to the awarding of contracts or the application of an accounting principle.

9.4 Safeguards

There are two broad categories of safeguards which may eliminate or reduce such threats to an acceptable level:

Safeguards created by the profession, legislation or regulation

Examples are:

- Educational, training and experience requirements for entry into the profession

- Continuing professional development requirements

- Corporate governance regulations

- Professional standards

- Professional or regulatory monitoring and disciplinary procedures

- External review by a legally empowered third party of reports, returns, communication or information produced by a professional accountant

- Effective, well-publicised complaints systems operated by the employing organisation, the profession or a regulator, which enable colleagues, employers and members of the public to draw attention to unprofessional or unethical behaviour

- An explicitly stated duty to report breaches of ethical requirements

Safeguards in the work environment

Examples are:

- The employing organisation's systems of corporate oversight or other oversight structures

- The employing organisation's ethics and conduct programmes

- Recruitment procedures in the employing organisation emphasising the importance of employing high calibre, competent staff

- Strong internal controls

- Appropriate disciplinary processes

- Leadership that stresses the importance of ethical behaviour and the expectation that employees will act in an ethical manner

- Policies and procedures to implement and monitor the quality of employee performance

- Timely communication to all employees of the employing organisation's policies and procedures, including any changes made to them, and appropriate training and education given on such policies and procedures

- Policies and procedures to empower and encourage employees to communicate to senior levels within the employing organisation any ethical issues that concern them without fear of retribution

- Consultation with another appropriate professional accountant

9.5 Ethical conflict resolution

When evaluating compliance with the fundamental principles, a professional accountant may be required to resolve a conflict in complying with the fundamental principles.

A professional accountant may face pressure to:

- Act contrary to law or regulation.

- Act contrary to technical or professional standards.

- Facilitate unethical or illegal earnings management strategies.

- Lie to, or otherwise mislead, others in particular:

  - The auditor of the employing organisation
  - Regulators

- Issue, or otherwise be associated with, a financial or non-financial report that materially misrepresents the facts, for example:

  - Financial statements
  - Tax compliance
  - Legal compliance
  - Reports required by securities regulators

When dealing with such a conflict resolution the following should be considered:

- Relevant facts
- Relevant parties
- Ethical issues involved
- Fundamental principles related to the matter in question
- Established internal procedures
- Alternative courses of action

In this case he/she should:

- Determine the appropriate course of action that is consistent with the fundamental principles.
- Weigh up the possible consequences of each course of action.
- Consult with other appropriate persons if the matter remains unresolved.
- Obtain professional advice from the Institute or legal advisers, if it cannot be resolved.
- Finally if it remains unresolved refuse to remain associated with the matter creating the conflict.

9.6 Preparation and reporting of information

Accountants will often be involved in the preparation and reporting of information that may be:

- Made public or
- Used by others inside or outside the employing organisation.

The accountant should:

- Prepare or present such information fairly, honestly and in accordance with relevant professional standards.

- Present financial statements in accordance with applicable financial reporting standards.

- Maintain information for which (s)he is responsible in a manner which:

    - Describes clearly the true nature of the business transactions, assets or liabilities
    - Classifies and records information in a timely and proper manner
    - Represents the facts accurately and completely in all material respects

9.7 Acting with sufficient expertise

An accountant should only undertake significant tasks for which (s)he has, or can obtain, sufficient specific training or expertise.

Circumstances that threaten the ability of the accountant to perform duties with the appropriate degree of professional competence and due care include:

- Insufficient time for properly performing or completing the relevant duties
- Incomplete, restricted or otherwise inadequate information for performing the duties properly
- Insufficient experience, training and/or education
- Inadequate resources for the proper performance of the duties

Safeguards that may be considered include:

- Obtaining additional advice or training.
- Ensuring that there is adequate time available for performing the relevant duties.
- Obtaining assistance from someone with the necessary expertise.
- Consulting where appropriate with:

    - Superiors within the employing organisation, or
    - Independent experts, or
    - ICAEW

9.8 Financial interests

An accountant may have financial interests, or may know of financial interests of immediate or close family members, that could in certain circumstances, threaten compliance with the fundamental principles.

Examples of circumstances that may create self-interest threats, are if the accountant or family member:

- Holds a direct or indirect financial interest in the employing organisation and the value of that interest could be directly affected by decisions made by the accountant.

- Is eligible for a profit related bonus and the value of that bonus could be directly affected by a decision made by the accountant.

- Holds, directly or indirectly, share options in the employing organisation, the value of which could be directly affected by decisions made by the accountant.

- Holds, directly or indirectly, share options in the employing organisation which are, or will soon be, eligible for conversion.

- May qualify for share options in the employing organisation or performance-related bonuses if certain targets are achieved.

Safeguards against such threats may include:

- Policies and procedures for a committee independent of management to determine the level or form of remuneration of senior management.

- Disclosure of all relevant interests and of any plans to trade in relevant shares to those charged with the governance of the employing organisation, in accordance with any internal policies.

- Consultation, where appropriate, with superiors within the employing organisation.

- Consultation, where appropriate, with those charged with the governance of the employing organisation or relevant professional bodies.

- Internal and external audit procedures.

- Up-to-date education on ethical issues and the legal restrictions and other regulations around potential insider trading.

9.9 Inducements

An accountant, or immediate or close family, may be offered an inducement such as:

- Gifts
- Hospitality
- Preferential treatment
- Inappropriate appeals to friendship or loyalty

An accountant should assess the risk associated with all such offers and consider whether the following actions should be taken:

- Immediately inform higher levels of management or those charged with governance of the employing organisation.

- Inform third parties of the offer for example a professional body or the employer of the individual who made the offer, or seek legal advice.

- Advise immediate or close family members of relevant threats and safeguards where they are potentially in positions that might result in offers of inducements (for example as a result of their employment situation).

- Inform higher levels of management or those charged with governance of the employing organisation where immediate or close family members are employed by competitors or potential suppliers of that organisation.

9.10 Conflicts of interest

An accountant should take reasonable steps to identify circumstances that could pose a conflict of interest.

Examples might be:

- An accountant in public practice, competing directly with a client, or having a joint venture or similar arrangement with a major competitor of a client.

- An accountant performing services for clients whose interests are in conflict.

- Clients are in dispute with each other in relation to the matter or transaction in question.

Safeguards should include:

- Notifying the client of the firm's business interest or activities that may represent a conflict of interest, and obtaining their consent to act in such circumstances.

- Notifying all known relevant parties that the professional accountant is acting for two or more parties in respect of a matter where their respective interests are in conflict and obtaining their consent to so act.

- Notifying the client that the accountant does not act exclusively for any one client in the provision of proposed services and obtaining their consent to so act.

9.11 General duty to report

Under the ICAEW's Bye-laws it is the duty of every member where it is in the public interest to do so, to report to the Institute any facts or matters indicating that a member and/or firm or provisional member may have become liable to disciplinary action. In determining whether it is in the public interest to report such facts or matters, regard shall be had to such guidance as the Council shall give from time to time.

This general duty to report to the Institute under the Bye-laws is separate from the duty to report money laundering (see above) to the National Crime Agency; this latter duty arises from legislation.

Worked example: Ethical considerations

You are a reporting accountant in a company. Your immediate manager is a very forceful, domineering individual and you have accepted his views over the last two years on the level of work in progress. He has given you specific assurance that work in progress has increased by 200% during the current reporting period and instructed you to report this level in the monthly management accounts. The year end draft financial accounts show that the organisation has only just met its business plan financial targets.

Evidence then becomes available (which you were not aware of when the draft accounts were produced) to indicate that the work in progress had not increased by anywhere near the rate advised by your manager.

How should you approach this?

Solution

Key fundamental principles

Integrity – Will you be able to demonstrate that the accounts are true and fair without re-drafting?

Objectivity – How would you maintain your objectivity given that your immediate manager is such a forceful character?

Professional competence and due care – Are the draft accounts prepared in accordance with technical and professional standards?

Professional behaviour – How should you proceed so as not to discredit yourself?

Discussion

Identify relevant facts: Consider the business' policies, procedures and guidelines, accounting standards, best practice, Code of Ethics, applicable laws and regulations. Is the evidence that work in progress is incorrectly stated supported by other documentation, for example, any hard copy relating to the valuation, or analytical review of cost of sales, margins and cash flows?

Identify affected parties: Key affected parties are you and your immediate manager. Other possible affected parties are the next levels of management, recipients of management accounts and the draft financial accounts, finance, purchasing, accounts payable, human resources, internal audit, audit committee, the Board, external auditors, shareholders and financial backers.

Who would be involved in resolution? Consider not just who should be involved but also for what reason and the timing of their involvement. Have you thought of contacting the ICAEW for advice and guidance? Have you discussed this matter with your immediate line manager in light of all the available evidence and possible consequences? Can you discuss this matter with recipients of the management and financial accounts? At what point will you consider involving other affected parties?

Possible course of action

Check the relevant facts by corroborating with other available documentation, for example, cost of sales calculations, margins, previous inventory counts and other financial information.

Discuss the matter with your immediate line manager to determine an appropriate course of action, for example, undertaking another inventory count.

If you feel that your manager's response is not appropriate, discuss the matter with recipients of the management accounts and draft financial accounts and the next level of management.

Next stages could include discussion with senior management, internal audit, audit committee, the board of directors, external auditors or other actions indicated in internal whistle-blowing procedures.

During the resolution process it may be helpful to document your involvement, the substance of the discussions held, who else was involved, what decisions were made and why.

Interactive question 3: Ethical considerations [Difficulty level: Intermediate]

Your employer has put you in charge of a project which when you considered it carefully requires expertise that you do not have. You are uneasy about doing the job given that you do not have the necessary expertise and are uncertain about what to say to your employer.

Fill in the proforma below.

Key fundamental principles

Discussion

Possible course of action

See **Answer** at the end of this chapter.

9.12 Practical significance

Accountants working within a financial reporting environment can come under pressure to improve the financial performance or financial position of their employer. Finance managers who are part of the team putting together the results for publication must be careful to withstand pressures from their non-finance colleagues to indulge in reporting practices which dress up short-term performance and position. Financial managers must be conscious of their professional obligations and seek appropriate assistance from colleagues, peers or independent sources.

Summary and Self-test

Summary

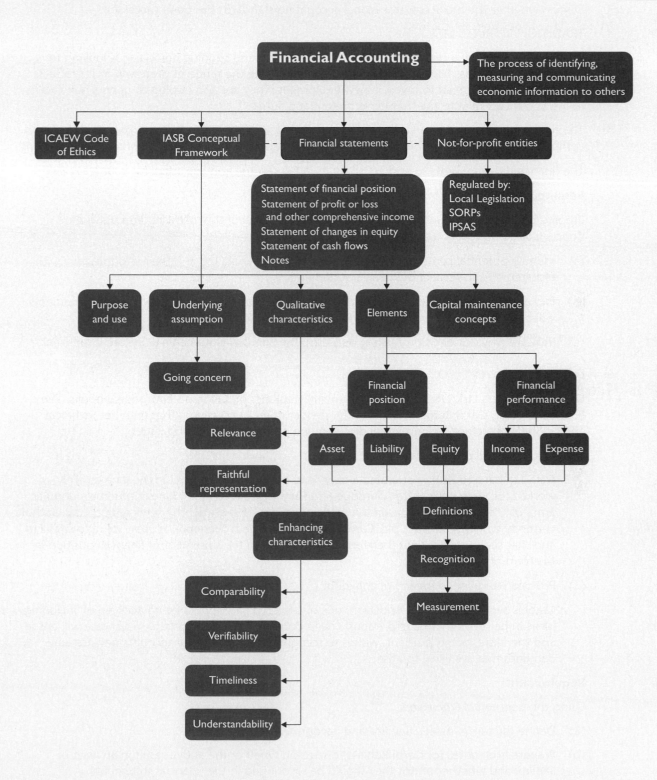

Self-test

Answer the following questions.

1   What are the conditions which the *Conceptual Framework* identifies as necessary if the going concern basis is to be used for the preparation of financial statements?

2   According to the *Conceptual Framework* what are the characteristics of information which is **faithfully represented**?

3   Discuss whether the move towards global accounting standards has been successful.

4   TRADITIONAL FRUITS LTD

Traditional Fruits Ltd, a Herefordshire based fruit bottling and canning company, is looking to expand its operations. The directors are hoping to increase the range of preserved fruit products and in doing so will need to invest in new equipment. They are also hoping to open a new facility in the South East near to the fruit farms of Kent and Surrey.

The finance director has been asked to prepare a résumé of the financial performance of the company in order that possible providers of finance can assess the future potential of the company.

The finance director wants to address all issues in her résumé and has asked for your assistance.

Requirements

Prepare brief notes for the finance director, addressing each of the following and using the *Conceptual Framework* as a source of reference.

(a)   Identify potential providers of finance for Traditional Fruits Ltd and their information requirements in respect of financial statements.

(b)   Explain the terms 'performance' and 'position' and identify which of the financial statements will assist the user in evaluating performance and position.

(c)   Indicate why, for decision-making purposes, the financial statements alone are insufficient.

5   DAVIES AND SAYERS LTD

Davies and Sayers Ltd (D&S Ltd) is a well-known publisher of children's educational books. The finance director, Carol Roberts, is known for her commercial acumen rather than her technical ability. She is therefore seeking your advice on two particular accounting issues.

(1)   Value of head of publishing

D&S Ltd have recently appointed a new head of publishing, Jane Lindsay. Jane recently worked for a key competitor, Surridge and Hughes plc (S&H plc). Jane is extremely popular amongst the leading authors in the market and is sure to attract the services of certain authors currently working for S&H plc. Carol believes that Jane is therefore of great value to D&S Ltd and that such value should therefore be recognised in the statement of financial position in the form of an asset.

(2)   Provision for alleged breach of copyright

Carol is aware that Poppy Anderson, one of D&S Ltd's authors, is being accused of 'including ideas in her texts that have previously been published'. Carol is certain a legal case will ensue and therefore, being prudent, wishes to recognise a liability in the accounts now for any damages that are likely to arise.

Requirements

Using the *Conceptual Framework*

(a)   Define the terms 'asset', 'liability' and 'recognised'.

(b)   Prepare brief notes for Carol Roberts, discussing whether the above result in an asset or liability and whether or not they should be recognised in the financial statements.

Note: You are **not** required to refer to specific IFRSs that may be relevant.

6   TATTANHOE PLC

You are the financial controller of Tattanhoe plc, a holding company listed on the UK stock exchange. Together with the finance director, you have held conversations with external consultants about accounting policy implementation issues. You have discussed a number of areas where the finance director believes the application of the requirements of an IFRS would not give a 'true and fair view' for users. The finance director has sent you the following extract from a note prepared by the consultants.

'Accounting policies

It is essential that the accounting policies selected when implementing IFRS result in financial statements that give a fair presentation. The application of the principle of substance over form is integral in achieving this.

The choice of accounting policies is a matter of judgement and careful consideration is required particularly where you wish to override the requirements of an accounting standard.'

Tattanhoe plc's UK subsidiaries prepare their financial statements in accordance with UK GAAP, but none of them are eligible to use the FRSSE. The UK Accounting Standards Board (ASB) approach to convergence will have a significant effect on the future accounting policies to be adopted by these subsidiaries.'

The finance director wishes to discuss the above extract with you. He has a strong personality and he is adamant that non-compliance with IFRS may be justified where it does not give a true and fair view.

Requirements

(a)   Prepare notes for your meeting with the finance director:

   (i)   Explaining the concept of 'fair presentation' and comparing it with 'true and fair view'.
   (2 marks)

   (ii) Explaining the concept of 'substance over form' and its relationship to 'fair presentation'.
   (2 marks)

   (iii) Explaining the circumstances in which non-compliance with the detailed provisions of an IFRS is justified.
   (2 marks)

   (iv) Describing the ASB's current proposals for convergence with IFRS and the reporting issues this will raise for Tattanhoe plc's UK subsidiaries.
   (3 marks)

(b)   Identify the ethical issues and actions, from the above scenario, that you should consider arising from the adoption of IFRS and your professional relationship with the finance director.
   (3 marks)

   (12 marks)

7   DARLAT LTD

You are the financial controller of Darlat Ltd which currently prepares financial statements in accordance with UK GAAP. Your finance director has been in discussions with your corporate reporting advisors about whether to move to reporting under IFRS and has forwarded to you the following note received from them:

'There are a number of differences between the UK GAAP and the IFRS recognition and measurement rules. Using information on our files, we have conducted a preliminary review of how your most recent financial statements might change if you had reported under IFRS. Below we show our estimate of the effect on equity at the end of the last year, together with brief notes on the different rules.

	£'000	£'000
Equity as reported under UK GAAP		6,688
Adjustments:		
Amortisation of goodwill acquired in business combination		250
Valuation of property measured under revaluation model	1,200	
Depreciation thereof	(350)	
		850
Development expenditure	180	
Amortisation thereof	(40)	
		140
Equity as reported under IFRS		7,928

Existing UK GAAP is now being replaced by FRS 102. As you are not eligible to use the FRSSE, you have the option to report under FRS 102 or under IFRS.

The following table shows the effect of this reporting move on recognition and measurement.

Recognition and measurement rules	Old UK GAAP	New UK GAAP	IFRS
Goodwill	You, like most UK companies, amortise goodwill over 20 years	Goodwill should normally be amortised over five years	Goodwill amortisation is prohibited
Property – revaluation model – basis of valuation	Existing use value, that is taking into account what you use it for	Fair value, that is the open market value taking account of all possible uses	Fair value, that is the open market value taking account of all possible uses
Development expenditure	You, like most UK companies, choose to write off development expenditure as incurred	You will still have the choice of whether to capitalise or write off	Recognition as an asset is compulsory when certain conditions are met

We would like to discuss these issues with you at an early date.'

Your finance director is aware that those making economic decisions use financial information for various purposes, including for the assessment of financial performance. He is pleased that the introduction of IFRS increases equity, remarking: 'if equity increases, then profit must increase both in the year of change and in future years. This will improve our performance. Shouldn't we move to IFRS as soon as possible?'

Requirement

In advance of a meeting with your finance director to discuss his remarks, prepare bullet-point notes about the likely effect on performance if Darlat Ltd adopts IFRS. **(8 marks)**

Now go back to the Learning objectives in the Introduction. If you are satisfied you have achieved these objectives, please tick them off.

Technical reference

Point to note: The whole of the *Conceptual Framework* and *Preface to International Financial Reporting Standards* is examinable. The paragraphs listed below are the key references you should be familiar with.

1 What is financial reporting?

- Financial reporting is the provision of financial information about a reporting entity that is useful to existing and potential investors, lenders and other creditors in making decisions about providing resources to the entity.
  Concept Frame (OB2)

- Financial statements comprise statement of financial position, statement of profit or loss and other comprehensive income, statement of changes in equity, statement of cash flows and notes.
  IAS 1 (10)

2 Purpose and use of financial statements

- Users' core need is for information for making economic decisions.
  Concept Frame (OB2)

- Objective is to provide information on financial position (the entity's economic resources and the claims against it) and about transactions and other events that change those resources and claims.
  Concept Frame (OB12)

- Financial position:
  Concept Frame (OB13)
  - Resources and claims
  - Help identify entity's strengths and weaknesses
  - Liquidity and solvency

- Changes in economic resources and claims:
  Concept Frame (OB15-16)
  - Help assess prospects for future cash flows.
  - How well have management made efficient and effective use of the resources.

- Financial performance reflected by accrual accounting.
  Concept Frame (OB17)

- Financial performance reflected by past cash flows.
  Concept Frame (OB20)

3 Qualitative characteristics of useful financial information

- Two fundamental qualitative characteristics are relevance and faithful representation.
  Concept Frame (QC5)

- Relevance = capable of making a difference to decisions
  Concept Frame (QC6)
  - Predictive and confirmatory values
    Concept Frame (QC7)
  - Materiality
    Concept Frame (QC11)

- Faithful representation
  Concept Frame (QC12)
  - Complete, neutral and free from error

- Four enhancing qualitative characteristics
  Concept Frame (QC19)
  - Comparability, verifiability, timeliness and understandability

4 Cost constraint on useful financial reporting

- Costs (of preparing and analysing) financial information must be justified by the benefits of reporting it.
  Concept Frame (QC35)

5 Underlying assumption

- Going concern
  Concept Frame (4.1)

6 Elements of financial statements

- **Asset**: A resource controlled by the entity as a result of past events and from which future economic benefits are expected to flow to the entity.

  Concept Frame (4.4)

- **Liability**: A present obligation of the entity arising from past events, the settlement of which is expected to lead to the outflow from the entity of resources embodying economic benefits.

  Concept Frame (4.4)

- **Equity**: The residual interest in assets less liabilities, that is net assets.

  Concept Frame (4.4)

- **Income** (comprising revenue and gains): Increases in economic benefits in the form of asset increases/liability decreases, other than contributions from equity.

  Concept Frame (4.25, 4.29)

- **Expenses** (including losses): Decreases in economic benefits in the form of asset decreases/liability increases, other than distributions to equity.

  Concept Frame (4.25, 4.33)

7 Recognition

- An asset or a liability should be recognised in financial statements if:

  Concept Frame (4.38)

  - It is probable that any future economic benefits associated with the item will flow to or from the entity, and
  - Its cost or value can be measured with reliability.

8 Measurement

- Historical cost
- Current cost
- Realisable value
- Present value

  Concept Frame (4.55)

9 Capital maintenance

- Financial capital:
  - Monetary
  - Constant purchasing power
- Physical capital

  Concept Frame (4.57)

10 IASB

- Objectives of IASB
- Scope and authority of IFRS
- Due process re IFRS development

  Preface (6)
  Preface (7-16)
  Preface (17)

11 Fair presentation

- Financial statements are required to give a fair presentation of the financial position, financial performance and cash flows of an entity.

  IAS 1 (15)

  In the UK financial statements must present a true and fair view.

  CA 2006

12 Not-for-profit entities

- Regulated by:
  - Local legislation
  - SORPs
  - IPSAS
- Wording and format of IAS 1 financial statements may not be suitable for not-for-profit entities.

  IAS 1 (5)

Answers to Interactive questions

Answer to Interactive question 1

Question	Answer
(a) Oak plc has purchased a patent for £40,000. The patent gives the company sole use of a particular manufacturing process which will save £6,000 a year for the next five years.	This is an asset, albeit an intangible one. There is a past event, control and future economic benefit (through cost saving).
(b) Elm plc paid John Brown £20,000 to set up a car repair shop, on condition that priority treatment is given to cars from the company's fleet.	This cannot be classed as an asset. Elm plc has no control over the car repair shop and it is difficult to argue that there are future economic benefits.
(c) Sycamore plc provides a warranty with every washing machine sold.	This is a liability. The business has an obligation to fulfil the terms of the warranty. The liability would be recognised when the warranty is issued rather than when a claim is made.

Answer to Interactive question 2

- Charities
- Friendly societies
- Public sector hospitals
- Public sector schools
- Clubs
- Associations
- Local councils
- Public services
- Trade unions
- Societies
- Housing associations
- Colleges

Answer to Interactive question 3

Key fundamental principles

Professional competence and due care – Do you have the necessary skills and experience to undertake the work?

Professional behaviour – How should you proceed so as not to discredit yourself?

Discussion

Identify relevant facts: Consider the business' policies, procedures and guidelines, accounting standards, best practice, Code of Ethics, applicable laws and regulations. Can you demonstrate your lack of expertise in this area, the potential impact on the organisation and offer alternatives? Can you make reference to the Institute's professional values and disciplinary process?

Identify affected parties: Key affected parties are you and your employer. Other possible affected parties are the human resources, internal audit, external auditors, shareholders and financial backers.

Who would be involved in resolution? Consider not just who should be involved but also for what reason and the timing of their involvement. Have you thought of contacting the Institute for advice and guidance? Do you have a trusted colleague with whom you can discuss your position? At what point will you consider involving the next level of management and human resources?

Possible course of action

Discuss your lack of expertise with your employer and suggest clearly defining the scope of the project and a course of action for addressing this issue, for example employing a person with the necessary expertise.

During the discussion, focus on the potential consequences to both the business and you personally of undertaking this project.

Explain that employing a person with the necessary expertise does not remove your obligation to ensure that the work is conducted in accordance with accounting standards, laws and regulations.

If your employer does not agree to the suggested course of action, it may be appropriate to discuss the matter with the next level of management.

If the response from management is not satisfactory, it may be necessary to involve the human resources department, the internal audit team or the Board.

During the resolution process it may be helpful to document your involvement, the substance of the discussions held, who else was involved, what decisions were made and why.

Answers to Self-test

1   Neither the intention nor the need to liquidate or curtail materially the scale of its operations.

2   It should be complete, neutral and free from error.

3   **Has the move towards global accounting standards been successful?**

The move towards global accounting standards has taken great strides in the last decade. International accounting standards themselves have improved, with the elimination of contradictory alternatives and the creation of an open and independent standard setting organisation. This in turn has led to greater acceptance of these standards, particularly in 2005 with the compulsory adoption of IFRS for consolidated financial statements by all quoted companies in the EU.

Since the EU successes there has been further progress on general global convergence. The IASB and the US FASB have been involved in the development of a common conceptual framework. There is also a Memorandum of Understanding between the IASB and FASB in respect of IFRS/US GAAP convergence. This has led to a number of short-term convergence projects between IFRS and US GAAP aimed to reduce differences in accounting practice such as the revised version of IAS 23 *Borrowing Costs,* which brings the IFRS more into line with the US method of capitalising appropriate borrowing costs. Progress has been such that non-US companies listed in the US no longer have to reconcile profit and equity in their IFRS financial statements to the equivalent figures under US GAAP.

The Securities and Exchange Commission (the US regulator) has published proposals (in the form of a 'roadmap') under which, subject to satisfactory progress being made in a number of areas, it would become compulsory in 2015 or 2016 for US entities to adopt IFRS in place of US GAAP. However progress on this has slowed in recent years.

Also, there is no global system of enforcement, and so it is too early to say if IFRS are being adopted properly. Some countries with their own highly developed accounting standards see the adoption of IFRS as a backward step, whereas other countries see IFRS as unnecessarily complicated.

There is also the assumption that the globalisation of accounting standards is a good thing. Recent developments in IFRS have focussed on quoted companies in the western world; they may not be suitable for all types and sizes of business organisation, or for all stages of economic development.

4   TRADITIONAL FRUITS LTD

(a) **Potential providers of finance**

- The existing shareholders of the company and potential new shareholders – through a new issue of share capital.
- Existing and future lenders and creditors to the company.

Information requirements

- The profit before interest of Traditional Fruits Ltd (TF Ltd), to determine risk.
- The trend of profitability of TF Ltd together with a history of dividend payments. This will enable them to assess return and risk of their investment.
- The financial structure of TF Ltd, to determine the level of debt finance as a measure of risk.
- TF Ltd's liquidity or ability to pay out dividends and redeem share capital.
- TF Ltd's ability to generate cash and the timing and certainty of its generation.
- The liquidity of TF Ltd and its ability to repay interest and capital instalments.
- The existing level of debt and any security over that debt.

(b) **Performance and position and the financial statements which assist in evaluation**

Performance

The financial performance of a company comprises the return it obtains on the resources it controls. Performance can be measured in terms of the profits of the company and its ability to generate cash flows.

Management will be assessed on their skill in achieving the highest level of performance, given the resources available to them.

Information on performance can be found in

- The statement of profit or loss and other comprehensive income.
- The statement of changes in equity.
- The statement of cash flows.

Position

The financial position of the company is evaluated by reference to:

(i) Its economic resources and claims.
(ii) Its capital structure, ie its level of debt finance and shareholders' funds.
(iii) Its liquidity and solvency.

The user of the financial statements can then make assessments on the level of risk, ability to generate cash, the likely distribution of this cash and the ability of the company to adapt to changing circumstances.

The statement of financial position is the prime source of information on a company's position but the statement of cash flows will also indicate a company's cash position over a period of time.

(c) **Financial statements – inherent limitations as a tool of decision-making**

Financial statements are prepared by reference to a relatively rigid set of accounting standards applicable to all companies, regardless of the sectors of the economy they operate in. As a result, information for individual and specialised companies may not be forthcoming. Further, the preparation of financial statements is based on estimates and judgements by the management and therefore are not a source of totally verifiable information.

Financial statements primarily use the historical cost convention. They can identify trends from the past which may be relevant to the future, but they are not forecasts and are therefore less helpful when making predictions.

In deciding whether or not to invest in a company, a decision-maker will also want access to non-financial data not contained in the financial statements such as

(i) A discussion of business risks and opportunities.
(ii) An evaluation of the quality of management.
(iii) A narrative analysis of position and performance.

5 DAVIES AND SAYERS LTD

(a) **Terms**

Asset

An asset is:

(i) A resource controlled by the entity
(ii) As a result of past events, and
(iii) From which future economic benefits are expected to flow into the entity.

Legal ownership is not an essential part of the definition of an asset, even though such ownership is indicative that the control criterion has been met. But the key is whether the entity controls a resource, so having the continued use of an item will often be sufficient evidence of control.

Liability

A liability is

(i) A present obligation of the entity
(ii) Arising from past events

(iii) The settlement of which is expected to result in an outflow from the entity of resources embodying economic benefits.

An obligation arises from a legally-enforceable contract, but it may also result from an entity's normal business practices.

Recognised

Recognition means that an item is recorded in the financial statements. An asset or liability is recognised if

(i) It is probable that any future economic benefit associated with the item will flow to or from the entity, and

(ii) The cost or value can be measured with reliability.

(b) Notes for Carol Roberts

(1) Value of head of publishing

Existence of an asset

If you apply the definition of an asset from the *Conceptual Framework* to the head of publishing, Jane Lindsay, it is possible to argue that she has the characteristics of an asset.

As a full-time employee, Jane is likely to have a contract which was signed prior to the end of the reporting period. The legal contract will prevent Jane working for any other company, giving D&S Ltd unrestricted access to any benefits she may provide.

If Jane is able to persuade new authors to join the D&S team, she is creating a flow of future economic benefits – on the assumption that the authors' new work will prove salesworthy.

However, there is uncertainty over

(i) The enforceability of Jane's contract: she may recruit new authors to D&S Ltd, but within a short period of time might leave and join a new company; her authors are then likely to follow her.

(ii) The revenue stream to result from the new authors: they have not as yet been recruited and it is only possible that they will be; there are also no guarantees as to the quality of their future work and therefore the level of revenue they are likely to generate.

Therefore, at this stage we cannot conclude that an asset exists.

Recognition of the asset

An item is recognised when it is included in the financial statements at a monetary value. Carol Roberts is proposing to include Jane Lindsay as an asset in the statement of financial position. However, certain criteria should be applied prior to recognition.

(i) Is there sufficient evidence of the existence of the asset?

(ii) Can the asset be measured at a monetary amount with sufficient reliability?

(2) Provision for breach of copyright

Existence of a liability

At this stage Poppy Anderson has been accused of breach of copyright. From the information given, there is no opinion from lawyers as to the strength of the case or estimate of the possible value of any claim. Therefore, whilst a past transaction has allegedly occurred, there is insufficient evidence of, and uncertainty over, whether an obligation exists.

Recognition of the liability

To recognise the liability in the financial statements there must be sufficient evidence of the existence of the liability and it should be probable that economic benefit will flow from the entity. In this case, there is insufficient evidence of a liability and we are unable to reliably measure any potential liability.

The case is at far too early a stage to estimate the possible loss. It would therefore be over-prudent and inappropriate to recognise the liability in the financial statements.

(a) **Notes for meeting**

(i)   **Fair presentation and true and fair view**

IAS 1 *Presentation of Financial Statements* describes the concept of fair presentation. Fair presentation involves representing faithfully the effect of transactions, other events and conditions in accordance with the definitions and recognition criteria in the *Conceptual Framework*.

This is developed by stating that the application of IFRS, interpretations and additional disclosures will result in fair presentation.

The traditional UK approach required financial statements to comply with the Companies Act (and therefore UK standards) and give a true and fair view. True could be approximated to 'represent faithfully' and fair to 'fair presentation'. IAS 1 links them by stating that compliance with standards will give a fair presentation. As a result there is unlikely to be any difference between the two.

(ii) **Substance over form and fair presentation**

Most transactions are reasonably straightforward and their substance (their commercial effect) is the same as their legal form. In some complex transactions the true substance may not be readily apparent. Their legal form may not adequately express the true commercial effect of such transactions.

Where this is the case, it may not be sufficient to account for them by merely recording their form. The financial statements should represent commercial substance, not just legal form (substance over form). If a transaction gives rise to an asset or liability (as defined in the *Conceptual Framework*), it should be accounted for on this basis even if this is different from its legal form. Applying the definitions of an asset and a liability identifies the appropriate accounting treatment.

The *Conceptual Framework* identifies faithful representation as one of the two fundamental qualitative characteristics of useful financial information. If information is to represent faithfully the transactions it purports to represent, then they should be accounted for in accordance with their substance and economic reality and not merely their legal form. The substance may not be consistent with the legal form of a transaction. An example is a sale and repurchase agreement.

(iii) **Non-compliance with IFRS**

IAS 1 allows non-compliance with a standard (or interpretation) only where management concludes that compliance would be so misleading as to conflict with the objectives of financial statements set out in the *Conceptual Framework*. However this is only where the relevant regulatory framework requires, or does not prohibit, such a departure.

The standard uses the phrase 'where management concludes' which may indicate that there is a margin for those preparing the financial statements to use this exception where they believe it is appropriate. However, IAS 1 talks about this coming about 'in extremely rare circumstances'. To all intents and purposes, these circumstances will never occur.

Inappropriate accounting policies or non-compliance are not rectified by disclosure of the policies adopted or by description in the notes to the financial statements.

The true and fair override is a UK concept and not permitted under IFRSs.

(iv) **Convergence proposals and practical implications**

FRS 100, FRS 101 and FRS 102 have now been issued with the intention of bringing financial reporting for UK companies into line with IFRS.

Because none of the subsidiaries can use the FRSSE, they will be affected by the new standards as follows:

*   They may be able to report under the Reduced Disclosure Framework set out in FRS 101.

*   As an alternative they will be able to report under FRS 102 based upon the IASB's IFRS for SMEs.

This will require all the subsidiaries to change their reporting processes from UK GAAP to IFRS. New systems will be necessary, with implications for IT and staff training.

(b) Issues and actions

The Finance Director has a strong personality. He may use his position to dominate. This may result in him exerting influence on those around him, including the financial controller, so they acquiesce to his requirements.

Whilst IFRS narrow down the range of possible alternatives, the adoption of accounting policies still requires judgement and much is left to the discretion of management. It is essential that accounting policy selections generate information that is free from bias and presents faithfully the substance of the transactions.

The financial controller needs to use his professional skills and judgement. It may be appropriate to consult the Code of Ethics, the local district society for confidential support or to take advice from the ethical help lines offered by the ICAEW.

7   DARLAT LTD

Notes for meeting with FD
Subject: **Performance measurement under IFRS**
Prepared by: **Financial controller**
Date: **xx/xx/xx**

- Comparability is one of the qualitative characteristics which makes financial statement information useful.

- Changing from one set of accounting rules to another will make the FRS 102 or IFRS figures for the current year not comparable with the UK GAAP figures for the previous year.

- Normal comparability rules require restatement of the previous period under IFRS or FRS 102, so the previous period equity will probably increase as well.

- So performance in the current year may not be assessed as having improved.

- Financial statement users have three key measures: cash flow, profitability and gearing
    - Cash flow: cash flows are unaltered by changing recognition/measurement rules for assets and liabilities in the statement of financial position.
      No performance improvement (no change at all).
    - Profitability: increase in equity = increase in capital employed, so, other things being equal, ROCE (profit before interest and tax as % of (equity and interest-bearing liabilities)) will go down, not up.
        - Profit will go up as a result of no goodwill amortisation if IFRS is adopted. However it should be reviewed for impairment.
        - Under FRS 102 amortisation will normally be over a shorter period and goodwill should still be reviewed for impairment. This could reduce profit.
        - Profit will go down as a result of higher property values – higher depreciation in future years.
        - It is not clear what effect recognising development expenditure as an asset will have in future years. Depreciation will go up, but perhaps by less than positive effect of capitalisation of expenditure written off under UK GAAP.
        - Net effect may be performance deterioration.
    - Gearing: equity goes up, but no change in interest-bearing liabilities. So gearing (interest-bearing liabilities as % of equity) goes down.
        - Improvement in performance

CHAPTER 2

Format of financial statements

Introduction

Examination context

Topic List

Introduction

Learning objectives

Tick off

- Explain the purpose and principles underlying IAS 1 *Presentation of Financial Statements* ☐

- Prepare and present the financial statements (or extracts), of an entity according to its accounting policies and appropriate IFRSs ☐

- Calculate the amounts to be included in the equity section of the statement of financial position of a not-for-profit entity ☐

- Prepare the statement of cash flows of an individual entity in accordance with IAS 7 ☐

Specific syllabus references for this chapter are: 2a, 2b, 2c, 2e, 2g, 2h.

Syllabus links

You will have been introduced to the basics of company accounts in the Accounting paper. In this paper however, you are expected to have a much more detailed understanding of the preparation of financial statements and a thorough knowledge of the regulation in this area. This knowledge will be assumed at the Advanced Stage.

Examination context

The ability to prepare financial statements for an individual entity (including the statement of cash flows) is a fundamental part of the Financial Accounting and Reporting syllabus and has a syllabus weighting of 60%.

In the examination, candidates may be required to:

- Discuss the way IAS 1 builds on the principles contained in the IASB *Conceptual Framework*, including the following matters:
  - Fair/faithful presentation
  - Accrual basis
  - Going concern
  - Materiality

- Draft, in accordance with IAS 1:
  - A statement of financial position
  - A statement of profit or loss
  - A statement of profit or loss and other comprehensive income
  - A statement of changes in equity
  - Notes to the financial statements

  Candidates may be provided with trial balance/nominal ledger information or draft financial statements may be provided which need finalising.

- Prepare the equity section of the statement of financial position of a not-for-profit entity from financial and other data

- Prepare a statement of cash flows in accordance with IAS 7, or extracts therefrom, from an entity's statement of profit or loss and statement of financial position or finalise a draft statement of cash flows

- Explain and illustrate the differences between the relevant treatment under IFRS and UK GAAP

1 IAS 1 *Presentation of Financial Statements*

Section overview

- IAS 1 applies to all general purpose financial statements.

- Financial statements provide information about:

  - Financial position
  - Financial performance
  - Cash flows

- Financial statements are also regulated by local laws and regulations.

1.1 Objective

IAS 1 *Presentation of Financial Statements* prescribes the basis for the presentation of financial statements, so as to ensure comparability with:

- The **entity's own financial statements** of previous periods, and
- The **financial statements of other entities**.

IAS 1 must be applied to all **general purpose financial statements** prepared in accordance with IFRSs, ie those intended to meet the needs of users who are not in a position to demand reports tailored to their specific needs. IAS 1 is concerned with overall considerations about the **minimum content** of a set of financial statements; detailed rules about recognition, measurement and disclosures of specific transactions are then contained in other standards.

Whilst the terminology used was designed for profit-orientated businesses, it can be used, with modifications, for **not-for-profit entities**.

1.2 Purpose of financial statements

The objective of general purpose financial statements is to provide information about the **financial position, financial performance and cash flows** of an entity that is useful to a wide range of users in making economic decisions. They also show the result of **management stewardship** of the resources of the entity. (This is very similar to the purpose stated by the *Conceptual Framework* covered in Chapter 1.)

In order to achieve this, information is provided about the following aspects of the entity's results:

- Assets
- Liabilities
- Equity
- Income and expenses (including gains and losses)
- Other changes in equity
- Cash flows

Additional information is contained in the notes.

IAS 1 looks at the statement of financial position and statement of profit or loss and other comprehensive income. We will not give all the detailed disclosures as some are outside the scope of your syllabus. Instead we will look at a **'proforma' set of accounts** based on the Standard.

1.3 Components of financial statements

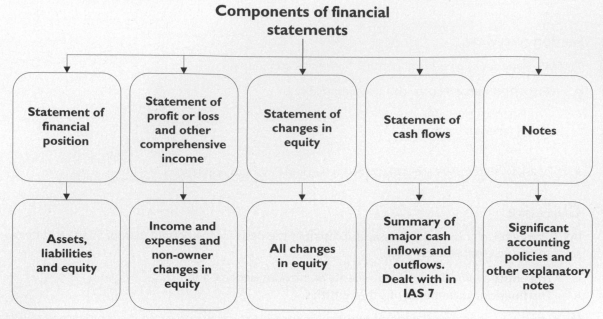

Although the financial statements may be included as part of a wider document IAS 1 requires that they should be **clearly identified and distinguished** from other information presented.

1.4 Fair presentation

Financial statements should **present fairly** the financial position, financial performance and cash flows of an entity as discussed in Chapter 1.

IAS 1 expands on this principle as follows:

- Compliance with IFRS should be **disclosed**.

- Financial statements can only be described as complying with IFRS if they comply with all **the requirements** of IFRS.

- Use of **inappropriate accounting** policies **cannot be rectified** either by disclosure or explanatory material.

1.5 Going concern

As we saw in Chapter 1 going concern is referred to by the *Conceptual Framework* as the **underlying assumption**. It means that an entity is normally viewed as continuing in operation for the **foreseeable future**. Financial statements are prepared on the going concern basis unless management either intends to liquidate the entity or to cease trading or has no realistic alternative but to do so.

IAS 1 makes the following points:

- In assessing whether the entity is a going concern management must look at least **12 months** into the future measured from the **end of the reporting period** (not from the date the financial statements are approved).

- **Uncertainties** that may cast significant doubt on the entity's ability to continue should be **disclosed**.

- If the going concern assumption is not followed that fact must be disclosed together with:
  - The **basis** on which financial statements have been prepared
  - The **reasons** why the entity is not considered to be a going concern

1.6 Accrual basis of accounting

Financial statements other than the statement of cash flows, must be prepared on the **accrual basis** of accounting.

Definition

Accrual basis of accounting: Items are recognised as assets, liabilities, equity, income and expenses when they satisfy the definitions and recognition criteria for those elements in the *Conceptual Framework*.

Point to note: The definition refers to the definitions and recognition criteria of the *Conceptual Framework*. The effect is that:

- Transactions are recognised **when they occur** (and not when the relevant cash is received or paid).
- They are **recorded** in the financial statements of the **periods to which they relate**.

According to the accrual assumption, then, in computing profit, revenue earned must be **matched** against the expenditure incurred in earning it. (This issue will be considered further when IAS 18 *Revenue* is dealt with in Chapter 6.)

1.7 Consistency of preparation

To maintain consistency, the presentation and classification of items in the financial statements should stay the same from one period to the next. There are two exceptions to this:

- Where there is a significant change in the **nature and operations** or a review of the financial statements presentation which indicates a **more appropriate presentation**. (This change is only allowed if the resulting information is a more faithful representation and more relevant than the previous presentation. If two presentations are equally appropriate then the current presentation must be retained.)
- Where a change in presentation is required by an IFRS.

Where a change of presentation and classification is made, figures for the previous period must be restated on the new basis, unless this is impracticable (ie not possible 'after making every reasonable effort').

Worked example: Consistency

Compare the following two statements of profit or loss prepared for a sole trader who wishes to show them to the bank manager to justify continuation of an overdraft facility.

Year ended 31 December 20X6

	£	£
Sales revenue		25,150
Less: production costs	10,000	
selling and administration	7,000	
		17,000
Gross profit		8,150
Less interest charges		1,000
Profit after interest		7,150

Year ended 31 December 20X7

	£
Sales revenue less selling costs	22,165
Less production costs	10,990
Gross profit	11,175
Less administration and interest	3,175
Net profit	8,000

Which accounting concept is being ignored here? Justify your choice.

How do you think the changes in the format of these financial statements affect the quality of the accounting information presented?

Solution

The accounting assumption breached here is that of **consistency**. This concept holds that accounting information should be presented in a way that facilitates comparisons from period to period.

In the statement of profit or loss for 20X6 sales revenue is shown separately from selling costs. Also interest and administration charges are treated separately.

The new format is poor in itself, as we cannot know whether any future change in 'sales revenue less selling costs' is due to an increase in sales revenue or a decline in selling costs. A similar criticism can be levelled at the lumping together of administration costs and interest charges. It is impossible to divide the two. (All material balances should be shown separately under IAS 1 and in fact, interest charges are required to be shown separately.)

It is not possible to 'rewrite' 20X6's accounts in terms of 20X7, because we do not know the breakdown in 20X6 between selling and administration costs.

The business's bank manager will not, therefore, be able to assess the business's performance, and might wonder if the sole trader has 'something to hide'. Thus the value of this accounting information is severely affected.

1.8 Materiality and aggregation

Each material class of items should be presented separately in the financial statements because such presentation is relevant to the understanding of the financial statements.

Amounts which are **immaterial** can be aggregated with amounts of a similar nature or function and need not be presented separately.

Definition

Materiality: Omissions or misstatements of items are material if they could, individually or collectively, influence the economic decisions of users taken on the basis of the financial statements. Materiality depends on the size and nature of the omission or misstatement judged in the surrounding circumstances. The size or nature of the item, or a combination of both, could be the determining factor.

An error which is too trivial to affect anyone's understanding of the financial statements is referred to as **immaterial**. However, the cumulative effects of many errors should also be taken into account. A number of immaterial errors taken together could be material to the financial statements as a whole. In preparing financial statements it is important to assess what is material and what is not, so that time and money are not wasted in the pursuit of excessive detail.

Determining whether or not an item is material is a very **subjective exercise**. There is no absolute measure of materiality. It is common to apply a convenient rule of thumb (for example to define material items as those with a value greater than 5% of the net profit disclosed by the financial statements). But some items disclosed in financial statements are regarded as particularly sensitive and even a very small misstatement of such an item would be regarded as a material error. An example in the financial statements of a limited liability company might be the amount of remuneration paid to directors of the company.

The assessment of an item as material or immaterial may **affect its treatment in the financial statements**. For example, the statement of profit or loss of a business shows the expenses incurred by the business grouped under suitable captions (heating and lighting expenses, rent and property taxes etc). However, in the case of very small expenses it may be appropriate to lump them together under a caption such as 'sundry expenses', because a more detailed breakdown would be inappropriate for such immaterial amounts.

In assessing whether or not an item is material, it is not only the amount of the item which needs to be considered. The **context** is also important.

Worked example: Materiality

If a statement of financial position shows non-current assets of £2 million and inventories of £30,000 an error of £20,000 in the depreciation calculations might not be regarded as material, whereas an error of £20,000 in the inventory valuation probably would be. In other words, the total of which the erroneous item forms part must be considered.

If a business has a bank loan of £50,000 and a £55,000 balance on bank deposit account, it might well be regarded as a material misstatement if these two amounts were displayed in the statement of financial position as 'cash at bank £5,000'. In other words, incorrect presentation may amount to material misstatement even if there is no monetary error.

Users are assumed to have a reasonable knowledge of business and economic activities and accounting and a willingness to study the information with reasonable diligence.

1.9 Offsetting

IAS 1 does not allow **assets and liabilities to be offset** against each other unless such a treatment is required or permitted by another IFRS.

Income and expenses can be offset only when:

- An IFRS requires/permits it, **or**
- Gains, losses and related expenses arising from the same/similar transactions are not material (in aggregate).

1.10 Comparative information

IAS I requires comparative information to be disclosed for the previous period for all **numerical information**, unless another IFRS permits/requires otherwise. Comparatives should also be given in narrative information where relevant to an understanding of the current period's financial statements.

Comparatives should be **reclassified** when the presentation or classification of items in the financial statements is amended.

Under IAS 8 a statement of financial position as at the beginning of the earliest comparative period is additionally required when an entity applies an accounting policy retrospectively or makes a retrospective restatement of items in its financial statements, or when it reclassifies items in its financial statements. (This will be covered in Chapter 3.)

1.11 Disclosure of accounting policies

There should be a specific section for accounting policies in the notes to the financial statements and the following should be disclosed there.

- **Measurement bases** used in preparing the financial statements
- Each **specific accounting policy** necessary for a proper understanding of the financial statements

To be clear and understandable it is essential that financial statements should disclose the accounting policies used in their preparation. This is because **policies may vary**, not only from entity to entity, but also from country to country. As an aid to users, all the major accounting policies used should be disclosed in the same place. This is normally referred to as the accounting policy note.

2 IAS 12 *Income Taxes*

Section overview

- Current tax is recognised as an expense (income) in profit or loss and as a liability (asset) in the statement of financial position.

- Adjustments should be made in the current period for tax over/under-charged in respect of prior periods.

- Tax liabilities and assets should be disclosed separately from other liabilities/assets.

- Tax expense (income) should be disclosed in the statement of profit or loss.

2.1 Introduction

Taxation is a major expense for business entities. In many developed countries taxation accounts for over 30% of corporate profits. This has a direct effect on cash flow and performance measures such as earnings per share and cash flow per share. Multinational entities use sophisticated tax planning techniques to minimise their tax costs. Tax planning may be through tax effective group structures, industry specific rules, optimisation of capital and revenue structures, and effective planning of acquisitions and disposals. Tax is an important planning consideration in significant business transactions.

With tax being such a significant cost to business, it is essential that an entity's financial statements include relevant information that enables users to understand historical, and predict future, taxation cash flows and liabilities.

2.2 Accounting for tax

The basic rule is that when a liability for tax arises it is recognised as an **expense** in profit or loss for the period. It is also recognised as a **liability** to the extent that it remains unpaid.

		£	£
DR	Income tax expense	X	
CR	Cash		X
CR	Current liabilities: taxation		X

2.3 Recognition of current tax liabilities and assets

The income tax due on the profit for any year cannot be finally determined until after the year end when the tax liability has been agreed with the tax authorities, something which takes months and, in some cases, years. So the amount of income tax on profits recognised each year is an estimate. When the tax due is later agreed with the tax authorities, an adjustment to the original estimate will normally be required. This adjustment will be recognised in profit or loss for the accounting period in which the estimate is revised.

IAS 12 requires any **unpaid tax** in respect of the current or **prior periods** to be recognised as a **liability** (resulting in an income tax expense being recognised in profit or loss).

Conversely, any **tax paid** in respect of current or **prior periods** in **excess of** what is due should be recognised as an **asset** (resulting in a reduction in the income tax expense recognised in profit or loss).

Worked example: Current tax

In 20X8 Darton Ltd had taxable profits of £120,000. In the previous year (20X7) income tax on 20X7 profits had been estimated as £30,000.

Calculate tax payable and the charge for 20X8 if the tax due on 20X7 profits was subsequently agreed with the tax authorities as:

(a) £35,000; or
(b) £25,000.

Any under or over payments are not settled until the following year's tax payment is due.

Assume a tax rate of 30%.

Solution

(a)

	£
Tax due on 20X8 profits (£120,000 × 30%)	36,000
Underprovision for 20X7 (£35,000 – £30,000)	5,000
Tax charge and liability	41,000

(b)

	£
Tax due on 20X8 profits (as above)	36,000
Overprovision for 20X7 (£25,000 – £30,000)	(5,000)
Tax charge and liability	31,000

Alternatively, the overprovision could be shown separately as income in profit or loss and as an asset in the statement of financial position. An offset approach like this is, however, most likely.

2.4 Measurement

Measurement of current tax liabilities (assets) for the current and prior periods is very simple. Liabilities (assets) are measured at the **amount expected to be paid to (recovered from) the tax authorities**. The tax rates (and tax laws) used should be those enacted (or substantively enacted) by the end of the reporting period.

2.5 Presentation

In the statement of financial position, **tax assets and liabilities** should be shown separately from other assets and liabilities.

Current tax assets and liabilities can be **offset**, but this should happen only when certain conditions apply.

(a) The entity has a **legally enforceable right** to set off the recognised amounts; **and**

(b) The entity intends to settle the amounts on a **net basis**, or to realise the asset and settle the liability at the same time.

The **tax expense (income)** related to the profit or loss from ordinary activities should be presented in **profit or loss**. An analysis of this figure would be provided in the notes to the financial statements showing the **major components** as follows.

	£
Current tax expense	X
Adjustment for current tax of prior periods	X/(X)
Income tax expense	X

3 Structure and content of financial statements

Section overview

In addition to giving substantial guidance on the form and content of published financial statements IAS 1 also covers a number of general points:

- The profit or loss must be calculated after taking account of all income and expense in the period (unless a standard or interpretation requires otherwise).
- Recommended formats are given but they are not mandatory.
- Readers of annual reports must be able to distinguish between the financial statements and other information.
- Financial statements should be prepared at least annually.

3.1 Profit or loss for the period

The statement of profit or loss and statement of profit or loss and other comprehensive income are the most significant indicators of a company's financial performance. So it is important to ensure that they are not misleading.

IAS 1 stipulates that all items of income and expense recognised in a period shall be included in profit or loss unless a **Standard** or an **Interpretation** requires otherwise.

Circumstances where items may be excluded from profit or loss for the current year include the correction of errors and the effect of changes in accounting policies. These are covered in IAS 8 *Accounting Policies, Changes in Accounting Estimates and Errors* (which is covered in Chapter 3).

3.2 How items are disclosed

IAS 1 specifies disclosures of certain items in certain ways:

- Some items must appear in the statement of financial position, statement of profit or loss, or in the statement of profit or loss and other comprehensive income.

- Other items can appear in a note to the financial statements instead.

- Illustrative formats are given which entities may or may not follow, depending on their circumstances.

Obviously, disclosures specified by **other standards** must also be made, and we will mention the necessary disclosures when we cover each IAS or IFRS in turn. Disclosures in both IAS 1 and other IAS or IFRS must be made either in the relevant statement or in the notes unless otherwise stated, ie disclosures cannot be made in an accompanying commentary or report.

3.3 Identification of financial statements

As a result of the above point, it is most important that entities **distinguish the financial statements** very clearly from any other information published with them. This is because all IASs/IFRSs apply *only* to the financial statements (ie the main statements and related notes), so readers of the annual report must be able to differentiate between the parts of the report which are prepared under IFRS, and other parts which are not.

The entity should **identify each component** of the financial statements very clearly. IAS 1 also requires disclosure of the following information in a prominent position. If necessary it should be repeated wherever it is felt to be of use to the reader in his understanding of the information presented.

- **Name** of the reporting entity (or other means of identification)

- Whether the accounts cover the **single entity** only or a group of entities

- The **end of the reporting period** or the period covered by the financial statements (as appropriate)

- The **reporting currency**

- The **level of rounding** used in presenting the figures in the financial statements

Judgement must be used to determine the best method of presenting this information. In particular, the standard suggests that the approach to this will be very different when the financial statements are communicated electronically.

The **level of rounding** is important, as presenting figures in thousands or millions of units makes the figures more understandable. The level of rounding must be disclosed, however, and it should not obscure necessary details or make the information less relevant.

3.4 Reporting period

It is normal for entities to present financial statements **annually** and IAS 1 states that they should be prepared at least as often as this. If (unusually) an entity's reporting period is changed, for whatever reason, the period for which the statements are presented will be less or more than one year. In such cases the entity should also disclose:

- The **reason(s) why** a period other than one year is used, and
- The fact that the comparative figures given **are not in fact comparable**.

3.5 Proforma accounts

IAS 1 looks at the statement of financial position, the statement of profit or loss, the statement of profit or loss and other comprehensive income and the statement of changes in equity. We will not give all the detailed disclosures as some are outside the scope of your syllabus. Instead we will look at a **'proforma' set of accounts** based on the Guidance on Implementing IAS 1 which accompanies the Standard. Note the description of this guidance as 'not part' of IAS 1 which means that it is **not mandatory**. So it shows ways in which financial statements **may** be presented. However, these are the formats that the Financial Accounting and Reporting paper is based on and therefore should be adopted in the exam.

4 Statement of financial position

Section overview

- IAS 1 provides guidance on the layout of the statement of financial position.
- IAS 1 specifies that certain items must be shown in the statement of financial position.
- Other information is required in the statement of financial position or in the notes.
- Both assets and liabilities must be separately classified as current and non-current.

4.1 Statement of financial position format

IAS 1 **suggests** a format for the statement of financial position although it does not prescribe the order or format in which the items listed should be presented. The layout below is consistent with the minimum requirements of IAS 1 and will be used throughout this Study Manual.

PROFORMA STATEMENT OF FINANCIAL POSITION

XYZ plc – Statement of financial position as at 31 December 20X7

	£'000	£'000
ASSETS		
Non-current assets		
Property, plant and equipment		350,700
Intangibles		308,270
Investments		242,650
		901,620
Current assets		
Inventories	135,230	
Trade and other receivables	91,600	
Investments	25,000	
Cash and cash equivalents	153,953	
	405,783	
Non-current assets held for sale	25,650	
		431,433
Total assets		1,333,053

CHAPTER 2

	£'000	£'000
EQUITY AND LIABILITIES		
Equity attributable to owners of the parent		
Ordinary share capital		600,000
Preference share capital (irredeemable)		30,000
Share premium account		20,000
Revaluation surplus		2,053
Retained earnings		243,900
		895,953
Non-controlling interest		72,950
		968,903
Non-current liabilities		
Preference share capital (redeemable)	28,000	
Finance lease liabilities	28,850	
Borrowings	120,800	
		177,650
Current liabilities		
Trade and other payables	115,100	
Dividends payable	7,500	
Taxation	34,500	
Provisions	5,000	
Borrowings	10,000	
Finance lease liabilities	14,400	
		186,500
Total equity and liabilities		1,333,053

4.2 Information which must be presented in the statement of financial position

IAS 1 specifies various items which must be presented in **the statement of financial position** as a minimum disclosure.

- Property, plant and equipment
- Investment property
- Intangible assets
- Financial assets
- Investments accounted for using the equity method (see Chapter 13)
- Assets classified as held for sale
- Inventories
- Trade and other receivables
- Cash and cash equivalents
- Trade and other payables
- Provisions
- Financial liabilities
- Current and deferred tax assets and liabilities
- Non-controlling interest (see Chapter 10)
- Issued capital and reserves attributable to owners of the parent

Any **other line items**, headings or sub-totals should be **shown in the statement of financial position** when it is necessary for an **understanding** of the entity's financial position.

This decision depends on judgements based on the assessment of the following factors.

- **Nature and liquidity of assets and their materiality**. Thus goodwill and assets arising from development expenditure will be presented separately, as will monetary/non-monetary assets and current/non-current assets.

- **Function within the entity.** Operating and financial assets, inventories, receivables and cash and cash equivalents are therefore shown separately.

- **Amounts, nature and timing of liabilities**. Interest-bearing and non-interest-bearing liabilities and provisions will be shown separately, classified as current or non-current as appropriate.

The standard also requires separate presentation where **different measurement bases** are used for assets and liabilities which differ in nature or function. According to IAS 16 *Property, Plant and Equipment*, for example, it is permitted to carry certain items of property, plant and equipment at cost or at a revalued amount. Property, plant and equipment may therefore be split to show classes held at historical cost separately from those that have been revalued.

4.3 Information presented either in the statement of financial position or in the notes

Certain pieces of information may be presented **either** in the statement of financial position **or** in the notes to the financial statements.

These comprise:

- Further sub-classification of line items from the statement of financial position. Disclosures will vary from item to item, which will in part depend on the requirements of IFRS. For example, tangible assets are classified by class of asset (eg land and buildings, plant and equipment) as required by IAS 16 *Property, Plant and Equipment*

- Details about each class of share capital

- Details about each reserve within equity

4.4 The current/non-current distinction

An entity must present **current and non-current assets and liabilities as separate classification**s in the statement of financial position. This is similar to the UK practice of separating current assets from fixed assets and amounts due within one year from amounts due after more than one year.

An alternative liquidity presentation which lists assets by reference to how closely they approximate to cash is permitted but only where this provides more reliable information, eg in the case of a financial institution such as a bank.

For all businesses which have a clearly identifiable **operating cycle**, it is the current/non-current presentation which is more meaningful, so this is the one which must be used. (See Section 4.5 below.)

In either case, the entity should disclose any portion of an asset or liability which is expected to be recovered or settled **after more than 12 months**.

Worked example: Amount receivable

For an amount receivable which is due in instalments over 18 months, the portion due after more than 12 months must be disclosed.

4.5 Operating cycle

Definition

Operating cycle: The time between the acquisition of assets for processing and their realisation in cash or cash equivalents.

The typical operating cycle of a manufacturing business is shown below.

This is an important term as it forms part of the definitions of current assets and current liabilities.

4.6 Current assets

Definition

Current asset: An asset shall be classified as **current** when it satisfies **any of the following criteria:**

- It is expected to be realised in, or is intended for sale or consumption in, the entity's normal operating cycle;

- It is held primarily for the purpose of being traded;

- It is expected to be realised within 12 months after the reporting period; or

- It is cash or a cash equivalent (as defined in IAS 7 *Statement of Cash Flows*), unless it is restricted from being exchanged or used to settle a liability for at least 12 months after the reporting period.

All other assets should be classified as non-current assets.

Current assets therefore include inventories and trade receivables that are sold, consumed and realised as part of the normal operating cycle. **This is the case even where they are not expected to be realised within 12 months**. It is the operating cycle which is the key.

Current assets will also include **marketable securities** if they are expected to be realised within 12 months of the end of the reporting period. If expected to be realised later, they should be included in non-current assets.

Point to note: There is no specific definition of non-current assets. These are merely all assets which are not current assets.

4.7 Current liabilities

Definition

Current liability: A liability shall be classified as **current** when it satisfies **any of the following criteria:**

- It is expected to be settled in the entity's normal operating cycle;

- It is held primarily for the purpose of being traded;

- It is due to be settled within 12 months after the reporting period; or

- The entity does not have an unconditional right to defer settlement of the liability for at least 12 months after the reporting period.

All other liabilities should be classified as non-current liabilities.

The categorisation of current liabilities is very similar to that of current assets. Thus, some current liabilities are part of the **working capital** used in the normal operating cycle of the business (ie trade payables and accruals for employee and other operating costs). Such items will be classed as current liabilities **even where they are due to be settled more than 12 months after the reporting period.**

There are also current liabilities which are not settled as part of the normal operating cycle, but which are due to be settled within 12 months of the reporting period. These include bank overdrafts, income taxes, other non-trade payables and the current portion of interest-bearing liabilities. Any interest-bearing liabilities that are used to finance working capital on a long-term basis, and that are not due for settlement within 12 months, should be classed as **non-current liabilities**.

4.8 Shares and dividends

A company statement of financial position will show **ordinary shares** but may also show **preference shares**. Preference shares may be **redeemable or irredeemable**. Redeemable, and some irredeemable, preference shares are accounted for as a liability, not as equity, and this also affects the treatment of the dividends, as we will see below (and in more detail in Chapter 8).

Dividends on ordinary and some irredeemable preference shares are treated as **appropriations of profit** (ie a reduction to retained earnings) and are therefore reflected in the statement of changes in equity (see later). An **interim ordinary dividend that has been declared in the period but is unpaid at the year end is not treated as a liability** in the statement of financial position. However, an **unpaid mandatory dividend on irredeemable preference shares** at the end of the reporting period is shown under current liabilities as a **dividend payable**.

The difference in treatment arises because an interim ordinary dividend declared by the directors before the end of the reporting period could be revoked before it is paid and therefore there is no obligation at the period end. Mandatory dividends on irredeemable preference shares are contractual obligations. A final ordinary dividend for a reporting period is declared at the following periods Annual General Meeting and is therefore binding from that date. However, as the AGM is usually held after the end of the reporting period, there will be no liability at the year end.

For the purposes of your exam studies it will be made clear if an ordinary dividend meets the definition of a liability.

Dividends on redeemable, and some irredeemable, preference shares are treated as an **expense** and recognised in profit or loss (as a finance cost). If they are unpaid at the year end, they are shown under current liabilities as **other payables**.

In an exam question it will be specified whether preference shares are redeemable or irredeemable and, if irredeemable, whether the dividend is mandatory or not (see Chapter 8 for more detail on the differences).

4.9 Accounting for dividends

- Payment of ordinary dividend:

		£	£
DR	Retained earnings	X	
CR	Cash		X

- Payment or declaration of interim or final dividend on redeemable preference shares:

		£	£
DR	Finance costs	X	
CR	Cash/other payables (current liability)		X

- Payment or declaration of mandatory dividend on irredeemable preference shares:

		£	£
DR	Retained earnings	X	
CR	Cash/dividends payable (current liability)		X

Worked example: Redeemable preference shares

On 1 January 20X1 a company issues 100,000 £1 5% redeemable preference shares. In the financial statements for 20X1 the preference shares and the 5% dividend that is declared, but unpaid, will be shown as follows.

Solution

Statement of financial position as at 31 December 20X1 (extract)

	£
Current liabilities	
Other payables (unpaid dividend)	5,000
Non-current liabilities	
Preference share capital	100,000

Statement of profit or loss for the year ended 31 December 20X1 (extract)

	£
Finance cost	5,000

4.10 Non-controlling interest

A parent company may own less than 100% of a subsidiary, in which case the amount not owned is described as the **non-controlling interest**. The detail of how to account for such holdings is dealt with in Chapter 10 onwards, so for the moment it is only necessary to note that:

- In the statement of financial position, equity must be split between the non-controlling interest and the amount attributable to the owners of the parent.

- In the statement of profit or loss, the allocation must be shown of the profit or loss for the period between the non-controlling interest and the owners of the parent.

- In the statement of changes in equity, the total comprehensive income for the period must be split between the non-controlling interest and the amount attributable to the owners of the parent.

This treatment is consistent with the *IASB Conceptual Framework's* definitions of the elements within financial statements. As there is no present obligation arising out of past events to settle the amount due to the non-controlling interest, it cannot be classified as a liability; instead it must be part of equity, which is the residual once liabilities have been deducted from assets.

Note: In Chapters 1–9 only the financial statements of single entities are covered. Non-controlling interests do not arise in the financial statements of single entities. However, as this chapter shows the complete formats per IAS 1, a non-controlling interest has been included for completeness.

5 Statement of profit or loss and other comprehensive income

Section overview

- IAS 1 requires all items of income and expense in a period to be presented either:
  - In a single statement of profit or loss and other comprehensive income, or
  - In two statements: a separate statement of profit or loss and a statement of profit or loss and other comprehensive income which begins with 'profit for the year'.
- Expenses can be classified by function or by nature.

5.1 Statement of profit or loss and other comprehensive income – format

The standard gives the following examples of the formats for the single statement and the two separate statements. The only items under 'other comprehensive income' which are included in your syllabus are valuation gains/losses, so where there is a gain or loss on non-current assets you may be required to show it in a separate statement of profit and loss and other comprehensive income.

Note that here the single statement format shows the classification of expenses in the statement of profit or loss by **function** and the two statement format shows expenses classified by **nature**. As expense classification by function is more common in practice, this is the method that will be tested in the exam for the preparation of a complete statement of profit or loss (ie from a trial balance or draft statements). However, expenses classified by nature may be tested in an extracts question or in an explain style question.

Single statement format

XYZ plc – statement of profit or loss and other comprehensive income for the year ended 31 December 20X7 (illustrating a single statement approach)

Illustrating the classification of expenses by function

	£'000
Revenue	390,000
Cost of sales	(245,000)
Gross profit	145,000
Other income	20,667
Distribution costs	(9,000)
Administrative expenses	(20,000)
Other expenses	(2,100)
Profit/(loss) from operations	134,567
Finance costs	(8,000)
Share of profits/(losses) of associates	35,100
Profit/(loss) before tax	161,667
Income tax expense	(40,417)
Profit/(loss) for the year from continuing operations	121,250
Profit/(loss) for the year from discontinued operations	–
Profit/(loss) for the year	121,250
Other comprehensive income:	
Gains on property revaluation	933
Income tax relating to component of other comprehensive income	(280)
Other comprehensive income for the year, net of tax	653
Total comprehensive income for the year	121,903
Profit attributable to:	
Owners of the parent	97,000
Non-controlling interest	24,250
	121,250
Total comprehensive income attributable to:	
Owners of the parent	97,653
Non-controlling interest	24,250
	121,903

Point to note: The sub-total 'profit/loss from operations' is not a current requirement of IAS 1. These Learning Materials use this description as it is used in practice and is not prohibited by IAS 1.

Revaluation of non-current assets will be dealt with in Chapter 4.

Two statement format

XYZ plc – Statement of profit or loss for the year ended 31 December 20X7 (illustrating the two statement approach)

Illustrating the classification of expenses by nature

	£'000
Revenue	390,000
Other income	20,667
Changes in inventories of finished goods and work in progress	(115,100)
Work performed by the entity and capitalised	16,000
Raw material and consumables used	(96,000)
Employee benefits expense	(45,000)
Depreciation and amortisation expense	(26,000)
Impairment of property, plant and equipment	(4,000)
Other expenses	(6,000)
Profit/(loss) from operations	134,567
Finance costs	(8,000)
Share of profit of associates	35,100
Profit before tax	161,667
Income tax expense	(40,417)
Profit for the year from continuing operations	121,250
Loss for the year from discontinued operations	–
Profit for the year	121,250
Profit attributable to:	
Owners of the parent	97,000
Non-controlling interest	24,250
	121,250

XYZ plc – statement of profit or loss and other comprehensive income for the year ended 31 December 20X7 (illustrating the two statement approach)

	£'000
Profit for the year	121,250
Other comprehensive income:	
Gains on property revaluation	933
Income tax relating to components of other comprehensive income	(280)
Other comprehensive income for the year, net of tax	653
Total comprehensive income for the year	121,903
Total comprehensive income attributable to:	
Owners of the parent	97,653
Non-controlling interest	24,250
	121,903

5.2 Information presented in the statement of profit or loss (under the two statement approach)

The standard lists the following as the **minimum** to be included in the statement of profit or loss (under the two statement approach).

- Revenue

- Finance costs

- Share of profits and losses of associates and joint ventures accounted for using the equity method (we will look at associates and joint ventures in Chapter 13)

- Income tax expense

- A single amount comprising the total of:
  - The post-tax profit or loss of discontinued operations.
  - The post-tax gain or loss recognised on the measurement to fair value less costs to sell or on the disposal of the assets constituting the discontinued operation.
- Profit or loss

The following items must be disclosed in the statement of profit or loss as allocations of profit or loss for the period.

- Profit or loss attributable to non-controlling interest
- Profit or loss attributable to owners of the parent

The allocated amounts must not be presented as items of income or expense. (These issues relate to group accounts, covered later in this text.)

Point to note: Income and expense items can only be **offset** in certain circumstances (see Section 1.9).

5.3 Information presented in the statement of profit or loss and other comprehensive income (under the two statement approach)

The standard lists the following as the **minimum** to be included in the statement of profit or loss and other comprehensive income (under the two statement approach).

- Each component of other comprehensive income
- Total comprehensive income

The following items must be disclosed in the statement of profit or loss and other comprehensive income as allocations of total comprehensive income for the period.

- Total comprehensive income attributable to non-controlling interest
- Total comprehensive income attributable to owners of the parent

5.4 Analysis of expenses

An analysis of expenses must be shown **either in the statement of profit or loss and other comprehensive income** (one statement format) **or separate statement of profit or loss** (two statement format) **or by note**, using a classification based on **either** the nature of the expenses or their function. This **sub-classification of expenses** indicates a range of components of financial performance; these may differ in terms of stability, potential for gain or loss and predictability.

Function of expense/cost of sales method	You are likely to be more familiar with this method. Expenses are classified according to their function as part of cost of sales, distribution or administrative activities. This method often gives **more relevant information** for users, but the allocation of expenses by function requires the use of judgement and can be arbitrary. Consequently, perhaps, when this method is used, entities should disclose **additional information** on the nature of expenses, including staff costs, and depreciation and amortisation expense.
Nature of expense method	Expenses are not reallocated amongst various functions within the entity, but are aggregated in the statement of profit or loss **according to their nature** (eg purchase of materials, depreciation, wages and salaries, transport costs). This may be the easiest method for smaller entities.

Which of the above methods is chosen by an entity will depend on **historical and industry factors**, and also the **nature of the organisation**. The choice of method should fairly reflect the main elements of the entity's performance. These Learning Materials will use the **functional analysis** in accordance with past UK practice.

5.5 Other information presented either in the statement of profit or loss or in the notes

These comprise:

- **'Exceptional items'**

  These are material items of income and expense which should be disclosed separately. These include:

  - Write downs of inventories to net realisable value
  - Write down of property, plant and equipment to recoverable amount
  - Disposals of property, plant and equipment
  - Restructuring of the activities of an entity and reversals of any provisions for the cost of restructuring
  - Disposals of investments
  - Discontinued operations
  - Litigation settlements
  - Other reversals of provisions

  IAS 1 does not specifically use the term 'exceptional'. However, it is a useful label for this type of item and is used in UK GAAP.

  (IAS 1 has prohibited the use of the UK term **'extraordinary'** in line with most jurisdictions.)

- Details, including per share amounts, of **dividends** recognised in the financial statements.

  Point to note: Dividends paid (on ordinary and irredeemable preference shares) are **not** shown as expenses in the **statement of profit or loss**; instead they should be shown in the statement of changes in equity.

  IMPORTANT NOTE: Where no items are involved which would be shown in a separate statement of profit or loss and other comprehensive income, this text refers to 'statement of profit or loss'.

6 Statement of changes in equity

Section overview

The statement of changes in equity shows the total comprehensive income for the period and the amounts of transactions with owners.

The statement of profit or loss and other comprehensive income is framed as a straightforward measure of financial performance, in that it shows all items of income and expense recognised in a period. It is then necessary to link this result with the results of transactions with owners such as share issues and dividends. The statement making the link is the **statement of changes in equity**. This must be presented as a separate component of the financial statements not just included in the notes.

The following should be shown in the statement:

(a) Total comprehensive income for the period, showing separately the total amounts attributable to owners of the parent and to non-controlling interest

(b) The effect of changes in accounting policy or correction of errors for each component of equity where these have been recognised during the period in accordance with IAS 8 (see Chapter 3)

(c) The amounts of transactions with owners in their capacity as owners, showing separately contributions by and distributions to owners

(d) For each component of equity, a reconciliation between the carrying amount at the beginning and end of the period, showing separately each change

Dividends to owners recognised during the period and the amount per share can be presented in the statement of changes in equity or in the notes.

Point to note: In most cases the 'total comprehensive income for the year' will be the profit for the period from the statement of profit or loss. Where an additional 'statement of profit or loss and other comprehensive income' has been prepared, the items comprising 'other comprehensive income' will be shown on the same line; for instance any revaluation gain will appear under 'revaluation surplus'.

Point to note: In extracts from the statement of changes in equity throughout this text we will show the correct terminology of 'total comprehensive income for the year' even though the figures may be taken from a simple statement of profit or loss.

XYZ group – Statement of changes in equity for the year ended 31 December 20X7

	Ordinary share capital £'000	Preference share capital (irredeemable) £'000	Share premium £'000	Retained earnings £'000	Revaluation surplus £'000	Total £'000	Non-controlling interest £'000	Total equity £'000
At 1 January 20X7	550,000	30,000	10,000	161,300	1,600	752,900	48,600	801,500
Changes in accounting policy	–	–	–	400	–	400	100	500
Restated balance	550,000	30,000	10,000	161,700	1,600	753,300	48,700	802,000
Issue of share capital	50,000	–	10,000	–	–	60,000	–	60,000
Final dividends on ordinary shares	–	–	–	(12,000)	–	(12,000)	–	(12,000)
Final dividends on irredeemable shares	–	–	–	(3,000)	–	(3,000)	–	(3,000)
Total comprehensive income for the year	–	–	–	97,000	653	97,653	24,250	121,903
Transfer to retained earnings	–	–	–	200	(200)	–	–	–
At 31 December 20X7	600,000	30,000	20,000	243,900	2,053	895,953	72,950	968,903

7 Statement of cash flows

Section overview

- The statement of cash flows shows movements in cash and cash equivalents.
- All entities are required to produce a statement of cash flows.

The statement of cash flows is covered more fully in the Accounting paper, so this section is just an overview.

7.1 Objective of IAS 7

The objective of IAS 7 *Statement of Cash Flows* is to provide **historical** information about changes in cash and cash equivalents, classifying **cash flows** between operating, investing and financing activities. This will provide information to users of financial statements about the entity's **ability to generate cash and cash equivalents**, as well as indicating the cash needs of the entity.

Statements of cash flows, particularly when they can be analysed over more than one year, are useful to creditors, lenders and investors, especially major investors such as pension funds. A company with good operating cash flows can finance both business operations and returns to investors.

Definition

Cash flows: These are inflows and outflows of cash and cash equivalents.

7.2 Scope

A statement of cash flows should be presented as an **integral part** of an entity's financial statements. All types of entity can provide useful information about cash flows as the need for cash is universal, whatever the nature of their revenue-producing activities. Therefore **all entities are required by the standard to produce a statement of cash flows.**

7.3 Benefits of cash flow information

Statements of cash flows should be used **in conjunction** with the rest of the financial statements. Users can gain further appreciation of:

- The change in net assets.

- The entity's financial position (liquidity and solvency).

- The entity's ability to adapt to changing circumstances and opportunities by affecting the amount and timing of cash flows.

Statements of cash flows **enhance comparability** as they are not affected by differing accounting policies used for the same type of transactions or events.

Cash flow information of a historical nature can be used as an indicator of the amount, timing and certainty of future cash flows. Past forecast cash flow information can be **checked for accuracy** as actual figures emerge. The relationship between profit and net cash flow and the impact of changing prices can be analysed over time.

7.4 Cash and cash equivalents

The statement of cash flows shows movements in **cash and cash equivalents**.

Definitions

Cash: Comprises cash on hand and demand deposits.

Cash equivalents: Short-term, highly liquid investments that are readily convertible to known amounts of cash and which are subject to an insignificant risk of changes in value.

IAS 7 expands on the definition of cash equivalents: they are not held for investment or other long-term purposes, but rather to meet short-term cash commitments. To fulfil the above definition, an investment's **maturity date should normally be within three months from its acquisition date**. It would usually be the case then that equity investments (ie shares in other companies) are **not** cash equivalents. An exception would be where preference shares were acquired with a very close maturity date.

Points to note

1   **Loans and other borrowings** from banks are classified as financing activities. In some countries, however, **bank overdrafts** are repayable on demand and are treated as part of an entity's total cash management system. In these circumstances an overdrawn balance will be included in cash and cash equivalents. Such banking arrangements are characterised by a balance which fluctuates between overdrawn and credit.

In the absence of other information you **should assume**, in the exam, that **bank overdrafts** are **repayable on demand** and should therefore be **classed as cash and cash equivalents.**

2   **Movements** between different types of cash and cash equivalent are not included in cash flows. The investment of surplus cash in cash equivalents is part of cash management, not part of operating, investing or financing activities.

7.5   Presentation

IAS 7 requires statements of cash flows to report cash flows during the period classified by:

- **Operating activities**: These are primarily derived from the principal revenue-producing activities of the entity and other activities that are not investing or financing activities.

- **Investing activities**: These are the cash flows derived from acquisition and disposal of non-current assets and other investments not included in cash equivalents.

- **Financing activities**: These are activities that result in changes in the size and composition of the equity capital and borrowings of the entity.

7.6   Example of a statement of cash flows

This is a proforma adapted from the example given in the standard.

Statement of cash flows for the year ended 31 December 20X7	£m	£m
Cash flows from operating activities		
Cash generated from operations	2,730	
Interest paid	(270)	
Income taxes paid	(900)	
Net cash from operating activities		1,560
Cash flows from investing activities		
Purchase of property, plant and equipment	(900)	
Proceeds from sale of property, plant and equipment	20	
Interest received	200	
Dividends received	200	
Net cash used in investing activities		(480)
Cash flows from financing activities		
Proceeds from issue of share capital	250	
Proceeds from issue of long-term borrowings	250	
Dividends paid	(1,290)	
Net cash used in financing activities		(790)
Net increase in cash and cash equivalents		290
Cash and cash equivalents at beginning of period		120
Cash and cash equivalents at end of period		410

Points to note

1   The headings in italics are necessary to comply with the standard.

2   The information to prepare a statement of cash flows can be obtained from the figures in the:

- Statement of financial position at the start of the period

- Statement of financial position at the end of the period

- Statement of profit or loss and statement of profit or loss and other comprehensive income for the period

- Supporting notes

Point to note: As full single entity statements of cash flows are tested in the Accounting paper it is more likely at this level that you will be asked to revise an existing statement of cash flows or prepare extracts. So in the next few sections we will look at the standard T-accounts that you will need to be able to produce.

7.7 Payments of interest and tax

The **adjustments** in the statement of cash flows to '**cash generated from operations**' to arrive at '**net cash from operating activities**' consist of **payments of interest and income tax**.

A similar method can be used to calculate the cash flows for interest paid and income tax paid. For each item, the information available might be:

- Opening balance at the start of the period (opening statement of financial position)
- Statement of profit or loss (the amount of the item, as reported)
- Closing balance at the end of the period (closing statement of financial position)

The cash flow is a balancing figure obtained from these three figures.

A T account can be used as a working.

Worked example: Interest paid

A company's financial statements show the following information:

	At 1 Jan 20X2 £	At 31 Dec 20X2 £	For the year 20X2 £
Interest payable	54,000	63,000	
Interest charge			240,000

Interest paid is calculated as follows.

INTEREST PAID

	£		£
Cash payment (balancing figure)	231,000	Balance b/d	54,000
Balance c/d	63,000	Profit or loss	240,000
	294,000		294,000

Alternatively, this could be calculated as follows:

(54,000 + 240,000 – 63,000) = £231,000

A similar technique can be used to calculate payments of income tax in the year. The taxation payment refers to payments of **income** tax, not to payments of sales tax (VAT) or tax paid by employees.

The opening and closing statements of financial position will show a liability for income tax. The income tax charge for the year is shown in the statement of profit or loss. The figure for income taxes paid during the year is derived as a balancing figure.

Interactive question 1: Income tax [Difficulty level: Easy]

A company had a liability for income tax at 31 December 20X6 of £940,000 and a liability for income tax at 31 December 20X7 of £1,125,000. The income tax charge for the year to 31 December 20X7 was £1,270,000. What amount of income tax was paid during the year?

INCOME TAX PAID

	£		£

See **Answer** at the end of this chapter.

7.8 Cash receipts from sales of property, plant and equipment

A T account can be used for calculating the cash receipts from sales of property, plant and equipment (PPE). The company's accounts will include the amount of any profit or loss on disposal. A note to the accounts on non-current assets will show the cost and the accumulated depreciation for property, plant and equipment disposed of during the year. The cash received from the sale is the balancing figure in the T account.

PROPERTY, PLANT AND EQUIPMENT – DISPOSAL ACCOUNT

	£		£
Cost/valuation of asset disposed of	X	Accumulated depreciation	X
Profit on disposal	X	Loss on disposal	X
		Cash received (balancing figure)	X
	X̲		X̲

Worked example: Cash receipts from sale of PPE

A company's statement of financial position as at the beginning and the end of the year showed the following.

Property, plant and equipment

Cost	£
At 1 January 20X7	760,000
Disposals	(240,000)
At 31 December 20X7	520,000

Depreciation	
At 1 January 20X7	270,000
Disposals	(180,000)
Charge for year	50,000
At 31 December 20X7	140,000

Carrying amount	
At 31 December 20X7	380,000
At 31 December 20X6	490,000

The property, plant and equipment was disposed of at a loss of £7,000. What was the cash flow from the disposal?

Solution

The balancing figure can be obtained by constructing a disposal of property, plant and equipment account as a working.

PROPERTY, PLANT AND EQUIPMENT – DISPOSAL ACCOUNT

	£		£
Cost	240,000	Accumulated depreciation	180,000
		Loss on disposal	7,000
		Cash received (balancing figure)	53,000
	240,000		240,000

7.9 Cash payments for purchase of property, plant and equipment

Purchase of property, plant and equipment during a period can be calculated by means of a T account or a working table.

PROPERTY, PLANT AND EQUIPMENT

	£		£
Balance b/d	X	Disposals	X
Additions (balancing figure)	X	Balance c/d	X
	X̲		X̲

Interactive question 2: Cash payments for PPE   [Difficulty level: Easy]

A company's accounts show that at 31 December 20X7, it had property, plant and equipment at cost of £6,800,000. During the year, it disposed of assets that had a cost of £850,000. At 31 December 20X6, the company's property, plant and equipment at cost had been £5,100,000.

What were purchases of property, plant and equipment during the year?

PROPERTY, PLANT AND EQUIPMENT

	£		£

See **Answer** at the end of this chapter.

7.10 Interest and dividends received

Returns received in cash from investments will include interest and dividends received. The cash flows can be calculated by using an interest received or dividends received T account. Both T accounts are very similar and are prepared as follows:

INTEREST/DIVIDENDS RECEIVED

	£		£
Balance b/d (receivable)	X	**Cash receipt** (balancing figure)	X
Profit or loss	X	Balance c/d (receivable)	X
	X̄		X̄

Interactive question 3: Interest received   [Difficulty level: Easy]

A company had interest receivable of £35,000 at the start of the year and interest receivable of £42,000 at the end of the year. The statement of profit or loss for the year shows interest income of £90,000. What were the cash receipts for interest received in the year?

INTEREST RECEIVED

	£		£

See **Answer** at the end of this chapter.

7.11 Cash received from issuing shares

The amount of cash received from new issues of shares can usually be calculated from the opening and closing statement of financial position figures for share capital and share premium.

As a general rule:

SHARE CAPITAL AND PREMIUM

	£		£
		Balance b/d	X
Balance c/d	X	**Cash receipt** (balancing figure)	X
	X̲		X̲

Bonus issues do not involve the movement of cash but the general rule will still apply where a bonus issue has been financed from the share premium account.

The rule does not apply fully when the company makes a bonus issue of shares during the year, and some of the new share capital is obtained by means of reducing **a reserve account other than the share premium**. To calculate cash receipts from share issues in the year, the amount transferred to share capital from the other reserve account should be subtracted.

Worked example: Cash received from share issue

Rustler plc's annual accounts for the year to 31 December 20X7 show the following figures.

	At 31.12.X7 £	At 31.12.X6 £
Share capital: Ordinary shares of 50p	6,750,000	5,400,000
Share premium	12,800,000	7,300,000

There were no bonus issues of shares during the year. What amount of cash was raised from shares issued during the year?

Solution

SHARE CAPITAL AND PREMIUM

	£		£
		Balance b/d (5,400,000 + 7,300,000)	12,700,000
Balance c/d (6,750,000 + 12,800,000)	19,550,000	**Cash receipt** (balancing figure)	6,850,000
	19,550,000		19,550,000

Interactive question 4: Bonus issue   [Difficulty level: Intermediate]

Groat plc's accounts for the year to 31 December 20X7 show the following figures.

	At 31.12.X7 £	At 31.12.X6 £
Share capital: Ordinary shares of 10p	22,500,000	10,000,000
Share premium	900,000	4,800,000

The company made a one for two bonus issue of shares at the start of the year. It used the share premium account and £200,000 from retained earnings to do this.

What amount of cash was raised from share issues during the year?

SHARE CAPITAL AND PREMIUM

	£		£

See **Answer** at the end of this chapter.

7.12 Dividends paid

Cash flows from dividends paid should be **disclosed separately**.

Dividends paid by the entity can be classified in **one of two ways**.

(a) As a **financing cash flow**, showing the cost of obtaining financial resources (as in the example statement of cash flows in Section 2 above). This is the presentation adopted in these Learning Materials.

(b) As a component of **cash flows from operating activities** so that users can assess the entity's ability to pay dividends out of operating cash flows.

Cash flows for dividends paid can be calculated using a T account.

Worked example: Dividends paid

A company has declared preference dividends for the year of £7,000 (based on its 7% £100,000 redeemable preference shares in issue). At the start of the year the statement of financial position included a liability of £3,500 for preference dividends payable. At the end of the year no amount was owing to preference shareholders in respect of dividends.

The preference dividend paid for the year is not simply the £7,000 declared and reflected in retained earnings as this amount needs to be adjusted for any opening and closing liabilities.

DIVIDENDS PAID

	£		£
Cash payment (balancing figure)	10,500	Balance b/d	3,500
Balance c/d	0	Retained earnings	7,000
	10,500		10,500

The cash paid during the year of £10,500 is the second half year preference dividend due from last year and the whole of this year's preference dividend (all paid during the year).

7.13 Preparing a statement of cash flows

Worked example: Preparing a statement of cash flows

Able plc's statement of profit or loss and statement of changes in equity for the year ended 31 December 20X7 and statements of financial position at 31 December 20X6 and 31 December 20X7 were as follows.

ABLE PLC
Statement of profit or loss for the year ended 31 December 20X7

	£'000	£'000
Revenue		720
Raw materials consumed	70	
Staff costs	94	
Depreciation	118	
Loss on disposal of non-current asset	18	
		(300)
Profit from operations		420
Finance cost		(28)
Profit before tax		392
Income tax expense		(124)
Profit for the year		268

ABLE PLC
Statements of financial position as at 31 December

	20X7 £'000	20X7 £'000	20X6 £'000	20X6 £'000
ASSETS				
Non-current assets				
Cost	1,596		1,560	
Depreciation	318		224	
		1,278		1,336
Current assets				
Inventory	24		20	
Trade receivables	76		58	
Bank	48		56	
		148		134
Total assets		1,426		1,470
EQUITY AND LIABILITIES				
Equity				
Share capital (£1 ordinary shares)	360		340	
Share premium	36		24	
Retained earnings	686		490	
		1,082		854
Non-current liabilities				
Long-term loans		200		500
Current liabilities				
Trade payables	42		30	
Taxation	102		86	
		144		116
Total equity and liabilities		1,426		1,470

ABLE PLC
Statement of changes in equity (extract) for the year ended 31 December 20X7

	Retained earnings £'000
At 1 January 20X7	490
Dividend paid on ordinary shares	(72)
Total comprehensive income for the year	268
At 31 December 20X7	686

During the year, the company paid £90,000 for a new piece of machinery.

Prepare a statement of cash flows for Able plc for the year ended 31 December 20X7 in accordance with the requirements of IAS 7, using the indirect method. The reconciliation of profit before tax to cash generated from operations should be shown as a note.

Solution

Step 1
Set out the proforma statement of cash flows with the headings required by IAS 7 and the reconciliation note. You should leave plenty of space. Ideally, use three or more sheets of paper, one for the main statement, one for the notes and one for your workings. It is obviously essential to know the formats very well.

Step 2
Begin with the **cash flows from operating activities** as far as possible. You will usually have to calculate such items as depreciation, loss on sale of non-current assets, interest paid and tax paid.

Step 3
Calculate the cash flow figures for **dividends paid, purchase or sale of non-current assets, issue of shares and repayment of loans** if these are not already given to you (as they may be).

Step 4

If you are not given the profit figure, open up a **working for the statement of profit or loss**. Using the opening and closing balances of retained earnings, the taxation charge and dividends paid, you will be able to calculate profit for the year as the balancing figure to put in the cash flows from operating activities section.

Step 5

You will now be able to **complete the statement** by slotting in the figures given or calculated.

ABLE PLC
Statement of cash flows for the year ended 31 December 20X7

	£'000	£'000
Cash flows from operating activities		
Cash generated from operations (see Note)	546	
Interest paid	(28)	
Tax paid (86 + 124 – 102)	(108)	
Net cash from operating activities		410
Cash flows from investing activities		
Purchase of property, plant and equipment	(90)	
Proceeds from sale of property, plant and equipment (W)	12	
Net cash used in investing activities		(78)
Cash flows from financing activities		
Proceeds from issue of share capital (360 + 36 – 340 – 24)	32	
Long-term loans repaid (500 – 200)	(300)	
Dividends paid	(72)	
Net cash used in financing activities		(340)
Decrease in cash and cash equivalents		(8)
Cash and cash equivalents at 1.1.X7		56
Cash and cash equivalents at 31.12.X7		48

Note to the statement of cash flows

Reconciliation of profit before tax to cash generated from operations for the year ended 31 December 20X7

	£'000
Profit before tax	392
Depreciation charges	118
Loss on sale of tangible non-current assets	18
Interest expense	28
Increase in inventories	(4)
Increase in receivables	(18)
Increase in payables	12
Cash generated from operations	546

WORKING

Non-current asset disposals

COST

	£'000		£'000
Balance b/d	1,560	Balance c/d	1,596
Purchases	90	Disposals (balancing figure)	54
	1,650		1,650

ACCUMULATED DEPRECIATION

	£'000		£'000
Balance c/d	318	Balance b/d	224
Depreciation on disposals (balancing figure)	24	Charge for year	118
	342		342

	£'000
Carrying amount of disposals (54 – 24)	30
Net loss reported	(18)
Proceeds of disposals	12

7.14 Disclosures

7.14.1 Cash and cash equivalents

The following disclosures are required:

- The components of cash and cash equivalents

- A reconciliation showing the amounts in the statement of cash flows reconciled with the equivalent items reported in the statement of financial position

- The accounting policy used in deciding the items included in cash and cash equivalents (IAS 1)

7.14.2 Other disclosures

All entities should disclose, together with a **commentary by management**, any other information likely to be of importance, for example:

- Restrictions on the use of or access to any part of cash equivalents

- The amount of undrawn borrowing facilities which are available

- Cash flows which increased operating capacity compared to cash flows which merely maintained operating capacity

7.14.3 Significant non-cash transactions

Many investing and financing activities do not have a direct impact on current cash flows although they do affect the capital and asset structure of an entity. Significant 'non-cash transactions' should be disclosed.

Examples include:

- The acquisition of assets either by assuming directly related liabilities or by means of a finance lease
- The acquisition of an entity by means of an issue of equity shares

7.14.4 Example: Notes to the statement of cash flows

The following shows how the required disclosures would be presented.

Note: Cash and cash equivalents

Cash and cash equivalents consist of cash on hand and balances with banks, and investments in money market instruments. Cash and cash equivalents included in the statement of cash flows comprise the following amounts from the statement of financial position.

	20X7 £m	20X6 £m
Cash on hand and balances with banks	40	25
Short-term investments	370	95
Cash and cash equivalents	410	120

The company has undrawn borrowing facilities of £2,000m of which only £700m may be used for future expansion.

Note: Property, plant and equipment

During the period the company acquired property, plant and equipment with an aggregate cost of £1,250m of which £900m was acquired by finance lease. Cash payments of £350m were made to purchase property, plant and equipment.

8 Notes to the financial statements

8.1 Contents of notes

The notes to the financial statements will **amplify** the information given in the statement of financial position, statement of profit or loss, statement of profit or loss and other comprehensive income, statement of changes in equity and statement of cash flows. We have already noted above the information which IAS 1 allows to be shown by note rather than in the statements. To some extent, then, the contents of the notes will be determined by the level of detail shown **in the statements**.

8.2 Structure

The notes to the financial statements should perform the following functions:

- Present information about the **basis on which the financial statements were prepared** and which **specific accounting policies** were chosen and applied to significant transactions/events

- Disclose any information, not shown elsewhere in the financial statements, which is **required by IFRSs**

- Provide any additional information not presented elsewhere in the financial statements which is relevant to an understanding of any of them

The way the notes are presented is important. They should be set out in a **systematic manner** and **cross-referenced** back to the related figure(s) in the statement of financial position, statement of profit or loss and/or statement of profit or loss and other comprehensive income, statement of cash flows or statement of changes in equity.

Notes to the financial statements will amplify the information shown therein by giving the following:

- More **detailed analysis** or breakdowns of figures in the statements

- **Narrative information** explaining figures in the statements

- **Additional information** where items are not included in the financial statements, eg contingent liabilities and commitments

IAS 1 suggests a **certain order** for the notes to the financial statements. This will assist users when comparing the statements of different entities. (Remember, comparability is one of the enhancing qualitative characteristics of useful information.)

- Statement of **compliance** with IFRSs

- Summary of significant accounting policies applied

- **Supporting information** for items presented in each of the main components of the financial statements in the same order as the financial statements and each line item within them

- Other disclosures, eg:

  - Contingent liabilities, commitments and other financial disclosures
  - Non-financial disclosures

The order of specific items may have to be varied occasionally, but a systematic structure is still required.

8.3 Disclosure of accounting policies

The accounting policies section should describe the following.

- The **measurement basis** (or bases) used in preparing the financial statements

- The **other accounting policies** used, as required for a proper understanding of the financial statements

- The judgements, apart from those involving estimations, made by management in applying the accounting policies

- The key assumptions made about the future and other key sources of estimation uncertainty which carry a significant risk of causing a material adjustment to the carrying amounts of assets and liabilities within the next financial year

This information may be shown in the notes or sometimes as a **separate component** of the financial statements.

The information on measurement bases used is obviously fundamental to an understanding of the financial statements. Where **more than one basis is used**, it should be stated to which assets or liabilities each basis has been applied.

8.4 Other disclosures

An entity must disclose in the notes:

- The amount of dividends proposed or declared before the financial statements were authorised for issue but not recognised as a distribution to equity holders during the period, and the amount per share.

- The amount of any cumulative preference dividends not recognised.

IAS 1 ends by listing some **specific disclosures** which will always be required if they are not shown elsewhere in the financial statements.

- The domicile and legal form of the entity, its country of incorporation and the address of the registered office (or, if different, principal place of business)

- A description of the nature of the entity's operations and its principal activities

- The name of the parent entity and the ultimate parent entity of the group

9 Not-for-profit entities

Section overview

IPSAS 1 *Presentation of Financial Statements* provides guidance on the presentation of financial information for public sector bodies.

9.1 Presentation of financial statements

A complete set of financial statements produced in accordance with IPSAS 1 comprise:

- Statement of financial position
- Statement of financial performance
- Statement of changes in net assets/equity
- Statement of cash flows, and
- Accounting policies and notes to the financial statements

9.2 Statement of financial position

The following example is provided by IPSAS 1.

Public sector entity – statement of financial position as of 31 December 20X2

	20X2 £'000	20X2 £'000	20X1 £'000	20X1 £'000
Assets				
Current assets				
Cash and cash equivalents	X		X	
Receivables	X		X	
Inventories	X		X	
Prepayments	X		X	
Other current assets	X		X	
		X		X
Non-current assets				
Receivables	X		X	
Investments	X		X	
Other financial assets	X		X	
Infrastructure, plant and equipment	X		X	
Land and buildings	X		X	
Intangible assets	X		X	
Other non-financial assets	X		X	
		X		X
Total assets		X		X
Liabilities				
Current liabilities				
Payables	X		X	
Short-term borrowings	X		X	
Current portion of long-term borrowings	X		X	
Provisions	X		X	
Employee benefits	X		X	
Superannuation	X		X	
		X		X
Non-current liabilities				
Payables	X		X	
Long-term borrowings	X		X	
Long-term provisions	X		X	
Employee benefits	X		X	
Superannuation	X		X	
		X		X
Total liabilities		X		X
Net assets		X		X
Net Assets/Equity				
Capital contributed by other government entities	X		X	
Reserves	X		X	
Accumulated surpluses/(deficits)	X		X	
		X		X
Non-controlling interest		X		X
Total net assets/equity		X		X

9.3 Statement of financial performance

This is essentially a statement of profit or loss and other comprehensive income. The following example is provided by IPSAS 1.

Public sector entity – statement of financial performance for the year ended 31 December 20X2
(illustrating the classification of expenses by function)

	20X2 £'000	20X1 £'000
Operating revenue		
Taxes	X	X
Fees, fines, penalties and licences	X	X
Revenue from exchange transactions	X	X
Transfers from other government entities	X	X
Total operating revenue	X	X
Operating expenses		
General public services	X	X
Defence	X	X
Public order and safety	X	X
Education	X	X
Health	X	X
Social protection	X	X
Housing and community amenities	X	X
Recreational, cultural and religion	X	X
Economic affairs	X	X
Environmental protection	X	X
Total operating expenses	X	X
Surplus/(deficit) from operating activities	X	X
Finance costs	(X)	(X)
Gains on sale of property, plant and equipment	X	X
Total non-operating revenue/(expenses)	(X)	(X)
Surplus/(deficit) from continuing activities	X	X
Non-controlling interest share of surplus/(deficit)	(X)	(X)
Net surplus/(deficit) for the period	X	X

Worked example: Not-for-profit entity

The statement of financial position at 31 December 20X8 of a local authority shows equity as:

	£m
Capital contributed by central government	3.1
Reserves	1.2
Accumulated deficit	(1.9)
	2.4

For the year ended 31 December 20X9 the statement of financial performance is as follows:

	£m
Operating revenue	
Council tax	1.8
Parking fines and fees	0.5
Rents received	2.4
Interest earned	0.6
	5.3
Operating expenses	
Housing	1.9
Cleansing services	0.6
Schools and libraries	2.1
General expenses	0.3
	(4.9)
Surplus from operating activities	0.4
Finance costs	(0.2)
Loss on sale of property	(1.4)
Net deficit for the period	(1.2)

The local authority has received an additional £2m from central government and withdrawn £1m from reserves.

Equity at 31 December 20X9 will be:

	£m
Capital contributed by central government (3.1 + 2.0)	5.1
Reserves (1.2 – 1.0)	0.2
Accumulated deficit (1.9 + 1.2 – 1.0)	(2.1)
	3.2

The local authority had equity b/f of £2.4m. It incurred a deficit for the period of £1.2m. This leaves a net position of £1.2m. It received an additional £2m from central government, giving a balance of £3.2m. (The transfer from reserves to reduce the deficit does not affect the overall figure.)

10 UK GAAP comparison

Section overview

- In the UK the presentation of financial statements is dealt with in the Companies Act 2006 and FRS 102 *The Financial Reporting Standard Applicable in the UK and Republic of Ireland*.

10.1 Presentation of financial statements

In the UK the presentation of financial statements is primarily dealt with by the following:

- Companies Act 2006
- FRS 102

In the UK the Companies Act sets out balance sheet and profit and loss account formats. In general terms the requirements are similar to those of IAS 1.

The key differences between international and UK formats are as follows:

- **Different terminology** is used.

International terminology	UK terminology
Statement of financial position	Balance sheet/statement of financial position
Statement of profit or loss	Income statement/profit and loss account
Revenue	Turnover
Receivables	Debtors
Payables	Creditors
Non-current assets	Fixed assets
Property, plant and equipment	Tangible fixed assets
Non-current liabilities	Creditors falling due after more than one year
Current liabilities	Creditors falling due within one year
Retained earnings	Profit and loss account (reserve)

- The profit and loss account formats require less detail than IAS 1, although IAS 1 allows some of the extra detail to be presented in the notes.

- The Companies Act balance sheet formats are **less flexible** than the IAS 1 formats.

  The formats in IAS 1 are contained in the *Guidance on Implementation* and are therefore not mandatory. The Companies Act formats are enshrined in law.

- The UK balance sheet (called statement of financial position in FRS 102) is usually prepared on a **net assets basis**.

  Fixed assets are added to net current assets (current assets less current liabilities) and long-term liabilities are deducted from the result. IAS 1 allows more flexibility in formats.

Under FRS 102 a complete set of financial statements comprises:

(a) A statement of financial position as at the reporting date

(b) Either a single statement of comprehensive income for the period, including both profit or loss items and items of other comprehensive income, or a separate income statement and statement of comprehensive income. The separate statement of comprehensive income begins with profit (or loss) for the year and then displays items of other comprehensive income.

(c) A statement of changes in equity for the reporting period

(d) A statement of cash flows for the reporting period

(e) Notes to the financial statements

If the only changes to equity during the period arise from profit or loss, payment of dividends, corrections of prior period errors and changes in accounting policy, an entity may present a single **statement of income and retained earnings** in place of the (separate) statement of comprehensive income and statement of changes in equity.

The statement of income and retained earnings presents, in addition to profit or loss and other comprehensive income amounts:

(a) Retained earnings at the beginning of the reporting period
(b) Dividends declared and paid or payable during the period
(c) Restatements of retained earnings for correction of prior period material errors
(d) Restatements of retained earnings for changes in accounting policy
(e) Retained earnings at the end of the reporting period

The **statement of financial position** follows the format of the CA 2006 balance sheet. Debtors and creditors falling due after more than one year can be combined on the face of the statement of financial position with amounts due within one year where the amount due after more than one year is not so material that a failure to separately disclose could lead to misinterpretation.

Under FRS 102 an exemption from the preparation of a statement of cash flows is available for a member of a group where the parent entity prepares publicly available consolidated financial statements and that member is included in the consolidation.

10.1.1 Extraordinary items

FRS 102 defines extraordinary items as: 'material items possessing a high degree of abnormality which arise from events or transactions that fall outside the ordinary activities of the reporting entity and which are not expected to recur'.

Extraordinary items would in theory be disclosed on the face of the income statement. In practice extraordinary items are unlikely to arise given the extremely broad definition of 'ordinary items'.

IAS 1 does not permit any item to be presented as extraordinary but simply says that material items of income and expense should be disclosed separately.

10.2 Statement of cash flows

The format of the statement of cash flows under FRS 102 is the same as the IFRS format.

Entities reporting under FRS 101 are exempt from preparation of a statement of cash flows. Entities eligible for disclosure exemptions under FRS 102 are also exempt from preparation of a statement of cash flows.

Summary

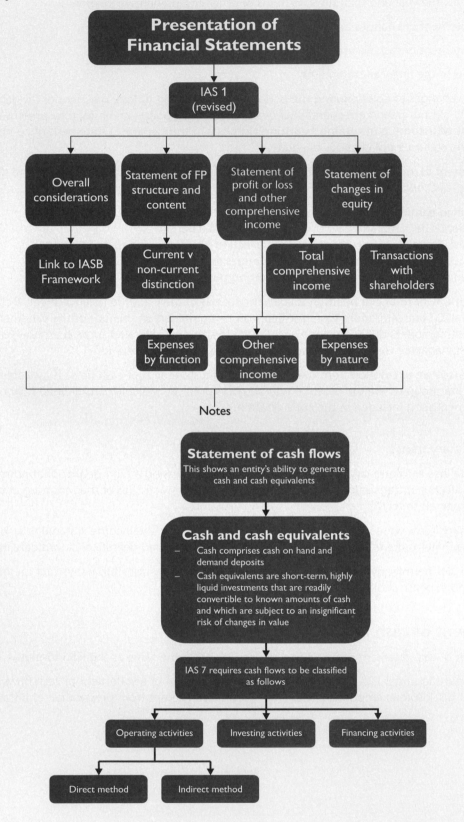

Presentation of Financial Statements

IAS 1 (revised)

- Overall considerations
- Statement of FP structure and content
- Statement of profit or loss and other comprehensive income
- Statement of changes in equity

- Link to IASB Framework
- Current v non-current distinction
- Total comprehensive income
- Transactions with shareholders

- Expenses by function
- Other comprehensive income
- Expenses by nature

Notes

Statement of cash flows
This shows an entity's ability to generate cash and cash equivalents

Cash and cash equivalents
- Cash comprises cash on hand and demand deposits
- Cash equivalents are short-term, highly liquid investments that are readily convertible to known amounts of cash and which are subject to an insignificant risk of changes in value

IAS 7 requires cash flows to be classified as follows

- Operating activities
- Investing activities
- Financing activities

- Direct method
- Indirect method

Self-test

Answer the following questions

1   The statement of profit or loss and other comprehensive income of Bell Holdings Ltd showed a total comprehensive income of £183,000 for the year ended 30 June 20X7. During the year the following transactions occurred.

   (1)   Equity dividends paid of £18,000.

   (2)   Capitalised development costs of £45,000 were written off directly to retained earnings as a result of a change in market conditions.

   (3)   Property with a carrying amount of £60,000 was revalued to £135,000, which gave rise to additional depreciation of £8,000.

   The total equity balance brought forward at 1 July 20X6 from the statement of changes in equity was £2,123,000.

   In accordance with IAS 1 *Presentation of Financial Statements* what is the total equity balance at 30 June 20X7 in the statement of changes in equity?

2   At 1 January 20X9 the opening statement of financial position of Dalston Ltd showed a credit balance on the tax payable account of £15,000. At 31 December 20X9 income tax on the profit for the year is estimated at £45,000.

   At the year end of 31 December 20X9 what amount will be shown as:

   (a)   The tax charge in the statement of profit or loss?
   (b)   The amount payable in the statement of financial position?

3   Information concerning the non-current assets of Ealing plc is detailed in the table. During the year non-current assets which had cost £80,000 and which had a carrying amount of £30,000 were sold for £20,000. Net cash from operating activities for the year was £300,000.

	Start of year £	End of year £
Cost	180,000	240,000
Aggregate depreciation	(120,000)	(140,000)
Carrying amount	60,000	100,000

   There was no other cash activity. By how much did cash increase over the year?

4   Information from the statement of cash flows and related notes of Gresham plc for the year ended 31 December 20X1 can be found in the table below.

	£
Depreciation	30,000
Profit on sale of property, plant and equipment	5,000
Proceeds from sale of property, plant and equipment	20,000
Purchase of property, plant and equipment	25,000

   If the carrying amount of property, plant and equipment was £110,000 on 31 December 20X0, what was it on 31 December 20X1?

5   TIGER LTD

The following extract has been taken from the trial balance at 31 December 20X9 of Tiger Ltd, a manufacturing company.

	£	£
Sales revenue		340,000
Raw material inventories at 1 January 20X9	43,000	
Finished goods inventories at 1 January 20X9	27,000	
Raw material purchases	72,000	
Factory wages	84,000	
Factory plant – cost	127,000	
Factory plant – accumulated depreciation at 1 January 20X9		21,000
Factory rent	65,000	
Office salaries	17,000	
Advertising and selling costs	1,800	

Additional information

Factory plant is depreciated at 20% pa on a reducing balance basis.

Closing inventory at 31 December 20X9 is:

	£
Raw materials	28,000
Finished goods	41,000

Requirement

Prepare the statement of profit or loss of Tiger Ltd down to 'profit from operations' using the 'expenses classified by nature' format.

6   HENDON LTD

For the year ended 15 July 20Y8 the accountant of Hendon Ltd has closed each of the ledger accounts to arrive at the following balances.

	£
At 16 July 20Y7	
Inventories	180,900
Retained earnings	170,555
Provision for depreciation	
Freehold buildings	20,000
Motor vehicles	28,000
Plant and machinery	22,100
Rental income	12,120
Sales	962,300
Trade receivables	112,870
Purchases	777,200
Trade payables	210,800
Discounts	
Allowed	53,400
Received	27,405
Sundry business expenses	
Wages	73,500
Salaries	74,000
Office	10,000
Directors' remuneration	30,000
Dividends	
Paid	40,000
Received	20,000
Interest	
Paid	12,500
Received	10,000
Freehold land	70,000
Freehold buildings	160,000
Motor vehicles	124,200
Plant and machinery	74,300

	£
10% debentures	
14 July 20Y9	35,000
14 July 20Z5	90,000
Share premium account	66,000
25p ordinary shares	200,000
Investments	58,000
Bank (debit)	61,410
New share issue account	38,000

Following a physical count closing inventories were determined to be £210,000.

In addition the accountant discovers the following.

(1) The debenture interest is payable in arrears on 14 July until maturity.

(2) One motor vehicle, stated in the accounts at cost of £8,000 with accumulated depreciation of £2,000, was stolen during the year. The insurance company has agreed to pay £7,000 in full settlement. No entries have been made in the books in respect of this matter.

(3) The company depreciates assets using the reducing balance method. The relevant rates are as follows.

	%
Freehold buildings	2
Plant and machinery	10
Motor vehicles	25

Freehold land is not depreciated.

(4) During the year the company issued 40,000 25p ordinary shares at 95 pence each. The proceeds have been credited to the new shares issue account and still need to be properly accounted for.

Requirements

Prepare a statement of profit or loss for the year ended 15 July 20Y8 and a statement of financial position as at 15 July 20Y8.

Note: Ignore comparatives and taxation.

7   OSCAR PLC

The following trial balance has been extracted from the books of account of Oscar plc as at 31 March 20X8.

	£'000	£'000
Administrative expenses	210	
Ordinary share capital		600
Trade receivables	470	
Bank overdraft		80
Provision for warranty costs		205
Distribution costs	420	
Non-current asset investments	560	
Investment income		75
Finance cost	10	
Freehold land and buildings at cost	200	
Plant and equipment		
At cost	550	
Accumulated depreciation (at 31 March 20X8)		220
Retained earnings (at 1 April 20X7)		180
Purchases	960	
Inventories (at 1 April 20X7)	150	
Trade payables		260
Revenue		2,010
20X7 final dividend paid	65	
20X8 interim dividend paid	35	
	3,630	3,630

Additional information

(1) Inventories at 31 March 20X8 were valued at £160,000.

(2) The following items are already included in the balances listed in this trial balance.

	Distribution costs £'000	Administrative expenses £'000
Depreciation charge for the year	27	5
Employee benefits	150	80

(3) The income tax charge for the year is estimated at £74,000.

(4) The warranty provision is to be increased by £16,000, charged to administrative expenses.

(5) Staff bonuses totalling £40,000 are to be provided for, charged equally to distribution costs and administrative expenses.

(6) In May 20X8 a final dividend for 20X8 of 10p per share was proposed on each of the company's 600,000 ordinary shares.

Requirement

Prepare Oscar plc's statement of profit or loss and statement of changes in equity for the year to 31 March 20X8, a statement of financial position at that date and notes in accordance with the requirements of IAS 1 *Presentation of Financial Statements* to the extent the information is available.

(10 marks)

8   MORTIMER LTD

The following draft financial statements for the year ended 31 August 20X9 have been prepared from the books of Mortimer Ltd

Draft statement of profit or loss for the year ended 31 August 20X9

	£
Revenue	3,290,000
Cost of sales	(2,606,000)
Gross profit	684,000
Distribution costs	(175,000)
Administrative expenses	(153,000)
Profit from operations	356,000
Finance cost	(22,000)
Investment income	5,000
Profit before tax	339,000

Draft statement of financial position at 31 August 20X9

	£	£
ASSETS		
Non-current assets		
Property, plant and equipment		
Cost – land and buildings	840,000	
– plant and machinery	714,000	
		1,554,000
Depreciation to 31.8.X8 – land and buildings	166,000	
– plant and machinery	368,000	
		(534,000)
		1,020,000
Current assets		
Inventories	179,000	
Trade and other receivables	107,000	
Cash and cash equivalents	24,000	
		310,000
		1,330,000
EQUITY AND LIABILITIES		
Equity		
Ordinary share capital	382,000	
Share premium account	199,000	
Retained earnings – at 31.8.X8	159,000	
– current year	339,000	
		1,079,000
Non-current liabilities		
Borrowings		148,000
Current liabilities		
Trade and other payables	84,000	
Provisions	19,000	103,000
		1,330,000

You also obtain the following information, which has not been reflected in the draft statements.

(1) Depreciation is to be provided on the straight-line method on buildings at 2% pa and on plant and machinery at 20% pa. The cost of buildings at 31 August 20X9 was £650,000.

(2) Borrowings comprise a bank loan of £58,000 and a mortgage which has £90,000 left to repay at 31 August 20X9. The original mortgage of £225,000 was taken out on 1 September 20X0 for a term of 15 years, repayable in equal monthly instalments on the 25th day of each month.

(3) Provision is to be made for income tax of £68,000, based on the results of the year.

(4) A transfer of £21,000 is to be made to the general reserve.

Requirements

(a) Redraft Mortimer Ltd's statement of profit or loss and statement of financial position for the year ended 31 August 20X9 to reflect (1) to (4) above and prepare the statement of changes in equity for the year in accordance with the requirements of IAS 1 *Presentation of Financial Statements* to the extent the information is available. You are *not* required to produce any notes thereto. **(15 marks)**

(b) Explain the concept of 'fair presentation'. **(2 marks)**

(17 marks)

9 MIDDLESEX LTD

The statement of financial position of Middlesex Ltd as at 30 June 20Y8, including comparative figures, is given below.

	20Y8 £	20Y8 £	20Y7 £	20Y7 £
ASSETS				
Non-current assets				
Property, plant and equipment		333,000		311,000
Less depreciation		(70,000)		(69,000)
		263,000		242,000
Investment		50,000		–
		313,000		242,000
Current assets				
Inventories	12,000		11,000	
Trade and other receivables	29,000		27,000	
Cash and cash equivalents	20,000		10,000	
		61,000		48,000
Total assets		374,000		290,000
EQUITY AND LIABILITIES				
Equity				
Ordinary share capital (£1 shares)		95,000		50,000
Share premium		15,000		10,000
Revaluation surplus		12,000		12,000
Retained earnings		149,000		115,000
		271,000		187,000
Non-current liabilities				
Interest-bearing borrowings (12% debentures 20Z1)		50,000		60,000
Current liabilities				
Provisions	–		2,000	
Trade and other payables	27,000		19,000	
Tax liabilities	7,000		3,000	
Accruals	19,000		19,000	
		53,000		43,000
Total equity and liabilities		374,000		290,000

You are also given the following information which is already reflected correctly in the accounts.

(1) During the year a bonus issue of 1 for 10 was made on the ordinary shares in issue at 30 June 20Y7, utilising available profits.

(2) New shares were issued on 1 July 20Y7. Part of the proceeds was used to redeem £10,000 12% debentures 20Z1 at par.

(3) During the year certain tangible non-current assets were disposed of for £20,000. The assets had originally cost £40,000 and had a net book value at the disposal date of £18,000.

(4) Trade and other payables include £5,000 for 20Y8 relating to the non-current asset purchases.

(5) The income tax charge for the year is £7,000.

Requirement

Prepare a statement of cash flows for the year ended 30 June 20Y8 and the note reconciling profit before tax with cash generated from operations. **(17 marks)**

10 HATCHBACK MOTOR COMPONENTS PLC

Hatchback Motor Components plc has prepared the summarised accounts as set out below.

Statements of profit or loss for the years ended 30 April

	20X7 £'000	20X6 £'000
Revenue	74,680	69,937
Cost of sales	(51,595)	(47,468)
Gross profit	23,085	22,469
Distribution and administrative costs	(17,681)	(16,920)
Profit before tax	5,404	5,549
Income tax expense	(2,634)	(1,093)
Net profit for the year	2,770	4,456

Statements of financial position at 30 April

	20X7 £'000	20X7 £'000	20X6 £'000	20X6 £'000
ASSETS				
Non-current assets				
Property, plant and equipment		26,146		25,141
Investments		7,100		–
		33,246		25,141
Current assets				
Inventories	16,487		15,892	
Trade and other receivables	12,347		8,104	
Cash and cash equivalents	863		724	
		29,697		24,720
Total assets		62,943		49,861
EQUITY AND LIABILITIES				
Equity				
Ordinary share capital (£1 ordinary shares)		13,000		10,000
Share premium		12,500		5,000
Revaluation surplus		2,650		2,650
Retained earnings		24,776		22,856
		52,926		40,506
Non-current liabilities (borrowings)		3,250		4,250
Current liabilities		6,767		5,105
Total equity and liabilities		62,943		49,861

Notes relating to the accounts

(1) Analysis of property, plant and equipment

	20X7 £'000	20X6 £'000
Freehold buildings	20,300	19,780
Fixtures and fittings	5,846	5,361
	26,146	25,141

(2) Depreciation has not been provided on freehold buildings. There were no disposals during the year.

(3) Additions to fixtures and fittings during the year totalled £1,365,000 at cost. There were no disposals.

(4) Current liabilities

	20X7 £'000	20X6 £'000
Trade and other payables	2,771	2,632
Accruals	1,200	1,235
Tax liability	2,796	1,238
	6,767	5,105

Taxation provided at 30 April 20X6 was settled at a figure lower than the amount provided.

(5) During the year the company made a rights issue of shares on the basis of three new shares for every ten shares held at a price of £3.50 per share. Pending the purchase of new plant part of the proceeds of the issue has been invested in shares in other UK companies.

Requirement

Prepare a statement of cash flows in accordance with IAS 7 *Statement of Cash Flows* under the indirect method, for the year ended 30 April 20X7.

11 VIRGIL LTD

You have been asked to correct the following draft statement of cash flows which has been prepared for Virgil Ltd:

Statement of cash flows for the year ended 30 June 20X2

	£'000	£'000
Net cash from operating activities		40
Cash flows from investing activities		
Development expenditure	(130)	
Purchase of property, plant and equipment (825 – 637 + 57)	(245)	
Proceeds of sale of property, plant and equipment	110	
Net cash used in investing activities		(265)
Cash flows from financing activities		
Proceeds of share issue (850 – 500)	350	
Proceeds from issue of loan notes	50	
Payment of finance lease liabilities	(56)	
Net cash from financing activities		344
Increase in cash and cash equivalents		119

The statements of financial position for the years ended 30 June 20X1 and 30 June 20X2 are as follows:

	20X2 £'000	20X1 £'000
Non-current assets		
Property, plant and equipment	825	637
Development expenditure	390	260
	1,215	897
Current assets		
Inventories	360	227
Trade receivables	274	324
Cash and cash equivalents	172	163
	806	714
Total assets	2,021	1,611
Equity		
Share capital – £1 ordinary shares	500	400
Share premium	350	100
Revaluation surplus	152	60
Retained earnings	285	300
	1,287	860
Non-current liabilities		
8% loan notes	150	100
Finance lease liabilities	100	80
	250	180
Current liabilities		
Finance lease liabilities	17	12
Other current liabilities	335	505
Bank overdraft	132	54
	484	571
Total equity and liabilities	2,021	1,611

It is immediately clear that the increase in cash and cash equivalents shown in the statement of cash flows does not agree with the cash movement shown in the statements of financial position.

You establish the following:

(1) The net cash flow from operating activities is correct.

(2) Amortisation of development expenditure, correctly adjusted for in the net cash from operating activities, was £60,000.

(3) One of the properties owned by Virgil Ltd was revalued upwards at the beginning of 20X2. Depreciation based on the year-end carrying amount of property, plant and equipment was £57,000, which was correctly added back in calculating net cash from operating activities. Depreciation based on historical cost would have been £49,000. Virgil Ltd has transferred the excess depreciation to retained earnings as allowed by IAS 16 *Property, Plant and Equipment*.

(4) Plant and equipment was sold during the year for £110,000 and yielded a profit of £7,000.

(5) New plant and equipment with a fair value of £56,000 was purchased during the year under a finance lease and this amount has been shown under financing activities.

(6) The share issue at full market price was preceded by a 1 for 8 bonus issue capitalising retained earnings.

(7) Profit after tax for the year ended 30 June 20X2 was £183,000.

Requirement

Prepare a corrected statement of cash flows for Virgil Ltd in accordance with IAS 7 *Statement of Cash Flows* for the year ended 30 June 20X2.

Notes to the statement of cash flows are not required.

12 OPTICA PLC

The following statement of cash flows has been prepared for Optica plc, an engineering company.

Statement of cash flows for the year ended 30 September 20X6

	£'000	£'000
Net cash from operating activities		275
Cash flows from investing activities		
Purchase of property, plant and equipment	(340)	
Purchase of non-current asset investments	(10)	
Net cash used in investing activities		(350)
Cash flows from financing activities		
Issue of 9% loan notes	120	
Redemption of 8% loan notes	(100)	
Equity share issue (200 share cap + 65 premium)	265	
Net cash from financing activities		285
Increase in cash and cash equivalents		210

Note: Reconciliation of profit before tax to net cash from operating activities

	£'000
Profit before tax	142
Depreciation	255
Finance costs	40
	437
Decrease in inventories	30
Decrease in receivables	110
Decrease in payables	(205)
Cash generated from operations	372
Interest paid	(40)
Income taxes paid	(57)
Net cash from operating activities	275

On looking this over you see that the decrease in cash does not agree back to the statements of financial position, which show cash and cash equivalents at 30 September 20X5 of £182,000 and cash and cash equivalents at 30 September 20X6 of £441,000.

You obtain the following further information:

(1) The figure included in the statement of cash flows for purchase of property, plant and equipment was calculated by taking the movement in the total PPE figure shown on the face of the statement of financial position. There were no disposals of PPE during the year.

(2) At 30 September 20X5 Optica plc completed installation of an offshore drilling rig. In five years' time the rig will have to be dismantled and the sea bed restored. The cost of decommissioning has been estimated and discounted at a rate of 8% to a present value of £300,000. This amount has been added to the cost of the rig and treated as a provision. Unwinding of the discount has been included in finance costs. There were no interest payments outstanding at 30 September 20X5 or 30 September 20X6.

(3) Land was revalued upward during the year. This was the only revaluation that took place during the year.

(4) On 1 April 20X6 a 1 for 3 bonus issue was made utilising as far as possible the share premium account. On 1 July 20X6 £100,000 of the 8% loan notes were converted to equity at the rate of one share per £2 of loan capital.

(5) A translation loss of £45,000 was recorded on the restatement of overseas investments at 30 September 20X6. This was charged to administrative expenses and has been correctly accounted for in arriving at the £10,000 net cash outflow on purchase of investments.

(6) No amounts were due to the tax authorities at 30 September 20X5 or 30 September 20X6.

(7) The equity sections of the statements of financial position are as follows:

		20X6		20X5
		£'000		£'000
Equity shares of £1		500		300
Share premium	150		85	
Revaluation surplus	60		25	
Retained earnings	950		965	
		1,160		1,075
		1,660		1,375

Requirement

Prepare a corrected statement of cash flows and note reconciling profit before tax to net cash from operating activities in accordance with IAS 7 *Statement of Cash Flows* for Optica plc for the year ended 30 September 20X6 taking account of (1) to (7) above.

Now, go back to the Learning objectives in the Introduction. If you are satisfied you have achieved these objectives, please tick them off.

Point to note: The whole of IAS 1 is examinable with the exception of paragraphs 134–136 and IG7 – IG11. The paragraphs listed below are the key references you should be familiar with.

1 IAS 1

- Applies to all general purpose financial statements.   IAS 1 (2–6)

- Links back to much in the *IASB Conceptual Framework*:

    - Fair/faithful presentation   IAS 1 (15)

    - Going concern   IAS 1 (25–26) Frame (4.1)

    - Accrual basis of accounting   IAS 1 (27–28) Frame (OB17)

    - Consistency of presentation   IAS 1 (45–46) Frame (QC22)

    - Materiality and aggregation   IAS 1 (29–31) Frame (QC11)

    - Offsetting   IAS 1 (32–35)

    - Comparative information   IAS 1 (38–44)

- Presentation and disclosure rules apply only to material items   IAS 1 (31)

- Statement of financial position:

    - Layout as in proforma above

    - Distinction between current and non-current   IAS 1 (60–65)

    - Linked to the operating cycle of the business, not just the next 12 months

    - Some items must be in the statement, others can be in the notes   IAS 1 (77–79)

- Statement of profit or loss:

    - Layout as in proformas above

    - Some items must be in the statement, others can be in the notes   IAS 1 (82–98)

    - No extraordinary items   IAS 1 (87)

    - No dividends paid or payable

    - Allocate net profit for the year between parent company owners and non-controlling interest   IAS 1 (83)

- Statement of changes in equity: IAS 1 (106–110)

    - Layout as in proforma above

    - Dividends recognised by end of the reporting period

- Notes

    - What must be included — IAS 1 (112)

    - The systematic manner in which it must be disclosed — IAS 1 (113)

    - The disclosure of the measurement bases (eg historical cost, fair value) and the other accounting policies used. Note the matters which an entity must consider when deciding what to disclose — IAS 1 (117)

    - The judgements made by management in applying the accounting policies — IAS 1 (122)

    - The key measurement assumptions made about the future which carry the significant risk of causing a material adjustment to assets and liabilities — IAS 1 (125)

    - The disclosure of ordinary dividends proposed or declared after the period end and not recognised in the accounting period. Such dividends do not fall within the definition of a liability at the period end, so cannot be recognised until the next accounting period — IAS 1 (137)

2 IAS 7 *Statement of Cash Flows*

- Objective of the statement of cash flows

    - The statement of cash flows should show the historical changes in cash and cash equivalents

    - Cash comprises cash on hand and demand deposits — IAS 7 (6)

    - Cash equivalents are short-term, highly liquid investments that are readily convertible to known amounts of cash and which are subject to an insignificant risk of changes in value — IAS 7 (6)

- Presentation of a statement of cash flows — Appendix A

    - Cash flows should be classified by operating, investing and financing activities — IAS 7 (10)

    - Cash flows from operating activities are primarily derived from the principal revenue-producing activities of the entity — IAS 7 (13–14)

    - Cash flows from investing activities are those related to the acquisition or disposal of any property, plant and equipment, intangible assets or trade investments together with returns received in cash from investments (that is dividends and interest) — IAS 7 (16)

- Financing activities include: — IAS 7 (17)

    - Cash proceeds from issuing shares

    - Cash proceeds from issuing debentures, loans, notes, bonds, mortgages and other short or long-term borrowings

    - Cash repayments of amounts borrowed

    - Dividends paid to shareholders

    - Principal repayments of amounts borrowed under finance leases

- Cash flows from operating activities

    There are two methods of presentation allowed:

    - Direct method — IAS 7 (19)

    - Indirect method — IAS 7 (20)

Answer to Interactive question 1

INCOME TAX PAID

	£		£
Cash payment (balancing figure)	1,085,000	Balance b/d	940,000
Balance c/d	1,125,000	Profit or loss	1,270,000
	2,210,000		2,210,000

Alternatively this could be calculated as follows:

(£940,000 + £1,270,000 – £1,125,000) = £1,085,000

Answer to Interactive question 2

PROPERTY, PLANT AND EQUIPMENT

	£		£
Balance b/d	5,100,000	Disposals	850,000
Additions (balance)	2,550,000	Balance c/d	6,800,000
	7,650,000		7,650,000

The company started the year with PPE at cost of £5,100,000. It bought a further £2,550,000 of PPE, giving a total of £7,650,000 at cost. However, there were disposals of PPE with a cost of £850,000, bringing the year-end figure down to £6,800,000.

Answer to Interactive question 3

INTEREST RECEIVED

	£		£
Balance b/d	35,000	Cash received (balancing figure)	83,000
Profit or loss	90,000	Balance c/d	42,000
	125,000		125,000

Answer to Interactive question 4

SHARE CAPITAL AND PREMIUM

	£		£
		Balance b/d	14,800,000
Balance c/d	23,400,000	Retained earnings	200,000
		Cash received (balance)	8,400,000
	23,400,000		23,400,000

1 The revaluation and additional depreciation of £8,000 will have already been accounted for in the statement of profit or loss and other comprehensive income.

	Equity £
B/f (2,123,000 – 45,000)	2,078,000
Total comprehensive income	183,000
Dividends paid	(18,000)
	2,243,000

2

		£
(a)	Tax charge on current year's profits	45,000
	Less overprovision in respect of previous year	(15,000)
	Tax charge in statement of profit or loss	30,000
(b)	Due to tax authority for current year	45,000

3 £180,000

NON-CURRENT ASSETS – COST

	£		£
Balance b/d	180,000	Disposals	80,000
Therefore purchases	140,000	Balance c/d	240,000
	320,000		320,000

	£
Cash from operations	300,000
Cash inflow: disposal proceeds	20,000
	320,000
Cash outflow: purchases of non-current assets	(140,000)
Therefore net cash increase	180,000

Note that adjustments for depreciation and loss on disposal will already be included in net cash from operating activities.

4 £90,000

PROPERTY (CARRYING AMOUNT)

	£		£
Balance b/d	110,000	Depreciation	30,000
Additions	25,000	Disposals (carrying amount)	15,000
		Balance c/d	90,000
	135,000		135,000

5 TIGER LTD

Statement of profit or loss for the year ended 31 December 20X9

	£
Revenue	340,000
Changes in inventories of finished goods (41,000 – 27,000)	14,000
Raw materials used (43,000 + 72,000 – 28,000)	(87,000)
Employee benefits expense (84,000 + 17,000)	(101,000
Depreciation ((127,000 – 21,000) × 20%)	(21,200)
Other expenses (65,000 + 1,800)	(66,800)
Profit from operations	78,000

6   HENDON LTD

Statement of profit or loss for the year ended 15 July 20Y8

	£
Revenue	962,300
Cost of sales (W8)	(753,320)
Gross profit	208,980
Other operating income (12,120 + 27,405)	39,525
Distribution costs (W8)	(21,550)
Administrative expenses (W8)	(243,700)
Loss from operations	(16,745)
Finance cost (W2)	(12,500)
Investment income (20,000 + 10,000)	30,000
Net profit for the year	755

Statement of financial position as at 15 July 20Y8

ASSETS		£
Non-current assets		
Property, plant and equipment (W9)		321,830
Investments		58,000
		379,830
Current assets		
Inventories	210,000	
Trade and other receivables (W7)	119,870	
Cash and cash equivalents	61,410	
		391,280
Total assets		771,110
EQUITY AND LIABILITIES		
Equity		
Ordinary share capital (W4)		210,000
Share premium (W5)		94,000
Retained earnings (W6)		131,310
		435,310
Non-current liabilities		
Interest-bearing borrowings		90,000
Current liabilities		
Trade and other payables	210,800	
Short-term borrowings	35,000	
		245,800
Total equity and liabilities		771,110

WORKINGS

(1) **Accumulated depreciation**

	Charge £	B/f £	Disposals £	C/f £
Freehold (160,000 – 20,000) × 2%)	2,800	20,000	–	22,800
Vehicles (((124,200 – 8,000) – (28,000 – 2,000)) × 25%)	22,550	28,000	(2,000)	48,550
Plant (74,300 – 22,100) × 10%	5,220	22,100	–	27,320

(2) **Finance cost**

	£
20Y9 debentures (35,000 × 10%)	3,500
20Z5 debentures (90,000 × 10%)	9,000
	12,500

∴ All interest due has been paid in year.

(3) **Cost of property, plant and equipment**

	£
Freehold (70,000 + 160,000))	230,000
Vehicles (124,200 – 8,000)	116,200

(4) **Ordinary share capital**

	£
Per TB	200,000
New issue (40,000 × 25p)	10,000
	210,000

(5) **Share premium**

	£
Per TB	66,000
New issue ((95p – 25p) × 40,000)	28,000
	94,000

(6)   RETAINED EARNINGS

	£		£
Dividends	40,000	B/d	170,555
C/d	131,310	Profit for the year	755
	171,310		171,310

(7) **Trade and other receivables**

	£
Trade receivables	112,870
Insurance claim	7,000
	119,870

(8) **Analysis of expenses**

	Cost of sales £	Distribution costs £	Administrative expenses £
Opening inventories	180,900		
Purchases	777,200		
Discounts allowed			53,400
Closing inventories	(210,000)		
Plant and machinery – depreciation charge (W1)	5,220		
Motor vehicles – depreciation charge (W1)		22,550	
Freehold buildings – depreciation charge (W1)			2,800
Profit on disposal of non-current assets		(1,000)	
Expenses (total sundry expenses)			187,500
	753,320	21,550	243,700

(9) **Analysis of property, plant and equipment**

	Cost or valuation (W3) £	Accumulated depreciation (W1) £	Carrying value £
Freehold buildings	230,000	22,800	207,200
Motor vehicles	116,200	48,550	67,650
Plant and machinery	74,300	27,320	46,980
	420,500	98,670	321,830

7 OSCAR PLC

Financial statements

Statement of profit or loss for the year ended 31 March 20X8

	£'000
Revenue	2,010
Cost of sales (960 + 150 – 160)	(950)
Gross profit	1,060
Distribution costs (420 + 20)	(440)
Administrative expenses (210 + 16 + 20)	(246)
Profit from operations	374
Finance cost	(10)
Investment income	75
Profit before tax	439
Income tax expense	(74)
Profit for the year	365

Statement of changes in equity for the year ended 31 March 20X8

	Share capital £'000	Retained earnings £'000	Total equity £'000
Balance at 1 April 20X7	600	180	780
Dividends		(100)	(100)
Total comprehensive income for the year	–	365	365
Balance at 31 March 20X8	600	445	1,045

Notes

(1) The profit from operations is arrived at after charging

	£'000
Depreciation (27 + 5)	32
Employee benefits (150 + 80 + 40)	270

(2) A final dividend for 20X8 of £60,000 (10p per share) is proposed.

Statement of financial position as at 31 March 20X8

	£'000	£'000
ASSETS		
Non-current assets		
Property, plant and equipment (200 + 550 – 220)		530
Investments		560
		1,090
Current assets		
Inventories	160	
Trade and other receivables	470	
		630
Total assets		1,720
EQUITY AND LIABILITIES		
Equity		
Ordinary share capital		600
Retained earnings		445
Total equity		1,045
Non-current liabilities		
Provision for warranty costs (205 + 16)		221
Current liabilities		
Trade and other payables (260 + 40)	300	
Taxation	74	
Borrowings	80	
		454
Total equity and liabilities		1,720

8   MORTIMER LTD

(a)   **Financial statements**

Statement of profit or loss for the year ended 31 August 20X9

	£
Revenue	3,290,000
Cost of sales (W1)	(2,748,800)
Gross profit	541,200
Distribution costs (W1)	(175,000)
Administrative expenses (W1)	(166,000)
Profit from operations	200,200
Finance cost	(22,000)
Investment income	5,000
Profit before tax	183,200
Income tax	(68,000)
Profit for the year	115,200

Statement of changes in equity for the year ended 31 August 20X9

	Share capital £	Share premium £	Retained earnings £	General reserve £	Total £
Balance at 1 September 20X8	382,000	199,000	159,000	–	740,000
Total comprehensive income for the year			115,200		115,200
Transfer to general reserve	–	–	(21,000)	21,000	–
Balance at 31 August 20X9	382,000	199,000	253,200	21,000	855,200

Statement of financial position as at 31 August 20X9

	£	£
ASSETS		
Non-current assets		
Property, plant and equipment (W2)		864,200
Current assets		
Inventories	179,000	
Trade and other receivables	107,000	
Cash and cash equivalents	24,000	
		310,000
Total assets		1,174,200
EQUITY AND LIABILITIES		
Equity		
Ordinary share capital		382,000
Share premium account		199,000
General reserve		21,000
Retained earnings		253,200
		855,200
Non-current liabilities		
Borrowings (148,000 – (225,000/15))		133,000
Current liabilities		
Trade and other payables	84,000	
Tax	68,000	
Provisions	19,000	
Borrowings (225,000/15)	15,000	
		186,000
Total equity and liabilities		1,174,200

(b) **Fair presentation**

IAS 1 *Presentation of Financial Statements* describes the concept of fair presentation. Fair presentation involves:

(i) Representing faithfully the effect of transactions, other events and conditions, and

(ii) In accordance with the definitions and recognition criteria in the *IASB Conceptual Framework*.

This is developed by stating that the application of IFRS, Interpretations and additional disclosures is presumed to result in fair presentation.

The *IASB Conceptual Framework* uses the description of fair presentation in its discussion of the application of the principal qualitative characteristics of financial information.

WORKINGS

(1) **Allocation of expenses**

	Cost of sales £	Distribution £	Administration £
Per Q	2,606,000	175,000	153,000
Depreciation			
Plant (714,000 × 20%)	142,800		
Buildings (650,000 × 2%)			13,000
	2,748,800	175,000	166,000

(2) **Property, plant and equipment**

	Land and buildings £	Plant and machinery £	Total £
Cost	840,000	714,000	
Depreciation			
At 1 September 20X8	166,000	368,000	
Charge for the year (W1)	13,000	142,800	
At 31 August 20X9	179,000	510,800	
Carrying amount	661,000	203,200	864,200

9   MIDDLESEX LTD

Statement of cash flows for the year ended 30 June 20Y8

	£	£
Cash flows from operating activities		
Cash generated from operations (Note)		71,000
Interest paid (W6)		(6,000)
Tax paid (W2)		(3,000)
Net cash from operating activities		62,000
Cash flows from investing activities		
Purchase of property, plant and equipment (W3)	(57,000)	
Proceeds from sale of property, plant and equipment	20,000	
Purchase of investments	(50,000)	
Net cash used in investing activities		(87,000)
Cash flows from financing activities		
Issues of ordinary shares (W4)	45,000	
Redemption of non-current interest-bearing borrowings	(10,000)	
Net cash from financing activities		35,000
Net change in cash and cash equivalents		10,000
Cash and cash equivalents brought forward		10,000
Cash and cash equivalents carried forward		20,000

Reconciliation of profit before tax to net cash generated from operations for the year ended 30 June 20Y8

	£
Profit before tax (W7)	46,000
Finance cost (W6)	6,000
Property, plant and equipment – depreciation charge (W1)	23,000
Profit on disposal of property, plant and equipment	(2,000)
Change in inventories (W5)	(1,000)
Change in trade and other receivables (W5)	(2,000)
Change in trade and other payables (W5)	3,000
Change in provision	(2,000)
Cash generated from operations	71,000

WORKINGS

(1)   PROPERTY, PLANT AND EQUIPMENT – ACCUMULATED DEPRECIATION

	£		£
Disposal (40,000 – 18,000)	22,000	B/f	69,000
C/f	70,000	Charge for year (β)	23,000
	92,000		92,000

(2)   TAX PAID

	£		£
Cash (β)	3,000	B/f	3,000
C/f	7,000	Charge for year	7,000
	10,000		10,000

(3)   PROPERTY, PLANT AND EQUIPMENT – COST OR VALUATION

	£		£
B/f	311,000	Disposal	40,000
Additions (β)	57,000	C/f	333,000
C/f	5,000		
	373,000		373,000

(4)   SHARE CAPITAL AND PREMIUM

	£		£
		B/f (50,000 + 10,000)	60,000
		Accumulated profit/losses (bonus issue) (50,000 ÷ 10)	5,000
C/f (95,000 + 15,000)	110,000	Cash (β)	45,000
	110,000		110,000

(5) Changes in current items

	£
Inventories (12,000 – 11,000)	(1,000)
Receivables (29,000 – 27,000)	(2,000)
Payables (27,000 – 5,000 – 19,000)	3,000

(6) Finance cost

£50,000 × 12% = £6,000

(7)   ACCUMULATED PROFIT/LOSS

	£		£
Bonus issue	5,000	B/f	115,000
Income tax	7,000	Net profit for the year (β)	46,000
C/f	149,000		
	161,000		161,000

10 HATCHBACK MOTOR COMPONENTS PLC

Statement of cash flows for the year ended 30 April 20X7

	£	£
Cash flows from operating activities		
Cash generated from operations (Note)		1,550,000
Tax paid (W4)		(1,076,000)
Net cash from operating activities		474,000
Cash flows from investing activities		
Purchase of property, plant and equipment (W3)	(1,885,000)	
Purchase of investments	(7,100,000)	
Net cash used in investing activities		(8,985,000)
Cash flows from financing activities		
Proceeds from issue of ordinary shares (W2)	10,500,000	
Redemption of non-current interest-bearing borrowings	(1,000,000)	
Dividends paid (W5)	(850,000)	
Net cash from financing activities		8,650,000
Net change in cash and cash equivalents		139,000
Cash and cash equivalents brought forward		724,000
Cash and cash equivalents carried forward		863,000

Note to the statement of cash flows

Reconciliation of profit before tax to cash generated from operations for the year ended 30 April 20X7

	£
Profit before tax	5,404,000
Property, plant and equipment – depreciation charge (W1)	880,000
Increase in inventories (W6)	(595,000)
Increase in trade and other receivables (W6)	(4,243,000)
Increase in trade and other payables (W6)	139,000
Decrease in accruals (W6)	(35,000)
Cash generated from operations	1,550,000

WORKINGS

(1)   FIXTURES AND FITTINGS (AT CARRYING AMOUNT)

	£		£
Balance b/d	5,361,000	Balance c/d	5,846,000
Additions	1,365,000	Depreciation charge (β)	880,000
	6,726,000		6,726,000

(2)   SHARE CAPITAL AND PREMIUM

	£		£
		Balance b/d	
Balance c/d		(10,000,000 + 5,000,000)	15,000,000
(13,000,000 + 12,500,000)	25,500,000	Cash received (β)	10,500,000
	25,500,000		25,500,000

(3)   FREEHOLD BUILDINGS

	£		£
Balance b/d	19,780,000	Balance c/d	20,300,000
Additions (β)	520,000		
	20,300,000		20,300,000

Total additions = 520,000 + 1,365,000 = £ 1,885,000

(4)   TAX PAID

	£		£
Cash paid (β)	1,076,000	Balance b/d	1,238,000
Balance c/d	2,796,000	Profit or loss	2,634,000
	3,872,000		3,872,000

(5)   RETAINED EARNINGS

	£		£
Dividends paid (β)	850,000	Balance b/d	22,856,000
Balance c/d	24,776,000	Net profit for the period	2,770,000
	25,626,000		25,626,000

(6)   Changes in current items

	£
Inventories (16,487 – 15,892)	(595,000)
Receivables (12,347 – 8,104)	(4,243,000)
Payables (2,771 – 2,632)	139,000
Accruals (1,235 – 1,200)	(35,000)

11   VIRGIL LTD

Statement of cash flows for the year ended 30 June 20X2

	£'000	£'000
Net cash from operating activities		40
Cash flows from investing activities		
Development expenditure (130 + 60)	(190)	
Purchase of property, plant and equipment (W1)	(192)	
Proceeds of sale of property, plant and equipment	110	
Net cash used in investing activities		(272)
Cash flows from financing activities		
Proceeds of share issue (850 – 500 – (400/8))	300	
Proceeds from issue of loan notes	50	
Payment of finance lease liabilities (W2)	(31)	
Dividends paid (W3)	(156)	
Net cash from financing activities		163
Net decrease in cash and cash equivalents		(69)
Cash and cash equivalents at beginning of period (163 – 54)		109
Cash and cash equivalents at end of period (172 – 132)		40

WORKINGS

(1)   PPE – CARRYING AMOUNT

	£'000		£'000
B/f	637	Depreciation	57
Revaluation (152 – 60 + 8*)	100	Disposals (110 – 7)	103
Additions under finance lease	56		
Cash additions (ß)	192	C/f	825
	985		985

* (57,000 – 49,000)

(2)   FINANCE LEASE

	£'000		£'000
Payments made (ß)	31	B/f – non-current	80
C/f – non-current	100	– current	12
– current	17	Additions	56
	148		148

(3)   RETAINED EARNINGS

	£'000		£'000
Bonus issue	50	B/f	300
Dividends paid (ß)	156	Excess depreciation (W1)	8
C/f	285	Profit for the year	183
	491		491

12 OPTICA PLC

Statement of cash flows for the year ended 30 September 20X6

	£'000	£'000
Net cash from operating activities		344
Cash flows from investing activities		
Purchase of property, plant and equipment (W1)	(260)	
Purchase of non-current asset investments	(10)	
Net cash used in investing activities		(270)
Cash flows from financing activities		
Dividends paid (W2)	(85)	
Issue of 9% loan notes	120	
Equity share issue (50 (W3) + 100 (W4))	150	
Net cash from financing activities		185
Increase in cash and cash equivalents		259
Cash and cash equivalents at 30 September 20X5		182
Cash and cash equivalents at 30 September 20X6		441

Note: Reconciliation of profit before tax to net cash from operating activities

	£'000
Profit before tax	142
Depreciation	255
Foreign exchange loss	45
Finance costs	40
	482
Decrease in inventories	30
Decrease in receivables	110
Decrease in payables	(205)
Cash generated from operations	417
Interest paid (40 – (300 × 8% re decommissioning))	(16)
Income taxes paid	(57)
Net cash from operating activities	344

WORKINGS

(1) **PROPERTY, PLANT AND EQUIPMENT – CARRYING AMOUNT**

	£'000		£'000
Revaluation (60 – 25)	35	Depreciation	255
Decommissioning provision	300		
Additions (ß)	260	Movement	340
	595		595

(2) **RETAINED EARNINGS**

	£'000		£'000
Bonus issue (100 – 85 (W4))	15	Balance b/f	965
Dividends paid (ß)	85	Profit after tax (142 – 57)	85
Balance c/f	950		
	1,050		1,050

(3) **SHARE CAPITAL**

	£'000		£'000
		Balance b/f	300
		Loan notes converted (100/2)	50
		Bonus issue (300/3)	100
Balance c/f	500	New issue (ß)	50
	500		500

(4)

SHARE PREMIUM

	£'000		£'000
Bonus issue	85	Balance b/f	85
		Loan notes converted (W3)	50
Balance c/f	150	New issue	100
	235		235

CHAPTER 3

Reporting financial performance

Introduction

Examination context

Topic List

Summary and Self-test

Technical reference

Answer to Interactive questions

Answers to Self-test

Learning objectives

- Understand the purpose and principles underlying IAS 8 *Accounting Policies, Changes in Accounting Estimates and Errors*

- Understand how accounting policies are selected and applied

- Apply accounting requirements for changes in accounting policies, changes in accounting estimates and prior period errors

- Disclose the results of a discontinued operation in accordance with IFRS 5 *Non-current Assets Held for Sale and Discontinued Operations*

- Calculate and account for currency conversion gains and losses and assets and liabilities arising from foreign currency transactions

- Explain the reasons for disclosure provisions concerning related parties

- Calculate basic earnings per share

- Define and calculate the distributable profits of an entity and allocations of distributable profit

- Identify any related ethical issues

- Identify and illustrate the main differences between international and UK requirements

Specific syllabus references for this chapter are: 2a, 2b, 2c, 2d, 2e, 2f.

Syllabus links

In the Accounting paper you will have looked briefly at IAS 8 in the context of preparing company accounts. In this paper those basic principles are developed. IFRS 5 and IASs 21, 24 and 33 are introduced at this level. The more complex aspects of these standards will be covered at the Advanced Stage.

Examination context

In the examination, candidates may be required to:

- Prepare financial statements or extracts including adjustments for:

    - Changes in accounting policies
    - Changes in accounting estimates
    - Prior period adjustments
    - Foreign currency transactions

    and be able to explain the required accounting treatment

- Identify and explain the circumstances in which an operation would meet the IFRS 5 definition of a discontinued operation

- Calculate basic EPS and comment on how it might be affected by different accounting policies

- Identify the distributable reserves for an entity and explain the rules surrounding the calculation

- Identify and discuss a related party situation

- Explain and illustrate the difference between the relevant treatment under IFRS and UK GAAP

1 IAS 8 *Accounting Policies, Changes in Accounting Estimates and Errors*

Section overview

IAS 8 is intended to enhance:

- Relevance
- Faithful representation
- Comparability

1.1 Introduction

The objective of IAS 8 *Accounting Policies, Changes in Accounting Estimates and Errors* is to prescribe the criteria for selecting and changing accounting policies, together with the accounting treatment and disclosure of changes in accounting policies, changes in accounting estimates and correction of errors. This enhances relevance, faithful representation and comparability. IAS 8 achieves this objective by ensuring that:

- Information is available about the accounting policies adopted by different entities.

- Different entities adopt a common approach to the distinction between a change in accounting policy and a change in an accounting estimate.

- The scope for accounting policy changes is constrained.

- Changes in accounting policies, changes in accounting estimates and corrections of errors are dealt with in a comparable manner by different entities.

Definition

Accounting policies: The specific principles, bases, conventions, rules and practices applied by an entity in preparing and presenting financial statements.

Accounting policies are normally developed by reference to the **applicable IFRS or Interpretation** together with any relevant Implementation Guidance issued by the IASB. The exception to this is where the effect of applying the accounting policy set out in the IFRS is immaterial.

Where there is no applicable IFRS or Interpretation management should use its judgement in developing an accounting policy ensuring that the resulting information is relevant and reliable. In practical terms management should refer to:

- The requirements and guidance in IFRS/Interpretations dealing with similar and related issues.

- The basic principles set down in the *Conceptual Framework*, for example, the recognition criteria and measurement concepts for assets, liabilities and expenses.

Management may also consider the most recent pronouncements of other standard setting bodies that use a similar conceptual framework to develop standards, other accounting literature and accepted industry practices if these do not conflict with the sources above.

1.2 Consistency of accounting policies

Once selected, accounting policies should be **applied consistently** for similar transactions, other events and conditions. The exception to this is where an IFRS requires or allows categorisation of items where different policies may be applied to each category.

The same accounting policies are usually adopted from period to period, to enhance comparability thereby allowing users to analyse trends over time in profit, cash flows and financial position. **Changes in accounting policy will therefore be rare** and should only be made if the change:

- Is required by an IFRS; or

- Will result in the financial statements providing reliable and more relevant information about the effects of transactions, other events or conditions on the entity's financial position, financial performance or cash flows (a voluntary change).

The standard highlights two types of event **which do not constitute changes in accounting policy**.

- Adopting an accounting policy for a **new type of transaction** or event not dealt with previously by the entity.

- Adopting a **new accounting policy** for a transaction or event which has not occurred in the past or which was not material.

In the case of tangible non-current assets, if a policy of revaluation is adopted for the first time then this is treated, not as a change of accounting policy under IAS 8, but as a revaluation under IAS 16 *Property, Plant and Equipment* (see Chapter 5). The following paragraphs do not therefore apply to a change in policy to adopt revaluations.

1.3 Changes in accounting policy

A change in accounting policy **must be applied retrospectively**.

Definition

Retrospective application: Applying a new accounting policy to transactions, other events and conditions as if that policy had always been applied.

In other words, at the earliest date such transactions or events occurred, the policy is applied from that date.

Any resulting adjustment should be reported as an **adjustment to the opening balance of retained earnings**. Comparative information should be restated unless it is **impracticable** to do so (see Section 1.13 below).

This means that all comparative information must be restated **as if the new policy had always been in force**. When an entity applies an accounting policy retrospectively or retrospectively restates or reclassifies items in its financial statements, IAS 1 (Revised) requires a minimum of three statements of financial position, ie as at:

(a) The end of the current period.
(b) The end of the previous period (beginning of the current period).
(c) The beginning of the earliest comparative period.

As implicit in 'reclassifies' above, IAS 1 also requires that when the **presentation or classification of items is changed** the comparative figures should be restated (unless it is impracticable to do so). This means that a change in the way an item is presented, such as now classifying depreciation charges as cost of sales instead of in administrative expenses **would also be a change in accounting policy**.

Although IAS 8 requires retrospective adjustment for changes in accounting policy it recognises that there may be circumstances where it is **impracticable** to determine the effect in a specific period or on a cumulative basis. Where this is the case the policy should be applied retrospectively to the earliest period for which it is practicable to do so.

In the **rare circumstance** where it is impracticable to restate retrospectively **any** financial results the new policy should be applied **prospectively.** (Impracticability is dealt with in more detail in Section 1.13 below.)

Definition

Prospective application of a change in accounting policy: Applying the new accounting policy to transactions, other events and conditions occurring after the date as at which the policy is changed.

1.4 Adoption of a new IFRS

Where a new IFRS is adopted, IAS 8 requires any transitional provisions in the new IFRS itself to be followed. If none are given in the IFRS which is being adopted, then the entity should follow the general principles of IAS 8.

1.5 Disclosure

Certain **disclosures** are required when a voluntary change in accounting policy has a material effect on the current period or any prior period presented, or when it may have a material effect in subsequent periods.

- Nature of the change

- Reasons for the change (why more reliable and relevant)

- Amount of the adjustment for the current period and for each prior period presented for each line item

- Amount of the adjustment relating to periods prior to those included in the comparative information

- The fact that comparative information has been restated or that it is impracticable to do so

An entity should also disclose information relevant to assessing the **impact of new IFRS** on the financial statements where these have **not yet come into force.**

1.6 Accounting estimates

Definition

Change in accounting estimate: An adjustment of the carrying amount of an asset or a liability or the amount of the periodic consumption of an asset, that results from the assessment of the present status of, and expected future benefits and obligations associated with, assets and liabilities. Changes in accounting estimates result from new information or new developments and, accordingly, are not corrections of errors.

Estimates arise in relation to business activities because of the **uncertainties inherent within them**. Judgements are made based on the latest available, reliable information. The use of such estimates is a necessary part of the preparation of financial statements and does **not** undermine their reliability. Here are some examples of accounting estimates.

- A necessary bad debt (receivables) allowance
- Useful lives of depreciable assets
- Adjustment for obsolescence of inventory

1.7 Accounting treatment

The rule here is that the **effect of a change in an accounting estimate** should be included in the determination of net profit or loss in:

- The period of the change, if the change affects that period only, or
- The period of the change **and** future periods, if the change affects both.

Changes may occur in the circumstances which were in force at the time the estimate was calculated, or perhaps additional information or subsequent developments have come to light.

An example of a change in accounting estimate which affects only the **current period** is the bad debt estimate. However, a revision in the life over which an asset is depreciated would affect both the **current and future periods**, via the amount of the depreciation expense.

The effect of a change in an accounting estimate should be included in the **same revenue or expense classification** as was used previously for the estimate. This rule helps to ensure **consistency** between the financial statements of different periods.

The effect of a change in an accounting estimate is to be recognised **prospectively**.

1.8 Disclosure

Where a change in an accounting estimate has a **material effect** in the current period (or which is expected to have a material effect in subsequent periods) the following should be disclosed.

- Nature of the change in accounting estimate
- Amount of change (if impracticable to estimate, this fact should be disclosed)

Worked example: Change in accounting estimate

Taking the example of a machine tool with an original cost of £100,000, an originally estimated useful life of 10 years and an originally estimated residual value of £nil, the annual straight line depreciation charge will be £10,000 per annum and the carrying amount after three years will be £70,000. If in the fourth year it is decided that as a result of changes in market conditions the remaining useful life is only three years (so a total of six years), then the depreciation charge in that year (and in the next two years) will be the carrying amount brought forward ÷ the revised remaining useful life, so £70,000 ÷ 3 = £23,333. There is no question of going back to restate the depreciation charge for the past three years.

The effect of the change (in this case an increase in the annual depreciation charge from £10,000 to £23,333) in the current year and the next two years must be disclosed.

1.9 Changes in policy versus changes in estimate

It can be difficult sometimes to distinguish between changes in accounting policies and changes in accounting estimates.

When there is doubt as to which type of change it is, IAS 8 requires it to be treated as a **change in accounting estimate**.

1.10 Prior period errors

Errors may be discovered during a current period which **relate to a prior period.**

If **immaterial**, these errors can be **corrected through net profit or loss for the current period**. Where they are **material prior period errors**, however, this is **not appropriate**.

Definition

Prior period errors: Are omissions from, and misstatements in, the entity's financial statements for one or more prior periods arising from a failure to use, or misuse of, reliable information that:

- Was available when financial statements for those periods were authorised for issue.

- Could reasonably be expected to have been obtained and taken into account in the preparation and presentation of those financial statements.

Such errors include the effects of mathematical mistakes, mistakes in applying accounting policies, oversights or misinterpretations of facts, and fraud.

1.11 Accounting treatment

Material prior period errors should be corrected **retrospectively**.

Definition

Retrospective restatement: Correcting the recognition, measurement and disclosure of amounts of elements of financial statements as if a prior period error had never occurred.

This involves:

- Either restating the comparative amounts for the prior period(s) in which the error occurred

- Or, if the error occurred before the earliest prior period presented, restating the opening balances of assets, liabilities and equity for the earliest prior period presented

so that the financial statements are presented **as if the error had never occurred**.

Only where it is **impracticable** to determine the cumulative effect of an error on prior periods can an entity correct a prior period error **prospectively**.

Worked example: Correction of prior period error

Mufti Ltd is producing its draft financial statements for 20X8. The draft statement of profit or loss is as follows:

	20X8 £'000
Revenue	33,600
Cost of sales	(27,900)
Gross profit	5,700
Expenses	(1,617)
Profit before tax	4,083
Income tax expense	(1,225)
Profit for the year	2,858

It has been discovered that items valued at £2.1m which were included in inventory at 31 December 20X7 had in fact been sold before that year end. Retained earnings at 31 December 20X7 were reported as £9,638,000. Cost of sales for 20X8 includes the £2.1m error in opening inventory. No dividends have been declared or paid.

Show the corrected statement of profit or loss for 20X8 and the corrected retained earnings extract from the statement of changes in equity. Ignore any effect on taxation.

Solution

Statement of profit or loss

	20X8 £'000
Revenue	33,600
Cost of sales (27,900 – 2,100)	(25,800)
Gross profit	7,800
Expenses	(1,617)
Profit before tax	6,183
Income tax expense	(1,225)
Profit for the year	4,958

Statement of changes in equity (extract)

	Retained earnings £'000
Balance at 1 January 20X8	9,638
Correction of prior period error	(2,100)
Restated balance	7,538
Total comprehensive income for the year	4,958
Balance at 31 December 20X8	12,496

1.12 Disclosures

Various **disclosures** are required:

- **Nature** of the prior period error

- For each prior period, to the extent practicable, the **amount** of the correction for each financial statement line item affected

- The amount of the correction at the **beginning of the earliest prior period** presented

- If **retrospective restatement is impracticable** for a particular prior period, the **circumstances** that led to the existence of that condition and a description of how and from when the error has been corrected

Subsequent periods need not repeat these disclosures.

1.13 Impracticability

As we have already mentioned, in some cases it may be **impracticable** to make **retrospective adjustments** for changes in accounting policies or prior period errors.

Definition

Impracticable: Applying a requirement is impracticable when the entity cannot apply it after making every reasonable effort to do so. It is impracticable to apply a change in an accounting policy retrospectively or to make a retrospective restatement to correct an error if one of the following apply.

- The effects of the retrospective application or retrospective restatement are not determinable.

- The retrospective application or retrospective restatement requires assumptions about what management's intent would have been in that period.

- The retrospective application or retrospective restatement requires significant estimates of amounts and it is impossible to distinguish objectively information about those estimates that:

  - Provides evidence of circumstances that existed on the date(s) at which the transaction, other event or condition occurred; and

  - Would have been available when the financial statements for that prior period were authorised for issue, from other information.

Where it is impracticable to determine the period-specific or cumulative effects of:

- Retrospective application of a changed accounting policy
- Prior period errors ranking for retrospective restatement

then no retrospective adjustments are made.

It is important not to use hindsight but to identify information for earlier periods which not only reflects the circumstances at the earlier date but also would have been available at that earlier date. If such information is not identifiable, then it is impracticable to make retrospective application or restatement.

2 IFRS 5 and discontinued operations

Section overview
The results of discontinued operations should be presented separately in the statement of profit or loss.

2.1 The problem

The ability to predict the future performance of an entity is hampered when the financial statements include activities which as a result of sale or closure will not continue into the future. While figures inclusive of those activities are a fair measure of past performance, they do not form a good basis for predicting the future cash flows, earnings-generating capacity and financial position. Separating out data about discontinued activities benefits users of financial statements, but leads to difficulties in defining such operations and in deciding when a discontinuance comes about. This problem is addressed by IFRS 5 *Non-current Assets Held for Sale and Discontinued Operations*.

2.2 The objectives of IFRS 5 regarding discontinued operations

Part of IFRS 5 is designed to deal with the problem by requiring entities to disclose in the statement of profit or loss and statement of cash flows the results of discontinued operations separately from those of continuing operations and to make certain disclosures in the statement of financial position. This chapter only deals with IFRS 5's definition of discontinued operations and its disclosure requirements; the other aspects are concerned with measurement and recognition of profits and losses on non-current assets held for sale and these are covered in Chapter 4.

There are two parts of the Chapter 4 coverage which are relevant to the disclosure rules dealt with in this chapter:

- The key criterion for the classification of a non-current asset as held for sale is that it is highly probable that it will be finally sold within **12 months of classification**.

- A non-current asset held for sale is measured at the **lower of carrying amount and fair value less costs to sell**. The effect is that if fair value less costs to sell is lower than the carrying amount of the asset, then the loss is recognised at the time the decision is made to dispose of the asset, not when the disposal actually takes place.

2.3 Discontinued operations

Definitions

Discontinued operation: A component of an entity that has either been disposed of, or is classified as held for sale, and

- Represents a separate major line of business or geographical area of operations,

- Is part of a single co-ordinated plan to dispose of a separate major line of business or geographical area of operations, or

- Is a subsidiary acquired exclusively with a view to resale.

Component of an entity: Operations and cash flows that can be clearly distinguished, operationally and for financial reporting purposes, from the rest of the entity.

As already noted, the separation of information about discontinued activities benefits users of financial statements by providing them with information about continuing operations which they can use as the basis for predicting the future cash flows, earnings-generating capacity and financial position. Management is therefore faced with the temptation to classify continuing, but underperforming, operations as discontinued, so that their performance does not act as a drag on the figures used as a basis for future predictions. This is why the definition of a discontinued operation is so important, but applying that definition requires difficult **judgements**.

Consider the following:

- The abrupt cessation of several products within an ongoing line of business: presumably a line of business must be defined by reference to the requirement in the definition for a component to be 'distinguished operationally and for financial reporting purposes'. But how many products have to be stopped before the line of business itself is stopped?

- Selling a subsidiary whose activities are similar to those of other group companies: how should 'similar' be defined?

2.4 When does a discontinuance come about?

IFRS 5 does not set out specific criteria for when a discontinuance comes about, despite its importance in terms of defining the accounting period in which disclosures must first be made. Instead, it relies on the definition of a discontinued operation, but this comes in two parts; it is a component of the entity which:

- **Has been disposed of**. In this case, the disclosures will first be made in the accounting period in which the disposal takes place, or

- **Is held for sale**. In this case the disclosures will first be made in the accounting period in which the decision to dispose of it is made, provided that it is highly probable that it will be **sold within 12 months of classification**.

If a business decides to discontinue operations and the non-current assets supporting these operations are to be abandoned (so scrapped or just closed down) rather than sold, the carrying amount of the assets will not be recovered principally through sale. So these assets cannot be classified as held for sale. As a result, these operations should not be disclosed as discontinued until the underlying assets actually cease to be used.

Point to note: Operations supported by assets which become idle because they are temporarily taken out of use may not be described as discontinued. This includes, for example, assets that are mothballed and may be brought back into use if market conditions improve.

2.5 Presenting discontinued operations: statement of profit or loss and statement of cash flows

An entity should disclose a **single amount in the statement of profit or loss** comprising the total of:

- The post-tax profit or loss of discontinued operations, and

- The post-tax gain or loss recognised on the measurement to fair value less costs to sell or on the disposal of the assets constituting the discontinued operation.

An entity should also **disclose an analysis of this single amount** into:

- The revenue, expenses and pre-tax profit or loss of discontinued operations.

- The related income tax expense.

- The gain or loss recognised on measurement to fair value less costs to sell or on disposal of the assets constituting the discontinued operation.

- The related income tax expense.

This analysis may be presented either:

- In the statement of profit or loss, or
- In the notes.

If it is presented in the statement of profit or loss it should be presented in a section identified as relating to discontinued operations, ie separately from continuing operations. (This analysis is not required where the discontinued operation is a newly acquired subsidiary that has been classified as held for sale.)

The disclosure of discontinued operations adopted in these Learning Materials is in line with Example 11 in the (non-mandatory) Guidance on Implementing IFRS 5. The main part of the statement of profit or loss is described as 'continuing operations', with the single amount in respect of 'discontinued operations' being brought in just above 'profit/(loss) for the year'.

XYZ PLC – Statement of profit or loss for the year ended [date]

	£m
Continuing operations	
Revenue	X
Cost of sales	(X)
...	...
...	...
Share of profits/(losses) of associates	X
Profit/(loss) before tax	X
Income tax expense	(X)
Profit/(loss) for the year from continuing operations	X
Discontinued operations (Note Y)	
Profit/(loss) for the year from discontinued operations	(X)
Profit/(loss) for the year	X

Note Y Discontinued operation

During the year the company disposed of its textile division.

Amounts attributable to the division for 20X9 were as follows:

	£m
Revenue	X
Expenses	(X)
Pre-tax profit	X
Income tax expense	(X)
	X
Loss recognised on disposal of non-current assets	(X)
Income tax	X
	(X)

In the **statement of cash flows** an entity should disclose the net cash flows attributable to the:

- Operating
- Investing, and
- Financing

activities of discontinued operations.

These disclosures may be presented either in the statement of cash flows or in the **notes**.

Points to note

1   The results and cash flows for any prior periods shown as comparative figures must be restated to be consistent with the continuing/discontinued classification in the current period. As an example, operations discontinued in the year ended 31 December 20X7 will have been presented as continuing in the 20X6 financial statements but will be re-presented as discontinued in the 20X6 comparative figures included in the 20X7 financial statements.

2   Some narrative descriptions are also required. Although this part of the IFRS does not specifically mention discontinued operations, it includes them through its requirement for these narratives in respect of non-current assets disposed of or classified as held for sale; many discontinued operations will include such non-current assets.

3   If in the current period there are adjustments to be made to operations discontinued in prior periods, their effect must be shown separately from the figures for operations discontinued in the current period.

4   If a part of the business is discontinued but it does not meet the criteria for a discontinued operation (ie it cannot be clearly distinguished), then its results must be included in those from continuing operations.

2.6   Presenting discontinued operations: statement of financial position

If the operation has finally been discontinued and all its assets have been disposed of, **there will be nothing relating to the discontinued operation still in the statement of financial position**. So there will be no disclosures required.

If non-current assets held for sale have not been finally disposed of, they must be shown in the statement of financial position **separately from all other assets**. In these circumstances there will be a separate line item immediately below the sub-total for current assets for the **non-current assets held for sale**. If an operation is being discontinued, then any non-current assets related to it will now be held with a view to disposal and it will be inappropriate for them to be shown as non-current assets.

The previous classification is retained for non-current assets being abandoned because, by definition, they are not held for sale.

Point to note: Any non-current assets now held for sale are not reclassified as held for sale in the statements of financial position for any prior periods shown as comparative figures.

2.7 Link with other IASs

As has already been noted, the part of IFRS 5 dealt with in this chapter is concerned purely with disclosure, not about recognition or measurement. But a decision to discontinue an operation would normally require management to immediately consider the recognition and measurement requirements of:

- IAS 36 *Impairment of Assets* (dealt with in Chapter 4) which may require an immediate reduction in the carrying amount of non-current assets.

- IAS 37 *Provisions, Contingent Liabilities and Contingent Assets* (dealt with in Chapter 9) which may require the recognition of provisions for reorganisation and restructuring costs.

It is also the case that, even if a component being disposed of or abandoned has to be treated as a continuing operation (because it does not meet all of the conditions for being classified as a discontinued operation), management should still consider whether the requirements of IAS 36 and IAS 37, together with that of IAS 1 (dealt with in Chapter 2) to make separate disclosure of 'exceptional' items, should be applied to that continuing operation.

Worked example: Business closure

On 20 October 20X7 the directors of a parent company made a public announcement of plans to close a steel works. The closure means that the group will no longer carry out this type of operation, which until recently has represented about 10% of its total revenue. The works will be gradually shut down over a period of several months, with complete closure expected in July 20X8. At 31 December output had been significantly reduced and some redundancies had already taken place. The cash flows, revenues and expenses relating to the steel works can be clearly distinguished from those of the subsidiary's other operations.

How should the closure be treated in the financial statements for the year ended 31 December 20X7?

Solution

Because the steel works is being closed, rather than sold, it cannot be classified as 'held for sale'. In addition, the steel works is not a discontinued operation. Although at 31 December 20X7 the group was firmly committed to the closure, this has not yet taken place and therefore the steel works must be included in continuing operations. Information about the planned closure should be disclosed in the notes to the financial statements.

Interactive question 1: Discontinued operation

[Difficulty level: Exam standard]

The statement of profit or loss for Grey plc for the year ended 31 December 20X7 is as follows:

	£
Revenue	300,000
Cost of sales	(100,000)
Gross profit	200,000
Distribution costs	(40,000)
Administrative expenses	(90,000)
Profit before tax	70,000
Income tax expense	(21,000)
Profit for the year	49,000

On 30 September 20X7 the company classified a manufacturing division as held for sale. It satisfies the definition of a discontinued operation in accordance with IFRS 5.

The results of the division are as follows:

	£
Revenue	32,000
Cost of sales	(15,000)
Distribution costs	(12,000)
Administrative expenses	(10,000)

These balances have been included in the statement of profit or loss of Grey plc above.

Requirement

Show how the discontinued operation would be treated in the statement of profit or loss.

Fill in the proforma below.

£

Continuing operations
Revenue
Cost of sales
Gross profit
Distribution costs
Administrative expenses
Profit before tax
Income tax expense
Profit for the year from continuing operations
Discontinued operations
Loss for the year from discontinued operations
Profit for the year

WORKING

	Continuing operations £	Discontinued operations £	Total £
Revenue			
Cost of sales			
Gross profit			
Distribution costs			
Administrative expenses			
Profit/(loss) from operations			
Income tax			
Net profit/(loss) for year			

See **Answer** at the end of this chapter.

3 IAS 21 *The Effects of Changes in Foreign Exchange Rates*

Section overview

- Foreign currency conversion gains and losses arise when transactions are undertaken in different currencies.

- At the end of a reporting period foreign currency assets and liabilities must be retranslated into the local or 'functional' currency of the reporting entity.

3.1 The issue

If a company trades overseas, it will buy or sell assets in foreign currencies. For example, an Indian company might buy materials from Canada, and pay for them in US dollars, and then sell its finished goods in Germany, receiving payment in Euros. If the company owes money in a foreign currency at the end of the accounting period, or holds assets which were bought in a foreign currency, those liabilities or assets must be translated into the local currency (in this Text £), in order to be shown in the books of account.

If foreign currency exchange rates remained constant, there would be no accounting problem. As you will be aware, however, foreign exchange rates are continually changing, and it is not inconceivable for example, that the rate of exchange between the Euro and sterling might be €1.4 to £1 at the start of the accounting year, and €1.2 to £1 at the end of the year (in this example, a 17% increase in the relative strength of the Euro).

There are two distinct types of foreign currency transaction, conversion and translation.

3.2 Foreign currency transactions

Foreign currency transactions arise when one foreign currency is exchanged for another foreign currency. For example, suppose a local company buys a large consignment of goods from a supplier in Germany. The order is placed on 1 May and the agreed price is €127,875. At the time of delivery the rate of foreign exchange was €1.50 to £1. The local company would record the amount owed in its books as follows.

DR	Inventory account (127,875 ÷ 1.5)	£85,250	
CR	Payables account		£85,250

When the local company comes to pay the supplier, it needs to obtain some foreign currency. By this time, however, if the rate of exchange has altered to €1.55 to £1, the cost of raising €127,875 would be (÷ 1.55) £82,500. The company would need to spend only £82,500 to settle a debt for inventories 'costing' £85,250. Since it would be administratively difficult to alter the value of the inventories in the company's books of account, it is more appropriate to record a profit on conversion of £2,750.

DR	Payables account	£85,250	
CR	Cash		£82,500
CR	Profit on conversion		£2,750

Profits (or losses) on conversion would be included in profit of loss for the year in which conversion (whether payment or receipt) takes place.

Suppose that another home company sells goods to a Chinese company, and it is agreed that payment should be made in Chinese Yuan at a price of Y116,000. We will further assume that the exchange rate at the time of sale is Y10.74 to £1, but when the debt is eventually paid, the rate has altered to Y10.8 to £1. The company would record the sale as follows.

DR	Receivables account (116,000 ÷ 10.74)	£10,800	
CR	Sales account		£10,800

When the Y116,000 are paid, the local company will convert them into £, to obtain (÷ 10.8) £10,740. In this example, there has been a loss on conversion of £60 which will be written off to profit or loss for the year:

DR	Cash	£10,740	
DR	Loss on conversion	£60	
CR	Receivables account		£10,800

3.3 Translation

Foreign currency translation does not involve the act of exchanging one currency for another. **Translation is required at the end of an accounting period when a company still holds assets or liabilities in its statement of financial position which were obtained or incurred in a foreign currency.**

These assets or liabilities might arise where an individual home company holds individual **assets** or **liabilities** originating in a foreign currency 'deal'.

3.4 Definitions

These are some of the definitions given by IAS 21.

> **Foreign currency.** A currency other than the functional currency of the entity.
>
> **Functional currency.** The currency of the primary economic environment in which the entity operates.
>
> **Exchange rate.** The ratio of exchange for two currencies.
>
> **Exchange difference.** The difference resulting from translating a given number of units of one currency into another currency at different exchange rates.
>
> **Closing rate.** The spot exchange rate at the year end date.
>
> **Spot exchange rate.** The exchange rate for immediate delivery.
>
> **Monetary items.** Units of currency held and assets and liabilities to be received or paid in a fixed or determinable number of units of currency. *(IAS 21)*

For most individual companies the functional currency will be the currency of the country in which they are located and in which they carry out most of their transactions.

3.5 Foreign currency transactions: initial recognition

IAS 21 states that a foreign currency transaction should be recorded, on initial recognition in the functional currency, by applying the exchange rate between the reporting currency and the foreign currency **at the date of the transaction** to the foreign currency amount.

An **average rate** for a period may be used if exchange rates do not fluctuate significantly.

3.6 Reporting at subsequent year ends

It is important to make the clear distinction between foreign currency monetary and non-monetary items, as the treatment for reporting these items is different at the year end. The main feature of a monetary item is that there is a right to receive (or an obligation to deliver) a fixed or determinable number of units of currency, for example, receivables, payables, loans, provisions to be settled in cash and cash in a foreign currency.

Conversely, the essential feature of a non-monetary item is the absence of a right to receive (or an obligation to deliver) a fixed or determinable number of units of currency, for example, intangible assets, property, plant and equipment and inventories.

The following rules apply at each subsequent year end.

(a) Report foreign currency **monetary items** using the **closing rate**.

(b) Report **non-monetary items** which are carried at **historical cost** in a foreign currency using the **exchange rate at the date of the transaction** (historical rate).

(c) Report **non-monetary items** which are carried at **fair value** in a foreign currency using the exchange rates that existed **when the values were measured**.

3.7 Recognition of exchange differences

Exchange differences occur when there is a **change in the exchange rate** between the transaction date and the date of settlement of monetary items arising from a foreign currency transaction.

Exchange differences arising on the settlement of monetary items or on translating an entity's monetary items at rates different from those at which they were translated initially, or reported in previous financial statements, should be **recognised in profit or loss** in the period in which they arise.

There are two situations to consider.

(a) The transaction is **settled in the same period** as that in which it occurred: all the exchange difference is recognised in that period.

(b) The transaction is **settled in a subsequent accounting period**: the exchange difference recognised in each intervening period up to the period of settlement is determined by the change in exchange rates during that period.

In other words, where a monetary item has not been settled at the end of a period, it should be **restated using the closing exchange rate** and any gain or loss taken to profit or loss.

When a gain or loss on a non-monetary item is recognised **in other comprehensive income** (for example, where property is revalued), any **related exchange differences** should also be **recognised in other comprehensive income**.

Interactive question 2: Exchange rate movements   [Difficulty level: Easy]

Watford Ltd, a company whose functional currency is the £, entered into the following foreign currency transaction.

31.10.20X8 Purchased goods from Mexico SA for 129,000 Mexican pesos

31.12.20X8 Mexico SA has not yet been paid

31.01.20X9 Payment made to Mexico SA

The exchange rates are as follows.

	Pesos to £1
31.10.X8	9.5
31.12.X8	10
31.01.X9	9.7

Requirement

Show how this transaction would be recorded in the books of Watford Ltd during the years ended 31 December 20X8 and 20X9.

See **Answer** at the end of this chapter.

4   IAS 24 *Related Party Disclosures*

Section overview

- Disclosure is required of the nature of any related party relationships and of any transactions between such parties.

- There are a number of ways in which one party may be related to another.

- The relationship between an entity and its parent and subsidiaries should be disclosed regardless of whether any transactions have taken place between them.

- An entity is required to disclose the name of its parent and, if different, that of the ultimate controlling party.

- An entity should disclose the salary and other compensation of key management personnel in total together with an analysis of this balance.

4.1   Introduction

The normal assumption is that directors of companies attempt to promote the interests of shareholders in their dealings with other entities. As a result **transactions are normally assumed to take place at arm's length values**.

However, companies are made up of a variety of stakeholders with different interests and incentives, which in some cases may lead to **a conflict of interest**. Examples might include:

- Transactions between companies under **common control** (for example a parent and a subsidiary)
- Transactions between the company and its directors

The two parties to the transactions referred to above are said to be related to each other and the transactions between them to be related party transactions.

In these circumstances the normal rules of commercial arrangements **may not** apply and as a result:

- The reported performance of the entity **may** be distorted
- Directors **may** face conflicting incentives.

IAS 24 enhances transparency by requiring **disclosure** to shareholders of these relationships and the transactions stemming from them.

Point to note: IAS 24 **does not** require any disclosures about whether related party transactions were carried out at prices other than open market prices.

4.2 Objective

The key emphasis of IAS 24 is **appropriate disclosure**. It aims to ensure that an entity's financial statements contain the disclosures necessary to draw attention to the possibility that its position and results may have been affected by the existence of related parties and transactions with them.

Related party transactions are, however, a normal feature of commerce and business, so IAS 24 does not attempt to prevent such relationships or to require any adjustments to the values of related party transactions carried out at non-market prices.

4.3 Scope

IAS 24 should be applied in:

(a) Identifying **related party relationships** and **transactions**
(b) Identifying **outstanding balances** between an entity and its related parties
(c) Identifying circumstances in which **disclosure** of the items in (a) and (b) is required, and
(d) **Determining the disclosures to be made** about those items

IAS 24 requires disclosure of related party relationships, transactions and outstanding balances in the separate financial statements of:

- A parent
- A venturer in a joint venture
- An investor in an associated entity

Related party transactions and outstanding balances with other entities in a group are disclosed in an **individual entity's financial statements**.

Intra-group related party transactions and outstanding balances **are eliminated on consolidation in the financial statements of the group** and are not disclosed.

Point to note: On many occasions IAS 24 uses the phrase 'outstanding balances, including commitments', commitments meaning undertakings to do something if a particular event occurs or does not occur in the future. In these notes this phrase had been shortened to 'outstanding balances'.

4.4 Identifying related parties

This depends on a number of key definitions in IAS 24.

Definitions

Related party: A person or entity that is related to the entity preparing its financial statements (the reporting entity).

(a) A person or a close member of that person's family (see definition below) is related to a reporting entity if that person:

(i) Has control or joint control over the reporting entity

(ii) Has significant influence over the reporting entity, or

(iii) Is a member of the key management personnel (see definition below) of the reporting entity or of a parent of the reporting entity.

(b) An entity is related to a reporting entity if any of the following conditions applies:

    (i)   The entity and the reporting entity are members of the same group.

    (ii)   One entity is an associate or joint venture of the other entity (or of a member of the group of which the other entity is a member).

    (iii) Both entities are joint ventures of the same third party.

    (iv) One entity is a joint venture of a third entity and the other entity is an associate of the third entity.

    (v)   The entity is a post-employment benefit plan for the benefit of employees of either the reporting entity or of an entity related to the reporting entity.

    (vi) The entity is controlled or jointly controlled by a person identified in (a) above.

    (vii) A person identified in (a) (i) above has significant influence over the entity or is a member of the key management personnel (see definition below) of the entity or of a parent of the entity.

Point to note: The definitions of a related party treat control and joint control differently from significant influence. So fellow subsidiaries and fellow joint ventures are related parties of each other under definitions (b)(i) and (b)(iii) respectively, but if the same investor has significant influence over two associates, those associates are not related parties of each other.

Close members of the family of a person: Those family members who may be expected to influence, or be influenced by, that person in their dealings with the entity. These include:

(a) That person's children and spouse or domestic partner;
(b) Children of that person's spouse or domestic partner, and
(c) Dependants of that person or that person's spouse or domestic partner.

Control: The power to govern the financial and operating policies of an entity so as to obtain benefits from its activities.

Joint control: The contractually agreed sharing of control over an economic activity.

Key management personnel: Those persons having authority and responsibility for planning, directing and controlling the activities of the entity, directly or indirectly, including any director (whether executive or otherwise) of that entity.

Significant influence: The power to participate in the financial and operating policy decisions of an entity, but not to control those policies. Significant influence may be gained by share ownership, statute or agreement.

4.5 Application of substance over form

Under IAS 24 attention should be directed to the **substance** of the relationship rather than focusing on its legal form. For example, the following **are not related parties:**

- Two entities **simply because they have a director** (or other member of key management personnel) **in common,** or because a member of key management personnel of one entity has significant influence over the other entity.

- Two venturers **simply because they share joint control over a joint venture**.

- Providers of finance, trade unions, public utilities and government departments and agencies of a government that does not control, jointly control or significantly influence the reporting entity **simply by virtue of their normal dealings with an entity.**

- A customer, supplier, franchisor, distributor, or general agent, with whom an entity transacts a significant volume of business, **simply by virtue of the resulting economic dependence.**

Worked example: Related parties

The following examples illustrate the application of the definition of a related party to practical situations:

(a) Person A owns 30% of Entity B and Entity C owns 40% of Entity B

Entity B is the reporting entity:

Person A is a related party under definition (a)(ii) and Entity C is a related party under definition (b)(ii)

Entity C is the reporting entity:

Entity B is a related party under definition (b)(ii)

(b) Person A and Entity B have joint control over Entity C

Entity B is the reporting entity:

Entity C is a related party under definition (b)(ii)

Entity C is the reporting entity:

Person A is a related party under definition (a)(i) and Entity B is a related party under definition (b)(ii)

(c) Person A is a non-executive director of Entity B

Entity B is the reporting entity:

Person A falls within the definition of Entity B's key management personnel and is a related party under definition (a)(iii)

(d) Person A owns 70% of Entity B and is a director of Entity C

Entity B is the reporting entity:

Person A is a related party under definition (a)(i) and Entity C is a related party under definition (b)(vii)

Entity C is the reporting entity:

Person A falls within the definition of Entity C's key management personnel and is a related party under definition (b)(iii)

Entity B is a related party under definition (b)(vi)

4.6 Related party transactions

Definition

Related party transaction: A transfer of resources, services or obligations between a reporting entity and a related party, regardless of whether a price is charged.

Note that this definition covers **any transaction that occurs between a reporting entity and a related party**

- It is common practice for a reporting entity's employees to receive goods or services at reduced prices or for free. If the employees fall within the definition of the reporting entity's key management personnel, they will be related parties and the entity should disclose these transactions.

- Even if every transaction with a related party takes place at the full arm's length price, the reporting entity should disclose them.

IAS 24 is based on the principle that **it is the identification of the related party relationship that triggers the disclosure requirements.**

Examples of transactions which should be disclosed include:

- **Transfers of resources for which no charge is made**

  It is common for parent companies not to make a charge for some services, such as for management services provided to a subsidiary. In practice, **it is very difficult to identify transactions for which there is no charge at all**; there is nothing for accounting systems to capture, so there is no easy place to go looking for the relevant information.

- **Transfers of resources for which an artificial charge is made**

  An example of an artificial charge would be where, under instructions from the parent, **sales** between group companies **are at above, or below, open market prices**.

- **Transfers of resources made at full, open market, prices (that is arm's length prices)**

  The reason for including these is that even if in the current year such transfers are made for full consideration, the related party relationship means that in a future year they might not be. Also, **the related party relationship itself is important information to users** in understanding the motivation of the relevant parties in the context of corporate governance.

  Disclosures that related party transactions were made on terms equivalent to those that prevail in arm's length transactions should be made **only if such terms can be substantiated**.

4.7 Disclosures

- **Disclosure is always required of the related party relationship between a parent and a subsidiary**, irrespective of whether there have been any transactions between the entities.

  Disclosure is required of the parent's name and, if different, the name of the ultimate controlling party.

  If the financial statements of the parent or ultimate controlling party are not publicly available, the entity is required to identify the next most senior parent in the group that does produce financial statements that are available to the general public.

  Point to note: The reason this relationship must be disclosed even if there have not been any such transactions in the current period, is that the control held by the parent means that there could be such transactions in future periods, if the parent decided this was appropriate.

- **Disclosure is always required of compensation**, being the consideration in exchange for their services, received by **key management personnel** in total and for each of the following five categories:

Category	Example
Short-term employee benefits	Salary and holiday pay
Post-employment benefits	Pensions
Other long-term benefits	Long-service awards or sabbatical leave
Termination benefits	Redundancy pay
Share-based payments	Shares and share options

- **Disclosures required only if there have been related party transactions during the period:**

  - The nature of the relationships (but remember this must always be disclosed in respect of a parent)

  - The amount of the transactions

  - The amount of any balances outstanding at the year end

  - The terms and conditions attaching to any outstanding balance (for example, whether security has been provided and what form the payment will take)

  - Details of any guarantees given or received

  - Any provision against any outstanding balances and the expense recognised in the period for bad or doubtful debts due from related parties

- **Disclosure** of the fact that transactions were on an **arm's length basis** is **voluntary**.

  This disclosure may be made only if such terms can be substantiated.

These disclosures should be made separately for different categories of related parties, although items of a similar nature may be disclosed together. Where aggregation results in key information necessary to understand the effect of the transactions on the financial statements being unavailable, separate disclosure should be made.

The different categories for which separate disclosures are required are identified as:

- The **parent**
- Entities with **joint control** or **significant influence** over the entity
- **Subsidiaries**
- **Associates**
- **Joint ventures** in which the entity is a **venturer** (see Chapter 13)
- **Key management personnel** of the entity or its parent
- **Other related parties**

Although information is required about the nature of related parties, there is no requirement to identify them by name.

4.8 Examples

The following are **examples of transactions that are disclosed** if they are **with a related party**:

- Purchases or sales of goods (finished or unfinished)
- Purchases or sales of property and other assets
- Rendering or receiving of services
- Leases
- Transfers of research and development
- Transfers under licence agreements
- Transfers under finance arrangements
- Provision of guarantees or collateral
- Commitments to do something if a particular event occurs or does not occur in the future
- Settlement of liabilities on behalf of the entity, or by the entity on behalf of another party

Interactive question 3: Related party disclosures   [Difficulty level: Exam standard]

Pinot is a company that complies with the minimum requirements of IAS 24.

Requirements

Explain whether related party relationships exist and what disclosures, if any, would be required by IAS 24 in the current year financial statements of Pinot, in respect of each of the following transactions.

(1)   Pinot sells goods on credit to Chablis, which is a company owned by the son of Mr Grigio. Mr Grigio is a director of Pinot. At the year end there was a trade receivable of £100,000 owing from Chablis to Pinot. It was decided to write off £30,000 of this receivable, and make full provision against the remainder. Debt collection costs incurred by Pinot during the year were £4,000.

(2)   During the year Pinot purchased goods from Merlot for £600,000, which was deemed to be an arm's length price. Pinot owns 40% of the ordinary share capital of Merlot.

(3)   At the year end an amount of £90,000 was due to one of Pinot's distributor companies, Shiraz.

(4)   During the year a house owned by Pinot, with a carrying amount of £200,000 and a market value of £450,000, was sold to one of its directors, Mrs Barolo, for £425,000. Pinot guaranteed the loan taken out by Mrs Barolo to purchase the property.

See **Answer** at the end of this chapter.

4.9 Judgements required

In practical terms the identification of related parties and the disclosure of transactions with them may not be straightforward. Reasons for this include the following:

- The application of the definitions of a related party can be **subjective** and will involve the use of **judgement**, for example whether someone is a close member of the family of an individual.

- Transactions may be difficult to identify, particularly where **no consideration** has changed hands.

- Directors and key management may be **sensitive** to the disclosure of certain transactions; this increases the risk of deliberate concealment.

- **Quantitative materiality** issues are not necessarily relevant. In many cases the existence of the relationship is the issue rather than the amounts involved.

An accountant preparing financial statements must ensure that **all relevant information is made available to him/her** and that the statements comply with the requirements of IAS 24, irrespective of any other pressures being applied.

5 IAS 33 *Earnings per share*

Section overview

- Basic earnings per share is calculated as the profit or loss attributable to the ordinary equity holders divided by the number of shares in issue.

- IAS 33 is only mandatory for listed entities.

5.1 Context

One of the most commonly used performance measures worldwide is basic earnings per share (EPS), which is calculated as the profit or loss attributable to the ordinary equity holders divided by the number of shares in issue.

In addition to being an important independent measure, it also is a component in the price earnings (P/E) ratio which often forms a pivotal role in the valuation of businesses. A meaningful comparison between entities, or against a benchmark figure, can only be made where entities measure their EPS figure on a consistent basis. IAS 33 prescribes what that consistent basis should be.

Standard EPS calculations assist in comparisons which are meaningful across entities, but they take account of all income and expenses that have been reported during the period, whether or not they are likely to recur in the future. These calculations provide a historical performance measure and do not purport to provide a measure of future performance. So entities frequently present alternative forms of EPS, based on income and expenses which have been adjusted to exclude non-recurring items; entities generally refer to the adjusted profit figure as 'maintainable earnings'. Industry or market standard EPS figures are also often reported. Both of these additional performance measures are claimed to provide a more realistic measure of the entity's performance in future periods.

Compliance with IAS 33 is mandatory for:

- The separate financial statements of entities whose ordinary shares are publicly traded or are in the process of being issued in public markets.

- The consolidated financial statements for groups whose parent has shares similarly traded/being issued.

Other entities need not present EPS (because their shares are not traded, there is no readily available market price which can be used to calculate the P/E ratio), but if they do voluntarily, they should comply with IAS 33.

IAS 33 requires the EPS to be presented in the statement of profit or loss.

5.2 Calculation

The calculation for basic EPS is profit or loss divided by the number of shares in issue.

The fully worded calculation is:

$$\frac{\text{Profit/(loss) attributable to ordinary equity holders of the parent}}{\text{Weighted average number of ordinary shares outstanding during the period}}$$

Shares are usually included in the weighted average number of shares from the date any consideration for them is receivable by the issuer. This is generally the date of their issue.

Point to note: The need for a weighted average number of shares is explained later in Section 5.4.

5.3 Calculating earnings

The earnings figure to be used is the profit or loss attributable to **the ordinary equity holders**. The statement of profit or loss presents the profit attributable to the **owners** of the entity. Usually this will be the amount attributable to ordinary equity holders, but in some cases a deduction should be made for the amount attributable to preference equity holders.

Whether such a deduction is needed depends upon the type of preference share:

- Redeemable preference shares should be classified as liabilities and the finance charge relating to them (both dividend and any premium on redemption adjustment) should already have been recognised in profit or loss as part of finance charges. No adjustment is needed.

- Some irredeemable preference shares are classified as equity and the dividend is deducted in the statement of changes in equity. An adjustment is needed; the dividend should be deducted from the profit figure taken from the statement of profit or loss to arrive at the profit attributable to the ordinary equity holders.

Interactive question 4: Dividend on irredeemable preference shares presented as equity

[Difficulty level: Easy]

	£m
Profit for the period	2,177
Attributable to:	
Owners of the parent	1,897
Non-controlling interests	280
	2,177
Dividends presented in statement of changes in equity	
On irredeemable preference shares	400
On ordinary shares	600

The weighted average number of ordinary shares in issue is 6,241 million.

Requirement

Calculate the basic EPS.

Fill in the proforma below.

£m

Profit attributable to owners of the parent
Less: dividend on irredeemable preference shares
Profit attributable to ordinary equity holders of the parent

EPS =

See **Answer** at the end of this chapter.

5.3.1 Cumulative dividends on irredeemable preference shares presented as equity

If the dividends on such shares are cumulative, any dividend not paid in the current year (due, for example, to lack of distributable profits) will be payable in subsequent years when distributable profits become available. All such arrears need to be paid off before any ordinary share dividend is paid.

The **treatment of such cumulative dividends** for EPS purposes is as follows.

- If the dividend is not paid in the year, then it should still be deducted from profit.
- When the arrears of dividend is subsequently paid, it should be excluded from the EPS calculation.

Interactive question 5: Cumulative dividend on irredeemable preference shares presented as equity

[Difficulty level: Intermediate]

	£m
Profit for the period	88

Attributable to:	
Owners of the parent	82
Non-controlling interest	6
	88

Dividends presented in statement of changes in equity	
On irredeemable preference shares (Note)	20
On ordinary shares	5

Note

This figure includes £15m in respect of arrears of cumulative dividend not paid in previous years due to lack of distributable profits.

The weighted average number of ordinary shares is 1,200 million.

Requirement

Calculate the basic EPS.

Fill in the proforma below.

£m

Profit
Less dividend on irredeemable preference shares
Profit attributable to ordinary equity holders of the parent

EPS =

See **Answer** at the end of this chapter.

5.4 Calculating the weighted average number of ordinary shares

If no additional shares have been issued during the year, or repurchased, there are no complications; the number of shares in issue at the start (or end) of the period is used.

If additional shares **have been issued** during the current period, the calculation of the weighted average number of shares depends upon whether:

- The resources of the entity have increased, for example an issue of shares for cash at full market price.

- The resources of the entity have not changed, for example a bonus issue.

If shares are repurchased during the period (treasury shares), the weighted average number of shares will again depend on whether:

- The repurchase was at market price
- The repurchase was other than at market price

5.5 Issue of shares for cash at full market price

Where shares are issued during the period for cash at full market price, the cash received is an **increase in the resources** of the entity. These additional resources will only have been available to increase earnings (the numerator in the EPS fraction) for part of the period, so the additional shares should only be included in the shares in issue (the denominator of the fraction) for part of the period. The number of new shares is 'weighted' for the proportion of the period they have been in issue.

Point to note

An issue of shares in an acquisition at market value is equivalent to an issue of shares for cash in these calculations.

The weighted average number of shares is calculated as follows.

- Start with the number of shares in issue **at the start of the year** and time-apportion it for the period **up to** the date the new shares were issued.

- Take the number of shares in issue **after** the new shares were issued and time-apportion it for the period **after** the date of issue.

- The total of these two is the weighted average number of shares in issue over the year.

Worked example: Issue of shares for cash at full market price

X plc has 10 million ordinary shares in issue at 1 January 20X4. Its accounting year end is 31 December. During 20X4 the following events occur:

1 April 20X4	2 million shares are issued to acquire a subsidiary
1 October 20X4	2 million shares are issued at full market price

What is the weighted average number of ordinary shares outstanding during the period?

Solution

The weighted average number of ordinary shares is calculated as follows.

		Weighted Av (million)
January to March	10 million × 3/12 =	2.5
April to September	12 million × 6/12 =	6.0
October to December	14 million × 3/12 =	3.5
		12.0

5.6 Bonus issue

When a bonus issue is made:

- Additional shares are issued to the ordinary equity holders in proportion to their current shareholding, for example one new share for each five shares already owned.

- No cash is received for these shares.

- Reserves are capitalised by a debit to share premium/retained earnings.

In this case the issuing entity has not received any additional resources to help increase earnings. Each shareholder has more shares, but still has the same proportionate interest in the entity. As an example, a shareholder owning 100,000 shares out of the 1 million in issue has a 10% interest. If the entity makes a 1 for 2 bonus issue, the shareholder will own 150,000 shares out of the 1.5 million now in issue, still a 10% interest.

For a bonus issue the treatment for the weighted average number of shares is to assume that the **shares have always been in issue**. This means that they should be treated as having been issued at the start of the earliest period for which results are reported, usually the start of the year presented as the comparative figures.

Worked example: Bonus issue

X plc has 10m ordinary shares in issue at 1 January 20X3. Its accounting year end is 31 December.

Earnings:

	£m
20X4	13
20X3	10

Two million bonus shares are issued on 1 October 20X4.

What basic EPS amount was presented in the 20X3 financial statements and what two basic EPS amounts should be presented in the 20X4 financial statements?

Solution

20X3 financial statements: EPS (£10m/10m shares)   100p

20X4 financial statements:

Basic EPS for both years should be calculated as if the bonus shares had always been in issue.

Basic EPS for 20X4 (£13m/(10 + 2)m)	108.3p
Basic EPS for 20X3 (£10m/(10 + 2)m)	83.3p

Point to note: An alternative adjustment to the 20X3 basic EPS as originally stated would be to multiply it by (shares before bonus/shares after bonus), so 100p × (10m/12m) = 83.3p

---

Interactive question 6: Bonus issue   [Difficulty level: Intermediate]

At 1 January 20X4 and 1 January 20X5 X plc had in issue 20 million ordinary shares.

During 20X5 the following events took place.

31 May 20X5	Issue of 6 million shares for cash at full market price
30 September 20X5	Bonus issue of 1 for 2

Earnings for the year ended 31 December 20X4 were £6m and for the year ended 31 December 20X5 were £8m.

Requirements

(a) Calculate the basic EPS originally reported in 20X4.
(b) Calculate the basic EPS reported in 20X5 including comparative.

See **Answer** at the end of this chapter.

5.7 Rights issue

A rights issue is:

- An issue of shares for cash to the existing ordinary equity holders in proportion to their current shareholdings.

- At a discount to the current market price.

Because the issue price is below the market price, a rights issue is in effect a combination of **an issue at full value and a bonus issue**.

In order to calculate the basic EPS number of shares when there has been a rights issue, an adjustment for the bonus element is required:

$$\text{Adjustment} = \frac{\text{Pre-rights issue price of shares}}{\text{Theoretical ex-rights price (TERP)}}$$

The pre-rights issue price of the shares is the market price immediately before the rights issue is announced. The TERP is the theoretical price at which the shares would trade after the rights issue and takes into account the diluting effect of the bonus element in the rights issue.

The adjustment is used to increase the number of shares in issue **prior to** the rights issue for the bonus element.

Point to note: The TERP is used because the market price at which the shares trade after the rights issue takes account of other factors; for example, it will go up above the TERP if investors interpret the rights issue as a positive sign for the development of the issuing company, and go down below it if they interpret it as a negative sign.

Worked example: TERP

A 1 for 3 rights issue is made at 132p when the market price is 220p.

What is the TERP?

Solution

	No.	Price	Total
		p	p
Pre-rights issue holding	3	220	660
Rights share	1	132	132
	4		792

TERP (792/4) = 198p

Point to note

To prove that a rights issue is a combination of an issue at full market price and a bonus issue, consider the effect if instead of this rights issue, an issue of 1 for 8 had been made at the full market price of 220p, followed immediately by a 1 for 9 bonus:

	No.	Price	Total
		p	p
Initial holding	8	220	1,760
Issue at full market price	1	220	220
Revised holding	9		1,980
Bonus issue	1	N/A	0
Revised holding	10		1,980

Theoretical price (1,980/10) = 198p

Worked example: EPS following a rights issue

The following information is available for an entity.

	£'000
Earnings	
20X2	1,000
20X3	1,300
20X4	1,500

Number of shares in issue at 1 January 20X2: 800,000

Rights issue: 1 for 4 at £5 each on 1 April 20X3 when the market value was £7

What are the basic EPS amounts for each of the three years **after** adjustment for the rights issue?

CHAPTER

3

Solution

Computation of theoretical ex-rights price (TERP):

	No.	Price p	Total p
Pre-rights issue holding	4	700	2,800
Rights share	1	500	500
	5		3,300

Therefore TERP = $\dfrac{3,300}{5}$ = 660p

Computation of bonus adjustment factor:

Adjustment = $\dfrac{\text{Value of shares before rights}}{\text{TERP}} = \dfrac{700p}{660p}$

Computation of EPS:

20X2

Earnings £1m/(800,000 shares × (700/660)) = 117.9p

20X3

Earnings = £1.3 million

		Total
Weighted average shares		
1 Jan – 31 Mar	800,000 × 700/660 × 3/12	212,121
1 Apr – 31 Dec	800,000 × ((4 + 1)/4) × 9/12	750,000
		962,121

Basic EPS $\dfrac{£1.3m}{962,121}$ = 135.1p

20X4 Basic EPS $\dfrac{£1.5m}{(800,000 \times (4+1)/4)}$ = 150.0p

---

Interactive question 7: Rights issue
[Difficulty level: Intermediate]

At 1 January 20X8 and 1 January 20X9 Box plc had in issue ten million ordinary shares. On 30 June 20X9 Box plc made a 1 for 4 rights issue at £2.40 per share. At that date the market price before the issue was announced was £3.20 per share. The earnings of the company were £4m for 20X8 and £4.8m for 20X9.

Requirement

Calculate the reported basic EPS for 20X9 (including the comparative).

See **Answer** at the end of this chapter.

5.8 Repurchase of shares

When shares are repurchased and held as treasury shares the number of shares in issue reduces but share capital remains unchanged as the treasury shares are shown in a separate reserve. An adjustment therefore needs to be made when calculating the weighted average number of shares as part of the EPS calculation.

If the shares are repurchased at market price, the resources expended on the repurchase are commensurate with the reduction in the number of shares. If the shares are repurchased for a price above market value, the resources expended will exceed the reduction in the number of shares. This reduces EPS and so the prior year EPS must be adjusted to reflect this.

In the exam a share repurchase will always be at market price.

Worked example: Weighted average following repurchase

An entity had ten million £1 ordinary shares in issue at 1 January 20X8 and on 30 September 20X8 entered into a repurchase arrangement to buy back two million £1 ordinary shares at market price. The repurchased shares are recognised in a separate reserve as treasury shares.

What is the number of shares that will be used to calculate EPS at 31 December 20X8?

Solution

The weighted average number of shares will be calculated as follows:

10 million × 9/12	7,500,000
8 million × 3/12	2,000,000
	9,500,000

6 Distributable profits

Section overview

- Distributable profits are calculated by reference to the individual entity, not the consolidated group.

- The rule for private companies is that distributable profits are net accumulated realised profits.

- Public companies also have to deduct any net unrealised losses.

- ICAEW/ICAS have issued technical releases in order to provide guidance on distributable profits.

6.1 Introduction

Distributable profits are the profits that under the Companies Act 2006 an entity is legally entitled to **distribute to its equity holders**. The rules are slightly different for private companies (Ltd) and public companies (plc).

For entities within a group, the calculation is made for each entity separately, not for the consolidated group.

Point to note: In a group it is the parent company which pays the dividends to group shareholders, so it is important that there are sufficient distributable profits in the parent company. If the parent does not trade but acts solely as an investment holding company, its only income, and only source of distributable profits, will be dividends passed up by its subsidiaries. An important part of year-end planning will be to make sure that sufficient dividends are passed up before the year end.

6.2 Rule for private companies

Distributable profits are measured as accumulated realised profits less accumulated realised losses.

Point to note

It is the accumulated position which is important, not the profits/losses arising in a particular year.

Generally this equates to the **retained earnings balance** determined under **generally accepted accounting principles**. There is specific guidance in the Companies Act 2006 that:

- A provision is a realised loss.

- A revaluation surplus is an unrealised profit.

- Any additional depreciation on revalued non-current assets can be added back to profits for determining distributable amounts.

- When a revalued asset is disposed of, the unrealised surplus or loss on revaluation becomes a realised profit or loss.

6.2.1 The effect of revaluations

When a revaluation of non-current assets takes place:

- Gains are unrealised unless they reverse a loss previously treated as realised.

- Losses are realised except where the loss

    - Offsets a previous surplus on the same asset, or

    - Arises on a revaluation of all non-current assets, or

    - Arises on a revaluation of some non-current assets where the directors consider that the assets not revalued are worth at least their book value.

6.3 Additional rules for public companies

Over and above the rule for private companies there is an additional restriction for public companies; they may not make a distribution if this reduces its net assets below the total of **called-up share capital and undistributable reserves**.

Undistributable reserves are:

- Share premium account

- Net unrealised profits

- Any other reserve specified by law or the company's constitution to be unrealised (for example a capital redemption reserve)

One way of calculating the distributable profits of a public company is:

	£
Distributable profits per rule for private companies	X
Less any excess of unrealised losses over unrealised profits	(X)
Distributable profits per rule for public companies	X

Worked example: Distributable profits

The summarised draft statement of financial position of a company at 31 March 20X0 was as follows.

	£'000
Non-current assets	
Land and buildings	1,500
Plant and machinery	60
Fixtures	15
	1,575
Net current assets	925
	2,500
Share capital	1,600
Retained earnings	900
	2,500

An independent professional valuation undertaken on 31 March 20X0 showed valuations of £1.4 million and £50,000 for the land and buildings and plant and machinery respectively, which the directors decided to incorporate into the company's accounting records from 1 April 20X0. They considered the value of fixtures was not less than £15,000.

Requirements

Calculate the maximum amount of distributable profit for the year ended 31 March 20X0 assuming the company is:

(a) A private company
(b) A public company

Solution

	(a) Private company £'000	(b) Public company £'000
Accumulated realised profits less accumulated realised losses	900	900
Less net unrealised losses (1,500 + 60 – 1,400 – 50)	N/A	(110)
	900	790

The £110,000 downward revaluation is treated as unrealised because the directors have reassessed the values of all non-current assets. This unrealised loss should be taken into account for the public company calculation, but not for the private company calculation.

Interactive question 8: Distributable profits
[Difficulty level: Intermediate]

Haver Ltd is a rapidly-expanding company which was incorporated two years ago to benefit from limited liability, issuing 10,000 £1 shares for £5 per share.

On 1 January 20X2 the company revalued its non-current assets to improve its statement of financial position, and thus help it to raise finance, giving a revaluation surplus of £400,000. The remaining useful life of these assets at the date of revaluation was 25 years.

At 1 January 20X2 retained earnings brought forward were £80,000 and profits for the year ended 31 December 20X2 were £40,000.

The directors, who are also equity holders, are considering taking dividends for the first time but are unsure how much they may distribute.

Requirements

(a) Explain the calculation of and calculate the distributable profits for Haver Ltd at 1 January 20X2.

(b) Explain the calculation of and calculate the distributable profits for Haver Ltd at 31 December 20X2.

(c) Explain how the revaluation surplus should be treated if in the future the assets are sold.

Fill in the proforma below.

(a)

(b)

(c)

See **Answer** at the end of this chapter.

6.4 Relevant accounts

For the purposes of calculating their distributable profits, entities should use the amounts shown in the 'relevant accounts', normally their last annual accounts.

If distributable profits shown in the last annual accounts are insufficient to justify a proposed distribution, then more recent interim accounts should also be used. The requirements as to their preparation are:

- For private companies: they should be sufficient to determine the legality of distribution.
- For public companies: they should be properly prepared under the Companies Act 2006.

6.5 ICAEW/ICAS Technical Release 02/10 – realised profits

As we have seen above, distributable profits are based upon generally accepted accounting practice and legal rules from the Companies Act.

The concept of realised profit is intended to be dynamic, changing with the development of generally accepted accounting principles. The ICAEW and ICAS have issued a number of technical releases over the years to assist practitioners in identifying realised profits. These have been consolidated into Technical Release 2/10, issued on 3 November 2010. TR 2/10 provides guidance on the determination of realised profits and losses in the context of distributions under the Companies Act 2006.

TR 02/10 sets out that the translation of monetary assets which comprises qualifying consideration or a liability denominated in a foreign currency is a realised profit. The Technical Release also confirms that goodwill arising in a company's individual financial statements will become a realised loss as the goodwill is amortised or written down for impairment in accordance with the relevant accounting standards. Conversely, negative goodwill (a gain on bargain purchase) up to the fair values of the non-monetary assets acquired should be treated as being realised in the periods in which the non-monetary assets are recovered, whether through depreciation or sale.

6.5.1 Principles of realisation

It is generally accepted that profits shall be treated as realised when realised in the form of cash or of other assets the ultimate cash realisation of which can be assessed with reasonable certainty. According to TR 02/10 this definition catches profits and losses arising from changes in fair values recognised in accordance with accounting standards, to the extent they are readily convertible into cash.

7 UK GAAP comparison

Section overview

FRS 101 grants exemptions from certain provisions of IAS 8, IAS 24 and IFRS 5.

There are some differences between FRS 102, IAS 24 and IFRS 5.

7.1 Reporting performance

Companies reporting under FRS 101 are exempt from the requirement in IAS 8 to disclose any non-application of a new IFRS that has been issued but is not yet effective.

FRS 102 states that a change to the cost model when a reliable measure of fair value is no longer available is not to be treated as a change of accounting policy. IAS 8 does not state this.

7.2 Continuing and discontinued operations

Under FRS 102 entities disclose discontinued operations in a separate column in the income statement, showing the amount for all income and expense lines attributable to discontinued operations.

FRS 102 does not have the category of 'held for sale'. Assets of a discontinued operation continue to be depreciated up to the date of disposal.

Entities reporting under FRS 101 follow the IFRS presentation and are exempt from having to disclose the cash flows relating to discontinued operations.

7.3 Foreign currency transactions

There are no exemptions granted by FRS 101 from the provisions of IAS 21 *The Effects of Changes in Foreign Exchange Rates.*

IAS 21 requires the cumulative amount of exchange differences to be presented in other comprehensive income as a separate component of equity. There is no such requirement in FRS 102.

7.4 Related party transactions

FRS 101 grants entities exemption from disclosing:

(a) Key management personnel compensation

(b) Related party transactions entered into between two or more members of a group, provided that any subsidiary involved is wholly-owned

However, **management compensation disclosures**, as well as disclosures on **loans and other transactions involving directors** are included in **Companies Act 2006**, so will have to be disclosed in any case.

FRS 102 does **not** require disclosure of transactions entered into between two or more members of a group as long as any subsidiary which is a party to the transaction is **wholly owned** by the other party to the transaction.

Disclosure is required of:

(a) Relationships between a parent and its subsidiaries
(b) Key management personnel compensation
(c) Related party transactions

7.5 Earnings per share

Entities reporting under FRS 102 are required to apply IAS 33 *Earnings per Share.* FRS 101 contains no exemption from IAS 33.

Summary

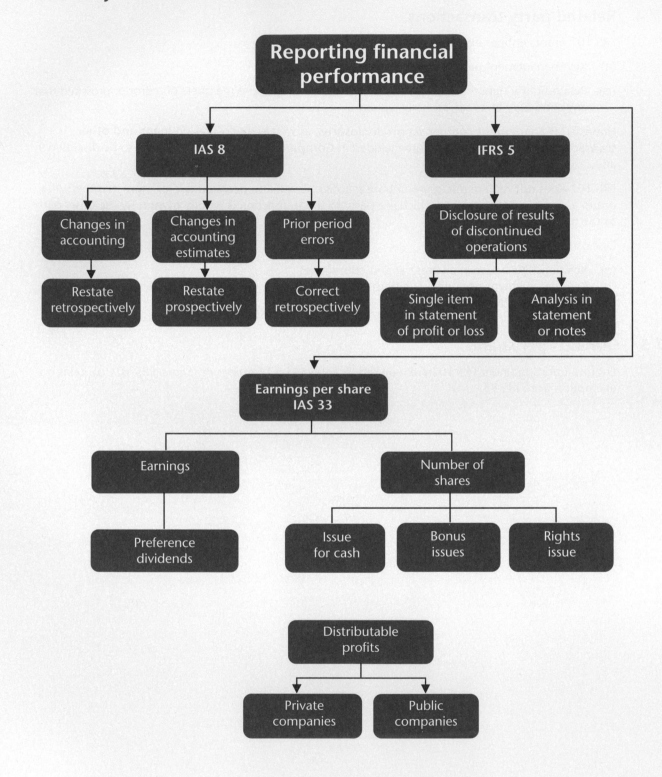

Self-test

Answer the following questions.

1 During the year to 30 September 20X6, the following events occurred in relation to Pipe Ltd.

   (1) A claim for tax relief, submitted in 20X3, was rejected by the General Commissioners of HMRC. No appeal will be made. The resulting liability of £15,000 was not provided at 30 September 20X5, since the company had expected the claim to succeed.

   (2) A cut-off error in respect of inventories at 30 September 20X5 was discovered which would have reduced the carrying amount of inventories by £24,000. This error is material but not fundamental.

   (3) Non-current assets which had been written down to their estimated realisable value of £17,000 at 30 September 20X5 were sold for £7,000.

   How much should be accounted for retrospectively as an adjustment to retained earnings brought forward at 1 October 20X5?

2 When considering IFRS 5 *Non-current Assets Held for Sale and Discontinued Operations*, which of the following statements is true?

   (1) A discontinued operation must have been disposed of by the end of the reporting period.

   (2) A discontinued operation must be a separate major line of business or geographical area of operation.

   (3) A discontinued operation must be clearly distinguished operationally and for financial reporting purposes.

3 During the financial year Alphabet plc carried out a reorganisation as follows.

   Division X, a UK division whose operations are being terminated and transferred to another UK division producing the same product.

   Division Y, the sole operator in South America whose business is being sold externally to the group.

   Activity W, (part of Division Z) whose operations have been closed down. W's results have not been reported separately.

   Which of these divisions could be a discontinued operation according to IFRS 5 *Non-current Assets Held for Sale and Discontinued Operations*?

4 During the year to 30 April 20X9 Grant plc carried out a major reorganisation of its activities as follows.

   Maynard was closed down on 1 January 20X9. Maynard was the only manufacturing division of the company, and as a result of the closure Grant's only activity will be the retail of artists equipment.

   On 30 March 20X9 it was decided to sell Lytton, the only division that operated in Europe. The company were confident of a sale within the year. The sale actually took place on 15 July 20X9.

   The activities carried on by Hobhouse were terminated during the period. Hobhouse was one of a number of smaller divisions which operated from the same location as the main headquarters of Grant. All these divisions use the same central accounting system and operating costs are allocated between them for the purpose of the management accounts.

   The accounts for the year ended 30 April 20X9 were approved on 7 July 20X9.

   Which of these divisions should be classified as discontinued operations in accordance with IFRS 5 *Non-current Assets Held for Sale and Discontinued Operations* in the financial statements of Grant plc for the year ended 30 April 20X9?

5 Abercorn Ltd, whose year end is 31 December, buys some goods from Prima SA of France on 30 September. The invoice value is €40,000 and is due for settlement in equal instalments on 30 November and 31 January. The exchange rate moved as follows.

	€ = £1
30 September	1.60
30 November	1.80
31 December	1.90
31 January	1.85

State the journal entries required to record this transaction in the books of Abercorn Ltd.

6   Sunbeam plc has the following individual draft statement of financial position at 31 December 20X9:

	£'000
Non-current assets	
Land and buildings	4,000
Plant and machinery	1,000
Equity investments	2,000
	7,000
Net current assets	1,500
	8,500
Share capital	2,000
Share premium	2,500
Revaluation surplus	500
Retained earnings	2,000
	7,000
Non-current liabilities	1,000
Current liabilities	500
	8,500

Land and buildings were revalued during the year, giving rise to the revaluation surplus. The additional depreciation arising on the buildings due to the revaluation is £25,000. Sunbeam plc has not made the transfer from the revaluation surplus to retained earnings which it is permitted to make in accordance with IAS 16.

An independent valuation of all non-current assets at the year end confirmed the carrying amount of land and buildings but valued plant and machinery at £700,000. The directors have decided to adjust the carrying amount of plant and machinery in the next financial year.

The directors estimate that an increase in the existing warranty provision of £200,000 is needed.

Calculate the maximum amount that can be distributed to shareholders in respect of the year ended 31 December 20X9.

7   Explain whether the following relationships are related party relationships under IAS 24 *Related Party Disclosures*.

(i)   Albert plc and James plc each have a board containing five directors, four of whom are common. There are no common shareholdings. Are the companies related entities?

(ii)   James plc has two associated companies, Hector Ltd and Frances Ltd. Is Hector Ltd a related party of Frances Ltd?

(iii) Fredrick Pearson is a director of Gambit plc and Frodsham Ltd – are these companies related?

(iv)   Giprock Ltd controls Jasper plc. Giprock Ltd also exerts influence over Kendal plc. Are Jasper plc and Kendal plc related entities?   **(8 marks)**

8   MITCHELL BROS PLC

Mitchell Bros plc had 14 million ordinary shares in issue on 1 January 20X4 and 20X5. In its financial year ended 31 December 20X5 it issued further shares as follows:

- On 1 April, four million shares in consideration for the majority holding in another entity; and

- On 1 July a rights issue of 1 for 6 at a price of £15 per share. The market price of Mitchell Bros shares immediately prior to the rights issue had been £20 per share.

A profit of £17 million attributable to the ordinary equity holders was reported for 20X5 and £14 million for 20X4.

The shares issued on the acquisition were issued at their full fair value.

Requirement

Calculate basic EPS for the year ended 31 December 20X5 and the basic EPS for the year ended 31 December 20X4, as restated in the 31 December 20X5 financial statements. **(5 marks)**

9   WESTERN ENTERPRISES PLC

Western Enterprises plc wholesales and distributes toys and models and provides distribution services to other organisations. The following balances have been extracted from its books of account as at 31 December 20X3.

	£'000
Ordinary shares	800
5% redeemable preference shares	200
Share premium account	350
Retained earnings at 1 January 20X3	2,000
Revenue	11,899
Purchases	8,935
Inventories at 1 January 20X3	974
Staff costs – distribution	270
Staff costs – administration	352
Depreciation charge for the year	
Freehold land and buildings	30
Distribution equipment	116
Other plant and equipment	160
General expenses	432
Interest receivable	41
Interest payable	35
Taxation – charge for the year	336
Paid dividends	
Ordinary shares – final regarding 20X2	60
Ordinary shares – interim regarding 20X3	30
5% redeemable preference shares – for 20X3	10
Patent rights	200
Freehold land and buildings – cost	1,200
Distribution equipment – cost	800
Other plant and equipment – cost	1,400
Accumulated depreciation at 31 December 20X3	
Freehold land and buildings	130
Distribution equipment	320
Other plant and equipment	250
Trade receivables	1,600
Trade payables	850
Cash and cash equivalents	300
Tax liability	400

Additional information

(1)   Included in revenue are invoices totalling £120,000 in relation to distribution services rendered under a contract to a customer who is very unhappy with the quality of the services provided. The overall outcome of the contract is uncertain and management believes that of the £90,000 costs incurred to date under the contract, probably only £65,000 will be reimbursed by this customer.

(2)   The patent was acquired during the year. Amortisation of £20,000 should be charged to administrative expenses.

(3)   Inventories at 31 December 20X3 were valued at £1,304,000.

(4)   Costs not specifically attributable to one of the profit or loss expense headings should be split 50:50 between distribution costs and administrative expenses.

(5) Inventories carried at £846,000 were purchased from Germany in euros and payment is due on 2 March 20X4. At the date of the transaction the exchange rate was €1.55 to £1. At 31 December 20X3 the exchange rate was €1.50 to £1.

(6) A final ordinary share dividend for 20X3 of £50,000 was proposed in May 20X4, payable on 28 June 20X4.

(7) £450,000 cash was received during the year as a result of a rights issue of ordinary shares. The nominal value of the shares issued was £100,000.

(8) On 1 June 20X3 the company made the decision to sell its loss-making soft toy division as a result of severe competition from the Far East. The company is confident that the closure will be completed by 30 April 20X4. The division's operations represent in 20X3 10% of revenue (after all adjustments), 15% of cost of sales, 10% of distribution costs and 20% of administrative expenses. No disclosures are necessary in the statement of financial position.

Requirement

Prepare Western Enterprises plc's statement of profit or loss and statement of changes in equity for the year to 31 December 20X3, a statement of financial position at that date and movements schedules and notes in accordance with the requirements of IFRS, to the extent the information is available. **(17 marks)**

Now go back to the Learning objectives in the Introduction. If you are satisfied you have achieved these objectives, please tick them off.

Technical reference

Point to note: The following sets out the examinability of the standards covered in this chapter.

IAS 8	All examinable
IFRS 5	References to disposal groups and implementation guidance (except 11 and 12) are not examinable
IAS 21	Only paragraphs 1-34 are examinable
IAS 24	All examinable except for 25-27
IAS 33	Only paragraphs 1-29 examinable

The paragraphs listed below are the key references you should be familiar with.

1 Accounting policies

- Definition — IAS 8 (5)
- Developed by reference to the relevant Standard/Interpretation where this is applicable — IAS 8 (7)
- Otherwise judgement applied — IAS 8 (10)
- Selection and application should be consistent — IAS 8 (13)

2 Change in accounting policies

- Only allowed if: — IAS 8 (14)
    - Required by a Standard/Interpretation, or
    - Results in relevant and more reliable information
- Changes should be applied: — IAS 8 (19–22)
    - In accordance with transitional provisions, or
    - Retrospectively if there are no transitional provisions or the change is voluntary
- Retrospective application is applying a new accounting policy as if that policy had always been applied — IAS 8 (5)
- If impracticable to determine the period specific effects: — IAS 8 (23–28)
    - Apply the new accounting policy from the earliest period for which retrospective application is practicable
    - Disclose this fact
- When changes are made to presentation or classification of items, comparative amounts should also be reclassified, unless impracticable — IAS 1 (41–42)

3 Changes in accounting estimates

- Definition — IAS 8 (5)
- Changes relating to assets, liabilities or equity are adjusted in the period of change — IAS 8 (37)
- All other changes should be applied prospectively: — IAS 8 (36)
    - In the period of change
    - In the period of change and future periods if both are affected
- Disclosure: — IAS 8 (39)
    - Nature of change
    - Amount

CHAPTER 3

4 Prior period errors

- Definition   IAS 8 (5)

- Correct retrospectively in the first set of financial statements authorised for issue after their discovery   IAS 8 (42)

- Disclose   IAS 8 (45)

  - Nature of the prior period error

  - Amount of the correction for each prior period presented

  - Amount of the correction at the beginning of the earliest period presented

- If impracticable to determine the period-specific effects or the cumulative effect of the error: IAS 8 (49)

  - Correct the error from the earliest period/date practicable
  - Disclose this fact

5 Discontinued operations

- Definition   IFRS 5 (31–32)

- Disclosures in the statement of profit or loss – a single amount comprising the total of: IFRS 5 (33(a))

  - The post-tax profit or loss of discontinued operations, and

  - The post-tax gain or loss recognised on related assets

- Disclosures in the statement of profit or loss or in the notes – an analysis of the single amount disclosed in the statement of profit or loss   IFRS 5 (33(b) (c))

- Comparative figures must be restated   IFRS 5 (34)

- Narrative disclosures are also required   IFRS 5 (41)

- If part of the business is discontinued but it does not meet the criteria then its results must be included in those from continuing operations   IFRS 5 (37)

6 Foreign currency transactions

- Definition: functional currency   IAS 21 (9)

- Initial recognition of foreign currency transactions   IAS 21 (20)

- Reporting at the ends of subsequent reporting periods   IAS 21 (23)

- Recognition of exchange differences   IAS 21 (27-34)

7 Related party disclosures

- Definition: related party   IAS 24 (9)

           : related party transaction   IAS 24 (9)

- Disclosure   IAS 24 (13–24)

8 Earnings per share

- Definition   IAS 33 (5)

- Basic earnings per share   IAS 33 (9–29)

Answer to Interactive question 1

Statement of profit or loss for the year ended 31 December 20X7

	£
Continuing operations	
Revenue (300 – 32)	268,000
Cost of sales (100 – 15)	(85,000)
Gross profit	183,000
Distribution costs (40 – 12)	(28,000)
Administrative expenses (90 – 10)	(80,000)
Profit before tax	75,000
Income tax expense	(21,000)
Profit for the year from continuing operations	54,000
Discontinued operations	
Loss for the year from discontinued operations (32 – 15 – 12 – 10)	(5,000)
Profit for the year	49,000

WORKING

	Continuing operations £	Discontinued operations £	Total £
Revenue	268,000	32,000	300,000
Cost of sales	(85,000)	(15,000)	(100,000)
Gross profit	183,000	17,000	200,000
Distribution costs	(28,000)	(12,000)	(40,000)
Administrative expenses	(80,000)	(10,000)	(90,000)
Profit/(loss) before tax	75,000	(5,000)	70,000
Income tax expense	(21,000)	–	(21,000)
Net profit/(loss) for year	54,000	(5,000)	49,000

Answer to Interactive question 2

		DR £	CR £
31.10.X8	Purchases (129,000 @ 9.50)	13,579	
	Payables		13,579
31.12.X8	Payables (W)	679	
	Profit or loss – exchange gains		679
31.01.X9	Payables	12,900	
	Profit or loss – exchange losses	399	
	Cash (129,000 @ 9.7)		13,299

WORKING

	£
Payables as at 31.12.X8 (129,000 @ 10)	12,900
Payables as previously recorded	13,579
Exchange gain	679

Answer to Interactive question 3

(1) Chablis is owned by one of the close members of the family of a member of Pinot's key management personnel, so it is a related party of Pinot. Disclosure should be made of the nature of the relationship, any transactions during the period and the fact that the £100,000 balance has been written off during the period.

There is no requirement to disclose the debt collection costs of £4,000, or the names of Chablis, the director of Pinot or his son.

(2) Merlot is very probably a related party of Pinot because Pinot's 40% shareholding in it appears to provide Pinot with significant influence over Merlot. Despite being an arm's length price, the value of the transaction should be disclosed (aggregated with similar transactions during the year if appropriate).

The company should only disclose that related party transactions were made on terms equivalent to those that prevail in arm's length transactions if these terms can be substantiated.

The nature of the relationship should be disclosed, but no names need to be disclosed.

(3) The distributor is not a related party of Pinot, thus no separate disclosure is required.

(4) Mrs Barolo is a member of the key management personnel of Pinot, so is one of its related parties. The nature of the relationship, details of the amount and nature of the transaction should be disclosed, along with the fact that Pinot is guaranteeing the loan of a related party. Any amount of the sale price still owed to Pinot at the year-end should be disclosed.

Answer to Interactive question 4

	£m
Profit attributable to owners of the parent	1,897
Less dividend on irredeemable preference shares	(400)
Profit attributable to ordinary equity holders of the parent	1,497

$$EPS = \frac{1,497}{6,241} = 24p \text{ per share}$$

Answer to Interactive question 5

	£m
Profit attributable to owners of the parent	82
Less one year's dividend on irredeemable preference shares (20 – 15)	(5)
Profit attributable to ordinary equity holders of the parent	77

$$EPS = \frac{77}{1,200} = 6.4p \text{ per share}$$

Answer to Interactive question 6

(a) EPS originally reported in 20X4 (£6m/20m) = 30p

(b) EPS reported in 20X5

The bonus issue is treated as having been issued at the start of 20X4 (the earliest reported period).

The adjusted weighted average number of shares for 20X4 is (20m × (2 + 1)/2) = 30m

The restated 20X4 EPS is (£6m/30m) = 20p

EPS for 20X5

Weighted average shares:

As the bonus issue came **after** the issue for cash at full market price, the 6 million new shares rank for the bonus issue.

	Weighted Av (million)
1 January – 31 May 20m × (2 + 1)/2 × 5/12	12.50
1 June – 31 December (20m + 6m) × ((2 + 1)/2) × 7/12 =	22.75
	35.25

EPS (£8m/35.25m) = 22.7p

Answer to Interactive question 7

Computation of theoretical ex-rights price (TERP).

	No	£
Pre-rights issue holding	4 @ 3.20	12.80
Rights share	1 @ 2.40	2.40
	5	15.20

$$\text{TERP} = \frac{£15.20}{5} = £3.04$$

Computation of bonus adjustment factor:

$$\text{Adjustment} = \frac{\text{Value of shares before rights}}{\text{TERP}} = \frac{320p}{304p}$$

Computation of basic EPS:

$$20X8 \text{ EPS} = \frac{£4m}{\left(10m \text{ shares} \times \left(^{320}\!/_{304}\right)\right)} = 38.0p$$

20X9 Earnings = £4.8 million

		Total
Weighted average shares		
1 Jan – 30 June	10m × 320/304 × 6/12	5,263,158
1 July – 31 Dec	10m × ((4 + 1)/4) × 6/12	6,250,000
		11,513,158

$$\text{EPS} = \frac{£4.8m}{11,513,158} = 41.7p$$

Answer to Interactive question 8

(a) **Distributable profits at 1 January 20X2**

As Haver Ltd is a private limited company the profits available for distribution are defined as accumulated realised profits less accumulated realised losses. This is usually the balance on retained earnings, so £80,000.

Haver Ltd also has a share premium account of £40,000 (10,000 × (£5 – £1)) and a current revaluation surplus of £400,000, both of which are non-distributable.

(b) **Distributable profits at 31 December 20X2**

The £80,000 balance at the start of the year is increased by the £40,000 profits earned during the year, to £120,000.

The additional depreciation in the year on non-current assets is £16,000 (£400,000/25) and this is added, making total distributable profits of £136,000.

(c) **Revaluation surplus**

Each year Haver Ltd should transfer the extra £16,000 depreciation to retained earnings from the revaluation surplus.

Any revaluation surplus remaining when these assets are finally sold would then be realised and should be transferred to retained earnings in the statement of changes in equity.

Answers to Self-test

1   A retrospective adjustment should be made for a decrease of £24,000 in retained earnings. Under IFRS items (1) and (3) arise from normal estimation errors and are recognised in the current accounting period. Item (2) results from an error which reduces retained earnings brought forward by £24,000.

2   Statements (2) and (3) are true. In order to be classified as discontinued, a component must either have been disposed of or be held for sale (provided that it is highly probable that it will be sold within 12 months of classification (IFRS 5 paragraph 8)).

3   Division Y could be a discontinued operation as a geographical area of operations is being sold.

        Division X is not a discontinued operation as a separate line of business is not being terminated – production is shifting from one division to another.

        Activity W is not discontinued, as it cannot be separately distinguished for financial reporting purposes.

4   Maynard and Lytton should both be classified as discontinued operations. Maynard amounts to the withdrawal from a particular line of business. Lytton amounts to the withdrawal from a geographical area of operation. The date of sale is irrelevant.

5   The purchase will be recorded in the books of Abercorn Ltd using the rate of exchange ruling on 30 September.

DR Purchases	£25,000	
CR Trade payables		£25,000

Being the £ cost of goods purchased for €40,000 (€40,000 ÷ €1.60/£1)

On 30 November, Abercorn Ltd must pay €20,000. This will cost €20,000 ÷ €1.80/£1 = £11,111 and the company has therefore made an exchange gain of £12,500 – £11,111 = £1,389.

DR Trade payables	£12,500	
CR Exchange gain: profit or loss		£1,389
CR Cash		£11,111

On 31 December, the year end, the outstanding liability will be recalculated using the rate applicable to that date: €20,000 ÷ €1.90/£1 = £10,526. A further exchange gain of £1,974 has been made and will be recorded as follows.

DR Trade payables	£1,974	
CR Exchange gain: profit or loss		£1,974

The total exchange gain of £3,363 will be included in the operating profit for the year ending 31 December.

On 31 January, Abercorn Ltd must pay the second instalment of €20,000. This will cost them £10,811 (€20,000 ÷ €1.85/£1).

DR Trade payables	£10,526	
Exchange loss: profit or loss	£285	
CR Cash		£10,811

6

	£'000
Accumulated realised profits less accumulated realised losses	2,000
Additional depreciation on revaluation	25
Less: additional warranty provision	(200)
net unrealised losses (1,000 – 700)	(300)
Maximum amount available for distribution	1,525

7   This question explores the nature of the relationships and attempts to contrast control and the exercise of influence. Two entities which are related parties of a third party are not necessarily related parties of each other.

(i)   All five directors of Albert plc are members of its key management personnel and are therefore its related parties. The same is the case for all five directors of James plc. Individually the four common directors do not have significant influence over either Albert plc or James plc, but together, as the clear majority of the board, they can control both of them. There is nothing in IAS 24's definitions of a related party which makes these entities related parties of each other. But IAS 24 requires consideration of the substance of situations, not just their legal form. If the four directors are acting in concert, then in substance they control both entities which are therefore related parties of each other.

(ii)   Hector Ltd and Frances Ltd are associates of the same investor. James plc has significant influence over each company, but not control. Hector Ltd and Frances Ltd would not normally be regarded as related parties of each other.

(iii)   Gambit plc and Frodsham Ltd have one director in common, but there is no information about shareholdings which would indicate that this director has control over either of them. They would not normally be regarded as related parties of each other.

(iv)   Kendal plc is an associate of Giprock Ltd and Jasper plc is a member of the Giprock Group, so Kendal plc and Jasper plc are related parties per IAS 24.9(b)(ii).

8   MITCHELL BROS PLC

The issue at full market price does not contain any bonus element (that is it is not expected to reduce/dilute the future earnings potential of each share). It is therefore simply time apportioned.

The rights issue is priced below market price, which will dilute the future earnings potential of each ordinary share. There will need to be a retrospective adjustment to EPS to allow for this. This is achieved by calculating the bonus fraction and retrospectively increasing the number of ordinary shares prior to the rights issue occurring.

The calculation of the weighted average number of shares in issue is as follows:

Date	No shares '000	Time	Bonus fraction	Weighted average
1 Jan 20X5	14,000	3/12	(W) 20/19.29	3,628,823
1 Apr 20X5	4,000			
	18,000	3/12	(W) 20/19.29	4,665,630
1 July 20X5	3,000			
	21,000	6/12		10,500,000
Weighted average				18,794,453

The basic EPS for 20X5 is therefore £17 million/18,794,453 = 90.45p.

The previous year's EPS should have been reported in the 20X4 financial statements as £14 million/14 million = 100p per share. This should be restated as 100p × 19.29/20 = 96.45p.

WORKING

Calculation of theoretical ex-rights price (TERP) and bonus element.

	No	Price £	Total £
Pre-rights holding	6	20	120
Rights share	1	15	15
Post-rights holding	7		135

TERP = £135/7 = £19.29

The bonus element of this issue is therefore 20/19.29. This means that future EPS is expected to be 19.29/20 of the amount before the rights issue at below market price.

9   WESTERN ENTERPRISES PLC

Statement of profit or loss for the year ended 31 December 20X3

	£'000
Continuing operations	
Revenue (W4)	10,660
Cost of sales (W4)	(7,314)
Gross profit	3,346
Distribution costs (W4)	(627)
Administrative expenses (W4)	(569)
Profit from operations	2,150
Finance cost (35 + 10)	(45)
Investment income	41
Profit before tax	2,146
Income tax expense	(336)
Profit for the year from continuing operations	1,810
Discontinued operations	
Loss for the year from discontinued operations (W3)	(319)
Profit for the year	1,491

Statement of changes in equity for the year ended 31 December 20X3

	Share capital £'000	Share premium £'000	Retained earnings £'000	Total £'000
Balance at 1 January 20X3	700		2,000	2,700
Changes in equity for 20X3:				
Issue of share capital	100	350		450
Dividends			(90)	(90)
Total comprehensive income for the year			1,491	1,491
Balance at 31 December 20X3	800	350	3,401	4,551

Notes

(1) The profit from operations is arrived at after charging

	£'000
Depreciation (30 + 116 + 160)	306
Amortisation of intangibles	20
Employee benefits (270 + 352)	622
Foreign exchange loss	28

(2) A final ordinary share dividend for 20X3 of £50,000 is proposed for payment on 28 June 20X4.

(3) On 1 June 20X3 the company classified its soft toy division as held for sale. The division had been loss-making for some time due to severe competition from the Far East. It is expected that the closure will be complete by 30 April 20X4.

Amounts in £000 attributable to this division in 20X3 were: revenue £1,184, expenses £1,503 and pre-tax loss £319.

Statement of financial position as at 31 December 20X3

	£'000	£'000
ASSETS		
Non-current assets		
Property, plant and equipment (see Note)		2,700
Intangibles (see note)		180
		2,880
Current assets		
Inventories	1,304	
Trade and other receivables (1,600 – 55 (W1))	1,545	
Cash and cash equivalents	300	
		3,149
Total assets		6,029
EQUITY AND LIABILITIES		
Equity		
Ordinary share capital		800
Share premium		350
Retained earnings		3,401
Total equity		4,551
Non-current liabilities		
Preference share capital		200
Current liabilities		
Trade and other payables (850 + 28 (W3))	878	
Taxation	400	
		1,278
Total equity and liabilities		6,029

NOTES

PROPERTY, PLANT AND EQUIPMENT

	Freehold land and buildings £'000	Distribution equipment £'000	Other plant and equipment £'000	Total £'000
Cost				
At 1 January 20X3	1,200	800	1,400	3,400
At 31 December 20X3	1,200	800	1,400	3,400
Depreciation				
At 1 January 20X3	100	204	90	394
Charge for the year	30	116	160	306
At 31 December 20X3	130	320	250	700
Carrying amount				
At 31 December 20X3	1,070	480	1,150	2,700
At 1 January 20X3	1,100	596	1,310	3,006

	£'000
INTANGIBLES	
Cost at 31 December 20X3	200
Amortisation	(20)
Carrying amount at 31 December 20X3	180

This patent was acquired during the year.

WORKINGS

(1) Revenue

	£'000	£'000
Per list of balances		11,899
Adjustment regarding contract under dispute		
Included in revenue	120	
Costs recoverable	(65)	
Adjustments to revenue and trade receivables		(55)
		11,844

(2) Analysis of expenses

	Cost of sales £'000	Distribution costs £'000	Administrative expenses £'000
Opening inventories	974		
Purchases	8,935		
Staff costs		270	352
Depreciation			
Land and buildings		15	15
Distribution equipment		116	
Other PPE		80	80
General expenses		216	216
Amortisation of patent			20
Foreign exchange loss			28
Closing inventories	(1,304)		
	8,605	697	711

(3) Foreign exchange loss

	£'000
Payable at date of transaction	846
Payable at year end date (846 × 1.55/1.5)	(874)
Exchange loss at end of reporting period	(28)

(4) Continuing/discontinued analysis

	Continuing operations £'000	Discontinued operations £'000	Total £'000
Revenue (W1 – 90:10)	10,660	1,184	11,844
Cost of sales (W2 – 85:15)	(7,314)	(1,291)	(8,605)
Gross profit	3,346	(107)	3,239
Distribution costs (W2 – 90:10)	(627)	(70)	(697)
Administrative expenses (W2 – 80:20)	(569)	(142)	(711)
Profit/(loss) from operations	2,150	(319)	1,831
Finance cost (35 + 10)	(45)	–	(45)
Investment income	41	–	41
Profit/(loss) before tax	2,146	(319)	1,827
Income tax	(336)	–	(336)
Net profit/(loss) for the year	1,810	(319)	1,491

CHAPTER 4

Property, plant and equipment

Introduction

Examination context

Topic List

Summary and Self-test

Technical reference

Answers to Interactive questions

Answers to Self-test

Learning objectives

- Relate the treatment of property, plant and equipment to the principles in the IASB *Conceptual Framework*

- Identify the accounting standards which apply to the treatment of property, plant and equipment

- Apply the accounting requirements for property, plant and equipment, including the effects of the following:

  - Property, plant and equipment measured under the cost and revaluation models
  - Borrowing costs
  - Depreciation of property, plant and equipment
  - Impairment
  - Derecognition
  - Disclosure

- Identify and consider appropriate actions for ethical issues involving non-current assets

- Identify and illustrate the main differences between International and UK requirements in relation to PPE, borrowing costs, impairment and non-current assets held for sale

Specific syllabus references for this chapter are: 1b, 2b, 2c, 2d, 2e.

Syllabus links

You will have a working knowledge of IAS 16 from the Accounting paper and will have applied it to straightforward situations.

In the Financial Accounting and Reporting paper we look at the more complex aspects of accounting for PPE and the issues of judgement that can be involved in applying IAS 16. We also cover the other accounting standards involved in this topic:

- IAS 23 *Borrowing Costs*
- IAS 36 *Impairment of Assets*
- IFRS 5 *Non-current Assets Held for Sale and Discontinued Operations*

The syllabus also covers in detail the alternative basis of accounting for property, plant and equipment referred to as the revaluation model.

Examination context

In the examination, candidates may be required to:

- Explain how the IASB *Conceptual Framework* applies to the recognition of property, plant and equipment

- Prepare and present financial statements or extracts therefrom in accordance with:
  - IAS 16 *Property, Plant and Equipment*
  - IAS 23 *Borrowing Costs*
  - IAS 36 *Impairment of Assets*
  - IFRS 5 *Non-current Assets Held for Sale and Discontinued Operations*

- Explain the accounting treatment of property, plant and equipment, borrowing costs, impairment and non-current assets held for sale

- Explain and illustrate the difference between the relevant treatment under IFRS and UK GAAP

- Identify and explain any ethical issues

1 Property, plant and equipment

Section overview

IAS 16 *Property, Plant and Equipment* provides guidance on the accounting treatment of non-current tangible assets.

1.1 What are property, plant and equipment?

Definition

Property, plant and equipment: Tangible items that are both:

- Held for use in the production or supply of goods or services, for rental to others or for administrative purposes.

- Expected to be used during more than one period.

In practice this definition causes few problems. Property, plant and equipment (PPE) includes **freehold and leasehold land and buildings** and **plant and machinery,** and forms the major part of assets of certain types of business, such as manufacturing and transport businesses.

1.2 Non-current v current

The main issue arising is whether the assets are held for use in the company's activities or intended for resale.

For example, cars held for resale by a motor dealer are inventories (a current asset) whereas cars held for use by employees on company business are PPE.

1.3 IAS 16 *Property, Plant and Equipment*

The objective of IAS 16 is to set out in relation to PPE the accounting treatment for:

- The recognition of assets.
- The determination of their carrying amounts.
- The depreciation charges and impairment losses relating to them.

This provides the users of financial statements with information about an entity's investment in its PPE and changes in such investments.

IAS 16 should be followed when accounting for PPE *unless* another IAS or IFRS requires a **different** treatment, eg IFRS 5 *Non-current Assets Held for Sale and Discontinued Operations.*

1.4 Underlying principles

The key elements in financial statements, identified in the IASB *Conceptual Framework,* which are relevant to PPE are:

Assets	Resources controlled by the entity as a result of past events and from which future economic benefits are expected to flow into the entity
Gains, which are a part of income	Increases in economic benefits through enhancements of assets or decreases in liabilities other than contributions from equity
Losses, which are included in expenses	Decreases in economic benefits through depletions of assets or additional liabilities other than distributions to equity participants

Gains and losses relate to the subsequent depreciation, revaluation, impairment and disposal of PPE.

2 Recognition of PPE

Section overview

- Items of PPE should be recognised where it is probable that future economic benefits will flow to the entity and their cost can be measured reliably.

- Subsequent costs:

    - Repairs and maintenance expenditure should not be capitalised.
    - Replacement parts should be capitalised.

- Items of PPE may be separated into components, each with a separate useful life.

2.1 Recognition

In this context, recognition simply means incorporation of the item in the entity's financial statements, in this case as a non-current asset. The recognition of PPE depends on two criteria both of which must be satisfied.

- It is **probable that future economic benefits associated with the item will flow to the entity**.
- The item's cost can be **measured reliably**.

Points to note

1 The asset is not defined in terms of the tangible piece of PPE (eg a building or a piece of production machinery) but in terms of the **economic benefits flowing from it**:

   - So components acquired for obligatory safety or environmental reasons can be treated as part of the cost of an item of PPE because they enable the item of PPE to **continue in operation**, thereby generating economic benefits.

   - **Legal ownership of an item of PPE is not necessary**, as long as the **economic benefits** flowing from it are enjoyed. An item held under a **finance lease** (see Chapter 7) is treated as an asset of the user of the item.

2 There is **no definition of what constitutes an 'item of PPE'**. It will be for each entity to develop its own definitions. It will be straightforward to decide that an individual motor vehicle should constitute an item. But when it comes to a blast furnace, should that be a single item or several items?

3 There is no mention of the 'acquisition' of an item of PPE. The whole of the definition revolves round the 'cost' of such an item. This means that the **definition must be applied at any time over the life of the item of PPE when expenditure on it is incurred**; it is not only applied on the initial acquisition or construction of the item.

2.2 Subsequent costs

In terms of costs incurred subsequently to add to, replace part of, or service the item, the practical application is that:

- **Repairs and maintenance expenditure should be recognised in profit or loss as incurred**, because it is not probable that there will be future economic benefits flowing from it, over and above the benefits flowing from the cost originally recognised when the item was first acquired.

- **Replacement parts should be capitalised, provided the original cost of the items they replace is derecognised (ie treated as disposed of) at the time of the replacement.**

    IAS 16 gives the example of a blast furnace which may require relining after a specified number of hours of use. The existing lining is derecognised and the new lining is capitalised and depreciated, separately from the body of the furnace, over its useful life.

    Another example is parts of an aircraft, such as seats or galleys, which may require replacement several times over the life of the airframe.

2.3 Separate components

This leads to the practice of treating the different parts of a bigger asset as **separate components**, with **separate lives**. These are then **depreciated separately** (see Section 6 below), so that they are carried at their residual value over their useful lives, not the useful life of the overall asset.

This component approach is also applied **where regular major inspections of an asset are a condition of continuing to use it**. The cost of each inspection is treated as a separate item of PPE, provided on original acquisition part of the purchase price was allocated as the cost of inspection and recognised in profit or loss over the period to the next inspection. If no separate inspection cost was incurred on original acquisition, this allocation may be made by reference to the estimated cost of the first inspection that is actually made.

For instance, a firm operates lorries which have to pass an inspection every six months. If a new vehicle is £20,000 and the cost of an inspection is £3,000, then £17,000 will be allocated to the actual vehicle and £3,000 to the first inspection. This £3,000 will be written off over the next six months and the £3,000 paid when the inspection takes place will then be capitalised and written off over the following six months.

3 Measurement at recognition

Section overview

- PPE should be measured at cost at recognition.

- Elements of cost include:
  - Purchase price
  - Directly attributable costs
  - Estimate of dismantling and site restoration costs

- Cost is measured as:
  - Cash or
  - Fair value if PPE items are exchanged

3.1 Measurement at recognition

An item of PPE qualifying for recognition is initially measured at its **cost**.

Definitions

Cost: This is the amount of cash or cash equivalents paid or the fair value of the other consideration given to acquire an asset at the time of its acquisition or construction.

Fair value: This is the amount for which an asset could be exchanged between knowledgeable, willing parties in an arm's length transaction.

3.2 Elements of cost of PPE

The cost of a PPE item comprises:

- **Purchase price**, including all non-recoverable duties and taxes but net of discounts.

- Costs **directly attributable to bringing the asset to the location and condition** necessary for it to be capable of operating in the manner intended by the management.

- The initial estimate of **dismantling and site restoration costs**.

Directly attributable costs include:

- **Employee benefits** arising directly from construction or acquisition of the item.

- **Site preparation, delivery, installation and assembly costs, costs of testing, and professional fees** (eg legal costs and architects' fees).

But note that certain costs associated with the item cannot be included in its cost:

- Some costs are **excluded** because they are **not directly attributable to the item**. Examples include:

  - The costs of opening a new facility
  - The cost of introducing new products
  - The cost of conducting business in a new location or with a new class of customer
  - Administration and general overhead costs

- **Capitalisation ceases when the item is capable of operating in the manner intended**. Costs incurred after this date have to be **excluded**. Examples include:

  - Costs incurred when the item is not yet in use or is operated at less than full capacity
  - Operating losses while demand for the output builds up (eg a new hotel)
  - Reorganisation costs

Points to note

1 Costs of testing would include flight testing a new aircraft and testing for the satisfactory output of a new plant. In this latter case, any proceeds from selling product generated during testing are deducted from the cost of the plant.

2 Where activities are undertaken that are incidental to the development of the PPE item, any revenue and expenses are recognised in profit or loss, not taken into account in arriving at the cost of the item.

3 Where as a result of the acquisition of an item of PPE an obligation arises to dismantle it at the end of its useful life and/or to restore its site then that obligation must be recorded as a liability at the same time as the asset is recognised (eg the decommissioning costs of nuclear power stations). We will look at this issue again in Chapter 9.

4 In the case of self-constructed assets:

   - **Internal profits and abnormal costs** (eg those relating to design errors, wasted resources or industrial disputes) are excluded from cost.

   - **Interest costs** incurred during the course of construction are capitalised under IAS 23 *Borrowing Costs*, where they are eligible for capitalisation.

Interactive question 1: Measuring cost   [Difficulty level: Intermediate]

A business incurs the following costs in relation to the construction of a new facility and the introduction to the market of its output:

	£'000
Site preparation	400
Net income while site used as a car park, prior to construction commencing	(50)
Materials used, inclusive of £0.3m recoverable VAT	2,000
Labour costs, inclusive of £0.5m incurred when a labour dispute meant that no construction work was carried out	4,000
Testing of facility's processes	300
Sale of by-products produced as part of testing process	(60)
Consultancy fees re installation and assembly	500
Professional fees	450
Opening of facility	100
Overheads incurred:	
– Construction	800
– General	600
Relocation of staff to new facility	350

The following estimates have been made:

(1) The cost of having to dismantle the facility at the end of its useful life — 750

(2) The facility has passed an initial safety inspection, the cost of which is subsumed within other costs. The next inspection is due in three years and thereafter every three years.

The cost of each future inspection is estimated at £150,000.

(3) While the overall life of the facility is 20 years, 40% of the costs other than those of safety inspections relate to items that will need replacing in eight years.

Requirement

Identify the total cost of the facility in accordance with IAS 16 and allocate it over the facility's components.

Fill in the proforma below.

Cost of facility

£'000

Site preparation
Net income while site used as a car park
Materials used
Labour costs
Testing of facility's processes
Sale of by-products
Consultancy fees re installation and assembly
Professional fees
Opening of facility
Overheads incurred:
–   Construction
–   General
Relocation of staff to new facility
Cost of dismantling facility

Allocated to components:

See **Answer** at the end of this chapter.

3.3 Measurement of cost

Cost is measured as the **cash price at the time of recognition**, with **discounting** if payment is deferred beyond normal credit terms.

Where there is an **exchange of items of PPE** such that there is no cash price, cost should be measured at **fair value**.

The **exception** to this is where:

- The exchange transaction lacks **commercial substance**, for example where the risk, timing and amount of the cash flows of the asset received differs from the risk, timing and amount of the cash flows of the asset transferred; or

- The fair value of neither asset exchanged can be **measured reliably**.

In this case the asset is measured at the **carrying amount** of the asset given up.

4 Borrowing costs

Section overview

- Under IAS 23 *Borrowing Costs* certain borrowing costs form part of the cost of a qualifying asset.
- Only the borrowing costs directly attributable to the acquisition/construction/production of the asset should be capitalised.
- If the funds used for the acquisition etc are the general funds of the business, a weighted average borrowing cost should be calculated.
- IAS 23 lays down requirements for the commencement and cessation of capitalisation of borrowing costs.

4.1 Introduction

If an entity constructs a substantial asset either for use itself or for resale, it is likely that additional funds in the form of loan capital will be required in order to finance the construction. The finance cost of these additional funds is a cost of the construction of the asset, in the same way that materials and labour are costs of the construction of the asset.

The question is therefore whether these finance costs incurred should be:

- Recognised as an expense in profit or loss, or
- Recognised as part of the cost of the asset carried in the statement of financial position.

Where borrowings have been acquired **specifically to finance the construction of a substantial asset**, a direct cost is incurred that would have been avoided had the construction not taken place. It therefore seems reasonable that the financing cost associated with such borrowings should form **part of the cost of the asset**, as are other costs incurred in the construction process. International standards now **require** this treatment for all 'directly attributable' borrowing costs.

'Directly attributable' borrowing costs should therefore be recognised as part of the cost of the asset and not treated as an expense in profit or loss.

4.2 IAS 23 core principle

Borrowing costs that are directly attributable to the acquisition, construction or production of a qualifying asset form part of the cost of that asset. Other borrowing costs are recognised as an expense.

Definition

A **qualifying asset** is an asset that necessarily takes a substantial period of time to get ready for its intended use or sale.

This could cover:

- Property, plant and equipment
- Investment properties under construction
- Inventories (such as construction of an aeroplane for sale)
- Construction contracts
- Intangible assets

The definition **excludes** an asset which is ready for use or sale at the time it is acquired.

Point to note

An entity is not required to apply IAS 23 to borrowing costs directly attributable to the acquisition, construction or development of:

- Assets which on initial recognition are measured at fair value

- Inventories that are manufactured or produced in large quantities on a repetitive basis even if they take a substantial period of time to get ready for use or sale.

4.3 Borrowing costs to be capitalised

Definition

Borrowing costs are interest and other costs that an entity incurs in connection with the borrowing of funds.

This definition includes:

- Interest expense calculated using the effective interest method as described in IAS 39 *Financial Instruments: Recognition and Measurement* (see Chapter 8).

- Finance charges in respect of finance leases.

However, only borrowing costs which are **directly attributable** to the acquisition, construction or production of the qualifying asset should be capitalised; these are the borrowing costs which would have been avoided if the expenditure on the qualifying asset had not been made.

If **funds are borrowed specifically** for the construction:

- The borrowing costs can be readily identified.

- If the funds are not all required immediately and some are invested, the borrowing costs capitalised should be reduced by the investment income received on the excess funds.

Worked example: Specific funds

An entity borrowed £1 million at 7.5% pa in order to finance the construction of a new building which would take 12 months to complete. As stage payments were to be made in respect of the construction costs, surplus funds were invested and during the 12-month period interest income of £35,000 was earned.

Solution

Borrowing costs to be capitalised = (£1,000,000 × 7.5%) – £35,000
= £40,000

If the construction is financed out of the **general borrowing** of the entity:

- The amount of borrowing costs to be capitalised should be calculated by reference to the weighted average cost of the general borrowings.

- The weighted average calculation excludes borrowings to finance a specific purpose or building.

If the entity is part of a group and funds are negotiated for the whole group rather than individual entities, then judgement is required as to which borrowings should be used in the calculation of the weighted average cost of (group) borrowings.

Worked example: Weighted average cost

An entity has the following loan finance in place during the year:

£1 million of 6% pa loan finance
£2 million of 8% pa loan finance

It constructed a new factory which cost £600,000 and this was funded out of the existing loan finance. The factory took eight months to complete.

What borrowing costs should be capitalised?

Solution

$$\text{Weighted average cost of loans} = \frac{(£1,000,000 \times 6\%) + (£2,000,000 \times 8\%)}{£3,000,000}$$

$$= 7.33\%$$

Borrowing costs to be capitalised = £600,000 × 7.33% × 8/12
= £29,320

The amount of borrowing costs capitalised may be **limited** because the total carrying amount of the asset (including borrowing costs) should not exceed the asset's recoverable amount.

4.4 Commencement of capitalisation

Capitalisation should commence when the entity first meets **all three** of the following conditions:

- It incurs expenditures for the asset
- It incurs borrowing costs
- It undertakes activities that are necessary to prepare the asset for its intended use or sale

Activities necessary to prepare the asset for use or sale include:

- Construction
- Drawing up plans
- Obtaining planning permissions
- Obtaining permissions from utility providers
- Obtaining other consents required

Simply holding an asset for development without any associated activities is not enough to qualify for capitalisation.

Interactive question 2: Commencement of capitalisation   [Difficulty level: Easy]

The following events take place:

- An entity buys some land on 1 December.

- Work is undertaken in December and January in preparing a planning application.

- Planning permission is obtained on 31 January.

- Payment for the land is deferred until 1 February.

- The entity takes out a loan to cover the cost of the land and the construction of the building on 1 February.

When should capitalisation of borrowing costs commence?

See **Answer** at the end of this chapter.

4.5 Cessation of capitalisation

The entity shall cease capitalising borrowing costs when substantially all the activities necessary to get the asset ready for its intended use or sale are complete.

Minor activities such as decoration of a building to a purchaser's specification do not form part of substantial activities, so capitalisation should cease before this work is started.

Point to note

It is the availability for use or sale which is important, not the actual use or sale. An asset is normally ready for use or sale when its physical construction is complete.

Where an asset is completed in parts:

- Where each part is capable of being used/sold separately while other parts continue to be constructed, the cessation of capitalisation of borrowing costs should be assessed on the completion of each part.

- Where no part is capable of being used/sold separately until all the other parts have been completed, cessation should take place when the last part is completed.

4.6 Disclosure

The entity should disclose:

- The costs which have been capitalised in the current period.
- The capitalisation rate used to determine the amount of borrowing costs eligible for capitalisation.

4.7 Judgements required

IAS 23 requires some significant judgements on the part of management, particularly in terms of how to define:

- 'A substantial period of time to get ready' which is a central part of the definition of a qualifying asset.

- The borrowing costs which are 'directly attributable' to work on the qualifying asset. In groups of companies with a central treasury function, it may be that some of the group borrowings are really attributable to activities other than the work on the qualifying asset.

- 'Activities necessary to prepare the qualifying asset'. This is central to identifying when capitalisation should commence.

- When 'substantially all the activities necessary... are complete', the point at which capitalisation should cease.

5 Measurement of PPE after initial recognition

Section overview

After initial recognition an item of PPE may be carried under:

- The cost model, or
- The revaluation model.

5.1 The two models

IAS 16 sets out **two** models, **without expressing a preference** for either:

- The **cost model**. An item of PPE is carried at cost (ie initial cost plus subsequent expenditure) less accumulated depreciation and impairment losses.

- The **revaluation model.** An item of PPE is carried at the revalued amount, being **fair value** less accumulated depreciation and impairment losses.

The choice of model is an **accounting policy choice**, which must be applied across an entire **class of PPE**.

5.2 Fair value

Fair value is normally taken to be market value:

Land and buildings	Fair value is determined from market-based evidence by appraisal by professionally qualified valuers.
Plant and equipment	Fair value is usually their market value determined by appraisal.
Specialised items of property, plant and equipment (which are rarely sold)	Fair value is determined by using a depreciated replacement cost (as there is no market-based evidence of fair value).

Worked example: Depreciated replacement cost

An asset that originally cost £30,000 and is halfway through its useful life will have a carrying amount of 50% of cost = £15,000; if it would cost £40,000 to buy a replacement asset with the same operating characteristics, then the depreciated replacement cost would be 50% of the replacement cost = £20,000.

5.3 Frequency of valuations

Revaluations should be made with **sufficient regularity** to ensure that the **carrying amount does not differ materially from that which would be determined using fair value at the end of the reporting period**.

So, the frequency of the valuation **depends on the volatility of the fair values** of individual items of PPE. The more volatile the fair value, the more frequently revaluations should be carried out.

The **maximum interval mentioned is five years**, but longer could be justified if movements were very small and slow.

The requirement for periodic revaluations is designed to **prevent companies from revaluing assets selectively**.

5.4 Classes of assets

Definition

Class of property, plant and equipment: A grouping of assets of a similar nature and use in an entity's operations.

Where an item of PPE is revalued, all other assets **in the same class** should also be revalued.

Again, this is designed to stop companies being selective about which items to revalue and to avoid financial statements including a mixture of costs and values for like items.

IAS 16 provides **examples** of separate classes including the following:

- Land
- Land and buildings
- Machinery
- Motor vehicles
- Furniture and fixtures
- Office equipment

6 Depreciation

Section overview

- Depreciation is a means of spreading the cost of a non-current asset over its useful life.

- Each significant part of an item of PPE must be depreciated separately.

- Land should be accounted for separately from buildings.

- Residual values and useful lives must be reviewed annually. Any change must be treated as a change in accounting estimate.

- There are a number of different methods of depreciation:

  - Straight-line
  - Diminishing balance (= reducing balance)
  - Sum of the units.

6.1 Objective of depreciation

Depreciation is an application of the **accrual concept**. Its objective is to charge to operating profit the cost of using PPE in each period, so that at the end of its useful life the whole of the cost has been written off. The cost of using an asset is the amount of economic benefits consumed.

Depreciation does not relate to the value of an asset as it is a cost-allocation concept, not a measure of value changes. An increase in the current value of an asset does not itself justify not depreciating that asset. The means of recognising an increase in value of an asset is to revalue the asset, which is a separate issue from depreciation.

Definitions

Depreciation: This is the systematic allocation of the depreciable amount of an asset over its useful life.

Depreciable amount: The cost of an asset, or other amount substituted for cost, less its residual value.

Useful life: This is:

- The period over which an asset is expected to be available for use by an entity, or
- The number of production or similar units expected to be obtained from the asset by an entity.

6.2 Calculation and recognition

Each significant part of an Item of PPE must be **depreciated separately**, although they may be grouped together for depreciation charge purposes if they have the same useful lives and depreciation methods. So an aircraft's engines will be depreciated separately from its airframe when they have different useful lives. This is a natural consequence of the initial process of analysing the cost of an asset over its component parts (see Section 2 above).

Land and buildings are separable assets and **accounted for separately**, even when acquired together. Land usually has an infinite life, whereas buildings do not. So **buildings are always depreciable assets, but land is not**; the exception is that if the initial cost of land includes a provision for dismantlement and restoration (see Section 3.2 above), then that part of its cost is depreciated over the period expected to benefit.

The **depreciation charge is recognised in profit or loss**, unless it can be included in the cost of an asset. The valuation of inventories under IAS 2 *Inventories* includes depreciation charges on manufacturing PPE.

Interactive question 3: Calculating depreciation   [Difficulty level: Intermediate]

Requirement

Using the costs from Interactive question 1 and assuming there are no residual values, calculate the annual depreciation charges for the facility.

Fill in the proforma below.

£'000

See **Answer** at the end of this chapter.

6.3   Depreciable amount and depreciation period

The **residual value and useful life** of an asset must be reviewed **at least each year end**; any change is a change in **accounting estimate** and must be accounted for prospectively under IAS 8 *Accounting Policies, Changes in Accounting Estimates and Errors*. The accounting policy remains one of taking account of residual values and useful lives; all that changes are the judgements as to what the values for these are.

Interactive question 4: Depreciation period   [Difficulty level: Intermediate]

An asset has a cost of £1,000, useful life of 10 years and residual value of £200. At the beginning of year 3 of its life, the remaining useful life was revised to four years, the residual value being unchanged.

Requirement

Calculate the depreciation charge for each of years 1 to 3 on the straight-line basis.

Fill in the proforma below.

	Year 1 (£)	Year 2 (£)	Year 3 (£)
Cost			
Accumulated depreciation			
Carrying amount			
Charge for the year (W)			

WORKING

See **Answer** at the end of this chapter.

Points to note

1   Depreciation continues to be recognised even if fair value (ie the open market price) is greater than the carrying amount. This is for two reasons: the entity has no intention of selling the asset (so market price is not relevant) and depreciation is, as has been noted, a cost-allocation concept, not a means of revaluing an asset;

2   Depreciation is zero if residual value exceeds the carrying amount. The reason is that there is no longer a depreciable amount.

6.4 Commencement of depreciation

Depreciation should commence **when the asset is in the location and condition necessary for it to be capable of operating in the manner intended**. This is the case even if the asset is actually put into use at a later date. Depreciation continues **even if the asset lies idle**, for example as a result of a fall in market demand for its output. Depreciation **only ceases when the asset is derecognised**; the treatment of assets held for sale is dealt with in Section 9 below.

6.5 Factors affecting useful life

There are many factors affecting the useful life of an asset.

These include:

- **Expected usage** of the asset measured by reference to the asset's expected capacity or physical output.

- Expected **physical wear and tear**.

- **Technical or commercial obsolescence** arising from changes or improvements in production, or from a change in market demand.

- **Legal or similar limits** on the use of the asset, such as expiry dates of related leases.

These factors should be considered by management on the initial assessment of the asset's useful life and on each subsequent annual review.

6.6 Depreciation method

IAS 16 requires that a **systematic basis** should be used to allocate the depreciable amount over the asset's useful life; the method should reflect the **pattern in which the future economic benefits are consumed**. A number of methods are identified, which you should be familiar with from your Accounting studies:

- **Straight-line**, whereby there is a constant charge each year, on the assumption that equal amounts of economic benefit are consumed in each year of the asset's life.

- **Diminishing (or reducing) balance**, whereby the depreciation rate is applied to the opening carrying amount. This method, which charges more depreciation in the early years of an asset's life than in later years, could be appropriate in circumstances where over its life the asset becomes less capable of producing a high-quality product.

- **Units output**, whereby the charge is calculated by reference to the output each year as a proportion of the total expected output over the asset's useful life.

6.7 Change in method

Depreciation methods must be reviewed at least **at each financial year end**. A change in the pattern of consumption of economic benefits may demand a change to the method. Any changes are **changes in an accounting estimate** and are accounted for **prospectively**. The carrying amount of the asset is depreciated under the new method over the remaining useful life, beginning in the period in which the change is made in accordance with IAS 8.

CHAPTER

4

Worked example: Change in depreciation method

Bord plc has a 31 December year end. On 1 January 20X3 it bought a machine for £100,000 and depreciated it at 15% per annum on the reducing balance basis. The residual value is nil.

On 31 December 20X6, the machine will be included in Bord plc's accounts at the following amount:

	£
Cost	100,000
Accumulated depreciation	(47,800)
Carrying amount	52,200

During 20X7, the company decided to change the basis of depreciation to straight-line over a total life of 10 years, ie six years remaining from 1 January 20X7.

$$\text{New annual charge from 20X7} = \frac{52,200}{6} = £8,700 \text{ pa.}$$

6.8 Impairment

IAS 16 requires the provisions of IAS 36 *Impairment of Assets* to be applied.

The provisions of IAS 36 are dealt with in Section 8. Any compensation received from third parties for impaired PPE is recognised in profit or loss (where the impairment loss is charged), not set against the cost of the PPE item.

7 Accounting for revaluations

Section overview

- Revaluation gains are recognised in other comprehensive income and form part of equity as a revaluation surplus.

- Revaluation losses are recognised as an expense in profit or loss unless they relate to an earlier revaluation surplus.

- After revaluation, depreciation is based on the revalued amount.

- An annual reserves transfer is allowed amounting to the excess of actual depreciation over the historical cost depreciation.

7.1 Increases in value

When the historical cost convention is used in accounting, assets are recorded at their original purchase cost. For many small businesses this is sufficient.

Non-current assets might have been purchased a long time ago, and risen in value over time, so that their historical cost (less accumulated depreciation) is no longer representative of the current value.

This is most noticeable in respect of freehold land and buildings. Property prices in the UK have tended to rise over time, and their historical cost may be much lower than their current value. Freehold property may have been purchased at different times, and each item of property cannot be properly compared with another on the basis of their historical cost. For example, suppose that a company purchased a freehold property for £1 million in 1980, another for £1 million in 1990 and a third for £1 million in 2000. Although all three properties originally cost £1 million, their current values will be substantially different. As long as property prices continue to rise, the oldest property will be worth more now than the most recently-purchased one because £1 million would have bought a more substantial property in 1980 than in 1990 or 2000.

Non-current assets may therefore be revalued using the **revaluation model**. This new value is then depreciated over the remainder of the useful life.

The basic rule is that increases in value on a revaluation are recognised in other comprehensive income and form part of equity under the heading of revaluation surplus. The effect of this is that they:

- Appear under 'other comprehensive income' in the statement of profit or loss and other comprehensive income.

- Appear in the statement of changes in equity as part of 'total comprehensive income', and hence are part of total equity.

- Are not recognised in profit or loss.

The exception is that where such an increase reverses an earlier revaluation decrease on the same asset that was recognised in profit or loss (see Section 7.3 below), then the surplus should be recognised in profit or loss, but only to the extent of the previous decrease. In practice, the surplus is treated so that the overall effect is the same as if the original downward revaluation recognised in profit or loss had not occurred. Any excess surplus is recognised in other comprehensive income as described above.

7.2 Accounting for increases in value

The commonly adopted method of accounting for upward revaluations to fair value is to **write the original cost to fair value** and **write back the accumulated depreciation to revaluation surplus**.

Journal entries for revaluation

- When undepreciated freehold land is revalued upwards, the journal entry increases the asset's cost to the revalued amount and creates a **revaluation surplus**.

DR	Freehold land – cost/valuation	£X	
CR	Revaluation surplus		£X

- When assets which have been depreciated are revalued upwards, we still increase the asset's cost to its new value, but we also remove the accumulated depreciation that has built up to date. Together these amounts create the revaluation account:

DR	Building – cost/valuation	£X	
DR	Building – accumulated depreciation	£X	
CR	Revaluation surplus		£X

- The **asset's** annual depreciation charge on the full amount after the revaluation is charged as an expense (the annual depreciation charge will rise after the revaluation):

DR	Profit or loss – depreciation on revalued amount	£X	
CR	Accumulated depreciation		£X

Worked example: Revaluation

A company has two non-current assets.

Asset A was bought for £1,400,000 some years ago and is now valued at £4,500,000. This asset is not depreciated.

Asset B was bought for £500,000 five years ago and has been depreciated at 10% on cost pa. It is now valued at £800,000. There is no change to its useful life.

Requirement

Show the journals to record the asset revaluations, and show the extracts from the statement of financial position for the non-current assets and the revaluation surplus.

Solution

Asset A

DR	Asset A – cost/valuation (£4.5m – £1.4m)	£3,100,000	
CR	Revaluation surplus		£3,100,000

Asset B

		£	£
DR	Asset B – cost/valuation (£800,000 – £500,000)	300,000	
DR	Asset B – accumulated depreciation (£500,000 × 10% × 5)	250,000	
CR	Revaluation surplus		550,000

Statement of financial position (extract)

	£
Property, plant and equipment (£4,500,000 + £800,000)	5,300,000
Revaluation surplus (£3,100,000 + £550,000)	3,650,000

Interactive question 5: Revaluation   [Difficulty level: Exam standard]

On 1 January 20X2, an asset has a carrying amount of £100 and a remaining useful life of 10 years, with a nil residual value. The asset is revalued on that date to £50 and the loss is recognised in profit or loss.

The asset is depreciated straight-line over the next five years, giving a carrying amount of £25 at 31 December 20X6. Then, on 1 January 20X7 when the remaining useful life is the unexpired five years, the asset is revalued to £60.

Requirement

State how much of the revaluation surplus on 1 January 20X7 is recognised in other comprehensive income and how much is recognised in profit or loss.

Fill in the proforma below.

The revaluation gain on 1 January 20X7 is £..

If the previous downward revaluation had not taken place the carrying amount on 31 December 20X6 would have been £..

The 'excess' revaluation surplus recognised in other comprehensive income is £..

The amount recognised in profit or loss is £..

See **Answer** at the end of this chapter.

7.3 Decreases in value

The basic rule is that decreases in value on a revaluation are **recognised as an expense** and charged to profit or loss.

The exception is where such a decrease **reverses an earlier revaluation increase** on the same asset that was recognised in other comprehensive income and is held in the revaluation surplus, then the **deficit should be recognised in other comprehensive income**, but only to the extent of the previous increase.

Worked example: Revaluation decrease

An item of land originally cost £15,000. Two years ago it was revalued to £20,000. Now the value has fallen to £13,000.

When the land was originally revalued two years ago, the revaluation surplus of £5,000 would have been recognised in other comprehensive income and accumulated in the revaluation surplus as part of equity.

The asset value has fallen by £7,000, of which £5,000 should reverse the previous revaluation surplus via other comprehensive income and the remaining £2,000 should be recognised in profit or loss.

The double entry would be:

		£	£
DR	Revaluation surplus	5,000	
DR	Profit or loss	2,000	
CR	Asset value		7,000

If the profit for the year before adjusting for this loss was £57,000, the extracts from the financial statements would show the following:

Statement of profit or loss and other comprehensive income

	£
Profit for the year (57,000 – 2,000)	55,000
Other comprehensive income:	
Loss on property revaluation	(5,000)
Total comprehensive income for the year	50,000

Statement of changes in equity

	Retained earnings £	Revaluation surplus £	Total £
Total comprehensive income for the year	55,000	(5,000)	50,000

7.4 Depreciation of revalued assets

Where an asset has been revalued, **the depreciation charge is based on the revalued amount, less residual value, from the date of revaluation**. The asset's residual value should also be **re-estimated on revaluation**.

Definition

Residual value: The estimated amount that an entity would currently obtain from disposal of the asset, after deducting the estimated costs of disposal if the asset were already of the age and in the condition expected at the end of its useful life.

Worked example: Revaluation and depreciation of non-current assets

Vann Ltd commenced trading on 1 January 20X1. On that date the company purchased a building for £120,000 to be depreciated over 30 years with no residual value. Vann Ltd uses a revaluation model for buildings.

After five years of trading on 1 January 20X6, the building has a fair value of £175,000. It still has a further 25 years of useful life remaining.

Calculate the annual depreciation charge to profit or loss in each year of the asset's life, and the revaluation surplus as at 1 January 20X6.

Solution

Before the revaluation, the annual depreciation charge is £4,000 pa on the building. This charge is made in each of the first five years of the asset's life.

The carrying amount of the asset will decline by £4,000 pa, to £120,000 less (5 × £4,000) £20,000 = £100,000 at 31 December 20X5.

When the revaluation takes place, the amount of the revaluation is:

	£
New asset value (to be shown in statement of financial position)	175,000
Carrying amount as at end of 20X5	(100,000)
Amount of revaluation	75,000

The carrying amount of the asset will be increased by £75,000 to £175,000 and £75,000 recognised in other comprehensive income and accumulated in the revaluation surplus as part of equity.

The accumulated depreciation of £20,000 built up over five years is no longer needed. On 1 January 20X6 we therefore

		£	£
DR	Non-current asset cost (175,000 – 120,000)	55,000	
DR	Accumulated depreciation (entire balance)	20,000	
CR	Revaluation surplus		75,000

After the revaluation, depreciation will be charged on the building at a new rate of:

$$\frac{£175,000}{25 \text{ years}} = £7,000 \text{ per year}$$

The carrying amount of the building will fall by £7,000 per year over 25 years, from £175,000 as at 1 January 20X6 to nil at the end of the 25 years, ie it will have been fully depreciated.

The whole of the depreciation charge is **recognised in profit or loss**. None is recognised in other comprehensive income and consequently set against the revaluation surplus. However, IAS 16 **permits,** and it is best practice to make, **a transfer between reserves,** of the 'excess' depreciation arising as a result of the revaluation.

The overall effect is that the statement of profit or loss shows the economic benefit consumed, measured by reference to the revalued figure for the asset, but distributable profits (ie those out of which dividends may be declared) are not affected by extra depreciation on revalued assets.

The transfer is recorded as follows:

Amount of transfer = actual depreciation charged less equivalent charge based on original historical cost of asset

Entry to record transfer:

DR	Revaluation surplus	X	
CR	Retained earnings		X

This transfer is shown in the statement of changes in equity.

Worked example: Reserve transfer

An item of PPE was purchased for £800,000 on 1 January 20X6. It is estimated to have a useful life of 20 years and is depreciated on a straight-line basis. On 1 January 20X8 the asset is revalued to £850,000. The useful life is unchanged. (Ignore residual value.)

	£
Actual depreciation for 20X8 based on revalued amount $\left(\dfrac{850,000}{18}\right)$	47,222
Depreciation for 20X8 based on historical cost $\left(\dfrac{800,000}{20}\right)$	(40,000)
Difference	7,222

In the statement of profit or loss for 20X8 a depreciation expense of £47,222 will be charged. A reserve transfer, which will be shown in the statement of changes in equity, may be performed as follows:

	£	£
DR Revaluation surplus	7,222	
CR Retained earnings		7,222

The closing balance on the revaluation surplus on 31 December 20X8 will therefore be as follows:

	£
Balance arising on revaluation (850 – 720)	130,000
Transfer to retained earnings	(7,222)
	122,778

7.5 Disposal of revalued assets

This is dealt with in Section 9.4 below.

8 Impairment of assets

Section overview

- An asset is impaired if its recoverable amount is less than its carrying amount.

- The recoverable amount is the higher of:

    - The asset's fair value less costs to sell, and
    - Its value in use.

- Internal and external sources provide indications of possible impairment.

- For assets held at historical cost an impairment loss should be charged to profit or loss.

- For assets held at a revalued amount the impairment loss is treated as a revaluation decrease.

8.1 Objective and scope of IAS 36 *Impairment of Assets*

Whenever an asset's recoverable amount falls to an amount less than its carrying amount, it is said to be impaired. Its carrying amount in the statement of financial position is therefore reduced to this recoverable amount and, in most cases, an expense is recognised in profit or loss. IAS 36 puts in place a detailed method for carrying out impairment reviews and related accounting treatments and disclosures.

IAS 36 applies to all assets apart from those specifically excluded from the standard. It most commonly applies to assets such as **property, plant and equipment** accounted for in accordance with IAS 16 and **intangible assets** accounted for in accordance with IAS 38 *Intangible Assets* (we will look at intangible assets in Chapter 5). The standard also applies to some financial assets, namely subsidiaries, associates and joint ventures. Impairments of all other financial assets are accounted for in accordance with IAS 39 *Financial Instruments: Recognition and Measurement,* the detail of which is outside your syllabus.

8.2 Basic principle

The basic principle underlying IAS 36 is relatively straightforward. If an asset's value in the financial statements is higher than its realistic value, measured as its 'recoverable amount', the asset is judged to have been **impaired.**

The value of the asset should be reduced by the amount of the **impairment loss.** This loss should be **charged to profit immediately**.

The main accounting issues to consider are therefore as follows:

- How is it possible to **identify when** an impairment loss may have occurred?
- How should the **recoverable amount** of the asset be **measured**?
- How should an impairment loss be **reported in the financial statements**?

8.3 Indications of impairment

An entity should assess at the end of each reporting period whether there are any indications of impairment to any assets. The concept of **materiality** applies, and only material impairment needs to be identified.

If there are indications of possible impairment, the entity is required to make a formal estimate of the **recoverable amount** of the assets concerned.

In assessing such indications of a possible impairment, IAS 36 requires an entity to consider, as a minimum, the following:

- **External sources of information**:

  - A fall in the asset's market value that is more significant than would normally be expected from passage of time over normal use.

  - A significant change in the technological, market, legal or economic environment of the business in which the assets are employed.

  - An increase in market interest rates or market rates of return on investments likely to affect the discount rate used in calculating value in use.

  - The carrying amount of the entity's net assets being more than its market capitalisation.

- **Internal sources of information**:

  - Evidence of obsolescence or physical damage
  - Adverse changes in the use to which the asset is put
  - Indications that the economic performance of an asset is, or will be, worse than expected

Even if there are no indications of impairment, the following assets must **always** be tested for impairment annually:

- An intangible asset with an **indefinite useful life**
- **Goodwill** acquired in a business combination

(Intangible assets are covered in Chapter 5.)

8.4 Measuring the recoverable amount of the asset

Definition

Recoverable amount of an asset: Is the **higher** of:

- Its fair value less costs to sell, and
- Its value in use

8.4.1 Fair value less costs to sell

Definition

Fair value less costs to sell: The amount obtainable from the sale of an asset in an arm's length transaction between knowledgeable, willing parties, less costs of disposal.

In other words an asset's **fair value less costs to sell** is the amount net of selling costs that could be obtained from the sale of the asset. Selling costs include sales transaction costs, such as legal expenses.

A **binding sales agreement** is the best evidence of an asset's fair value less costs to sell. Where there is no binding sales agreement the following bases will be used:

- If there is **an active market** in the asset, the net selling price should be based on the **market price less costs to sell**, or on the price of recent transactions in similar assets.

- If there is **no active market** in the asset it might be possible to **estimate** a net selling price using best estimates of what 'knowledgeable, willing parties' might pay in an arm's length transaction and deducting costs of disposal.

Selling costs cannot include any **restructuring or reorganisation expenses**, or any costs that have already been recognised in the financial statements as liabilities.

8.4.2 Value in use

An asset's fair value less costs to sell is compared with its **value in use** in order to determine the recoverable amount (see above).

Definition

Value in use: the present value of the future cash flows expected to be derived from an asset.

The detailed guidance provided as to how to arrive at this value is not in the syllabus, but the following general points should be noted:

- Calculations should be based on **reasonable and supportable assumptions**.

- Projections should be based on the **most recent budgets etc approved by management** over a **maximum of five years**, unless a longer period can be justified.

- **Inflows and outflows should be estimated separately**, based upon the asset's current condition (so ignoring the benefits of restructurings not committed to and future performance enhancements).

- Financing and tax costs should be **excluded**.

- Account should be taken of net cash flows expected to arise on the asset's **ultimate disposal**.

Note the practical point that **if one of the two elements in the recoverable amount has been estimated as in excess of the asset's carrying amount, then the asset is not impaired and there is no need to estimate the value of the other element**. So if fair value less costs to sell exceeds carrying amount, as it well might in the case of freehold and leasehold properties, then there is no need to estimate value in use. This is useful in relation to assets for which there is an active market, **because fair values can be estimated quickly and cheaply**.

8.5 Accounting treatment of impairments

If the recoverable amount of an asset is less than the carrying amount, the difference is the impairment loss.

It should be described as such in the financial statements but the accounting treatment is similar to increases and decreases arising on a revaluation (see Section 7 above) whereby:

- An impairment loss **for assets at a historical cost** is treated as **a decrease on revaluation and is recognised as an expense** in profit or loss.

- If the impairment loss relates to **an asset that has previously been revalued**, then it is treated as a **revaluation decrease** and not as an impairment loss. So in line with Section 7.3 above it can first be set against any balance relating to the same asset standing on the revaluation surplus, with any excess being recognised in profit or loss.

- Depreciation charges in future accounting periods will be set to write off **the revised carrying amount**, less residual value, over its remaining useful life.

In certain circumstances impairment losses incurred in one accounting period may be reversed in a later period, but the relevant rules are outside the Financial Accounting and Reporting syllabus.

CHAPTER

4

Property, plant and equipment   189

Worked example: Impairment

The following details relate to a freehold property:

	£
Carrying amount (at date of revaluation)	1,000,000
Revalued to	1,600,000
Amount recognised in the revaluation surplus	600,000
Current carrying amount	1,500,000
Fair value	600,000
Value in use	800,000

The recoverable amount of the asset is £800,000 (ie the higher of fair value and value in use).

An impairment loss of £700,000 has occurred (1,500,000 – 800,000)

The impairment will be accounted for as follows:

		£	£
DR	Revaluation surplus	600,000	
DR	Profit or loss	100,000	
CR	Property (carrying amount)		700,000

8.6 Disclosure

For all impairments, disclosure must be made for **each class of assets** of:

- The amount of any impairment loss recognised in profit or loss and the line item where it has been included.

- The equivalent information about any impairment loss recognised directly in equity.

If an impairment loss for **an individual asset is material to the financial statements** as a whole, there must be **additional disclosure** of:

- The events that led to the recognition of the loss

- The amount

- The nature of the asset

- Whether the recoverable amount is fair value less costs to sell or value in use

- The basis used to determine fair value less costs to sell (where the recoverable amount is fair value less costs to sell)

- The discount rate used in the current estimate and any previous estimate of value in use (where the recoverable amount is value in use)

If impairment losses are **material only in aggregate**, then a **reduced** amount of additional information should be given. The following details must be disclosed:

- The main classes of assets affected by impairment losses
- The main events and circumstances that led to the recognition of these impairment losses

9 Derecognition of PPE

Section overview

- When the decision is made to sell a non-current asset it should be classified as 'held for sale'.

- An asset held for sale is valued at the lower of:

  - Its carrying amount
  - Its fair value less costs to sell

- No depreciation is charged on a held for sale asset.

9.1 General rule

An item of PPE shall be **removed from the statement of financial position** (ie derecognised) when it is **disposed** of or when **no future economic benefits** are expected from its use or disposal (ie **it is abandoned**).

The gain or loss on the disposal of an item of PPE is **included in the profit or loss** of the **period in which the derecognition occurs**. The gain or loss is calculated as the difference between the net sale proceeds and the carrying amount, whether measured under the cost model or the revaluation model. Gains may not be included in revenue in the statement of profit or loss.

The process of selling an item of PPE involves the following stages:

- Making the decision to sell the item
- Putting the item on the market, agreeing the selling price and negotiating the contract for sale
- Completing the sale

The issue is at what stage through this process should any gain or loss on the sale be recognised. These matters are dealt with in IFRS 5 and there are different required treatments depending on whether the item of PPE is measured under the cost model or the revaluation model.

9.2 Disposal of PPE measured under the cost model

Following the principle that any loss should be recognised immediately but any gain should only be recognised when it is realised, IFRS 5's requirements in respect of PPE measured under the cost model are that:

- When the carrying amount of a non-current asset **will be recovered principally through sale** (rather than through continuing use), the asset must be classified as **held for sale**. In most cases, **this classification will be made at the time of the decision to sell**.

- A non-current asset held for sale is measured at the lower of:

  - Its **carrying amount**
  - Its **fair value less costs to sell** (ie its net selling price)

  The effect is that any loss (ie where the former value exceeds the latter) is recognised at the time of classification as held for sale. But any gain (ie where the latter value exceeds the former) is not; instead it is recognised according to the general rule in Section 9.1 above.

- A non-current asset held for sale **is presented separately from all other assets** in the statement of financial position. IFRS 5 does not specify where this 'separate presentation' should be made, but these learning materials follow the IASB's (non-mandatory) guidance on implementing IFRS 5 by presenting it immediately below the sub-total for current assets.

- **No depreciation is charged** on a held for sale asset. The new valuation basis of fair value less costs to sell approximates to residual value, so there is now no depreciable amount.

- **The loss is an impairment loss**, dealt with in the same way as other impairment losses under IAS 36.

On ultimate disposal, any difference between carrying amount and disposal proceeds is treated **as a loss or gain under IAS 16**, not as a further impairment loss or reversal of the original impairment loss.

Interactive question 6: Asset held for sale I [Difficulty level: Intermediate]

An item of PPE was acquired on 1 January 20X5 at a cost of £100,000. A residual value of £10,000 and a useful life of 10 years was assumed for the purpose of depreciation charges.

On 1 January 20X8 the asset was classified as held for sale. Its fair value was estimated at £40,000 and the costs to sell at £2,000.

The asset was sold on 30 June 20X8 for £38,000.

Requirements

(a) Show an extract from the PPE table for 20X8 relating to the asset held for sale.

(b) Show the journal entry to record the classification as held for sale.

(c) Show the entry in the statement of profit or loss for the year ended 31 December 20X8.

(d) Describe how the answer to (c) would change if the sales proceeds on 30 June 20X8 were £32,000.

Fill in the proforma below.

(a) **Note showing movements on PPE (extract)**

	£'000
Cost or valuation:	
At 1 January 20X8	
Classified as held for sale	————
At 31 December 20X8	═══════
Depreciation:	
At 1 January 20X8	
Impairment loss	
Classified as held for sale	————
At 31 December 20X8	═══════

(b) **Journal entries to record the classification as held for sale**

Recognising the impairment

	£'000	£'000
DR Profit or loss		
CR PPE – accumulated depreciation		

(This is shown as an impairment loss in the PPE table)

Classification as held for sale

	£'000	£'000
DR Non-current assets held for sale		
DR PPE – accumulated depreciation		
CR PPE – cost		

(c) **Statement of profit or loss for the year ended 31 December 20X8**

	£'000
Impairment loss on reclassification of non-current asset as held for sale	

(d) **Statement of profit or loss for the year ended 31 December 20X8**

In the statement of profit or loss:

(i)

(ii)

See **Answer** at the end of this chapter.

Interactive question 7: Asset held for sale II   [Difficulty level: Intermediate]

These facts are as detailed in Interactive question 6, except that on classification as held for sale, the fair value was estimated at £80,000 and the costs to sell at £3,000.

The asset was sold on 30 June 20X8 for £77,000.

Requirements

(a) Show the journal entry to record the classification as held for sale.
(b) Show the entry in the statement of profit or loss for the year ended 31 December 20X8.

Fill in the proforma below.

(a) **Journal entry to record the classification as held for sale**

	£'000	£'000
1 January 20X8		
DR PPE – accumulated depreciation		
DR Non-current assets held for sale		
CR PPE – cost		

(b) **Statement of profit or loss for the year ended 31 December 20X8**

	£'000
Gain on disposal of non-current assets held for sale	

See **Answer** at the end of this chapter.

9.3 Classification as held for sale

For the classification as held for sale to be made detailed criteria must be met:

- The asset must be **available for immediate sale** in its present condition.
- Its sale must be **highly probable** (ie significantly more likely than probable).

For the sale to be highly probable:

- Management must be **committed** to a plan to sell the asset.

- There must be an active programme to **locate a buyer**.

- The asset must be marketed for sale at **a price that is reasonable** in relation to its current fair value.

- The sale should be expected to take place **within one year** from the **date of classification**.

- It is unlikely that significant changes to the plan will be made or that the plan will be **withdrawn**.

Other points to note

1   An asset can still be classified as held for sale, **even if the sale has not actually taken place within one year**. However, the delay must have been caused by events or circumstances beyond the entity's control and there must be sufficient evidence that the entity is still committed to sell the asset.

2   If the end of a reporting period intervenes between the classification as held for sale and the final disposal, fair value less costs to sell may have fallen below or risen above the figure used on original classification. Any fall is accounted for as a **further impairment loss**, while any rise goes to **reduce the amount of the original impairment loss**, but cannot write the asset's carrying amount above its original level.

3   The rules for disposal groups (where an operation comprising assets and liabilities is being sold) fall outside the Financial Accounting and Reporting syllabus.

C H A P T E R

4

9.4 Disposal of PPE measured under the revaluation model

For an item of PPE measured after recognition under the revaluation model and subsequently classified as held for sale, there is a different accounting treatment of the difference between carrying amount and fair value less costs to sell at the time of classification:

- Consistently with the accounting policy chosen, the asset must be **revalued at fair value** under IAS 16 **immediately before the classification**.

- 'Revaluation' means that **either a gain or loss will be recognised** (whereas, as explained in Section 9.2, for assets measured under the cost method, only a loss is recognised at the time of classification). If the previous carrying amount is greater than fair value, there will be a loss; if it is less than fair value, there will be a gain.

- Such a gain or loss is dealt with under IAS 16 (see Section 7 above), so **a gain is recognised in other comprehensive income and accumulated in revaluation surplus** (except to the extent it reverses a loss previously charged to the profit or loss) and **a loss in profit or loss** (except to the extent it reverses a gain previously recognised in other comprehensive income and held in revaluation surplus).

- Once revalued in this way, the measurement is then adjusted to the normal basis for held for sale assets, so fair value less costs to sell. The effect is that the **costs to sell are immediately recognised in profit or loss as an impairment loss**.

Interactive question 8: Disposal of revalued PPE   [Difficulty level: Exam standard]

Land, which is not depreciated, was acquired on 1 January 20X2 at a cost of £200,000 and revalued to £250,000 on 1 January 20X5. On 1 January 20X8 the asset was classified as held for sale. Its fair value was estimated at £235,000 and the costs to sell at £5,000.

Requirements

(a) Show the journal entry to record the revaluation on 1 January 20X5.
(b) Show the journal entry to record the classification as held for sale on 1 January 20X8.

Fill in the proforma below.

(a) **Journal entry to record the revaluation**

	£'000	£'000
1 January 20X5		
DR PPE – at valuation		
CR Revaluation surplus		

(b) **Journal entry to record the classification as held for sale**

	£'000	£'000
1 January 20X8		
DR Non-current assets held for sale – fair value less costs to sell		
DR Profit or loss – costs to sell		
DR Revaluation surplus		
CR PPE – at valuation		

See **Answer** at the end of this chapter.

9.5 Disposal and gains held in revaluation surplus

If there is still a credit balance on the revaluation surplus relating to an asset that has been disposed of, this balance should be **transferred to retained earnings as a reserve transfer** (the same treatment and presentation as for the reserve transfer in respect of extra depreciation). The accounting entry is:

DR Revaluation surplus	£X	
CR Retained earnings		£X

Interactive question 9: Summary   [Difficulty level: Intermediate]

On 1 January 20X1, Tiger Ltd buys for £120,000 an item of property, plant and equipment which has an estimated useful life of 20 years with no residual value. Tiger Ltd depreciates its non-current assets on a straight-line basis. Tiger Ltd's year-end is 31 December.

On 31 December 20X3, the asset will be carried in the statement of financial position as follows:

	£
Property, plant and equipment at cost	120,000
Accumulated depreciation (3 × (120,000 ÷ 20))	(18,000)
	102,000

On 1 January 20X4, the asset is revalued to £136,000. The total useful life remains unchanged.

On 1 January 20X8 the asset is classified as held for sale, its fair value being £140,000 and its costs to sell £3,000. On 1 May 20X8 the asset is sold for £137,000.

Requirements

(a) Show the journal to record the revaluation.

(b) Calculate the revised depreciation charge and show how it would be accounted for, including any permitted reserve transfers.

(c) Show the journal to record the classification as held for sale.

(d) Explain how these events will be recorded in the financial statements for the year ended 31 December 20X8.

Fill in the proforma below.

(a) **Journal to record the revaluation**

	£	£
1 January 20X4		
DR PPE cost/valuation		
DR PPE accumulated depreciation		
CR Revaluation surplus		

(b) **Revised depreciation charge**

	£	£
Annual charge from 20X4 onwards		
DR Profit or loss depreciation expense		
CR PPE accumulated depreciation		
Annual reserve transfer		
DR Revaluation surplus		
CR Retained earnings		

Being the difference between the actual depreciation charge and the charge based on historical cost.

Shown in the statement of changes in equity as follows:

	Revaluation surplus £	Retained earnings £
Brought forward	X	X
Profit for the year	–	X
Transfer of realised profits		
Carried forward	X	X

(c) **Journal to record classification as held for sale**

At 1 January 20X8, balances relating to the asset will be as follows:

	£
Property, plant and equipment at valuation	
Accumulated depreciation	
Carrying amount	
Revaluation surplus	

C
H
A
P
T
E
R

4

	£'000	£'000

1 January 20X8
DR   PPE – accumulated depreciation
DR   Non-current assets held for sale – fair value less costs to sell
DR   Profit or loss – costs to sell
CR   PPE – cost/valuation
CR   Revaluation surplus (ß)

(d) **Financial statements for the year ended 31 December 20X8**

In the statement of profit or loss:

(i)

(ii)

In the statement of profit or loss and other comprehensive income:

Remaining balance on revaluation surplus is transferred to retained earnings as a reserve transfer in the statement of changes in equity:

	Revaluation surplus £	Retained earnings £
Brought forward	X	X
Retained profit for the year	–	X
Transfer of realised profits		
Carried forward	X	X

See **Answer** at the end of this chapter.

9.6   Abandonment of non-current assets

All these requirements within IFRS 5 which we have looked at so far apply to non-current assets classified as held for sale because their carrying amounts will be recovered principally through a sale transaction. They **do not apply to non-current assets which are to be abandoned**, for example by being scrapped. Because there will be no sales proceeds, any recovery of the carrying amounts of such assets will principally be through continued use.

Such assets continue to be measured and presented under IAS 16, with the effect that:

*   The assets remain **classified within their existing non-current asset category**.

*   **Depreciation charges continue to be recognised.**

*   Any **profit or loss on abandonment is recognised at the time of abandonment** rather than at the (usually earlier) time of the decision to abandon them.

IAS 16, not IFRS 5, also applies to the measurement and presentation of an asset taken out of use but not scheduled for disposal; this might be the case if demand for its outputs has temporarily fallen away.

10   Disclosures

Section overview

IAS 16 requires a number of detailed disclosures.

10.1   IAS 16 requirements

As might be expected for items frequently that form such a large part of the statement of financial position and where management has to make so many important judgements (eg re residual values and useful lives), the financial statements disclosure provisions are wide-ranging. All of the following must be shown for each class of PPE by way of note:

- The measurement basis used (either cost model or revaluation model)

- The depreciation methods

- The useful lives or depreciation rates

- Gross carrying amounts and accumulated depreciation at the start and end of the period

- A reconciliation of the net carrying amounts at the start and end of the period by reference to:
  - Additions
  - Disposals
  - Acquisitions through business combinations
  - The effects of revaluations
  - Impairment losses
  - Exchange differences
  - Other changes, eg assets classified as held for sale

- Details of assets pledged as security for loans and of contractual commitments to acquire PPE

- Changes in accounting estimates in accordance with IAS 8

- For assets which have been revalued:
  - The effective date(s)
  - Whether an independent valuer was involved
  - The methods and significant assumptions underlying the fair value estimates
  - The extent to which fair values were determined by reference to prices in active markets or recent arm's length transactions
  - The carrying amount under the cost model
  - The total revaluation surplus, together with any movements in the period

There are further, voluntary disclosures. These include:

- The carrying amount of temporarily idle PPE.

- The gross carrying amount of any fully depreciated PPE that is still in use.

- The carrying amount of PPE retired from active use and not classified as held for sale in accordance with IFRS 5.

- When the cost model is used, the fair value of PPE when this is materially different from the carrying amount.

Interactive question 10: Disclosure [Difficulty level: Exam standard]

(1) RSBH Ltd's statement of financial position at its year end 31 December 20X6 includes the following property, plant and equipment amounts:

	Cost £'000	Accumulated depreciation £'000
Freehold property	1,000	300
Plant and machinery	700	330
Fixtures and fittings	300	180

(2) On 1 January 20X7 RSBH Ltd revalued its existing freehold property to its market value of £1.2m and bought additional freehold property at a cost of £100,000. As a result of no depreciation being charged on the land element, the effective rate of depreciation is 2% per annum on cost/valuation, assuming no residual value.

(3) On 1 April 20X7 RSBH Ltd classified as held for sale a machine with an original cost of £360,000 and a carrying amount at 31 December 20X6 of £100,000. The machine's fair value at 1 April

20X7 was estimated at £80,000 with £5,000 costs to sell. The company also bought plant and machinery at a cost of £400,000. Depreciation is to be charged at the rate of 10% per annum on cost, assuming no residual value.

(4) On 1 July 20X7 RSBH Ltd scrapped fixtures and fittings with an original cost of £40,000 and accumulated depreciation at 31 December 20X6 of £25,000 and bought new fixtures at a cost of £80,000. Depreciation is to be charged at 15% per annum on cost, assuming no residual value.

Requirement

Prepare the note showing the movements on property, plant and equipment, including accumulated depreciation, which would be included in the financial statements of RSBH Ltd for the year ended 31 December 20X7.

Complete the proforma below.

RSBH Ltd: Note showing movements on property, plant and equipment for the year ended 31 December 20X7

	Freehold property £'000	Plant and machinery £'000	Fixtures and fittings £'000	Total £'000
Cost/valuation				
At 1 January 20X7				
Revaluation				
Additions				
Classified as held for sale				
Disposals				
At 31 December 20X7				
Depreciation				
At 1 January 20X7				
Revaluation				
Charge for the year				
Classified as held for sale				
Impairment loss				
Disposals				
At 31 December 20X7				
Carrying amount				
At 31 December 20X7				
At 31 December 20X6				

WORKINGS

	Plant and machinery £'000	Fixtures and fittings £'000
(1) **Depreciation charge for the year**		
Items reclassified/disposed of during year		
Items owned throughout year		
Items acquired during year		
(2) **Accumulated depreciation on items reclassified/disposed of**		
Brought forward		
Charge for year		
(3) **Impairment loss on items reclassified**		
Cost		
Accumulated depreciation		
Carrying amount on classification as held for sale		
Fair value less costs to sell		
Impairment loss		

See **Answer** at the end of the chapter.

11 UK GAAP comparison

Section overview

FRS 101 allows a limited exemption from the disclosure requirements of IAS 16.

There are no material differences between IAS 16 and FRS 102.

11.1 Property, plant and equipment

Under FRS 101 entities do not have to present comparative information in respect of the reconciliation of property, plant and equipment amounts at the beginning and end of the period.

There are no significant differences between FRS 102 and IAS 16.

11.2 Borrowing costs

FRS 101 grants no exemptions from the provisions of IAS 23.

Differences between FRS 102 and IAS 23 are as follows:

FRS 102	IAS 23
Entities are allowed the **choice** of whether to **capitalise** borrowing costs **or** to **recognise them as an expense** as incurred.	Capitalisation is **required**.

11.3 Impairment

FRS 101 allows exemption from disclosures regarding estimates used to measure recoverable amounts of cash-generating units (CGUs) containing goodwill or intangible assets with indefinite useful lives.

CGUs are not in the Financial Accounting and Reporting syllabus.

Summary

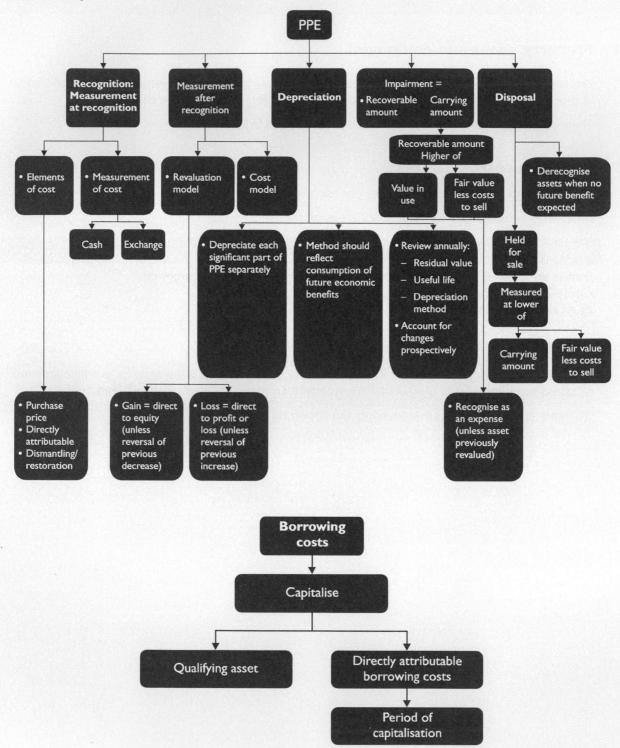

Self-test

Answer the following questions

1 Per IAS 16 *Property, Plant and Equipment,* which of the following should be capitalised as part of the cost of an asset?

    (1)   Stamp duty
    (2)   Employee costs related to site selection activities
    (3)   Cost of site preparation and clearance
    (4)   Installation costs

2 Max plc has incurred the following expenditure in 20X0 in respect of its non-current assets.

	£
Servicing of plant and equipment	25,000
Repainting of warehouse	40,000
Modification of an item of plant in order to increase its capacity	12,000
Upgrading of machine parts to improve quality of product	7,500

In 20X0 what will be the charge for repairs and maintenance in the statement of profit or loss in accordance with IAS 16 *Property, Plant and Equipment?*

3 Lakeland purchased freehold land and buildings on 1 July 20W3 for £380,000 including £80,000 for the land. The buildings had been depreciated at the rate of 4% per annum on cost for each of the ten years to 30 June 20X3. On 1 July 20X3 the property was professionally revalued at £800,000 including £200,000 for the land, an amount which was reflected in the books. At 1 July 20X3 it was estimated that the building had a remaining useful life of 20 years and a residual value of £100,000.

    (a)   In accordance with IAS 16 *Property, Plant and Equipment* what should the surplus on revaluation be on 1 July 20X3?

    (b)   In accordance with IAS 16 *Property, Plant and Equipment* what is the carrying amount of the freehold land and buildings on 30 June 20X4?

4 On 1 January 20X9 Rolax plc borrowed £3m to finance the production of two assets, both of which were expected to take a year to build. Work started during 20X9. The loan facility was drawn down and incurred on 1 January 20X9, and was utilised as follows, with the remaining funds invested temporarily.

	Asset A	Asset B
	£'000	£'000
1 January 20X9	500	1,000
1 July 20X9	500	1,000

The loan rate was 9% pa and Rolax plc can invest surplus funds at 7% pa.

Calculate the borrowing costs which may be capitalised for each of the assets and consequently the cost of each asset as at 31 December 20X9.

5 Webster plc had the following loans in place at the beginning and end of 20X6.

	1 January 20X6	31 December 20X6
	£m	£m
10% Bank loan repayable 20X8	120	120
9.5% Bank loan repayable 20X9	80	80

On 1 January 20X6, Webster plc began construction of a qualifying asset, an industrial machine, using existing borrowings. Expenditure drawn down for the construction was: £30m on 1 January 20X6, £20m on 1 October 20X6.

What is the amount of borrowing costs that can be capitalised for the machine?

6   Baboon plc adopts the revaluation model for its property, plant and equipment. It has collected the following information.

	Existing use value £	Open market value £
Office building	250,000	300,000
Warehouse (1)	175,000	200,000
Warehouse (2) (which is classified as held for sale)	150,000	210,000

None of the above assets are considered to be impaired and costs to sell are immaterial.

In accordance with IAS 16 *Property, Plant and Equipment,* at what total amount should the three properties be carried in Baboon plc's statement of financial position?

7   Paris Ltd has a freehold property carried at a revalued amount of £175,000. Due to a slump in property prices its recoverable amount is now estimated to be only £150,000. Its historical cost carrying amount is £160,000.

How should the above fall in value be reflected in the financial statements in accordance with IAS 16 *Property, Plant and Equipment*?

8   On 1 June 20X6 Dempster Ltd bought a new factory. The building has an estimated useful life of 50 years, but the roof will require replacing after 25 years. The cost of replacement is currently £100,000. The total price of the factory was £1,000,000.

In accordance with IAS 16 *Property, Plant and Equipment* what should the depreciation charge be for the year ended 31 May 20X7?

9   The following figures relate to an asset with a five-year life purchased on 1 January 20X1.

	£
Cost	100,000
Residual value at acquisition	10,000
Residual value at the end of 20X1 (taking into account current price changes)	15,000

What amount will be recognised in profit or loss as depreciation in the year to 31 December 20X1?

10   On 1 January 20X1 Lydd Ltd purchased production machinery costing £100,000, having an estimated useful life of 20 years and a residual value of £2,000. On 1 January 20X7 the remaining useful life of the machinery is revised and estimated to be 25 years, with an unchanged residual value.

In accordance with IAS 8 *Accounting Policies, Changes in Accounting Estimates and Errors* what should the depreciation charge on the machinery be in the year ended 31 December 20X7?

11   Propane plc are undertaking an impairment review of assets following IAS 36 *Impairment of Assets.* Investigations have uncovered the following:

Asset R has a carrying amount of £60,000, a value in use of £65,000 and a fair value less costs to sell of £30,000.

Asset Q has a carrying amount of £100,000, a value in use of £92,000 and a fair value less costs to sell of £95,000.

In accordance with IAS 36 *Impairment of Assets* what amount should be recognised as an impairment loss in relation to these two assets?

12   Gandalf Ltd has a year end of 31 December. On 30 October 20X4 it classified an item of plant as held for sale. At that date the plant had a carrying amount of £13,200 and had been accounted for according to the cost model. Its fair value was estimated at £11,100 and the costs to sell at £500.

On 15 December 20X4 the plant was sold for £10,500.

In accordance with IFRS 5 *Non-current Assets Held for Sale and Discontinued Operations* what amounts should be recognised as impairment loss and loss on disposal in profit or loss for the year to 31 December 20X4?

13 Merlin Ltd has a year end of 30 June. On 1 October 20X3 it classified one of its leasehold properties as held for sale. At that date the property had a carrying amount of £98,500 and had been accounted for according to the cost model. Its fair value was estimated at £120,100 and the costs to sell at £2,500.

On 15 June 20X4 the property was sold for £115,500.

In accordance with IFRS 5 *Non-current Assets Held for Sale and Discontinued Operations* what amounts should be recognised as gain on reclassification and gain on disposal in profit or loss for the year to 30 June 20X4?

14 Dumbledore Ltd has a year end of 30 June. On 1 June 20X5 it classified one of its freehold properties as held for sale. At that date the property had a carrying amount of £567,000 and had been accounted for according to the revaluation model. Its fair value was estimated at £725,000 and the costs to sell at £3,000.

In accordance with IFRS 5 *Non-current Assets Held for Sale and Discontinued Operations* what amounts should be recognised in the financial statements for the year to 30 June 20X5?

15 Arnold Ltd bought an asset on 1 October 20X1 for £200,000. It was being depreciated over 20 years on the straight-line basis. On 1 October 20X3, the asset was revalued to £270,000. Subsequently, on 30 September 20X7 the asset was classified as held for sale. Its fair value was estimated at £190,000 with costs to sell of £5,000.

(a) In accordance with IAS 16 *Property, Plant and Equipment* and best practice, what should the balance on the revaluation surplus be at the year end of 30 September 20X4?

(b) In accordance with IFRS 5 *Non-current Assets Held for Sale and Discontinued Operations* what should the loss recognised in profit or loss for the year ended 30 September 20X7 be on classification as held for sale?

16 The following information was disclosed in the financial statements of Maine Ltd for the year ended 31 December 20X2.

	Plant and equipment	
	20X2	20X1
	£	£
Cost	735,000	576,000
Accumulated depreciation	(265,000)	(315,000)
Carrying amount	470,000	261,000

During 20X2	£
Expenditure on plant and equipment	512,000
Impairment loss on reclassification of old plant as held for sale	50,000
Loss on the disposal of old plant	57,000
Depreciation charge on plant and equipment	143,000

In accordance with IFRS 5 *Non-current Assets Held for Sale and Discontinued Operations* what were the sales proceeds received on the disposal of the old plant?

17 The following information relates to the classification as held for sale of two machines by Halwell Ltd.

	Machine 1	Machine 2
	£	£
Cost	120,000	100,000
Fair value less costs to sell	90,000	40,000
Anticipated gain/(loss) on sale (based on fair value)	30,000	(20,000)

In accordance with IFRS 5 *Non-current Assets Held for Sale and Discontinued Operations* what was the total accumulated depreciation on both machines classified as held for sale?

18 On 1 January 20X2 Dulson Ltd purchased a freehold office block for £2.5 million. At the date of acquisition the useful life was estimated to be 50 years and the residual value £250,000. The company policy is to depreciate freehold property on the straight-line basis. On 31 December 20X7 the residual value of the offices was estimated at £450,000 due to an increase in commercial property prices. The estimated useful life of the property remained unchanged.

What amount will be recognised in profit or loss as depreciation in respect of the freehold property in the year to 31 December 20X7?

19 PORSCHE PLC

Porsche plc has the following non-current assets at 1 January 20X7.

	Cost £'000	Accumulated depreciation £'000	Carrying amount £'000
Freehold factory	1,440	144	1,296
Plant and equipment	1,968	257	1,711
Motor vehicles	449	194	255
Office equipment and fixtures	888	583	305
	4,745	1,178	3,567

You are given the following information for the year ended 31 December 20X7.

(1) The factory was acquired on 1 January 20X2 and is being depreciated over 50 years.

(2) Depreciation on other items is provided on cost on a straight-line basis. The rates used are 20% for fixtures and fittings, 25% for cars and 10% for equipment.

(3) On 1 January 20X7 the factory was revalued to an open market value of £2.2 million and an extension costing £500,000 became available for use. The directors wish to incorporate the revaluation into the accounts.

(4) The directors decided to change the method of depreciating motor vehicles to 30% reducing balance to give a more relevant presentation of the results and of the financial position.

(5) Two cars costing £17,500 each were bought on 1 January 20X7. Plant and fittings for the factory extension cost £75,000 and £22,000 respectively.

(6) When reviewing the expected lives of its non-current assets, the directors felt that it was necessary to reduce the remaining life of a two year old grinding machine to four years when it is expected to be sold for £8,000 as scrap. The machine originally cost £298,000 and at 1 January 20X7 had related accumulated depreciation of £58,000.

Requirements

(a) Prepare the disclosure notes for property, plant and equipment for the year ended 31 December 20X7 required by IFRSs.   **(14 marks)**

(b) Briefly explain the qualitative characteristics of financial information contained in the IASB *Conceptual Framework* illustrating your answer with references to the provisions of IAS 16 *Property, Plant and Equipment*.   **(7 marks)**

(21 marks)

20 PLOVER PLC

Plover plc is a car manufacturing group and during the year ended 30 September 20X9 the following transactions relating to property, plant and equipment took place.

(1) New factory premises were finally completed and were ready for occupation on 1 March 20X9. Production was not transferred to the factory until 31 August 20X9 due to a dispute with the labour force arising from proposed redundancies.

Capitalised costs relating to the factory were £1.1 million (including land of £600,000) at 1 October 20X8 and the following costs have been incurred since then.

	£'000
Further construction costs	125
Additional legal fees	25
Management and supervision costs (allocation)	75

(2) On 1 March 20X9, plant and machinery for a new highly computerised production and assembly line became available for use in the factory. The external costs relating to this were £800,000 and in addition the company also incurred the following.

- Labour costs of £80,000 in installing the line (these were 20% higher than budgeted because of the impact of industrial disputes).

- Management and supervision costs (allocation) of £15,000.

- Start-up costs of £30,000 incurred in testing the new process. £20,000 of these were necessary to ensure the line operated correctly. The remaining £10,000 was incurred when the directors held an 'open day' for their bankers to demonstrate the efficiency of the new system.

(3) The company still owns and uses part of the old factory but on 30 September 20X9 it was classified as held for sale. It is expected to be sold by 31 December 20X9 for £200,000 (after spending £25,000 to generally improve the property). The carrying amount of the factory at 1 October 20X8 is £310,000 (cost £500,000).

Depreciation rates are:

Freehold land and buildings –   2% pa
Plant and machinery   –   20% pa

(4) Plover plc's head office building was acquired on 1 October 20X2 for £1.5 million and depreciated at 2% per annum.

On 1 October 20X6 it was revalued to £2.1 million. Plover plc did not make any reserve transfers for the additional depreciation.

Following a severe fall in the property market, Plover's valuers advised at 30 September 20X9 that the building was worth £1.7 million.

Requirements

(a) Prepare extracts from the statement of financial position in relation to the above as at 30 September 20X9 and draft the note showing the movements on property, plant and equipment for the year (working to the nearest £000).   **(11 marks)**

(b) Calculate the impairment loss arising on classifying the old factory as held for sale.   **(2 marks)**

(c) Plover plc had profit for the year ended 30 September 20X9 of £25.6 million, before adjusting for the impairment loss on the old factory.

Prepare the separate statement of profit or loss and other comprehensive income for the year.
(2 marks)

(15 marks)

Now, go back to the Learning objectives in the Introduction. If you are satisfied you have achieved these objectives, please tick them off.

C
H
A
P
T
E
R

4

Technical reference

Point to note: The following sets out the examinability of the standards covered in this chapter.

IAS 16	All examinable
IAS 23	References to suspension of capitalisation are not examinable
IAS 36	Paragraphs 1–64 (excluding paragraph 54), 126–128, and 130–131 are examinable. The Appendices are not examinable
IFRS 5	References to disposal groups and implementation guidance (except paragraphs 11 and 12) are not examinable

The paragraphs listed below are the key references you should be familiar with.

Property, plant and equipment recognition

- Recognise items of PPE, provided future economic benefits and reliable measurement of cost.   IAS 16 (7)

    - Initial costs to acquire or construct.   IAS 16 (10)
    - Subsequent costs to add to, replace part of, or service.

- Separate into components, with different lives, eg inspections.   IAS 16 (13)

Measurement at recognition

- At cost.   IAS 16 (15)
    - Purchase price.   IAS 16 (16)
    - Costs directly attributable to bringing asset into location and condition necessary for it to be capable of working as intended, including testing.   IAS 16 (16-17)
    - Costs to dismantle/restore.   IAS 16 (16)
- Some costs excluded because not directly attributable or after item is capable of working as intended, eg abnormal costs, general overheads, initial losses, internal profits.   IAS 16 (19–22)

- Can include interest.   IAS 16 (22)

Measurement after recognition

- Choice of model: cost or revaluation to fair value.   IAS 16 (29–31)

- Frequency: to ensure carrying amount not materially different from updated fair value.   IAS 16 (31)
    - Maximum interval 5 years?   IAS 16 (34)
- All assets in a single class must be treated in the same way.   IAS 16 (36)

Accounting for revaluations

- Gain recognised in other comprehensive income and accumulated in equity as part of revaluation surplus, so in statement of changes in equity – if reverse previous decrease, take to profit or loss to extent of that decrease.   IAS 16 (39)

- Loss direct to profit or loss – if reverse previous increase, recognised in other comprehensive income and reduce revaluation surplus to extent of that increase.   IAS 16 (40)

- Depreciation charge based on revalued amount.

- Annual reserve transfer re excess of actual depreciation over historical cost depreciation.   IAS 16 (41)

Depreciation

- Each significant part of PPE item depreciated separately.   IAS 16 (43)

- Charge to profit or loss, unless included in inventory, construction contract or other PPE.   IAS 16 (48)

- Depreciate depreciable amount (ie cost less residual value (RV)) over estimated useful life (UL).   IAS 16 (6)

  - RV is current estimate of disposal proceeds, net of disposal costs, if item already of the age and in condition expected at the end of UL.   IAS 16 (6)

  - UL is period over which asset expected to be available for use, commencing with when asset is available for use.   IAS 16 (6 and 55)

- Method should allocate depreciable amount systematically over useful life, so as to reflect consumption of future economic benefits.   IAS 16 (60-61)

- Annual reviews of RVs, ULs and depreciation methods.   IAS 16 (51 and 61)

  - Any changes accounted for prospectively.   IAS 16 (51 and 61)

Derecognition

- Derecognise non-current asset when classified as held for sale or when no future economic benefits expected.   IAS 16 (67)

  - Separate procedures where held for sale – see below

- Proceeds less carrying amount (current NBV) taken to profit or loss.   IAS 16 (68)

- Revalued assets:
  - Recycling of gains on disposal not permitted.   IAS 16 (41)
  - Reserve transfer re previously recognised gains now realised.

Disclosures
                                                                                 IAS 16 (73,74 and 77)

- Measurement bases.

- Depreciation methods.

- Useful lives or depreciation rates.

- Gross, accumulated depreciation and net amounts at start and end of period.

- Additions, disposals, acquisitions through business combinations, revaluations, impairments, depreciation, classification as held for sale.

- Assets pledged as security for loans and contractual commitments to acquire PPE.

- For revalued assets, the dates, whether independent valuer used, assumptions, reference to active markets/recent transactions, carrying amount under historical cost convention, revaluation surplus.

Borrowing costs

- Core principle   IAS 23 (1 and 8)
- Directly attributable borrowing costs   IAS 23 (10–11)
- Commencement of capitalisation   IAS 23 (17–19)
- Cessation of capitalisation   IAS 23 (22–25)
- Disclosure

Impairment

- At each reporting date assess whether indication of impairment: IAS 36 (9)

  - If so, estimate recoverable amount.

  - Recoverable amount is higher of fair value less costs to sell and value   IAS 36 (6)
    in use (present value of future cash flows in use and on disposal).

- Review both external and internal information for evidence of impairment.   IAS 36 (12)

- Calculation of value in use to be on reasonable and supportable bases.   IAS 36 (33)

- Impairment loss where carrying amount exceeds recoverable amount.   IAS 36 (59)

- Treat impairment loss as a revaluation loss: IAS 36 (60–61)

  - Treat as revaluation gain if impairment loss subsequently reversed.

- Depreciate revised carrying amount over remaining useful life.   IAS 36 (63)

- Disclosures:

  - All impairments: IAS 36 (126)

    - The amount of any impairment loss recognition/reversal in profit
      or loss (and the line item where included) and in statement of
      changes in equity.

  - For a material impairment on an individual asset: IAS 36 (130)

    - The events which led to the recognition/reversal.

    - The amount.

    - The nature of the asset and, if relevant, the reportable segment
      to which it belongs.

    - Whether the recoverable amount is the fair value less costs to sell
      or its value in use, with information about how it was calculated.

Non-current assets held for sale

- Non-current asset classified as held for sale when carrying amount   IFRS 5 (6)
  recovered principally through sale.

  - Must be available for immediate sale and sale (within 12 months of   IFRS 5 (7)
    classification) must be highly probable.

  - If meet criteria after end of the reporting period, a non-adjusting   IFRS 5 (12)
    event under IAS 10.

- Measured at lower of carrying amount and fair value less costs to sell.   IFRS 5 (15)

  - Any loss accounted for under IAS 36 (any gain is recognised on actual   IFRS 5 (20)
    disposal).

  - Not depreciated.   IFRS 5 (25)

- Presented separately from all other assets, immediately below the sub-total   IFRS 5 (38)
  for current assets.

- Different rules if asset previously revalued: IFRS 5 (18)

  - Revalue before classification, with gain/loss accounted for under
    IAS 16.

  - Costs to sell = impairment loss.

- Measurement and presentation of non-current assets to be abandoned per   IFRS 5 (13)
  IAS 16, not IFRS 5.

Answers to Interactive questions

Answer to Interactive question 1

Cost of facility

		£'000
Site preparation		400
Net income while site used as a car park	Incidental, so taken to profit or loss	–
Materials used	(2,000 – 300)	1,700
Labour costs	(4,000 – 500)	3,500
Testing of facility's processes		300
Sale of by-products		(60)
Consultancy fees re installation and assembly		500
Professional fees		450
Opening of facility		–
Overheads incurred:		
– Construction		800
– General		–
Relocation of staff to new facility		–
Cost of dismantling facility		750
		8,340
Allocated to components:		
Safety inspection		150
To be replaced in 8 years	(40% × (8,340 – 150))	3,276
Remainder		4,914
		8,340

Answer to Interactive question 2

In this scenario the key dates are as follows:

- Expenditure on the acquisition is incurred on 1 February.

- Borrowing costs start to be incurred from 1 February.

- Activities to prepare the building for intended use/sale (work on planning permission) were carried out during December and January.

The earliest date when all three of these conditions were met is 1 February.

Answer to Interactive question 3

		£'000
Annual charge re:		
Over 3 years	(150/3)	50
Over 8 years	(3,276/8)	410
Over 20 years	(4,914/20)	246
		706

Answer to Interactive question 4

	Year 1 £	Year 2 £	Year 3 £
Cost	1,000	1,000	1,000
Accumulated depreciation	(80)	(160)	(320)
Carrying amount	920	840	680
Charge for the year (W)	80	80	160
WORKING	$\dfrac{1,000-200}{10}$	$\dfrac{1,000-200}{10}$	$\dfrac{840-200}{4}$

Answer to Interactive question 5

The revaluation gain on 1 January 20X7 is £35 (60 – 25).

If the previous downward revaluation had not taken place the carrying amount on 31 December 20X6 would have been £50 (£100 less five years' depreciation at £10 each year).

The 'excess' revaluation surplus recognised in the other comprehensive income is £10 (60 – 50).

The amount recognised in profit or loss is £25 (50 – 25).

Answer to Interactive question 6

(a)   **Note showing movements on PPE (extract)**

	£'000
Cost or valuation:	
At 1 January 20X8	100
Classified as held for sale	(100)
At 31 December 20X8	–
Depreciation:	
At 1 January 20X8 ((100 – 10) × 3/10)	27
Impairment loss	35
Classified as held for sale	(62)
At 31 December 20X8	–

(b)   **Journal entries to record the classification as held for sale**

   Recognising the impairment

		£'000	£'000
DR	Profit or loss	35	
CR	PPE – accumulated depreciation		35

   Classification as held for sale

		£'000	£'000
DR	Non-current assets held for sale	38	
DR	PPE – accumulated depreciation	62	
CR	PPE – cost		100

(c)   **Statement of profit or loss for the year ended 31 December 20X8**

	£'000
Impairment loss on reclassification of non-current assets held for sale ((100 – 27) – 38)	35

(d)   **Statement of profit or loss for the year ended 31 December 20X8**

   With sales proceeds of £32,000

   (i)   The impairment loss would remain the same
   (ii)   A loss on disposal of £6,000 (38,000 – 32,000) would be included

Answer to Interactive question 7

(a)   **Journal entry to record the classification as held for sale**

	£'000	£'000
1 January 20X8		
DR PPE – accumulated depreciation (30% × (100 – 10))	27	
DR Non-current assets held for sale (β)	73	
CR PPE – cost		100

   As fair value less costs to sell is greater than carrying amount, there is no impairment loss at the time of classification.

(b)   **Statement of profit or loss for the year ended 31 December 20X8**

	£'000
Gain on disposal of non-current assets held for sale (77 – 73)	4

Answer to Interactive question 8

(a) Journal entry to record the revaluation

	£'000	£'000
1 January 20X5		
DR PPE – at valuation	50	
CR Revaluation surplus		50

(b) Journal entry to record the classification as held for sale

	£'000	£'000
1 January 20X8		
DR Non-current assets held for sale – fair value less costs to sell (235 – 5)	230	
DR Profit or loss – costs to sell	5	
DR Revaluation surplus (250 – 235)	15	
CR PPE – at valuation		250

Answer to Interactive question 9

(a) Journal to record the revaluation

	£	£
1 January 20X4		
DR PPE cost/valuation (136,000 – 120,000)	16,000	
DR PPE accumulated depreciation	18,000	
CR Revaluation surplus (136,000 – 102,000)		34,000

(b) Revised depreciation charge

Annual charge from 20X4 onwards

	£	£
DR Profit or loss – depreciation expense (136,000 ÷ 17)	8,000	
CR PPE accumulated depreciation		8,000
Annual reserve transfer		
DR Revaluation surplus	2,000	
CR Retained earnings		2,000

Being the difference between the actual depreciation charge and the charge based on historical cost (£6,000).

Shown in the statement of changes in equity as follows:

	Revaluation surplus £	Retained earnings £
Brought forward	X	X
Profit for the year	–	X
Transfer of realised profits	(2,000)	2,000
Carried forward	X	X

(c) Journal to record classification as held for sale

At 1 January 20X8, balances relating to the asset will be as follows:

	£
Property, plant and equipment at valuation	136,000
Accumulated depreciation (4 × 8,000)	(32,000)
Carrying amount	104,000
Revaluation surplus (34,000 – (4 × 2,000))	26,000

	£'000	£'000
1 January 20X8		
DR PPE – accumulated depreciation	32	
DR Non-current assets held for sale – fair value less costs to sell	137	
DR Profit or loss – costs to sell	3	
CR PPE – cost/valuation		136
CR Revaluation surplus (ß)		36
	172	172

(d) **Financial statements for the year ended 31 December 20X8**

In the statement of profit or loss:

(i) A charge of £3,000 will be made for the costs to sell, classified as an impairment loss.

(ii) No profit or loss on disposal will be shown, as the asset is sold for its fair value less costs to sell.

In the statement of profit or loss and other comprehensive income:

The revaluation surplus arising from the classification as held for sale will be recognised:

	£
Profit for the year	X
Gain on property revaluation	36,000
Total comprehensive income	X

Remaining balance on revaluation surplus is transferred to retained earnings as a reserve transfer in the statement of changes in equity:

	Revaluation surplus £	Retained earnings £
Brought forward	X	X
Retained profit for the year	–	X
Transfer of realised profits (26 + 36)	(62,000)	62,000
Carried forward	X	X

Answer to Interactive question 10

RSBH Ltd: Note showing movements on property, plant and equipment for the year ended 31 December 20X7

	Freehold property £'000	Plant and machinery £'000	Fixtures and fittings £'000	Total £'000
Cost/valuation				
At 1 January 20X7	1,000	700	300	2,000
Revaluation	200	–	–	200
Additions	100	400	80	580
Classified as held for sale	–	(360)	–	(360)
Disposals	–	–	(40)	(40)
At 31 December 20X7	1,300	740	340	2,380
Depreciation				
At 1 January 20X7	300	330	180	810
Revaluation	(300)	–	–	(300)
Charge for the year (W1)	26	73	48	147
Classified as held for sale				
(269 (W2) + 16 (W3))	–	(285)	–	(285)
Impairment loss (W3)	–	16	–	16
Disposals (W2)	–	–	(28)	(28)
At 31 December 20X7	26	134	200	360
Carrying amount				
At 31 December 20X7	1,274	606	140	2,020
At 31 December 20X6	700	370	120	1,190

	Plant and machinery £'000	Fixtures and fittings £'000
(1) Depreciation charge for the year		
Items reclassified/disposed of during year		
(360 × 10% × 1/4) and (40 × 15% × 1/2)	9	3
Items owned throughout year		
((700 − 360) × 10%) and ((300 − 40) × 15%)	34	39
Items acquired during year (400 × 10% × 3/4) and (80 × 15% × 1/2)	30	6
	73	48
(2) Accumulated depreciation on items reclassified/disposed of		
Brought forward	260	25
Charge for year (as above)	9	3
	269	28

	£'000
(3) Impairment loss on items reclassified	
Cost	360
Accumulated depreciation (W2)	(269)
Carrying amount on classification as held for sale	91
Fair value less costs to sell (80 − 5)	(75)
Impairment loss	16

1   Per IAS 16 paragraph 16 (1), (3) and (4) should be capitalised.

2   The profit or loss charge will be:

	£
Servicing	25,000
Repainting	40,000
	65,000

Plant modification and upgrading creates future economic benefits from the asset and should be capitalised (IAS 16 paragraph 7).

3   (a)   The revaluation surplus is £540,000

   (b)   The total carrying amount of freehold land and buildings is £775,000.

   WORKING

	Land £'000	Buildings £'000	Total £'000
Cost on 1 July 20W3	80	300	380
10 years' depreciation (300 × 4% × 10)		(120)	(120)
	80	180	260
Revaluation surplus	120	420	540
	200	600	800
Depreciation (600 – 100) / 20		(25)	(25)
	200	575	775

4

	Asset A £	Asset B £
Borrowing costs		
To 31 December 20X6 £1,000,000/£2,000,000 × 9%	90,000	180,000
Less investment income		
To 30 June 20X6 £500,000/£1,000,000 × 7% × 6/12	(17,500)	(35,000)
	72,500	145,000
Cost of assets		
Expenditure incurred	1,000,000	2,000,000
Borrowing costs	72,500	145,000
	1,072,500	2,145,000

5   The amount of borrowing costs to be capitalised is £3.43m.

$$\text{Capitalisation rate} = \text{weighted average rate} = (10\% \times \frac{120}{120+80}) + (9.5\% \times \frac{80}{120+80}) = 9.8\%$$

Borrowing costs = (£30m × 9.8%) + (£20m × 9.8% × 3/12) = £3.43m

6   Per IAS 16, under the revaluation model assets should be carried at fair value, which is usually open market value (IAS 16, paragraph 32).

	£
Office building	300,000
Warehouse 1	200,000
Warehouse 2*	210,000
	710,000

* Since classified as held for sale, this would be presented separately from all other assets.

7   £10,000 should be debited to profit or loss and £15,000 should be debited to other comprehensive income.

If an asset has previously been revalued, we recognise the revaluation loss down to depreciated historic cost (175,000 – 160,000 = £15,000) in other comprehensive income, the balance (160,000 – 150,000 = £10,000) in profit or loss (IAS 16 paragraph 40).

8   Each significant part of an item of PPE must be depreciated separately (IAS 16 paragraph 43).
£900,000/50 years = £18,000
£100,000/25 years = £4,000
Total depreciation £18,000 + £4,000 = £22,000

9   Residual value is the year-end estimate of the disposal value of the asset (IAS 16.51 and IAS 8.36(b)).

(£100,000 – £15,000)/5 years = £17,000

10 Depreciable amount at 31 December 20X6 = (100,000 – 2,000) × 14/20 = 68,600
Depreciation charge in 20X7 = 68,600 × 1/25 = £2,744

11 An asset is impaired when the recoverable amount is lower than the carrying amount of the asset. To determine whether an asset is impaired, compare the recoverable amount to the carrying amount. The recoverable amount is the greater of the value in use and the fair value less costs to sell.

Asset R is not impaired as recoverable amount is greater than carrying amount. Asset Q is impaired as recoverable amount of £95,000 is lower than the carrying amount of £100,000.
An impairment loss of £5,000 should be recognized.

12 An impairment loss should be recognised when the asset is classified as held for sale. This will be the difference between the carrying amount (£13,200) and its fair value less costs to sell (£11,100 – £500 = £10,600). An impairment loss of £2,600 (13,200 – 10,600) is therefore recognised at this point.

When the asset is actually sold any further loss or gain is treated as a loss or gain on disposal. Here there is a further loss of £100 (10,600 – 10,500).

13 Although an impairment loss is recognised when a non-current asset measured under IAS 16's cost model is classified as held for sale, any gain is only recognised when the asset is actually derecognised (ie sold). Hence the only gain recognised is that on sale of £17,000 (115,500 – 98,500).

14 Where an asset has been held under the revaluation model and is subsequently classified as held for sale the asset must be revalued to fair value immediately before the reclassification. Any gain will be taken to the revaluation surplus and any loss to profit or loss (except to the extent that it reverses a gain held in the revaluation surplus). So here, a revaluation gain is recognised of £158,000 (725,000 – 567,000).

Once revalued in this way, the measurement is then adjusted to the normal basis for held for sale assets, so fair value less costs to sell. The effect is that the costs to sell (here £3,000) are recognised in profit or loss as an impairment loss.

15 (a) The balance on the revaluation surplus will be £85,000.

	Revaluation surplus £
Gain on revaluation (W)	90,000
Reserve transfer:	
New depreciation – old depreciation to 30/9/X4 $\left(\dfrac{270,000}{18} - \dfrac{200,000}{20}\right)$	(5,000)
Balance at 30/9/X4	85,000

WORKING

	£
Cost	200,000
Less depreciation (200,000 × 2/20)	(20,000)
Carrying amount at revaluation	180,000
Gain on revaluation	90,000
Valuation	270,000

(b) The loss recognised in profit or loss will be £5,000.

	£
At 30/9/X7:	
Revalued amount	270,000
Depreciation (270,000 × 4/18)	(60,000)
Carrying amount on reclassification	210,000
Revalue to fair value	(190,000)
Loss to revaluation surplus	20,000
Revaluation surplus at 30/9/X4	85,000
Reserve transfer	
New depreciation – old depreciation (5,000 × 3)	(15,000)
Revaluation surplus at 30/9/X7	70,000
Impairment loss	(20,000)
Balance c/f (transfer to retained earnings on disposal)	50,000

Because there was a sufficient balance on the revaluation surplus in respect of this asset to which the loss could be charged, the only impairment loss taken to profit or loss is the costs to sell of £5,000.

16   The disposal proceeds were £53,000.

PLANT ACCOUNT (CARRYING AMOUNT)

	£		£
B/f	261,000	Depreciation	143,000
Additions	512,000	Loss on disposal	57,000
		Impairment loss	50,000
		Disposal proceeds (ß)	53,000
		C/f	470,000
	773,000		773,000

17

	Machine 1	Machine 2
	£	£
Fair value less costs to sell	90,000	40,000
Carrying amount (ß)	(60,000)	(60,000)
Anticipated gain/(loss) on sale	30,000	(20,000)
Cost	120,000	100,000
Carrying amount	(60,000)	(60,000)
Accumulated depreciation	60,000	40,000

Total accumulated depreciation £60,000 + £40,000 = £100,000

18   Depreciation 20X7

$$\frac{2,500,000 - 225,000 - 450,000}{45} = £40,556$$

19   PORSCHE PLC

(a) **Notes to the financial statements for the year ended 31 December 20X7 (extracts)**

1   **Accounting policies**

Property, plant and equipment

Freehold land and buildings are stated at a valuation. Other tangible non-current assets are stated at cost, together with any incidental expenses of acquisition.

Depreciation is calculated so as to write off the net cost or valuation of tangible non-current assets over their expected useful lives. Depreciation charges commence when an asset becomes available for use. The rates and bases used are as follows.

Asset	% pa	Basis
Freehold land and buildings	2%	Straight-line
Plant and equipment	10%	Straight-line
Office equipment and fixtures	20%	Straight-line
Motor vehicles	30%	Reducing-balance

2 **Profit from operations is stated after charging**

	£
Depreciation of property, plant and equipment	562,000

3 **Property, plant and equipment**

	Freehold land and buildings £'000	Plant and equipment £'000	Motor vehicles £'000	Office equipment and fixtures £'000	Total £'000
Cost or valuation					
At 1 January 20X7	1,440	1,968	449	888	4,745
Additions	500	75	35	22	632
Revaluations (W1)	760	–	–	–	760
At 31 December 20X7	2,700	2,043	484	910	6,137
Depreciation					
At 1 January 20X7	144	257	194	583	1,178
Revaluation adjustment (W1)	(144)	–	–	–	(144)
Charge for year	60 (W2)	233 (W5)	87 (W3)	182 (W4)	562
At 31 December 20X7	60	490	281	765	1,596
Carrying amount					
At 31 December 20X7	2,640	1,553	203	145	4,541
At 1 January 20X7	1,296	1,711	255	305	3,567

(i) Freehold land and buildings were valued for the purposes of the 20X7 accounts at open market value, with subsequent additions at cost. Their historical cost is £1,940,000 (W6) and the related accumulated depreciation is £183,000 (W6).

(ii) The company's depreciation policy on motor vehicles has been changed from a rate of 25% pa on cost to a rate of 30% pa on reducing balance in order to give a more relevant presentation of the results and of the financial position. The effect of this change has been to reduce the depreciation charge for the year by £34,000 (£121,000 – £87,000).

(b) **Qualitative characteristics and IAS 16**

Understandability

Information must be readily understandable to users so that they can perceive its significance. This is dependent on how information is presented and how it is categorised.

For example, IAS 16 requires disclosures to be given by each class of property, plant and equipment so it will be clear what type of assets have been purchased during the year and what types of assets have been sold. If this information were merged over one class it would be less understandable.

Relevance

Information is relevant if it influences the economic decisions of users.

The choice of the revaluation model as a measurement model in IAS 16 provides relevant information by showing up-to-date values. This will help give an indication as to what the entity's underlying assets are worth.

Faithful representation

Information is a faithful representation if it is free from error or bias, complete and portrays events in a way that reflects their reality.

Although the revaluation model gives relevant information this information is generally seen to be less reliable than the cost model – the other measurement model allowed by IAS 16. The cost model is based on historic costs, which are not the most relevant costs on which to base future decisions. However, historic cost is a faithful representation being based on fact.

Comparability

Users must be able to compare information with that of previous periods or with that of another entity. Comparability is achieved via consistency and disclosure.

IAS 16 allows comparability between the cost and the revaluation model (for example, to facilitate comparisons between two companies who have adopted different models) by requiring equivalent cost information to be disclosed under the revaluation model. It also requires disclosures (in accordance with IAS 8) of the effect of a change in an accounting estimate such as useful lives or depreciation rates. This facilitates comparison between different periods.

WORKINGS

(1) **Freehold land and buildings revaluation**

	£'000	£'000
DR Freehold land and buildings (ß)	760	
DR Accumulated depreciation (1,440 × 5 / 50)	144	
CR Revaluation surplus (2,200 – 1,296)		904

(2) **Freehold land and buildings depreciation charge**

Valuation/cost at 1 January 20X7	£2,700,000
Remaining useful life	45 years

$$\text{Annual depreciation charge} = \left(\frac{2,700,000}{45 \text{ years}}\right) \qquad \text{£60,000}$$

(3) **Motor vehicles depreciation charge**

	£'000
Carrying amount at 1 January 20X7	255
Additions	35
	290
Depreciation – reducing balance method @ 30%	87

(4) **Fixtures and fittings depreciation charge**

	£'000
Cost at 31 December 20X7	910
Depreciation – straight-line method @ 20%	182

(5) **Plant and equipment depreciation charge**

	£'000
Cost at 1 January 20X7	1,968
Less Grinding machine	(298)
Add Purchases for factory extension	75
	1,745
Depreciation – straight-line method @ 10%	175
Grinding machine – cost less residual value (298 – 8)	290
Accumulated depreciation at 1 January 20X7	(58)
Carrying amount	232

The carrying amount must be written off over the machine's remaining useful life of four years.

	£
Depreciation charge $\left(\dfrac{232,000}{4 \text{ years}}\right)$	<u>58,000</u>

	£000
Total depreciation charge for plant	
Grinding machine	58
Other plant	<u>175</u>
	<u>233</u>

(6) **Historical cost depreciation on freehold land and buildings**

	£'000
Cost at 1 January 20X7	1,440
Addition – extension	<u>500</u>
Cost at 31 December 20X7	<u>1,940</u>
Accumulated depreciation at 1 January 20X7	144
Depreciation charge at 2%	<u>39</u>
Accumulated depreciation at 31 December 20X7	<u>183</u>

20 PLOVER PLC

(a) **Financial statement extracts**

Statement of financial position as at 30 September 20X9

	£'000	£'000
ASSETS		
Non-current assets		
Property, plant and equipment (Note)		3,726
		<u>X</u>
Current assets	X	
Non-current assets held for sale (200 – 25)	<u>175</u>	<u>X</u>
		<u>X</u>
EQUITY		
Revaluation surplus (720 – 263 (W5))		<u>457</u>

Notes to the financial statements

Property, plant and equipment

	Head office £'000	Factory premises £'000	Plant and equipment £'000	Assets in the course of construction £'000	Total £'000
Cost/valuation					
At 1 October 20X8	2,100	500	–	1,100	3,700
Additions (W1 & W2)	–	–	887	150	1,037
Transfers	–	1,250	–	(1,250)	–
Classified as held for sale	–	(500)	–	–	(500)
Revaluation loss (W5)	(400)	–	–	–	(400)
At 30 September 20X9	1,700	1,250	887	–	3,837
Depreciation					
At 1 October 20X8 (W4, 5)	91	190	–	–	281
Charge for the year (W3)	46	18	103	–	167
Impairment loss (b)	–	125	–	–	125
Classified as held for sale	–	(325)	–	–	(325)
(125 (b) + 200 (W4))					
Revaluation loss (W5)	(137)	–	–	–	(137)
At 30 September 20X9	–	8	103	–	111
Carrying amount					
At 30 September 20X9	1,700	1,242	784	–	3,726
At 1 October 20X8	2,009	310	–	1,100	3,419

(b) **Impairment loss**

	£'000
Carrying amount brought forward	310
Depreciation to 30 September (W3)	(10)
	300
Recoverable amount (200 – 25)	(175)
Charge to profit or loss	125

(c) **Statement of profit or loss and other comprehensive income for the year ended 30 September 20X9**

	£'000
Profit for the year (25,600 – 125)	25,475
Other comprehensive income:	
Loss on property revaluation (400 – 137)	(263)
Total comprehensive income for the year	25,212

WORKINGS

(1) **Additions to new factory**

	£'000
Construction costs	125
Legal fees	25
	150

(2) **Additions to plant and equipment**

	£'000
External costs	800
Labour (80,000 × 100/120)	67
Start-up costs	20
	887

(3) **Depreciation**

	£'000
Head office (W5)	46
New factory ((1,250 – 600) × 2% × 7/12)	8
Old factory (500 × 2%)	10
	18
Plant and equipment (887 × 20% × 7/12)	103

(4) **Old factory accumulated depreciation**

	£'000
Brought forward at 1 October 20X8 (500 – 310)	190
Charge for year (W3)	10
	200

(5) **Head office revaluation**

	£'000
Original cost	1,500
Depreciation (4 years at 2%)	(120)
Carrying amount at 1 October 20X6	1,380
Revaluation gain	720
Revalued amount at 1 October 20X6	2,100
Depreciation (2,100/46 × 2)	(91)
Balance at 1 October 20X8	2,009
Depreciation (2,100/46)	(46)
Revaluation loss (400 – 91 – 46)	(263)
Carrying amount 30 September 20X9	1,700

Point to note: As the carrying amount has not fallen below original cost less depreciation to date on original cost, the fall in value will be debited to the revaluation surplus and recognised in other comprehensive income.

CHAPTER 5

Intangible assets

Introduction

Examination context

Topic List

Summary and Self-test

Technical reference

Answer to Interactive question

Answers to Self-test

Introduction

Learning objectives

Tick off

- Relate the treatment of intangible assets to the principles in the IASB *Conceptual Framework* ☐

- Identify the accounting standards which apply to the treatment of intangible assets ☐

- Apply the accounting requirements for intangible assets, including the effects of the following:

  – Separately acquired intangible assets ☐

  – Intangible assets acquired as part of a business combination ☐

  – Internally generated intangible assets including research and development expenditure ☐

  – Internally generated and purchased goodwill ☐

- Identify and consider appropriate actions for ethical issues involving intangible assets ☐

- Identify and illustrate the main differences between International and UK requirements in relation to non-current assets ☐

Specific syllabus references for this chapter are: 1b, 2b, 2c, 2d, 2e.

Syllabus links

In the Accounting paper you will have had an introduction to accounting for intangible assets. In this paper you are required to develop a sound understanding of the accounting guidance in this area, provided by IAS 38 *Intangible Assets* and appreciate the impact that intangible assets can have on the way that financial information is interpreted.

Examination context

In the examination, candidates may be required to:

- Explain how the IASB *Conceptual Framework* applies to the recognition of intangible assets

- Prepare and present financial statements or extracts therefrom in accordance with:

  – IAS 38 *Intangible Assets*
  – IAS 36 *Impairment of Assets*

- Explain the accounting treatment of intangible assets

- Explain and illustrate the difference between the relevant treatment under IFRS and UK GAAP

- Identify and explain any ethical issues

1 What are intangible assets?

Section overview

The key issues affecting intangible assets are:

- Recognition – is the definition of an asset met?
- Measurement – can cost or value be measured reliably?

1.1 Intangibles

Definition

Intangible asset: An identifiable non-monetary asset without physical substance.

One of the principal distinctions between property, plant and equipment (PPE) and intangible assets is that whilst the former have physical substance, the latter do not.

The following are examples of categories of expenditure that **might** be capitalised as an intangible asset:

- Brand names
- Publishing titles
- Computer software
- Patents
- Copyrights
- Motion picture films
- Customer lists
- Fishing licences
- Import quotas
- Franchises
- Customer or supplier relationships
- Customer loyalty
- Market share
- Marketing rights

The key issue affecting the treatment of this type of expenditure is whether it should be **recognised as an asset** and if so, how it should be **measured**. IAS 38 *Intangible Assets* provides guidance in this area.

1.2 Underlying principles

The underlying principles of the IASB *Conceptual Framework* are reflected in IAS 38.

The key element in financial statements, identified in the IASB *Conceptual Framework*, which is relevant to intangible assets is:

- Asset: a resource controlled by the entity as a result of past events and from which future economic benefits are expected to flow to the entity.

Also relevant are the definitions of:

- Gains, which are a part of income: increases in economic benefits through enhancements of assets or decreases in liabilities other than contributions from equity.

- Losses, which are a part of expenses: decreases in economic benefits through depletions of assets or increases in liabilities other than distributions to equity.

And the recognition criteria set out in the *Conceptual Framework* whereby an element is only recognised if:

- It is probable that any future economic benefit associated with the item will flow to or from the entity, and

- The item has a cost or value that can be measured with reliability.

2 IAS 38: objective and scope

Section overview

IAS 38 applies to almost all intangibles, the key exception being goodwill acquired in a business combination.

2.1 Objective

The objective of IAS 38 is to prescribe the accounting treatment of intangible assets not covered by other IFRS, in terms of:

- **Recognition** if, and only if, certain criteria are met
- **Measurement**
- **Disclosures**

2.2 Scope

IAS 38 applies to **all intangible assets** with certain exceptions. Examples of assets **specifically excluded** from IAS 38 include:

- **Goodwill acquired in a business combination**, which is accounted for under IFRS 3 (Revised) *Business Combinations*.

- **Financial assets** as defined in IAS 39 *Financial Instruments: Recognition and Measurement*.

- **Mineral extraction, related exploration and development expenditure** incurred.

2.3 Context for IAS 38

Historically, corporate success has been built on physical assets and improving manufacturing efficiency; this is in contrast with leading businesses in the new economy which use ideas and market positions. The most important assets for many businesses are now brands, market positions, knowledge capital and people, although these are rarely recognised in financial statements.

Active strategies have been pursued by some businesses to develop intangible asset management as the core success of the business. One of Coca-Cola's Chief Financial Officers once described the entity's market capitalisation as being the sum of the values of its brand and its management systems. The importance of intangible assets was once highlighted by Microsoft:

'The law requires circa 40 pages of figures in the annual company report but these figures represent only 3% of the company's value and assets. The remaining 97% are the company's intangible assets.'

In an increasingly fast moving business environment, analysing business performance involves understanding corporate culture, knowledge management systems, product delivery processes, innovation and technological sustainability. Current financial reporting practices are often cited as out of date and unhelpful. The use of historical cost accounting based on past cash flows does not report the strength or value created by modern businesses. This can create challenges for users of financial statements.

It is widely recognised that the quality of employees has a direct effect on future cash flows of an organisation. Indeed, many CEOs describe employees as their most important assets. Cost-based reporting principles mean that it is rare that employee assets appear in corporate statements of financial position. A number of initiatives, such as the Accounting for People Report in the UK, have tried to address the specific issues of accounting for people. Many alternative measurement techniques, including current values, have been suggested, but none has received acceptance by standard setters. As current trends in business management and corporate practice develop, this is an area that standard setters may be forced to revisit.

3 The definition of intangible assets

Section overview

An intangible asset must be:

- 'Identifiable'
- Under the control of the entity

3.1 Identifiability

As we saw in the definition in Section 1.1 above an intangible asset must be '**identifiable**'. IAS 38 includes this identifiability requirement to distinguish intangible assets from goodwill, which arises on the acquisition of a subsidiary. (We will look at the issue of goodwill in more detail in Section 9 of this chapter.)

An intangible asset is identifiable if it meets at least one of the two following criteria:

- It is **separable**
- It arises from **contractual or other legal rights**

An asset is separable if it can be sold, transferred, exchanged, licensed or rented to another party on its own rather than as part of a business.

It is likely that all of the examples of intangibles listed in Section 1.1 are separable, in that the owner can sell them to others (even though some of them may fail other parts of the recognition test).

Most of these examples also meet the second condition, that of arising from contractual or other legal rights. Clearly, patents, copyrights, motion picture films, fishing licences and import quotas arise from such rights. But this second condition is designed to cover items that are not separable, but are nevertheless valuable. The argument is that:

- If in a group of assets most are tangible,

- If economic benefits cannot be obtained from the tangible assets without the transfer of a legal right, and

- If the legal right is of no benefit without the tangible assets to which they relate then that legal right is non-separable but is still identifiable.

That part of the definition of an intangible asset which requires it to be identifiable is of fundamental importance, because an identifiable intangible which has a finite useful life is subject to annual amortisation, whereas an item which is not identifiable is either not recognised at all or, if it is subsumed in goodwill acquired in a business combination, not amortised but subject to annual impairment reviews.

There are few problems in identifying intangibles which meet the identifiability criterion of being separable. To be separable, they should be capable of being disposed of on their own, with the remainder of the business being retained.

Goodwill can only be disposed of as part of the sale of a business, so is not separable.

The other way in which an asset is to be regarded as identifiable is if it arises from contractual or other legal rights and is not separable. An example would be where an entity controls both unique PPE to produce a unique product and the right to manufacture and distribute that product in a particular territory. The unique PPE is worthless without the distribution rights and vice versa, so the distribution rights are non-separable but still identifiable.

Point to note: It is the lack of identifiability which prevents internally generated goodwill being recognised. It is not separable (see above) and does not arise from contractual or other legal rights.

3.2 Control

An **intangible asset** must also satisfy the **basic definition of an asset**.

One of the characteristics of an asset (according to the definition in the IASB *Conceptual Framework*) is that it is under the **control** of the entity. The entity must therefore be able to enjoy the future economic benefits from the asset, and prevent the access of others to those benefits. A **legally enforceable right** is evidence of such control, but not always a **necessary** condition. The following should be noted:

- Control over technical knowledge or know-how only exists if it is protected by a legal right.

- The skills of employees, arising out of the benefits of training costs, are most unlikely to be recognised as an intangible asset, because an entity does not control the future actions of its staff.

- Similarly, an entity normally has insufficient control over market share and customer loyalty for those to meet the definition of an intangible asset. However, the exception to this would be where the entity has the ability to exchange a customer relationship, for example, where a customer list can be traded, or separate rights provided for its use by a third party. This provides reliable evidence that the entity has control over the future economic benefits flowing from that relationship, and therefore meets the definition of an intangible asset.

4 Initial recognition and measurement

Section overview

- An intangible asset should be recognised if:
  - It is probable that future economic benefits from the asset will flow to the entity.
  - The cost of the asset can be measured reliably.

- At recognition the intangible should be recognised at cost.

- Separately acquired intangibles and intangibles acquired as part of a business combination are normally considered to meet the recognition criteria of IAS 38.

- An intangible asset acquired as part of a business combination should be recognised at fair value.

4.1 Recognition: basic principle

An item should only be recognised as an intangible asset if **economic benefits** are expected to flow in the future from ownership of the asset. Economic benefits may result in increased revenue, but may also result in the **reduction of costs** (cost savings).

An intangible asset should be recognised if, and only if, both the following occur:

- It is **probable** that the future economic benefits that are attributable to the asset will flow to the entity.

- The cost can be measured **reliably**.

Management has to **exercise judgement** in assessing the degree of certainty attached to the flow of economic benefits to the entity, giving greater weight to **external** evidence.

An intangible asset should initially be measured at its **cost**.

4.2 Subsequent expenditure

Subsequent expenditure should **rarely be recognised** in the carrying amount of an asset. This is because in most cases the expenditure is incurred to maintain the expected future economic benefits embodied in an existing asset. In addition it is often difficult to attribute subsequent expenditure directly to a particular intangible asset rather than to the business as a whole.

4.3 Separately acquired intangible assets

In most cases, separately acquired intangibles **satisfy the IAS 38 recognition criteria**.

Brands, mastheads, publishing titles, licences, computer software, copyrights, patents and airport landing slots are all examples of assets that can be acquired externally and should be capitalised.

As we saw in Section 4.1 above an intangible asset should initially be measured at cost.

Cost for these purposes comprises:

- **Purchase price** (including duties and non-refundable taxes)
- Any **directly attributable** costs of preparing the asset for its intended use

Directly attributable costs include:

- **Costs of employees** working directly to bring the asset to its working condition
- **Legal and professional fees**
- **Costs of testing**

The following expenditure is excluded from the cost of the intangible asset:

- Costs of introducing a new product or service including costs of advertising and promotional activities.

- Costs of conducting business in a new location or with a new class of customer (including staff training).

- Administration and other general overhead costs.

(These expenses are also excluded from the cost of PPE.)

Capitalisation of costs should **cease** when the asset is ready for use, irrespective of whether it is put into use immediately or not.

Worked example: Cost of separately acquired intangibles

Data Ltd acquires new technology that will revolutionise its current manufacturing process. Costs incurred are as follows:

	£
Original cost of new technology	1,200,000
Discount received	120,000
Staff training incurred in operating the new process	60,000
Testing of the new manufacturing process	12,000
Losses incurred whilst other parts of the plant stood idle	24,000

The cost that should be capitalised as part of the intangible asset is:

	£
Cost	1,200,000
Less discount	(120,000)
Plus testing of process	12,000
Total	1,092,000

4.4 Intangible assets acquired as part of a business combination

When an entity purchases another business entity the consideration given will normally exceed the value of the individual assets and liabilities bought. This excess is normally referred to as **goodwill**.

The Illustrative Examples in IFRS 3 (Revised) *Business Combinations* include a list of items acquired in a business combination that should be recognised as intangible assets separately from goodwill, under five headings:

- Marketing-related intangible assets, such as **trademarks**
- Customer-related intangible assets, such as **customer lists**
- Artistic-related intangible assets, such as **motion picture films**
- Contract-based intangible assets, such as **franchise agreements**
- Technology-based intangible assets, such as **computer software**

The effect of recognising these intangible assets is to reduce to a minimum the amount ascribed to the goodwill acquired in a business combination.

Intangible assets acquired as part of a business combination are normally considered to **meet the recognition criteria** of IAS 38. The cost of an intangible asset acquired as part of a business combination should be measured at its **fair value** at the date it was acquired.

Definition

Fair value: The price that would be received to sell an asset or paid to transfer a liability in an orderly transaction between market participants at the measurement date.

Fair value may be observable from an active market or recent similar transactions. Other methods may also be used. If fair value cannot be ascertained reliably, then the asset has failed to meet the recognition criteria. In this situation no separate intangible asset would be recognised, resulting in an increase in the value of goodwill acquired in the business combination.

4.5 Recognition of an expense

Expenditure on intangibles should be recognised as an expense unless:

- It is part of the cost of an asset which meets the recognition criteria; or

- It arises in a business combination but cannot be recognised as an asset. (This will form part of the goodwill arising at the acquisition date.)

Examples of expenditure which should be treated as an expense include:

- Start up costs
- Training costs
- Advertising and promotional costs
- Business relocation and reorganisation costs

5 Internally generated assets

Section overview

- Internally generated goodwill should not be recognised.
- Expenditure incurred in the research phase should be expensed as incurred.
- Expenditure incurred in the development phase should be recognised as an intangible asset provided certain criteria are met.
- IAS 38 prohibits the recognition of internally generated brands.
- If recognised, internally generated assets should be measured at cost.

5.1 Recognition of internally generated assets

Internally generated goodwill should **not be recognised** as an asset.

The key difficulties in deciding whether **other internally generated intangible assets** should be recognised are:

- Fixing the time when an identifiable asset comes into **existence**.
- Measuring its costs **reliably**, as it may be difficult to distinguish the costs of generating it from those of maintaining or enhancing the day-to-day operations of the business.

So additional requirements and guidance apply.

The evolution of such assets is split into the **research phase** and the **development phase**. Note that these phases relate to **all intangibles**, not just what would normally be regarded as 'research and development expenditure'.

Also note that when there is doubt regarding into which phase expenditure falls, it should be allocated to the research phase.

5.2 Research phase

All expenditure that arises in the research phase should be recognised as an expense when it is incurred. No costs should be recognised as an intangible asset. The rationale for this treatment is that at this stage there is insufficient certainty that the expenditure will generate future economic benefits.

Examples of research costs include:

- Activities aimed at obtaining new knowledge
- The search for, evaluation and final selection of applications of research findings or other knowledge
- The search for alternatives for materials, devices, products, processes, systems or services
- The formulation, design, evaluation and final selection of possible alternatives for new or improved materials, devices, products, processes, systems or services

5.3 Development phase

Development costs **should be recognised** as intangible assets provided that the entity can demonstrate that all the following **strict criteria** are met:

- The technical feasibility of completing the intangible asset so that it will be available for use or sale
- The intention to complete the intangible asset and use or sell it
- The ability to use or sell the intangible asset
- How the intangible asset will generate probable future economic benefits. Among other things, the entity should demonstrate the existence of a market for the output of the intangible asset or the intangible asset itself or, if it is to be used internally, the usefulness of the intangible asset
- The availability of adequate technical, financial and other resources to complete the development and to use or sell the intangible asset
- Its ability to measure reliably the expenditure attributable to the intangible asset during its development

If the above conditions are met development expenditure **must be capitalised**. In contrast with research costs, development costs are incurred at a later stage in a project, and the probability of success should be more apparent. Examples of development costs include the following.

- The design, construction and testing of pre-production or pre-use prototypes and models
- The design of tools, jigs, moulds and dies involving new technology
- The design, construction and operation of a pilot plant that is not of a scale economically feasible for commercial production

CHAPTER

5

- The design, construction and testing of a chosen alternative for new or improved materials, devices, products, processes, systems or services

5.4 Other internally generated intangible assets

The standard **prohibits** the recognition of **internally generated brands, mastheads, publishing titles and customer lists** and similar items as intangible assets. The reason for this is that these costs cannot be identified separately from the cost of developing the business as a whole. They can be seen as being component parts of internally generated goodwill, the recognition of which is also prohibited (see Section 5.1).

5.5 Cost of an internally generated intangible asset

If an internally generated intangible asset is recognised it should be measured at **cost**. The costs allocated to an internally generated intangible asset should be only costs that can be **directly attributed** or allocated on a reasonable and consistent basis to creating, producing or preparing the asset for its intended use. Such costs include:

- Materials and services consumed
- Employment costs of those directly engaged in generating the asset
- Legal and patent or licence registration fees

The principles underlying the costs that should or should not be included are similar to those for other non-current assets and inventory.

The cost of an internally generated intangible asset is the sum of the **expenditure incurred from the date when** the intangible asset **first meets the recognition criteria**. If, as often happens, considerable costs have already been recognised as expenses before management can demonstrate that the criteria have been met, **this earlier expenditure should not be retrospectively recognised** at a later date as part of the cost of an intangible asset.

Worked example: Treatment of expenditure

Douglas Ltd is developing a new production process. During 20X7, expenditure incurred was £100,000, of which £90,000 was incurred before 1 December 20X7 and £10,000 between 1 December 20X7 and 31 December 20X7. Douglas Ltd can demonstrate that, at 1 December 20X7, the production process met the criteria for recognition as an intangible asset. The recoverable amount of the know-how embodied in the process is estimated to be £50,000.

How should the expenditure be treated?

Solution

At the end of 20X7, the production process should be recognised as an intangible asset at a cost of £10,000. This is the expenditure incurred since the date when the recognition criteria were met, that is, 1 December 20X7. The £90,000 expenditure incurred before 1 December 20X7 is expensed, because the recognition criteria were not met. It will never form part of the cost of the production process recognised in the statement of financial position.

6 Measurement of intangible assets after recognition

Section overview

- After initial recognition an entity can choose between two models:
    - The cost model
    - The revaluation model
- In practice few intangible assets are revalued.
- An intangible asset with a finite useful life should be amortised over this period.
- An intangible asset with an indefinite useful life should not be amortised.

6.1 Cost model

The standard allows two methods of measuring intangible assets after they have been first recognised.

Applying the **cost model**, an intangible asset should be **carried at its cost**, less any accumulated amortisation and any accumulated impairment losses.

6.2 Revaluation model

The **revaluation model** requires an intangible asset to be carried at a revalued amount, which is its **fair value** at the date of revaluation, less any subsequent accumulated amortisation and any subsequent accumulated impairment losses.

Points to note

1   The fair value should be determined by reference to an **active market** in that type of asset. (See definition of an active market below.)

2   The **entire class** of intangible assets of that type should be revalued at the same time (to prevent selective revaluations).

3   If an intangible asset in a class of revalued intangible assets cannot be revalued because there is **no active market** for this asset, the asset should be carried at its **cost less any accumulated amortisation and impairment losses**.

4   Revaluations should be made with such **regularity** that the carrying amount does not differ materially from its fair value.

5   Where an intangible asset is revalued, subsequent amortisation is based on the revalued amount.

Definition

Active market: A market in which all the following conditions exist:

- The items traded are homogeneous
- Willing buyers and sellers can normally be found at any time
- Prices are available to the public

In practice there **will not usually be an active market** in an intangible asset; therefore the revaluation model **will usually not be available**. For example, although copyrights, publishing rights and film rights can be sold, each has a unique sale value. In such cases, revaluation to fair value would be inappropriate. A fair value might be obtainable, however, for assets such as fishing rights or quotas or taxi cab licences, where one is identical to the next.

6.3 Revaluation: accounting treatment

The treatment of revaluation gains and losses for intangibles follows the same rules as for PPE (see Chapter 4). This can be summarised as follows:

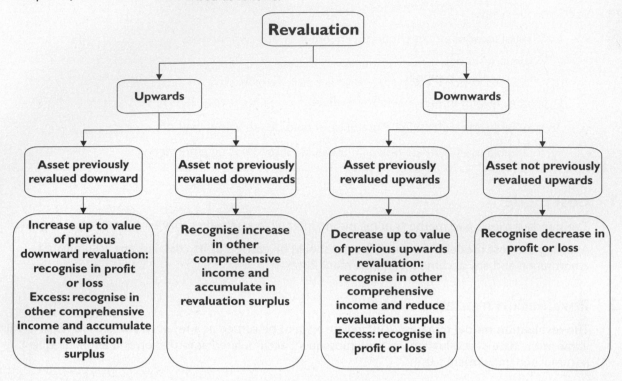

Worked example: Revaluation

An intangible asset is carried by a company under the revaluation model. The asset was revalued by £800 in 20X6; this was recognised in other comprehensive income, so that there is a revaluation surplus of £800 in the statement of financial position. At the end of 20X7, the asset is revalued downward by £1,000.

State the accounting treatment for the downward revaluation.

Solution

In this example, the downward valuation of £1,000 should first be recognised in other comprehensive income and set against the revaluation surplus of £800. The revaluation surplus should be reduced to zero and a charge of £200 recognised as an expense in the statement of profit or loss in 20X7.

6.4 Useful life

Under both measurement models an entity should **assess** the useful life of an intangible asset, which may be **finite or indefinite**. An intangible asset has an indefinite useful life when there is **no foreseeable limit** to the period over which the asset is expected to generate net cash inflows for the entity.

Many factors should be considered in determining the useful life of an intangible asset, including:

- Expected usage
- Typical product life cycle
- Technical, technological, commercial or other types of obsolescence
- The stability of the industry
- Expected actions by competitors
- The level of maintenance expenditure required
- Legal or similar limits on the use of the asset, such as the expiry dates of related leases

Computer software and many other intangible assets normally have short lives because they are susceptible to technological obsolescence. However, uncertainty does not justify choosing a life that is unrealistically short.

The useful life of an intangible asset that arises from **contractual or other legal rights** should not exceed the period of the rights, but may be shorter depending on the period over which the entity expects to use the asset.

6.5 Amortisation period and amortisation method

An intangible asset with a finite useful life should be amortised over its **expected useful life**.

- Amortisation should start when the asset is **available for use**.

- Amortisation should cease at the earlier of the date that the asset is classified **as held for sale** in accordance with IFRS 5 *Non-current Assets Held for Sale and Discontinued Operations* and the date that the asset is **derecognised**.

- The amortisation method used should reflect the **pattern in which the asset's future economic benefits are consumed**. If such a pattern cannot be predicted reliably, the straight-line method should be used.

- The amortisation charge for each period should normally be recognised **in profit or loss**.

The **residual value** of an intangible asset with a finite useful life should be **assumed to be zero** unless a third party is committed to buying the intangible asset at the end of its useful life or unless there is an active market for that type of asset (so that its expected residual value can be measured) and it is probable that there will be a market for the asset at the end of its useful life.

The amortisation period and the amortisation method used for an intangible asset with a finite useful life should be **reviewed at each financial year end**.

6.6 Intangible assets with indefinite useful lives

An intangible asset with an indefinite useful life **should not be amortised**. Instead the asset should be reviewed annually to assess whether there has been a fall in its value in accordance with IAS 36 *Impairment of Assets*.

7 Disposals

 Section overview

On disposal of an intangible asset the gain or loss should be recognised in profit or loss.

7.1 Accounting treatment

An intangible asset should be derecognised from the statement of financial position when it is disposed of or when there is no further economic benefit expected from its future use or disposal. On disposal the gain or loss arising from the **difference between the net disposal proceeds and the carrying amount** of the asset should be recognised in profit or loss as a gain or loss on disposal.

 Worked example: Disposal

Marketpro Ltd has been trading for ten years and has built up a substantial customer base. The directors estimate that the customer list is worth £25,000. The company moves into a different line of business and sells its customer list to a competitor for £20,000.

How will the sale be recorded in the financial statements?

Solution

The customer list was an internally-generated intangible asset and internally-generated customer lists are one of the items whose recognition is prohibited by IAS 38. So it will never have appeared in the financial statements prior to the sale. There will therefore be no impact on non-current assets in the statement of financial position and the whole £20,000 will be recorded as other income in the statement of profit or loss.

8 Disclosure

Section overview

IAS 38 requires detailed disclosures:

- For each class of intangible asset.
- For intangibles accounted for at revalued amounts.

8.1 Disclosure requirements

The standard has fairly extensive disclosure requirements for intangible assets. The financial statements should disclose the **accounting policies** for intangible assets that have been adopted.

For **each class of intangible assets**, disclosure is required of the following distinguishing between internally-generated intangibles and other intangibles.

- The method of amortisation used

- The useful life of the assets or the amortisation rates used

- The gross carrying amount, and any accumulated amortisation (aggregated with accumulated impairment losses) at the beginning and the end of the period

- The line item(s) of the statement of profit or loss in which any amortisation of intangible assets is included

- A reconciliation of the carrying amount as at the beginning and at the end of the period (additions, retirements/disposals, revaluations, impairment losses, amortisation charge for the period)

The financial statements should also disclose the following.

- In the case of intangible assets that are assessed as having an indefinite useful life, the carrying amounts and the reasons supporting the assessment of an indefinite useful life

- A description, the carrying amount, nature and remaining amortisation period of any individual intangible asset that is **material to the financial statements of the entity as a whole**

- The existence (if any) and carrying amounts of intangible assets whose **title is restricted** and of intangible assets that have been **pledged as security** for liabilities

- The amount of any contractual **commitments for the future acquisition of intangible assets**

Where intangible assets are accounted for under the revaluation model, disclosure is required of the following by class of intangible assets.

- The **effective date of the revaluation**

- The **carrying amount** of revalued intangible assets

- The carrying amount that would have been recognised **if the cost model had been used,** and the amount of amortisation that would have been charged

Also:

- The amount of any **revaluation surplus** on intangible assets, as at the beginning and end of the period, and movements in the surplus during the year (and any restrictions on the distribution of the balance to shareholders).

- The methods and significant assumptions applied in estimating the assets' fair values.

- The amount of research and development expenditure that has been recognised as an expense in the period should be disclosed.

Interactive question: Intangible assets [Difficulty level: Intermediate]

In preparing its accounts for the year ended 30 June 20X7 NS plc has to deal with a number of matters.

(1) An advertising campaign has just been completed at a cost of £1.5m. The directors authorised this campaign on the basis of the evidence from NS plc's advertising agency that it would create £4m of additional profits over the next two years.

(2) A staff training programme has been carried out at a cost of £250,000, the training consultants having demonstrated to the directors that the additional profits to the business over the next 12 months will be £400,000.

(3) A new product has been developed during the year. The expenditure totals £1.2m, of which £750,000 was incurred prior to 31 December 20X6, the date on which it became clear the product was technically feasible. The new product will be launched in the next three months and its recoverable amount is estimated at £600,000.

Requirement

Calculate the amounts which will appear as assets in NS plc's statement of financial position at 30 June 20X7.

Fill in the proforma below.

The treatment in NS plc's statement of financial position at 30 June 20X7 should be as follows:

(1) **Advertising campaign:**

....

....

(2) **Staff training programme:**

....

....

(3) **New product:**

....

....

See **Answer** at the end of the chapter.

C
H
A
P
T
E
R

5

9 Goodwill

Section overview

- Internally generated goodwill should not be recognised.
- Acquired goodwill should be recognised.
- Acquired goodwill should not be amortised but is tested for impairment at least annually.

9.1 What is goodwill?

Goodwill can be thought of as being the excess of the value of a business over the sum of its identifiable net assets. It can be created in many different ways, such as **by good relationships** between a business and its customers:

- By building up a **reputation** (by word of mouth perhaps) for high quality products or high standards of service.

- By **responding promptly and helpfully** to queries and complaints from customers.

- Through the **personality of the staff** and their attitudes to customers.

The value of goodwill to a business might be **extremely significant**. However, goodwill is not usually recognised in the accounts of a business at all, and we should not normally expect to find an amount for goodwill in its statement of financial position.

On reflection, we might agree with this omission of goodwill from the accounts of a business.

(a) The goodwill is **inherent** in the business but it has not been paid for, and it does not have an 'objective' value. We can guess at what such goodwill is worth, but such guesswork would be a matter of individual opinion, and not based on hard facts.

(b) Goodwill **changes** from day to day. One act of bad customer relations might damage goodwill and one act of good relations might improve it. Staff with a favourable personality might retire or leave to find another job, to be replaced by staff who need time to find their feet in the job, etc. Since goodwill is continually changing in value, it cannot realistically be recorded in the accounts of the business.

The result of this is that **internally generated goodwill should not be recognised as an asset**.

9.2 Purchased goodwill

There is one exception to the general rule that goodwill has no objective valuation. This is **when a business is acquired**. People wishing to set up in business have a choice of how to do it – they can either buy their own long-term assets and inventory and set up their business from scratch, or they can buy up an existing business from a proprietor willing to sell it. When a buyer purchases an existing business, he/she may have to purchase not only its long-term assets and inventory (and perhaps take over its accounts payable and receivable too) but also the goodwill of the business.

Purchased goodwill is shown in the acquirer's statement of financial position because it has been paid for. It has no tangible substance, and so it is an **intangible non-current asset**.

Point to note: At this stage we are referring to goodwill arising on the acquisition of an **unincorporated** business. Goodwill arising on the acquisition of companies is reported in consolidated financial statements and will be explained when we deal with group accounting in Chapter 10 onwards.

Worked example: Goodwill

Andrew is a sole trader. At 31 December 20X7 he has total net assets in his statement of financial position amounting to £150,000. On 1 January 20X8 Brian purchases Andrew's business for £175,000.

The summarised statement of financial position of Brian at 1 January 20X8 would be as follows:

	£
Total net assets	150,000
Intangible asset – goodwill (175 – 150)	25,000
	175,000
Capital introduced	175,000

Goodwill is calculated as the difference between the consideration transferred of £175,000 and the value of the net assets (equity) acquired of £150,000. The goodwill is recognised in the statement of financial position of Brian as it is purchased goodwill. It would not have been recognised in the financial statements of Andrew.

10   UK GAAP comparison

Section overview

- FRS 101 allows a limited exemption from IAS 38.
- FRS 102 differs from IAS 38 in a number of respects.

FRS 102 and IAS 38 can be compared as follows:

- Under FRS 102 an entity can choose whether or not to capitalise development costs. IAS 38 requires all eligible development costs to be capitalised.

- FRS 102 treats all intangible assets as having a finite useful life with a rebuttable presumption that this should not exceed five years. Under IFRS intangible assets can have an indefinite life.

Entities applying FRS 101 are exempt from the IAS 38 requirement to disclose a reconciliation of carrying amounts of intangible assets at the beginning and end of the period when presenting comparative information.

Summary

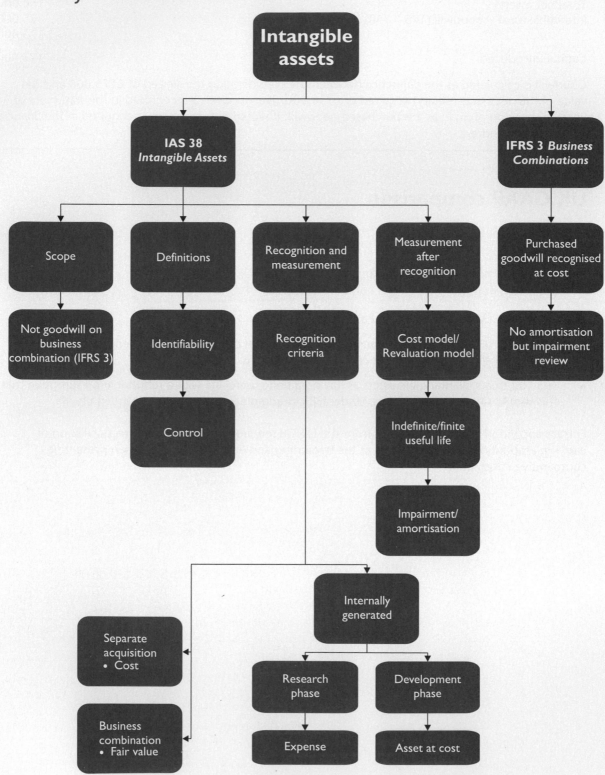

Intangible assets

- IAS 38 *Intangible Assets*
  - Scope
    - Not goodwill on business combination (IFRS 3)
  - Definitions
    - Identifiability
      - Control
  - Recognition and measurement
    - Recognition criteria
      - Separate acquisition
        - Cost
      - Business combination
        - Fair value
      - Internally generated
        - Research phase
          - Expense
        - Development phase
          - Asset at cost
  - Measurement after recognition
    - Cost model/ Revaluation model
      - Indefinite/finite useful life
        - Impairment/ amortisation
- IFRS 3 *Business Combinations*
  - Purchased goodwill recognised at cost
    - No amortisation but impairment review

ICAEW

Self-test

Answer the following questions.

1 During 20X7 Plex Ltd incurred the following expenditure on research and development activities, none of which related to the cost of tangible non-current assets.

   (1) £20,000 on investigating methods of separating raw materials into chemicals A, B and C.

   (2) After the technical viability of converting chemical B into a new medicine for sensitive teeth had been proved, £150,000 on the conversion process.

   Commercial production and sales of the medicine commenced on 1 April 20X7 and are expected to produce steady profitable income during a 10-year period before being replaced. Adequate resources exist to achieve this. No commercial uses have been discovered for chemicals A and C.

   What is the development expenditure that should be carried forward at 31 December 20X8 in accordance with IAS 38 *Intangible Assets*?

2 Henna plc was incorporated on 1 January 20X6. At 31 December 20X6 the following items had arisen.

(1)	Purchase of laboratory equipment for research purposes	£80,000
(2)	Goodwill purchased for valuable consideration	£100,000
(3)	Goodwill created by the company	£80,000
(4)	Patents purchased for valuable consideration	£70,000
(5)	Costs incurred by the company in developing brands	£60,000

   Prior to amortisation, what amount should be carried as intangible assets in the statement of financial position of Henna plc at 31 December 20X6 in accordance with IAS 38 *Intangible Assets*?

3 In accordance with IAS 38 *Intangible Assets* how should these types of expenditure be treated in the financial statements?

   (1) Tangible assets acquired in order to provide facilities for research and development activities
   (2) Legal costs in connection with the registration of a patent
   (3) Costs of searching for possible alternative products
   (4) Salaries of personnel solely engaged in finalising a new product

4 MINBAD PLC

   Minbad plc is a company operating in media and communications. It owns a number of newspapers and monthly magazine titles, which were acquired when the company acquired the assets of Newsmedia. The consideration totalled £130 million, of which £100 million was attributed to identifiable net assets (£60 million specifically for the newspaper and magazine titles). The acquisition occurred on 1 January 20X7. The newspaper and magazine titles are assessed as having indefinite lives. Goodwill arising on the acquisition is estimated to have a useful life of 20 years. However, an impairment review at 31 December 20X7 showed that goodwill had fallen in value by £1 million during 20X7.

   The newspapers and magazines have all shown increasing circulation since the acquisition. Accordingly, in considering the financial statements to 31 December 20X7 the directors wish to revalue the titles to £133 million, which represents the sum of amounts it is estimated could be realised if each title and its associated rights were sold separately in the market at 31 December 20X7. The directors estimate that this approximates closely to current cost.

   On 1 January 20X7 the company decided to expand its printing capacity by investing in new high tech machinery costing £20 million. This machinery had been developed by a French company and Minbad plc had to pay £20 million to acquire the patent allowing it sole use of the technology for ten years. In addition Minbad plc has also developed a range of greeting cards to be sold alongside, and advertised in, the monthly magazines. These cards will all be sold under a newly developed brand name which Minbad plc has developed at a cost of £6 million in 20X7.

   Requirements

   (a) Assuming that IAS 38 *Intangible Assets* and IFRS 3 (Revised) *Business Combinations* are complied with, prepare the table of movements and accounting policy notes for intangible assets for inclusion in the financial statements of Minbad plc for the year ended 31 December 20X7.

(b) Comment on your treatment of Minbad plc's intangible assets in (a) above in the light of the IASB *Conceptual Framework*. **(4 marks)**

(10 marks)

5 PHARMORIA PLC

Pharmoria plc operates in the pharmaceutical business. The following information relates to the company's activities in research and development for the year ended 31 October 20X7.

(1) Commercial production started on 1 June 20X3 for Formula A. By 31 October 20X6 £43,000 had been capitalised in respect of development expenditure on this product. During the year a further £10,000 was spent on development of this product.

Pharmoria plc has taken out a patent in respect of Formula A which will last for 10 years. Legal and administrative expenses in relation to this of £2,000 were incurred on 1 November 20X6.

In the current year, sales of Formula A amounted to £50,000. Sales are expected to be made over the next three years of £150,000, £200,000 and £100,000 respectively.

(2) The development of Formula B is at an earlier stage. Although the company believes it has a reasonable expectation of future benefits from this project it has not as yet been able to demonstrate this with sufficient certainty. Expenditure on this project in the current year was £20,000.

Requirements

(a) Calculate the total amount to be recognised in profit or loss in respect of the above in the year ended 31 October 20X7. **(2 marks)**

(b) Draft the table showing the movement on intangible assets which should appear in the notes to the financial statements of Pharmoria plc for the year ended 31 October 20X7. **(4 marks)**

(6 marks)

6 DRONFIELD LTD

IAS 38 *Intangible Assets* defines an intangible asset as an **identifiable** non-monetary asset without physical substance. An asset is a resource:

- **Controlled** by an entity as a result of past events, and
- From which **future economic** *benefits* are expected to flow to the entity.

IAS 38 requires an entity to recognise an intangible asset in its financial statements if it meets the recognition criteria.

Dronfield Ltd is a large company which researches, develops and manufactures pharmaceutical products. The company has in the past prepared its financial statements using UK GAAP and is considering changing to using IFRS. The company invests heavily in the following areas.

(1) Research into alternative chemically active ingredients that may have therapeutic benefit. The research activities identify chemical compounds that have commercial application possibilities.

(2) Development of chemical compounds by applying research findings to design new drug therapies. At the end of the development phase each new compound must be successful in a series of regulatory trials before production can commence.

(3) The investment in marketing and brand development of new pharmaceutical products. This includes the significant launch costs of new drugs and the on-going brand development activities.

(4) The acquisition, either directly or through business combinations, of pharmaceutical patents and brands at the fully licensed stage.

Requirements

(a) Discuss the IAS 38 definition of an intangible asset with specific reference to the three terms in italics. **(3 marks)**

(b) Explain and justify the required accounting treatment for each of the above four areas by considering the recognition criteria for internally developed and acquired intangible assets.

(4 marks)

(c) Outline the key differences between UK GAAP and IFRS in respect of intangible assets other than goodwill.

(3 marks)

(10 marks)

7   STANNINGTON PLC

Stannington plc is 'knowledge led' and its management has initiated a strategy of investment in areas such as brands, advertising, media, technology, business processes and employee training. The business has few items of property, plant and equipment and the management are concerned that last year's statement of financial position did not reflect the value of these intangibles. The following events have occurred during the year ended 31 December 20X3.

(1) On 1 January 20X3 the company acquired a cable television franchise for £10 million. The franchise allows Stannington plc the exclusive right to provide cable television to two million viewers in the Sheffield area for the next 20 years.

A twenty year franchise covering a similar number of viewers in Liverpool was sold by a competitor to a third party on 31 December 20X3 for £30 million. A franchise consultant has provided the management with an independent report that supports an equivalent market value for the Sheffield franchise. The company has measured the franchise rights in its statement of financial position at the valuation of £30 million.

(2) The company is developing a new production process. In previous years £2 million incurred on the project had been recognised as an expense in profit or loss as research costs. On 1 July 20X3 the company was able to demonstrate that the process met the IAS 38 criteria for recognition as an intangible asset. At 31 December 20X3 the company has recognised the intangible asset at a cost of £4.5 million comprising the following:

	£'000
Research costs from prior years	2,000
Costs incurred in the six months to 30 June 20X3	1,000
Costs incurred in the six months to 31 December 20X3	1,500
	4,500

At the end of 20X3 the development process was nearing completion and a competitor submitted a written offer to acquire the process for £6 million.

(3) On 1 January 20X3 Stannington plc acquired a publishing title for £25 million. The title complemented the company's existing portfolio of four similar publishing titles. During 20X3 £10 million of expenditure was incurred on marketing and promotional activities which management hope has enhanced the value of the publishing portfolio and £2 million has been added to the carrying amount of the acquired publishing title.

The long-term strategic plans for the business show that Stannington plc will invest significantly in the future development of the titles. The management believe this will enhance the value of the titles and that the titles have an indefinite life.

Requirements

(a) Compare the recognition criteria for acquired and internally generated intangible assets.

(4 marks)

(b) Explain the required accounting treatment of the above issues, preparing calculations where appropriate and setting out the presentation requirements.

(12 marks)

(16 marks)

Now, go back to the Learning objectives in the Introduction. If you are satisfied you have achieved these objectives, please tick them off.

Technical reference

Point to note: The following sets out the examinability of the standards covered in this chapter.

IAS 38	All examinable except paragraphs 42-47 and the illustrative examples.
IFRS 3	All examinable except the following: paragraphs 41 and 42. Appendix B1–B4, B13–B27 and the illustrative examples are also excluded.

The paragraphs listed below are the key references you should be familiar with.

1 Scope and definition

- Scope of IAS 38: excludes what other IFRSs cover, eg goodwill acquired in a business combination (IFRS 3). IAS 38 (2 and 3)

- Intangible asset: an identifiable, non-monetary asset without physical substance. IAS 38 (8)

- Identifiability the key:

    - Separable – could be sold separately from entity which owns it IAS 38 (12(a))

    - Arises from contractual or other legal rights IAS 38 (12(b))

- Control is an essential part of the definition of an asset. Many items excluded because not controlled by a business: IAS 38 (13)

    - Staff (always)

    - Customers (very often)

2 Recognition and initial measurement

- Reliable measurement – the recognition criteria disallow: IAS 38 (21)

    - Internally generated goodwill IAS 38 (48)

    - Similar items such as internally generated brands, mastheads and customer lists IAS 38 (63)

    - Advertising IAS 38 (69)

- Initial measurement at cost. IAS 38 (24)

- Separate acquisition:

    - Always – future economic benefits are probable IAS 38 (25)

    - Usually – cost reliably measurable IAS 38 (26)

    - Cost includes licences, etc IAS 38 (27)

- Part of business combination

    - Always – future economic benefits are probable IAS 38 (33)

    - Almost always – cost reliably measurable IAS 38 (35)

    - Cost = fair value IAS 38 (33)

    - Includes acquiree's unrecognised intangibles, such as in-process research and development IAS 38 (34)

- Internally generated: at cost, but:

  - Research expenditure (seeking new knowledge) written off as incurred (including subsequent expenditure on business combination research) — IAS 38 (54 and 42)

  - Development expenditure (application of research findings) capitalised if it meets stringent conditions as to future economic benefit — IAS 38 (57 and 42)

  - Development expenditure includes materials, staff costs and licences but not general overheads — IAS 38 (66 and 67)

  - Only development expenditure incurred after recognition criteria met is to be capitalised. No subsequent capitalisation of earlier expenditure already recognised in profit or loss — IAS 38 (65 and 71)

- Subsequent expenditure almost always written off, because most expenditure relates to maintenance, not enhancement, and is non-separable from that on business as a whole. — IAS 38 (20)

3 Measurement after recognition

- Cost or revaluation models — IAS 38 (72)

  - Revaluation only if active market (homogeneous products, always trading, prices available to public) — IAS 38 (75 and 78)

- Useful life:

  - Indefinite – no amortisation, but annual impairment and useful life reviews — IAS 38 (107-109)

  - Finite – annual amortisation, with impairment review if indication of impairment. Residual value almost always nil — IAS 38 (97, 100, 111)

4 Disclosure

- Disclosures specific to intangibles (otherwise follow IAS 16):

  - Whether useful lives are indefinite or finite (in which case amortisation rates must be disclosed) — IAS 38 (118(a))

  - For intangibles with indefinite useful lives, their carrying amount and the reasons supporting the indefinite life assessment — IAS 38 (122(a))

  - Individual assets material to financial statements as a whole — IAS 38 (122(b))

  - Amount of research and development expenditure recognised as an expense in the period. — IAS 38 (126)

5 Goodwill

- Goodwill: non-current asset at excess of consideration over net assets acquired — IFRS 3 (32)

- No amortisation but subject to annual impairment reviews — IAS 36 (10)

CHAPTER

5

Answer to Interactive question

The treatment in NS plc's statement of financial position at 30 June 20X7 should be as follows:

(1) Advertising campaign: no asset should be recognised, because it is not possible to identify future economic benefits that are attributable only to this campaign. The whole expenditure should be recognised in profit or loss.

(2) Staff training programme: no asset should be recognised, because staff are not under the control of NS plc and when staff leave, the benefits of the training, whatever they may be, also leave. The whole expenditure should be recognised in profit or loss.

(3) New product: the development expenditure appearing in the statement of financial position should be measured at £450,000.

    The expenditure prior to the date on which the product becomes technically feasible should be recognised in profit or loss. The remaining £450,000 is less than the recoverable amount, so no impairment issues arise.

Answers to Self-test

1   (1)   Relates to research so should be written off as an expense in 20X7.

    (2)   Relates to development so should be capitalised once the recognition criteria (IAS 38 paragraph 57) are met.

	£
Capitalised as at 1 April 20X7	150,000
Amortised up to 31 December 20X8 (21/120 ×150,000)	(26,250)
C/f as at 31 December 20X8	123,750

2   £170,000

(1) should be carried forward as property, plant and equipment under IAS 16.

(2) and (4) should be carried forward as intangible assets under IAS 38.

(3) and (5) should not be carried as intangible assets – per IAS 38 (paragraphs 48 and 63).

3   (1) Capitalised under IAS 16.

(2) and (4) Capitalised as part of the cost of an internally-generated intangible (IAS 38 paragraphs 66–67).

(3) should be written off to profit or loss as research expenditure.

4   MINBAD PLC

(a)   **Notes to the financial statements at 31 December 20X7 (extracts)**

Intangible assets

	Goodwill £m	Patents £m	Publishing titles £m	Total £m
Cost				
At 1 January 20X7	–	–	–	–
Additions	30	20	60	110
At 31 December 20X7	30	20	60	110
Amortisation/impairment				
At 1 January 20X7	–	–	–	–
Charge for year (20 ÷ 10)	1	2	–	3
At 31 December 20X7	1	2	–	3
Carrying amount				
At 1 January 20X7	–	–	–	–
At 31 December 20X7	29	18	60	107

Note: Of the additions during the year totalling £110 million the goodwill and publishing titles were acquired through a business combination. The patents were separately acquired.

Accounting policy note

Purchased intangibles are recognised at the fair value of consideration paid and separately from goodwill.

Patents are amortised on a straight-line basis over the life of the legal agreement.

Publishing titles are considered to have an indefinite life and are not amortised but are subject to annual impairment reviews.

Goodwill is not amortised but is subject to annual impairment reviews.

Note: This analysis shown under the heading 'Note' is required by IAS 38 paragraph 118 (e) (i)

(b) **IASB** *Conceptual Framework*

Under the IASB *Conceptual Framework* an asset is a resource controlled by the entity as a result of past events from which future economic benefits are expected.

Here, Minbad plc has control over all the intangibles as it has either legally purchased them (the goodwill, newspaper titles and patents) or developed them internally (the brand).

However, an additional requirement of the *Conceptual Framework* is that items can only be recognised as intangible assets if

(i) There is a probable inflow of economic benefits, and
(ii) The cost/value can be measured reliably.

Acquired intangibles meet this requirement, but, as IAS 38 clearly identifies, it is not possible to separate out reliably the cost of internally generated brands from the costs to develop the business as a whole.

Other sections of the *Conceptual Framework* highlight the importance of providing relevant information to users of financial statements. It could be argued that users would find the value of internally generated intangibles of great relevance when assessing/evaluating a business.

With regard to the proposed revaluation, although under IAS 38 either the cost or revaluation model can be used, intangibles should only be revalued where there is an 'active market' for them. This must be a market where all items traded are homogeneous, which clearly cannot be true for assets such as magazine titles.

5 PHARMORIA PLC

(a) **Total amount to be charged to profit or loss in the year ended 31 October 20X7**

	£
Formula B (not yet qualifying as development phase)	20,000
Amortisation of development costs (Formula A) (W)	5,300
Amortisation of patent (2,000 ÷ 10)	200
	25,500

(b) **Notes to the financial statements as at 31 October 20X7 (extracts)**

Intangible assets

	Development costs £	Patents £	Total £
Cost			
At 1 November 20X6	43,000	–	43,000
Additions	10,000	2,000	12,000
At 31 October 20X7	53,000	2,000	55,000
Amortisation			
At 1 November 20X6	–	–	–
Charge for year	5,300	200	5,500
At 31 October 20X7	5,300	200	5,500
Carrying amount			
At 1 November 20X6	43,000	–	43,000
At 31 October 20X7	47,700	1,800	49,500

WORKING

Amortisation of development costs for Formula A

Sales in year ÷ total sales × £53,000

$50,000/(50,000 + 150,000 + 200,000 + 100,000) \times £53,000 = £5,300$

6 DRONFIELD LTD

(a) **IAS 38 definitions**

The definition of an intangible asset in IAS 38 *Intangible Assets* (para 8) is consistent with the *Conceptual Framework* asset definition.

The key aspects of the definition are set out below.

Identifiable – an intangible asset should be identifiable so that it can be distinguished from goodwill. Concluding on whether a resource is identifiable is not straightforward.

IAS 38 states that an asset is identifiable when:

- It is separable, that is it is capable of being sold, transferred, rented or exchanged individually or with related items, or

- It arises from contractual or other legal rights, regardless of whether those rights are transferable or separable by the entity from other rights and obligations.

A separable asset is individual and the acquirer does not require other assets to be acquired with it. Examples could be quotas, franchises and licences.

An example of an asset arising from legal rights would be the legal right to operate some plant and equipment in circumstances where the assets cannot generate economic benefits without the transfer of the legal right to do so, and the legal right is of no benefit without the plant and equipment to which it relates.

Control – an entity can demonstrate control of an asset through:

- Being able to obtain future economic benefits from it, and
- Restricting the access of others to those benefits.

This control usually arises from the ability to enforce legal rights in a court of law, for example through the ownership of a patent. However, legal enforceability is not a necessary condition. For example, trade secrets confidentially known to a few people will give access to future benefits and restrict their use by others.

Human resources and market share are examples of intangible resources that fail to meet the control test in the definition of an asset, since they cannot be legally protected or controlled.

Future economic benefits may flow from an increase in revenues or a reduction in costs from the use of the asset. These benefits could arise from the product itself or from the use of the intellectual property as part of the production process.

(b) **Required accounting treatments**

Dronfield Ltd invests in four key business areas. The intangible resources it develops or acquires would meet the definition of an intangible asset. The issue is whether they meet the recognition criteria and should be included in the statement of financial position.

IAS 38 requires an entity to recognise an intangible asset if future economic benefits are probable and the cost can be measured reliably.

(1) **Research activities**

Dronfield Ltd's own research activities are planned investigations that try to identify new scientific knowledge. They meet the IAS 38 definition of a research phase of activity.

IAS 38 does not allow the recognition of intangible assets arising from the research phase. An entity cannot demonstrate that it is probable that future economic benefits will be generated. Hence the costs incurred do not meet the recognition criteria and should be recognised as an expense in profit or loss.

(2) **Development activities**

Dronfield Ltd's own development activities apply those research findings to design specific therapies that could be commercially beneficial. This is a development phase because it is further advanced than the research phase.

An intangible asset from the development phase should be recognised if, and only if, the entity can demonstrate that a number of stringent conditions have been met. In summary, the entity should be able to demonstrate the following.

- The technical feasibility of completing, and the intention to complete, the asset and the ability to use or sell it (this demonstrates completion of the process that will generate economic benefits).

- How the intangible asset will generate future economic benefits, either through the existence of an external market or its use internally, and the availability of resources to complete it (this demonstrates the generation of economic benefits required by the recognition criteria).

- The ability to measure the development expenditure reliably (recognition criteria requirement).

In practice the criteria severely restrict the ability of entities to recognise development phase costs as assets. Assets should only be recognised from the date that the recognition criteria are met and retrospective recognition of costs previously expensed is not allowed.

The existence of regulatory trials means that costs incurred before the successful outcome of these trials should not be recognised as an asset, because prior to the completion of these trials, technical feasibility cannot be demonstrated. Hence, it is extremely unlikely that any development phase costs should be recognised as an asset by Dronfield Ltd.

(3) Marketing and brand development costs

IAS 38 states that internally generated brands and marketing costs should never be recognised as intangible assets.

The standard takes the view that costs of developing market positions and brands cannot be distinguished from the cost of developing the business as a whole. Hence the costs cannot be measured reliably and the recognition criteria cannot be met.

(4) Acquired intangibles

IAS 38 states that it is always probable that future economic benefits will arise from acquired intangibles. The basis for this is that if there were no such future benefits, the acquirer would not have bothered to acquire them; the probability that they will arise is adjusted for in the price offered: the greater the probability, the higher the price, and *vice versa*.

IAS 38 also states that the cost of separately acquired intangibles can usually be measured reliably, particularly when the purchase consideration is in the form of cash or other monetary assets. The cost of intangibles acquired through a business combination should also be capable of reliable measurement, for example by reference to the way the acquirer built up the acquisition price. There is a rebuttable presumption of reliable measurement when such intangibles have finite useful lives.

(c) Key differences between UK GAAP and IFRS with regard to intangibles

- IFRS 3 requires the recognition of all the acquiree's intangible assets provided they can be reliably measured. (The test that economic benefits are expected to flow to the acquirer is automatically met in a business combination.) IFRS 3 suggests many examples of such intangibles, for example customer contracts, customer relationships and order backlogs. As these are to be recognised separately from goodwill, their carrying amount should go to reduce the carrying amount of goodwill. Under UK GAAP, only intangible assets that can be sold separately from the business are recognised in an acquirer's financial statements. As compared with calculations under UK standards, intangibles will be higher, and goodwill lower, under IFRS 3.

- IAS 38 requires the recognition as assets of all development expenditure meeting the relevant recognition criteria. Under UK GAAP it is an accounting policy choice whether to capitalise or to expense costs that meet the recognition criteria.

- The criteria for recognising development costs are more restrictive under IAS 38 because there is a requirement to demonstrate (rather than have a reasonable expectation of) future benefits.

7 STANNINGTON PLC

(a) Recognition criteria

Initial or subsequent expenditure on an item should be recognised as an intangible asset if it will give rise to future economic benefits and if its cost or value can be measured reliably.

For acquired intangibles the probability of expected future benefits is reflected in the price paid, so this condition is automatically met. This is the case whether the asset has been purchased separately or as part of a business combination. So the recognition criteria are fully met if the acquiring entity can measure the cost of the intangibles reliably.

IAS 38 outlines the criteria that need to be met for an entity to recognise the costs associated with an internally generated asset (such as technical feasibility, and probable future economic benefits). Costs should only be capitalised from the date that the recognition criteria are met. Costs written off before this point should never be subsequently capitalised. In practice this restricts the capitalisation of costs to the later stages of development when the technical and economic viability of a project is virtually certain. For example, where companies require regulatory approval for developed products, no costs should be recognised as an asset until that approval is successful. This is usually the point at which development is complete.

IAS 38 does not allow the recognition of internally generated goodwill, brands, mastheads, publishing titles and so on, because the costs of individual assets cannot be separated from the development of the business as a whole and then measured reliably. However, such items should be recognised if acquired separately or as part of a business combination. An acquisitive company's statement of financial position would probably present more intangible assets than a company which has invested in their internal generation.

(b) Accounting treatment

(1) Cable television franchise

The cable television franchise should be recognised at cost of £10 million on 1 January 20X3 provided the management believe cost is reliably measurable. The processes involved in determining whether to acquire the asset should provide sufficient evidence.

The intangible asset should be amortised over its useful life. The rights cover a period of twenty years and so an amortisation expense of £0.5 million per annum should be recognised, such that the carrying amount becomes £9.5 million at the end of the year.

The management have revalued the asset to £30 million at the year end. The revaluation model is allowed by IAS 38 provided

- All assets of the same class are revalued, and

- Fair values can be determined by reference to an active market for the intangible asset.

An active market is one where the items traded in it are homogeneous, willing buyers and sellers can be readily found and prices are available to the public. It is unusual for such a market to exist for many intangible assets and it does not exist for television franchises. The franchises are not homogeneous – they are unique as they cover specific areas and demographics. Also, franchises are not offered at prices available to the public.

As no active market exists the franchise should not be revalued.

(2) New production process

All costs incurred before the production process met the IAS 38 criteria for recognition as an intangible asset should be written off as an expense. Such costs cannot be subsequently capitalised. The asset should be initially measured in the statement of financial position at cost of £1.5 million, the expenditure after 1 July 20X3.

The production process is unique and whilst an offer has been received from a competitor that provides evidence of fair value, it should continue to be recognised at cost, as the £6 million value is not determined by reference to an active market.

However, as the asset is not ready for use IAS 36 requires an impairment review (that is estimate of recoverable amount) to be made at least annually. The offer from the competitor provides evidence of the recoverable amount and that no impairment has been incurred.

(3) **Publishing title**

The publishing title should be recognised as an asset initially at a cost of £25 million. The usual recognition criteria for intangibles should be applied to any subsequent expenditure, that is it is recognised in profit or loss unless it is probable that the expenditure will lead to future economic benefits and the expenditure can be reliably measured.

The £2 million expenditure does not meet the recognition criteria, as no persuasive evidence is available that future economic benefits are probable. In addition, it is difficult to attribute the expenditure to that asset rather than to the publishing portfolio or business as a whole. It appears that the £2 million is an apportionment of the total amount across the five titles. The £2 million should be recognised in profit or loss and the asset carried at £25 million.

The significant investment in the development of all the titles is powerful evidence that the acquired titles have indefinite lives. There should be no amortisation charges but annual impairment reviews are required, even if there is no indication of any impairment.

CHAPTER 6

Revenue and inventories

Introduction

Examination context

Topic List

Summary and Self-test

Technical reference
Answers to Interactive questions
Answers to Self-test

Introduction

Learning objectives

- Relate the treatment of revenue to the principles in the IASB *Conceptual Framework*

- Understand and apply the main provisions of IAS 18 *Revenue*, which sets out the requirements in relation to the recognition and measurement of revenue, in particular
  - Sale of goods
  - Rendering of services
  - Investment income

- Understand and apply the main provisions of IAS 2 *Inventories*, which sets out requirements in relation to the measurement of inventories

- Identify and consider appropriate actions for ethical issues involving revenue and inventories

Specific syllabus references for this chapter are: 1b, 1f, 2b, 2c, 2d, 2e.

Syllabus links

Revenue

You will have come across the accounting treatment of revenue in your earlier studies without necessarily being aware of this. In your Accounting studies you will have been introduced to the basic double entry for both a cash and a credit sale. With a credit sale the revenue is recognised in advance of the cash being received.

The Financial Accounting and Reporting syllabus builds on this basic knowledge by putting the topic into the context of IAS 18 *Revenue*. This sets out the basic principles of revenue recognition and introduces more complex transactions.

Inventories

In the Accounting paper you will have covered the basic principles of inventory valuation, ie inventory is valued at the lower of cost and net realisable value. You will also have dealt with the accounting entry for inventories as a year-end adjustment to a trial balance being:

DR   Inventories (Asset in the statement of financial position)
CR   Cost of sales (profit or loss)

The Financial Accounting and Reporting syllabus looks in more detail at the guidance provided by IAS 2 *Inventories*, particularly the calculation of cost and net realisable value.

Examination context

In the examination, candidates may be required to:

- Prepare and present financial statements or extracts therefrom in accordance with:

  - IAS 18 *Revenue*
  - IAS 2 *Inventories*

- Explain the accounting treatment of revenue and inventories

- Explain the differences between the accounting treatment using the accrual basis and the cash basis in relation to revenue recognition

- Know that the principles of revenue and inventory measurement and recognition are the same under IFRS and UK GAAP

- Identify and explain any ethical issues

1 Introduction

Section overview

- Both revenue recognition and accounting for inventories are affected by the application of the accrual basis of accounting.

- The key issue affecting revenue is the timing of recognition.

- The key issue affecting inventories is the identification of which costs should be:

  - Carried forward in the statement of financial position.
  - Expensed as part of cost of sales.

1.1 Background issues

Financial statements are prepared on the underlying assumption of the **accrual basis** of accounting, whereby effects of transactions are recognised **when they occur** and not when the cash associated with them is received or paid.

But this raises questions about **when** a transaction 'occurs':

- Is it when the buyer takes possession of the goods, in circumstances where the contract for sale contains clauses that seek to ensure that ownership does not pass to the customer until the seller has been paid in full?

- Is it when services are provided, in circumstances where the seller undertakes to come back to do additional work without charge if needed, eg remedial work carried out by a building contractor?

- When does the profit arise on a contract for the provision of services to a customer over time, such as under a maintenance contract of two years' duration? Only at the start, only in the middle, only at the end, or over the period of two years?

In addition there are issues about **which costs** to include in the carrying amount for inventories, in the statement of financial position:

- Should the amount include only those variable costs that are incurred in the manufacture? After all, fixed costs are incurred regardless of volume of activity and perhaps should be recognised in profit or loss as incurred.

- Or should the amounts include fixed costs? And if so, which? Should general administration costs be included?

Finally there is the issue of how to **identify the cost of goods** which must be removed from the carrying amount of inventories when they are sold:

- Should it be the cost of the goods manufactured longest ago?
- Should it be the cost of those manufactured most recently?
- Or should some sort of average cost be used?

The **timing of the recognition of revenue** is critical to the timing of profits, while the amount of **year-end inventories has a £ for £ effect on the profits earned in the period**. So the way these are calculated is vital to any real understanding of the financial performance in the period.

1.2 Context

Revenue is often the largest single item in the financial statements. US studies have shown that over half of all financial statement frauds and requirements for restatements of previously published financial information involved revenue manipulation.

The most blatant recent example was the Satyam Computer Services fraud in 2010, in which false invoices were used to record fictitious revenue amounting to $1.5bn. Revenue recognition fraud also featured in the Enron and WorldCom cases.

The directors of Enron inflated the value of 'agency' services by reporting the entire value of each of its trades as revenue, rather than just the agency commission on the sale. Other energy companies then adopted this 'model' in a bid to keep up with Enron's results.

WorldCom was an entity in which all executive bonuses were tied to revenue targets and dubious accounting adjustments were constantly made to keep revenue 'on target'. By the time WorldCom filed for bankruptcy, revenue had been overstated by about $960m.

There is definitely a need for thorough guidance in this area. Robust principles for recognition and measurement should be applied. A consistent approach to revenue recognition is essential if financial statements are to present fairly the true economic activity of an entity. One of the main issues is the reporting of revenue within discrete periods, when under a single contract services are provided in the current and future periods. This allocation of revenue has a direct impact on the earnings for each period.

2 IAS 18 *Revenue*

Section overview

- Revenue is income arising in the normal course of an entity's activities.

- Revenue should be recognised when it is probable that future economic benefits will flow to the entity and when these benefits can be measured reliably.

- IAS 18 *Revenue* provides guidance on the recognition of revenue arising in the following transactions:

  - Sale of goods
  - Rendering of services
  - The use by others of entity assets yielding interest, royalties and dividends

- Although detailed rules apply to the above, generally revenue is recognised when the entity has transferred to the buyer the significant risks and rewards of ownership and when that revenue can be measured reliably.

2.1 Objective and scope

IAS 18 prescribes the accounting treatment of revenue recognition in common types of transaction. It states that in general terms revenue should be recognised:

- When it is **probable that future economic benefits will flow to the entity** and
- These benefits can be **measured reliably**.

IAS 18 applies to:

- Sale of goods (manufactured items and items purchased for resale).

- The rendering of services (which typically involves the performance by the entity of a contractually agreed task over an agreed period of time).

- The use by others of entity assets yielding interest, royalties and dividends.

The standard specifically excludes various types of revenue arising from leases, construction contracts, insurance contracts, changes in value of financial instruments or other current assets, natural increases in agricultural assets and mineral ore extraction.

2.2 Revenue

Income is defined in the IASB's *Conceptual Framework* as 'increases in economic benefits in the form of inflows or enhancements of assets or decreases of liabilities that result in increases in equity.' **Revenue is simply income arising in the ordinary course of an entity's activities** and it may be called different names such as:

- Sales
- Turnover
- Interest
- Dividends
- Royalties

Revenue is defined by IAS 18 as follows:

Definition

Revenue: The gross inflow of economic benefits during the period arising in the course of the ordinary activities of an entity when those flows result in increases in equity, other than increases relating to contributions from equity participants.

Points to note

1 The reference to 'gross' inflow requires revenue to be shown **gross of the costs associated with earning it** (an example of the general prohibition against netting off in financial statements).

2 The reference to 'increases in equity' precludes the inclusion in revenue of amounts collected on behalf of others, eg **sales tax** (VAT in the UK) and **amounts collected by agents** on behalf of a principal.

2.3 Measurement

When a transaction takes place, the amount of revenue is usually decided by the **agreement** of the buyer and the seller. The revenue, however, should be measured at the **fair value** of the consideration received or receivable.

Definition

Fair value: The price that would be received to sell an asset or paid to transfer a liability in an orderly transaction between market participants at the measurement date.

Fair value will take into account any **trade discounts** and **volume rebates** allowed by the seller.

In straightforward situations the requirement to measure revenue at fair value provides few problems. So sales on credit terms of 30 days will be measured at the amount receivable in 30 days, net of all sales allowances such as quantity discounts.

Problems can arise where much longer credit intervals are allowed.

2.4 Sale of goods

Revenue should only be recognised when all of the following conditions are satisfied.

- The entity has **transferred the significant risks and rewards of ownership** of the goods to the buyer.

- The seller **no longer has management involvement or effective control** over the goods.

- The amount of **revenue** can be **measured reliably**.

- It is **probable** that the economic benefits associated with the transaction will flow to the entity.

- The **costs incurred** in respect of the transaction can be **measured reliably**.

Points to note

1 In most cases **the transfer of risks and rewards of ownership coincides with the transfer of legal title,** or the passing of possession to the buyer. This is the case for most retail sales.

2   If the entity retains **significant risks of ownership**, the transaction is **not** a sale and **revenue is not recognised**.

Examples of this type of situation include the following:

- When the seller retains some obligation for unsatisfactory performance which is outside a normal warranty cover.

- If the receipt of the revenue from a particular sale depends on the buyer receiving revenue from his own sale of the goods.

- When the goods are shipped subject to installation and the installation is a significant part of the contract which has not yet been completed by the seller (revenue should not be recognised until the installation has been completed).

3   It is possible for the seller to retain only an insignificant risk of ownership and for the sale and revenue to be recognised. Common examples include the following situations:

- Where the seller retains title only to ensure collection of what is owed on the goods.
- Where an item may be returned and a refund provided.

4   The **probability** of the entity receiving the revenue arising from the transaction **must be assessed**. For example, in most cases revenue in relation to credit sales is recognised before actual payment is received. However, where collectability is called into doubt and recovery has ceased to be probable, the amount should be recognised as an expense and **not** an adjustment to revenue previously recognised.

5   **Matching** should take place, ie revenue and expenses relating to the same transaction should be recognised at the same time. In some cases expenses may need to be estimated at the date of sale, eg warranty costs. Where they cannot be estimated reliably, then revenue cannot be recognised; any consideration that has already been received is treated as a liability.

Worked example: Sale of goods

Morgan Motors Ltd sells a car for £15,000 with one year's free credit. There is a three-year manufacturer's warranty on the vehicle.

Revenue will be recognised at the time of sale, but:

- The £15,000 receivable will be split between interest earned and the cash sale price.

- The cash sale price will be recognised in the period the sale is made.

- The interest income will be recognised over the period of free credit.

- The production and selling costs of the car will be set against the cash sale price. At the same time a charge to profit or loss will be made to set up a warranty provision for the expected costs of carrying out the expected amount of warranty work over the three-year warranty period.

- Costs incurred on the warranty work over the three years will be charged to the provision, with any over-provision being written back (and any under-provision being charged) to the profit or loss.

Interactive question 1: Publishing revenue   [Difficulty level: Easy]

A magazine publisher launched a new monthly magazine on 1 January 20X7. During January it received £48,000 in annual subscriptions in advance. It has despatched four issues by the year end 31 March 20X7.

What revenue should be recognised for the year ended 31 March 20X7?

See **Answer** at the end of this chapter.

Interactive question 2: Advance sales [Difficulty level: Intermediate]

A DIY store is about to sell a new type of drill. Customer demand is high and the store has taken advance orders for the drill. The selling price of the drill will be £50 and so far two hundred customers have paid an initial 10% deposit on the selling price of the drill. No drills are yet held in inventory.

What amount should be recognised as revenue?

See **Answer** at the end of this chapter.

2.5 Deferred consideration

In some sectors of the retail industry it is common practice to provide interest-free credit to customers in order to encourage sales of, for example, furniture and new cars.

Where an extended period of credit is offered, the revenue receivable has two separate elements:

*   The fair value of the goods on the date of sale, for example the cash selling price
*   Financing income

In order to separate these two elements the future receipts are discounted to present value at an imputed interest rate, identified as either:

*   The prevailing rate for lending to a customer with a credit rating similar to that of the customer or
*   The rate of interest which discounts the receivable back to the current cash selling price.

The effect on the timing of the revenue recognition is that:

*   The fair value of the goods is recognised on delivery of the goods.
*   The finance element is recognised over the period that the financing is provided.

Worked example: Deferred consideration

A car retailer sells its new cars by requiring a 20% deposit followed by no further payments until the full balance is due after two years. The price of the cars is calculated using a 10% per annum finance charge.

On 1 January 20X7 a car was sold to a customer for £20,000.

How should the revenue be recognised in the year ended 31 December 20X7 and what should the carrying amount of the customer receivable be on that date?

Solution

Revenue to be recognised

	£
Sale of goods (£4,000 + £13,223 (W))	17,223
Financing income (£13,223 (W) × 10%)	1,322
Carrying amount of receivable (£13,223 (W) × 1.10)	14,545

WORKING

The deposit is £4,000 (£20,000 × 20%), so the amount receivable in two years is £16,000.

This is discounted at 10% for two years to £13,223 (£16,000 × $1/1.10^2$).

Worked example: Deferred consideration

Comfy Couches Ltd sells an item of furniture to a customer on 1 September 20X7 for £2,500 with a one-year interest-free credit period. The fair value of the consideration receivable is £2,294. (In other words, if the company tried to sell this debt, this is the amount it would expect to receive now.)

In this case the transaction would be split into two components:

- Interest revenue of £206 (2,500 – 2,294), which would be recognised over the period of credit
- Sales revenue of £2,294, which would be recognised on 1 September 20X7

When goods or services are 'swapped' for those of similar nature and value, **then no revenue is created** (and no additional cost recorded), because all that is really taking place is the substitution of one good or service by something very similar. Such transactions are quite common in the sale of commodities.

When the goods/services are dissimilar, then there are transactions which generate revenue and cost, measured by reference to the fair value of what is received.

2.6 Rendering of services

When the outcome of a transaction involving the rendering of services can be estimated reliably, the associated revenue should be recognised by reference to the **stage of completion of the transaction** at the end of the reporting period. The outcome of a transaction can be estimated reliably when **all** of the following conditions are satisfied.

- The amount of revenue can be **measured reliably**.

- It is probable that the **economic benefits** associated with the transaction will flow to the entity.

- The **stage of completion** of the transaction at the end of the reporting period can be measured reliably.

- The **costs incurred** for the transaction and the **costs to complete** the transaction can be measured reliably.

The recognition criteria above are similar to those for the sale of goods. One of the key differences is the need to be able to **determine the stage of completion** of the transaction. This is of particular relevance when the completion of a contract for services **straddles more than one accounting period**. The following methods of assessing the stage of completion are referred to in IAS 18:

- Surveys of work performed
- Services performed to date as a percentage of total services to be performed
- The proportion that costs incurred to date bear to the estimated total costs of the transaction

Progress payments and advances received from customers often do not reflect the services performed. As a result it is normally inappropriate to recognise revenue based on payments received.

If the overall outcome of a services transaction cannot be estimated reliably, then revenue is only recognised to the extent of those costs incurred that are recoverable from the client.

Interactive question 3: Rendering of services   [Difficulty level: Easy]

A £210,000 fixed-price contract is entered into for the provision of services. At the end of 20X7, the first accounting period, the contract is thought to be 33% complete and costs of £45,000 have been incurred in performing that 33% of the work.

Requirements

Calculate the revenue to be recognised in 20X7 on the alternative assumptions that:

(a) The costs to complete are reliably estimated at £90,000; and

(b) The costs to complete cannot be reliably estimated and it is thought that £40,000 of the costs incurred are recoverable from the customer.

See **Answer** at the end of this chapter.

Interactive question 4: Service contract [Difficulty level: Intermediate]

An entity entered into a contract for the provision of services over a two year period. The total contract price was £150,000 and the entity initially expected to earn a profit of £20,000 on the contract. In the first year costs of £60,000 were incurred and 50% of the work was completed. The contract did not progress as expected and management was not sure of the ultimate outcome but believed that the costs incurred to date would be recovered from the customer.

What revenue should be recognised for the first year of the contract?

See **Answer** at the end of this chapter.

2.7 Goods and services provided in one contract

One marketing tool frequently used is to bundle together into one transaction both goods and services. For example a car dealer may sell new cars with one year's free servicing and insurance.

In such cases:

- The components of the package which could be sold separately should be identified; and
- Each should be measured and recognised as if sold separately.

IAS 18 does not specifically state how each component should be measured but general principles require that each component should be:

- Measured at its fair value.
- Recognised as revenue only when it meets the recognition criteria.

If the total of the fair values exceeds the overall price of the contract, an appropriate approach would be to apply the same discount percentage to each separate component.

Worked example: Goods and services

A car dealer sells a new car, together with 50 litres of fuel per month for a year and one year's servicing, for £27,000. The fair values of these components are: car £28,000, fuel £1,200 and servicing £800.

How should the £27,000 be recognised as revenue?

Solution

The total fair value of the package is £30,000 (28,000 + 1,200 + 800) but is being sold for £27,000, a discount of £3,000 or 10%.

The discounted fair value of the car should be recognised as revenue upon delivery:

£28,000 × 90% = £25,200

The discounted fair value of the fuel should be recognised as revenue on a straight line basis over the next 12 months:

£1,200 × 90% = £1,080

The discounted fair value of the servicing should be recognised as revenue at the earlier of when the servicing is provided and the end of the year:

£800 × 90% = £720

Interactive question 5: Goods and services [Difficulty level: Intermediate]

An entity sells an item of equipment to a customer on 1 January 20X7 for £1.5m. Due to the specialised nature of the equipment the entity has agreed to provide free support services for the next two years, despite the cost to the entity of that support being estimated at £120,000 in total. The entity usually earns a gross margin of 20% on such contracts.

How much revenue should the entity recognise for the year ended 30 April 20X7?
Fill in the proforma below.

£

Revenue

WORKINGS

See **Answer** at the end of this chapter.

2.8 Investment income

When others use the entity's assets yielding interest, royalties and dividends, the revenue should be recognised when:

(a) It is probable that the **economic benefits** associated with the transaction will flow to the entity; and
(b) The amount of the revenue can be **measured reliably**.

The revenue is recognised on the following bases.

*   **Interest** is recognised on a time proportion basis that takes into account the effective yield on the asset.

*   **Royalties** are recognised on an accrual basis in accordance with the substance of the relevant agreement.

*   **Dividends** are recognised when the shareholder's right to receive payment is established.

2.9 Disclosure

The following items should be disclosed.

*   The **accounting policies** adopted for the recognition of revenue, including the methods used to determine the stage of completion of transactions involving the rendering of services

*   The amount of each **significant category of revenue** recognised during the period including revenue arising from:

    –   The sale of goods
    –   The rendering of services
    –   Interest
    –   Royalties
    –   Dividends

*   The amount of revenue arising from **exchanges of goods or services** included in each significant category of revenue

Any **contingent gains or losses**, such as those relating to warranty costs, claims or penalties should be treated according to IAS 37 *Provisions, Contingent Liabilities and Contingent Assets* (covered in Chapter 9).

2.10 Practical application

IAS 18 includes an appendix, which demonstrates the application of its concepts to particular types of transactions. These include the following:

Consignment sales	Under such arrangements, the buyer of the goods undertakes to sell them on, but on behalf of the original seller. So the buyer is effectively acting as an agent on behalf of the original seller. The original seller only recognises his sale **when his buyer sells them on to a third party.**
	This treatment also applies to sale and return transactions.
Lay away sales	Under these arrangements, the goods are only delivered once the final instalment has been received, so it is only then that the risks and rewards of ownership move from seller to buyer and revenue can be recognised.
	However, when experience indicates that most such sales are completed, revenue may be recognised when a significant deposit is received provided the goods are ready for delivery to the buyer.
Sale and repurchase agreement	This is an agreement whereby the seller concurrently agrees to repurchase the same goods at a later date, or where there are call or put options in place.
	The **terms of the agreement** need to be considered to determine whether there is a sale in **substance**. Where legal title has been transferred but the risks and rewards of ownership have been retained by the seller revenue is not recognised and the transaction is treated as a financing arrangement. (We looked at the principle of substance over form in Chapter 1.)
Subscriptions to publications	Where a series of publications is subscribed to and each publication is of a similar value, eg a monthly magazine, revenue is recognised on **a straight-line basis** over the period in which the publications are despatched.
	Where the value of each publication varies revenue is recognised on the basis of the sales value of the item despatched in relation to the estimated sales value of all items covered by the subscription.
Servicing fees included in the price of the product	When an item's sales price includes 'free' servicing, revenue in relation to that servicing should be **deferred and recognised over the servicing period**. The amount deferred should be sufficient to cover both the cost of servicing and a reasonable profit.
Tuition fees	Revenue should be recognised over a period of time (the period of instruction), **in line with the way the services are provided** over that period of time.
Advertising commissions	Media commissions, eg payment for a series of adverts, should be recognised **when the related advertisement or commercial appears before the public.**

2.11 Agent v principal

The appendix to IAS 18 was amended for the 2009 *Annual Improvements to IFRSs* and now provides guidance on how to recognise and account for an agency-principal relationship.

Individually or in combination, the following criteria indicate that the entity is acting as a principal:

- The entity has the primary responsibility for providing the goods or services to the customer or for fulfilling the order.

- The entity has the inventory risk before or after the customer order, during shipping or on return.

- The entity has latitude in establishing prices, either directly or indirectly.

- The entity bears the customer's credit risk on the amount due from the customer.

Worked example: Agent or principal?

An entity runs a website which enables customers to buy goods from a range of suppliers. Prices are set by suppliers and payments are processed through the entity's website. Customers pay in advance and goods are delivered directly from the supplier to the customer.

The entity receives a commission of 10% of the sales price and has no further obligation to the customer after arranging for the products to be shipped.

Is the entity an agent or the principal?

Solution

The entity is acting as an agent based on the following points:

- Goods travel directly from the supplier to the customer, so the entity never has physical custody of them and does not bear the associated risk.

- The supplier, not the entity, has the obligation to the customer.

- The entity does not set prices or bear credit risk.

- The payment received by the entity is in the form of commission.

So the entity should only recognise as revenue the commission received from suppliers.

2.12 Faithful representation/substance over form

The decision about when to recognise revenue on the sale of goods requires consideration of whether the risks and rewards of ownership have been transferred to the buyer, the seller retaining neither management involvement in, nor effective control over, the asset sold.

For the decision to result in faithful representation of the transaction it is critical that the substance of arrangements for the sale of goods is clearly identified and then accounted for. Merely examining the form of arrangements is insufficient. One of the greatest difficulties is establishing whether or not there are arrangements, such as an option, whereby the seller can at a fixed or determinable future date for a fixed or determinable amount repurchase the asset being sold.

In such circumstances, and particularly if the seller retains use of the asset between the sale and repurchase dates, the arrangement is probably in substance a secured loan, not a sale at all.

Worked example: Faithful representation

An entity sold an investment property to a financial institution for £4 million when the fair value of the property was £5 million. Further investigation uncovered an agreement whereby the entity could repurchase the property after one year for £4.32 million.

How should this transaction be accounted for?

Solution

The sale of the property at 20% below fair value is sufficient to cast doubt on whether a real sale has been made. Also, the repurchase price is below fair value at the date of sale and represents a return to the financial institution of 8% ((£4.32m – 4m) as a percentage of £4m) on the amount paid out.

The substance of the arrangement appears to be that the financial institution has granted the entity a one year loan secured on the property, charging interest at 8%.

The transaction should be accounted for by:

- Continuing to recognise the property as an asset.
- Crediting the £4 million received to a liability account.
- Recognising £0.32m as a finance cost in profit or loss and crediting it to the liability account.
- Derecognising the liability when the £4.32 million cash is paid out.

Interactive question 6: Sale and repurchase   [Difficulty level: Exam standard]

Builder Ltd specialises in building high quality executive flats in city centres. On 1 March 20X6 it sells a plot of building land to Finance plc, an unconnected company, for £1.5m. Builder Ltd retains rights of access and supervision over the plot, the right to build on this land until 28 February 20X8 and the right to buy the plot back again on that date for £1.9m. On 1 March 20X6 the plot is valued at £2.5m.

Requirement

Explain how this sale transaction would be dealt with in Builder Ltd's financial statements for the year ended 28 February 20X7.

-
-
-
-
-
-
-

See **Answer** at the end of this chapter.

Interactive question 7: Servicing fees   [Difficulty level: Exam standard]

On the last day of its current accounting period, Computer Ltd completes the handover of a new system to a client and raises an invoice for £800,000. This price includes after-sales support for the next two years, which is estimated to cost £35,000 each year. Computer Ltd normally earns a gross profit margin of 17.5% on such support activity.

Requirement

Calculate the revenue to be included in Computer Ltd's current year statement of profit or loss in respect of this sale.

Fill in the proforma below.

	£
After-sales support	
Remainder	
Total selling price	
So the revenue from the sale in the current year is	

See **Answer** at the end of this chapter.

2.13 Judgements required

The key judgements required of management include:

- When do the risks and rewards of ownership of goods pass to the buyer?
- In what circumstances is management involvement in the asset retained?
- How is a decision made as to whether the stage of completion of a service transaction can be measured reliably?

Because revenue has such a direct impact on earnings and because many investors focus on revenue growth as an important measure of performance, management may well be tempted to be very optimistic in its judgements, in order that the amount of revenue recognised is maximised. Chartered Accountants need to be very clear about the need to ensure that there are robust internal policies for the recognition of revenue and that they are applied consistently from one period to another.

2.14 Relevance of information for users

IAS 18 requires only limited information about revenue to be disclosed: the accounting policies for recognition of revenue (including the methods for determining the stage of completion for service transactions) and the amount of revenue from goods, services, interest, royalties and dividends. Accounting policies that are disclosed tend to lack detail.

So users are not very well served, a particular weakness when:

- Revenue has a £1 for £1 effect on profit and therefore the return on capital employed calculation.
- Every extra £1 of profit reduces gearing.

2.15 Ethical issues

One of the easiest ways to increase profit is to overstate revenue. The timing of recognition is crucial, as often this is a judgement area. For example, cash may have been received although the services may not yet have been delivered. Increased profit allows the payment of larger dividends and often triggers the payment of executive bonuses. In addition, the advancement of revenue and hence inflated profit for a particular period may be beneficial if the company is looking to expand or attract new owners.

The most blatant revenue fraud of the last decade was perpetrated at Satyam Computer Services in India and uncovered in January 2009. The Satyam chairman confessed that the company's financial statements had been falsified to overstate revenue by $1.47 billion.

3 IAS 2 *Inventories*

Section overview

- Inventories should be measured at the lower of cost and net realisable value (NRV).

- Cost comprises the costs of:

    - Purchase
    - Conversion
    - Bringing the inventories to their present location and condition

- The comparison of cost and NRV should be performed on an item-by-item basis although similar items may be grouped together.

3.1 Objective and scope

The objective of IAS 2 *Inventories* is to prescribe the accounting treatment for inventories. In particular it provides guidance on the **determination of cost** and its subsequent recognition as an expense, including any write-down to **net realisable value**.

IAS 2 applies to all inventories except the following:

- Work in progress under construction contracts
- Financial instruments (eg shares, bonds)
- Biological assets

Construction contracts and biological assets are outside the scope of the Financial Accounting and Reporting syllabus.

Certain inventories are exempt from the standard's measurement rules, ie those held by:

- Producers of agricultural, forest and mineral products
- Commodity-broker traders

3.2 Revision of Accounting material

IAS 2 is covered in some detail in the Accounting syllabus, so this section is mainly revision.

Definition

Inventories: Assets which are:

- Held for sale in the ordinary course of business;

- In the process of production for such sale; or

- In the form of materials or supplies to be consumed in the production process or in the rendering of services.

Inventories can include:

- **Goods purchased and held for resale**
- **Finished goods**
- **Work in progress** being produced
- **Raw materials** awaiting use

3.2.1 Measurement of inventories

Inventories should be measured at the **lower of cost and net realisable value (NRV)**.

Definitions

Cost: Comprises all costs of purchase, costs of conversion and other costs incurred in bringing the inventories to their present location and condition.

Net realisable value: The estimated selling price in the ordinary course of business less the estimated costs of completion and the estimated costs necessary to make the sale.

A write-down of inventories would normally take place on an **item-by-item basis**, but similar or related items may be **grouped together**. This grouping is acceptable for, say, items in the same product line, but it is not acceptable to write-down inventories based on a whole classification (eg finished goods) or a whole business.

3.2.2 Cost of inventories

As we have seen from the definition of cost in Section 3.2.1:

The cost of inventories will consist of:

- **Cost of purchase**
- **Costs of conversion**
- **Other costs** incurred in bringing the inventories to their **present location and condition**

Costs of purchase

IAS 2 lists the following as comprising the costs of purchase of inventories.

- **Purchase price plus**

- **Import duties** and other non-recoverable taxes **plus**

- Transport, handling and any other costs **directly attributable** to the acquisition of finished goods, services and materials **less**

- **Trade discounts**, rebates and other similar amounts.

Costs of conversion

Costs of conversion of inventories consist of two main parts.

- Costs **directly related** to the units of production, eg direct materials, direct labour

- Fixed and variable **production overheads** that are incurred in converting materials into finished goods, allocated on the basis of normal production capacity

You may have come across the terms 'fixed production overheads' or 'variable production overheads' elsewhere in your studies.

Definitions

Fixed production overheads: Those indirect costs of production that remain relatively constant regardless of the volume of production, such as depreciation and maintenance of factory buildings and equipment, and the cost of factory management and administration.

Variable production overheads: Those indirect costs of production that vary directly, or nearly directly, with the volume of production, such as indirect materials and labour.

IAS 2 emphasises that fixed production overheads must be allocated to items of inventory on the basis of the **normal capacity of the production facilities**. This is an important point.

- **Normal capacity** is the expected achievable production based on the average over several periods/seasons, under normal circumstances.
- The above figure should take account of the capacity lost through **planned maintenance**.
- If it approximates to the normal capacity then the **actual level of production** can be used.
- The allocation of variable production overheads to each unit is based on the **actual use** of production facilities.

As a result:

- **Low production** or **idle plant** will **not** result in a higher fixed overhead allocation to each unit.
- **Unallocated overheads** must be recognised as an expense in the period in which they were incurred.
- When production is **abnormally high**, the fixed production overhead allocated to each unit will be reduced, so avoiding inventories being stated at more than cost.

Worked example: Fixed production overheads

A business plans for fixed production overheads of £50,000 and annual production of 100,000 items in its financial year. So the planned overhead recovery rate is 50p per item.

A fire at the factory results in production being only 75,000 units, with no saving in fixed production overheads.

Inventory should still be valued on the basis of 50p per item, leading to a recovery of £37,500 of overheads. The £12,500 balance of overhead cost must be recognised as an expense in the year.

Other costs

Any other costs should only be recognised if they are incurred in bringing the inventories to their **present location and condition**.

IAS 2 lists types of cost that **would not be included** in cost of inventories. Instead, they should be recognised as an **expense** in the period in which they are incurred.

These include:

- **Abnormal amounts** of wasted materials, labour or other production costs.
- **Storage costs** (except costs that are necessary in the production process before a further production stage).
- **Administrative overheads** not incurred to bring inventories to their present location and condition.
- **Selling costs**.

Interactive question 8: Cost of inventories

[Difficulty level: Exam standard]

A manufacturing business incurs the following expenditure.

	Include in cost of inventories	Recognised as an expense as incurred
Supplier's gross price for raw materials		
Quantity discounts allowed by supplier		
Purchase taxes and duties charged by supplier and recoverable from taxing authorities		
Costs of transporting materials to the business' premises		
Labour costs directly incurred in the processing of raw materials		
Variable costs, such as power, incurred in the processing of raw materials		
Fixed production costs/overheads, such as rent for the processing factory and depreciation charges on the plant used in the processing		
Costs of holding finished goods in inventory		
Costs of transporting goods to customer on sale		
Purchase taxes charged to customer on sale		
Commission payable to salesmen on sale of the goods		
Allowance for bad and doubtful debts in relation to trade receivables		
Costs of accounts department		
Head office costs relating to the overall management of the business		

Requirement

Identify in the table above the expenditures to be included in the cost of inventories and those to be recognised as an expense as incurred.

Fill in the proforma above.

Commentary on Interactive question 8

- In terms of the normal operating cycle of a business, all costs up to the time goods are taken into inventory will be costs incurred in bringing items **to their present location and condition**. But all costs of holding goods in inventory, selling the goods and collecting outstanding receivables are not incurred for this reason; nor are the general costs of accounting for and managing the business.

- Fixed production costs/overheads are to be included in inventory values, but only at the rates based upon **normal levels of output**. These rates should not be increased as a result of production being below expected levels, as a result of plant failures, for example.

See **Answer** at the end of this chapter.

Techniques for the measurement of cost

Two techniques are mentioned by the standard, both of which produce results that **approximate to cost**, and so both of which may be used for convenience.

(a) **Standard costs**: These are set up to take account of normal levels of raw materials used, labour time etc. They are reviewed and revised on a regular basis.

(b) **Retail method**: This is often used in the retail industry where there is a large turnover of inventory items, which nevertheless have similar profit margins. The only practical method of inventory valuation may be to take the total selling price of inventories and deduct an overall average profit margin, thus reducing the value to an approximation of cost. The percentage will take account of reduced price lines. Sometimes different percentages are applied on a departmental basis.

Worked example: Retail method

A retailer identifies inventories at the end of an accounting period as follows:

- Department A: inventories with a selling price of £30,000. This department makes a 25% gross profit on its sales.

- Department B: inventories with a selling price of £21,000. This department sets its selling prices at cost plus 50%.

Requirement

Calculate the value of inventories in each department.

Solution

Department A: Selling price of inventories £30,000 less gross profit 25% = £22,500

Department B: If selling price is cost plus 50%, then selling price must be 150% of cost
and the gross profit margin must be 50/150 = 33.3%
Selling price of inventories £21,000 less gross profit 33.3% = £14,000

3.2.3 Cost formulae

It is possible to attribute specific costs to items that are not interchangeable and to items produced for specific projects or customers and it is these costs which are used in arriving at inventory valuations.

But **many inventories include items that are interchangeable** with each other, in which case **it is not possible to identify a specific cost for a specific item**. In these cases, **cost formulae** should be used, which make assumptions about which of the items produced have been sold and which are still held in inventory, and therefore about the cost of inventory.

Only two cost formulae are allowed under IAS 2:

First-in, first-out (FIFO)	Weighted average cost
This assumes a **physical flow of items** whereby **those produced earliest are the first to be sold**. The items produced most recently are the ones in inventory, to be measured at the most recent production cost.	This formula calculates an **average cost of production** (either at the end of each period or after each new batch has been produced, depending on the circumstances of the company) and measures inventories at that average cost.

Points to note

1 The last-in, first-out (LIFO) formula (which makes an assumption about the physical flows of items that is the opposite of FIFO) is not permitted by IAS 2. The reasoning, not included in the IAS, is that LIFO is not a reliable representation of the actual flow of items into and out of inventory.

2 The same cost formula must be used for all inventories having a similar nature. This limitation on management choice is aimed to ensure that like items are accounted for in like ways.

3.3 Net realisable value

As a general rule assets should not be carried at amounts **greater than those to be realised from their sale or use**. This applies to inventory **where NRV falls below cost**. There are a number of reasons why this may be the case, including the following:

- An **increase in costs** or a **fall in selling price**
- A **physical deterioration** in the condition of inventory
- **Obsolescence** of products
- A **strategic decision** to manufacture and sell products at a loss
- **Errors** in production or purchasing

Where NRV falls below cost the inventory is written down to its recoverable amount and **the fall in value is charged to profit or loss**. The write-down may be of such size, incidence or nature that it must be **disclosed separately**.

Points to note

1   In the case of **incomplete items**, NRV must take account of **costs to complete**.

2   In the absence of a contractually agreed selling price, the **best estimate** must be made of the likely selling price and then appropriate deductions made from it.

3   Materials to be incorporated into a finished product should only be written down **if that finished product will be sold at below its cost**.

4   Net realisable value must be **reassessed at the end of each period** and compared again with cost. This may result in the **reversal** of all or part of the original write-down.

3.4 Recognition as an expense

Once an item has been sold, it cannot remain in inventories as it no longer meets the IASB *Conceptual Framework* definition of an asset. Its carrying amount is recognised as an **expense** in the accounting period in which the item is sold and the **related revenue recognised**.

3.5 Disclosure

The financial statements should disclose the following:

- **Accounting policies** adopted in measuring inventories, including the cost formula used.

- **Total carrying amount of inventories** and the carrying amount in classifications appropriate to the entity (eg merchandise, production supplies, materials, work in progress, finished goods).

- **Carrying amount** of inventories carried at fair value less costs to sell.

- The amount of inventories **recognised as an expense** in the period.

- The amount of any **write-down** of inventories **recognised as an expense** in the period.

- The amount of any **reversal of any write-down** that is recognised as a reduction in the amount of inventories recognised as an expense in the period.

- **Circumstances or events** that led to the reversal of a write-down of inventories.

- Carrying amount of inventories **pledged as security for liabilities**.

The financial statements must also disclose one of two things:

- The **cost of inventories** recognised as an expense during the period.

- The **operating costs**, applicable to revenues, recognised as an expense during the period, classified by their nature.

The choice reflects differences in **the way the statement of profit or loss can be presented** (see Chapter 2).

4 UK GAAP comparison

Section overview

There are some differences between UK GAAP and IFRS treatment of inventories.

Companies reporting under FRS 101 have no exemption from the provisions of IAS 18 *Revenue* or IAS 2 *Inventories*.

There are no significant differences between FRS 102 and IAS 18.

Differences between FRS 102 and IAS 2 are as follows:

- FRS 102 requires inventories held for distribution at no or nominal consideration, or through a non-exchange transaction, to be measured at adjusted cost. IAS 2 includes no such requirement.

- Under FRS 102 impairment losses on inventory can be reversed if the circumstances which led to the impairment no longer exist, or if economic circumstances change. No such guidance is provided in IAS 2.

Summary and Self-test

Summary

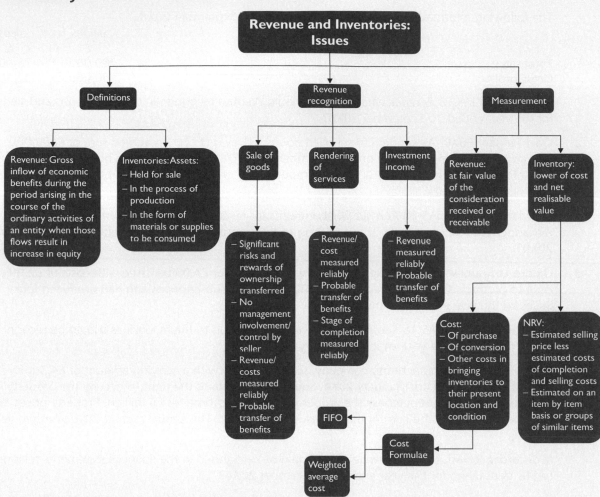

Self-test

Answer the following questions

1   Webber sells two types of product, the sleigh and the sled. Webber sells the sleigh as an agent of Caplin receiving commission of 15% on selling price. Webber sells the sled as principal at a gross margin of 30%.

The following information relates to the year ended 30 September 20X8.

	Sleighs £	Sleds £
Total sales	200,000	75,000
Gross profit	60,000	22,500

According to IAS 18 *Revenue* what revenue should Webber recognise in total for sleighs and sleds for the year ended 30 September 20X8?

2   On 1 January 20X0, Alexander Ltd supplied goods to David Ltd for an agreed sum of £600,000. This amount becomes payable on 31 December 20X2. David Ltd could have bought the goods for cash of £450,000 on 1 January 20X0. The imputed rate of interest to discount the receivable to the cash sales price is 10%.

In accordance with IAS 18 *Revenue* what amounts for revenue and interest income should Alexander Ltd record in profit or loss relating to this transaction for the year ended 31 December 20X0?

3   Oxford Ltd publishes a monthly magazine, which is sold for £4.00 per issue with costs of £2.00 per issue to produce. Oxford Ltd received £48,000 in annual subscriptions and had produced four issues by the year end of 31 January 20X8.

In accordance with IAS 18 *Revenue* what revenue in relation to the magazines should be recognised by Oxford Ltd for the year ended 31 January 20X8?

4   Southwell Ltd, a manufacturing company, sold a property with a carrying amount of £4.5m for £5m to Financier Ltd on 1 January 20X4. Southwell Ltd retains the right to occupy the property and has an option to repurchase the property in two years' time for £6 million. Property prices are expected to rise and the current market value is £8 million. The annual rate for 20% over two years is 9.5%.

In accordance with IAS 18 *Revenue* what should be recognised in the financial statements relating to this transaction for the year ended 31 December 20X4?

5   Space Ltd sells a specialised piece of equipment to Planet Ltd on 1 September 20X7 for £1.5m. Due to the specialised nature of the equipment, Space Ltd has additionally agreed to provide a support service for the next two years. The cost to Space Ltd of providing this service will be £120,000. Space Ltd usually earns a gross margin of 20% on such contracts.

What revenue should be included in the statement of profit or loss of Space Ltd for the year ended 31 December 20X7 according to IAS 18 *Revenue*?

6   Major Ltd has entered into a contract for the provision of services over a two-year period. The total contract price is £150,000. In the first year costs of £60,000 have been incurred and 50% of the work has been completed. The contract has not progressed as expected and Major Ltd is not sure of the ultimate outcome, but believes that the costs incurred to date will be recovered from the customer. Major Ltd initially expected to earn a profit of £20,000 on the contract.

According to IAS 18 *Revenue* what revenue should be recognised in the first year of the contract?

7   White Goods Ltd sells an electrical appliance for £2,400 on 1 October 20X7 making a mark up on cost of 20%. The customer is given a one-year interest-free credit period. White Goods Ltd has a cost of capital of 9%.

In accordance with IAS 18 *Revenue*, what amount should the company recognise as revenue from the sale of the appliance in profit or loss for the year ended 31 December 20X7?

8   Taunton plc manufactures spare parts for a range of agricultural equipment. These are sent from its UK factory to its various distribution centres in the United Kingdom and Eire.

According to IAS 2 *Inventories*, which of the following expenses should be included as part of the cost of finished goods inventories?

(1) Rectification costs of a lorry-load of parts that were badly damaged in an accident en route to one of the UK distribution centres.

(2) Expenses paid to the firm's lorry-drivers for transporting parts from the distribution centres to customers.

(3) Shipping costs for drivers and lorries to the Eire distribution centre.

(4) Subsistence and accommodation expenses relating to the return journey from Eire.

9   Quick Ltd absorbs its production overheads on the basis of units produced. Cost data relating to units of production for the year to 31 December 20X3 are as follows.

Material (for 10,000 units actually produced)	£10,000
Sub-contract labour	£20,000
Fixed production overheads	£50,000

There are 1,000 units in inventories at the year end. Production was half the normal activity level.

In accordance with IAS 2 *Inventories* what should be the figure for inventories in the statement of financial position on 31 December 20X3?

10 The normal selling price of an item included in year end inventories is £21 per unit. The item originally cost £15 per unit, but could only be sold at the normal selling price after modifications were made after the year end at a cost of £5 per unit. The scrap value of the item is £11 per unit.

Under IAS 2 *Inventories* at what amount should the item be included in the financial statements?

11 Hunt Ltd has prepared the following schedule in respect of two items held in inventory.

	Purchase price of raw materials £	Attributable production overheads incurred £	Attributable distribution overheads to be incurred £	Expected selling price £
Item X	80	10	12	85
Item Z	20	5	10	40
	100	15	22	125

According to IAS 2 *Inventories* what is the aggregate amount at which inventories of these items should be stated in the statement of financial position of Hunt Ltd?

12 Greenmore Ltd is making a product for a customer. The cost to date is £35,000. Owing to a change in government regulations an additional £12,000 will need to be spent before the product can be sold. The customer agrees to pay half of this. The initially agreed selling price was £40,000.

At what amount should inventories be carried in the financial statements of Greenmore Ltd according to IAS 2 *Inventories*?

13 PARSON PLC

Parson plc has entered into the following transactions during the year ended 31 December 20X3.

(1) On 1 October 20X3 Parson plc received £400,000 in advance subscriptions. The subscriptions are for 20 monthly issues of a magazine published by Parson plc. Three issues of the magazine had been despatched by the year end. Each magazine is of the same value and costs approximately the same to produce.

(2) A batch of unseasoned timber, which had cost £250,000, was sold to Banko plc for £100,000 on 1 January 20X3. Parson plc has an option to repurchase the timber in 10 years' time. The repurchase price will be £100,000 plus interest charged at 8% per annum from 1 January 20X3 to the date of repurchase. The market value of the timber is expected to increase as it seasons.

(3) Parson plc made a major sale on 1 January 20X3 for a fee of £450,000, which related to a completed sale and after-sales support for three years. The cost of providing the after-sales support is estimated at £50,000 per annum, and the mark-up on similar after-sales only contracts is 20% on cost.

(4) The food division of Parson plc operates its retail outlets on a franchise basis. On 1 January 20X3 a new outlet was opened, the franchisee paying a fee of £500,000 to cover the initial services. The franchise is for five years, and the franchisee will pay an additional annual fee of £60,000 commencing on 1 January 20X3 to cover marketing, managerial and other support services provided by Parson plc during the franchise period. Parson plc has estimated that the cost of providing these services is £80,000 per annum, and has achieved a gross margin of 20% on providing similar services on other contracts.

Requirements

(a) Prepare extracts from Parson plc's financial statements for the year ended 31 December 20X3, clearly showing how each of the above would be reflected. Notes to the financial statements are not required. **(10 marks)**

(b) With reference to transaction (2) above explain the concept of 'substance over form'.**(4 marks)**

(14 marks)

14 SCRAMJET

Scramjet is a UK-based airline which has traditionally operated in the low cost sector, but which is trying to attract a greater proportion of business travellers.

The airline sells tickets in different booking classes, each of which has a different set of booking conditions concerning changes, refunds, and so on.

The further in advance flights are paid for and the more restrictive the booking conditions (such as not allowing changes or refunds in any circumstances), the less the flights cost.

At the company's year end of 31 December 20X6, there are a large number of passengers who have paid in advance for their flights. A sample of three passengers below illustrates some of the booking conditions.

Barbara booked flights to and from Reus for travel in August 20X7 in booking class N. This is the most restrictive booking class and does not allow any refunds or changes whatever. If Barbara misses her flight, Scramjet will not provide any refund or move her booking to another flight. On 1 November 20X6, Barbara booked a flight out to Reus and one back a week later, each at a sales price of £40.

On 1 December 20X6, Denise booked a one-way flight to Paris in booking class Y, at a price of £150. This is the most flexible booking class and allows Denise to take any flight operated by Scramjet to Paris within six months of the booking being made. At the year-end, Denise had not used her one-way ticket.

On 7 August 20X6, Dave booked two flights for the new year holiday from Stansted to Prague. The outward flight was on 28 December 20X6 and the return flight was on 3 January 20X7. His tickets are in booking class N (see above for restrictions). He paid £70 for the flight in each direction, so that Scramjet has received £140 from him by its year-end.

Requirement

Applying IAS 18, explain how each of the above transactions should be reported in the financial statements of Scramjet at 31 December 20X6. State any criticisms you may have of the accounting treatment that IAS 18 requires. **(6 marks)**

15 AIRPHONE

Airphone is a mobile phone company that offers a package price of £800 for a portable email and data service, comprising the following separable components:

	Fair value £
Handset	300
One year's subscription to the network	100
120 free megabytes of data transfer per month for one year – see below	600
Total fair value of individual components of package	1,000

Payment is due in full upon signing the contract.

The promotion offers 120 free megabytes (MB) of data transfer per month with unused MB each month being rolled over to the following month. Analysis of similar past promotions shows that on average subscribers use only 1,200 MB over the year with 400 MB used evenly over the first six months and 800 MB used evenly over the second six months. The fair value of the data transfer is estimated from past experience as £0.50 per MB of data.

Requirement

Assuming that a customer signs up for the package above on 1 December 20X6, explain, with supporting calculations how this transaction should be reflected in Airphone's financial statements to 31 December 20X6.

(6 marks)

16 **LATENTILE LTD**

Latentile Ltd is a newly-formed company, which uses a chemical process to manufacture a revolutionary new roof covering, which it sells at a mark up of 25% on cost. Its inventories consist of raw material, work in progress and finished goods, and at the end of its first year of trading it is having problems valuing inventories.

You ascertain the following information.

(1) **Raw material**

(i) The process needs at least 100,000 kgs of clay to continue working, but a physical inventory count reveals that the machinery contains 108,000 kgs.

(ii) The original cost of the initial 100,000 kgs to set up the process was 30p per kg and you find an invoice to show that the last consignment of 20,000 kgs cost 31p per kg. All other consignments in the year (a total of 200,000 kgs) cost 32p per kg.

(2) **Work in progress**

(i) The work in progress is currently all 60% complete and you discover that there are 50,000 units currently going through the process.

(ii) The total number of complete units for the period was, as anticipated, 800,000.

(iii) The costs for the process for the period were as follows.

	£'000
Raw materials	200
Direct labour	242
Factory overheads	191
Administrative expenses attributable to production	114
Distribution costs	90

(3) **Finished goods**

(i) There were 70,000 units in inventories.

(ii) Of (i) above, it was intended to sell 20,000 units at 75p per unit, a discount of one third on normal selling price, in a future promotional campaign (a further 10p per unit distribution cost is to be incurred).

Requirements

(a) Explain how IAS 2 *Inventories* applies the accrual and the going concern bases of accounting.

(4 marks)

(b) For each of the above categories of inventory, suggest a method of valuation and show the value as it would appear in the statement of financial position.

(6 marks)

(c) If the information regarding costs for the period were not available, suggest an alternative method of valuing finished goods.

(2 marks)

(12 marks)

Now, go back to the Learning objectives in the Introduction. If you are satisfied you have achieved these objectives, please tick them off.

Technical reference

Point to note: The following sets out the examinability of the standards covered in this chapter.

IAS 18	All paragraphs examinable except examples 9, 10, 13 & 14 in the Appendix.
IAS 2	All paragraphs examinable.

The paragraphs listed below are the key references you should be familiar with.

1 IAS 18 *Revenue*

- Revenue recognised when: IAS 18 Objective

  - Probable that future economic benefits will flow to the entity; and
  - These benefits can be measured reliably.

- Apply principle of substance over form.

- Revenue defined as gross inflows that result in increase in equity.   IAS 18 (7)

  - Sales taxes (eg VAT) and amounts collected by agent on behalf of   IAS 18 (8)
    principal are excluded.

- Measured as fair value of consideration – discounted where appropriate.   IAS 18 (9-11)

- Recognition of sale of goods: when buyer has obtained significant   IAS 18 (14)
  risks/rewards of ownership.

- Recognition of rendering of services: can take account of stage of completion,   IAS 18 (20)
  if over a long period:

  - Include pro-rata costs and consider costs to complete;
  - If overall outcome cannot be estimated reliably, revenue limited to costs   IAS 18 (26)
    recoverable from customer.

- Practical considerations, including 'free' servicing, where revenue deferred to   IAS 18 Appendix (all
  cover both cost and reasonable profit.   but 9, 10, 13 and 14)

2 IAS 2 *Inventories*

- Measurement and disclosure, but not recognition.   IAS 2 (1)

- Inventories are to be measured at the lower of cost and net realisable value.   IAS 2 (9)

- Cost = expenditure incurred in bringing the items to their present location   IAS 2 (10)
  and condition, so the cost of purchase and the cost of conversion.

  - Fixed costs included by reference to normal levels of activity.   IAS 2 (13)

- Cost formulae: FIFO or weighted average.   IAS 2 (25)

  - Use same formula for all inventories with similar nature.

- Net realisable value takes costs to complete into account, as well as selling   IAS 2 (6)
  costs.

- Disclosures include accounting policies, carrying amounts and amounts   IAS 2 (36 and 38)
  recognised as an expense.

Answers to Interactive questions

Answer to Interactive question 1

Magazine revenue   £16,000

Explanation

Revenue for the magazines should be recognised in the periods in which they are despatched, assuming the items are of similar value in each period. Thus the revenue to be recognised in the year ended 31 March 20X7 is £48,000 × 4/12 = £16,000.

Answer to Interactive question 2

Revenue   £nil

Explanation

Revenue should be recognised when the drills are delivered to the customer. Until then no revenue should be recognised and the deposits should be carried forward as deferred income.

Answer to Interactive question 3

(a) **Costs to complete are £90,000**

As each of the total revenue, the costs incurred and the costs to complete can be estimated reliably, revenue can be recognised by the percentage of completion method, so 33.3% of £210,000 = £70,000.

Note. The project is profitable overall (total revenue £210,000, total costs £135,000), so no provision for a contract loss need be made.

(b) **Costs to complete cannot be estimated reliably**

As the outcome of the overall contract cannot be estimated reliably, revenue is recognised to the extent of the costs incurred which are recoverable, ie £40,000. The current period therefore recognises the contract loss to date of £5,000.

Answer to Interactive question 4

Contract revenue   £60,000

Explanation

If the outcome of a services transaction cannot be estimated reliably, revenue should only be recognised to the extent that expenses incurred are recoverable from the customer.

Answer to Interactive question 5

	£
Revenue – sale of goods (W)	1,350,000
– sale of services (W)	25,000
Total	1,375,000

WORKING

	£
After-sale support (120,000/(100% – 20%))	150,000
Remainder = sale of goods (bal fig)	1,350,000
Total revenue	1,500,000

Revenue for sale of services recognised in the four months to 30 April 20X7 should be £150,000/2 years × 4/12 = £25,000

Answer to Interactive question 6

- In substance, this is a secured loan; no revenue should be recognised in profit or loss.

- Through the rights of access and supervision, together with the right to build on the land, Builder Ltd has retained the risks and rewards of ownership over the building plot, so should continue to show it as an asset in its statement of financial position.

- The fact that the consideration for the sale on 1 March 20X6 is so far below the valuation is further evidence that the transaction is in substance a two-year loan, with the £400,000 difference between the selling and repurchase prices being interest on the loan.

- The right to repurchase in the future for much less than the current valuation (making the exercise of the repurchase right almost a certainty) is further evidence that this is not a real sale.

- So Builder Ltd will show the building plot in its 28 February 20X7 statement of financial position as a current asset (as it will be realised in the normal course of its operating cycle) at its original acquisition cost (not given in the Interactive Question).

- In the same statement of financial position it will show the £1.5m received on 1 March 20X6 as a current liability (as it will be settled in the normal course of its operating cycle – the fact that it is repayable more than 12 months after the end of the reporting period is not relevant), together with any unpaid part of the £400,000 interest which is attributable to the first year of the loan.

- The appropriate part of the total interest will be charged to profit or loss for the year ended 28 February 20X7.

Answer to Interactive question 7

	£
After-sales support (2 × (35,000/82.5%))	84,848
Remainder	715,152
Total selling price	800,000
So the revenue from the sale in the current year is	715,152

This allocation is in line with IAS 18 Appendix paragraph 11.

Answer to Interactive question 8

	Include in cost of inventories	Recognised as an expense as incurred
Supplier's gross price for raw materials	Yes	
Quantity discounts allowed by supplier	Yes	
Purchase taxes and duties charged by supplier and recoverable from taxing authorities	n/a, because recoverable	n/a, because recoverable
Costs of transporting materials to the business' premises	Yes	
Labour costs directly incurred in the processing of raw materials	Yes	
Variable costs, such as power, incurred in the processing of raw materials	Yes	
Fixed production costs/overheads, such as rent for the processing factory and depreciation charges on the plant used in the processing	Yes, but see commentary in text	
Costs of holding finished goods in inventory		Yes
Costs of transporting goods to customer on sale		Yes
Purchase taxes charged to customer on sale		No, assuming they are recoverable

	Include in cost of inventories	Recognised as an expense as incurred
Commission payable to salesmen on sale of the goods		Yes
Allowance for bad and doubtful debts in relation to trade receivables		Yes
Costs of accounts department		Yes
Head office costs relating to the overall management of the business		Yes

1

	£
Revenue recognised as agent (£200,000 × 15%)	30,000
Revenue recognised as principal	75,000
Total revenue	105,000

2 At the time of supply, revenue is recognised for the cash sale price of £450,000. Interest will then be accrued until payment is made. For the year ended 31 December 20X0 the interest charge is £450,000 × 10% = £45,000.

3 Revenue for the magazines should be recognised over the period in which the magazines are despatched, provided the items are of similar value in each time period. Thus revenue recognised in the year ended 31 January 20X8 is £48,000 × 4/12 = £16,000.

4 The substance of this transaction is that of a secured loan as Southwell Ltd retain the risks and rewards of ownership and given that property prices are rising, it is highly likely that the repurchase option will be exercised.

Initial loan:	DR Cash £5m	
	CR Loan £5m	
Interest:	DR Interest (Profit or loss) (5m x 9.5%)	£0.475m
	CR Loan	£0.475m

Total loan liability is £5.475m

5 The sale of equipment of £1.5m is recognised immediately.

The provision of the support service is recognised over the period of service: two years.

£120,000/0.80 = £150,000 total value of service contract.

Recognised in current period: £150,000/2 years × 4/12 = £25,000

Total revenue: £1.5m + £0.025m = £1.525m

6 If the outcome cannot be estimated reliably then recognise revenue to the extent that expenses incurred are recoverable. In this case £60,000 can be recognised.

7 The amount receivable discounted to present value = £2,400 × 1/1.09 = £2,202

This is recognised as income on 1 October 20X7. The difference between this and the sale proceeds (2,400 – 2,202 = 198) is treated as interest and will be recognised over the 12-month interest-free credit period.

8 Cost comprises all costs of purchase, conversion and other costs incurred in bringing the inventories to their present location and condition (IAS 2 paragraph 10). Only (3) meets this definition of costs. Abnormal costs such as (1) are effectively excluded by IAS 2 paragraph 16(a).

9

		£
Material	$\dfrac{£10,000}{10,000} =$	1.0
Labour	$\dfrac{£20,000}{10,000} =$	2.0
Overheads*	$\dfrac{£50,000}{(10,000 \div 50\%)} =$	2.5
		£5.5 × 1,000 £5,500

* based on normal production capacity (IAS 2 paragraph 13)

10   Inventories should be measured at the lower of cost and NRV.

Cost = £15

NRV = (21 – 5) = £16

The inventories should be carried at £15 per unit.

11   Inventories should be measured at the lower of cost and NRV.

	Cost £	NRV £	Lower £
Item X	90	73	73
Item Z	25	30	25
Total			98

12   Cost   = £35,000

NRV   = 40,000 – 12,000 costs to complete + 6,000 customer contribution = £34,000

Inventories should therefore be carried at £34,000.

13   PARSON PLC

(a)   **Financial statement extracts**

Statement of financial position as at 31 December 20X3

	£
EQUITY AND LIABILITIES	
Non-current liabilities	
Borrowings (100,000 + 8,000)	108,000
Deferred income (W2)	280,000
Current liabilities	
Deferred income (W2)	340,000

Statement of profit or loss for the year ended 31 December 20X3

	£
Revenue (W1)	790,000
Finance cost (8% × 100,000)	8,000

(b)   **Transaction (2) and substance over form**

In a straightforward transaction its commercial effect is the same as its legal form. However, in more complex transactions the true substance of the transaction may be different from its legal form, with one party having the risks and rewards of ownership but another party having legal title to the asset.

In such circumstances recording the legal form of the transaction would not be sufficient to provide a fair presentation in the financial statements

This transaction appears unusual as the initial sale is below fair value, which raises questions about its substance. Parson plc has a call option significantly below the current fair value which is expected to increase over time. The terms of the transaction are that it is almost certain that the timber will be reacquired, hence this is essentially a sale and repurchase agreement.

Parson plc has retained the risks and rewards of ownership, even though legal title has passed. The transaction is effectively a financing agreement secured on the timber, and does not give rise to revenue. The proceeds of £100,000 are therefore recognised as borrowings in non-current liabilities. In the year to 31 December 20X3 Parson plc should recognise a finance cost of £8,000 (8% of £100,000) which will increase the borrowings.

WORKINGS

(1) **Revenue**

	£
Transaction (1) (3/20 × 400,000)	60,000
Transaction (3)	
Sale (450,000 − (50,000 × 120% × 3))	270,000
After-sales support Year 1 (50,000 × 120%)	60,000
Transaction (4)	
Initial fee (500,000 − (40,000 (W2) × 5))	300,000
Continuing fee Year 1 (80,000 × 100/80)	100,000
	790,000

(2) **Deferred income**

	Current £	Non-current £
Transaction (1) (400,000 × 12/20, 5/20)	240,000	100,000
Transaction (3) (50,000 × 120% for Years 2 and 3)	60,000	60,000
Transaction (4) (100,000 − 60,000 for Years 2 to 5)	40,000	120,000
	340,000	280,000

14 SCRAMJET

IAS 18 requires that revenue from rendering of services is recognised by reference to the stage of completion of the transaction at the end of the reporting period. IAS 18 takes an approach which is focused on the statement of profit or loss rather than the statement of financial position. This means that Scramjet may have taken bookings which are entirely non-refundable but the revenue associated with payments for tickets should be held in the statement of financial position as deferred income until either the flight is taken or the ticket expires.

Barbara

Barbara's flight resulted in Scramjet receiving £80 in November 20X6, which it will be entitled to keep without any further conditions. Both outbound and return flights are after the year-end date and so all this £80 should be recognised as deferred revenue in the statement of financial position, rather than as revenue in the year to 31 December 20X6.

Denise

Denise's flight has also not been taken at the year-end and so the £150 received should also be recognised as deferred income in the statement of financial position at 31 December 20X6. The Framework principles for income and asset recognition would also give this same conclusion since Scramjet is not yet unconditionally entitled to the income as it may need to refund the flexible ticket.

Dave

Under IAS 18 revenue for the outbound flight should be recognised as that part of the service has been completed. £70 should thus be recognised in profit or loss and £70 should remain in the statement of financial position as deferred income until Dave's flight back is completed.

15 AIRPHONE

Revenue from the sale of the handset should be recognised when the risks and rewards of ownership pass to the buyer, which will normally be on delivery to the customer.

Access to the network (subscription) and free data transfer represent the rendering of services; the subscription should normally be recognised on a straight-line basis and the free data transfer should be recognised based on past experience as set out in the question.

The bundled package represents a £200 discount (£1,000 total fair value of the individual components less package price of £800). In the absence of any specific discounting strategy, a reasonable basis is to recognise the £200 discount on a pro rata basis.

	Fair value £	%	Discount £	Revenue £
Handset	300	30	60	240
Subscription	100	10	20	80
Free data	600	60	120	480
Total	1,000	100	200	800

The revenue per MB attributable to free data transfer should be calculated by reference to the expected take-up of 1,200 MB, not the contractually allowed take-up of 1,440 MB. The amount is £0.40 per MB (£480/1,200 MB).

The total revenue recognised in the current year for this contract should be:

	£
Handset	240.00
Subscription (£80/12)	6.67
Free data transfer (£0.40 × (400/6))	26.67
	273.34

The balance of £526.66 should be recognised as a current liability in the statement of financial position (deferred income).

16 **LATENTILE LTD**

(a) **IAS 2**

Accrual basis of accounting

The cost of unsold or unconsumed inventories is incurred in the expectation of future economic benefits. When such benefits will not arise until a subsequent accounting period, the related costs should be carried forward and matched with the revenue when it arises. The recognition of year-end inventories achieves this carry forward.

Going concern basis of accounting

The very act of recognising closing inventories as assets implies that the business intends to continue in operational existence for the foreseeable future.

If the business did not intend to continue trading, its inventories would have to be written off as an item of expenditure during the period, unless there was clear evidence that they could be sold as part of the breaking up of the business. In this case, the selling price should be determined and inventories measured at the lower of cost and net realisable value in the usual way.

(b) **Suggested methods of valuing inventories**

Given the limited information the following methods would be appropriate in the circumstances.

Raw material

IAS 2 allows either a first in, first out (FIFO) formula or a weighted average cost (WAC) formula.

Given the fact that clay is presumably continually added to the machinery, WAC would seem the most appropriate basis.

	£
100,000 kgs @ 30p	30,000
200,000 kgs @ 32p	64,000
20,000 kgs @ 31p	6,200
320,000	100,200

= 31.3p per kg

Closing raw materials would therefore be measured at £33,804 (108,000 × 31.3p).

Work in progress

This could be measured using a weighted average cost, given that total cost and total output are known.

Total output (800,000 + (60% × 50,000))	830,000 units
Total costs (excluding distribution costs)	£747,000

Thus average cost per unit $\dfrac{£747,000}{830,000}$ = 90p

Carrying amount of WIP (50,000 × 60% × 90p)	£27,000

Finished goods

Again, a weighted cost could be used of 90p per unit. This would be applicable to 50,000 units, with the remaining 20,000 units being measured at net realisable value of 65p (75p – 10p).

	£
50,000 at 90p	45,000
20,000 at 65p	13,000
	58,000

Thus inventories would appear as follows.

	£
Raw material	33,804
Work in progress	27,000
Finished goods	58,000
	118,804

(c) **Alternative valuation method for finished goods**

If details regarding total costs were not known, adjusted selling price could be used since the cost structure is known.

	p
Normal selling price (75p discounted price × 3/2)	112.5
Less gross profit (112.5 × 25/125)	(22.5)
Cost re 50,000	90.0

Thus finished goods inventories would be measured as before.

IAS 2 allows the above practice, used by the retail industry, on the basis that the result can be a very close approximation to cost.

CHAPTER 7

Leases

Introduction

Examination context

Topic List

Summary and Self-test

Technical reference

Answers to Interactive questions

Answers to Self-test

Learning objectives

Tick off

- Understand the purpose and principles underlying IAS 17 *Leases*

- Classify leases as finance or operating and explain the classification

- Apply accounting requirements for:

    - Finance leases, including initial recognition, allocation of finance charges and presentation and disclosure

    - Operating leases, including disclosures and incentives

    - Sale and leaseback transactions

- Identify and consider appropriate actions for ethical issues involving leasing

- Identify and illustrate the main differences between International and UK requirements in relation to leases

Specific syllabus references for this chapter are: 2b, 2c, 2d, 2e.

Syllabus links

In the Accounting paper, you covered the purchase of non-current assets and the relevant entries in the statement of financial position. You will have also dealt with renting such assets and the relevant entries to the statement of profit or loss.

As you will see, many of these accounting entries will be relevant as you go on to consider finance leases and operating leases in this paper.

In Financial Accounting and Reporting you are only expected to be familiar with the accounting treatment of leases from the lessee's point of view (ie the user of the asset).

Sale and leaseback arrangements are also covered in this syllabus.

Lease accounting also raises the issue of substance over form which you will encounter in various contexts in this paper and at the Advanced Stage.

Examination context

In the examination, candidates may be required to:

- Explain and apply the principle of substance over form

- Prepare and present financial statements or extracts therefrom in accordance with IAS 17 *Leases*

- Explain the accounting treatment of lessee accounting including sale and leaseback transactions and prepare relevant financial statement extracts

- Explain and illustrate the differences between relevant treatment under IFRS and UK GAAP

- Identify and explain the judgements to be made relating to the classification and treatment of leases and sale and leaseback transactions

- Identify and explain any ethical issues

1 Obtaining non-current assets

> **Section overview**
>
> - Certain types of contracts where a company leases an asset from another company are very similar in substance to the outright purchase of that asset.
>
> - If these leases are accounted for in accordance with their strict legal form, a company's assets and liabilities are likely to be understated.
>
> - Failing to record the true substance of the transaction is an example of 'off-balance sheet' financing.
>
> - IAS 17 *Leases* states that the substance of the transaction takes precedence over the legal form even if the legal title never passes from lessor to lessee.

1.1 Using assets

There are many different ways of gaining use of an asset: for example, you can buy a car or hire it. In both cases, you are able to drive the car, but your rights over the car differ in each case.

As far as this chapter is concerned in effect you have two choices.

Buy the asset	Simply, you pay to own the asset, in order to access the benefits it can give you.
	• You are legally the owner of the asset (ie you have legal title).
	• You can do what you like with it, and you get all the risks and rewards of owning the asset.
	In the financial statements, the asset will be treated as a non-current asset. For relevant accounting issues, see Chapter 4.
	Of course, the company might pay for the asset a couple of months later, on standard credit terms. This is then a simple credit purchase.
Hire or lease the asset	If you hire or lease an asset, you are paying someone else for the use of that asset. It is the owner's property, but you are getting the benefits from using it. (In a hire purchase agreement, ownership only transfers to you once you have paid for it, and this is typically over a long period.)
	The accounting treatment depends on the circumstances:
	• Say a company hires a car for one of its staff for a couple of days; the car is not an asset of the company, it is just being hired for a couple of days, and the owner retains the benefit of owning the car (eg to hire it out to other people) over the rest of the asset's useful life.
	• However, a company might lease the car for a guaranteed period of three years or so, and has sole use of it, be responsible for maintaining it and so on. The company may also be obliged to enter a long-term agreement to pay the supplier. The company might end up owning the car at the end of the period.

The example of a long-term lease above shows that, for practical purposes, the company has acquired the use of a non-current asset, and all the risks and rewards of owning it. The car is being used as if it is a non-current asset, even though, legally speaking, it belongs to a third party. In many ways this is similar to purchasing the asset outright.

1.2 Leasing agreements

As we have said, one way by which businesses can obtain the use of an asset is by a leasing agreement.

Definition

Lease: An agreement whereby the lessor conveys to the lessee in return for a payment or series of payments the right to use an asset for an agreed period of time.

In a leasing transaction, there is a contract between the lessor and the lessee for the hire of an asset.

- The **lessor** is owner and supplier of the asset.
- The **lessee** is the user of the asset.

The lessor retains legal ownership but transfers to the lessee the right to use the asset for an agreed period of time in return for specified payments.

1.3 Substance over form

It is a principle of accounting that the **commercial substance of a transaction** should be reflected in financial statements rather than the legal form. This is a consequence of the IASB *Conceptual Framework* requirement to represent transactions **faithfully**.

There are many types of leasing arrangements. By entering into certain sorts of lease, a company is, in effect, gaining the use of a non-current asset whilst incurring a long-term liability. Where the commercial substance of the transaction is the purchase of a non-current asset, this should be reflected in the accounting treatment despite the legal form of the rental agreement.

IAS 17 gives guidance as to the accounting treatment depending on the terms of the leasing transaction, which are discussed in Section 2.

2 Types of lease

Section overview

- IAS 17 recognises two types of lease:
  - Finance leases, in which the risks and rewards of ownership are transferred from the lessor to the lessee, and
  - Operating leases: all other leases.
- Inception is when the parties become committed to the lease: commencement is when the lessee can use the leased asset (and when the values agreed at inception are recognised in the financial statements).
- For leases of land and buildings, land is normally treated as an operating lease, buildings as a finance lease.

2.1 Classification of a lease

As mentioned above, there are two types of leases.

Definitions

Finance lease: A lease that transfers substantially all the risks and rewards incidental to ownership of an asset. Title may or may not eventually be transferred.

Operating lease: A lease other than a finance lease.

From these definitions you can see that the classification of a lease is based on the extent to which the risks and rewards of ownership lie with the legal owner, the lessor, or are transferred to the user, the lessee.

If a lease transfers **substantially all the risks and rewards** normally associated with the **ownership of an asset** it should be classified as a **finance lease**. **All other leases** should be classified as **operating leases**.

IAS 17 provides the following examples of the key risks and rewards incidental to ownership of an asset.

Risks	Possibility of losses arising from:
	• **Idle capacity**
	• **Technological obsolescence**
	• **Falls in value** due to changing economic conditions
Rewards	Potential gains arising from:
	• **Profitable use of the asset over its economic life**
	• **Future sale of the asset** where it has increased in value

2.2 Identifying finance leases

IAS 17 also provides examples of situations that individually or in combination would normally lead to a lease being classified as a finance lease.

These include the following circumstances where:

• The terms of the lease are such that **ownership of the asset transfers to the lessee by the end of the lease term** eg a hire purchase agreement.

• The lessee has the **option to purchase the asset** at such a price that it is **reasonably certain** from the outset that the option will be exercised.

• The **lease term** is for the **major part of the economic life of the asset** even if legal title is never transferred (see Section 2.5 below).

• At the **inception of the lease the present value of the minimum lease payments amounts to at least substantially all of the fair value of the leased asset** (see Sections 2.3 and 2.4 below).

• The leased assets are of such **a specialised nature** that only the lessee can use them without major modifications.

Other indicators listed by IAS 17 that could **also lead to the lease being classified as a finance lease** are:

• Whether **cancellation losses** are borne by the lessee.

• Whether **fluctuations in fair value at the end of the lease accrue to the lessee**.

• Whether the lessee has the **option to extend the lease for a secondary period at a 'peppercorn rent'** (ie below market rent).

2.3 Present value of the minimum lease payments

A persuasive factor in classifying a lease as a **finance lease** is if at the inception of the lease the **present value** of the **minimum lease payments amounts to at least substantially all of** the **fair value** of the leased asset.

Definition

Minimum lease payments: Payments over the lease term that the lessee is or can be required to make, excluding contingent rent, costs for services and taxes to be paid by and reimbursed to the lessor, together with any amounts guaranteed by the lessee or by a party related to the lessee.

The **minimum lease payments** are what the **lessee** (or a party related to the lessee) **has to make over the life of the lease**. However, as these payments are some time in the future, a **discount factor** is applied to reach a '**present value**' of these amounts, in other words a cash equivalent.

This is then compared to the asset's **fair value**.

Definition

Fair value: The price that would be received to sell an asset or paid to transfer a liability in an orderly transaction between market participants at the measurement date.

Worked example: Fair value

Alpha Ltd agrees to pay Beta Ltd a sum of £1,000 each year for four years, a total of £4,000. Assuming prevailing interest rates at the time of the agreement were 5%, the present value would be £3,546. If the present value at the date of the agreement is more than or 'substantially all' of the fair value then this would indicate a finance lease. Effectively, Alpha Ltd is buying an asset from Beta Ltd, who is providing loan finance.

Point to note: In the examination you will not be expected to calculate the present value of the minimum lease payments. Where relevant the information in the question will include the discounted figure.

Interactive question 1: What type of lease?   [Difficulty level: Easy]

Classify the following situations as finance or operating leases. You will have to do some thinking here.

Question	Fill in your answer
(a) A company leases machine tools. Legal title is transferred after three years.	
(b) A company leases a photocopier. The present value of minimum lease payments is £2,000 but the fair value of the asset is £10,000.	
(c) A company leases a car for a sales representative for a five-year period, after which the car will have come to the end of its useful economic life.	
(d) A company acquires some equipment made bespoke to its specifications. To sell the equipment to a third party would require substantial modification.	

See **Answer** at the end of this chapter.

2.4   When does a lease actually begin?

A lease should be classified as operating or finance at **inception**.

There is a difference between **commencement** and **inception**.

Definition

Inception: This is when the terms of the lease, including the financial settlement, are agreed (which may be the contract signing date or, if earlier, the date when the main terms were agreed).

For example, a company might agree to lease equipment, with agreed payments every year. However, it may be some time before the company uses the equipment – especially if it is new.

At inception:

- The lease is classified as a finance or operating lease
- The values, in the case of a finance lease, are determined

Definition

Commencement: This is the date when the lessee can **use** the leased asset. For example, a company leasing a building may move in several months after the lease contract was agreed. The commencement date is also the date when the values determined at inception are recognised in the financial statements.

In many cases, the dates are not far apart. Remember, however, that the **value** of the leased **asset** and consequent **liability** shown in the financial statements are normally those at the **inception** of the lease.

2.5 The lease term

Once classified, the classification should remain throughout the lease term.

In a leasing transaction, the **lease term** is the length of the agreement between lessor and lessee.

Definition

Lease term: The non-cancellable period for which the lessee has contracted to lease the asset together with any further terms for which the lessee has the option to continue to lease the asset, with or without further payment, when at the inception of the lease it is reasonably certain that the lessee will exercise the option.

With a finance lease the lease term might be divided into two periods.

Primary period	During the **primary period** the lease will either be non-cancellable or will be cancellable only under certain conditions, for example on the payment of a heavy settlement figure.
	The **rentals** payable during the primary period will be sufficient to **repay to the lessor** the cost of the equipment plus interest thereon.
Secondary period	The **secondary period** is usually cancellable at any time at the lessee's option.
	The **rentals** during the secondary period will be of a **nominal amount**. (Sometimes referred to as a 'peppercorn rent'.)
	If the lessee wishes to **terminate the lease** during the **secondary** period, the equipment will be sold and substantially all of the sale proceeds will be paid to the **lessee** as a rebate of rentals.

3 Accounting for finance leases

Section overview

- In the statement of financial position, assets held under finance leases are treated as non-current assets and payables or finance lease liabilities.
- The asset is depreciated and otherwise treated as any other non-current asset.
- Lease payments reduce the liability and cover any accrued interest.
- The lessee has to allocate the finance charge between accounting periods.
- The finance charge is recognised in profit or loss.

3.1 Setting up accounts in the statement of financial position

IAS 17 requires that, when an asset changes hands under a **finance lease**, the accounting treatment should reflect the **substance of the transaction**. In the lessee's books therefore:

DR	Asset account	The amount to be recorded in this way is the lower of the fair value and the present value of the minimum lease payments at the inception of the lease
CR	Payables: Finance lease liabilities	

The **initial** deposit, if any, counts as one of the lease payments and hence is included in the cost of the asset.

Points to note

1   The entries are made at the **commencement** of the lease term, with the **values** determined at **inception** (see Section 2.4 above).

2   The present value of the minimum lease payments is derived by discounting them at the **interest rate implicit in the lease**. If it is not practicable to determine the interest rate implied in the lease, then the lessee's **incremental borrowing rate** can be used.

3   Initial direct costs can be treated as part of the cost of the asset – provided they are directly attributable to activities performed by the lessee to obtain the finance lease.

4   Although interest is payable under the lease, this is accrued over time. The justification is that the capital could, in theory, be paid off at any time, with cancellation charges. These charges could be avoided, so they are not a 'true' long term liability. **Interest is therefore recognised as it accrues**.

3.2 Depreciating the asset

DR	Depreciation expense	The asset should be depreciated over the shorter of the lease term or the asset's useful life
CR	Accumulated depreciation	

Points to note

1   Depreciation policies adopted should be consistent with other non-current assets.

2   As with other non-current assets, impairment reviews must be conducted in accordance with IAS 36 *Impairment of Assets*.

3   If there is reasonable certainty that the lessee will eventually own the asset, then it should be depreciated over its estimated useful life.

4   The lease term comprises the period for which the lessee has contracted to lease the asset and any further terms for which there is reasonable certainty at the inception of the lease that the lessee will exercise the option. (See Section 2.5.)

3.3 Making the payment

Every period, the payments are accounted for as follows.

DR	Payables: Finance lease liabilities	Each lease payment is comprised partly of a repayment of capital and partly of an interest charge for the period. (See Section 3.4 below.)
CR	Cash	

3.4 Finance charge

The finance charge is dealt with as follows.

DR	Profit or loss: Finance cost	With the amount of the interest accrued over the period
CR	Payables: Finance lease liabilities	

4 Allocating and calculating finance charges

Section overview

The finance charge is calculated and allocated to accounting periods using the actuarial method.

4.1 How much interest is payable in total?

This is relatively easy to calculate.

	£
Total lease payments	X
Less initial cost of asset (as calculated in Section 3.1)	(X)
Total finance charge (= interest)	X

The finance charge is allocated to profit or loss over the period for which the finance is provided, from the commencement of the lease term until the last payment is made. (If payments are made in advance, the last payment might be made before the end of the lease term.)

4.2 Allocating the interest charge to accounting periods

IAS 17 requires the total finance charge to be allocated to each period during the lease term so as to produce a **constant periodic rate of interest** on the outstanding lease obligation.

As the lessee pays off the capital sum, the total capital owed falls from period to period. You would therefore also expect a reduction in the total interest payable, too, on the outstanding balance.

For example, if you owe £10,000 and pay 15%, the interest will be £1,500. After you have paid off, say, £8,000 of the capital, interest would be £300 (on £2,000). The monthly payments remain the same, but the mix of interest and capital changes over the life of the loan.

There are three possible methods of allocating the interest.

Actuarial method	Interest is charged at a constant percentage on the outstanding liability, thus matching interest to the 'loan' balance.
	This method is specified by IAS 17, as it is the most accurate. However, to apply it, the rate of interest implicit in the lease is required.
'Sum of digits' method	This method is a 'reasonable' approximation to the actuarial method where the implicit rate of interest is not known.
	The **sum of digits** method splits the total interest (without reference to a rate of interest) in such a way that the greater proportion falls in the earlier years. The procedure is as follows.
	(a) Assign a digit to each instalment. The digit 1 should be assigned to the final instalment, 2 to the penultimate instalment and so on.
	(b) Add the digits. A quick method of adding the digits is to use the formula $\frac{n(n+1)}{2}$ where n is the number of periods of borrowing. If there are 12 instalments paid in arrears, then the sum of the digits will be 78. For this reason, the sum of the digits method is sometimes called the **rule of 78**.
	(c) Calculate the interest charge included in each instalment. Do this by multiplying the total interest accruing over the lease term by the fraction: $$\frac{\text{Digit applicable to the instalment}}{\text{Sum of the digits}}$$
Straight line method	A constant amount of interest is charged each period, hence interest does not match the amount outstanding of the loan. Therefore this method is not normally allowed, except where the amounts involved are immaterial.

Worked example: Rentals in arrears

A Ltd has a year end of 31 December.

A finance lease commences on 1 January 20X1. Lease payments comprise three payments of £10,000 annually, commencing on 31 December 20X1. The asset would have cost £24,869 to buy outright.

The implicit interest rate is 10%.

You are required to calculate the interest charge and the year-end liability for each year of the lease under:

(a) Straight line method
(b) Actuarial method
(c) Sum of digits method

Solution

Total finance charges to be allocated:

	£
Total lease payments	30,000
Less initial cost of asset	(24,869)
Total finance charge (interest)	5,131

(a) **Straight line method**

Allocation of interest to periods:

$$20X1 - 20X3 = \frac{5,131}{3} = 1,710$$

Lease liability

	CR Balance b/f 1 Jan £	CR Interest accrued 31 Dec £	DR Payment 31 Dec £	CR Balance c/f 31 Dec £
20X1	24,869	1,710	(10,000)	16,579
20X2	16,579	1,710	(10,000)	8,289
20X3	8,289	1,711	(10,000)	–
		5,131	30,000	

(b) **Actuarial method**

Lease liability

	CR Balance b/f 1 Jan £	CR Interest accrued @10% 31 Dec £	DR Payment 31 Dec £	CR Balance c/f 31 Dec £
20X1	24,869	2,487	(10,000)	17,356
20X2	17,356	1,736	(10,000)	9,092
20X3	9,092	908	(10,000)	–
		5,131	30,000	

(c) **Sum of digits method**

Each period of borrowing is allocated a digit as follows:

Period of borrowing	Digit
1st (20X1)	3
2nd (20X2)	2
3rd (20X3)	1
	6

Or using the formula $\dfrac{3 \times 4}{2} = 6$

Point to note

In this example, as the instalments are paid in **arrears** the number of periods of borrowing (n in the formula) are **equal** to the number of instalments.

The £5,131 interest charges can then be apportioned

		£
1st period of borrowing	£5,131 × 3/6	2,566
2nd period of borrowing	£5,131 × 2/6	1,710
3rd period of borrowing	£5,131 × 1/6	855
		5,131

	CR Balance b/f 1 Jan £	*Lease liability* CR Interest accrued 31 Dec £	DR Payment 31 Dec £	CR Capital balance c/f 31 Dec £
20X1	24,869	2,566	(10,000)	17,435
20X2	17,435	1,710	(10,000)	9,145
20X3	9,145	855	(10,000)	–
		5,131	30,000	

Point to note: The year-end liability for 20X1 is £17,435. This balance is **all capital**. Any interest which has accrued during the year has been **settled** by the first instalment because the instalment was paid on the last day of the year.

Point to note: In your exam only the **actuarial method** will be tested as this is the most accurate method and the method that companies use in practice.

4.3 Instalments in advance

As we have seen in the examples above, interest accrues over time and is included in the payment at the end of each period of borrowing. However, where instalments are **paid in advance**:

* The first instalment **repays capital only** as no time has yet elapsed for interest to accrue.

* At the end of each accounting period the year-end liability will include **capital and interest** that has accrued to date but which has not been paid.

Worked example: Rentals in advance

A Ltd has a year end of 31 December.

A finance lease commences 1 January 20X1. Lease payments comprise four payments of £10,000 annually, commencing on 1 January 20X1. The asset would have cost £34,869 to buy outright.

The interest rate implicit in the lease is 10%.

Requirements

Calculate the lease interest charge for each year of the lease using the actuarial method.

Also calculate the year end liability for each year of the lease.

Solution

Point to note:

The last payment is made on 1.1.X4. This is **three** years after the start of the lease. Therefore the 'loan' is in existence for three years and interest is charged over this period, ie in the statement of profit or loss for 20X1, 20X2 and 20X3.

	CR Balance b/f 1 Jan	DR Payment 1 Jan	*Lease liability* CR Capital balance remaining 1 Jan	CR Interest accrued @ 10% 31 Dec	CR Balance c/f 31 Dec
	£	£	£	£	£
20X1	34,869	(10,000)	24,869	2,487	27,356
20X2	27,356	(10,000)	17,356	1,736	19,092
20X3	19,092	(10,000)	9,092	908	10,000
20X4	10,000	(10,000)	–	–	–
		40,000		5,131	

Points to note

1   As the first instalment is paid on 1 January 20X1 it is purely a repayment of capital **as no time has passed for interest to accrue**.

2   The year-end liability is made up of the **capital outstanding plus any interest accrued to date**.

3   The payment of £10,000 on 1 January 20X2 will pay the **interest accrued in 20X1 (£2,487)** with the balance repaying capital.

5   Disclosure

Section overview

The key disclosures in the statement of financial position are:

* The split and analysis of the finance lease liability.
* The carrying amount of non-current assets held under finance leases.

5.1   Finance lease liability

The liability at each reporting date needs to be split between:

* The **current liability**
* The **non-current liability**

Point to note

The non-current liability will comprise only capital outstanding. No interest will be included as any interest due at the end of the next year will not yet have accrued.

The steps to split the liability are therefore:

Step 1
Identify the capital balance remaining in **one year's time**. (This can be found in the lease calculation table.)

Step 2
Deduct the capital balance remaining in one year's time from the total liability at the end of the reporting period. This will give the amount due within one year as **a balancing figure**.

Interactive question 2: Rentals in arrears [Difficulty level: Exam standard]

(a) Using the facts from the Worked example: Rentals in arrears, part (b), show the split of the lease liability at the end of 20X1.

Fill in the gaps in the extract below.

The lease liability extract from the Worked example: Rentals in arrears, part (b) is as follows:

	Lease liability			
	CR *Balance* *b/f* *1 Jan*	*CR* *Interest* *accrued* *@10%* *31 Dec*	*DR* *Payment* *31 Dec*	*CR* *Capital* *balance* *c/f* *31 Dec*
	£	*£*	*£*	*£*
20X1 (current period)	24,869	2,487	(10,000)	17,356
20X2 (future periods)	17,356	1,736	(10,000)	9,092

Total lease liability at 31 December 20X1 = £ ☐

Capital > 1 year = £ ☐   < 1 year (β) = £ ☐

(b) Prepare journals to show accounting entries in respect of the lease during 20X1.

See **Answer** at the end of this chapter.

Interactive question 3: Rentals in advance [Difficulty level: Exam standard]

Requirement

(a) Using the facts from the Worked example: Rentals in advance, show the split of the lease liability at the end of 20X1.

Fill in the gaps in the extract below.

The lease liability extract from the Worked example: Rentals in advance is as follows:

	Lease liability				
	CR *Balance* *b/f* *1 Jan*	*DR* *Payment* *1 Jan*	*CR* *Capital* *balance* *remaining* *1 Jan*	*CR* *Interest* *accrued* *@10%* *31 Dec*	*CR* *Balance* *c/f* *31 Dec*
	£	*£*	*£*	*£*	*£*
20X1 (current period)	34,869	(10,000)	24,869	2,487	27,356
20X2 (future periods)	27,356	(10,000)	17,356	1,736	19,092

Total lease liability at 31 December 20X1 = £ ☐

Capital > 1 year = £ ☐   < 1 year (β) = £ ☐

(b) Prepare journals to show accounting entries in respect of the lease during 20X1.

See **Answer** at the end of this chapter.

5.2 Other disclosures

Point to note

The leased assets and lease liabilities may not be netted off against each other.

Non-current assets

- Disclosure must be made of the carrying amount of assets held under finance leases as follows:

  'Of the total carrying amount of £X, £Y relates to assets held under finance leases.'

- All other IAS 16 *Property, Plant and Equipment* disclosures are required, together with IAS 36 impairment tests (both dealt with in Chapter 4).

Liabilities

- Finance lease liabilities must be **split** between their **current and non-current components** (as we saw in Section 5.1).

- IAS 17 also requires disclosure of future lease payments, split between amounts due:

  - Within one year
  - Within two to five years
  - After more than five years

This disclosure can be given **either**:

- On a **gross basis**, ie showing gross future lease payments for each of the three categories, then deducting as a single figure the future periods' finance charges to arrive at the net figure included in liabilities.

- On a **net basis**, ie excluding from each of the three categories the finance charges allocated to future periods (and hence not yet accrued).

Interactive question 4: Disclosure
[Difficulty level: Exam standard]

The facts are as detailed in Interactive question 4.

Requirement

Show the disclosure of the analysis of finance lease liabilities at the end of 20X1 on **both** the gross and net basis.

Complete the proforma below.

(a) **Gross basis**

	£
Finance lease liabilities include:	
Gross lease payments due within:	
One year	
Two to five years	____
Less finance charges allocated to future periods	____
	====

(b) **Net basis**

	£
Finance lease liabilities include:	
Amounts due within:	
One year	
Two to five years	____
	====

See **Answer** at the end of this chapter.

Other disclosures

- In the case of most entities, the IAS 1 *Presentation of Financial Statements* requirement to disclose significant accounting policies would result in the disclosure of the policy in respect of finance leases.

- IAS 17 requires a general description of material leasing arrangements to be included.

6 Finance leases: other issues

Section overview

Other issues include:

- Secondary periods and peppercorn rentals
- Non-annual payments
- Initial deposit

6.1 Secondary periods and peppercorn rentals

A finance lease may contain an option for the lessee to extend the lease for a secondary period at a nominal ('peppercorn') rental. This rental will be **immaterial** and can be ignored in the calculations.

However, the optional extension period **counts as part of the lease term** if the lessee is reasonably certain at the outset to exercise the option to extend the lease. This therefore impacts on the **depreciation calculations**, because the secondary period is counted when identifying the asset's useful life. (See Section 3.2.)

6.2 Non-annual payments

Many leases in practice have monthly, quarterly or six-monthly payments. The lease calculations must be performed for **each credit period** (interval between payments).

6.3 Initial deposit

A lease may include an initial deposit payment prior to the commencement of the regular lease payments. This initial payment counts as part of the minimum lease payments and therefore as **part of the cost of the asset**.

In the lease calculations, **deduct the initial deposit from the initial liability**.

The recording at the commencement of the lease term will therefore be in two steps:

Step 1
Record liability and non-current asset

	£	£
DR Non-current assets – cost	X	
CR Payables: Finance lease liabilities		X

Step 2
Reduce initial liability by amount of deposit paid

	£	£
DR Payables: Finance lease liabilities	X	
CR Cash		X

Interactive question 5: Summary   [Difficulty level: Exam standard]

A company leases an asset on 1 January 20X1. The terms of the lease are to pay a non-refundable deposit of £575 followed by seven annual instalments of £2,000 payable in arrears. The fair value of the asset (equivalent to the present value of minimum lease payments) on 1 January 20X1 is £10,000.

Requirements

Calculate the interest charge to profit or loss and the finance lease liability in the statement of financial position for the year ended 31 December 20X1 using the actuarial method, where the interest rate implicit in the lease is 11%:

Fill in the proforma below.

£

Statement of profit or loss (extract)

Finance costs (W)

Statement of financial position (extract)

Non-current liabilities

    Finance lease liability (W)

Current liabilities

    Finance lease liability (W)

WORKING

See **Answer** at the end of this chapter.

7 Operating leases

Section overview

Operating lease rentals are charged to profit or loss on a straight-line basis over the lease term.

7.1 Accounting for operating leases

As we saw in Section 2 an **operating lease is a lease other than a finance lease.**

Operating leases do not really pose an accounting problem as the **substance** and the **legal situation** are the **same,** ie the lessee does not own the leased asset either legally or in substance. The lessee is simply renting the asset and the rental expense is charged to **profit or loss.**

7.2 Balance in the statement of financial position and profit or loss charge

IAS 17 requires the lease payments under an operating lease to be charged on a **straight-line basis** over the lease term, **even if the payments are not made on such a basis**, unless another systematic and rational basis is more representative of the time pattern of the user's benefit. Hence, if lease payments are not made evenly, an **accrual or prepayment** will be recorded in the statement of financial position.

Worked example: Operating leases

Under an operating lease agreement, Williamson plc pays a non-returnable deposit of £100,000 and then three years' rental of £100,000 per annum on the first day of each year.

You are required to calculate the charge to profit or loss for each year, and any balance in the statement of financial position at the end of the first year.

Solution

$$\text{Profit or loss charge} = \frac{100,000 + 300,000}{3 \text{ years}}$$

$$= £133,333$$

Statement of financial position at end of year 1:

	£
Paid in year	200,000
Charged to profit or loss	(133,333)
Prepayment	66,667

Note: A premium paid for the lease of land and buildings would be treated in the same way as this non-returnable deposit.

7.3 Disclosures

IAS 17 and other IASs require disclosure of:

- The **accounting policy** for operating leases.

- Operating lease payments **charged as an expense** for the period.

- In respect only of **non-cancellable** operating leases, a **commitments note** showing the total lease payments that the lessee is committed to paying in the coming years, analysed by amounts due:

    - Within one year
    - Within two to five years
    - After more than five years

    Note that this disclosure is both similar to but different from that for finance leases in Section 5.2 above:

    - The disclosures are the same in terms of the time periods over which the payments must be analysed.

    - They are different in that for finance leases the analysis is of amounts appearing in the statement of financial position within liabilities, whereas for operating leases the analysis is just of commitments. Note also that for operating leases there can be no separate disclosure of any equivalent of the finance charges for finance leases.

- A general description of **significant** leasing arrangements.

Interactive question 6: Operating leases
[Difficulty level: Exam standard]

Stone plc has the following outstanding non-cancellable operating lease commitments at the end of its reporting period:

- Rental on buildings of £100,000 pa for 15 years
- Rental on plant of £30,000 pa for three years
- Rental on cars of £40,000 payable over the next 11½ months

Requirement

Complete the operating lease commitment note to be included in Stone plc's accounts.

Fill in the proforma below.

The minimum lease payments under non-cancellable operating leases are:

	£
Within one year	
Within two to five years	
After five years	_____
	======

See **Answer** at the end of this chapter.

8 Operating lease incentives

Section overview

Operating lease incentives should be recognised on a straight-line basis over the lease term.

8.1 Basic issue

Operating lease incentives are dealt with by SIC 15 *Operating Lease – Incentives.*

In negotiating a new or renewed operating lease, the lessor may provide **incentives** for the lessee to enter into the agreement. Examples of such incentives are:

- An up-front payment to the lessee
- The reimbursement of costs of the lessee
- Initial rent-free or reduced rent periods

All incentives for the agreement of a new or renewed operating lease should be **recognised as an integral part of the net amount agreed** for the use of the leased asset, **irrespective of the incentive's nature, form or the timing of payments**.

8.2 Treatment

The lessee	Should normally recognise the aggregate benefit of incentives **as a reduction of rental expense over the lease term, on a straight-line basis**

Interactive question 7: Operating lease incentives
[Difficulty level: Easy]

On 1 January 20X7 Whittaker Ltd entered into an operating lease for a retail unit. Lease payments were £4,000 per month in advance for a period of five years. As an incentive however, Whittaker Ltd was given the first five months as a rent-free period.

Requirement

Calculate the operating lease expense which should be recognised in Whittaker Ltd's statement of profit or loss for the year ended 31 December 20X7 and any amounts to be recognised in its statement of financial position at that date.

See **Answer** at the end of this chapter.

9 Land and buildings

Section overview

When dealing with a lease of land and buildings, the land and buildings elements need to be considered separately.

Leases of land and buildings are classified as operating or finance leases **in the same way as the leases of other assets**. However due to the differing characteristics of land and buildings IAS 17 requires that the **land and buildings elements of a single lease are considered separately for classification purposes.**

Land	A characteristic of land is that it normally has an **indefinite economic life**. As a result, paragraphs 14 and 15 of IAS 17 originally stated that a lease of land should be treated as an operating lease unless title is expected to pass at the end of the lease term. The IASB reconsidered this and decided that in substance, for instance in a long lease of land and buildings, the risks and rewards of ownership do pass to the lessee regardless of transfer of title. An amendment was issued in 2009 cancelling paragraphs 14 and 15, so that a lease of land can be regarded as a finance lease if it meets the existing criteria.
Buildings	A lease of a building **may** be treated as a **finance lease** depending on the full terms of the lease (see Sections 2.1 and 2.2 above).

Problem	Solution
If you are not told, how do you work out how much of the minimum lease payments to allocate to buildings and how much to land?	Work out the relative fair values of the leasehold interests at the inception of the lease, and split the payment according to these proportions.
What happens if you cannot allocate the minimum lease payments between land and buildings?	Treat everything as a finance lease (unless clear that both elements are operating leases).
What happens if the land is immaterial?	Treat everything as buildings.

Worked example: Lease of land and buildings

Amber Ltd entered into a 40-year lease for land and buildings on 1 January 20X7. The following information is available:

Lease payments:	£60,000 pa made annually in advance
Fair value of the leasehold interest:	£600,000 of which £50,000 relates to land
Interest rate implicit in the lease:	10%
Present value of the minimum lease payments in respect of buildings:	£591,633
Present value of the minimum lease payments in respect of land:	£53,785

Under IAS 17 the land and buildings element are considered separately. This is a relatively long lease and in both cases the present value of the minimum lease payments amounts to 'substantially all' of the fair value of the asset.

It will therefore be correct to treat the whole lease as a finance lease, combined for land and buildings. In this case, as the present value of the minimum lease payments is above fair value, the lease is capitalised at fair value.

The £60,000 will be treated as a repayment of a finance lease as follows:

	B/f £	Payment £	Capital £	Interest @ 10% £	C/f £
20X7	600,000	(60,000)	540,000	54,000	594,000
20X8	594,000	(60,000)	534,000	53,400	587,400

At 31 December 20X7 interest of £54,000 will be charged to profit or loss. The liability of £594,000 will be disclosed in the statement of financial position split between the current element of £6,600 (594,000 – 587,400) and the non-current element of £587,400.

Note that the land and buildings will appear separately under property, plant and equipment, as only the buildings will be depreciated.

Worked example: Lease of land and buildings

Opal Ltd entered into a 20-year lease for land and buildings on 1 January 20X7.

The following information is available:

Lease payments:	£37,000 paid annually in arrears – £32,000 in respect of buildings and £5,000 in respect of land
Interest rate implicit in the lease:	10%
Fair value of leasehold interest:	Land £100,000
	Buildings £300,000
Present value of minimum lease payments:	Land £42,550
	Buildings £272,320

In this case, the fair value of the minimum lease payments amounts to substantially all of the fair value in respect of the buildings. This is not the case in respect of the land.

It will therefore be correct to treat the buildings lease as a finance lease and the land lease as an operating lease.

The finance lease will be accounted for as follows:

	B/f	Interest 10%	Payment	C/f
	£	£	£	£
20X7	272,320	27,232	(32,000)	267,552
20X8	267,552	26,755	(32,000)	262,307

At 31 December 20X7 the finance cost of £27,232 will be charged to profit or loss. The liability of £267,552 will be presented as a current liability of £5,245 (267,552 – 262,307) and a non-current liability of £262,307.

The land lease payment of £5,000 will be charged to profit or loss.

Interactive question 8: Land and buildings [Difficulty level: Intermediate]

On 1 January 20X8 an entity acquired a land and buildings lease with a term of 30 years at an annual rental of £50,000 payable in advance. Other details of the lease were as follows:

- The lease is renewable at the end of the lease term at a reduced rent.

- The interest rate implicit in the lease was 7.5% and the present value of £50,000 pa payable in advance over 30 years is £630,000.

- The fair value of the leasehold interest was £660,000, of which £66,000 is attributable to the land element.

Calculate the amounts to be recognised in the entity's statement of profit or loss for the year ended 31 December 20X8 and its statement of financial position at that date.

See **Answer** at the end of this chapter.

---

10 Sale and leaseback transactions

Section overview

- A sale and leaseback may result in:
    - A sale and finance leaseback
    - A sale and operating leaseback

- The accounting for a sale and finance leaseback results in any profit being recognised over the lease term.

- The accounting for a sale and operating leaseback depends on the relationship between the sale price and fair value.

10.1 Introduction

Companies can raise finance in a number of different ways. These include short-term measures such as a bank overdraft, medium-term measures such as loans or finance leases and longer-term measures including secured loans.

Another option is a **sale and leaseback transaction**. This is a common feature of certain industries, including retailing and hotels. It involves **the original owner of the asset selling it**, typically to a finance house or bank, **and immediately leasing it back,** thereby raising cash and retaining the use of the asset. Such arrangements provide entities with the opportunity to release capital caught up in the business for investment in other opportunities or to return it to shareholders. In essence, an entity acquires cash in exchange for a commitment to make regular lease payments without losing use of the asset.

The sale and leaseback transaction can result in either **a finance lease** or **an operating lease**, as determined by applying the principle of substance over form. As the accounting treatment depends on this categorisation, **this decision is critical**.

10.2 Sale and leaseback as a finance lease

This transaction is essentially a financing arrangement. The seller (who is subsequently the lessee) does not dispose of the risks and rewards of ownership (because the leaseback is through a finance lease) and no profit should be recognised immediately on disposal.

The accounting entries are:

- Derecognise the carrying amount of the asset now sold

- Recognise the sales proceeds

- Calculate the profit on sale as proceeds less carrying amount and recognise it as deferred income

- Recognise the finance lease asset and the associated liability and measure them in the normal way (at the lower of fair value and the present value of the minimum lease payments)

- Amortise the profit on sale as income over the lease term

The effect is to adjust the expense recognised in profit or loss to an amount equal to the depreciation expense before the leaseback transaction.

Point to note: If the carrying amount exceeds fair value, the asset should be written down to fair value prior to the sale and leaseback and the loss recognised as an impairment loss.

Interactive question 9: Sale and finance leaseback [Difficulty level: Intermediate]

Frayn plc entered into a sale and finance leaseback arrangement on 1 January 20X1, when:

- The carrying amount of the asset was £70,000.
- The sale proceeds were at fair value of £120,000.
- The remaining useful life of the asset was five years.

The lease provided for five annual rentals of £30,000 payable in arrears on 31 December of each year. The interest rate implicit in the lease was 8% and the present value of the minimum lease payments was £120,000.

Requirement

Set out the journal entries at the date of disposal and calculate the amounts to be recognised in profit or loss in the year to 31 December 20X1 and in the statement of financial position at that date.

See **Answer** at the end of this chapter.

10.3 Sale and leaseback as an operating lease

Some businesses arrange sales and operating leasebacks to give them the capital to build a replacement asset while occupying the original one for a short period of time. For example, a football club might sell its stadium and then lease it back for just one year, using the sale proceeds to fund the construction over that year of its new stadium.

The substance of the transaction is that **a sale has taken place** both in terms of the legal transfer of ownership and because the risks and rewards of ownership are not subsequently substantially reacquired when the leaseback is an operating lease. There is a genuine profit or loss to be recognised.

If the **sale price is at fair value**, the profit or loss measured as proceeds (fair value) less carrying amount should be recognised immediately in profit or loss.

If **the sale is different from fair value** (possibly for one of the reasons set out below), different rules apply.

- If the sale price is below fair value **and future lease payments are at market levels**, any profit or loss shall be recognised immediately.

  Even though lease payments are set at market levels, the sale price might be below fair value because the entity is desperate for cash, and so accepts a low sale price to alleviate its liquidity problems. Under these circumstances it is appropriate that the whole loss on disposal should be immediately recognised.

- If the sale price is below fair value **and** the loss is compensated for by **future lease payments at below market levels**, the loss should be deferred and amortised in proportion to the lease payments over the period for which the asset is expected to be used.

- If the sale price is above fair value, the excess over fair value should be deferred and amortised over the period for which the asset is expected to be used.

The following table summarises these rules.

Sale price at fair value

	Carrying amount equal to fair value	Carrying amount below fair value	Carrying amount above fair value
Profit	No profit	Recognise profit immediately	N/A
Loss	No loss	N/A	Recognise loss immediately

Sale price below fair value

	Carrying amount equal to fair value	Carrying amount below fair value	Carrying amount above fair value
Profit	No profit	Recognise profit immediately	No profit (Note 1)
Loss not compensated for by future lease rentals below market rate	Recognise loss immediately	Recognise loss immediately	(Note 1)
Loss compensated for by future lease rentals below market rate	Defer and amortise loss	Defer and amortise loss	(Note 1)

Sale price above fair value

	Carrying amount equal to fair value	Carrying amount below fair value	Carrying amount above fair value
Profit	Defer and amortise profit	Defer and amortise (sale price less fair value) Recognise immediately (fair value less carrying amount)	Defer and amortise profit (Note 2)
Loss	No loss	No loss	(Note 1)

Notes

1   IAS 17 requires the carrying amount of an asset to be written down to fair value (and an impairment loss recognised) before the sale and leaseback is accounted for.

2   Profit is the difference between fair value and sale price because the carrying amount would have been written down to fair value in accordance with IAS 17.

Interactive question 10: Sale and operating leaseback   [Difficulty level: Intermediate]

Six different companies each sell an asset and immediately enter into an operating leaseback for five years. There are different sets of circumstances with respect to each asset for the six companies:

	Carrying amount £	Proceeds generated £	Fair value £
Company (1)	360,000	300,000	400,000
Company (2)	400,000	300,000	360,000
Company (3)	300,000	360,000	400,000
Company (4)	300,000	400,000	360,000
Company (5)	360,000	400,000	300,000
Company (6)	400,000	360,000	300,000

Requirement

Assess the impact of the sale and operating leaseback arrangement on profit or loss for each of the six companies for all years affected by the arrangement.

See **Answer** at the end of this chapter.

11 UK GAAP comparison

Section overview

FRS 101 grants no exemptions in respect of leases.

There are no significant differences between FRS 102 and IAS 17.

An entity reporting under FRS 101 is reporting in line with IAS 17. FRS 101 does not grant any disclosure exemptions in respect of leasing.

FRS 102 sets out reduced disclosures in comparison with IAS 17. There are no other differences.

Summary and Self-test

Summary

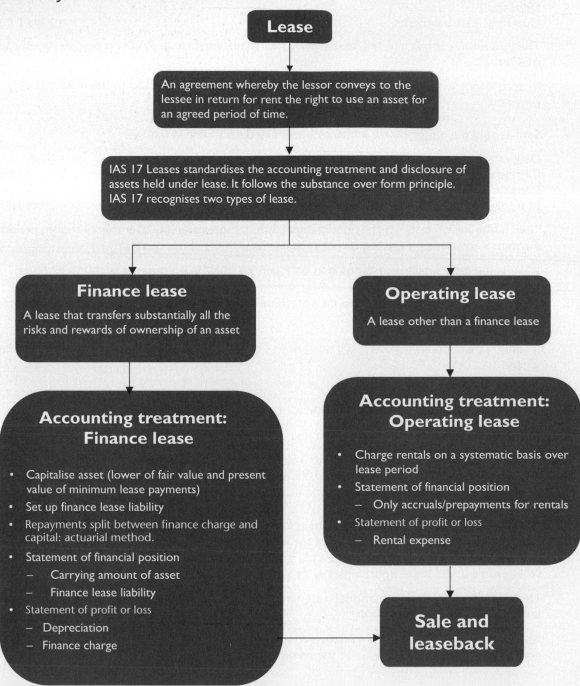

Lease

An agreement whereby the lessor conveys to the lessee in return for rent the right to use an asset for an agreed period of time.

IAS 17 Leases standardises the accounting treatment and disclosure of assets held under lease. It follows the substance over form principle. IAS 17 recognises two types of lease.

Finance lease

A lease that transfers substantially all the risks and rewards of ownership of an asset

Operating lease

A lease other than a finance lease

Accounting treatment: Finance lease

- Capitalise asset (lower of fair value and present value of minimum lease payments)
- Set up finance lease liability
- Repayments split between finance charge and capital: actuarial method.
- Statement of financial position
  - Carrying amount of asset
  - Finance lease liability
- Statement of profit or loss
  - Depreciation
  - Finance charge

Accounting treatment: Operating lease

- Charge rentals on a systematic basis over lease period
- Statement of financial position
  - Only accruals/prepayments for rentals
- Statement of profit or loss
  - Rental expense

Sale and leaseback

Self-test

Answer the following questions

1   Henry acquired a lorry on a finance lease. The details were as follows.

Date of acquisition	1 January 20X8
Cash price	£20,000
Deposit	£5,000
Quarterly lease payments	12 @ £1,800

    The interest rate implicit in the lease is 20% pa. The payments are made on the last day of each quarter.

    In accordance with IAS 17 *Leases* how much interest would be allocated to the third quarterly payment?

2   Sam acquired a motor car on a finance lease. The details were as follows.

Date of acquisition	1 July 20X6
Cash price	£5,000
Deposit	£1,000
Monthly lease payments	24 @ £200

    The charge for interest, which is not material, is to be spread evenly over the 24-month period. The payments are made on the last day of each month.

    What is the total liability outstanding as on 1 January 20X7 in accordance with IAS 17 *Leases*?

3   On 1 January 20X7 Melon plc bought a machine on a finance lease. The terms of the contract were as follows.

	£
Cash price	18,000
Deposit	(6,000)
	12,000
Interest (9% for two years)	2,160
Balance – two annual payments commencing 31 December 20X7	14,160

    The rate of interest implicit in the contract is approximately 12%.

    Applying the provisions of IAS 17 *Leases* calculate the finance charge in the statement of profit or loss for the year ended 31 December 20X7 and prepare journals to show the accounting entries in 20X7 in respect of the lease.

4   Alpha plc enters into a lease with Omega Ltd for an aircraft, which had a fair value of £240,000 at the inception of the lease. The terms of the lease require Alpha plc to make ten annual lease payments of £36,000 in arrears. Alpha plc is totally responsible for the maintenance of the aircraft, which has a useful life of approximately 11 years.

    The present value of the ten annual lease payments of £36,000 discounted at the interest rate implicit in the lease is £220,000.

    Applying the provisions of IAS 17 *Leases* to this lease, by how much will the property, plant and equipment of Alpha plc increase at the commencement of the lease?

5   Cambridge plc leases an asset on a five-year lease. The fair value of the asset is £500,000, while the present value of the minimum lease payments derived by discounting at the rate of interest implicit in the lease is £480,000. The asset has a five-year life, with Cambridge plc responsible for maintenance and insurance. The asset will be scrapped at the end of five years.

    Cambridge plc uses the sum of digits method of depreciation.

    In accordance with IAS 17 *Leases* what is the carrying amount of the asset in the accounts of Cambridge plc at the end of the second year?

6   On 1 January 20X3 Tile Ltd took out a finance lease to purchase production equipment with a cash price of £750,000. The terms of the lease required five lease payments of £200,000 to be paid annually in advance. These lease payments have been charged to profit or loss as administrative expenses. The equipment is expected to have a five-year life with no residual value. The error in the treatment of the finance lease was discovered when preparing the financial statements for the year ended 31 December 20X5.

The interest rate implicit in the lease is 22% pa. All depreciation is on a straight-line basis.

Applying the provisions of IAS 17 *Leases* to this lease what amount will be shown as an adjustment to retained earnings brought forward?

7   Pont Ltd enters into a four-year operating lease on 1 January 20X6. Although the annual lease payments were originally agreed at £50,000 a year, Pont Ltd managed to negotiate a lease 'holiday' and will pay nothing in 20X6.

In accordance with IAS 17 *Leases* what should appear in the financial statements of Pont Ltd as at 31 December 20X7 in respect of the rental charge to profit or loss and any accrual in the statement of financial position?

8   SNOW PLC

On 1 January 20X1 Snow plc entered into the following finance lease agreements.

(1) **Snow machine**

To lease a snow machine for five years from Slush plc. The snow machine cost Slush plc £150,000 and is estimated to have a useful life of five years.

Snow plc has agreed to make five annual payments of £35,000, payable in advance, commencing on 1 January 20X1.

The interest rate implicit in the lease is 8.36%.

(2) **Snowplough**

To lease a snowplough for three years from Ice plc. The machine had cost Ice plc £35,000.

A deposit of £2,000 was payable on 1 January 20X1 followed by six half-yearly payments of £6,500, payable in arrears, commencing on 30 June 20X1. The interest rate implicit in the lease is 10% pa.

Requirements

Calculate the amounts to be included in the financial statements of Snow plc for the year ended 31 December 20X1 in respect of the above and draft the reconciliation note for property, plant and equipment, and the analysis of finance lease liabilities note required by IAS 17 *Leases* on **both** the gross and net basis.   **(13 marks)**

9   FEENEY PLC

Feeney plc is considering replacing a piece of machinery that is coming towards the end of its life. Its value is negligible. The finance director has asked you for your advice as to the financial accounting and disclosure implications of each of the options. The new machine has a purchase price of £80,000 and an estimated life of five years and will be acquired on the first day of next year. The options are given below.

(1) Lease the machine for a two year period for a lease payment of £2,000 per month in arrears. A non-refundable deposit of £6,000 has to be paid on order. The lessor remains liable for maintenance.

(2) Lease the machine for a five-year period for a lease payment of £9,900 half-yearly in advance.

Requirements

Prepare a memorandum to the finance director, which:

(a) Sets out the extent to which IAS 17 *Leases* provides information that is relevant, faithfully represented, comparable and understandable. **(4 marks)**

(b) Briefly explains how each of the options should be accounted for and shows the figures to be included in the statement of profit or loss and statement of financial position for the first year. Allocate interest on an actuarial basis using an interest rate of 5% per half year. **(11 marks)**

(15 marks)

10 RICHARDS PLC

You are the financial controller for Richards plc, a company listed on the London Stock Exchange.

The Chairman has asked you to explain a number of matters relating to the substance of transactions and the reporting of lease transactions in financial statements. He has approached you as you have recently attended a number of training courses on IFRS and are in the process of preparing the draft financial statements for the year ended 31 May 20X6 in accordance with IFRS.

Richards plc recently entered into a lease contract for a new piece of machinery. The new machine could have been purchased for a cash price of £150,000. The terms of the lease are:

- The lease is for four years.

- An initial deposit of £30,000 was payable on 1 June 20X5 followed by eight half-yearly payments thereafter of £20,000 payable on 1 December and 1 June each year, commencing on 1 December 20X5.

The estimated useful life of the equipment is four years. The interest rate implicit in the lease is 14.4% pa.

Requirements

(a) Prepare notes for a meeting with the Chairman, which:

(i) Explain the concept of 'substance over form', and

(ii) Discuss the application of 'substance over form' and asset recognition to:
- The accounting by a lessee for a finance lease; and
- The accounting by a lessee for an operating lease. **(7 marks)**

(b) Prepare financial statement extracts and supporting disclosure notes that show how the machinery lease transaction should be presented in the financial statements of Richards plc for the year ended 31 May 20X6. **(7 marks)**

(14 marks)

11 ASTLEY

Astley Co owns a distribution depot which it is considering selling to Newton, a property development company, under a sale and leaseback arrangement. Astley intends moving into newer premises on a different site in approximately three years' time. When Astley moves out, Newton intends demolishing the current buildings and replacing them with flats. The current market value of the premises is approximately £4 million and the current carrying amount of the depot in Astley's statement of financial position is £3.4 million.

The market rental for Astley's depot is estimated to be £350,000 per year and Newton has offered Astley the following two options:

	Option 1	Option 2
Period of leaseback	3 years	3 years
Annual rental payable by Astley	£300,000	£450,000
Purchase price payable by Newton	£3.85 million	£4.3 million

Requirement

Explain the accounting treatment and hence impact on Astley's profit or loss of each of the above options. **(6 marks)**

Now, go back to the Learning objectives in the Introduction. If you are satisfied you have achieved these objectives, please tick them off.

Technical reference

Point to note: The following aspects of IAS 17 are not examinable: lessor accounting, paragraphs 36-57 and the implementation guidance. The paragraphs listed below are the key references you should be familiar with.

1 Lease classification

- If substantially all of the risks and rewards of ownership are transferred to the lessee, then a lease is a finance lease. Factors:

  IAS 17(4)

  - Ownership passing at end of term

    IAS 17(10–11)
  - Bargain purchase option
  - Lease term the major part of asset's life
  - Very substantial charges for early cancellation
  - Peppercorn rent in secondary period
  - PV of minimum lease payments substantially all of asset's fair value.

    IAS 17(10(d))

- Otherwise, an operating lease.

  IAS 17(4)

- Classify at inception.

  IAS 17(13)

- Can be a lease even if lessor obliged to provide substantial services.

  IAS 17(3)

2 Finance lease

- Non-current asset and liability for the asset's fair value (or PV of minimum lease payments, if lower):

  IAS 17(20)

  - Measured at inception of lease

    IAS 17(4)
  - Recognised at commencement of lease term

    IAS 17(4)

- Depreciate asset over its useful life, or the lease term if shorter and no reasonable certainty that lessee will obtain ownership at end of lease.

  IAS 17(27)

- Consider whether IAS 36 impairment procedures needed.

  IAS 17(30)

- Debit lease payments to liability, without separating into capital and interest.

- Charge lease interest to profit or loss and credit lease liability.

- Charge interest so as to produce constant periodic rate of charge on reducing liability – approximations allowed.

  IAS 17(25)

- Disclosures:

  - Show carrying value of each class of leased assets

    IAS 17(31)
  - In the statement of financial position split the liability between current and non-current

    IAS 17(23)
  - Show analysis of total liability over amounts payable in 1, 2 to 5 and over 5 years

    IAS 17(31(b))
  - General description of material leasing arrangements

    IAS 17(31(e))
  - Other IAS 16 disclosures re leased PPE assets

    IAS 17(32)

3 Operating lease

- Charge lease payments to profit or loss on straight-line basis, unless some other systematic basis is more representative of user's benefit.   IAS 17(33)

- The aggregate benefit of operating lease incentives should be recognised as a reduction of rental expense over the lease term, on a straight line basis.   SIC 15

- Disclosures:

    - Lease payments charged as expense in the period   IAS 17(35(c))

    - In a 'commitment' note, show analysis of amounts payable in 1, 2 to 5 and over 5 years, even though not recognised in statement of financial position   IAS 17 (35(a))

    - General description of significant leasing arrangements   IAS 17(35(d))

4 Land and buildings

- Land and buildings elements within a single lease are classified separately. (Note: Together, usually as operating lease, for UK GAAP)   IAS 17(16–17)

5 Sale and finance leaseback

- Recognise excess sale proceeds as deferred income and amortise over the lease term.   IAS 17 (59–60)

6 Sale and operating leaseback

- If the fair value at the time of the sale and leaseback is less than the carrying amount of the asset, the loss (carrying amount – fair value) is recognised immediately.   IAS 17 (63)

- Treatment of any profit or loss depends on relationship between sale price and fair value: IAS 17 (61)

    - Sale price at fair value
    - Sale price below fair value
    - Sale price above fair value

Answer to Interactive question 1

(a)	A company leases machine tools. Legal title is transferred after three years.	Finance lease, because title is transferred and the company enjoys the risks and rewards of ownership before-hand.
(b)	A company leases a photocopier. The PV of minimum lease payments is £2,000 but the fair value of the asset is £10,000.	Operating lease, as the fair value of the asset is a lot more than the minimum lease payments.
(c)	A company leases a car for a sales representative for a five-year period, after which the car will have come to the end of its useful economic life.	Finance lease, as the lease term is for the major part (in this case the whole) of the economic life of the asset.
(d)	A company acquires some equipment made bespoke to its specifications. To sell the equipment to a third party would require substantial modification.	Finance lease, as the asset is of such a specialised nature that only the lessee can use it without major modification.

Answer to Interactive question 2

	Lease liability			
	CR Balance b/f 1 Jan	CR Interest accrued @ 10% 31 Dec	DR Payment 31 Dec	CR Capital balance c/f 31 Dec
	£	£	£	£
20X1 (current period)	24,869	2,487	(10,000)	17,356
20X2 (future periods)	17,356	1,736	(10,000)	9,092

Total lease liability at 31 December 20X1 = £17,356

Capital > 1 year = £9,092   < 1 year (β) = £8,264

		£	£
DR	Non-current asset	24,869	
CR	Finance lease liability		24,869
	Being purchase of asset under finance lease		
DR	Finance charge (profit or loss)	2,487	
CR	Finance lease liability		2,487
	Being interest on finance lease		
DR	Finance lease liability	10,000	
CR	Cash		10,000
	Being payment in respect of finance lease		

Answer to Interactive question 3

	CR Balance b/f 1 Jan	DR Payment 1 Jan	*Lease liability* CR Capital balance remaining 1 Jan	CR Interest accrued @10% 31 Dec	CR Balance c/f 31 Dec
	£	£	£	£	£
20X1 (current period)	34,869	(10,000)	24,869	2,487	27,356
20X2 (future periods)	27,356	(10,000)	17,356	1,736	19,092

Total lease liability at 31 December 20X1 = £27,356

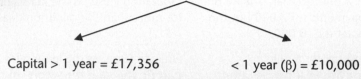

Capital > 1 year = £17,356   < 1 year (β) = £10,000

		£	£
DR	Non-current asset	34,869	
CR	Finance lease liability		24,869
CR	Cash (deposit)		10,000
	Being purchase of asset under finance lease		
DR	Finance charge (profit or loss)	2,487	
CR	Finance lease liability		2,487
	Being interest on finance lease		
DR	Finance lease liability	10,000	
CR	Cash		10,000
	Being payment in respect of finance lease		

Answer to Interactive question 4

(a) **Gross basis**

	£
Finance lease liabilities include:	
Gross lease payments due within:	
One year	10,000
Two to five years	20,000
	30,000
Less finance charges allocated to future periods (β)	2,644
	27,356

(b) **Net basis**

	£
Finance lease liabilities include:	
Amounts due within:	
One year	10,000
Two to five years (β)	17,356
	27,356

Answer to Interactive question 5

Statement of profit or loss (extract)

	£
Finance costs (W)	1,037

Statement of financial position (extract)

	£
Non-current liabilities	
Finance lease liability (W)	7,393
Current liabilities	
Finance lease liability (W)	1,069

WORKING

	CR Bal b/f 1 Jan	CR Interest accrued at 11%	DR Payment 31 Dec	CR Bal c/f 31 Dec
	£	£	£	£
20X1	(10,000 – 575) = 9,425	1,037	(2,000)	8,462
20X2	8,462	931	(2,000)	7,393

Total lease liability at 31 December 20X1 = £8,462

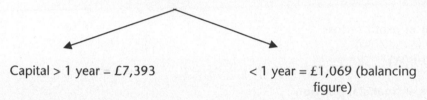

Capital > 1 year – £7,393   < 1 year = £1,069 (balancing figure)

Answer to Interactive question 6

The minimum lease payments under non-cancellable operating leases are:

	£
Within one year (£100,000 + £30,000 + £40,000)	170,000
Within two to five years ((£100,000 × 4) + £30,000 × 2)	460,000
After more than five years (£100,000 × 10)	1,000,000
	1,630,000

Answer to Interactive question 7

	£
Statement of profit or loss	
Operating lease rentals (W1)	44,000
Statement of financial position	
Non-current liabilities	
Operating lease liability (W2)	12,000
Current liabilities	
Operating lease liability (W2)	4,000

WORKINGS

(1) **Operating lease rentals**

Total due under lease £240,000 (£4,000 × 12 × 5) – rent free £20,000 (5 × £4,000) = £220,000

Over five years = £44,000 per year

(2) Operating lease liability

		£
Profit or loss charge (W1)		44,000
Paid in year (7 × £4,000)		(28,000)
Liability		16,000
Current liability: amount payable in 20X8 ((12 × £4,000) – 44,000)		4,000
Non-current liability (balance)		12,000

Answer to Interactive question 8

The land and buildings elements should be measured by reference to the fair value of the leasehold interests, so

* £66,000 (which is 10% of £660,000) is allocated to the land
* £594,000 (the 90% remainder) is allocated to the buildings

In the case of both the land and the buildings the present value of the minimum lease payments amounts to substantially all of the fair value of the asset. Also, this lease is renewable at a reduced rent, suggesting that both elements should be treated as finance leases.

* The land: the lower of the £66,000 fair value allocated to the land and £63,000 (£630,000 × 10%) present value of minimum lease payments is recognised as a non-current asset and as a liability.

* The building: the lower of the £594,000 fair value allocated to the building and the £567,000 (£630,000 × 90%) present value of the minimum lease payments so allocated should be recognised as a non-current asset and as a liability.

	£
Statement of profit or loss	
Depreciation (567/30)	18,900
Finance cost (W)	43,500
Statement of financial position	
Property, plant and equipment	
Cost (567,000 + 63,000)	630,000
Depreciation	(18,900)
	611,100
Non-current liabilities	
Finance lease obligations (W)	573,500
Current liabilities	
Finance lease obligations (W)	50,000

WORKING

	Balance	Lease payment	Balance	Finance cost at 7.5%	Balance
	£	£	£	£	£
20X8	630,000	(50,000)	580,000	43,500	623,500
20X9	623,500	(50,000)	573,500	43,013	616,513

Answer to Interactive question 9

Journal entries at date of disposal

		£	£
DR	Cash	120,000	
CR	Non-current asset (carrying amount)		70,000
	Deferred income (120,000 – 70,000)		50,000
DR	Non-current asset	120,000	
CR	Lease liability		120,000

Statement of profit or loss

	£
Depreciation (120,000/5)	(24,000)
Interest (120,000 × 8%)	(9,600)
Release of deferred profit (50,000/5)	10,000

Statement of financial position

	£
Non-current assets	
Carrying amount at 1 January 20X1	120,000
Depreciation	(24,000)
Carrying amount at 31 December 20X1	96,000
Non-current liabilities	
Obligations under finance leases (W)	77,568
Deferred income (50,000 × 3/5)	30,000
Current liabilities	
Obligations under finance leases (30,000 – 7,968 (W))	22,032
Deferred income (50,000/5)	10,000

WORKING

	Balance	Finance cost at 8%	Lease payment	Balance
	£	£	£	£
20X1	120,000	9,600	(30,000)	99,600
20X2	99,600	7,968	(30,000)	77,568

Point to note: The net expense for the year in respect of the asset (excluding the financing cost) is £14,000 (24,000 – 10,000), the same as if the asset had not been sold (70,000/5).

Answer to Interactive question 10

(1) Loss of £60,000 (carrying amount less proceeds = £360,000 – £300,000) should be recognised immediately unless lease rentals are below market rentals in which case it should be deferred and amortised over the five years lease period at £12,000 per year.

(2) An impairment loss of £40,000 based on fair value (carrying amount – fair value = £400,000 – £360,000) should be recognised immediately. The remaining £60,000 of the loss (fair value – proceeds = £360,000 – £300,000) should also be recognised immediately unless the future rentals payable are below market levels, in which case it should be deferred and amortised over the lease term.

(3) The profit of £60,000 (proceeds – carrying amount = £360,000 – £300,000) should be recognised immediately.

(4) A profit of £60,000 based on fair value (fair value – carrying amount = £360,000 – £300,000) should be recognised immediately. The remaining £40,000 of the profit (proceeds – fair value = £400,000 – £360,000) should be deferred and recognised over the five years lease period at £8,000 per year.

(5) An impairment loss of £60,000 based on fair value (carrying amount – fair value = £360,000 – £300,000) should be recognised immediately. The profit of £100,000 (proceeds – fair value = £400,000 – £300,000) should be deferred and recognised over the five years lease period at £20,000 per year.

(6) An impairment loss of £100,000 based on fair value (carrying amount – fair value = £400,000 – £300,000) should be recognised immediately. The profit of £60,000 (proceeds – fair value = £360,000 – £300,000) should be deferred and recognised over the five years lease period at £12,000 per year.

1   Third interest payment is £642

Quarter	B/f	Interest 20%/4	Payment	C/f
	£	£	£	£
1	15,000	750	(1,800)	13,950
2	13,950	698	(1,800)	12,848
3	12,848	642		

2   The outstanding liability is £3,000.

	£
Total lease payments (24 × £200)	4,800
Deposit	1,000
Less capital (cash price)	(5,000)
Total interest	800

Interest per payment = 800/24 = £33.3

	£
Cash price	5,000
Deposit	(1,000)
	4,000
Interest – 6 × £33.3	200
Payments – 6 × £200	(1,200)
Liability at 1 January 20X7	3,000

3   Finance charge for 20X7 = 12% × 12,000
                         = £1,440

		£	£
DR	Non-current asset	18,000	
CR	Finance lease liability		12,000
CR	Cash (deposit)		6,000
	Being purchase of asset under finance lease		
DR	Finance charge (profit or loss)	1,440	
CR	Finance lease liability		1,440
	Being interest on finance lease		
DR	Finance lease liability	7,080	
CR	Cash		7,080
	Being payment in respect of finance lease		

4   The information suggests that a transference of risks and rewards has taken place. Therefore the lease is a finance lease and should be capitalised at present value of minimum lease payments (as this is lower than fair value), ie £220,000. So PPE will increase by this amount.

5   The terms of the agreement indicate that this is a finance lease.

	£
Initially recorded at present value of minimum lease payments	480,000
Years 1 and 2 depreciation $\frac{5+4}{15^*}$	(288,000)
Carrying amount	192,000

$$* \text{ SOTD} = \frac{5 \times (5+1)}{2} = 15$$

6   Retained earnings will be debited by £125,000.

Cumulative adjustment to profit at 1 January 20X5

	£'000	£'000
Lease payments charged to date (2 × 200)		400
Depreciation to date (2 × $^{750}/_5$)	(300)	
Finance charges to date (W)	(225)	
		(525)
		(125)

WORKING

Year ended	B/f £'000	Payment £'000	Balance £'000	Interest 22% £'000	C/f £'000
31.12.X3	750	(200)	550	121	671
31.12.X4	671	(200)	471	104	575
				225	

7   At the end of 20X7 there will be a charge to profit or loss of £37,500 and an accrual of £25,000.

Year	Cash £	Expense £	Accrual £
20X6	–	37,500	37,500
20X7	50,000	37,500	25,000
20X8	50,000	37,500	12,500
20X9	50,000	37,500	–
	150,000	150,000	

8   **SNOW PLC**

(i)   **Amounts to be included in the financial statements of Snow plc for the year ended 31 December 20X1**

Statement of profit or loss

	£
Depreciation of leased assets (Note)	41,667
Finance lease interest (9,614 + 1,650 + 1,407) (W1 & W2)	12,671

Statement of financial position

	£
Non-current assets	
Property, plant and equipment (Note)	143,333
Current liabilities	
Finance lease liabilities (W3)	45,962
Non-current liabilities	
Finance lease liabilities (W3)	101,709

(ii)   **Notes**

Property, plant and equipment

	Plant and machinery £
Cost	
At 1 January 20X1	–
Additions (35,000 + 150,000)	185,000
At 31 December 20X1	185,000
Accumulated depreciation	
At 1 January 20X1	–
Charge for year $\left(\dfrac{35,000}{3}+\dfrac{150,000}{5}\right)$	41,667
At 31 December 20X1	41,667
Carrying amount	
At 31 December 20X1	143,333
At 1 January 20X1	–

Analysis of finance lease liabilities

£

Gross basis

Finance lease liabilities include

Gross lease payments due within:

	£
One year (£35,000 + £13,000)	48,000
Two to five years (3 × £35,000) + £13,000	118,000
	166,000
Less finance charges allocated to future periods (β)	(18,329)
	147,671

Net basis

Finance leases liabilities include

Amounts due within:

	£
One year (W3)	45,962
Two to five years (W3)	101,709
	147,671

WORKINGS

(1) **Snow machine**

Period ended	B/f £	Payment £	Capital £	Interest @ 8.36% £	C/f £
31 December 20X1	150,000	(35,000)	115,000	9,614	124,614
31 December 20X2	124,614	(35,000)	89,614	7,492	97,106

Total liability
£124,614

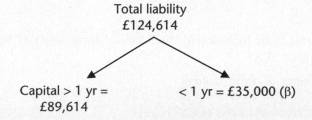

Capital > 1 yr = £89,614   < 1 yr = £35,000 (β)

(2) **Snowplough**

Liability table

Period ended	B/f £	Interest (10%/2) £	Payment £	Capital £
30 June 20X1	33,000	1,650	(6,500)	28,150
31 December 20X1	28,150	1,407	(6,500)	23,057
30 June 20X2	23,057	1,153	(6,500)	17,710
31 December 20X2	17,710	885	(6,500)	12,095

Total liability
£23,057

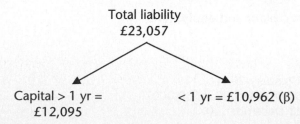

Capital > 1 yr = £12,095   < 1 yr = £10,962 (β)

(3) **Finance lease liabilities**

	Snow machine (W1) £	Snowplough (W2) £	Total £
< 1 year	35,000	10,962	45,962
> 1 year	89,614	12,095	101,709
	124,614	23,057	147,671

9 FEENEY PLC

MEMORANDUM

To   Finance Director, Feeney plc
From Financial Accountant
Date 30 March 20X4
Subject Accounting and disclosure implications of replacement of machinery

(a) Information provided

The key terms 'relevant', 'faithfully represented', 'comparable' and 'understandable' are concerned with the quality of financial information as discussed in the IASB *Conceptual Framework*. They can be applied to IAS 17 as follows.

(i) **Relevant.** Information is relevant if it can influence the economic decisions of users. By showing the true substance of finance leases, companies are forced to bring debt into the statement of financial position and this could influence other potential lenders. Also, the commitments note for operating leases and the liabilities note for finance leases have predictive value by warning lenders of existing contractual obligations and how long they are likely to last.

(ii) **Faithfully represented.** This means that information represents the economic phenomena that it purports to represent, ie all the rights and liabilities arising from a transaction must be identified and assessed. IAS 17 clearly does this via its overriding requirement to account for substance.

(iii) **Comparable.** Comparability implies consistency between different companies and from year to year. IAS 17 gives detailed guidance on how to identify a finance lease. However, there will always be a certain element of subjectivity in assessing 'risks and rewards'.

A key benefit of IAS 17 is that the financial statements of a company acquiring the use of an asset through a finance lease will be comparable, in terms of tangible assets, borrowings, gearing, return on capital employed, etc, with those of a company taking out a loan to acquire legal title to an asset.

In addition, disclosure of the detailed accounting policy (including how interest is allocated) will assist in comparability.

(iv) **Understandable.** Although some users might assume that the assets in the statement of financial position are owned by the company, the accounting policy note should explain the inclusion of leased assets. Also, preparers of accounts are entitled to assume that users have a reasonable level of knowledge.

(b) Accounting for each option

Option (1)

(i) Because the lease is only for two years and the asset has a life of five years, Feeney plc is not obtaining substantially all the rewards of ownership.

(ii) Because the lessor is liable for maintenance, Feeney plc is not bearing substantially all the risks of ownership.

(iii) This lease is therefore an operating lease and thus the asset is not capitalised nor the liability recognised in the statement of financial position.

Statement of profit or loss

	£
Operating lease rental (W1)	27,000

Statement of financial position

	£
Trade and other receivables (W2)	3,000

Option (2)

(i)   As the machine will be leased for the whole of its life, it is an asset acquired under a finance lease.

(ii)   IAS 17 requires the non-current asset to be capitalised (and depreciated over the shorter of the lease term and its useful life), a liability to be created, and certain detailed disclosures to be made.

Statement of profit or loss

	£
Depreciation (W3)	16,000
Interest charge (3,505 + 3,185) (W4)	6,690

Statement of financial position

	£
Total property, plant and equipment held under finance leases	
Cost	80,000
Depreciation (W3)	(16,000)
Carrying amount	64,000
Non-current liabilities	
Finance lease liabilities (W4)	49,940
Current liabilities	
Finance lease liabilities (W4)	16,950

WORKINGS

(1) **Rental**

$$\frac{\text{Total payable}}{\text{Life of lease}} = \frac{6,000 + (24 \times 2,000)}{2 \text{ years}} = £27,000 \text{ pa}$$

(2) **Operating lease prepayment**

	£	£
DR Profit or loss	27,000	
DR Trade and other receivables (bal fig)	3,000	
CR Cash (6,000 + (12 × 2,000))		30,000

(3) **Depreciation**

$$\frac{£80,000}{5 \text{ years}} = £16,000 \text{ pa}$$

(4) **Lease creditor**

Year	Period	B/f £	Payment £	Capital £	Interest @ 5% £	C/f £
1	1	80,000	(9,900)	70,100	3,505	73,605
	2	73,605	(9,900)	63,705	3,185	66,890
2	1	66,890	(9,900)	56,990	2,850	59,840
	2	59,840	(9,900)	49,940	2,497	52,437

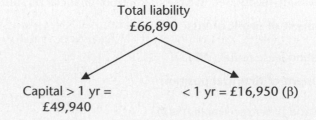

Total liability
£66,890

Capital > 1 yr =   < 1 yr = £16,950 (β)
£49,940

10 RICHARDS PLC

(a) **Notes for meeting with chairman**

(i) **Concept of substance over form**

In a straightforward transaction its commercial effect is the same as its legal form. However, in more complex transactions the true substance of the transaction may be different from its legal form, with one party having the risks and rewards of ownership but another party having legal title to the asset.

In such circumstances recording the legal form of the transaction would not be sufficient to provide a fair presentation in the financial statements. The financial statements are required to meet the qualitative characteristic of faithful representation.

Where a transaction gives rise to an asset that asset should be recognised even if legally the entity does not own it. For example, where an entity has the sole use of an asset for the majority of its economic life the asset should be recognised in the entity's financial statements even if legally it is owned by a third party.

(ii) **Application of substance over form and asset recognition to finance lease**

Under a finance lease, the lessor retains the legal title to the asset. However, the lessee has use of the asset during substantially the whole of the asset's useful life. During this period the lessee is controlling the asset and has the benefit of the economic benefits being generated from the asset's use.

In addition, the present value of the minimum lease payments amounts to at least substantially all of the fair value of the leased asset, thereby suggesting that the lessee is actually paying the current market price for the asset under a financing arrangement. The cost of the asset is therefore known. The legal title of the asset may or may not pass to the lessee at the end of the lease term.

In essence the lessee has all the risks and rewards of ownership and therefore should recognise the leased asset in its statement of financial position along with a liability even though it may not have legal title to the asset.

Operating lease

Under an operating lease, the lessee will have use of the asset for only part of its useful life and does not therefore have access to the economic benefits generated by the asset over its useful life.

Under an operating lease the lease payments will be substantially less than the fair value of the asset and at the end of the lease term the asset may be used by the owner or leased to another third party.

The lessee does not have the substantial risks and rewards of ownership and therefore the lessee does not recognise the asset or liability in its financial statements. The lessee will instead recognise the lease rentals on a straight-line basis over the period of the lease in its statement of profit or loss.

(b) **Financial statement extracts**

Statement of financial position

Property, plant and equipment

	£
Cost	150,000
Accumulated depreciation (150,000/4 years)	(37,500)
Carrying amount	112,500
Current liabilities	
Finance lease liability (W)	33,055
Non-current liabilities	
Finance lease liability (W)	83,407

Note: Finance lease liability

Gross basis

	£
Finance lease liabilities include:	
Gross lease payments due within:	
One year	40,000
Two to five years	100,000
	140,000
Less finance charges allocated to future periods (β)	(23,538)
	116,462 (W)

Note: The liability could also be presented on the net basis:

Net basis

	£
Finance lease liabilities include:	
Amounts due within:	
One year (W)	33,055
Two to five years	83,407
	116,462 (W)

WORKING

Liability table

Period ending	B/f £	Payment £	Capital £	Interest (14.4%/2) £	C/f £
30 November 20X5	120,000*	–	120,000	8,640	128,640
31 May 20X6	128,640	(20,000)	108,640	7,822	116,462
30 November 20X6	116,462	(20,000)	96,462	6,945	103,407
31 May 20X7	103,407	(20,000)	83,407	6,005	89,412

* (150,000 – 30,000)

Total lease liability at 31 May 20X6 = £116,462

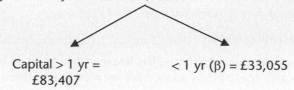

Capital > 1 yr = £83,407   < 1 yr (β) = £33,055

11 ASTLEY

Option 1

The profit on sale of £450,000 (£3.85 million sales price less £3.4 million carrying amount) should be recognised immediately in profit or loss. This sales price is below the £4 million fair value and the £300,000 annual rental is below the £350,000 market rental, but IAS 17 does not require any adjustment to the profit as calculated above.

This profit should be recognised immediately and the subsequent rentals should be recognised in profit or loss each year at £300,000. This will have the following effect over the three years on profit or loss:

	Year 1 £'000	Year 2 £'000	Year 3 £'000	Total £'000
Profit on derecognition of depot	450	0	0	450
Rental expense recognised	(300)	(300)	(300)	(900)
Total income/(expense)	150	(300)	(300)	(450)

Option 2

This option generates a profit on sale of £900,000 as the £4.3 million sales price is above the £3.4 million carrying amount. This sales price is £300,000 above the £4 million fair value, but this seemingly generous extra consideration appears to be clawed back by Newton planning to charge above market rentals for the following three years.

This excess profit should initially be recognised as deferred income and released to profit or loss over the three years of the leaseback. The profit recognised immediately should be the difference between the £4 million fair value and the £3.4 million carrying amount. The effect on profit or loss will be:

	Year 1 £'000	Year 2 £'000	Year 3 £'000	Total £'000
Profit on derecognition of depot	600	0	0	600
Rentals expense recognised	(450)	(450)	(450)	(1,350)
Deferred income released to profit	100	100	100	300
	(350)	(350)	(350)	(1,050)
Total income/(expense)	250	(350)	(350)	(450)

The total expense is the same over the three years, but the timing of its recognition is different under the two leases.

CHAPTER 8

Financial instruments

Introduction

Examination context

Topic List

Introduction

Learning objectives

- Prepare and present extracts of financial statements in respect of financial instruments

- Formulate accounting and reporting policies in respect of financial instruments

- Explain and illustrate the main differences between international and UK requirements

- Identify and consider appropriate actions for ethical issues involving financial instruments

Specific syllabus references for this chapter are: 1d, 2a, 2b, 2c, 2d, 2e.

Syllabus links

These are the International Financial Reporting Standards relating to this area:

- IAS 32 Financial Instruments: Presentation
- IAS 39 Financial Instruments: Recognition and Measurement
- IFRS 7 Financial Instruments: Disclosures
- IFRS 13 Fair Value Measurement

The majority of IAS 32 is examinable at Financial Accounting and Reporting with the standard examined at level B. However only the more basic areas of IAS 39, IFRS 7 and IFRS 13 are examinable at this stage. These three standards will be examined in more detail at the Advanced Stage.

Examination context

In the examination, candidates may be required to:

- Describe the recognition and derecognition criteria for financial instruments

- Calculate the liability and equity elements of compound financial instruments

- Classify financial instruments and prepare extracts of financial statements for basic financial instruments

- Calculate the carrying amount of a financial asset or liability measured at amortised cost using the effective interest method

- Recognise the correct accounting treatment of a variety of financial instruments

- Describe the disclosure requirements for financial instruments and their usefulness to users of financial statements

- Identify ethical issues and professional judgements involving financial instruments and the effect this may have on financial performance and financial position

Points to note:

Knowledge of derivatives is not required. Only those types of financial instruments included in this chapter and in the revision questions and answers will be included in examination questions.

Hedge accounting is excluded from the Professional Stage syllabus.

1 Financial instruments – introduction

Section overview

- The extensive financial reporting requirements for financial instruments are covered by IAS 32, IAS 39 and IFRS 7.

- A number of common definitions are used in all three standards and IFRS 13.

1.1 Introduction

The increasing diversity of businesses and the wider development and availability of financial instruments has increased the use of complex financial transactions by entities in order to reduce their exposure to risks. The existence of financial instruments has a significant effect on the risk profile of organisations. Such instruments can have a significant effect on profits, solvency and cash flow.

Common financial instruments include:

- Cash and timed deposits
- Trade payables and receivables
- Loans payable and receivable
- Debt and equity investments
- Derivatives such as interest rate swaps and foreign exchange contracts
- Redeemable and irredeemable preference shares
- Convertible debt instruments
- Investments in shares issued by other entities

As a result of this widespread use of financial assets and financial liabilities as part of an entity's ordinary activities, International Financial Reporting Standards have been published to deal with:

- Recognition
- Measurement
- Presentation and disclosure

1.2 Relevant accounting standards

The relevant accounting standards for financial instruments are:

- IAS 32 *Financial Instruments: Presentation*
- IAS 39 *Financial Instruments: Recognition and Measurement*
- IFRS 7 *Financial Instruments: Disclosures*
- IFRS 13 *Fair Value Measurement*

The individual standards cannot be studied in isolation. A number of terms and definitions are used across the standards and an understanding of financial instruments requires an understanding of the key concepts in each standard.

1.3 What is a financial instrument?

The definition of a financial instrument is consistent throughout the accounting standards covering financial instruments. It is introduced in IAS 32.

Definition

A **financial instrument** is any contract that gives rise to a financial asset of one entity and a financial liability or equity instrument of another entity.

Note that a financial instrument has **two parties**. It should be recognised as an **asset** by one party and either a **liability or equity** by the other. The classification of a financial instrument as a financial liability or equity is particularly important as it will have an effect on gearing.

1.4 What is a financial asset?

Definition

A **financial asset** is any asset that is:

- Cash

- An equity instrument of another entity

- A contractual right:
    - To receive cash or another financial asset from another entity; or
    - To exchange financial assets or financial liabilities with another entity under conditions that are potentially favourable to the entity; or

- A contract that will or may be settled in the entity's own equity instruments and which is:
    - A non-derivative for which the entity is or may be obliged to receive a variable number of the entity's own equity instruments; or
    - A derivative that will or may be settled other than by exchange of a fixed amount of cash or another financial asset for a fixed number of the entity's own equity instruments. For this purpose the entity's own equity instruments do not include instruments that are themselves contracts for the future receipt or delivery of the entity's own equity instruments.

The key here is that financial assets are cash, a **contractual right** to receive cash or another financial asset (such as shares) or to exchange financial assets or liabilities on favourable terms, or holdings of equity instruments (such as shares).

IAS 32 makes it clear that the following items are *not* financial instruments.

- **Physical assets**, eg inventories, property, plant and equipment, leased assets and **intangible assets** (patents, trademarks, etc).

- **Prepaid expenses**, deferred revenue and most warranty obligations.

- Liabilities or assets that are **not contractual** in nature.

- Contractual rights/obligations that **do not involve transfer of a financial asset**, eg commodity futures contracts.

Worked example: Definitions

List the reasons why physical assets and prepaid expenses do not qualify as financial instruments.

Solution

Refer to the definitions of financial assets and liabilities given above.

(a) **Physical assets**: control of these creates an opportunity to generate an inflow of cash or other assets, but it does not give rise to a present right to receive cash or other financial assets.

(b) **Prepaid expenses, etc**: the future economic benefit is the receipt of goods/services rather than the right to receive cash or other financial assets.

Assets that have physical substance, such as plant and machinery, are not financial assets and neither are intangible assets, such as patents and brands. These assets generate future economic benefits for an entity although there is no contractual right to receive cash or another financial asset. Examples of financial assets include cash, a trade receivable and equity investments.

Worked example: Financial asset

An entity deposits £20,000 of cash with a bank for a fixed term of three years. The £20,000 is a financial asset of the entity as it has a contractual right to receive the cash in three years' time.

1.5 What is a financial liability?

Definition

A **financial liability** is any liability that is:

- A contractual obligation:

    - To deliver cash or another financial asset to another entity; or

    - To exchange financial assets or financial liabilities with another entity under conditions that are potentially unfavourable to the entity; or

- A contract that will or may be settled in the entity's own equity instruments and which is:

    - A non-derivative for which the entity is or may be obliged to deliver a variable number of the entity's own equity instruments; or

    - A derivative that will or may be settled other than by exchange of a fixed amount of cash or another financial asset for a fixed number of the entity's own equity instruments. For this purpose the entity's own equity instruments do not include instruments that are themselves contracts for the future receipt or delivery of the entity's own equity instruments.

The key to this definition is that a financial liability is a **contractual obligation** to deliver cash or another financial asset, or a contractual obligation to exchange financial assets or liabilities on potentially unfavourable terms.

This terminology is consistent with the *Conceptual Framework* in which financial liabilities are defined in terms of obligations. Note that the IAS 32 definition requires the obligations to be contractual.

Examples of financial liabilities include trade payables, loans and redeemable preference shares. A bank overdraft is a financial liability as it is repayable in cash. A warranty provision would not be a financial liability because the obligation is to deliver additional goods or services, not cash.

We should clarify some points arising from these definitions. Firstly, one or two terms above should be themselves defined.

- A '**contract**' need not be in writing, but it must comprise an agreement that has 'clear economic consequences' and which the parties to it cannot avoid, usually because the agreement is enforceable in law.

- An '**entity**' here could be an individual, partnership, incorporated body or government agency.

The definitions of **financial assets** and **financial liabilities** may seem rather circular, referring as they do to the terms financial asset and financial instrument. The point is that there may be a chain of contractual rights and obligations, but it will lead ultimately to the receipt or payment of cash *or* the acquisition or issue of an equity instrument.

Worked example: Financial liability

In 20X2 an entity entered into a contract that required it to issue shares to the value of £10,000 on 1 January 20X5.

This is a financial liability since the entity is required to settle the contract by issuing a variable number of shares based on a fixed monetary amount.

If the number of shares were fixed, it would not meet the definition of a financial liability and should be presented as an equity instrument.

1.6 What is an equity instrument?

Definition

An **equity instrument** is any contract that evidences a residual interest in the assets of an entity after deducting all of its liabilities.

In applying all these definitions it is essential to establish whether or not there is in existence a contractual right to receive, or a contractual obligation to deliver, which is enforceable by law.

The definitions of financial assets, financial liabilities and equity instruments are necessarily complex. For the Financial Accounting and Reporting examination it is necessary for you to understand the basic points of each definition and the challenges that these definitions represent for financial reporting.

Worked example: Ordinary shares

Holders of ordinary shares in a company own equity instruments. Although they own the residual interest in a company, they have no **contractual right** to demand any of it to be delivered to them, for example by way of a dividend. Equally, the company has issued an equity instrument, not a financial liability, because the company has no **contractual obligation** to distribute the residual interest.

An entity that invests in the ordinary shares of another entity holds a financial asset, because an equity interest in another entity falls within the definition of a financial asset.

Interactive question 1: Financial instruments   [Difficulty level: Easy]

Identify which of the following are financial instruments, financial assets, financial liabilities or equity instruments and for which party.

(1)   Offertake Ltd sells £5,000 of inventory to Guideprice Ltd on 30-day payment terms.
(2)   Ashdell Ltd pays £20,000 in advance for a 12-month insurance policy.
(3)   Wellbeck Ltd issues 100,000 ordinary shares which are acquired by Keeload Ltd.
(4)   Cashlow plc borrows £200,000 under a mortgage from Norbert plc.

See **Answer** at the end of this chapter.

2   IAS 39 *Financial Instruments: Recognition and Measurement*

Section overview
- A financial instrument should initially be measured at fair value, usually including transaction costs.
- Financial assets and liabilities should be remeasured either at fair value or at amortised cost.

2.1   Introduction

The purpose of IAS 39 is to establish the principles by which financial assets and financial liabilities should be recognised and measured in financial statements.

2.2   Initial recognition and measurement

In general a **financial asset or financial liability** should be:

- **Recognised** when an entity enters into the contractual provisions of the financial instrument.

- Initially **measured** at its fair value.

  The general rule is that transaction costs, such as brokers' and professional fees, should be included in the initial carrying amount. The **exception** is that transaction costs for financial instruments classified as at fair value through profit or loss should be recognised as an expense in profit or loss, however these are not included in the Financial Accounting and Reporting syllabus.

IAS 39 requires the recognition of all financial instruments in the statement of financial position.

Fair value is defined as follows by IFRS 13 *Fair Value Measurement*. It is an important definition.

Definition

Fair value: The price that would be received to sell an asset or paid to transfer a liability in an orderly transaction between market participants at the measurement date.

IFRS 13 provides extensive guidance on how the fair value of assets and liabilities should be established.

This standard requires that the following are considered in determining fair value:

(a) The asset or liability being measured

(b) The principal market (ie that where the most activity takes place) or where there is no principal market, the most advantageous market (ie that in which the best price could be achieved) in which an orderly transaction would take place for the asset or liability

(c) The highest and best use of the asset or liability and whether it is used on a standalone basis or in conjunction with other assets or liabilities

(d) Assumptions that market participants would use when pricing the asset or liability

Having considered these factors, IFRS 13 provides a hierarchy of inputs for arriving at fair value. It requires that level 1 inputs are used where possible:

Level 1   Quoted prices in active markets for identical assets that the entity can access at the measurement date

Level 2   Inputs other than quoted prices that are directly or indirectly observable for the asset

Level 3   Unobservable inputs for the asset

If an entity has investments in **equity instruments that do not have a quoted price** in an active market and it is not possible to calculate their fair values reliably, they should be measured at cost.

The fair value on initial recognition is normally the transaction price. However, if part of the consideration is given for something other than the financial instrument, then the fair value should be estimated using a valuation technique.

Worked example: Initial fair value

An entity enters into a marketing agreement with another organisation. As part of the agreement the entity makes a two year £5,000 interest free loan. Equivalent loans would normally carry an interest rate of 6%, given the borrower's credit rating. The entity made the loan in anticipation of receiving future marketing and product benefits.

The fair value of the loan can be determined by discounting the future cash flows to present value using the prevailing market interest rate for a similar instrument with a similar credit rating. The present value of the cash flow in two years time at 6% is £4,450 (£5,000 × (1/1.06^2)). On initial recognition of the financial asset the entity should recognise a loss of £550 as follows:

DR	Loan	£4,450	
DR	Loss (finance expense)	£550	
CR	Cash		£5,000

The difference between this initial amount recognised of £4,450 and the final amount received of £5,000 should be treated as interest received and recognised in profit or loss over the two-year period.

2.3 Subsequent measurement of financial assets

After initial recognition at fair value the subsequent measurement of financial assets and the treatment of profits and losses depends upon how they were categorised. However, for the purposes of your Financial Accounting and Reporting studies all financial assets will be assumed to be held to maturity and should therefore be measured at **amortised cost** using the **effective interest method**.

Amortised cost is:

- The initial amount recognised for the financial asset
- Less any repayments of the principal sum
- Plus any amortisation

The amount of amortisation should be calculated by applying the effective interest method to spread the financing cost (that is the difference between the initial amount recognised for the financial asset and the amount receivable at maturity) over the period to maturity. The amount amortised in respect of a financial asset should be recognised as income in profit or loss.

Definition

The **effective interest rate** is the rate that exactly discounts estimated future cash payments or receipts through the expected life of the instrument or, when appropriate, a shorter period to the net carrying amount of the financial asset or financial liability.

If required, the effective interest rate will be given in the examination. You will not be expected to calculate it.

Worked example: Amortised cost

An entity acquires a zero coupon bond with a nominal value of £20,000 on 1 January 20X6 for £18,900. The bond is quoted in an active market and broker's fees of £500 were incurred in relation to the purchase. The bond is redeemable on 31 December 20X7 at a premium of 10%. The effective interest rate on the bond is 6.49%.

Set out the journals to show the accounting entries for the bond until redemption if it is classified as a held-to-maturity financial asset. The entity has a 31 December year end.

Solution

On 1 January 20X6

DR	Financial asset (£18,900 plus £500)	£19,400	
CR	Cash		£19,400

On 31 December 20X6

DR	Financial asset (£19,400 × 6.49%)	£1,259	
CR	Interest income		£1,259

On 31 December 20X7

DR	Financial asset ((£19,400 + £1,259) × 6.49%)	£1,341	
CR	Interest income		£1,341
DR	Cash	£22,000	
CR	Financial asset		£22,000

2.3.1 Loans and receivables

A financial asset classified as a loan or receivable should also be measured at **amortised cost** using the effective interest method.

Amortisation should be recognised as an income in profit or loss.

Most financial assets that meet this classification are simple receivables and loan transactions.

Interactive question 2: Loans and receivables　　　[Difficulty level: Exam standard]

Hallowes plc has agreed to lend a customer £9,500 on 1 January 20X2 subject to the following terms:

- The loan is repaid on 31 December 20X4 in full.
- Three interest payments of £1,000 are paid on 31 December each year.

Hallowes plc incurred £250 of legal fees in agreeing the loan documentation with the customer. The effective rate of interest on the loan is 9.48%.

Demonstrate by journal entries how the loan should be recorded in the financial statements of Hallowes plc for the year ended 31 December 20X2 and subsequent years.

See **Answer** at the end of this chapter.

2.4 Subsequent measurement of financial liabilities

Most financial liabilities should be measured at **amortised cost using the effective interest method.** This includes redeemable and irredeemable preference shares which have been recognised as liabilities. Note that the effective interest rate will be equal to the actual interest rate for irredeemable preference shares as there is no redemption premium.

Interactive question 3: Financial liabilities　　　[Difficulty level: Exam standard]

Bonds with a nominal value of £200,000 were issued at £157,763 on 1 January 20X1. The coupon rate is 4% while the effective interest rate is 9.5%. Interest is paid annually in arrears. Redemption is at par in five years. Issue costs are immaterial.

Calculate the carrying amount of the bonds in the statement of financial position at 31 December 20X1 and at each subsequent year end until redemption.

The carrying amount of the bonds at 31 December in the years 20X1 to 20X5 is as follows:

Period end	Amount borrowed £	Interest (at 9.5%) £	Repaid £	Carrying amount £
20X1				
20X2				
20X3				
20X4				
20X5				

See **Answer** at the end of this chapter.

3　IAS 32 *Financial Instruments: Presentation*

Section overview

- Financial instruments should be presented as assets, liabilities or equity in the statement of financial position.

- Compound financial instruments should be split between their liability and equity components.

- Interest, dividends, gains and losses should be presented in a manner consistent with the classification of the related financial instrument.

- Financial assets and financial liabilities can only be offset in limited circumstances.

3.1 Objectives and scope of IAS 32

The objective of IAS 32 *Financial Instruments: Presentation* is to enhance a user's understanding of the way in which financial instruments affect an entity's financial performance, financial position and cash flows. IAS 32 sets out the presentation requirements for financial instruments and their related interest or dividends, and specifies the circumstances in which they should be offset.

The principles that underlie the standard are consistent with, and complement, those in IAS 39, which addresses recognition and measurement criteria.

The scope of IAS 32 is that it applies to **all entities** and to all types of financial instruments except where another standard is more specific. Examples of areas which are outside the scope of IAS 32 are:

- Subsidiaries accounted for under IAS 27 and IFRS 10
- Associates and joint ventures accounted for under IAS 28

Worked example: Investments in subsidiaries

Greatdane plc acquired 40,000 ordinary shares in Subtime Ltd which represents 80% of its issued ordinary share capital. Whilst these ordinary shares are a financial asset of Greatdane plc, in its consolidated financial statements IAS 32 (and IAS 39) does not apply; the provisions of IFRS 10 *Consolidated Financial Statements* should be applied.

In the separate (company only) financial statements of Greatdane plc, IAS 27 *Separate Financial Statements* allows a choice of accounting treatment. The investment may be accounted for either at cost or in accordance with IAS 39 (as a financial asset).

In practice most companies account for investments in subsidiaries, associates and jointly controlled entities at cost in their separate financial statements. Therefore, the provisions of IAS 32 (and IAS 39) are generally only applied to minor investments where the investor does not have control, significant influence or joint control.

3.2 Presentation of equity and liabilities

When an entity issues a financial instrument, it should classify it according to the **substance** of the contract under which it has been issued. It should be classified as:

- A financial asset; or
- A financial liability; or
- An equity instrument.

The characteristics of the financial instrument should be considered to ensure that it is appropriately classified. If the financial instrument meets any of the **criteria** set out in the definition of a **financial liability**, then it should be classified as a liability and not as an equity instrument. The classification should be made at the time the financial instrument is issued and not changed subsequently.

The classification is important as it changes the perceived risk of the entity. The classification of an instrument as a financial liability will potentially have an adverse effect on the gearing ratio of a company and may reduce its ability to obtain further debt funding.

The classification of a financial instrument as a liability or as equity depends on the following:

- The **substance of the contractual arrangement** on initial recognition
- The **definitions** of a financial liability and an equity instrument

How should a financial liability be distinguished from an equity instrument? The critical feature of a liability is an obligation to transfer economic benefit. Therefore, the financial instrument is a financial liability if there is:

- A **contractual obligation** on the issuer to deliver cash/another financial asset, or
- A **contractual right** for the holder to receive cash/another financial asset.

Where this feature is **not** met, then the financial instrument is an **equity instrument**.

Worked example: Classification of financial instruments

Alpha Ltd issues 100,000 £1 ordinary shares.

These would be classified as an equity instrument:

- The shareholders own an equity instrument because although they own a residual interest in the company, they have no contractual right to demand any of it to be delivered to them, eg by way of dividend.

- The company has issued an equity instrument because it has no contractual obligation to distribute that residual interest.

3.3 Preference shares

Preference shares provide the holder with the right to receive an annual dividend (usually of a predetermined and unchanging amount) out of the profits of a company, together with a fixed amount on the ultimate liquidation of the company or at an earlier date if the shares are redeemable. The legal form of the instrument is equity.

IAS 32 treats most preference shares as **liabilities**. This is because they are, in substance, loans.

| Fixed annual dividend | = | 'interest' |
| Fixed amount on redemption/liquidation | = | 'repayment of loan' |

In substance the fixed level of dividend is interest and the redemption amount is a repayment of a loan. Because financial reporting focuses on the substance of the transactions, redeemable preference shares should be presented as liabilities.

However, where preference shares are not redeemable at the option of the preference shareholder they are known as irredeemable preference shares and the classification depends on other terms related to the preference shares, such as the rights to dividends. If dividends on the irredeemable preference shares are mandatory and cumulative, then the entity has a contractual obligation to pay the dividends to the preference shareholders and therefore the shares should be presented as liabilities. If there is no mandatory requirement to pay (or defer) dividends on irredeemable preference shares ie the payment of dividends is discretionary, then there is no contractual obligation to deliver cash (or another financial asset) and instead the irredeemable preference shares should be presented as equity.

Therefore in practical terms preference shares are only treated as part of equity when:

- They will never be redeemed, or

- The redemption is solely at the option of the issuer and the terms are such that it is very unlikely at the time of issue that the issuer will ever decide on redemption, **and**

- The payment of dividends is discretionary.

For the purposes of your exam, you will be told whether the payment of dividends is discretionary or mandatory in relation to irredeemable preference shares.

Interactive question 4: Liabilities and equity   [Difficulty level: Intermediate]

Moorgate Ltd issued 10,000 preference shares. The preference shares are redeemable only at the option of Moorgate Ltd. A preference share dividend is payable at the same amount per share as any ordinary share dividend declared during that year.

Explain the presentation requirements for Moorgate Ltd's preference shares.

See **Answer** at the end of this chapter.

Interactive question 5: Redeemable preference shares [Difficulty level: Intermediate]

On 1 January 20X3 Philo plc issued 300,000 £1 6% redeemable preference shares. The shares were issued at a discount of 5% and the effective interest rate is 7%. Dividends are paid annually in arrears.

Calculate the carrying amount of the shares in the statement of financial position of Philo plc as at 31 December 20X4.

See **Answer** at the end of this chapter.

3.4 Compound financial instruments

A compound or 'hybrid' financial instrument is one that contains both a **liability component** and an **equity component**. As an example, an issuer of a **convertible bond** has:

- The obligation to pay annual interest and eventually repay the capital – the liability component

- The possibility of issuing equity, should bondholders choose the conversion option – the equity component

In substance the issue of such a bond is the same as issuing separately a non-convertible bond and an option to purchase shares.

At the date of issue the components of such instruments should be classified separately according to their substance. This is often called 'split' accounting. The amount received on the issue (net of any issue expense) should be allocated between the separate components as follows:

- The fair value of the liability component should be measured at the present value of the periodic interest payments and the eventual capital repayment assuming the bond is redeemed. The present value should be discounted at the market rate for an instrument of comparable credit status and the same cash flows but without the conversion option

- The fair value of the equity component should be measured as the remainder of the net proceeds

Note that the rate of interest on the convertible will be lower than the rate of interest on the comparable instrument without the convertibility option, because of the value of the option to acquire equity.

The allocation should not be revised for subsequent changes in market interest rates, share prices or other events that have changed the likelihood that the conversion option will be exercised. This is the case even if the terms become so disadvantageous that it is extremely unlikely that the option will be exercised.

Worked example: Convertible bonds

Instead of issuing a 7% loan repayable in ten years' time an entity issues a 5% convertible bond for £50,000 that is repayable in cash in ten years or convertible at that time into 5,000 ordinary shares in the company.

In such a case the company could have issued two separate instruments, a 7% loan repayable in ten years' time and a warrant or option to subscribe for 5,000 ordinary shares on that date.

Note that the cash flows of the instrument are the same regardless of its accounting treatment, but the accounting treatment may affect the user's perception of risk.

Worked example: Compound instruments

A company issued 3,000 convertible 6% ten year bonds at £100 each. The present value of the redemption value and interest payments determined at market yields for an investment without the conversion option was £275,000.

What amounts should be attributed to the liability and equity components?

Solution

	£
Net proceeds on issue (3,000 × £100)	300,000
Fair value of liability component	(275,000)
Equity component	25,000

Therefore the following should be recognised in the statement of financial position:

Liability	£275,000
Equity (Other reserves)	£25,000

Note how the treatment of a convertible bond in this way improves a company's gearing as compared to treating the whole £300,000 as debt.

Interactive question 6: Compound financial instruments [Difficulty level: Exam standard]

On 1 January 20X7 an entity issued 10,000 6% convertible bonds at a par value of £100. Each bond is redeemable at par or convertible into four shares on 31 December 20X8.

Interest is payable annually in arrears. The market rate of interest for similar debt without the conversion option is 8%.

Using the proforma below measure the liability and equity components of these bonds on 1 January 20X7.

Year	Cash flow £	Discount factor	Present value £
20X7			
20X8			
Total liability component			
Net proceeds			
Equity element			

See **Answer** at the end of this chapter.

Subsequently the annual interest expense recognised in profit or loss should be calculated by reference to the interest rate used in the initial measurement of the liability component.

If all or part of the compound financial instrument is eventually converted into equity, the relevant proportion of the carrying amount of the financial liability should be reclassified as equity, being added to the equity amount initially recognised. No gain or loss should be recognised on conversion of the instrument.

Worked example: Compound instruments

In Interactive question 3 the liability component is £964,335. The subsequent accounting for the liability component should be as follows.

Year	Opening balance £	Interest expense (8%) £	Interest paid £	Closing balance £
20X7	964,335	77,147	(60,000)	981,482
20X8	981,482	78,518	(60,000)	1,000,000

Note how the £77,147 interest expense is greater than the £60,000 (6% × 10,000 × £100) interest paid because it includes the amortisation of the discount attributable to the liability element. Only the interest actually paid should be presented in the statement of cash flows.

If on 31 December 20X8 all the bond holders elect to convert into equity, then the £1 million liability should be reclassified to equity, making £1,035,665 in total. The double entry should be:

DR	Financial liability	£1 million	
CR	Equity		£1 million

If none of the bonds are converted to equity, the liability of £1 million will be extinguished by the cash repayment. However, the amount already included in equity of £35,665 should remain there. The double entry should be:

DR	Financial liability	£1 million	
CR	Cash		£1 million

3.5 Interest, dividends, losses and gains

Interest, dividends, losses and gains arising in relation to a financial instrument that is classified as a financial liability should be recognised in profit or loss for the relevant period.

The costs of servicing the financing of a company must be treated **consistently** with the way that the underlying instrument has been treated:

- Dividends on ordinary shares and irredeemable preference shares where the payment of dividends is discretionary will be shown as an **appropriation of profit** (in the statement of changes in equity).

- The cost of servicing loans will be shown as **interest payable** as a finance cost (in profit or loss).

- Dividends on redeemable preference shares and irredeemable preference shares where the payment of dividends is mandatory will be shown alongside **interest payable** as part of the finance cost (in profit or loss).

Distributions, such as dividends, paid to holders of a financial instrument classified as equity should be charged directly against equity (as part of the movement on retained earnings in the statement of changes in equity).

The classification will not affect the cash flows which are the same regardless of the presentation.

Interactive question 7: Dividends

[Difficulty level: Intermediate]

Dorehouse Ltd has declared the following dividends during the year:

(1) An ordinary dividend of £4 million
(2) A £3 million dividend on preference shares redeemable in 20X9

Explain the presentation requirements for Dorehouse Ltd's dividends in the financial statements for the year.

See **Answer** at the end of this chapter.

When equity shares are issued, the transaction costs should be deducted from equity, net of any related income tax benefit. The transaction costs to be deducted are only those incremental costs attributable to the equity transaction that otherwise would have been avoided.

Worked example: Issue costs

An entity issued 100,000 new £1 ordinary shares which have a fair value of £2.50 per share for cash.

Professional fees in respect of the share issue were £50,000. The management of the entity estimates that costs incurred internally for time incurred working on the share issue are £25,000.

How should these transactions be recorded in the financial statements?

Solution

The internal costs should be recognised as an expense in profit or loss as they were not incremental costs; they would have been incurred in any event. The professional fees were directly attributable to the transaction and £50,000 should be deducted from equity.

The double entry to record this transaction should be:

DR	Cash (£250,000 less £50,000)	£200,000	
CR	Share capital		£100,000
CR	Share premium		
	((100,000 × (£2.50 less £1.00)) less £50,000)		£100,000

3.6 Offsetting

Financial assets and financial liabilities should generally be presented as separate items in the statement of financial position. However, offset is required if:

- The entity has a legal right of offset, and
- The entity intends to settle on a net basis.

It may be the case that one entity both owes money to and is due money from another entity. A frequently occurring example of this is where a company has several accounts with a single bank, some of which are in credit and some overdrawn. The presentation issue is whether these amounts should be shown separately or whether they should be netted off against each other and a single figure for the resulting net asset (or liability) shown.

IAS 32 looks to see whether there is a **legally enforceable** right to make the set off. But it then goes further, by taking account of the entity's intentions. If there is a legal right to make a set off and the entity **intends to settle the amounts on a net basis**, then the set off must be made.

On this basis an entity with credit and overdrawn bank balances would not set them off against each other (even if it had the legal right to do so) because in the normal course of business it is keeping these accounts separate, so it cannot claim that it 'intends' to settle on a net basis.

Worked example: Offsetting

Herdings plc and Intake Ltd trade with each other. Herdings plc has recognised in its financial statements trade receivables of £40,000 and trade payables of £20,000 in respect of Intake Ltd. Herdings plc and Intake Ltd have an informal arrangement to periodically offset balances and settle on a net basis.

Herdings plc should not offset the trade receivables and trade payables as no legal right of offset exists. Whilst its custom and practice is to settle on a net basis, no formal right of setoff exists.

3.7 Treasury shares

It is becoming increasingly popular for companies to reacquire their own shares as an alternative to making dividend distributions and/or as a way to return excess capital to shareholders. Equity instruments reacquired by the entity which issued them are known as treasury shares.

The treatment of these treasury shares is that:

- They should be deducted from equity (shown as a separate reserve) and the original share capital and share premium amounts remain unchanged.

- No gain or loss should be recognised in profit or loss on their purchase, sale, issue or cancellation.

- Consideration paid or received should be recognised directly in equity.

- Although the shares are shown separately in equity, they are deducted in the weighted average number of shares calculation for the purposes of calculating EPS (see Chapter 3).

The amount of treasury shares held should be disclosed either in the statement of financial position or in the notes to the financial statements in accordance with IAS 1 *Presentation of Financial Statements*.

Worked example: Treasury shares

An entity entered into a share buyback scheme. It reacquired 10,000 £1 ordinary shares for £2 cash per share. The shares had originally been issued for £1.20 per share.

The entity should record the reacquired shares as a debit entry of £20,000 in equity. The original share capital and share premium amounts of £10,000 and £2,000 remain unchanged.

		£	£
DR	Treasury shares	20,000	
CR	Cash		20,000

4 IFRS 7 *Financial Instruments: Disclosures*

Section overview

- The disclosures required by IFRS 7 are extensive.

- They are designed to show the significance of financial instruments for the entity's financial position and performance.

- They should indicate the nature and extent of risks arising from financial instruments to which the entity is exposed during the period and at the reporting date, and how the entity manages those risks.

4.1 The risks associated with financial instruments

The use of financial instruments by entities is widespread and the risk associated with such instruments can be significant. As financial instruments become more complex and commonplace, clear and full disclosure becomes increasingly important. Financial instruments may or may not be recognised in an entity's financial statements, depending upon their nature. However, an entity's exposure to risk associated with unrecognised instruments may still be significant, and therefore disclosure is even more important.

The disclosure of information about financial instruments held by an entity is essential as an entity increases the use of such instruments, for example entities operating in the financial services sector. Over the last decade entities have changed the way in which they use financial instruments and manage their exposure to risk. As a result a fundamental review of what information should be disclosed by entities in relation to their financial instruments was undertaken by the IASB.

4.2 Objectives of IFRS 7

Information concerning an entity's exposure to risk and how the entity manages that risk continues to be important when assessing an entity's financial position and performance. The IASB issued IFRS 7 because it felt that existing standards needed to be improved to ensure that disclosures made in this area provided greater transparency of information, to allow users to better assess the risks that an entity is exposed to.

The objective of IFRS 7 is to require entities to provide disclosures in their financial statements which enable users to evaluate:

- The **significance of financial instruments** for the entity's financial position and performance, and

- The **nature and extent of risks** arising from financial instruments to which the entity is exposed during the period and at the reporting date, and how the entity manages those risks.

4.3 Assessing financial performance and financial position

As set out above, one of the overall objectives of IFRS 7 is to ensure that users of financial statements can adequately evaluate the significance that financial instruments have in the assessment of financial position and performance of an entity. To meet this objective IFRS 7 sets out detailed disclosure requirements in relation to both the statement of financial position and the statement of profit or loss and other comprehensive income.

Either in the statement of financial position or in the notes the carrying amounts of **each category of financial instruments** should be disclosed.

The fair values of each class of financial instrument should also be disclosed.

As well as monetary (**quantitative**) disclosures, **narrative commentary** by issuers is encouraged. This is to enable users to understand management's **attitude to risk**.

The standard sets out the following categories of risk:

Definitions

Credit risk is the risk that one party to a financial instrument will cause a financial loss for the other party by failing to discharge an obligation.

Liquidity risk is the risk that an entity will encounter difficulty in meeting obligations associated with financial liabilities that are settled by delivering cash or another financial asset.

Market risk is the risk that the fair value or future cash flows of a financial instrument will fluctuate because of changes in market prices. Market risk includes interest rate risk and currency exchange rate risk.

Worked example: Extract from the financial statements of Centrica plc 2011

Liquidity risk

Cash forecasts identifying the Group's liquidity requirements are produced regularly and are stress-tested for different scenarios, including, but not limited to, reasonably possible increases or decreases in commodity prices and the potential cash implications of a credit rating downgrade. The Group seeks to ensure that sufficient financial headroom exists for at least a 12-month period to safeguard the Group's ability to continue as a going concern. It is the Group's policy to maintain............an average term to maturity in the recourse long-term debt portfolio greater than five years.

Interest rate risk management

In the normal course of business the Group borrows to finance its operations. The Group is exposed to interest rate risk because the fair value of fixed rate borrowings and the cash flows associated with floating rate borrowings will fluctuate with changes in interest rates. The Group's policy is to manage the interest rate risk on long-term borrowings by ensuring the exposure to floating interest rates remains within a 30% to 70% range, including the impact of interest rate derivatives. A sensitivity analysis that is intended to illustrate the sensitivity of the Group's financial position and performance to changes in interest rates is provided…

5 Ethical and judgement issues

Section overview

The application of accounting standards to financial instruments requires significant judgement.

The failure to report transactions involving financial instruments appropriately has contributed to a number of recent accounting scandals. The complexity of many financial instruments presents challenges for financial reporting. This is evidenced by the length of the accounting standards and the detailed application guidance.

The greatest risks come from derivatives held off-balance sheet. One of the purposes of IAS 39 was to regulate this and require all derivatives to be recognised in the financial statements. This makes it possible for users to assess the risks to which the entity is exposed. An obvious example of what can happen when financial instruments are repackaged and resold in a way which masks the level of risk attached is the US subprime mortgage crisis which led into the recession of 2008.

Derivatives are **not in your syllabus**. However, even the application of the accounting standards to the simple financial instruments in this chapter requires significant judgements to be made by management. These include:

- Determining fair values using other valuation mechanisms where market values are not readily available.

- Determining whether financial instruments are financial liabilities or equity.

- Ensuring qualitative disclosures of treasury policies are consistent with the actual transactions undertaken.

6 UK GAAP comparison

Section overview

There are some differences in accounting for financial instruments under UK GAAP.

Entities reporting under FRS 101 are exempt from the following provisions of IFRS 7 and IFRS 13:

- All requirements of IFRS 7 *Financial Instruments: Disclosures*, provided that equivalent disclosures are included in the consolidated financial statements of the group in which the entity is consolidated.

- The disclosure requirements of IFRS 13 *Fair Value Measurement* provided that equivalent disclosures are included in the consolidated financial statements of the group in which the entity is consolidated.

Entities reporting under FRS 102 measure financial assets or liabilities initially at transaction price (this will include transaction costs unless measurement is at fair value through profit or loss). Under IAS 39 initial measurement is at fair value.

Measurement after initial recognition is generally at amortised cost or fair value through profit or loss, whereas IAS 39 provides more categories.

Summary and Self-test

Summary

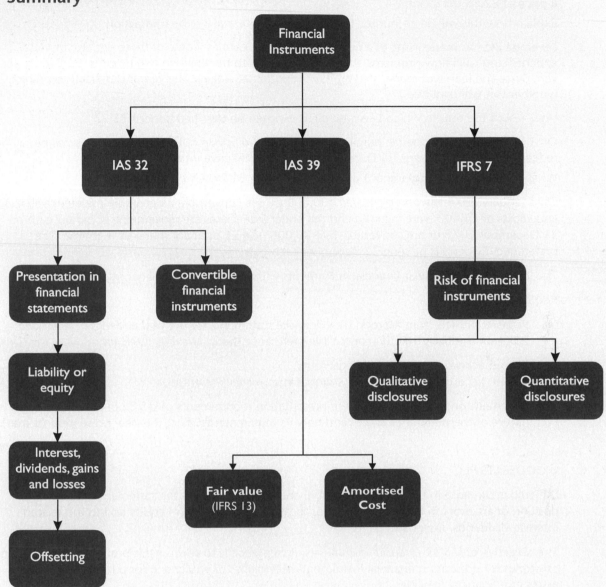

Self-test

Answer the following questions.

1   According to IAS 32 *Financial Instruments: Presentation*, what is the correct treatment for dividends on redeemable preference shares and dividends on ordinary shares in financial statements?

2   Cashrich plc has decided that it will utilise surplus funds to reacquire 100,000 of its equity shares at a price of £2.15 per share.

   Explain how this will be accounted for and show the journal for the transaction.

3   Leverage plc has made loans to a number of different entities. Some of those entities are now experiencing cash flow problems. Another loan is due to be repaid in two months' time in Japanese yen. Since the loan was made, sterling has strengthened against the yen. It is difficult to predict whether this will continue.

   How would the risks to which Leverage plc is exposed be classified under IFRS 7?

4   On 1 January 20X5 Beppe plc purchases £150,000 of 6% loan notes. The loan notes will be redeemed at a premium on 31 December 20X8. The effective interest rate is 7.5%.

   What will be the carrying amount of the loan notes at 31 December 20X6?

5   On 1 January 20X4 Maroon plc issued 100,000 £1 6% convertible redeemable preference shares. Issue costs of £5,000 were incurred and the preference shares are redeemable at par for cash on 31 December 20X8 or are convertible into 20,000 new £1 ordinary shares at that time. The preference dividend is paid on 31 December each year.

   The interest rate on similar financial instruments without the convertibility option is 8%.

   Requirements

   (a)   Prepare extracts from Maroon plc's financial statements for the year ended 31 December 20X4 on the basis that the convertible preference shares are accounted for:

   (i)   In accordance with their legal form
   (ii)   In accordance with IAS 32 *Financial Instruments: Presentation*   **(5 marks)**

   (b)   Comment on the usefulness of the presentation requirements of IAS 32 in understanding the nature of the preference shares and how its requirements affect the view presented. **(3 marks)**

                                                                                            (8 marks)

6   WOODSEATS PLC

   Difficulties can arise in the presentation of financial instruments in the statement of financial position of an entity in relation to their classification as liabilities and equity and to the related interest, dividends, losses and gains.

   The objective of IAS 32 *Financial Instruments: Presentation* is to address this problem by establishing principles for presenting financial instruments as liabilities or equity and for offsetting financial assets and financial liabilities.

   On 1 January 20X3 Woodseats plc had only 50m £1 ordinary shares in issue, which had been in issue for many years. During the year ended 31 December 20X3 Woodseats plc entered into the following financing transactions.

   (1)   On 1 January 20X3 Woodseats plc issued 20 million 8% £1 preference shares at par. The preference shares are redeemable at par on 30 June 20X8. The appropriate dividend in respect of these shares was paid on 31 December 20X3.

   (2)   On 30 June 20X3 Woodseats plc issued 10 million 12% £1 irredeemable preference shares at par. Dividends are discretionary and non-cumulative. The appropriate dividend in respect of these shares was paid on 31 December 20X3.

   In reviewing the draft financial statements of Woodseats plc the auditors drew attention to an error which had begun in the previous year's financial statements. Expenditure had been capitalised as an intangible asset which did not meet the criteria in IAS 38. The carrying amount of the intangible asset included in the draft statement of financial position was as follows.

	£m
At 1 January 20X3	4.5
Costs incurred during 20X3	2.0
Amortisation charge	(0.5)
At 31 December 20X3	6.0

The draft profit for 20X3, before adjusting for these capitalised costs, was £15 million. Retained earnings at 1 January 20X3 were £75 million.

Requirements

(a) Describe the concept of 'substance over form' and its application to the presentation of financial liabilities under IAS 32 *Financial Instruments: Presentation*. **(3 marks)**

(b) Prepare extracts from the financial statements of Woodseats plc for the year ended 31 December 20X3 to the extent the information is available, showing how the above would be reflected in those financial statements.

Notes to the accounts are not required. Ignore taxation. **(7 marks)**

(10 marks)

Now, go back to the Learning objectives in the Introduction. If you are satisfied you have achieved these objectives, please tick them off.

Technical reference

IAS 32 *Financial Instruments: Presentation*

1 Presentation of equity and liabilities

- Classification as financial asset, financial liability or equity instrument   IAS 32 (15–16)
- Definitions   IAS 32 (11)
- Contractual obligation and substance of instrument   IAS 32 (17–18)
- Settlement options   IAS 32 (26–27)
- Treasury shares   IAS 32 (33–34)
- Interest, dividends, losses and gains   IAS 32 (35–36)
- Offsetting   IAS 32 (42)

2 Compound instruments

- Recognising liability and equity elements   IAS 32 (28)
- Example of convertible bonds   IAS 32 (29–30)
- Calculation of liability and equity elements   IAS 32 (31–32)

IAS 39 *Financial Instruments: Recognition and Measurement*

1 Recognition

- Fair value   IAS 39 (9)
- Amortised cost and effective interest method   IAS 39 (14)

2 Measurement

- Initial measurement of financial assets and financial liabilities   IAS 39 (43)
- Subsequent measurement of financial assets   IAS 39 (45–46)
- Subsequent measurement of financial liabilities   IAS 39 (47)
- Determining fair value   IAS 39 (48–49)

4 Treatment of gains and losses

- Financial assets/liabilities at fair value   IAS 39 (55)
- Financial assets/liabilities at amortised cost   IAS 39 (56)

IFRS 13 *Fair Value Measurement*

Definition, measurement framework and required disclosures   IFRS 13 (App and 11–91)

IFRS 7 *Financial Instruments: Disclosures*

Nature and extent of risks arising from financial instruments

- Purpose of disclosures   IFRS 7 (31–32)
- Qualitative disclosures   IFRS 7 (33)
- Quantitative disclosures   IFRS 7 (34)

Answer to Interactive question 1

(1) The inventory is not a financial instrument as it is a physical asset. Guideprice Ltd should recognise a trade payable in its financial statements; this is a financial liability because there is a contractual obligation to pay the amount in cash. Conversely, Offertake Ltd records a trade receivable for £5,000, which is a financial asset as it has the contractual right to receive cash.

(2) Ashdell Ltd has paid for services in advance. The £20,000 should be recorded as a prepayment. The future economic benefit is the right to receive insurance services rather than cash, ordinary shares or another financial asset. Therefore, prepayments are not financial instruments.

(3) The ordinary shares are an equity instrument of Wellbeck Ltd as they give the holder a residual interest in the assets of Wellbeck Ltd after deducting the liabilities. The ordinary shares are a financial asset of Keeload Ltd.

(4) Cashlow plc has entered into a mortgage. The contractual obligation to repay £200,000 to Norbert plc is a financial liability. Norbert plc has a financial asset as it has the contractual right to receive £200,000 cash.

Answer to Interactive question 2

1 January 20X2

DR	Loan (£9,500 + £250)	£9,750	
CR	Cash		£9,750

31 December 20X2

DR	Cash	£1,000	
CR	Interest income (£9,750 × 9.48%)		£924
CR	Loan (bal fig)		£76

Note: loan balance is now £9,674 (£9,750 – £76)

31 December 20X3

DR	Cash	£1,000	
CR	Interest income (£9,674 × 9.48%)		£917
CR	Loan (bal fig)		£83

Note: loan balance is now £9,591 (£9,674 – £83)

31 December 20X4

DR	Cash (£9,500 + £1,000)	£10,500	
CR	Interest income (£9,591 × 9.48%)		£909
CR	Loan (bal fig)		£9,591

Answer to Interactive question 3

The carrying amount of the bonds at 31 December in the years 20X1 to 20X5 is as follows:

Period end	Amount borrowed £	Interest (at 9.5%) £	Repaid (4% × £200,000) £	Carrying amount £
20X1	157,763	14,988	(8,000)	164,751
20X2	164,751	15,651	(8,000)	172,402
20X3	172,402	16,378	(8,000)	180,780
20X4	180,780	17,174	(8,000)	189,954
20X5	189,954	18,046	(8,000)	200,000
			(200,000)	–

Answer to Interactive question 4

Preference shares redeemable at the issuer's option are classified as equity because there is no obligation to transfer financial assets (for example cash) at some future time. However, if Moorgate Ltd notifies the holders of an intention to redeem the preference shares at some future time, then an obligation arises and the preference shares should be reclassified as financial liabilities.

The rights attaching to the shares should be considered, to establish the substance of the instruments for classification. The dividends are not contractual obligations as they are only paid when ordinary share dividends are declared. In substance they are at the discretion of Moorgate Ltd and this confirms the classification as equity.

Answer to Interactive question 5

Year	Opening balance £	Interest expense 7% £	Dividend paid 6% £	Closing balance £
20X3	285,000	19,950	(18,000)	286,950
20X4	286,950	20,086	(18,000)	289,036

Answer to Interactive question 6

Year	Cash flow £	Discount factor	Present value £
20X7	60,000	1/1.08	55,556
20X8	1,060,000	$1/1.08^2$	908,779
Total liability component			964,335
Total proceeds 10,000 × £100			1,000,000
Equity element			35,665

Answer to Interactive question 7

Dividends payable should be classified according to the underlying financial instrument:

- Dividends payable on ordinary shares (an equity instrument) should be charged directly against equity. Dorehouse Ltd's £4 million ordinary dividend should be recognised in the statement of changes in equity.

- Dividends payable on redeemable preference shares (a financial liability) should be recognised as an expense in profit or loss. Dorehouse Ltd's £3 million preference dividend should be recognised in profit or loss. The dividend may be presented as part of the finance cost or as a separate line item.

1 Equity dividends paid are recognised in the statement of changes in equity. Equity dividends proposed after the year-end are not a liability at the end of the reporting year so are not recognised. Dividends on redeemable preference shares are recognised in profit or loss as a finance cost.

2 IAS 32 requires shares which have been repurchased to be shown separately in the statement of financial position as a deduction from equity. No gain or loss on the transaction is recognised so there is no impact on profit or loss.

The journal entry will be:

		£'000	£'000
DR	Treasury shares (equity section)	215	
CR	Cash		215

3 Leverage plc is exposed to two types of risk:

- Credit risk. The risk that one of the entities to whom it has advanced a loan will be unable to repay the money.

- Market risk. The risk in this case of an exchange loss on the transaction. If sterling is stronger against the yen when the loan matures than it was when the loan was made, then the amount that Leverage plc receives in yen will buy less sterling.

4 The carrying amount of the loan notes at 31 December 20X6 will be £154,669.

WORKING

	B/f	Interest	Interest received	C/f
	£	7.5%	6%	£
1 January 20X5	150,000	11,250	(9,000)	152,250
1 January 20X6	152,250	11,419	(9,000)	154,669

5 (a) **Extracts from financial statements for the year ended 31 December 20X4**

	(i)	(ii)
	Legal Form	IAS 32
Statement of profit or loss		
Finance cost (W2)	–	7,361
Statement of changes in equity		
Dividends paid	6,000	–
Statement of financial position		
Non-current liabilities		
Borrowings (W2)	–	93,376
Equity		
Equity element of convertible debt (W1)	–	2,985
Convertible preference shares (100,000 – 5,000)	95,000	–
Statement of cash flows		
Cash flows from operating activities		
Interest paid	–	(6,000)
Dividends paid	(6,000)	–
Cash flows from financing activities		
Proceeds from issue of convertible, redeemable		
preference shares	95,000	95,000

Note: IAS 7 *Statement of Cash Flows* allows flexibility in the presentation of interest paid and dividends paid.

WORKINGS

(1) Splitting the liability and equity components on initial recognition

Payments	Amount £	Discount factor (Note)	Present value £
20X4	6,000	0.9259	5,556
20X5	6,000	0.8573	5,144
20X6	6,000	0.7938	4,763
20X7	6,000	0.7350	4,410
20X8	106,000	0.68058	72,142
Liability component			92,015
Equity component (Bal fig)			2,985
Total (£100,000 less £5,000)			95,000

Note: The discount factors are calculated using the $1/(1+r)^n$ formula.

(2) Calculating the liability carrying amount at year end

	£
Liability at 1 January 20X4	92,015
Interest expense at 8% (8% × 92,015)	7,361
Cash paid	(6,000)
Liability at 31 December 20X4	93,376

(b) The legal form of the preference shares is equity. They are a type of share capital. If the transaction is accounted for in accordance with its legal form, the preference shares are included in equity and the dividends are presented as part of the movement in equity.

The substance of redeemable preference shares is that they are debt as there is a contractual obligation to make repayments of interest and capital. These terms meet the definition of a financial liability.

However, the convertibility option means that the preference shares also have an equity component. The same effect could have been achieved by issuing warrants and redeemable preference shares separately.

The requirements of IAS 32 reflect the substance of the transaction, focusing on the economic reality that in effect two financial instruments have been issued. These preference shares are a compound financial instrument and split accounting should be applied.

The requirements of IAS 32 will increase the amount of borrowings in the financial statements compared with if the preference shares had been accounted for in accordance with their legal form. As a result gearing will be higher and it may be more difficult for Maroon plc to obtain further borrowing.

Should the legal form be accounted for, the preference share dividend should be recognised in the statement of changes in equity. Under IAS 32 the amount should be recognised as an expense in profit or loss. The IAS 32 expense is higher than the dividend paid as it includes the amortisation of the discount of the liability. Earnings under IAS 32 will be lower than under the legal form.

The cash flows are the same in both sets of circumstances, although they will be categorised differently as interest and dividends paid. However, users of financial statements may perceive a different level of risk.

Point to note: Convertible bonds are another type of compound financial instrument. Their legal form is debt. For convertible bonds, gearing would be higher if the legal form was applied.

6 WOODSEATS PLC

(a) **Substance over form and the presentation of financial liabilities under IAS 32** *Financial Instruments: Presentation*

Under the IASB *Conceptual Framework for Financial Reporting*, information must be relevant and faithfully represented. Faithful representation means that financial information represents the substance of an economic phenomenon rather than merely representing its legal form.

The substance is not always consistent with the legal form of a transaction. This is often the case when an arrangement involves a number of linked transactions or components.

IAS 32 uses the substance of a financial liability rather than its legal form to determine the classification in the statement of financial position. Some financial instruments take the legal form of equity but are liabilities in substance as they include contractual obligations to transfer economic benefits to the holder. This approach is consistent with the definition of a liability in the IASB *Conceptual Framework* and such financial liabilities are classified in liabilities and not equity.

More complex financial instruments may combine features of both equity instruments and financial liabilities. IAS 32 looks at the substance of the components of the instrument and classifies them separately.

(b) **Financial statement extracts**

Statement of financial position as at 31 December 20X3

	£m
EQUITY AND LIABILITIES	
Equity	
Ordinary share capital	50
Preference share capital (irredeemable)	10
Non-current liabilities	
Preference share capital (redeemable)	20

Statement of profit or loss for the year ended 31 December 20X3

	£m
Cost of sales (2m – 0.5m)	(1.5)
Finance cost (20m × 8%)	(1.6)

Statement of changes in equity for the year ended 31 December 20X3

	Ordinary share capital £m	Irredeemable preference share capital £m	Retained earnings £m	Total £m
Balance at 1 January 20X3	50	–	75	125
Correction of prior period error	–	–	(4.5)	(4.5)
Restated balance	50	–	70.5	120.5
Issue of share capital		10		10
Dividends paid (10 × 12% × 6/12)			(0.6)	(0.6)
Total comprehensive income (15 – 1.5)			13.5	13.5
Balance at 31 December 20X3	50	10	83.4	143.4

CHAPTER 9

Other standards

Introduction

Examination context

Topic List

Summary and Self-test

Technical reference

Answers to Interactive questions

Answers to Self-test

Introduction

Learning objectives

- Explain the definitions and recognition criteria of IAS 37 *Provisions, Contingent Liabilities and Contingent Assets* within the context of the IASB *Conceptual Framework*

- Apply the accounting and disclosure requirements of IAS 37 including:

    - Recognition, measurement and disclosure of provisions; and

    - Disclosure of contingent liabilities and contingent assets

- Apply the accounting and disclosure requirements of IAS 10 *Events After the Reporting Period* including the distinction between:

    - Events after the reporting period that require adjustment; and

    - Those that require disclosure only

- Prepare and present extracts of financial statements in respect of government grants and explain the financial reporting treatment

- Identify and consider appropriate actions for related ethical issues

- Identify and illustrate the main differences between International and UK requirements in relation to IAS 37, IAS 10 and IAS 20

Specific syllabus references for this chapter are: 1d, 2b, 2c, 2d, 2e.

Syllabus links

You will have a general knowledge of IAS 37 from your Accounting syllabus. In the Financial Accounting and Reporting syllabus this standard is covered at a higher level, requiring an understanding of the issues which can be involved in applying it and the professional judgement required. IAS 10 and IAS 20 are both introduced for the first time in this syllabus. All three standards are examined at level A in this paper. This level of knowledge will also be relevant to the Advanced Stage.

Examination context

In the examination, candidates may be required to:

- Explain the IASB *Conceptual Framework* definitions and recognition principles and explain how they relate to IAS 37

- Prepare extracts from the financial statements and notes to the financial statements in respect of provisions and contingencies and explain the financial reporting treatment required

- Prepare financial statements or extracts taking into account the effect of events after the reporting period and explain the financial reporting treatment required

- Explain the accounting treatment of government grants

- Draft financial information including government grants

- Explain and illustrate the difference between the relevant treatment under IFRS and UK GAAP

- Identify and explain any ethical issues

1 Provisions and contingencies

Section overview

IAS 37 *Provisions, Contingent Liabilities and Contingent Assets* provides guidance on when provisions and contingencies should be recognised and if so, at what amount.

1.1 Issues

As we have seen in many of the previous chapters, amounts in the financial statements often result from the exercise of judgement, for example the carrying amount of property, plant and equipment. Accounting for provisions and contingencies, however, is particularly problematic due to the **increased level of uncertainty**. The key issues include:

- **Whether** a provision or contingency should be recognised
- If it is recognised at **what amount** it should be recorded

The situation is further complicated by the fact that these decisions may be affected by events occurring after the reporting period.

1.2 IAS 37 *Provisions, Contingent Liabilities and Contingent Assets*

Objective

IAS 37 aims to ensure that:

- **Appropriate recognition criteria and measurement bases are applied** to provisions, contingent assets and contingent liabilities; and

- **Sufficient information is disclosed** in the notes to the financial statements to enable users to understand their nature, timing and amount.

Scope

Although IAS 37 has wide scope, there are two limited exceptions:

Executory contracts (except where the contract is onerous – see Section 4.2)	Executory contracts are contracts under which neither party has performed any of its obligations or both parties have partially performed their obligations to an equal extent. For example, an unfulfilled order for the purchase of goods, where at the end of the reporting period, the goods have neither been delivered nor paid for.
Where the accounting treatment is covered by another accounting standard	For example, IFRS 3 *Business Combinations* deals with the recognition of an acquiree's contingent liabilities at the time of a business combination (see Chapter 10).

2 Provisions: definition and recognition

Section overview

A provision is recognised when all of the following conditions are met:

- A present obligation exists as a result of a past event
- An outflow of resources is probable
- The amount can be estimated reliably

2.1 Definition

The key aim of IAS 37 is to ensure that provisions are only recognised when there are valid grounds for doing so.

Definitions

A **provision** is a liability of uncertain timing or amount.

A **liability** is a present obligation of the entity arising from past events, the settlement of which is expected to result in an outflow from the entity of resources embodying economic benefits.

Points to note

1 IAS 37 views provisions as a **sub-class of liabilities**.

2 Provisions can be distinguished from other liabilities such as trade payables and accruals, because of the **degree of uncertainty** as to their timing or amount.

3 The definition of a liability used in IAS 37 is the **same as the definition contained in the IASB** *Conceptual Framework* (see Chapter 1).

2.2 Recognition

IAS 37 states that a provision should be recognised when:

- An entity has a **present obligation** (legal or constructive) as a result of **a past event**;

- It is **probable** that an outflow of resources embodying economic benefits will be required to settle the obligation; and

- A **reliable estimate** can be made of the amount of the obligation.

Points to note

1 **If one or more of these criteria is not met**, a provision is not recognised (although as we will see later in this chapter a contingent liability may exist).

2 The recognition criteria of IAS 37 **are very similar to the criteria for the recognition of a liability contained in the IASB** *Conceptual Framework* (see Chapter 1). These also refer to the **probable** outflow of economic benefit and the need for **reliable** measurement.

2.3 A present obligation as a result of a past event

To establish whether an entity has a present obligation which arose from a past event, identification of an 'obligating event' is required.

An obligating event occurs where the entity has no realistic alternative to settling the obligation created by the event. IAS 37 recognises that this can occur:

- Where the settlement **can be enforced by law**; or

- In the case of a **constructive obligation**, where the event creates **valid expectations** in other parties that the entity will discharge the obligation (see Section 2.4 below).

Points to note

1 The event must be **past**, ie it must have occurred at the end of the reporting period. No provision is made for costs that may be incurred in the future but where no obligation yet exists.

2 Only obligations arising from past events **existing independently of an entity's future actions** (ie the future conduct of its business) are recognised as provisions. If management can avoid incurring expenditure by changing the entity's future operations, no provision arises.

3   An obligation always involves **another party to whom the obligation is owed**. However, the exact identity of that other party need not be known, eg the obligation may be to the public at large.

4   A board or management decision **does not give rise to an obligation** unless it has been communicated before the end of the reporting period to those affected by it so as to raise a **valid expectation** that the entity will discharge its responsibilities. In the absence of such communication, the board could change its mind and hence would be under no obligation.

5   Sometimes, the existence of an obligation will be uncertain, eg where there is a legal dispute. In these cases, IAS 37 deems a past event to give rise to a present obligation if it is **more likely than not** that an obligation exists at the end of the reporting period. However, if it is possible rather than probable that an obligation exists, a **contingent liability** will exist, not a provision (see Section 6 below).

Worked example: Present obligation as a result of a past event

Company A carries out quarrying activities. A condition of the planning consent is that environmental damage caused by quarrying must be remedied on completion of the quarrying. In this case, an obligation exists independently of the company's future conduct in relation to damage already caused at the end of the reporting period, because the company cannot avoid having to pay for remedial action. By contrast, no obligation exists in relation to expected further damage from continued quarrying because the company could decide not to quarry in the future.

Company B operates aircraft that need periodic overhauls if they are to continue in operation. No obligation exists in relation to future overhauls because the company could decide to sell or scrap the aircraft rather than overhaul them.

2.4   Legal and constructive obligations

You should be familiar with the concept of a legal obligation.

Definition

Legal obligation: An obligation that derives from:

* A contract (through explicit or implicit terms);
* Legislation; or
* Other operation of law.

An example of a legal obligation would be a **warranty** provided at the time of sale to undertake necessary repairs for a specified period of time.

A constructive obligation may be a less familiar term.

Definition

Constructive obligation: An obligation that derives from an entity's actions where:

* By an established pattern of past practice, published policies or a sufficiently specific current statement, the entity has indicated to other parties that it will accept certain responsibilities; and

* As a result, the entity has created a valid expectation on the part of those other parties that it will discharge those responsibilities.

Constructive obligations are more difficult to identify with certainty than legal obligations. In practice they are recognised **where the situation has much the same commercial effect as a legal obligation**. In other words, in practice, the entity cannot avoid settling the obligation.

For example there is likely to be a constructive obligation where failure to do something would result in **unacceptable damage to an entity's reputation or future business.**

Worked example: Constructive obligation

A retail store operates a policy of giving refunds to customers that goes beyond the company's legal obligations. The policy is long established and widely known. It is likely that this policy creates a constructive obligation, as a significant breach of the policy would damage the company's reputation considerably.

2.5 Probable outflow of resources

A provision is recognised only where the obligation will lead to a **probable** outflow of resources. Probable is defined for these purposes as **more likely than not** to occur. In practical terms this means that there is a **greater than 50% chance** that an entity will have to transfer resource to another party.

Point to note: Where there are a number of similar obligations (eg product warranties) the probability should be based on considering the class of obligation as a whole.

Worked example: Probable outflow

If a company has entered into a warranty obligation then the probability of outflow of economic benefits may well be extremely small in respect of one specific item. However, when considering the class of obligation as a whole, the probability of some outflow of economic benefits is likely to be much higher. If there is a **greater than 50% probability** of some transfer of economic benefits then a **provision** should be made for the **expected amount.**

2.6 Reliable estimate

A provision should be recognised only if a **reliable estimate** of the obligation can be made.

Points to note

1   Where an entity can determine a range of possible outcomes, a sufficiently reliable estimate can be made, even if the exact amount cannot be quantified.

2   In the extremely rare case where no reliable estimate can be made, a liability exists that cannot be recognised. That liability is disclosed as a contingent liability. IAS 37 provides no example of such an extremely rare case. In effect, 'extremely rare' means, 'almost never'.

3 Measurement and subsequent treatment

Section overview

- A provision should be measured at the best estimate of the expenditure required to settle the obligation.

- Where there is a large population an expected value will be calculated.

- The amount of the provision should be discounted where the time value of money is material.

- Reimbursement should be recognised as a separate asset when it is virtually certain that it will be received.

3.1 Basic rule

The amount provided should be the **best estimate** of the expenditure required to settle the present obligation at the end of the reporting period. This is the amount that an entity would rationally pay to settle the obligation at the end of the reporting period or to transfer it to a third party at that time. In making a best estimate account should be taken of:

- Information provided by **events after the reporting period**.

- **Management judgement/experience** of similar transactions.

- Guidance from independent **experts**.

- The **risks and uncertainties** surrounding the situation. Care is needed both to avoid understating provisions and to avoid excessively prudent provisioning.

3.2 Single obligation

Uncertainties surrounding the amount to be recognised as a provision are dealt with by various means **according to the circumstances**.

Worked example: Single obligation

If the expenditure for a single obligation is estimated at £10,000 and there is a 55% chance of the expenditure being incurred, then £10,000 is provided for. The process of estimating the amount involves two separate steps:

Step 1

Is it probable that there will be an outflow of economic resources (arising from a present obligation)? Yes, there is in this case, as there is a 55% probability.

Step 2

What reliable estimate can be made? £10,000 in this case.

Points to note

An **expected value** calculation (see next section) is **not** relevant for a **single obligation**.

Where a single obligation is being measured, the individual most likely outcome may be the best estimate of the liability. However, even in this case, the entity should consider **other outcomes**. Where other possible outcomes are either mostly higher or mostly lower than the most likely outcome, the best estimate will be a higher or lower amount.

CHAPTER

9

3.3 Expected values

Where there is a **large population of items**, the obligation is estimated by weighting all possible outcomes by their associated probabilities, to arrive at the **expected value**.

Interactive question 1: Expected values   [Difficulty level: Exam standard]

X plc sells goods which carry a one-year repair warranty. If minor repairs were to be required for all goods sold in 20X7, the cost would be £100,000. If major repairs were to be needed for all goods sold in 20X7, the cost would be £500,000.

X plc estimates that 80% of goods sold in 20X7 will have no defects, 15% will have minor defects and 5% will have major defects.

Requirement

Calculate the provision for repairs required at 31 December 20X7.

See **Answer** at the end of this chapter.

3.4 Future events

Future events such as changes in technologies, efficiency improvements and changes in legislation may have a significant impact on the **measurement of provisions**. These should be taken into account where there is **sufficient objective evidence** that they will occur.

3.5 Expected disposal of assets

Gains from the expected disposal of assets **should not be taken into account in measuring a provision** even if the expected disposal is closely linked to the event giving rise to the provision. Instead, such gains are accounted for under the relevant **IFRS**, ie IAS 16 *Property, Plant and Equipment* and IFRS 5 *Non-current Assets Held for Sale and Discontinued Operations* for PPE.

3.6 Discounting

Where the effect of the **time value of money** is **material**, the amount of the provision should be **discounted**. In other words it should be recorded at the **present value** of the expenditure required to settle the obligation. This is likely to be an issue when there is a significant period of time between the end of the reporting period and settlement of the obligation.

The discount rate used should be the **pre-tax rate** that reflects **current market assessments** of the time value of money and the **risks specific to the liability**.

Over the period between the recognition of a provision and its ultimate settlement, the provision should be increased each year by the discount rate. The increase should be recognised as a finance cost in profit or loss, not as a further expense under the line item where the original provision was charged.

The double-entry will be:

DR Finance costs (profit or loss)

CR Provision

Points to note

1   The entity's average borrowing rate **should not** be used as the discount rate. The discount rate should be pre-tax and reflect current market rates of the time value of money and the risks specific to the liability.

2   The discount rate should not be risk-adjusted if the cash flows already take account of this.

     This is relevant when risk is being incorporated directly in cash flows (for example a potential outflow may be increased to reflect its greater risk). When this has been done, adding a risk premium to the discount rate would be double-counting the risk effect.

3   Disclosure should be made of the **increase during the period in the discounted amount** arising from the passage of time and the **effect of any change** in the discount rate.

Worked example: Discounting

A company has a present obligation at 31 December 20X6, which it expects to settle in three years' time for £100,000. The rate which reflects the time value of money and the risks specific to the liability is 10%.

At what amount should the provision be measured at 31 December 20X6? How much should be recognised as a finance charge in each of the three years ending 31 December 20X7, 20X8 and 20X9? What accounting entry is required to record the finance charge in the year ending 31 December 20X7?

Solution

The provision should be measured at its present value at 31 December 20X6, that is £100,000/$(1.1)^3$ = £75,131.

The finance charge in each of the three years is calculated as:

	Balance b/f £	Finance cost @ 10% £	Balance c/f 31 Dec £
20X7	75,131	7,513	82,644
20X8	82,644	8,264	90,908
20X9	90,908	9,092	100,000

The accounting entry to record the finance charge in 20X7 is:

DR	Finance costs in profit or loss	£7,513	
CR	Provisions		£7,513

Interactive question 2: Discounting   [Difficulty level: Intermediate]

At 31 December 20X8 a company has an obligation in respect of costs that will be payable in 10 years' time arising from the restoration of land subject to quarrying and which satisfies the criteria for a provision as set out in IAS 37. The costs in 10 years' time are estimated at £1.2m.

Some asset disposals are anticipated that should help defray some of the anticipated costs and they are estimated at £0.2m in 10 years' time. It is possible that new site-cleaning technology might reduce the anticipated costs to £1m. The relevant discount rate has been assessed as 9%.

Requirement

Calculate the finance cost to be recognised as an expense in the year ended 31 December 20X9.

See **Answer** at the end of this chapter.

3.7   Reimbursements

In some cases, an insurance company or a supplier under a warranty may reimburse all or part of a company's expenditure to settle a provision. If so **the reimbursement should be recognised only when it is virtually certain that reimbursement will be received if the entity settles the obligation**. IAS 37 requires that the reimbursement should be:

*   Treated as an **asset** in the statement of financial position **separate from the provision**; and

*   Recognised in the statement of financial position **at an amount not exceeding the amount of the provision**.

The double entry will be:

DR Reimbursement receivable (current asset)
CR Expense account (profit or loss)

Points to note

1 Where an asset is recognised, it is presented separately from the liability, because in the unlikely event that the asset is not recovered, the company would still remain liable for its obligation.

2 In the statement of profit or loss, the expense relating to a provision may be presented net of the amount recognised for a reimbursement.

3 Note the different approaches to the recognition of assets and liabilities throughout this standard. An asset can be recognised only if an inflow of resources is virtually certain (and therefore not contingent), whereas a liability is recognised if an outflow of resources is more likely than not to occur.

If the likelihood of receiving reimbursement is not virtually certain then the amount should be disclosed as a **contingent asset**, assuming that receipt is probable (see Section 6 below).

3.8 Changes in provisions and judgements required

Provisions are inherently uncertain and IAS 37 requires that they should be **reviewed at the end of each reporting period** and adjusted to reflect the current best estimate. If a transfer of economic benefit is no longer probable, the provision should be reversed.

The application of the principles of IAS 37 in setting up and revising the amounts of provisions requires a great deal of estimation and judgement on the part of management. This is an area where it is vital that clear and comprehensive policies and procedures are laid down and then applied consistently from one period to another.

Even then, the carrying amounts of provisions are estimates of the effect of uncertain future events, so it is entirely legitimate for different people to take different views. The important objective is to make estimates which are neutral in terms of the information provided, rather than designed to achieve a pre-determined profit or net asset figure.

Prior to the introduction of IAS 37, there was no accounting standard dealing with provisions. Companies wanting to present their year-on-year results in the most favourable light would make large one-off provisions in years where a high level of profits was generated. These provisions were then available to shield expenditure in years where profits were lower. This created the misleading impression that profits were smoothly rising from year to year, with no peaks and troughs.

IAS 37 was introduced to end such abuses and the principle that provisions are only made where there are valid grounds for them must be maintained. This applies equally to any changes made to provisions. The integrity of management as a factor in financial statement preparation can never be overlooked.

3.9 Use of provisions

IAS 37 specifies that a provision should be used **only for expenditures for which the provision was originally recognised**.

If a provision is no longer required for its originally intended purpose, it should be reversed and not used to conceal the impact of other unrelated expenditure. The reversal is a **change of accounting estimate** and is recognised in profit or loss in the year of reversal. The entry to record the reversal is:

DR   Provisions   X
CR   Profit or loss for the year   X

3.10 Recognising an asset when recognising a provision

In some cases, an obligation may arise from a past event before an entity has obtained economic benefits from the event concerned, but the entity reasonably expects to obtain such future benefits.

In this case the **amount of the provision is also recognised as an asset**, to be written off over the period of the asset's useful life. An example of this is the way that under IAS 16 a provision for the initial estimates of dismantling and removing an item of PPE and restoring the site on which it is located is included in the cost of the item.

Interactive question 3: Provision for environmental damage
[Difficulty level: Exam standard]

A company establishes a new quarry and has a legal obligation to restore environmental damage once quarrying is completed. Before rock can be extracted for sale, the overlying material (the overburden) must be removed, causing environmental damage. The overburden itself has no commercial value. The estimated cost of remedying the damage caused by removal of the overburden is £50,000 (ignore discounting).

Requirement

Show and explain the accounting entry to record the provision for environmental damage rectification arising out of removal of the overburden.

Fill in the proforma below.

The entry to record the provision for environmental damage on removal of the overburden will be:

DR

CR

See **Answer** at the end of this chapter.

4 Specific applications

Section overview

- Future operating losses should not be provided for.

- A provision should be made for the unavoidable costs of meeting an onerous contract.

- Provisions for a restructuring should only be made where there is an obligation at the end of the reporting period.

4.1 Future operating losses

Provisions should not be recognised for future operating losses as they do not meet the definition of a liability (as they arise from future, not past events) or the general recognition criteria set out in IAS 37.

Point to note: This treatment is consistent with that required under IFRS 3 for expected future losses of an acquired business (see Chapter 10). IFRS 3 specifies that such losses should not be taken into account when calculating any goodwill acquired in a business combination but must be dealt with as post-acquisition items in the group accounts.

4.2 Onerous contracts

Definitions

An **onerous contract** is a contract in which the unavoidable costs of meeting the obligations under the contract exceed the economic benefit expected to be received under it.

The **unavoidable costs** under a contract are the lower of the cost of fulfilling the contract and any compensation or penalties arising from failure to fulfil it. In other words, it is the lowest net cost of exiting from the contract.

If an entity has a contract that is onerous, the present obligation under the contract should be **recognised and measured as a provision**. An example might be vacant leasehold property.

Worked example: Onerous contract

A company rents a building under an operating lease, but vacates the building shortly before the end of its reporting period, due to business relocation. The lease on the vacated building has three years to run and cannot be cancelled. The building cannot be sub-let.

In this case, the conditions for making a provision are met as:

- A present obligation exists as a result of a past event (the signing of the lease);

- An outflow of resources embodying economic benefit in settlement is probable (rentals for the remainder of the lease term); and

- The amount can be measured reliably (the future rentals, discounted if material).

Interactive question 4: Onerous contract   [Difficulty level: Intermediate]

You have a contract to buy 300 metres of silk from India Co each month for £18 per metre. From each metre of silk you make one silk dress. You also incur labour and other direct variable costs of £16 per dress.

Usually you can sell each dress for £40 but in late July 20X8 the market price falls to £28. You are considering ceasing production since you think that the market may not improve.

If you decide to cancel the silk purchase contract without two months' notice, you must pay a cancellation penalty of £2,400 for each of the next two months.

Requirements

(a) Is there a present obligation at 31 July 20X8?

(b) What amounts should be recognised in respect of the contract in your financial statements for the period ending 31 July 20X8?

See **Answer** at the end of this chapter.

4.3 Restructuring

Definition

A **restructuring** is a programme that is planned and controlled by management, and materially changes either:

- The scope of a business undertaken by an entity; or
- The manner in which that business is conducted.

Examples of events that may fall under the definition of restructuring include:

- **Sale or termination** of a line of business
- **Closure** of business locations or the **relocation** of business activities
- Changes in **management structure**
- **Fundamental reorganisations** that have a material effect on the nature and focus of the entity's operations

Point to note: The IAS 37 requirements apply to the recognition and measurement of provisions on discontinuance, as well as other restructurings. In the case of a discontinuance, IFRS 5 (dealt with in Chapter 3) provides additional disclosure requirements.

4.3.1 Criteria for making a provision

The key accounting issue is **whether**, and if so, **when**, to recognise a provision for a planned restructuring.

IAS 37 treats a restructuring as creating a **constructive obligation** (and therefore as requiring recognition as a provision) only when an entity:

- Has a **detailed formal plan** identifying at least:
  - The **business concerned**
  - The **principal locations**
  - The **employees affected**
  - The **expenditure required**
  - The **timing**; and

- Has raised a **valid expectation** in those affected that it will carry out the restructuring by starting implementation or announcing its main features.

A **management or board decision** taken before the end of the reporting period in itself **does not give rise to a constructive obligation** at the end of the reporting period **unless** the entity has:

- Already **begun implementation**; or
- **Made a public announcement** of the main features sufficient to establish a constructive obligation.

Point to note:

A similar decision taken after, not before, the end of the reporting period will normally require disclosure as a non-adjusting event after the reporting period, under IAS 10 (see Section 7 below).

4.3.2 Measurement

A provision should include only the **direct expenditures** arising from the restructuring, which are both:

- **Necessarily entailed** by the restructuring; and
- **Not** associated with **ongoing activities**.

This therefore excludes indirect costs, for example retraining or relocating staff in a continuing operation. Provisions for future losses of the restructured operation are also not permitted, unless they relate to onerous contracts.

4.3.3 Sale of an operation

Where an operation is to be sold, no obligation arises for the sale until the entity is committed to the sale, ie **there is a binding sale agreement**.

A decision to sell does not itself create an obligation. Without a binding agreement, there is no past event independent of the entity's future actions, as management may change its mind or be unable to find a purchaser.

4.4 Other examples

Appendix C of IAS 37 includes a number of examples of the way in which the recognition criteria would be applied to specific situations. Several of these have already been referred to in this chapter. You should read through the Appendix and attempt Interactive question 5 below to confirm your understanding.

 Interactive question 5: Provisions [Difficulty level: Exam standard]

In which of the following circumstances might a provision be recognised?

(a) On 13 December 20X9 the board of an entity decided to close down a division. The accounting date of the company is 31 December. Before 31 December 20X9 the decision was not communicated to any of those affected and no other steps were taken to implement the decision.

(b) As (a) above except that the board agreed a detailed closure plan on 20 December 20X9 and details were given to customers and employees.

(c) A company is obliged to incur clean up costs for environmental damage (that has already been caused).

(d) A company intends to carry out future expenditure to operate in a particular way in the future.

See **Answer** at the end of this chapter.

5 Disclosures relating to provisions

 Section overview

IAS 37 requires a number of numerical and narrative disclosures.

5.1 IAS 37 requirements

IAS 37 disclosures are examinable in full. The main requirements in relation to provisions are set out below. These are followed by an illustration of a provisions 'table' with supporting explanation.

Key IAS 37 numerical disclosures for each class of provision are:

- **Carrying amounts** at the beginning and end of the period.

- **Movements** during the period, including:

  - Amounts provided
  - Amounts used (ie incurred and charged against the provision)
  - Unused amounts reversed
  - Increases due to unwinding of a discount
  - Effect of changes in the discount rate

Key IAS 37 narrative disclosures for each class of provision are:

- A brief description of the **obligation** and **expected timing of any outflows** of resources embodying economic resources.

- An indication of the **uncertainties** involved.

- The amount of any **expected reimbursement**, including the amount of any asset that has been recognised.

Point to note: In extremely rare cases, **disclosure may seriously prejudice the company's position** in a dispute with other parties on the subject matter of the provision. In such cases, the **information need not be disclosed**, but the general nature of the dispute, together with the reason why the information has not been disclosed, should be stated.

5.2 Example of a provisions table

The following illustrates the way in which the key IAS 37 disclosures are normally met – by way of a provisions 'table', with supporting narrative, included in the notes to the financial statements.

Note X: Provisions

	Warranty provision £'000	Returns provision £'000	Total £'000
At 1 April 20X7	50,000	22,000	72,000
Additions	32,000	10,000	42,000
Amounts used during year	(51,000)	(20,000)	(71,000)
At 31 March 20X8	31,000	12,000	43,000

The warranty provision relates to estimated claims on those products sold in the year ended 31 March 20X8 which come with a one year warranty. A weighted average method is used to provide a best estimate. It is expected that the expenditure will be incurred in the next year.

The returns provisions relates to an open returns policy offered on all goods. Customers are given 28 days in which to return goods and obtain a full refund. The provision at the year end is based on a percentage, using past experience, of the number of sales made in March 20X8.

What the above table shows, for example for the warranty provision, is that at the end of last year a provision of £50m had been made. During the year, £51m was paid out in warranty costs. At the end of the year the company estimated that a provision of £31m was needed. This gives a balancing figure of £32m which represents the addition to the provision and will be charged to profit or loss.

The table above is essentially a glorified T account, with a column for each class of provision. For example, the warranty provision column in the table equates to a T account as set out below:

WARRANTY PROVISION

	£'000		£'000
Utilised (balancing figure)	51,000	Brought forward 1 April 20X7	50,000
Carried forward 31 March 20X8	31,000	Addition	32,000
	82,000		82,000

6 Contingent liabilities and contingent assets

Section overview

Contingent liabilities and assets should not be recognised but may require disclosure.

6.1 Contingent liabilities

Definition

A **contingent liability** is either:

* A possible obligation that arises from past events and whose existence will be confirmed only by the occurrence or non-occurrence of one or more uncertain future events not wholly within the control of the entity, or

* A present obligation that arises from past events but is not recognised because:

    - It is not probable that an outflow of resources embodying economic benefits will be required to settle the obligation; or

    - The amount of the obligation cannot be measured with sufficient reliability.

Points to note

1 Note the distinction between a provision and a contingent liability. A contingent liability arises when **some, but not all**, of the criteria for recognising a provision are met. The criteria for recognising a provision were covered in Section 2.2 above.

2 If an obligation is probable it is not a contingent liability – instead a provision is needed, assuming a reliable estimate can be made of the amount of the obligation.

6.2 Treatment of contingent liabilities

Contingent liabilities **should not be recognised in the financial statements**, but may require **disclosure** (see Section 6.3 below).

Because contingent liabilities are inherently uncertain, they should be **assessed continually** to identify whether the criteria for recognising a provision have been met. If this occurs, a provision should be recognised in the period in which the criteria are met. This would represent **a change of accounting estimate** regarding the likely outcome of an uncertain situation.

6.3 Disclosure of contingent liabilities

Unless the possibility of any outflow in settlement is **remote**, the following disclosures should be made for **each class of contingent liability at the end of the reporting period**:

- A brief description of its **nature**; and

- Where practicable:

    - An **estimate of the financial effect** (measured in the same way as a provision);
    - An indication of the **uncertainties**; and
    - The possibility of any **reimbursement**.

No specific guidance is provided in IAS 37 on the meaning of 'remote' but it should be interpreted as meaning **extremely unlikely**. This means that the probability of an event occurring should be **so small that it can be ignored**.

Worked example: Contingent liability

A company has provided a guarantee to a third party which, if it were to be called on to honour it, would undermine the going concern basis. In such a situation, even a 5% or 10% chance that the guarantee will be enforced should not be considered remote as this could potentially destroy the entire company.

6.4 Exemption

If the disclosure requirements of IAS 37 are not met because it is not practicable to do so, this fact should be stated. The same 'seriously prejudicial' disclosure exemption applies for contingent liabilities as for provisions (see Section 5 above).

6.5 Relationship between provisions and contingent liabilities

This can be summarised in the following flow chart which has been reproduced from Appendix B of IAS 37.

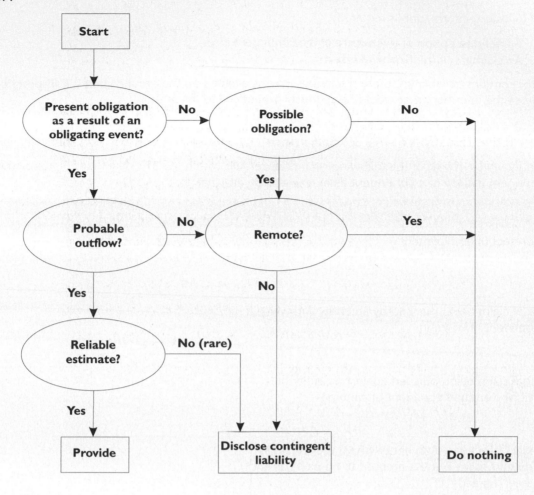

6.6 Contingent assets

Definition

A **contingent asset** is a possible asset that arises from past events and whose existence will be confirmed only by the occurrence or non-occurrence of one or more uncertain future events not wholly within the control of the entity.

An example of a contingent asset is the possible gain arising from a pending legal action or other claim.

6.7 Treatment of contingent assets

A contingent asset **must not be recognised**. Only when the realisation of the related economic benefits is **virtually certain** should recognition take place because, at that point, the asset is no longer contingent.

Contingent assets should be **assessed continually** to identify whether the uncertainty has been removed. If events confirm the existence of an asset, it should be **recognised** provided that it can be **measured reliably**.

6.8 Disclosure of contingent assets

Where an inflow of economic benefits is **probable**, ie more likely than not, the contingent asset must be disclosed.

The following information is required:

- A brief description of the **nature** of the contingent asset.
- An estimate of the **financial effect**.

As for contingent liabilities, these disclosures may be avoided on the grounds that it is **impractical** to provide the information or would be **seriously prejudicial** to the entity.

Interactive question 6: IAS 37 definitions   [Difficulty level: Easy]

Identify which, if any, of the following circumstances falls within IAS 37's definitions of a provision, a contingent liability or a contingent asset, explaining your answer:

Circumstance	Position under IAS 37
A contract of employment	
A legal claim being pursued by an entity and which it is confident of winning	
A legal claim being pursued against an entity but which the entity is confident of winning	
A legal claim against an entity where the entity has accepted liability but the amount to be paid has not yet been agreed	
Legislation enacted but coming into effect next year which will require substantial retraining of staff	
The reinstatement of land once quarrying has ceased, where there is no legal obligation. The entity's published policy in relation to environmental protection is that it will reinstate any environmental damage caused by its activities	
The reinstatement of land once quarrying has ceased, where there is no legal obligation, the entity has no published policy in relation to environmental protection and this is the first quarrying venture it has entered into	
Restructurings where the detailed plan has been developed, announced and agreed with employees' representatives	
Restructurings where the detailed plan has been developed and announced	

Circumstance	Position under IAS 37
Restructurings where the detailed plan has been developed and agreed by the board, but no announcement has been made	
Future reinstatement work under guarantees to be provided to customers in relation to future sales	

See **Answer** at the end of this chapter.

Interactive question 7: Application of IAS 37 [Difficulty level: Easy]

For each of the following circumstances identify when, if ever, an asset or liability should be recognised under IAS 37. In each case, is any disclosure required by IAS 37 prior to any asset/liability recognition?

Circumstance	Application of IAS 37
A legal claim in relation to a past event is pursued against an entity over several years. The entity makes the following judgements about outflows of resources in settlement:	
• Year 1: there will be no outflow	
• Year 2: an outflow is remote	
• Year 3: an outflow is possible	
• Year 4: an outflow is probable	
• Year 5: an outflow is virtually certain	
A legal claim in relation to a past event is pursued by an entity over several years. The entity makes the following judgements about inflows of resources in settlement:	
• Year 1: there will be no inflow	
• Year 2: an inflow is remote	
• Year 3: an inflow is possible	
• Year 4: an inflow is probable	
• Year 5: an inflow is virtually certain	

See **Answer** at the end of this chapter.

Interactive question 8: Recognition and measurement [Difficulty level: Intermediate]

(1) Conditional Ltd issued a one year guarantee for faulty workmanship on a single item of specialist equipment that it delivered to a customer. At the company's year end, the company is being sued by the customer for refusing to replace or repair the item of equipment within the guarantee period. Conditional believes the fault is not covered by the guarantee, but instead has arisen because the customer did not follow the operating instructions.

The company's lawyer has advised Conditional that it is more likely than not that the company will be found liable. This would result in the company being forced to replace or repair the equipment plus pay court costs and damages amounting to approximately £20,000.

Based on past experience with similar items of equipment, the company estimates that there is a 70% chance that the central core would need to be replaced, which would cost £80,000, and a 30% chance that the repair would only cost about £30,000.

(2) The company also manufactures small items of equipment which it sells via a retail network. The company sold 15,000 items of this type this year, which also carry a one year guarantee against failure. Based on past experience, 5% of items sold are returned for repair or replacement. In each case, one third of the items returned can be repaired at a cost of £100, while the remaining two-thirds are scrapped and replaced. The manufacturing cost of a replacement item is £300.

Requirement

Discuss the accounting treatment of the above situations.

See **Answer** at the end of this chapter.

7 IAS 10 *Events After the Reporting Period*

Section overview

- Events after the reporting period may be:

    - Adjusting events
    - Non-adjusting events

- The effect of adjusting events should be reflected in the year end financial statements.

- Where the effect of non-adjusting events is material they should be disclosed.

7.1 Purpose of IAS 10

Financial statements are prepared to the end of the reporting period. The preparation of financial statements however, will normally continue for a period after this date. During this time lag, events may occur which **provide additional information** that is relevant to the preparation of the financial statements. The objective of IAS 10 *Events After the Reporting Period* is to prescribe when financial statements **should be adjusted** for these events and any **disclosures** that may be required.

7.2 Events after the reporting period

Definition

Events after the reporting period are those events, favourable and unfavourable, that occur between the end of the reporting period and the date when the financial statements are authorised for issue.

Points to note

1   The date the financial statements are **authorised for issue** is the key cut off point. Any event which takes place **after** this date is outside the scope of IAS 10.

2   The process involved in authorising the financial statements may vary:

- Where an entity is required to submit its financial statements to its shareholders for approval after the financial statements have been issued, the financial statements are authorised for issue **on the date of issue** (not the date when the shareholders approve the financial statements).

- Where the management is required to issue the financial statements to a supervisory board (made up solely of non-executives) for approval, the financial statements are authorised for issue **when the management authorises them for issue to the supervisory board**.

3   The date of authorisation may be **after** a preliminary announcement has been made of profits or other information.

4   The date on which the financial statements are authorised for issue must be **disclosed,** so that users know the date up to which events and transactions have been taken into account.

There are two different classes of events after the reporting period:

*   **Adjusting events**
*   **Non-adjusting events**

We will look at these in detail below.

7.3   Adjusting events

Definition

Adjusting events: Those that provide evidence of conditions that existed at the end of the reporting period.

As the name suggests adjusting events lead to the **adjustment** of the financial statements. They require either:

*   **Adjustments to amounts already recognised** in the financial statements; or
*   Recognition of items **which did not previously meet the recognition criteria**.

Examples include:

*   The **settlement of a court case** outstanding at the end of the reporting period. (This is an example of an event which might require either adjustment to an amount already recognised in the financial statements as a liability or the recognition of something which prior to that would have been only a contingent liability.)

*   **Bankruptcy of a customer**, requiring adjustment to the amount receivable.

*   Proceeds or other evidence concerning **the net realisable value of inventories**.

*   Subsequent determination of **the purchase price or of the proceeds of sale** of assets purchased or sold before the end of the reporting period.

Worked example: Adjusting event

A pressing machine with a budgeted carrying amount at 31 December 20X6 of £20,000 is classified as held for sale in December 20X6. Its fair value less costs to sell is then estimated as £18,000 and it is sold for £16,500 on 28 February 20X7. The 20X6 financial statements are authorised for issue by the board on 15 March 20X7.

The machine should be measured at £16,500 as a held for sale asset in the 20X6 financial statements.

Point to note:

As the financial statements will have been adjusted for an adjusting event there is **no specific requirement to disclose the event.**

However, where the adjusting event affects an item which was not previously recognised but was disclosed, the disclosure will need to be updated. For example, the contingent liability for damages under a court case may need to be updated for new information.

7.4 Non-adjusting events

Definition

Non-adjusting events: Those that are indicative of conditions that arose after the reporting period.

Examples include:

*   A **fall in the market value of investments**
*   Plans to discontinue operations **announced after the reporting period**
*   Major **purchases of assets**
*   Losses on non-current assets or inventories **as a result of a catastrophe such as fire or flood**
*   Restructurings not provided for **as they were announced after the reporting period**

Adjustments to amounts in the financial statements are **not made to reflect non-adjusting events**.

However, where the effect of the non-adjusting event is **material**, such that non-disclosure could influence users' economic decisions the following **information should be provided in the notes** to the financial statements for each event:

*   The **nature** of the event; and
*   An estimate of the **financial effect**.

7.5 Dividends

Dividends on equity shares proposed or declared after the reporting period should be treated as follows:

*   They **cannot be shown as a liability** as there is **no obligation** at the end of the reporting period.
*   The amount of dividends payable should be **disclosed** in the notes to the financial statements.

Equity dividends **paid** are reflected in the statement of changes in equity.

7.6 Going concern

If management determines after the reporting period that it **intends to liquidate the entity or to cease trading, or that it has no realistic alternative but to do so**, then the financial statements **must not be prepared on the going concern basis**.

Points to note

1   Management intentions are taken into account.

2   A change from the going concern basis is so all-pervasive in its effects on financial statements that a fundamental change to the basis of accounting is required, not just adjustments to the figures prepared on the going concern basis. No guidance is given in any IFRS as to the basis of accounting which should be used in these circumstances, but it is likely that the break-up basis will be adopted (see Chapter 1). All assets will need to be measured at their net realisable values; amounts receivable from customers will need to take account of the period available for their collection – the shorter the period, the lower the value.

Interactive question 9: Building defects   [Difficulty level: Intermediate]

A routine inspection of an entity's main freehold building two weeks after its year end of 30 June 20X8 and before the accounts were authorised for issue revealed substantial cracks in the walls. A more detailed review was immediately undertaken by specialist professionals, who reported that there were major problems with the foundations. In their view these problems must have arisen several years ago, even though the visible evidence had only now come to light.

Requirement

Explain how this event should be dealt with in the financial statements for the year ended 30 June 20X8.

See **Answer** at the end of this chapter.

Interactive question 10: Inventories   [Difficulty level: Easy]

At its year end of 30 June 20X8 an entity held in inventories 4,000 units of a particular product line at a cost of £550 each. The product had been selling well, at £750 each with selling costs of £100 each.

Early in its new financial year the entity learnt that competitor action was such that it could only sell its product for £605, with selling costs unchanged.

Requirement

Explain how this event should be dealt with in the financial statements for the year ended 30 June 20X8.

See **Answer** at the end of this chapter.

7.7 Context and relevance of information for users

Financial statements are, by their very nature, prepared to a specific historical date. The process of preparing them can lead to a significant amount of time passing between the end of the reporting period and the publication date. Regardless of how quickly the financial statements are published, there will be a period of time before publication during which further events and transactions will take place.

Events that take place after the reporting period often provide further information on the financial position at the end of the reporting period. It is therefore reasonable that such information should be reflected in the financial statements.

Events may also arise prior to the publication of the financial statements that do not provide information on the financial position at the end of the reporting period but do have an impact on the operations of the entity in future periods. Where non-disclosure of such events is likely to influence the economic decisions of users of the financial statements, an explanation of the events should be included in the financial statements. For example, the sale of a significant operation after the year end could be key information for a user who is basing future earnings, cash flow and solvency forecasts on the financial statements.

IAS 10's requirement to disclose not just the nature but the financial effect of events occurring after the reporting period provides information which users should evaluate carefully.

8 IAS 20 *Accounting for Government Grants and Disclosure of Government Assistance*

Section overview

- A government grant is one type of government assistance.

- A government grant should only be recognised when there is reasonable assurance that:

  - The entity will comply with the conditions of the grant
  - The entity will receive the grant

- Grants related to income should be recognised over the period in which the associated costs are incurred.

- Grants related to assets may be presented by either:

  - Setting up the grant as deferred income or
  - Netting off the grant from the cost of the asset

- Grants received in the form of non-monetary assets should be recognised at fair value.

- Repayment of a grant should be treated as a change in accounting estimate.

8.1 Introduction

It is common for entities to receive government assistance for various purposes. In these terms the reference to 'government' is a **broad concept** including government agencies and similar bodies, whether local, national or international.

Government assistance can take many different forms and there are various motives for governments in providing such aid, including:

- **Geographical** – to stimulate employment in poorer regions
- **Industrial** – to support key industries (such as defence, IT and energy)
- **Inward investment** – to promote investment from overseas
- **New start-ups** – to help infant entities gain a foothold in a market

To ensure that the objective of providing the assistance is met by the recipient entity, there are often **a variety of criteria and conditions** attached to their receipt. Conditions, for example, may require a minimum investment to be provided or a minimum level of employment to be sustained over a specified period by the entity.

In a **financial reporting context** it is important to **disclose adequate information** in relation to government assistance, to ensure that **an entity's performance is accurately interpreted**. The identification of government assistance allows **a fair comparison** to be made with other entities in a similar industry that have not received such assistance.

Definition

Government assistance is action by government designed to provide an economic benefit specific to an entity or range of entities qualifying under certain criteria.

Government assistance does not include benefits provided **indirectly** to an entity, for example the provision of infrastructure in development areas.

Government grants are a form of government assistance.

The title of IAS 20 *Accounting for Government Grants and Disclosure of Government Assistance* explains its purpose. However, IAS 20 does not apply to the following situations:

- Government assistance given in the form of 'tax breaks', such as accelerated depreciation allowances and reduced rates of tax.

- Government acting as **part-owner** of the entity.

Definition

Government grants are assistance by government in the form of transfers of resources to an entity in return for past or future compliance with certain conditions relating to the operating activities of the entity. They exclude those forms of government assistance which cannot reasonably have a value placed upon them and transactions with government which cannot be distinguished from the normal trading transactions of the entity.

Point to note

Certain forms of government assistance are **excluded** from the above definition and should not be recognised. These include:

- Free technical or marketing advice

- The provision of guarantees

- Transactions with government that cannot be distinguished from the normal trading transactions of the enterprise, for example a government procurement policy that is responsible for a portion of the entity's sales

8.2 Recognition

A government grant (including a non-monetary grant at fair value) should only be recognised when there is **reasonable assurance** that:

- The entity will **comply with any conditions** attached to the grant.
- The entity **will actually receive the grant**.

Points to note

1   Receipt of the grant in itself does not prove that the conditions attached to it have been or will be fulfilled.

2   The manner in which a grant is received does not affect the accounting method adopted, so a grant is accounted for in the same way whether it is received in cash or as a reduction in a liability to the government.

8.3 Measurement

IAS 20 identifies **two methods** which could be used to account for government grants:

- **Capital approach**: recognise the grant outside profit or loss
- **Income approach**: the grant is recognised in profit or loss over one or more periods

IAS 20 requires grants to be recognised under the **income approach**, that is grants should be recognised in profit or loss over the periods in which the entity recognises as expenses the costs which the grants are intended to compensate.

It would be against the accrual principle to recognise grants in profit or loss on a receipts basis, so a **systematic basis of matching** must be used. A receipts basis would only be acceptable if no other basis was available.

It will usually be relatively easy to identify the costs related to a government grant, and thereby the period(s) in which the grant should be recognised in profit or loss.

8.3.1 Depreciating assets

Where grants are received in relation to a depreciating asset, the grant should be recognised over the periods in which the asset is depreciated **and** in the same proportions.

Interactive question 11: Grants for depreciating assets   [Difficulty level: Easy]

Arthur Ltd receives a government grant representing 50% of the cost of a depreciating asset which cost £40,000 and has a nil residual value. How should the grant be recognised if Arthur Ltd depreciates the asset:

- Over four years straight line, or
- At 40% reducing balance?

See **Answer** at the end of this chapter.

8.3.2 Non-depreciating assets

In the case of **grants for non-depreciable assets**, certain obligations may need to be fulfilled, in which case the grant should be recognised in profit or loss **over the periods in which the cost of meeting the obligation is incurred**. For example, if a piece of land is granted on condition that a building is erected on it, then the grant should be recognised in profit or loss over the building's life.

8.4 Presentation of grants

8.4.1 Grants related to assets

Grants related to assets are used to acquire or construct specific long term assets.

Government grants related to assets (including non-monetary grants at fair value) should be presented in the statement of financial position either:

- By setting up the grant as deferred income, or
- By deducting the grant in arriving at the carrying amount of the asset (that is netting off).

8.4.2 Deferred income method

The deferred income method sets up the grant as deferred income in the statement of financial position, which is recognised in profit or loss on a systematic and rational basis over the useful life of the asset. Normally this corresponds to the method of depreciation on the related asset.

8.4.3 Netting-off method

The netting-off method deducts the grant in arriving at the carrying amount of the asset to which it relates. The grant is recognised in profit or loss over the life of a depreciable asset by way of a reduced depreciation charge.

Worked example: Grants related to assets

An entity purchased an item of equipment for £50,000 on 1 January 20X5. It will depreciate this machinery on a straight-line basis over its useful life of five years, with a zero residual value. Also on 1 January 20X5, the entity received a government grant of £5,000 to help finance this equipment.

Under the **netting-off method** the grant and the equipment should be presented in the statement of profit or loss for the year to 31 December 20X5 and in the statement of financial position at that date as follows:

Statement of financial position

	£
Equipment	
Cost (50 – 5)	45,000
Depreciation	(9,000)
Carrying amount	36,000

Statement of profit or loss

Charge: depreciation	£9,000

Under the **deferred income method** the grant and the equipment should be presented in the statement of profit or loss for the year to 31 December 20X5 and in the statement of financial position at that date as follows:

Statement of financial position

	£
Equipment	
Cost	50,000
Depreciation	(10,000)
Carrying amount	40,000
Deferred income – non-current	3,000
Deferred income – current (the amount to be recognised in profit or loss in 20X6)	1,000
	4,000

(Total deferred income = 5,000 grant less 1,000 recognised in profit or loss = 4,000)

Statement of profit or loss

Charge:	Depreciation	£10,000
Credit:	Deferred income	£1,000

Points to note

1   There are less likely to be impairment issues if the grant has been deducted from the cost of the asset as this reduces the carrying amount. In addition, the financial statements will be less comparable with those of a similar entity that has not received government assistance.

2   Deferred income (recognised when using the deferred income method) should be split between current and non-current portions for disclosure purposes.

Interactive question 12: Grants related to assets: Deferred income method
[Difficulty level: Easy]

An entity purchased a new item of machinery for £320,000 on 1 January 20X7. It will depreciate this machinery at 25% per annum on the reducing balance basis, as this most closely resembles the pattern of benefits receivable from the asset. Also on 1 January 20X7, a government grant of £160,000 was received to help finance this machinery.

Requirement

Show the amounts to be recognised in profit or loss for the year ended 31 December 20X7 if the entity uses IAS 20's deferred income method for government grants.

See **Answer** at the end of this chapter.

8.4.4   Grants related to income

Government grants related to income are defined as those not related to assets and can be presented in two ways:

*   A credit in profit or loss (either separately, or under a general heading such as 'other income') or
*   A deduction from the related expense.

Treating the grant as a deduction from the related expense (the net treatment) results in the statement of profit or loss being less comparable with those of similar entities that have not received such grants. This treatment may also lead to the particular category of expenditure being excessively low in one year, or in comparison with other categories of expenditure during that period. Disclosure of grants received will therefore be important to assist comparison and understanding (see Section 8.6).

8.5   Other issues

8.5.1   Conditions and compensation

There may be a **series of conditions** attached to a grant. An entity must take care to identify precisely those conditions which give rise to costs which in turn determine the periods over which the grant will be earned. When appropriate, **the grant should be split and the parts allocated on different bases**.

An entity may receive a grant as compensation for expenses or losses which it has **already incurred**. Alternatively, a grant may be given to an entity simply to provide immediate financial support where no future related costs are expected. In cases such as these, the grant should be recognised in profit or loss in the period in which it becomes receivable.

Point to note: If it is possible that one or more of the conditions attaching to the grant will not be met, a contingent liability should be disclosed. If it turns out that one or more has not been met, then a provision should be recognised for the amount repayable.

8.5.2   Non-monetary government grants

A non-monetary asset may be transferred by government to an entity as a grant, for example a piece of land, or other resources. The **fair value** of such an asset is usually assessed and this is used to account for both the asset and the grant. Alternatively, both may be valued at a nominal amount.

8.5.3 Repayment of government grants

A government grant that becomes repayable should be accounted for as a change in an accounting estimate (see IAS 8 *Accounting Policies, Changes in Accounting Estimates and Errors*).

Repayment of a grant related to income should be applied in the following order:

* Against any **unamortised deferred credit** set up in respect of the grant

* To the extent that the **repayment exceeds any such deferred credit**, or **where no deferred credit exists**, the repayment should be **recognised immediately as an expense**

Repayment of a grant related to an asset should be recognised by either:

* Increasing the carrying amount of the asset or
* Reducing the deferred income balance by the amount repayable.

The cumulative additional depreciation that would have been recognised to date as an expense in the absence of the grant should be recognised immediately as an expense.

Interactive question 13: Grant recognition   [Difficulty level: Intermediate]

Determine if the following grants should be recognised and, if so, the period over which they should be recognised in profit or loss:

(1) A cash grant is available to private child nurseries to spend on toys in urban regeneration areas that qualify for such support. The only condition attaching to the grant is that the money should be spent immediately.

(2) A manufacturing entity receives a grant of £1 million when it creates 50 jobs. £0.5 million is payable when the figure is reached with the remaining £0.5 million payable at the end of four years should the 50 jobs still be in existence. There is reasonable assurance that the employment levels will be maintained when reached.

(3) Free testing equipment is available to new motor emission businesses being set up in a region that qualifies for special government support.

(4) A government department offers a grant in the form of free technical advice to entities setting-up businesses overseas to help export growth.

See **Answer** at the end of this chapter.

8.6   Disclosure

The disclosure requirements in IAS 20 help a user of the financial statements to understand the extent and effect of government grants on an entity during a particular period.

The following matters should be disclosed:

* The accounting policy adopted for government grants, including the methods of presentation

* The nature and extent of government grants recognised in the financial statements

* An indication of other forms of government assistance from which the entity has directly benefited

* Unfulfilled conditions and other contingencies attaching to government assistance that have been recognised

8.7   Judgements required

IAS 20 is one of the more straightforward reporting standards. Management judgement is only required in limited circumstances, such as:

* Whether to account for non-monetary grants at fair value or at a nominal amount.

- How to deal with a grant to defray the costs of a project if the project involves both capital and revenue expenditure. Some allocation to the different components would be appropriate, because it is likely that the two types of expenditure will be recognised in profit or loss over different periods.

8.8 Relevance of information for users

Users will wish to be aware of any significant amounts of government grants received so that they can:

- Take account of the effect on financial performance and position if further grants are not to be received in future periods.

- Compare the financial performance and position of a grant-receiving entity with that of an entity not eligible for grants.

The disclosures required by IAS 20 are very useful in this respect, particularly those in respect of the deferred income method of accounting for capital grants.

9 UK GAAP comparison

Section overview

- There are no significant differences in the treatment of provisions under UK GAAP.

- There are some differences in the treatment of events after the reporting period and government grants.

FRS 101 does not allow any exemptions from IAS 37 *Provisions, Contingent Liabilities and Contingent Assets,* IAS 10 *Events after the Reporting Period* or IAS 20 *Accounting for Government Grants and Disclosure of Government Assistance.*

There are some differences between FRS 102 and these standards:

- Under IAS 10 an equity dividend declared after the year end is not recognised but is disclosed in the notes. Under FRS 102 the dividend is not recognised as a liability but may be presented as a segregated component of retained earnings.

- FRS 102 does not permit the IAS 20 capital approach where government grants are deducted from the carrying amount of the asset.

- Under FRS 102 entities can account for grants using either the performance model or the accrual model. This choice is made on a class by class basis. IAS 20 allows a capital or an income approach.

- Unlike IAS 20, FRS 102 provides no guidance on accounting for repayment of a government grant.

CHAPTER

9

Summary

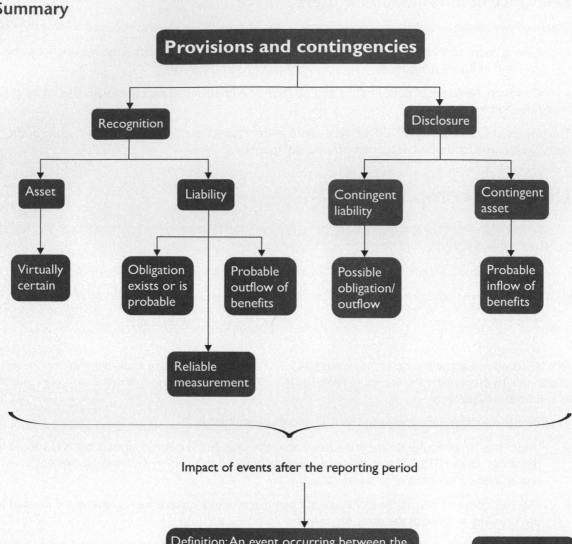

Provisions and contingencies

- Recognition
  - Asset
    - Virtually certain
  - Liability
    - Obligation exists or is probable
    - Probable outflow of benefits
    - Reliable measurement
- Disclosure
  - Contingent liability
    - Possible obligation/ outflow
  - Contingent asset
    - Probable inflow of benefits

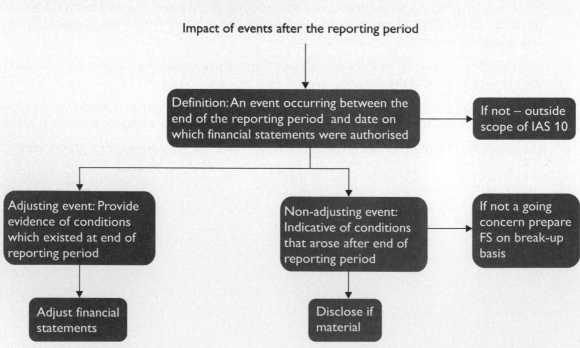

Impact of events after the reporting period

Definition: An event occurring between the end of the reporting period and date on which financial statements were authorised

If not – outside scope of IAS 10

Adjusting event: Provide evidence of conditions which existed at end of reporting period

Non-adjusting event: Indicative of conditions that arose after end of reporting period

If not a going concern prepare FS on break-up basis

Adjust financial statements

Disclose if material

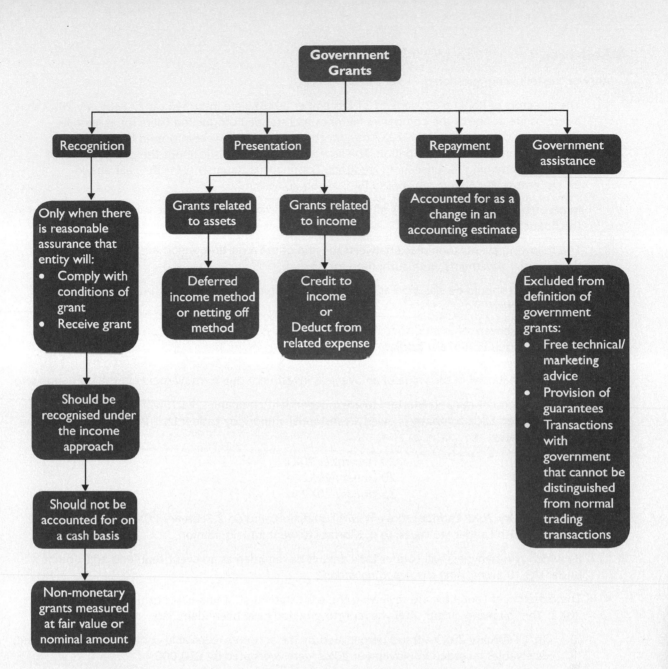

Government
Grants

Recognition

Only when there
is reasonable
assurance that
entity will:
• Comply with
  conditions of
  grant
• Receive grant

Should be
recognised under
the income
approach

Should not be
accounted for on
a cash basis

Non-monetary
grants measured
at fair value or
nominal amount

Presentation

Grants related
to assets

Grants related
to income

Deferred
income method
or netting off
method

Credit to
income
or
Deduct from
related expense

Repayment

Accounted for as a
change in an
accounting estimate

Government
assistance

Excluded from
definition of
government
grants:
• Free technical/
  marketing
  advice
• Provision of
  guarantees
• Transactions
  with
  government
  that cannot be
  distinguished
  from normal
  trading
  transactions

Self-test

Answer the following questions.

1   The directors of Robin plc (year end 31 December 20X6) were informed on 27 February 20X7 that a serious fire at one of the company's factories had stopped production there for at least six months to come. On 3 March 20X7 the directors of Robin plc were informed that a major customer had gone into liquidation. The liquidator was pessimistic about the prospect of recovering anything for unsecured creditors. The financial statements for the year ended 31 December 20X6 were authorised for issue on 20 March 20X7.

In accordance with IAS 10 *Events After the Reporting Period* how should the two events be treated in the financial statements?

2   The following events took place between the end of the reporting period and the date on which the financial statements were authorised for issue.

Which event should be classified as an adjusting event in accordance with IAS 10 *Events After the Reporting Period*?

(1)   The discovery of a fraud that shows the financial statements were incorrect
(2)   The acquisition of a subsidiary
(3)   A rights issue
(4)   A dramatic fall in the value of an overseas investment due to movements in the exchange rate

3   Brick Ltd, Cement Ltd and Mortar Ltd are independent companies, each with a year end of 31 December. Each company is owed a substantial amount by Ladder Ltd. The debts arose on the following dates.

Brick Ltd   20 December 20X1
Cement Ltd   20 January 20X2
Mortar Ltd   25 January 20X2

On 31 January 20X2 Ladder Ltd went into liquidation, and on 2 February 20X2, as a result of the amount which Ladder Ltd owed to it, Mortar Ltd went into liquidation.

By which company(ies) will Ladder Ltd's default be regarded as an event requiring adjustment under IAS 10 *Events After the Reporting Period*?

4   The directors of Laurel plc are reviewing the draft statement of financial position at 31 December 20X2. The following events after the reporting period have been identified.

(i)   On 1 February 20X3 a fraud perpetrated by the accounts receivable controller was discovered. Receivables recorded in November 20X2 were overstated by £30,000.

(ii)   Property, plant and equipment with a carrying amount of £25,000 was destroyed by a fire on 15 January 20X3. No insurance recovery is expected.

(iii) A claim brought by a customer which was under negotiation at the end of the reporting period was settled in court on 12 January 20X3. A payment of £20,000 in full settlement was made on 24 January 20X3.

Which of these events would be regarded as an adjusting event according to IAS 10 *Events After the Reporting Period*?

5   Porter plc is finalising its financial statements for the year ended 30 September 20X3.

A former employee of Porter plc has initiated legal action for damages against the company after being summarily dismissed in October 20X3. Porter plc's legal advisers feel that the employee will probably win the case and have given the company a reasonably accurate estimate of the damages which would be awarded. Porter plc has not decided whether to contest the case.

In accordance with IAS 37 *Provisions, Contingent Liabilities and Contingent Assets* how should this item be classified in the financial statements of Porter plc for the year ended 30 September 20X3?

6   Mulroon plc, a publishing company, is being sued for £1 million in a libel action in respect of a book published in January 20X4. On 31 October 20X4, the end of the reporting period, the directors believed that the claim had a 10% chance of success. On 30 November 20X4, the date the accounts were authorised for issue, the directors believed that the claim had a 30% chance of success.

In accordance with IAS 37 *Provisions, Contingent Liabilities and Contingent Assets* what amount should be accrued in the financial statements to 31 October 20X4?

7   Westbridge plc has constructed a power plant for a utility company. Under the terms of the contract Westbridge plc must repair free of charge any faults that arise in the plant during its first five years of operation.

The expected cost of any repair is 6 days at £100,000, giving a total of £600,000. But there is a significant chance that the first repair attempt will not succeed and further repair attempts will need to be made.

In accordance with IAS 37 *Provisions, Contingent Liabilities and Contingent Assets* how should Westbridge plc decide what amount should be accrued in the financial statements?

8   Construction plc was awarded a contract to build a tunnel under the Thames by a government department. Construction plc delegated some aspects of the contract to other companies. One of the sub-contractors, Underwater Ltd, was negligent in the performance of its contract with Construction plc, which caused delay in the completion of the tunnel.

As a result of the delay, the government department is claiming damages of £10 million against Construction plc. In turn, Construction plc has commenced proceedings against Underwater Ltd. The lawyers have advised Construction plc that both actions are likely to be successful.

In accordance with IAS 37 *Provisions, Contingent Liabilities and Contingent Assets* how should Construction plc account for the legal claims?

9   As a result of new banking regulations, Intrepid plc will need to retrain a large proportion of its financial services division in order to ensure continued compliance with banking regulations. At the end of the reporting period no retraining of staff has taken place. However, the head of the financial services division has announced that he is committed to a completion of the retraining programme by the end of the following year.

Carefree plc is also subject to the same banking regulations. By the end of the reporting period Carefree plc has contracted a training organisation to undertake the retraining programme with a start date of 15 January, two weeks after the reporting period. Staff have been notified of their training session dates.

In accordance with IAS 37 *Provisions, Contingent Liabilities and Contingent Assets* how should each company account for the cost of retraining their staff?

10   On 1 January 20X2 Delta Ltd began working a new mine. Legislation requires the owner to restore any environmental damage at the end of the three-year licence. The cost of restoration includes:

(i)   The replacement of the landscape, which had to be removed before mining could commence. The restoration cost is estimated at £6 million.

(ii) Damage that is progressively created as mining progresses. The total cost of this damage is estimated at £3 million. Environmental experts believe that the damage is created proportionately with time.

What provision for environmental remediation should be created at 31 December 20X2 in accordance with IAS 37 *Provisions, Contingent Liabilities and Contingent Assets*?

11   A government grant related to income can be credited to profit or loss or deducted from the related expense. What are the possible disadvantages of treating the grant as a deduction from the expense?

12   A housebuilding company receives a government grant to provide social housing as part of its new development. Under the terms of the grant 10% of the dwellings must be social housing. The construction is expected to take three years.

How should the conditions attached to the grant be reflected in the accounting treatment?

13 An entity purchased an item of machinery for £500,000 on 1 April 20X5 at which time it received a government grant of 20% of the cost of the machinery. The machinery is being depreciated at 25% per annum on the reducing balance basis.

Show how the machinery and the grant should be presented in the financial statements for the year ended 31 March 20X7 using the deferred income method.

14 VACS LTD

Vacs Ltd is a manufacturing company which prepares financial statements to 30 September each year. Before the draft financial statements for the year ended 30 September 20X3 can be finalised and approved by the directors, the following points need to be addressed. Draft net assets at 30 September 20X3 were £2 million.

(i)   Vacs Ltd has renewed the unlimited guarantee given in respect of the bank overdraft of a company in which it holds a significant investment. That company's overdraft amounted to £300,000 at 30 September 20X3 and it has net assets of £1 million.

(ii) A former director, who was dismissed from the company's service on 1 September 20X3 for acting outside his authority, has given notice of his intention to claim substantial damages for loss of office. On 1 November 20X3 a claim was received for £150,000. The company's legal advisers have been negotiating with the former director and believe that the claim will probably be settled at £100,000.

(iii) On 15 November 20X3 the company sold its former head office building, Whitley Wood, for £2.7 million. At the end of the reporting period the building was unoccupied and Vacs Ltd had not intended to sell the property for at least another year. The building's carrying amount (based on cost less accumulated depreciation) was £3.1 million at the end of the reporting period.

(iv) At 1 October 20X2 Vacs Ltd took out a three-year lease on a piece of land on which it erected temporary buildings to house some of its manufacturing processes. At the end of the three-year period the buildings will have to be removed and the land restored to grassland. The cost of carrying out this work had a present value at 1 October of £274,000. The appropriate discount rate is 8%.

Requirements

(a) Explain the definition of a liability from the IASB *Conceptual Framework* in the context of accounting for provisions and contingencies. **(5 marks)**

(b) Prepare extracts from the statement of financial position of Vacs Ltd as at 30 September 20X3, including any relevant notes to the financial statements. **(8 marks)**

(13 marks)

15 PROVISO PLC

Proviso plc is organised into several divisions. The following events relate to the year ended 31 December 20X2.

(i)   The computer division supplied a computer to a customer during the year that exploded, causing a fire. Proviso plc is being sued for damages. Lawyers have advised that there is a 30% chance of successfully defending the claim. Otherwise the damages are expected to cost £10 million (present value £9.5 million). The lawyers have investigated the cause of the problem with a team of accident consultants. They have concluded that parts supplied to the computer division by Moor Ltd contributed to the fire. Lawyers have estimated that Moor Ltd's contributory negligence amounted to 40% of the total damages. Negotiations have started with Moor Ltd and the lawyers believe that a claim is likely to succeed.

(ii) On 15 December 20X2, the directors of Proviso plc minuted their decision to close the operations of the loss making space technology division. The decision and an outline of a plan were immediately announced to employees and a press release was issued. The closure, which began on 4 January 20X3, has an estimated date for completion, including the sale of the non-current assets of the division, of 30 June 20X3. The costs associated with the closure include the following.

	£'000
Employee redundancy costs	12,000
Lease termination costs	4,000
Relocating continuing staff to other divisions	3,000
Impairment losses	2,000
	21,000

(iii) Proviso plc's retail division provides one-year warranties to its customers. Experience has shown that, on average, 10% of sales from this division result in a warranty claim. Revenue from this division in 20X2 was £8 million. At 1 January 20X2 Proviso plc had a warranty provision in place of £1 million. During the year claims of £600,000 were settled by the company.

Requirement

Prepare the provisions and contingencies notes for the financial statements of Proviso plc for the year ended 31 December 20X2. **(8 marks)**

16 FORDHAM LTD

Fordham Ltd receives an EU grant to cover 20% of the cost of an asset which has a fair value of £90,000 and a three year life. Annual profits before accounting for depreciation on the asset are expected to be £60,000 for each of the three years.

Show the effect on the statement of financial position and on profit or loss for each of the three years if the grant is accounted for by:

(a) Deducting it from the cost of the asset; and
(b) Treating it as deferred income **(10 marks)**

Now, go back to the Learning objectives in the Introduction. If you are satisfied you have achieved these objectives, please tick them off.

Technical reference

Point to note: All of IAS 10, IAS 37 and IAS 20 are examinable. The paragraphs listed below are the key references you should be familiar with.

1–2 Provisions – recognition

- Provisions are liabilities of uncertain timing or amount. — IAS 37 (10)

- A provision is recognised only when all of the following are met at the end of the reporting period: — IAS 37 (14)

  - A present obligation exists (legal or constructive) as a result of a past event

  - An outflow of resources embodying economic benefits in settlement is probable

  - Amount can be estimated reliably

- There is a useful decision tree in Appendix B — IAS 37 (App B)

3 Provisions – measurement and use

- Measure at best estimate of expenditure required to settle obligation at reporting date. — IAS 37 (36)

- Discount where material. — IAS 37 (45)

- Do not take into account gains from expected disposal of assets. — IAS 37 (51)

- Treat reimbursements as separate assets, recognised only where virtually certain, and only up to amount of provision. — IAS 37 (53)

  Expense in profit or loss may be shown net of reimbursement — IAS 37 (54)

- Review provisions at each reporting date and adjust to current best estimate. — IAS 37 (59)

- Use a provision only for the expenditures for which it was created. — IAS 37 (61)

4 Provisions – specific applications

- Do not provide for future operating losses. — IAS 37 (63)

- Provide for unavoidable costs of meeting onerous contracts. — IAS 37 (66)

- Provide for restructuring only where legal or constructive obligation exists at reporting date, and provision covers only costs: — IAS 37 (72 & 80)

  - Necessarily entailed by restructuring; and

  - Not associated with ongoing activities.

- No obligation arises on sale of an operation until there is a binding sale agreement. — IAS 37 (78)

- A useful set of examples is given in Appendix C. — IAS 37 (App C)

5 Disclosures

- Disclosure for each class of provision — IAS 37 (84–85)

- Disclosure for contingent liability — IAS 37 (86)

6 Contingent liabilities

- A contingent liability is either: IAS 37 (10)

  - A possible obligation arising from past events whose existence will be confirmed only by uncertain future events not wholly within the entity's control; or

  - A present obligation arising from past events not recognised because an outflow of resources embodying economic benefit is not probable or amount cannot be measured reliably.

- Do not recognise contingent liabilities but disclose unless possibility of outflow is remote. IAS 37 (27 & 86)

6 Contingent assets

- A contingent asset is a possible asset arising from past events whose existence will be confirmed only by uncertain future events not wholly within the entity's control. IAS 37 (10)

- Do not recognise contingent assets but disclose where inflow is probable (ie more likely than not). IAS 37 (31 & 89)

7 Events after the reporting period

- Events after the reporting period are events occurring between the end of the reporting period and date of authorisation of the financial statements. Two categories are: IAS 10 (3)

  - Adjusting events, which provide evidence of conditions existing at the end of the reporting period

  - Non-adjusting events, which are indicative of conditions arising after the end of the reporting period

- Financial statements are adjusted for:

  - Adjusting events IAS 10 (8)

  - Non-adjusting events that indicate that going concern assumption is not appropriate IAS 10 (14)

- Disclose, without adjustment, material non-adjusting events which could affect users' economic decisions taken on the basis of the financial statements. IAS 10 (21)

- Disclose date on which the financial statements are authorised for issue. IAS 10 (17)

8 Government grants

Treatment

- Should only be recognised if reasonable assurance that: IAS 20 (7)

  - Entity will comply with conditions

  - Grant will be received

- Manner in which received does not affect accounting method adopted IAS 20 (9)

- Should be recognised in profit or loss over periods necessary to match with related costs IAS 20 (12)

- Grants should not be accounted for on a cash basis IAS 20 (16)

- Grants in recognition of specific expenses recognised in profit or loss in same period as expense IAS 20 (17)

- Grants related to depreciable assets usually recognised in proportion to depreciation IAS 20 (17)

- Grants related to non-depreciable assets requiring fulfilment of certain obligations recognised in profit or loss over periods which bear the cost of meeting obligations

  IAS 20 (18)

- Grant received as compensation for expenses already incurred recognised in profit or loss in period in which receivable

  IAS 20 (20)

- Non-monetary grants should be measured at fair value or at nominal amount

  IAS 20 (23)

Presentation of grants related to assets

- Can be presented in the statement of financial position by:

  IAS 20 (24)

  - Setting up the grant as deferred income; or

  - Netting it off against the carrying amount of the asset

Presentation of grants related to income

IAS 20 (29)

- Either:

  - Recognised in profit or loss separately or under a general heading; or

  - Deducted in arriving at the amount of the related expense recognised in profit or loss

Repayment of government grants

- Accounted for as a change in an accounting estimate

  IAS 20 (32)

Government assistance

- The following forms of government assistance are excluded from the definition of government grants:

  IAS 20 (34-35)

  - Assistance which cannot reasonably have a value placed on it

  - Transactions with government which cannot be distinguished from the normal trading transactions of the entity

Disclosures

- Required disclosures

  IAS 20 (39)

Answers to Interactive questions

Answer to Interactive question 1

The expected cost of repairs will be:

$(80\% \times 0) + (15\% \times 100) + (5\% \times 500) = £40,000$

Answer to Interactive question 2

Measurement of the amount payable in 10 years' time:

- Anticipated asset disposals: these should not be used to reduce the amount payable

- Possible site-cleaning technology: this is said to be 'new' and there is no expert, independent evidence to support its likely availability. It should not be used to reduce the amount payable

The amount to be provided for is therefore £1.2m. This will arise after ten years and the relevant discount rate is 9%. The finance cost to be recognised in the year ended 31 December 20X9 is:

		£
Provision at 31 December 20X9	$£1.2m/1.09^9$	552,513
Provision at 31 December 20X8	$£1.2m/1.09^{10}$	506,893
Increase = finance cost		45,620

Answer to Interactive question 3

The entry to record the provision for environmental damage on removal of the overburden will be:

DR Non-current asset – Cost of establishing quarry	£50,000	
CR Provision for environmental costs		£50,000

When the overburden is removed, the company has yet to realise the economic benefits from extraction of the rock. However, the removal of the overburden is a past event giving rise to an obligation. Therefore a provision for restoration costs is recognised at this point. The debit entry is added to the non-current asset for the cost of establishing the quarry rather than being expensed immediately. The cost passes to profit or loss as the asset for the establishment of the quarry is depreciated over its life.

Answer to Interactive question 4

(a) The contract having been signed, there is a present obligation arising out of past events to pay the unavoidable costs under the contract.

(b)

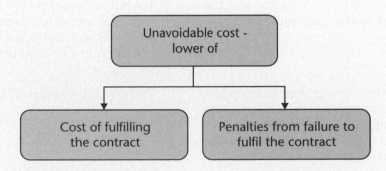

Take deliveries of silk and scrap it	Stop silk deliveries and pay penalties
Costs (300m × £18 × 2 months) £(10,800)	Penalties (£2,400 × 2 months) £(4,800)

Take deliveries of silk and make and sell dresses

Revenue (300m × £28 × 2 months)   £16,800

Costs (300m × (£18 + £16)) × 2 months £(20,400)

Loss   (£3,600)

Therefore the unavoidable cost is £3,600.

This should be recognised as a provision in the statement of financial position and as an expense in profit or loss.

Disclosure notes will give a brief description of the circumstances and of the obligation as well as an indication of the uncertainties about the timing of payments, amounts and assumptions.

Answer to Interactive question 5

(a) No provision would be recognised as the decision had not been communicated by the end of the reporting period.

(b) A provision would be made in the 20X9 financial statements.

(c) A provision for such costs would be made as the damage has already been caused.

(d) No present obligation exists and under IAS 37 no provision would be appropriate. This is because the entity could avoid the future expenditure by its future actions, maybe by changing its method of operation.

Answer to Interactive question 6

Circumstance	Position under IAS 37
A contract of employment	Obligations still have to be performed by both parties, so it is an executory contract. As there is no indication that it is an onerous contract, it falls outside the scope of IAS 37
A legal claim being pursued by an entity and which it is confident of winning	There is a possible asset and as the claim is being pursued, it must arise from past events. So a contingent asset
A legal claim being pursued against an entity but which the entity is confident of winning	There is a possible obligation and as the claim is being pursued, it must arise from past events. So a contingent liability
A legal claim against an entity where the entity has accepted liability but the amount to be paid has not yet been agreed	Liability has been admitted so the obligation exists and arises from past events. A provision
Legislation enacted but coming into effect next year which will require substantial retraining of staff	The obligation arises from future events (the legislation comes into force in the future) and both provisions and contingent liabilities require the obligation to arise from past events. Outside the scope of IAS 37
The reinstatement of land once quarrying has ceased, where there is no legal obligation. The entity's published policy in relation to environmental protection is that it will reinstate any environmental damage caused by its activities	There is a constructive obligation. A provision
The reinstatement of land once quarrying has ceased, where there is no legal obligation. The entity has no published policy in relation to environmental protection and this is the first quarrying venture it has entered into	There is no obligation. Outside the scope of IAS 37

Circumstance	Position under IAS 37
Restructurings where the detailed plan has been developed, announced and agreed with employees' representatives	There is a constructive obligation. A provision
Restructurings where the detailed plan has been developed and announced	There is a constructive obligation. A provision
Restructurings where the detailed plan has been developed and agreed by the board, but no announcement has been made	There is no obligation as the board could reverse its decision and not announce it. Outside the scope of IAS 37
Future reinstatement work under guarantees to be provided to customers in relation to future sales	The obligation arises from future sales. Outside the scope of IAS 37

Answer to Interactive question 7

Circumstance	Application of IAS 37
A legal claim in relation to a past event is pursued against an entity over several years. The entity makes the following judgements about outflows of resources in settlement:	This claim may result in the existence of a liability
• Year 1: there will be no outflow	Year 1: neither recognition nor disclosure
• Year 2: an outflow is remote	Year 2: neither recognition nor disclosure
• Year 3: an outflow is possible	Year 3: contingent liability disclosed
• Year 4: an outflow is probable	Year 4: provision recognised
• Year 5: an outflow is virtually certain	Year 5: provision retained
A legal claim in relation to a past event is pursued by an entity over several years. The entity makes the following judgements about inflows of resources in settlement:	This claim may result in the existence of an asset
• Year 1: there will be no inflow	Year 1: neither recognition nor disclosure
• Year 2: an inflow is remote	Year 2: neither recognition nor disclosure
• Year 3: an inflow is possible	Year 3: neither recognition nor disclosure
• Year 4: an inflow is probable	Year 4: contingent asset disclosed
• Year 5: an inflow is virtually certain	Year 5: asset recognised

Answer to Interactive question 8

(1) At the end of the reporting period, Conditional disputes liability (and therefore whether a present obligation exists).

However, the lawyer's advice is that it is more likely than not that Conditional will be found liable. A present obligation should be assumed to exist (IAS 37 paras 15–16).

Given that a single obligation is being measured, a provision is made for the outflow of the most likely outcome (IAS 37 para 40).

Consequently a provision should be recognised for £20,000 court costs and damages + £80,000 repair costs = £100,000.

(2) A present obligation exists at the end of the reporting period based on historical evidence of items being repaired under the guarantee agreement.

Here, a large population of items is involved. A provision should therefore be recognised for the expected value of the outflow:

	£
15,000 × 5% × 1/3 × £100	25,000
15,000 × 5% × 2/3 × £300	150,000
	175,000

Answer to Interactive question 9

The cracks in the walls are clear evidence of a change in the building's condition.

The specialist professionals have provided their opinion that the problems must have arisen several years ago (not since the year end), thus providing evidence as to the building's condition at the end of the reporting period.

The draft financial statements should be adjusted to take account of this change in condition. A full impairment review under IAS 36 *Impairment of Assets* should be carried out and any impairment loss should be recognised in the June 20X8 financial statements.

Point to note: It is highly likely that expenditure on repairs will be needed in the 30 June 20X9 financial year to rectify the damage and that the cost may be significant. But no provision for these repairs should be recognised at 30 June 20X8. There is a past event (the faults now identified) but at the end of the reporting period there is no obligation to incur the expenditure on repairs; so no provision should be recognised.

Answer to Interactive question 10

The reduction in selling price is evidence of the inventory's net realisable value at the end of the reporting period. It is therefore an adjusting event.

The net realisable value of the inventory is (£605 – £100) × 4,000 = £2,020,000.

The inventory is currently measured at a cost of £550 × 4,000 = £2,200,000, so it should be written down to the lower amount.

Answer to Interactive question 11

The grant should be recognised in the same proportion as the depreciation.

(a) **Straight line**

Year	Depreciation expense £	Grant recognised in profit or loss £
1 (40 ÷ 4) and 50% thereof	10,000	5,000
2 (40 ÷ 4) and 50% thereof	10,000	5,000
3 (40 ÷ 4) and 50% thereof	10,000	5,000
4 (40 ÷ 4) and 50% thereof	10,000	5,000

(b) **Reducing balance**

Year	Depreciation expense £	Grant recognised in profit or loss £
1 (40 × 40%) and 50% thereof	16,000	8,000
2 ((40 – 16) × 40%) and 50% thereof	9,600	4,800
3 ((40 – 16 – 9.6) × 40%) and 50% thereof	5,760	2,880
4 (remainder)	8,640	4,320

Answer to Interactive question 12

As the grant is half of the cost of the asset, then the credit in respect of deferred income will be half of the annual depreciation charge.

The depreciation charge for the year ending 31 December 20X7 is £320,000 × 25% = £80,000

The release of deferred income from the grant in 20X7 (50% × depreciation) is 50% × £80,000 = £40,000

Alternative calculation:

Deferred income released £160,000 × 25% = £40,000

Answer to Interactive question 13

(1) **Nursery toys**

This is a cash grant, so it ranks as a government grant which should be recognised. As it is given as immediate financial support to the entity, it should be recognised in profit or loss immediately.

(2) **Job creation**

This is a government grant which should be recognised.

£0.25 million should be recognised in profit or loss for each year from the date the grant becomes receivable (when 50 jobs have been created). This matches the grant with the related costs. Because this does not match the cash receipts, deferred income and a receivable will appear in Years 1 and 3 respectively.

(3) **Testing equipment**

This is a grant of a non-monetary asset. The usual treatment would be to account for both grant and the asset at the fair value of the equipment and recognise the grant in profit or loss over the period the asset is depreciated.

(4) **Technical advice**

Free technical advice is likely to be a grant which cannot reasonably have a value placed upon it. As a result it should not be recognised.

1   The fire is non-adjusting but should be disclosed in the notes, whereas the liquidation is adjusting.

2   Only (1), the discovery of the fraud, affects the conditions existing at the end of the reporting period.

3   Adjustments will need to be made by Brick Ltd and Mortar Ltd

   Brick Ltd   The debt arose before the end of the reporting period, so this would be an adjusting event.

   Cement Ltd   The debt arose after the reporting period, so that this would be a non-adjusting event.

   Mortar Ltd   As for Cement Ltd – a non-adjusting event, but of such significance that Mortar Ltd is no longer a going concern. Thus adjustments will be made to the accounts.

4   (i) and (iii) would be regarded as adjusting events (IAS 10 paragraphs 9 and 22).

5   This is a non-adjusting event after the reporting period. The legal action does not relate to conditions existing at the end of the reporting period as the cause arose subsequently.

6   Loss is not probable, therefore no accrual is required.

7   IAS 37 states that where there is a significant chance that more expenditure will be required, in this case that the first repair attempt will not succeed, a provision for a larger amount should be made. So Westbridge should accrue an amount in excess of £600,000 to allow for this.

8   The claim against Construction plc represents a probable loss and should be provided for. The claim against Underwater Ltd represents a contingent asset which is probable and should be disclosed.

9   At the end of the reporting period neither company has an obligation to pay for training as no training has been carried out.

10 £7 million should be provided for – £6 million for the landscape replacement and one year's charge for environmental damage (IAS 37 paragraph 19).

11 Treating the grant as a deduction from expense will reduce the amount of that expense category for the year and may make it appear excessively low compared to other expense categories. This may also reduce comparability with similar entities that have not received grants. If this method is used it will be important to disclose the receipt of the grant in the notes so that users are fully informed.

12 An entity receiving such a grant should identify precisely those conditions which give rise to costs. This will determine the period over which the grant is earned and it may be necessary to split the grant and allocate parts on different bases.

   In this case there will be a cost associated with building social housing which will be less profitable than private housing. If social housing plots are inserted at different phases of the development, then the grant should be split among these plots and recognised as each of them are completed.

   If it appears possible at any time that one or more of the social housing plots will not be provided, then a contingent liability for repayment of that proportion of the grant must be disclosed. If it is probable that one or more plots will not be built, then a provision should be recognised.

13 Note that 20X7 is the second year of the asset's ownership, so at 1 April 20X6 the carrying amounts of both the asset and the deferred income will have been reduced to 75% of their initial amounts.

Statement of profit or loss extract – year ended 31 March 20X7

	£
Depreciation ((£500,000 × 75%) × 25%)	(93,750)
Government grant income ((£100,000 × 75%) × 25%)	18,750

Statement of financial position extract – as at 31 March 20X7

	£
Non-current assets	
Machinery (£500,000 × 75% × 75%)	281,250
Non-current liabilities	
Deferred income (£100,000 × 75% × 75% × 75%)	42,187
Current liabilities	
Deferred income (£100,000 × 75% × 75% × 25%)	14,063

14 VACS LTD

(a) **Definition of a liability and accounting for provisions and contingencies**

The IASB *Conceptual Framework* defines a liability as:

(i)   A present obligation of the entity.

(ii) Arising from past events.

(iii) The settlement of which is expected to result in an outflow of resources which can be measured reliably.

This definition can be illustrated by looking at item (ii) in the question.

The claim is a present obligation because settlement of the claim can be enforced by law. Ultimately, a court will decide whether or not an outflow of resources will result.

The claim has arisen from past events because the action which gave rise to the claim (ie the dismissal) took place before the end of the reporting period (even though the company was not aware of this claim until after the reporting period). Hence this claim potentially needs recognising as a provision (a liability of uncertain timing and amount) in the financial statements as at 30 September 20X3.

If the event had not taken place until after the reporting period then it would not arise from past events and so no liability would be recognised (though disclosure as a non-adjusting event after the reporting period may be necessary).

For the claim to be recognised it must be expected to result in an outflow of resources which can be measured reliably. IAS 37 effectively defines 'expected' as 'more likely than not'. Here, the claim is recognised at an amount of £100,000 because the legal advisors believe the claim will 'probably be settled at £100,000'.

If the legal advisers believed that it was unlikely that the case would succeed (ie settlement is not probable) then the matter would not be recognised as a liability in the financial statements. However, disclosure as a contingent liability (contingent on the outcome of the future court case) would be necessary if the possibility of settlement was other than 'remote'. A contingent liability therefore arises when some, but not all, of the criteria for recognising a provision are met.

(b) **Financial statement extracts**

Statement of financial position as at 30 September 20X3 (extract)

	£
ASSETS	
Non-current assets	
Property, plant and equipment (3,100,000 + 274,000)	3,374,000
EQUITY AND LIABILITIES	
Non-current liabilities	
Provisions (Note 1) (100,000 + 295,200)	395,920

Notes to the financial statements as at 30 September 20X3 (extracts)

(1) Provisions

Compensation claim

	£
At 1 October 20X2	–
Profit or loss charge	100,000
At 30 September 20X3	100,000

This provision is in respect of a claim made by a director who was dismissed on 1 September 20X3 for acting outside his authority. It represents the amount at which the company's legal advisers believe the claim will be settled.

Decommissioning provision

	£
At 1 October 20X2	274,000
Unwinding of discount (274,000 × 8%)	21,920
At 30 September 20X3	295,920

This provision is in respect of an obligation to demolish temporary buildings and restore landscape on 1 October 20X5, discounted to present value at 8%.

(2) Contingent liabilities

The company has guaranteed the overdraft in respect of a company in which it holds a significant investment. It is not considered likely that this guarantee will be called upon. That company's overdraft was £300,000 at 30 September 20X3.

(3) Events after the reporting period

Following an offer made to the company after the reporting period, on 15 November 20X3 the company sold its former head office building for £2.7 million, realising a loss of £400,000. This loss will be reflected in the company's financial statements to 30 September 20X4.

Point to note: In part (a) it is not essential to use item (ii) in the question to illustrate. Any other appropriate example could have been used.

---

15 PROVISO PLC

Notes to the financial statements as at 31 December 20X2 (extracts)

(a) Provisions

	Warranty provision £'000	Compensation claim £'000	Provision for closure of division £'000	Total £'000
At 1 January 20X2	1,000	–	–	1,000
Utilised in the year	(600)	–	–	(600)
Profit or loss charge (bal fig)	400	9,500	16,000	25,900
At 31 December 20X2 (W1 and W2)	800	9,500	16,000	26,300

The warranty provision is in respect of warranties provided to customers. The provision is based on the level of past claims.

The compensation claim provision is in respect of a claim made by a customer for damages as a result of a faulty computer supplied by the company. It represents the present value of the amount at which the company's legal advisers believe the claim is likely to be settled.

On 15 December 20X2, Proviso plc announced that it would be closing its loss making space technology division. Details of the closure have been fully communicated to those affected. The cost of the closure, which began on 4 January 20X3, is estimated at £16 million and completion is expected by 30 June 20X3.

(b) **Contingent assets**

A counter-claim in respect of the compensation claim provided for above has been made against the supplier of parts for the affected computer. Lawyers have advised that this claim is likely to succeed and should amount to around 40% of the total damages (£3.8 million).

WORKINGS

(1) **Provision for closure of division**

	£'000
Employee redundancy costs	12,000
Lease termination costs	4,000
	16,000

> **Tutorial note:**
> The impairment losses of £2m would be offset against the carrying amount of the related non-current assets in accordance with IAS 36 *Impairment of Assets*.

(2) **Warranty provision**

£8 million × 10% = £800,000

16 FORDHAM LTD

(a) Deducting the grant from the cost of the asset

Statement of financial position

	Year 1 £	Year 2 £	Year 3 £
Non-current asset (90,000 × 80%)	72,000	72,000	72,000
Accumulated depreciation (72,000 / 3)	(24,000)	(48,000)	(72,000)
	48,000	24,000	–

Profit or loss

	Year 1 £	Year 2 £	Year 3 £	Total £
Profit for the year	60,000	60,000	60,000	180,000
Depreciation	(24,000)	(24,000)	(24,000)	(72,000)
	36,000	36,000	36,000	108,000

(b) Treating the grant as deferred income

Statement of financial position

	Year 1 £	Year 2 £	Year 3 £
Non-current asset	90,000	90,000	90,000
Accumulated depreciation (90,000 / 3)	(30,000)	(60,000)	(90,000)
	60,000	30,000	–
Deferred income (liability)	(12,000)	(6,000)	–
	48,000	24,000	–

Profit or loss

	Year 1 £	Year 2 £	Year 3 £	Total £
Profit for the year	60,000	60,000	60,000	180,000
Depreciation	(30,000)	(30,000)	(30,000)	(90,000)
	30,000	30,000	30,000	90,000
Grant	6,000	6,000	6,000	18,000
	36,000	36,000	36,000	108,000

The overall effect on the financial statements is the same whichever method is used.

Companies may prefer the deferred income method as it does not affect the carrying amount of the asset.

CHAPTER 10

Group accounts: basic principles

Introduction

Examination context

Topic List

Summary and Self-test

Technical reference

Answers to Interactive questions

Answers to Self-test

Learning objectives

Tick off

- Identify the financial effects of group accounting in the context of the IASB *Conceptual Framework* ☐

- Explain and demonstrate the concepts and principles surrounding the consolidation of financial statements including:

    – The single entity concept ☐

    – Substance over form ☐

    – The distinction between control and ownership ☐

- Identify and describe the circumstances in which an entity is required to prepare and present consolidated financial statements ☐

- Identify the laws, regulations and accounting standards applicable to the consolidated financial statements of an entity ☐

- Identify whether an entity should be treated as a subsidiary of a parent entity ☐

- Calculate goodwill including the measurement of identifiable assets and liabilities in relation to the acquisition of a subsidiary ☐

- Explain the accounting treatment of goodwill in consolidated financial statements ☐

- Explain the accounting treatment of subsidiaries in consolidated financial statements ☐

- Illustrate the application of the concepts and principles of consolidation through the preparation of simple consolidated statements of financial position and consolidated statements of profit or loss ☐

Specific syllabus references for this chapter are: 1d, 1h, 3a, 3b, 3c, 3f.

Syllabus links

Group accounts is a key part of the Financial Accounting and Reporting syllabus with a syllabus weighting of 30%. The syllabus covers:

- Consolidated statement of financial position (Chapter 11)
- Consolidated statements of financial performance (Chapter 12)
- Associates and joint ventures (Chapter 13)
- Disposals (Chapter 14)
- Consolidated statement of cash flows (Chapter 15)

More complex issues are covered at the Advanced Stage including control gained in stages, disposals of associates, partial disposals of subsidiaries and overseas subsidiaries, and the analysis and interpretation of group financial statements.

Examination context

Because the preparation of consolidated financial statements makes up 30% of the syllabus, each paper will feature questions requiring either a consolidated statement of financial position or a consolidated statement of profit or loss. Some papers may also include questions requiring a consolidated statement of cash flows and extracts from consolidated financial statements.

In the examination candidates may be required to:

- Explain and demonstrate the concepts and principles surrounding the consolidation of financial statements

- Prepare the consolidated statement of financial position or statement of profit or loss (or extracts) including the results of the parent entity and one or more subsidiaries from individual financial statements or draft consolidated financial statements

- Prepare the consolidated statement of cash flows (or extracts) from consolidated financial statements or finalise a draft consolidated statement of cash flows

1 Context for group accounts

Section overview

- A group includes a parent and one or more subsidiaries.
- A subsidiary is an entity controlled by the parent.
- Forming a group is a means of organising a business.
- Group accounts 'consolidate' the results of the individual companies.

1.1 What is a group?

In simple terms a group is created where one company, the **parent (P)** buys shares in another company, the **subsidiary (S)**, such that the parent company **controls** the subsidiary. A group may include one or many subsidiaries.

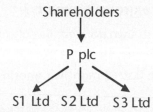

The shareholders (owners) of P plc may be individuals and/or institutions such as pension funds.

1.2 What is a subsidiary?

Definition

A **subsidiary** is an entity, including an unincorporated entity such as a partnership, that is controlled by another entity (known as the parent).

Control is defined by IFRS 3 as the power to **govern** the **financial and operating policies** of an entity so as to obtain benefits from its activities. This definition has now been expanded by IFRS 10 and will be covered further in Section 3.

Control is **presumed** where the parent acquires more than **50% of the other entity's voting rights**, unless it can be demonstrated otherwise.

In certain circumstances control may be achieved by other means. We will look at these circumstances in Section 5. For now we will assume that if a parent holds **more than 50% of the ordinary shares** in another entity **this constitutes control**. (Voting rights are normally attached to ordinary shares.)

1.3 Why form a group?

A business may operate in **several different markets** with different characteristics. These different markets will present different issues for management to address in terms of operations and finance and so on.

It would be possible for different activities to be carried out within a **single limited company**, where **separate divisions** could be established for each activity. The owners would then receive one set of accounts for that company, reflecting all its activities.

Alternatively, each activity could be carried out within a **separate company** (the subsidiaries), each of which is controlled by the parent.

There are a number of reasons why the business might be structured in this way:

- **Accountability of each group of managers can be made more precise**, as they can be identified more easily with the activities of the subsidiary which employs them.

- **Financing may be made easier**, as lenders can see audited financial statements for the individual company for which they are providing finance.

- The assets of one subsidiary can be **pledged as security for its borrowings**, leaving the assets of other subsidiaries unpledged.

- **Disposal of a business** may be made easier.

1.4 Why prepare group accounts?

This is best illustrated by the following worked example.

Worked example: Why prepare group accounts?

P Ltd (the parent) does not trade on its own account. Its only major asset is the ownership of all the shares in S Ltd (the subsidiary) and its only income is dividends from S Ltd.

Statements of profit or loss for the last 12 months (ignoring tax):

	P Ltd £m	S Ltd £m
Revenue	–	100
Cost of sales	–	(85)
Gross profit	–	15
Other costs	(1)	(40)
Loss from operations	(1)	(25)
Dividends received	11	–
Profit/(loss) for the year	10	(25)

Statement of changes in equity (extract) for the last 12 months:

	Retained earnings	
	P Ltd £m	S Ltd £m
Brought forward	1	45
Dividends	(6)	(11)
Total comprehensive income for the year	10	(25)
Carried forward	5	9

Without provisions requiring the preparation of group accounts (which put together, ie 'consolidate', the activities of the parent and subsidiaries), the owners would only legally be entitled to receive the financial statements of the parent company as an individual company.

In this case, they could well think that things were going well, because the dividend income for the period covers the expenses of P Ltd and provides for a £6m dividend. They would not be aware that:

- The £11m dividend income all came from profits earned by S Ltd in previous years.
- The trading activity controlled by P Ltd's management is currently loss-making.

As will be demonstrated later in this chapter, the effect of consolidation is to produce a fair picture of P Ltd and S Ltd taken together, which is that on revenue of £100m (S Ltd only), there is a loss for the year of £26m (S Ltd's net loss of £25m plus P Ltd's other costs of £1m).

1.5 Accounting principles

The key issue underlying group accounts is therefore the need to reflect the **economic substance** (see Chapter 1) of the relationship between companies where one (a parent) has control over another (a subsidiary), which together comprise a group.

Producing consolidated accounts that present the group as though it were a **single economic entity** reflects this economic substance.

As we will see in Section 3, the consolidated accounts also reflect another key principle (dealt with in the IASB *Conceptual Framework* – see Chapter 1), that of the distinction between:

- The resources controlled and the results they produce; and
- The ownership of those resources and results.

Point to note: The terms 'group accounts', 'consolidated accounts', 'group financial statements' and 'consolidated financial statements' can be thought of as meaning the same thing and are used interchangeably in the UK.

1.6 Composition of group accounts

Group accounts comprise:

- Consolidated statement of financial position (CSFP)
- Consolidated statement of profit or loss (CSPL)
- Consolidated statement of profit or loss and other comprehensive income (CSCI)
- Consolidated statement of changes in equity (CSCE)
- Consolidated statement of cash flows
- Notes to the accounts and comparative figures

Points to note

1   The consolidated statement of financial position is presented **in addition to** the parent's own individual statement of financial position.

2   The consolidated statement of profit or loss is usually presented **instead of** the parent's own individual statement of profit or loss.

3   The parent's own statement of financial position shows its **investment in subsidiaries** in **non-current asset investments (usually at cost)**.

4   The parent's own individual statement of profit or loss shows the **dividend income** received and receivable from subsidiaries.

1.7 Summary of investments

A parent may hold other investments apart from subsidiaries. These can be summarised as follows:

Investment	Criterion	Treatment in group accounts
Subsidiary	Control (>50%)	Consolidation
Associate (Chapter 13)	Significant influence (20%+)	Equity method
Joint venture (Chapter 13)	Joint control	Equity method
Investment	Asset held for accretion of wealth	Usually at cost

This chapter and Chapters 11–15 deal with the underlying principles and techniques involved in the preparation of group accounts.

2 The single entity concept

> **Section overview**
>
> - Group accounts are prepared on the basis that the parent and subsidiaries are a single entity.
> - This reflects the economic substance of the group arrangement.
> - The investment in a subsidiary's shares shown in the parent's own statement of financial position is replaced in the consolidated statement of financial position by the net assets of the subsidiary.
> - The dividend income from the subsidiary recognised in the parent's own statement of profit or loss is replaced in the consolidated statement of profit or loss by the subsidiary's revenues and costs.

2.1 The effect of consolidation

Group accounts consolidate the results and net assets of group members to present the group to the parent's shareholders as a **single economic entity**. This reflects the **economic substance** and contrasts with the **legal form**, where each company is a **separate legal person**.

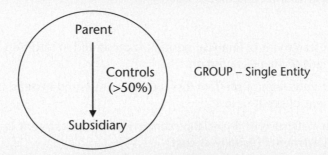

The effect of consolidation can be illustrated by comparing buying an unincorporated business from its existing proprietor with buying a controlling interest in a company from its existing shareholders.

2.2 Buying an unincorporated business

When a company invests in an unincorporated business, it pays cash to the proprietor and in exchange acquires legal title to all the assets and all the liabilities (ie the net assets) of the business.

Worked example: Buying an unincorporated business

Draft statements of financial position of Panther Ltd and Seal, a sole trader, at 31 December 20X1 are as follows:

	Panther Ltd £	Seal £
Cash	4,000	–
Sundry other assets	13,000	6,000
	17,000	6,000
Share capital/Capital	2,000	4,000
Retained earnings	12,000	–
Equity	14,000	4,000
Liabilities	3,000	2,000
	17,000	6,000

Panther Ltd then buys the net assets and business of Seal on 31 December 20X1 for £4,000 in cash.

In 20X2 Panther Ltd itself made sales of £6,000 with costs of £4,500. Panther Ltd also carried on Seal's trade, which made sales of £3,000 with costs of £1,000. There are no other changes in net assets in 20X2.

You are required to prepare the statement of profit or loss of Panther Ltd for the year ended 31 December 20X2 and the statement of financial position as at that date, reflecting the above information.

Solution

Panther Ltd
Statement of profit or loss for the year ended 31 December 20X2

	£
Revenue (6,000 + 3,000)	9,000
Costs (4,500 + 1,000)	(5,500)
Profit	3,500

Statements of financial position as at 31 December

	20X1 £	20X2 £
Sundry other assets (20X1: 13,000 + 6,000)	19,000	22,500
(20X2: P (13,000 + 6,000 – 4,500 = 14,500) +		
S (6,000 + 3,000 – 1,000 = 8,000))		
Share capital (P only)	2,000	2,000
Retained earnings (20X1: P only)	12,000	15,500
(20X2: P (12,000 + 6,000 – 4,500 = 13,500) +		
S post-acq (3,000 – 1,000))		
Equity	14,000	17,500
Liabilities (3,000 + 2,000)	5,000	5,000
Total equity and liabilities	19,000	22,500

Points to note

1. Seal's net assets at the date of acquisition are incorporated into Panther Ltd's books and Panther Ltd's cash is reduced by the cost of the acquisition.

2. All Seal's trading in 20X2 (and the increase in net assets attributable to it) is recorded in Panther Ltd's books.

2.3 Buying a company

When a company (A Ltd) invests in another company (B Ltd) the legal position is very different. Companies have their own legal identity separate from that of their owners. The investing company therefore pays cash to B Ltd's shareholders to buy their shares. It does not acquire legal title to the net assets of B Ltd; this remains with B Ltd.

Worked example: Buying a company

Draft statements of financial position of Panther Ltd and Seal Ltd at 31 December 20X1 are as follows:

	Panther Ltd £	Seal Ltd £
Cash	4,000	–
Sundry other assets	13,000	6,000
	17,000	6,000
Share capital	2,000	1,000
Retained earnings	12,000	3,000
Equity	14,000	4,000
Liabilities	3,000	2,000
	17,000	6,000

Panther Ltd then buys all the shares of Seal Ltd on 31 December 20X1 for £4,000 in cash. In 20X2 Panther Ltd itself made sales of £6,000 with costs of £4,500. Seal Ltd continued to trade and made sales of £3,000 with costs of £1,000. There are no other changes to net assets in 20X2.

You are required to:

(a) Prepare the statements of financial position as at 31 December 20X1 and 20X2 for Panther Ltd, Seal Ltd and the Panther Ltd group, reflecting the above information.

(b) Prepare the statements of profit or loss for the year ended 31 December 20X2 for Panther Ltd, Seal Ltd and the Panther Ltd group, reflecting the above information.

Solution

(a) **Statements of financial position as at**

	31 December 20X1			31 December 20X2		
	Panther Ltd	Seal Ltd	Consolidated	Panther Ltd	Seal Ltd	Consolidated
	£	£	£	£	£	£
Investment in Seal Ltd	4,000	–	–	4,000	–	–
Sundry other assets	13,000	6,000	19,000	14,500	8,000	22,500
	17,000	6,000	19,000	18,500	8,000	22,500
Share capital	2,000	1,000	2,000	2,000	1,000	2,000
Retained earnings	12,000	3,000	12,000	13,500	5,000	15,500
Equity	14,000	4,000	14,000	15,500	6,000	17,500
Liabilities	3,000	2,000	5,000	3,000	2,000	5,000
Total equity and liabilities	17,000	6,000	19,000	18,500	8,000	22,500

(b) **Statements of profit or loss for the year ended 31 December 20X2**

	Panther Ltd	Seal Ltd	Consolidated
	£	£	£
Revenue	6,000	3,000	9,000
Costs	(4,500)	(1,000)	(5,500)
Profit	1,500	2,000	3,500

Points to note

1   The investment in the shares of Seal Ltd in Panther Ltd's books **has been replaced by the underlying net assets of Seal Ltd.** The net assets of Seal Ltd at the date of acquisition (represented by its share capital and reserves at that date) are **cancelled out** against the investment in Panther Ltd's books. (Note that the situation where the net assets of a subsidiary at acquisition do not equal the cost of investment is covered in Chapter 11.)

2   As the net assets of Seal Ltd increase post-acquisition (an increase attributable to Panther Ltd's **control** of Seal Ltd) this increase has been reflected in net assets and retained earnings.

3   The profits of Seal Ltd are **combined** with those of Panther Ltd in the consolidated accounts from the date of acquisition, as post-acquisition profits of the subsidiary are earned under the parent's **control**. This is also reflected in the consolidated statement of financial position, where group retained earnings include Seal Ltd's **post-acquisition retained earnings**.

4   **Consolidated** statements of financial position and statements of profit or loss have been produced.

5   These are the same as those produced when Seal Ltd was unincorporated. This is because Panther Ltd and Seal Ltd have been treated, not as two separate legal entities, but as a **single entity**.

6   The two companies can be viewed as a **single entity** because Panther Ltd (the parent) **controls** Seal Ltd, its subsidiary. Together the companies form a **group**.

2.4   Summary

So far we have looked at the following key points:

*   Group = parent (P) + subsidiary(ies) (S)
*   Subsidiary(ies) = undertaking(s) under P's control

- The objective of group accounts is to present a true and fair view of the group to P's shareholders
- Mechanics of consolidation:

    - The investment in S shown in P's own statement of financial position is replaced in the consolidated statement of financial position (CSFP) by the line-by-line addition of S's net assets to P's to show the group's resources.

    - Dividend income in P's own statement of profit or loss is replaced in the consolidated statement of profit or loss (CSPL) by the line-by-line addition of S's revenue and costs to P's to show the group's performance.

    - The investment in S in P's statement of financial position is cancelled out against S's share capital and reserves at acquisition.

3 Control and ownership

Section overview

- Group accounts reflect both control and ownership.

- Ownership of more than 50% of the ordinary shares in a subsidiary normally gives control to the parent.

- The net assets and results not owned by the parent are reflected in the non-controlling interest.

3.1 Control

Usually a holding of **over 50%** of the **ordinary shares** in S will give P **control** of S.

As we saw in Section 1, control means **the ability to govern financial and operating policies of S** with a view to gaining economic benefits from its activities. This is an extension of the basic concept of control, introduced in Chapter 1 in the context of the definition of assets.

IFRS 10 *Consolidated Financial Statements* defines control as consisting of three elements:

- Power
- Exposure to variable returns
- An investor's ability to use power to affect its amount of variable returns

In an **individual company**, the assets are under the **direct control** of the company. In **a group**, the subsidiary's assets are under **indirect control** through the parent's control of the subsidiary.

IFRS 10 states that an investor controls an investee if, and only if, it has all of the following:

(i)   Power over the investee;
(ii) Exposure, or rights, to variable returns from its involvement with the investee; and
(iii) The ability to use its power over the investee to affect the amount of the investor's returns.

Power is defined as **existing rights that give the current ability to direct the relevant activities of the investee.** There is no requirement for that power to have been exercised.

In some cases assessing power is straightforward, for example where power is obtained directly and solely from having the majority of voting rights or potential voting rights, and as a result the ability to direct relevant activities.

Relevant activities include:

- Selling and purchasing goods or services
- Managing financial assets
- Determining a funding structure or obtaining funding

In other cases, the assessment of power is more complex. IFRS 10 gives the following examples of **rights**, other than voting rights or potential voting rights which can give an investor power:

- Rights to appoint, reassign or remove key management personnel who can direct the relevant activities.

- Rights to appoint or remove another entity that directs the relevant activities.

- Rights to direct the investee to enter into, or veto changes to, transactions for the benefit of the investor.

- Other rights, such as those specified in a management contract.

Variable returns have the potential to vary as a result of the investee's performance. Examples are dividends, potential losses from loan guarantees given on behalf of the investee, residual interests on liquidation.

3.2 Ownership

Equity, as defined in Chapter 1, is the **residual amount** found by deducting all of the entity's liabilities from all of the entity's assets. It is also described as the **ownership interest**.

In an individual company's accounts, there is only one ownership interest, ie that of the shareholders in that individual company, represented by the capital and reserves (which equal net assets).

In a group, it is possible for the parent to have control of a subsidiary **without owning 100% of it**.

That part of S's net assets and results included in the consolidation which is not owned by P is owned by the **non-controlling interest** (NCI).

Worked example: Ownership

P Ltd owns 75% of the ordinary shares of S Ltd.

In this case, P Ltd **controls** 100% of S Ltd as it owns more than 50% of the ordinary shares.

However, P Ltd only **owns** 75%. The **NCI owns the remaining 25%**.

In group accounts, the ownership interest of both P's shareholders and the NCI needs to be reflected, and the part of the group net assets in which P's shareholders do not have the ownership interest needs to be distinguished from that in which they do.

As both P's shareholders and the NCI own equity (in (P + S) and S, respectively), the sum of their respective ownership interests is described as **equity** in the consolidated statement of financial position.

3.3 Reflecting control and ownership in group accounts

When preparing the consolidated accounts, P's control of S and the ownership interest of P and NCI in S need to be reflected.

Group accounts reflect both control and ownership.

Consolidated statement of financial position (CSFP)

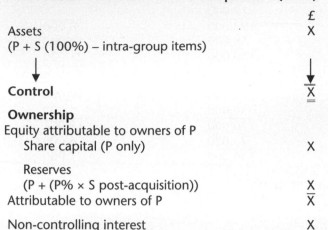

	£
Assets	X
(P + S (100%) – intra-group items)	
↓	↓
Control	X̲

Ownership
Equity attributable to owners of P

Share capital (P only)	X
Reserves	
(P + (P% × S post-acquisition))	X
Attributable to owners of P	X̲
Non-controlling interest	X
(NCI% × S's net assets)	
Total equity	X̲
Liabilities	X
	X̲

(Ownership: P% = P's share; NCI% = NCI share)

Consolidated statement of profit or loss (CSPL)

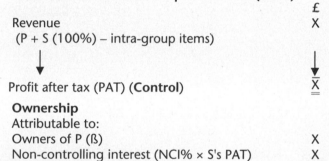

	£
Revenue	X
(P + S (100%) – intra-group items)	
↓	↓
Profit after tax (PAT) (**Control**)	X̲

Ownership
Attributable to:

Owners of P (ß)	X
Non-controlling interest (NCI% × S's PAT)	X
	X̲

(Ownership: P% = P's share; NCI% = NCI share)

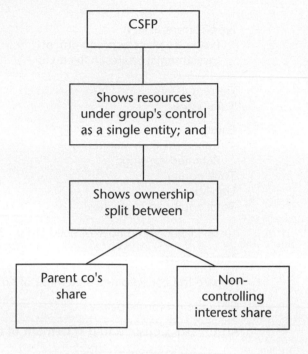

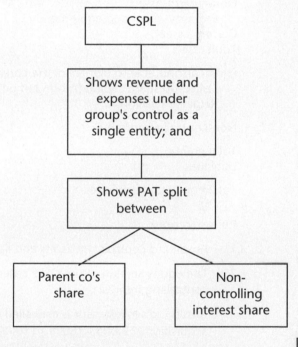

3.4 Reserves

The CSFP includes **P's reserves plus P's share of S's post acquisition reserves**, as these reserves are generated under P's control. S's reserves at acquisition (pre-acquisition reserves), along with its share capital, are cancelled against P's cost of investment in S.

The same basic calculation is used for each reserve separately (eg revaluation surplus, retained earnings).

The following interactive question brings together the points we have made so far.

Interactive question 1: Control and ownership

[Difficulty level: Easy]

The statements of financial position of two companies at 31 December 20X7 are as follows:

	Austin Ltd £	Reed Ltd £
Non-current assets		
Property, plant and equipment	80,000	8,000
Investments: Shares in Reed Ltd	12,000	–
	92,000	8,000
Current assets	58,000	13,000
Total assets	150,000	21,000
Equity		
Called up share capital	100,000	10,000
Retained earnings	30,000	5,000
Total equity	130,000	15,000
Liabilities	20,000	6,000
Total equity and liabilities	150,000	21,000

Austin Ltd acquired 80% of Reed Ltd on 31 December 20X7.

Requirement

Prepare the consolidated statement of financial position of Austin Ltd as at 31 December 20X7.

Fill in the proforma below.

Austin Ltd: Consolidated statement of financial position as at 31 December 20X7

£

Non-current assets
    Property, plant and equipment
Current assets
Total assets _____

Equity attributable to owners of the parent
    Called up share capital (Austin Ltd only)
    Retained earnings _____

Non-controlling interest _____

Total equity
Liabilities _____

Total equity and liabilities _____

Points to note

1   Austin Ltd controls the assets and liabilities of Reed Ltd. The CSFP reflects this.

2   The equity section of the CSFP reflects ownership (80% by Austin Ltd and 20% by the non-controlling interest).

3   Austin Ltd's investment is cancelled against the net assets (ie assets less liabilities) of Reed Ltd at acquisition (12,000 – (80% × (10,000 + 5,000))).

4   The remaining net assets are owned by the non-controlling interest.

5   Retained earnings are Austin Ltd's only, because Reed Ltd has, as yet, earned nothing under Austin Ltd's control. All of Reed Ltd's retained earnings are pre-acquisition.

See **Answer** at the end of this chapter.

Interactive question 2: Control and ownership   [Difficulty level: Easy]

Continuing from the facts in Interactive question 1, in the year ended 31 December 20X8 the two companies traded as follows.

	Austin Ltd £	Reed Ltd £
Revenue	20,000	5,000
Costs	(15,000)	(3,000)
Profit	5,000	2,000

The statements of financial position as at 31 December 20X8 are as follows.

	Austin Ltd £	Reed Ltd £
Non-current assets		
Property, plant and equipment	82,000	9,000
Investments: Shares in Reed Ltd	12,000	–
	94,000	9,000
Current assets	81,000	20,000
Total assets	175,000	29,000
Equity		
Called up share capital	100,000	10,000
Retained earnings	35,000	7,000
Total equity	135,000	17,000
Liabilities	40,000	12,000
Total equity and liabilities	175,000	29,000

Requirement

Prepare the consolidated statement of profit or loss of Austin Ltd for the year ended 31 December 20X8 and the consolidated statement of financial position at that date.

Fill in the proforma below.

Austin Ltd
Consolidated statement of profit or loss for the year ended 31 December 20X8

£

Revenue
Costs
Profit _____
Attributable to:
    Owners of Austin Ltd
    Non-controlling interest _____
_____

Consolidated statement of financial position as at 31 December 20X8

£

Non-current assets
    Property, plant and equipment
Current assets
Total assets _____
_____

Equity attributable to owners of the parent
    Share capital
    Retained earnings

_____

Non-controlling interest _____
Total equity
Liabilities
Total equity and liabilities _____
_____

C H A P T E R

10

Points to note

Consolidated statement of profit or loss

1   Down to 'Profit after tax' this reflects **control**.

2   To reflect ownership, this profit is then **allocated** between the non-controlling interest (in Reed Ltd) and the owners of Austin Ltd (Austin Ltd's profit plus that part of Reed Ltd's profit (80%) owned by Austin Ltd).

Consolidated statement of financial position

1   The assets and liabilities in the statement of financial position represent **control**.

2   The equity part of the CSFP represents **ownership**. This time the retained earnings are Austin Ltd's plus that part of Reed Ltd's (80%) that has arisen since acquisition, ie **post-acquisition earnings**. The non-controlling interest owns their share of Reed Ltd's equity at the end of the reporting period.

See **Answer** at the end of this chapter.

Finally, let us look at how the movement during the year would be reflected in the consolidated statement of changes in equity (CSCE). The consolidated statement of changes in equity is dealt with in Chapter 12. Here we will just look at the group retained earnings and non-controlling interest columns.

The retained earnings column shows group retained earnings and the non-controlling interest column shows the non-controlling share of the subsidiary's total comprehensive income (which will usually be net profit).

For Austin and Reed, these columns would be as follows:

	Retained earnings £	Non-controlling interest £
At 1 January 20X8 / (15,000 × 20%)	30,000	3,000
Total comprehensive income for the year		
(5,000 + (2,000 × 80%)) / (2,000 × 20%)	6,600	400
At 31 December 20X8	36,600	3,400

You can see that the carried forward totals correspond to the totals in the consolidated statement of financial position at 31 December 20X8.

Note that this is the first year of consolidation, so the opening retained earnings are simply the retained earnings of the parent. For subsequent years the opening retained earnings will include the parent's share of the subsidiary's post-acquisition retained earnings.

Now that we have looked at the mechanics of consolidation it is time to look in more detail at the requirements of the relevant standards, most importantly IFRS 3 *Business Combinations*.

4   IFRS 3 *Business Combinations*

Section overview

- All business combinations should be accounted for using the acquisition method.

- The acquirer should be identified for all business combinations.

4.1   Objective

The objective of IFRS 3 is to set out **the accounting and disclosure requirements** for a **business combination**. In practice business combinations can be structured in all sorts of different ways, usually for reasons which are peculiar to the parties to the combination and/or to suit the legal and tax environments in which they operate.

In an area of such potential complexity IFRS 3 looks beyond the legal form of the transaction to the underlying substance. This can be seen in the definitions below.

Definitions

Business combination: A transaction or other event in which an **acquirer** obtains control of one or more **businesses**.

Business: An integrated set of activities and assets capable of being conducted and managed for the purpose of providing:

(a) A return in the form of dividends; or
(b) Lower costs or other economic benefits directly to investors or other owners.

A business generally consists of inputs, processes applied to those inputs, and resulting outputs that are, or will be, used to generate revenues. If goodwill is present in a transferred set of activities and assets, the transferred set is presumed to be a business.

All business combinations result in one entity, the acquirer, obtaining **control** of one or more other businesses. We will look at the issue of control in Section 5.

The type of business combination with which you need to be familiar is **the acquisition of one company by another resulting in a parent-subsidiary relationship.**

Point to note: If assets alone are purchased, such as a fleet of motor vehicles, these will be accounted for under IAS 16 *Property, Plant and Equipment* not IFRS 3.

Definitions

Parent: An entity that has one or more subsidiaries

Subsidiary: An entity that is controlled by another entity

4.2 Scope

IFRS 3 applies to all business combinations except those for which there are or will be separate IFRSs. None of these excluded combinations fall within the syllabus.

4.3 Acquisition method of accounting

All business combinations should be accounted for by applying the **acquisition method**. This involves five key steps:

- **Identifying the acquirer**

- Determining the **acquisition date**

- Measuring the consideration transferred

- Recognising and measuring the **identifiable assets acquired**, the **liabilities assumed** and any **non-controlling interest** in the acquiree

- Recognising and measuring **goodwill** or a gain from a bargain purchase

We will look at these steps in more detail in the rest of this chapter.

4.4 Identifying the acquirer

IFRS 3 states that **the acquirer should be identified for all business combinations.**

Definitions

Acquiree: The business or businesses that the **acquirer** obtains control of in a **business combination**.

Acquirer: The entity that obtains control of the **acquiree**.

Control: The power to govern the financial and operating policies of an entity or business so as to obtain benefits from its activities.

In practical terms the simplest way in which control can be achieved is for the acquirer (P) to gain **more than half of the voting rights** in the acquiree (S) ie rights relating to votes of the shareholders in general meeting. These rights are normally attached to the ordinary shares. IFRS 3 states that in this case **control should be assumed** unless it can be demonstrated otherwise.

In most business combinations it should be relatively straightforward to identify that a business combination has taken place. Where this is not the case the Application Guidance in IFRS 3 provides a number of examples of ways in which a business combination could be structured as follows:

- One or more businesses become subsidiaries of an acquirer or the net assets of one or more businesses are legally merged into the acquirer

- One combining entity transfers its net assets to another combining entity

- All the combining entities transfer their net assets to a newly formed entity

- A group of former owners of one of the combining entities obtains control of the combined entity

4.5 Determining the acquisition date

Definition

Acquisition date: The date on which the acquirer obtains control of the acquiree.

General rule

The date on which the acquirer obtains control of the acquiree is normally the **closing date** of the transaction. This is the date on which the acquirer legally:

(a) Transfers the consideration;
(b) Acquires the assets; and
(c) Assumes the liabilities of the acquiree.

5   Measuring the consideration transferred

Section overview

- The consideration transferred comprises the fair values at the acquisition date of assets given, liabilities incurred or assumed and equity instruments issued by the acquirer.

- The amount of the consideration may not be fixed at the acquisition date; some may be contingent on future events.

- Quoted equity investments should be valued at their market price.

- Deferred consideration should be discounted.

- Acquisition-related costs should be expensed in the period in which they are incurred.

5.1 General rule

The cost of the business combination is:

- The total of the **fair values of the consideration transferred**.

5.2 Fair value of consideration

IFRS 3 requires that consideration given should be measured at **fair value** at the **acquisition date**.

Definition

Fair value: The price that would be received to sell an asset or paid to transfer a liability in an orderly transaction between market participants at the measurement date.

The Financial Accounting and Reporting syllabus includes only combinations achieved through a single exchange transaction (not a gradual build up of control through successive transactions to acquire shares in the acquiree).

The acquisition date should be used to split **pre and post-acquisition profits**.

Points to note

1 Consideration given may be in the form of cash or other assets, liabilities assumed or incurred and equity instruments (eg shares) issued by the acquirer.

2 The **fair value of any quoted equity investments** (marketable securities) forming part of the purchase consideration should be the **market price at the acquisition date,** except in extremely rare circumstances.

3 Future losses or other costs expected to be incurred as a result of the combination should not be included as part of the cost of the combination.

5.3 Deferred consideration

Part of the consideration for an acquisition may not pass to the acquiree's shareholders at the acquisition date but be deferred until a later date.

Deferred consideration should be measured at its **fair value at the acquisition date.** The fair value depends on the form of the deferred consideration.

Where the deferred consideration is in the form of **equity shares**:

- Its fair value should be measured at the acquisition date market price.

- The deferred amount should be recognised as part of equity, under a separate heading such as 'shares to be issued'.

Where the deferred consideration is payable in cash:

A **liability** should be recognised at the **present value** of the amount payable.

Points to note

1 The market price of shares at the date the consideration is recognised is regarded as the present value of all the future benefits arising from those shares, so no adjustment should subsequently be made for any change in the market price over the period until any deferred consideration in the form of equity shares is issued.

2 As with other present value remeasurements, the increase in a liability for deferred consideration over the period until it is issued should be recognised in profit or loss as a finance cost.

Worked example: Deferred consideration

The acquisition date for Winter plc's purchase of the whole of the share capital in Summer Ltd was 1 July 20X5. The consideration comprised 1,000,000 shares in Winter plc to be issued on 1 July 20X5, £10 million in cash payable on 1 July 20X5, 200,000 shares in Winter plc to be issued on 1 January 20X6 and £5 million in cash payable on 1 July 20X6.

The market price of one Winter plc share was 450p on 1 July 20X5, 475p on 1 January 20X6 and 480p on 1 July 20X6. A discount rate of 7% was appropriate.

What is the total consideration for this acquisition?

Solution

	£m
1,000,000 shares issued on 1 July 20X5 at 450p	4.50
200,000 shares to be issued on 1 January 20X6 at 450p	0.90
Cash payable on 1 July 20X5	10.00
Cash payable on 1 July 20X6 – £5m/1.07	4.67
	20.07

5.4 Contingent consideration

Definition

Contingent consideration is an obligation of the acquirer to transfer additional consideration to the former owners of the acquiree if specified future events occur or conditions are met.

The acquiree's shareholders may have a different view from the acquirer as to the value of the acquiree.

- The acquiree may be the subject of a legal action which the acquiree's shareholders believe will be settled at no cost, but is believed by the acquirer to be likely to result in an expensive settlement

- The two parties may have different views about the likely future profitability of the acquiree's business

In such cases it is often agreed that additional consideration may become due, depending on how the future turns out (for example, the settlement of the legal actions at a cost lower than that expected by the acquirer and future earnings being higher than the acquirer expected). Such consideration is 'contingent' on those future events/conditions.

Contingent consideration agreements result in the acquirer being under a legal obligation at the acquisition date to transfer additional consideration, should the future turn out in specified ways. IFRS 3 therefore requires contingent consideration to be recognised as part of the consideration transferred and measured at its fair value at the acquisition date.

Point to note

Estimates of the amount of additional consideration and of the likelihood of it being issued are both taken into account in estimating this fair value.

As with deferred consideration

- If the contingent consideration is to be in shares, the amount should be measured by reference to the market price at the acquisition date.

- If the contingent consideration is to be in cash, the amount should be **discounted to its present value** at the acquisition date.

It may turn out that the amount of the contingent consideration actually transferred is different from the original estimate of fair value. In terms of the examples given above, the legal action may be settled at no cost to the acquiree and the acquiree's profits may be higher than the acquirer expected.

IFRS 3 treats such subsequent adjustments to the **quantity** of the contingent consideration in ways familiar from IAS 10 *Events after the Reporting Period*:

- If (and this will be very rare) the adjustments result from additional information becoming available about conditions at the acquisition date, they should be related back to the acquisition date, provided the adjustments are made within the measurement period (however, adjustments made within the measurement period are outside of the Financial Accounting and Reporting syllabus).

- If (and this will be common) the adjustments result from events occurring after the acquisition date, they are treated as changes in accounting estimates; they should be accounted for prospectively and the effect usually recognised in profit or loss. This will be the treatment required for the additional consideration due after the legal action was settled/the earnings being higher than expected.

Measurement of the contingent consideration should be reassessed at fair value each year and the difference taken to profit or loss unless the contingent consideration is in shares. If the contingent consideration is in shares (ie classified as equity) then it should not be remeasured but its subsequent settlement should instead be recognised as part of equity.

Worked example: Contingent consideration

On 1 January 20X7 A acquired 100% of the shares of B when the fair value of B's net assets was £25 million. The consideration was 4 million shares in A issued at 1 January 20X7 when their market value was £6 per share and a cash payment of £6 million on 1 January 20X9 if the cumulative profits of B exceeded a certain amount by that date. At 1 January 20X7 the probability of B hitting that earnings target was such that the fair value of the possible cash payment was £2 million.

At 31 December 20X7 the probability that B would exceed the required profit level had risen and the fair value of the contingent consideration was judged to be £4 million.

At 31 December 20X8 it was clear that B had exceeded the profit target and the whole amount would be payable.

Show calculations of the amounts to be recognised in the statements of financial position and in profit or loss for the two years ended 31 December 20X8.

Solution

The contingent consideration should be recognised at the acquisition date. It should then be remeasured at fair value each year end until ultimate settlement of the amount. Changes in fair value should be recognised in profit or loss.

Statement of financial position at 31 December 20X7

		£'000
Non-current assets – goodwill		
Consideration transferred	– 4 million shares × £6	24,000
	– contingent at fair value	2,000
		26,000
Net assets acquired		(25,000)
Goodwill		1,000
Non-current liabilities – contingent consideration		4,000

Profit or loss for year ended 31 December 20X7	
Additional contingent consideration	2,000

Statement of financial position at 31 December 20X8	
Non-current assets – goodwill (unchanged)	1,000
Current liabilities – contingent consideration	6,000

Profit or loss for year ended 31 December 20X8	
Additional contingent consideration	2,000

Interactive question 3: Contingent consideration   [Difficulty level: Exam standard]

Autumn plc acquired 100% of Spring Ltd on 1 January 20X5 when the fair value of Spring Ltd's identifiable assets net of liabilities assumed was £20 million. The consideration was:

- Eight million shares in Autumn plc issued on 1 January 20X5 when the market price of Autumn plc's shares was 350p.

- A further payment of cash on 31 December 20X6:

    - £700,000 if Spring Ltd's profits for the year then ended were no less than £2 million; or
    - £1,750,000 if Spring Ltd's profits for the year then ended were no less than £3 million.

At 1 January 20X5 the fair value of the contingent consideration was £100,000.

At 31 December 20X5 the fair value of the contingent consideration was £1.2 million.

At 31 December 20X6 Spring Ltd's 20X6 profits per draft financial statements were £3.5 million.

Requirement

Show calculations of the amounts to be recognised in the statements of financial position and in profit or loss for the two years ended 31 December 20X6.

See **Answer** at the end of this chapter.

5.5 Acquisition-related costs

Acquisition-related costs such as professional and other fees relating specifically to the individual transaction eg accountants' fees and legal costs are **required to be recognised as expenses in the period in which they are incurred**.

Exception: **The costs of arranging financial liabilities (eg loans) and issuing equity are deducted from the liability/equity.**

6 Recognising and measuring the net assets acquired

Section overview

- The acquiree's identifiable assets and liabilities should be recognised at fair value at the date of acquisition.

- Where certain criteria are met the acquiree's assets and liabilities should be recognised separately.

- Provisions for future reorganisation plans and future losses should not be recognised as liabilities at the acquisition date.

- Contingent liabilities which can be measured reliably and for which there is a present obligation as a result of a past event should be recognised as liabilities at the acquisition date.

- An intangible asset should only be recognised if it is separable or arises from contractual or other legal rights and can be measured reliably.

- IFRS 3 provides guidance on the measurement at fair value of specific assets and liabilities.

- Any non-controlling interest in the acquiree is recognised separately.

6.1 Basic principle

IFRS 3 requires that the **acquiree's identifiable assets and liabilities should be recognised at fair value at the date of acquisition**.

The exception to this is non-current assets that are classified as held for sale in accordance with IFRS 5 *Non-current Assets Held for Sale and Discontinued Operations*. These are recognised at **fair value less costs to sell**.

What constitutes the acquiree's identifiable assets and liabilities is important as the difference between the consideration transferred in the business combination plus the value of any non-controlling interest and the net assets acquired represents **goodwill**. The higher the total value of net assets, the lower the total value of goodwill and vice versa.

6.2 Identification of net assets acquired

Separate recognition of the acquiree's assets and liabilities is required where they meet specific criteria at the acquisition date. The criteria are based on the IASB *Conceptual Framework* definitions of an asset and a liability, covered in Chapter 1. These are as follows:

Assets other than intangible assets	Where it is **probable** that any associated **future economic benefits** will flow to the acquirer, and their **fair value** can be measured **reliably**.
Liabilities other than contingent liabilities	Where it is **probable** that an **outflow of resources** embodying economic benefits will be required to settle the obligation, and its **fair value** can be measured **reliably**.
Intangible assets	Where they meet the **definition of an intangible asset** in accordance with IAS 38 *Intangible Assets* and their **fair value** can be measured **reliably**.
Contingent liabilities	Where there is a present obligation as a result of a past event and their **fair value** can be measured **reliably**.

6.3 Recognition of liabilities

An acquirer may only recognise an acquiree's liabilities if they exist at the acquisition date. This application of the normal IASB *Conceptual Framework* definition of a liability **prohibits** any account being taken at that time of two factors which may have depressed the price the acquirer is prepared to pay for the acquiree:

- **Reorganisation plans** devised by the acquirer which will only be put into effect once control over the acquiree is gained.

- Acquirers often plan to create value by changing the cost structure of the acquiree so that the post-acquisition cost base is less than the sum of the acquirer's and acquiree's existing cost bases. The acquirer will evaluate the one-off costs of making these changes when deciding what lower price to offer for the acquiree, but as these costs are **neither a liability nor a contingent liability** of the acquiree prior to the date control is gained, **they cannot be set up as provisions at the time of acquisition.**

- **Future losses** to be incurred as a result of the business combination (this covers future losses to be incurred by the acquirer as well as by the acquiree).

- An acquirer will often target a loss-making business, in the expectation that after reorganisation and with new management it will become profitable. But it often takes some time for the benefits of such changes to emerge, during which time further trading losses will be incurred. The reorganisation process may also cause short-term losses within the acquirer. The total of such losses will depress the price to be offered by the acquirer. But no account can be taken of them, because **future losses relate to future, not past, events.**

Point to note: Contrast the first of these situations with contractual obligations put in place by the acquiree (not the acquirer) prior to the acquisition date and conditional on being taken over. (Such contractual obligations are sometimes put together on a large scale by the acquiree's management, precisely to deter acquirers. In these cases they are often described as 'poison pill' defences.) Prior to the acquisition date **these are present obligations** arising from past events but outflows of resources are

not probable. So they will be dealt with as **contingent liabilities** by the acquiree up to the moment when a business combination becomes probable. At that point they meet the recognition criteria for a liability and must be recognised as one of the acquiree's **liabilities.**

6.4 Recognition of intangible assets

As already noted above, intangible assets should be recognised when they can be **reliably measured**. But even before that test, **they must meet the definition of an intangible asset** under IAS 38 *Intangible Assets*. This IAS was dealt with in detail in Chapter 5, but the following points are relevant here:

- An intangible asset is a non-monetary asset without physical substance. It must be **separable or arise from contractual or other legal rights**. 'Separable' means that the asset can be sold separately from the entity owning the asset, while 'contractual or other legal rights' provides evidence of the existence of the asset.

- The illustrative examples which accompany IFRS 3 (but which are not an integral part of it) list the following examples of intangible assets which could be recognised on a business combination:

  - **Separable assets:**
    - Customer lists
    - Non-contractual customer relationships
    - Databases

    Customer lists are often leased (ie used for a period without ownership being gained) for mailing purposes by entities wanting to try to acquire new customers. **Customer relationships** are details of customers together with their past buying profiles which can be sold, on the basis that even though these customers have no outstanding commitments to make purchases, the probability is that a number of them will place future orders. A value can then be put on this probability.

  - **Assets arising from contractual or other legal rights:**
    - Trademarks
    - Internet domain names
    - Newspaper mastheads
    - Non-competition agreements
    - Unfulfilled contracts with customers
    - Copyrights over plays
    - Books, music, videos, etc
    - Leases
    - Licences to broadcast television and/or radio programmes
    - Licences to fish in certain waters
    - Licences to provide taxi services
    - Patented technology
    - Computer software

- The definition also covers **research and development projects** which are in process at the acquisition date. These will often not be recognised in the acquiree's statement of financial position.

6.5 Contingent liabilities

IFRS 3 requires an acquirer **to recognise an acquiree's contingent liabilities where their amount can be measured reliably**. This is in spite of the fact that **they will not have been recognised in the statement of financial position of the acquiree** (under IAS 37 *Provisions, Contingent Liabilities and Contingent Assets*).

Once recognised, contingent liabilities should be carried **at the higher of the amount under IAS 37** (which will be nil until they become liabilities) **and their value at the acquisition date, less any subsequent amortisation.**

Points to note

1   If these cannot be measured reliably, their value, whatever it is, will be **subsumed within goodwill** or gain on bargain purchase on acquisition. But **full disclosure** must still be made.

2   **Even if recognised**, the normal IAS 37 **disclosures** re contingent liabilities should be made.

6.6   Consequences of recognition at fair value

The consequences of the recognition of the acquiree's assets and liabilities at the acquisition date are that:

- The acquirer's consolidated statement of profit or loss should include the acquiree's profits and losses **from the same date**.

- The fair values of the acquiree's net assets form the basis of all the **subsequent accounting** in the consolidated financial statements even where fair values are not incorporated into the acquiree's single entity financial statements. For example, depreciation should be based on the fair values of property, plant and equipment which may not be the same as the carrying amount in the acquiree's statement of financial position.

- Any **non-controlling interest** in the acquiree is based on the non-controlling interest share of the **net assets at their fair values**.

7   Goodwill

Section overview

- Goodwill is calculated as the excess of the fair value of the consideration transferred plus any non-controlling interest over the fair value of the net assets acquired.

- Goodwill acquired in a business combination should be recognised as an intangible asset in the consolidated statement of financial position.

- Goodwill should be tested for impairment at least annually.

- If a bargain purchase arises the measurement of the fair value of net assets acquired should be checked.

- If the bargain purchase remains the gain should be recognised in profit or loss in the accounting period in which the acquisition is made.

7.1   Calculation

When consolidation is carried out, the investment in the parent's statement of financial position is **cancelled** against the net assets of the subsidiary at acquisition.

Worked example: Cancellation

Using the facts from Interactive question 1, we had the following information:

	£
Consideration transferred to acquire an 80% investment in Reed Ltd (in Austin Ltd's statement of financial position)	12,000
Non-controlling interest (15,000 × 20%)	3,000
Net assets of Reed Ltd at acquisition	15,000

If you compare the consideration transferred (£12,000) plus the value of the non-controlling interest with the net assets acquired you can see that this cancels exactly. Austin Ltd has paid an amount which is equal to its share of the assets and liabilities of Reed Ltd at acquisition.

In practice this is not likely to be the case. The parent company will often pay **more** for the subsidiary than the value of its net assets, recognising that the subsidiary has attributes that are not reflected in its statement of financial position. The extra amount paid by the parent is **goodwill**.

7.2 Goodwill at acquisition

In accordance with IFRS 3 any excess of the consideration transferred plus the value of any non-controlling interest over the fair value of the net assets acquired should be:

- Described as **goodwill**; and
- **Recognised as an asset** (as it meets the recognition criteria).

Definition

Goodwill: An asset representing the future economic benefits arising from other assets acquired in a business combination that are not individually identified and separately recognised.

Point to note

Any goodwill carried in the acquiree's statement of financial position becomes subsumed in the goodwill arising on acquisition, because:

- It is **excluded** from identifiable assets (see Section 6.4 above);
- This reduces the net assets at acquisition; and
- Must therefore increase the goodwill arising on consolidation.

Interactive question 4: Goodwill   [Difficulty level: Easy]

P plc pays £10,000 to buy 75% of the share capital of S Ltd. The statement of financial position of S Ltd at the date of acquisition shows the following.

	£
Assets	16,000
Share capital	1,000
Retained earnings	11,000
Equity	12,000
Liabilities	4,000
	16,000

Requirement

Calculate the goodwill arising on P plc's acquisition of S Ltd.

Fill in the proforma below.

	£
Consideration transferred	
Plus non-controlling interest at acquisition	
Less net assets at acquisition	
Goodwill	

Point to note: For the purposes of calculating goodwill net assets at acquisition are normally calculated as share capital plus retained earnings (and other reserves, if any) at the acquisition date.

See **Answer** at the end of this chapter.

Interactive question 5: Measuring fair value   **[Difficulty level: Exam standard]**

Kelly plc acquired 75% of Eclipse plc on 1 July 20X7. The consideration comprised:

- Five million 25p ordinary shares of Kelly plc (market value 60p) to be issued on 1 July 20X7 (issue costs of £10,000 were paid to a merchant bank)

- £1 million cash payable on 1 July 20X7

- A further 1 million 25p ordinary shares of Kelly plc to be issued on 1 July 20X8

The fair value of the identifiable assets and liabilities recognised by Eclipse plc at 1 July 20X7 is £3,628,000. The financial statements of Eclipse plc have for some years disclosed a contingent liability with a potential amount of £2 million. The fair value of this contingent liability at 1 July 20X7 has been reliably estimated at £200,000.

Requirement

Show the entries in Kelly plc's books to record the investment in Eclipse plc, and calculate goodwill acquired in the business combination.

Fill in the proforma below.

	£'000	£'000
Recording investment in Eclipse plc		
Shares to be issued 1 July 20X7		
DR		
CR		
CR		
CR		
Cash		
DR		
CR		
Shares to be issued 1 July 20X8		
DR		
CR		

Goodwill on consolidation of Eclipse plc

	£'000	£'000
Consideration transferred		
Shares		
Cash		
Shares to be issued	_____	
Non-controlling interest		_____
Identifiable assets and liabilities acquired		
Per books of Eclipse plc		
Contingent liability		
		_____
Goodwill		_____

See **Answer** at the end of this chapter.

C
H
A
P
T
E
R

10

7.3 Summary

Goodwill arising from a business combination is calculated as follows:

	£	£
Fair value of consideration transferred		X
Non-controlling interest at acquisition		X
Less: Fair value of tangible assets	X	
Fair value of intangible assets	X	
Fair value of assets	X	
Fair value of liabilities	(X)	
Fair value of contingent liabilities	(X)	
Fair value of net assets		(X)
Goodwill/(Gain from a bargain purchase)		X/(X)

7.4 Goodwill subsequent to acquisition

After initial recognition, goodwill should be:

- Carried in the statement of financial position at **cost less accumulated impairment losses**
- **Tested for impairment** at least annually in accordance with IAS 36 *Impairment of Assets*

If goodwill has suffered an impairment **the loss will be recognised in the consolidated statement of profit or loss. Retained earnings** in the consolidated statement of financial position will also be **reduced**.

If the NCI has been measured at **fair value** (see Section 8) then part of the impairment loss will be **allocated to the NCI**, based on the NCI percentage shareholding.

Point to note

Retained earnings will be reduced by the total impairments recognised to date, not just the fall in value which relates to the current year.

This is because goodwill is a **consolidation adjustment**, ie it only affects the group accounts. The single entity accounts which are used as the basis of the consolidated statement of financial position will not reflect any impairments in goodwill arising on consolidation.

7.5 Bargain purchases

In certain circumstances the parent entity may pay **less** to acquire a subsidiary than represented by its share of the subsidiary's net assets.

These circumstances might include the following:

- The subsidiary has a poor reputation.
- It suffers from inherent weaknesses not reflected in its assets and liabilities.
- The parent company has negotiated a good deal.

A gain on a bargain purchase arises if the fair value of the net assets acquired **exceeds** the total of the consideration transferred and the value of any non-controlling interest, ie there is 'negative goodwill'.

IFRS 3 is based on the assumption that this usually arises because of **errors in the measurement of the acquiree's net assets** and/or the consideration transferred. So the first action is always to **reassess the identification and measurement of the net assets and the measurement of the consideration transferred**, checking in particular whether the fair values of the net assets acquired correctly reflect future costs arising in respect of the acquiree.

If the gain still remains once these reassessments have been made, then it is attributable to **a bargain purchase**, ie the acquirer has managed to get away with paying less than the full value for the acquiree. This gain does **not** meet the *Conceptual Framework's* definition of a liability, so it must be **part of equity**. It should therefore be **recognised in profit or loss** in the same accounting period as the acquisition is made.

7.6 Initial accounting

Initial accounting for goodwill is the process of identifying and determining the fair values of:

- The acquiree's identifiable assets and liabilities;

- The consideration transferred, ie the assets given, liabilities assumed and equity instruments issued; and

- Any non-controlling interest at acquisition.

Note

IFRS 3 allows the option to measure the non-controlling interest at acquisition at either the NCI share of the subsidiary's net assets or at **fair value**. We will be looking at the issue of **non-controlling interest measured at fair value** in the next section.

Whilst every effort should be made to complete this initial process by the end of the accounting period in which the combination is effected, **it may be that in some cases only provisional values can be established by that time**. This is often true of the valuation of non-current assets, including intangibles. In such cases:

- **Provisional values** should initially be used.

- **Adjustments** to the values of the net assets and/or the consideration transferred made **within one year of the acquisition** date, known as the measurement period, should be **backdated** to the acquisition date. Changes in these values may therefore lead to a **restatement of the provisional values for goodwill or the gain on bargain purchase on acquisition**.

- **Comparative figures** for the previous period (the one in which the combination was effected) **should be restated** as if these adjustments had been made as part of the initial accounting. So depreciation charges in the previous period in respect of PPE may have to be restated.

Point to note: This one year period can **only be used to reassess fair values**. It **cannot** be used to **backdate the recognition of acquired assets and liabilities** which did not meet the recognition criteria at the acquisition date but do so during this period, because this would involve taking account of events **after** the acquisition date. As an example, major pollution damage resulting from an accident taking place within the one year period may result in new types of liabilities being identified, types which were unknown at the acquisition date. No such liabilities should be recognised at the acquisition date as they were not known at that time.

7.7 Subsequent adjustments

The need for further adjustments may emerge later but to allow them to be backdated to the acquisition date might result in continual changes to previously published data in a way which is not helpful to users of financial statements. For example, a large group might make several acquisitions every year; adjustments to fair values at the date of each acquisition might result in annual adjustments to comparative figures and not just for acquisitions in the immediate prior period. So fair value adjustments made after the end of the one year period are to be treated as follows:

- In limited circumstances, they are **backdated** to the acquisition date with restatement of goodwill or gain on bargain purchase on acquisition and all comparative figures. These circumstances are if they arise as a result of an error, as defined by IAS 8 *Accounting Policies, Changes in Accounting Estimates and Errors* (dealt with in Chapter 4). But **such errors will be very rare**.

- In **all other circumstances**, such adjustments are to be treated as **changes in accounting estimates**, as defined in IAS 8. There is **no backdating** to the acquisition date and **no restatement** of comparative figures. These adjustments are recognised as **income or expenses in the accounting period in which they arise**. So if a trade receivable which had a fair value of nil at the acquisition date (ie it had been recognised as an expense in profit or loss) is recovered in full two years afterwards, **it is treated as income, not as a reduction in goodwill**.

8 Measurement of non-controlling interest

Section overview

- IFRS 3 allows two methods of measuring the non-controlling interest (NCI) at the acquisition date:
    - At the NCI's share of the acquiree's net assets (proportionate basis)
    - At its fair value

- The fair value method results in the NCI's share of goodwill being recognised.

8.1 Measurement of non-controlling interest at acquisition date

- The traditional method of measuring the NCI at the acquisition date is to measure it at the NCI's share of the acquiree's net assets, known as the proportionate basis throughout the Financial Accounting and Reporting materials.

    This method results in goodwill being in effect the difference between the cost of the parent's investment and its share of the net assets acquired. The rationale is that the market transaction which is the business combination has only provided evidence of the amount of the parent entity's goodwill; there has been no market transaction to provide evidence of the amount of goodwill attributable to the NCI. Hence only the acquirer's share of the goodwill is recognised.

    This method is the one adopted in the UK, and by international standards prior to 2007.

- The alternative approach works on the basis that the goodwill attributable to the NCI can be calculated from the estimate of the fair value of the NCI itself. It is an approach which is consistent with the rest of IFRS 3 which requires the consideration transferred, the assets acquired and the liabilities acquired all to be measured at fair value.

    This method was the one adopted in the US by the FASB.

    The fair value method usually results in a higher amount for the NCI; the difference between this and the amount as traditionally measured is added to the goodwill acquired in the business combination and is the goodwill attributable to the NCI at the acquisition date.

Note: The choice of method is available for each business combination separately. The choice in respect of one combination is **not binding** for subsequent combinations.

Worked example: Measurement of NCI (1)

The consideration transferred by National plc when it acquired 800,000 of the 1,000,000 £1 equity shares of Locale Ltd was £25 million. At the acquisition date Locale Ltd's retained earnings were £20 million and the fair value of the 200,000 equity shares in Locale Ltd not acquired was £5 million.

Calculate the goodwill acquired in the business combination on the basis that the NCI in Locale Ltd is measured using:

(a) Proportionate basis
(b) Fair value

Solution

	NCI on proportionate basis £'000	NCI at fair value £'000
Consideration transferred	25,000	25,000
NCI – 20% × £21 million/fair value	4,200	5,000
	29,200	30,000
Net assets acquired (£1 million + £20 million)	(21,000)	(21,000)
Goodwill acquired in business combination	8,200	9,000

The only difference between the results of the two methods at the acquisition date is that the NCI and goodwill are higher by £0.8 million, the amount by which the fair value of the NCI exceeds its share of the acquired net assets.

Point to note

There is always likely to be a difference between the fair values per share of an equity holding which provides control over another entity and a holding which does not, because buyers are prepared to pay a higher price per share if they end up gaining control of the other entity. This higher price is sometimes referred to as the 'control premium'. In the above example:

- The controlling interest is valued at £31.25 per share (25,000/800)
- The NCI is valued at £25.00 per share (5,000/200)

8.2 Subsequent measurement of NCI in statement of financial position

If NCI was measured at the acquisition date at fair value, then the carrying amount at the end of each subsequent period should take that fair value into account. This is best achieved by adapting the standard consolidation working (4) along the lines of equity accounting for associates, as follows

Consolidation working (4) – Non-controlling interest

	£
Fair value of NCI at acquisition date	X
Share of post acquisition profits and other reserves	
(NCI% × post acquisition (W2))	X
	X

Where NCI has been **measured at fair value** and there is an impairment of goodwill, part of that impairment will be **charged to the NCI** at the end of the reporting period, based on the NCI %.

For instance, if the goodwill in the worked example in Section 8.1 above was impaired by £1,000, the impairment would be charged as follows:

Proportionate basis

	£	£
DR Group retained earnings	1,000	
CR Goodwill		1,000

Fair value basis

	£	£
DR Group retained earnings (1,000 × 80%)	800	
DR Non-controlling interest (1,000 × 20%)	200	
CR Goodwill		1,000

Where NCI has been measured using the proportional basis, notional goodwill should be calculated for the NCI share. This is used to compare the carrying amount of a cash-generating unit (CGU) including goodwill to its recoverable amount. However, as CGUs do not form part of the Financial Accounting and Reporting syllabus, the notional goodwill for the NCI is ignored in this manual. This will instead be covered at the Advanced Stage.

Therefore, where the proportionate method of calculating goodwill and NCI has been used students should assume that any impairment given relates to the proportion of goodwill recognised and no adjustment to the figure will be necessary.

Worked example: Measurement of NCI (2)

Continuing with the immediately preceding worked example, Locale Ltd's retained earnings three years later were £23 million.

Calculate the carrying amount of the non-controlling interest three years later on the basis that at acquisition it was measured using:

(a) Proportionate basis
(b) Fair value

Solution

Consolidation working (2) – Net assets of Locale Ltd

	At period end £'000	At acquisition £'000	Post-acquisition £'000
Share capital	1,000	1,000	–
Retained earnings	23,000	20,000	3,000
	24,000	21,000	3,000

Consolidation working (4) – Non-controlling interest

	NCI on proportionate basis £'000	NCI at fair value £'000
NCI at acquisition date – share of net assets (20% × Column 2 (W2))/fair value	4,200	5,000
Share of post acquisition profits – (20% × post acquisition Column 3 (W2))	600	600
	4,800	5,600

Interactive question 6: Subsequent measurement of NCI

[Difficulty level: Exam standard]

On 1 January 20X8 Foot plc acquired 75,000 equity shares in Belt Ltd for £750,000. Belt Ltd's issued equity share capital was 100,000 £1 shares and at 1 January 20X8 the fair value and the carrying amount of its net assets was £600,000. On the same date the fair value of the equity shares in Belt Ltd not acquired by Foot plc was estimated at £175,000.

On 31 December 20X8 the summarised statements of financial position of the two entities were as follows:

	Foot plc £	Belt Ltd £
ASSETS		
Non-current assets		
Property, plant and equipment	150,000	500,000
Investments	750,000	–
	900,000	500,000
Current assets	1,700,000	680,000
Total assets	2,600,000	1,180,000
EQUITY AND LIABILITIES		
Equity		
Ordinary share capital (£1 shares)	500,000	100,000
Retained earnings	1,500,000	880,000
	2,000,000	980,000
Current liabilities	600,000	200,000
Total equity and liabilities	2,600,000	1,180,000

Requirement

Prepare the consolidated statement of financial position of Foot plc and its subsidiary Belt Ltd as at 31 December 20X8 on the basis that at acquisition the non-controlling interest was measured using:

(a) Proportionate basis
(b) Fair value

See **Answer** at the end of this chapter.

9 IFRS 10 *Consolidated Financial Statements*

Section overview

- With limited exceptions, all parent entities must present consolidated financial statements.
- Consolidated financial statements must include the parent and all the entities under its control.
- The IAS 27 provisions relating to consolidated financial statements have been replaced by IFRS 10.
- The investment in the subsidiary is carried at cost in the parent's statement of financial position.

9.1 Scope

IFRS 10 is to be applied **in the preparation of the consolidated financial statements** (CFS) of the group.

Definitions

A group: A parent and all its subsidiaries.

Consolidated financial statements: The financial statements of a group in which the assets, liabilities, equity, income, expenses and cash flows of the parent and its subsidiaries are presented as those of a single economic entity.

Non-controlling interest: The equity in a subsidiary not attributable, directly or indirectly, to a parent.

9.2 Background

IFRS 10 *Consolidated Financial Statements* was published in May 2011 and replaced the consolidation provisions of IAS 27 *Consolidated and Separate Financial Statements*. The IASB stressed that the purpose of IFRS 10 was to build upon rather than replace the IAS 27 requirements and concepts but the new provisions are clearly designed to eliminate the divergent practices which had been possible under IAS 27.

Like IAS 27, IFRS 10 bases its consolidation model on **control**, but it seeks to define control in a way which can be applied to all investees. IAS 27 defined control as 'the power to govern the financial operating policies of an entity so as to obtain benefits from its activities'. In practice, this had focussed attention on size of shareholding. IFRS 10 gives a more detailed definition of control and seeks in that way to reduce the opportunities for reporting entities to avoid consolidation. It expands upon the limited guidance in IAS 27 regarding the possibility of control without the majority of voting rights.

The IFRS 10 definition of control was explained in Section 3.1.

9.3 Presentation of CFS

With one exception, a **parent must present CFS**.

A parent need not prepare CFS if and only if **all** of the following hold:

- The parent is itself **a wholly-owned subsidiary** or it is a partially owned subsidiary of another entity and its other owners, including those not otherwise entitled to vote, have been informed about, and do not object to, the parent not presenting consolidated financial statements;

- Its securities are **neither publicly traded nor in the process of being issued to the public**; and

- IFRS-compliant CFS are prepared by the **immediate or ultimate parent company**.

9.4 Scope of CFS

The CFS **must include the parent and all subsidiaries**, both foreign and domestic, other than:

- Those held for sale in accordance with IFRS 5
- Those held under such long-term restrictions that control cannot be operated

IFRS 10 is clear that a subsidiary should not be excluded from consolidation simply because it is loss making or its business activities are dissimilar to those of the group as a whole.

9.5 Consolidation procedures

The following consolidation procedures are necessary to present the group as a single economic entity. These were explained in earlier sections of this chapter, ie:

- **Eliminating** the **carrying amount of the parent's investment** against its share of the **equity in its subsidiaries**, with **goodwill** being the resultant figure.

- **Calculating the non-controlling interest** and presenting it as a separate figure:

    - In the statement of financial position, within total equity but separately from the parent shareholders' equity.

    - In the statement of profit or loss.

In addition **intra-group balances, transactions, profits and losses should be eliminated in full** (ie not just the parent's share).

Point to note

Under IFRS 10 total comprehensive income is attributed to the parent and the non-controlling interests even if this results in the non-controlling interests having a deficit balance. This is consistent with the idea that the non-controlling interests are part of the equity of the group. If there is a non-controlling interest in cumulative preference shares which are classified as equity, the non-controlling interest must be allocated their share of the relevant dividends even if they have not been declared.

There are additional requirements that:

- Where the parent and subsidiary have **different reporting dates**, that difference should be **not more than three months** (remember that, because it has control, the parent can dictate a reporting date to the subsidiary) **and adjustments must be made for major transactions between the two dates**. An example of such an adjustment would be if the subsidiary with cash appearing in its statement of financial position at an earlier date lent it to the parent so that the same cash was in the parent's statement of financial position at the later date. An adjustment must be made to eliminate this double-counting.

- **Uniform accounting policies must be applied** to all companies in preparing the CFS. If they are not adopted in the subsidiaries' own financial statements, then **adjustments should be made as part of the consolidation**. It might be the case that certain group companies take advantage of the alternative accounting treatments allowed in some areas by IFRSs, but these should be made uniform on consolidation.

Changes in the composition of the group are accounted for as follows:

- **Acquisitions are accounted for under IFRS 3,** by bringing into the consolidated statement of profit or loss the new subsidiary's income and expenses from the date of acquisition.

- In the case of disposals, the **income and expenses to the date of disposal** (ie the date control is lost) **are included in the CFS**, as is the difference between the **proceeds of sale** and the **carrying amount in the consolidated statement of financial position** at that date (which will be the parent's share of the subsidiary's net assets at the date of disposal plus any remaining goodwill relating to that subsidiary – this is dealt with in Chapter 14).

10 IFRS 12 *Disclosure of Interests in Other Entities*

Section overview

- IFRS 12 sets out the required disclosures for group accounting.

10.1 Overview

IFRS 12 *Disclosure of Interests in Other Entities* was issued in May 2011 as part of a package of five standards relating to consolidation. It provides comprehensive disclosure requirements regarding a reporting entity's interests in other entities. The disclosure requirements in IAS 27 had been criticised as being too limited. The information required by IFRS 12 is intended to help users to evaluate the nature of, and risks associated with, a reporting entity's interest in other entities and the effects of those interests on its financial position, financial performance and cash flows. It replaces the disclosure requirements of all other standards relating to group accounting. The standard requires disclosure of:

- The significant judgements and assumptions made in determining the nature of an interest in another entity or arrangement, and in determining the type of joint arrangement in which an interest is held.

- Information about interests in subsidiaries, associates, joint arrangements and structured entities that are not controlled by an investor.

10.2 Interests in subsidiaries

The following disclosures are required in respect of subsidiaries:

- The interest that non-controlling interests have in the group's activities and cash flows, including the name of relevant subsidiaries, their principal place of business and the interest and voting rights of the non-controlling interests.

- The nature and extent of significant restrictions on an investor's ability to use group assets and liabilities.

- The nature of the risks associated with an entity's interests in consolidated structured entities.

- The consequences of changes in ownership interest in subsidiaries (possible loss of control).

IFRS 12 also requires specific disclosures in respect of associates and joint arrangements. These are explained in Chapter 13.

11 IAS 27 *Separate Financial Statements*

Section overview

- IAS 27 has been reissued covering just the requirements for a parent's separate financial statements.

IAS 27 *Separate Financial Statements* was reissued in May 2011 dealing only with the single entity financial statements of the parent, the consolidation provisions having been transferred to IFRS 10.

It outlines the accounting and disclosure requirements for the separate financial statements of the parent or the investor, in which the relevant investments will be accounted for either at cost or in accordance with IFRS 9 (IAS 39).

The exception to this is investments held for sale which will be accounted for in accordance with IFRS 5 *Non-current Assets Held For Sale and Discontinued Operations*.

In its separate financial statements an entity will recognise dividends from other entities, rather than recognising a share of their profits. An entity recognises a dividend from a subsidiary, joint venture or associate when its right to receive the dividend is established.

Summary

```
                                    ┌─────────────────┐                    ┌──────────────────────────┐
                                    │ Group accounts  │────────────────────│ Subsidiary: An entity     │
                                    │     (P + S)     │                    │ that is controlled by     │
                                    └─────────────────┘                    │ another entity            │
                                             │                             └──────────────────────────┘
                                             │
                                    ┌─────────────────────────┐            ┌──────────────────────────┐
                                    │ Single entity concept   │            │ Legal form: Each company  │
                                    │ applying substance over │────────────│ is a separate legal person.│
                                    │ form                    │            │ Substance: Group is a     │
                                    └─────────────────────────┘            │ single economic entity    │
                                             │                             └──────────────────────────┘
                                    ┌─────────────────┐
                                    │ Control and     │
                                    │ ownership       │
                                    └─────────────────┘
```

- Group accounts (P + S)
  - Subsidiary: An entity that is controlled by another entity
- Single entity concept applying substance over form
  - Legal form: Each company is a separate legal person. Substance: Group is a single economic entity
- Control and ownership

Consolidated statement of profit or loss
- Shows revenue and expenses under group control by the line-by-line addition of S's revenue and costs
- And shows ownership split between
  - Parent company's share
  - Non-controlling interest share
  - Of PAT

Consolidated statement of financial position
- Shows resources under group control by the line-by-line addition of S's net assets
- And shows ownership split between
  - Parent company's share
  - Non-controlling interest share
  - Of equity

Self-test

Answer the following questions

1   Vaynor plc acquired 100,000 ordinary shares in Weeton Ltd and 40,000 ordinary shares in Yarlet Ltd some years ago.

Extracts from the statements of financial position of the three companies as on 30 September 20X7 were as follows.

	Vaynor plc £'000	Weeton Ltd £'000	Yarlet Ltd £'000
Ordinary shares of £1 each	500	100	50
Retained earnings	90	40	70

At acquisition Weeton Ltd had retained losses of £10,000 and Yarlet Ltd had retained earnings of £30,000.

What were the consolidated retained earnings of Vaynor plc on 30 September 20X7?

2   The summarised statements of financial position of Peep Ltd and Pitti Ltd at 31 December 20X6 are as follows.

	Peep Ltd £	Pitti Ltd £
Net assets	300,000	160,000
Share capital (£1 shares)	100,000	100,000
Retained earnings	200,000	60,000
	300,000	160,000

On 31 December 20X6 Yum plc purchased for cash 90% of Peep Ltd's shares for £360,000 and 75% of Pitti Ltd's shares for £100,000. The carrying amounts of the assets in both companies are considered to be fair values and non-controlling interest is valued on the proportionate basis.

What amounts in respect of goodwill/gain on a bargain purchase will arise from these acquisitions?

3   Wolf plc acquired 80,000 £1 ordinary shares in Fox plc on 1 April 20X5 at a cost of £77,000. Fox plc's retained earnings at that date were £50,000 and its issued ordinary share capital was £100,000. Non-controlling interest is valued at fair value of £32,000.

What is the amount of the gain on a bargain purchase arising on the acquisition?

4   Ling plc purchased 80% of the ordinary shares of Moy Ltd on 1 June 20X0 for £5,400,000. The summarised statement of financial position of Moy Ltd on this date showed the following.

	£'000
Ordinary share capital	1,000
Share premium account	500
Revaluation surplus	400
Retained earnings	2,700
	4,600

The fair value of the identifiable net assets of Moy Ltd exceeded their carrying amount by £150,000. The statement of financial position of Moy Ltd included goodwill of £500,000. Ling plc has chosen to use the proportionate basis to measure the goodwill and non-controlling interest arising on the acquisition of Moy Ltd.

In accordance with IFRS 3 (Revised) *Business Combinations* what is the amount of goodwill acquired in the business combination?

5   Sansom plc has two subsidiaries, Mabbutt Ltd and Waddle Ltd. It purchased 10,000 £1 shares in Mabbutt Ltd on 1 January 20X1 for £35,000 when the retained earnings of Mabbutt Ltd stood at £21,000 and the fair value of the NCI was £13,000. It purchased 15,000 £1 shares in Waddle Ltd for £20,000 on 31 December 20X1 when the retained earnings of Waddle Ltd stood at £16,000 and the fair value of the NCI was £10,000. Non-controlling interests at the acquisition date are to be measured at their fair value.

The issued share capital of the two subsidiaries is as follows.

Mabbutt Ltd	£15,000
Waddle Ltd	£20,000

By the end of 20X4 goodwill impairment losses totalled £4,400.

What is the carrying amount of goodwill in the consolidated statement of financial position at 31 December 20X4?

6   Tom plc has purchased all the share capital of Jerry Ltd during the year.

Which of the following items should Tom plc take into account when calculating the fair value of the net assets acquired in accordance with IFRS 3 (Revised) *Business Combinations*?

(1)   A possible loss dependent on the outcome of a legal case which has not been provided for in Jerry Ltd's books. The acquisition date fair value of the loss can be estimated reliably.

(2)   A provision required to cover the costs of reorganising Jerry Ltd's departments to fit in with Tom plc's structure.

(3)   A warranty provision in Jerry Ltd's books to cover the costs of commitments made to customers.

7   Wilsons plc purchased 70% of Watneys Ltd for £20,000 on 30 June 20X2. The fair value of the non-controlling interest at that date was £7,000. The statements of financial position of Watneys Ltd are as follows.

	30 September	
	20X2	20X1
	£	£
Ordinary share capital	1,000	1,000
Share premium	2,000	2,000
Retained earnings	21,000	12,000
	24,000	15,000

Profits accrue evenly over the year. Wilsons plc uses fair value wherever possible as a preferred method of accounting.

What is the goodwill acquired in the business combination?

8   Leeds Ltd acquired the whole of the issued share capital of Cardiff Ltd for £12 million in cash. In arriving at the purchase price Leeds Ltd had taken into account future costs for reorganising Cardiff Ltd of £1 million and Cardiff Ltd's anticipated future trading losses of £2 million. The fair value of the net assets of Cardiff Ltd before taking into account these matters was £7 million.

In accordance with IFRS 3 (Revised) *Business Combinations*, what is the amount of goodwill acquired in the business combination?

9   Castor plc acquires 75% of the share capital of Pollux Ltd on 1 December 20X1. The consideration transferred is £1 million in cash and 300,000 £1 ordinary shares of Castor plc. The market value of each of Castor plc's shares on 1 December 20X1 is 300 pence. On 1 December 20X1 the fair value of Pollux Ltd's net assets is £1 million. Castor plc intends to recognise the non-controlling interest in Pollux Ltd at its fair value on 1 December 20X1 of £280,000.

In accordance with IFRS 3 *Business Combinations* what is the amount of goodwill acquired in the business combination to be dealt with in Castor plc's consolidated accounts?

10   In accordance with IFRS 3 *Business Combinations* the timetable for the acquisition of a subsidiary will usually include the following four dates.

(1)   The date on which consideration passes

(2)   The date on which an offer becomes or is declared unconditional

(3)   The date from which the acquiring company has the right to share in the profits of the acquired business under the agreement

(4)   The date on which control passes

What will be the effective date for accounting for the business combination?

11 Sam Ltd has a share capital of £10,000 split into 2,000 A ordinary shares of £1 each and 8,000 B ordinary shares of £1 each. Each A ordinary share has ten votes and each B ordinary share has one vote. Both classes of shares have the same rights to dividends and on liquidation. Tom plc owns 1,500 A ordinary shares in Sam Ltd. Dick plc owns 5,000 B ordinary shares in Sam Ltd.

All three companies conduct similar activities and there is no special relationship between the companies other than that already stated. The shareholdings in Sam Ltd are held as long-term investments and are the only shareholdings of Tom plc and Dick plc.

In accordance with IFRS 10 *Consolidated Financial Statements* which company(ies) should prepare consolidated financial statements?

12 ANDRESS LTD

The statement of profit or loss and statement of financial position for the year 20X0 for Andress Ltd and Bacall Ltd are given below.

Statements of profit or loss for the year ended 31 December 20X0

	Andress Ltd £	Bacall Ltd £
Revenue	10,000	7,000
Cost of sales	(6,000)	(2,000)
Gross profit	4,000	5,000
Expenses and tax	(3,000)	(2,000)
Profit	1,000	3,000

Statements of financial position as at 31 December 20X0

	Andress Ltd £	Bacall Ltd £
ASSETS		
Non-current assets		
Property, plant and equipment	25,300	9,000
Investments (3,200 shares in Bacall Ltd at cost)	3,200	–
	28,500	9,000
Current assets	22,500	7,000
Total assets	51,000	16,000
EQUITY AND LIABILITIES		
Equity		
Ordinary share capital	10,000	4,000
Share premium account	4,000	–
Retained earnings	2,000	7,000
Total equity	16,000	11,000
Non-current liabilities	10,000	2,000
Current liabilities	25,000	3,000
Total equity and liabilities	51,000	16,000

Andress Ltd has owned 80% of Bacall Ltd since incorporation.

Requirement

Prepare, for Andress Ltd, the consolidated statement of profit or loss for the year ended 31 December 20X0 and the consolidated statement of financial position at that date.

13 CRAWFORD LTD PART 1

The statements of financial position and statements of profit or loss for Crawford Ltd and Dietrich Ltd are given below.

Statements of financial position as at 30 June 20X0

	Crawford Ltd £	Dietrich Ltd £
ASSETS		
Non-current assets		
Property, plant and equipment	27,000	12,500
Investments (2,000 £1 shares in Dietrich Ltd at cost)	2,000	–
	29,000	12,500
Current assets	25,000	12,000
Total assets	54,000	24,500
EQUITY AND LIABILITIES		
Equity		
Ordinary share capital	20,000	3,000
Share premium account	6,000	–
Retained earnings	9,000	14,000
Total equity	35,000	17,000
Non-current liabilities	12,000	–
Current liabilities	7,000	7,500
Total equity and liabilities	54,000	24,500

Crawford Ltd acquired its shares in Dietrich Ltd five years ago when Dietrich's retained earnings were nil. At the start of the current year retained earnings were £2,000 and £4,000 respectively.

Statement of profit or loss for the year ended 30 June 20X0

	Crawford Ltd £	Dietrich Ltd £
Revenue	24,000	30,000
Cost of sales	(9,000)	(11,000)
Gross profit	15,000	19,000
Distribution costs	(2,300)	(1,300)
Administrative expenses	(1,500)	(2,700)
Profit from operations	11,200	15,000
Finance cost	(1,200)	–
Profit before tax	10,000	15,000
Income tax expense	(3,000)	(5,000)
Profit for the year	7,000	10,000

Requirement

(a) Briefly explain the objectives of producing group accounts. **(3 marks)**

(b) Briefly explain the following words/phrases.

  (i) Single entity concept
  (ii) Control
  (iii) Equity **(6 marks)**

(c) Prepare, for Crawford Ltd, the consolidated statement of profit or loss and the consolidated statement of changes in equity (retained earnings and the non-controlling interest columns only) for the year ended 30 June 20X0 and the consolidated statement of financial position as at that date. **(12 marks)**

(21 marks)

Now, go back to the Learning objectives in the Introduction. If you are satisfied you have achieved these objectives, please tick them off.

Technical reference

Point to note: The following sets out the examinability of the standards covered in this chapter.

IFRS 3   All paragraphs but excluding paragraphs 24–30, 41–44, 54–55, 57 and 67. Appendix B is excluded except for B5–B11, B31–B34 and B64–B67 and the illustrative examples are also excluded.

The paragraphs listed below are the key references you should be familiar with.

1 IFRS 3 *Business Combinations*

Basics

- Definitions: control, acquirer, acquiree, acquisition date, goodwill.   IFRS 3 (App A)
- Acquisition method: acquirer, cost of combination, allocation over identifiable assets, liabilities and contingent liabilities.   IFRS 3 (5)

Acquisition date

- Date that control passes.   IFRS 3 (8–9)

Consideration transferred

- Measured at fair value of assets given, liabilities assumed and equity instruments issued.   IFRS 3 (37–38)
- Subsequent adjustment to cost:
  - Subsequent adjustments within measurement period affect goodwill   IFRS 3 (45–50)
  - If after initial accounting complete, then in current period

Recognition and measurement of identifiable net assets acquired

- Identifiable assets – exist at acquisition date and:
  - May or may not have been recognised in the acquiree's own financial statements   IFRS 3 (10–14)
- Identifiable contingent liabilities – exist at acquisition date and:
  - Reliably measurable   IFRS 3 (23)
  - Normal IAS 37 disclosures   IFRS 3 (B64)
  - Subsequently carried at higher of IAS 37 value and value at acquisition date   IFRS 3 (56)

Goodwill

- Non-current asset   IFRS 3 (32)
- No amortisation but subject to annual impairment reviews.   IAS 36 (10)

Gain on bargain purchase

- Reassess identification and measurement of the net assets acquired and measurement of consideration transferred.   IFRS 3 (36)
- Any remaining amount recognised in profit or loss in period the acquisition is made.   IFRS 3 (34)

Initial accounting

- At acquisition date or within 12 months thereof.   IFRS 3 (45)
- Subsequently: errors accounted for retrospectively, everything else prospectively.   IFRS 3 (50)

Disclosures

IFRS 3 (B64–B67)

- Business combinations effected in the accounting period or after its finish but before financial statements authorised for issue (in the latter case, by way of note).

- Gains, losses, errors and other adjustments which relate to combinations effected in the current or previous periods.

- Changes in the carrying amount of goodwill during the period.

2 IFRS 10 *Consolidated Financial Statements*

Scope

- An entity that is a parent shall present consolidated financial statements, unless:
IFRS 10 (4)

    - Wholly or partially-owned subsidiary and all other owners do not object to no CFS

    - Debt or equity instruments not publicly traded

    - Not in the process of filing financial statements with any regulatory body for the purpose of making a public offering

    - Ultimate or intermediate parent publishes consolidated financial statements compliant with IFRS

Control

- An investor controls an investee when it is exposed, or has rights, to variable returns from its involvement with the investee and has the ability to affect those returns through its power over the investee.
IFRS 10 (6)

- An investee has power over an investee when the investor has existing rights that give it the current ability to direct the **relevant activities** ie the activities that significantly affect the investee's returns
(IFRS 10)

Accounting requirements

- A parent shall present consolidated financial statements using uniform accounting policies for like transactions and other events in similar circumstances.
IFRS 10 (19)

- Non-controlling interest to be presented in the consolidated statement of financial position within equity, but separately from owners' equity.
IFRS 10 (22)

Appendix A

Definitions: control, group, non-controlling interest, parent, power, relevant activities, subsidiary

3 IAS 27 *Separate Financial Statements*

Definitions – as per IFRS 10
IAS 27 (5)

Parent's separate financial statements

- Investments in subsidiaries, joint ventures and associates should be accounted for either at cost or in accordance with IFRS 9 (IAS 39), unless they are classified as held for sale.
IAS 27 (10)

- A dividend from a subsidiary, joint venture or associate shall be recognised when the right to receive the dividend is established.
IAS 27 (12)

Disclosures

- When a parent elects not to prepare consolidated financial statements, it shall disclose
IAS 27 (16)

    (a) Details of the entity and a statement that the exemption from consolidation has been used

    (b) A list of significant investments in subsidiaries, joint ventures and associates

    (c) A description of the method used to account for these investments

4 IFRS 12 *Disclosure of Interests in Other Entities*

- Deals with disclosure requirements for an entity that has an interest in subsidiaries, joint ventures or associates.

  IFRS 12 (5)

- An entity shall disclose information about **significant judgements and assumptions** it has made in determining that it has control, joint control or significant influence.

  IFRS 12 (7)

- An entity shall disclose information regarding:

  - Its interests in subsidiaries

    IFRS 12 (10)

  - The interests that non-controlling interests have in the group's activities and cash flows

    IFRS 12 (11)

Answer to Interactive question 1

Austin Ltd: Consolidated statement of financial position as at 31 December 20X7

	£
Non-current assets	
Property, plant and equipment (80,000 + 8,000)	88,000
Current assets (58,000 + 13,000)	71,000
Total assets	159,000
Equity attributable to owners of the parent	
Called up share capital (Austin Ltd only)	100,000
Retained earnings (Austin Ltd only)	30,000
	130,000
Non-controlling interest (20% × Reed Ltd's 15,000)	3,000
Total equity	133,000
Liabilities (20,000 + 6,000)	26,000
Total equity and liabilities	159,000

(Retained earnings are Austin Ltd's only, because Reed Ltd has, as yet, earned nothing under Austin Ltd's control.)

Answer to Interactive question 2

Austin Ltd

Consolidated statement of profit or loss for the year ended 31 December 20X8

	£
Revenue (20,000 + 5,000)	25,000
Costs (15,000 + 3,000)	(18,000)
Profit	7,000
Profit attributable to:	
Owners of Austin Ltd (ß)	6,600
Non-controlling interest (20% × 2,000)	400
	7,000

Consolidated statement of financial position as at 31 December 20X8

	£
Non-current assets	
Property, plant and equipment (82,000 + 9,000)	91,000
Current assets (81,000 + 20,000)	101,000
Total assets	192,000
Equity attributable to owners of parent	
Called up share capital (Austin Ltd only)	100,000
Retained earnings	
(35,000 + (80% × (7,000 – 5,000))	36,600
(ie Austin Ltd + its share of Reed Ltd post-acquisition)	
	136,600
Non-controlling interest (20% × Reed Ltd's 17,000)	3,400
Total equity	140,000
Liabilities (40,000 + 12,000)	52,000
Total equity and liabilities	192,000

Answer to Interactive question 3

	£'000

Statement of financial position at 31 December 20X5
Non-current assets – goodwill

		£'000
Consideration transferred	– 8 million shares × £3.50	28,000
	– contingent at fair value at acquisition date	100
		28,100
Net assets acquired		(20,000)
Goodwill		8,100
Current liabilities – contingent consideration at fair value at period end		1,200

Profit or loss for year ended 31 December 20X5

	£'000
Additional consideration for acquisition	1,100

Statement of financial position at 31 December 20X6

	£'000
Non-current assets – goodwill	8,100

Profit or loss for year ended 31 December 20X6

	£'000
Additional consideration for acquisition – (£1.75 million paid – £1.2 million))	550

Note that the contingent consideration of £1.75 million was settled in cash on 31 December 20X6 so there is no liability to be recognised at the end of 20X6.

Answer to Interactive question 4

P plc has paid £10,000 to buy 75% of S Ltd's net assets of (16,000 – 4,000) = £12,000

	£
Consideration transferred	10,000
Plus non-controlling interest at acquisition (12,000 × 25%)	3,000
Less net assets at acquisition	(12,000)
Goodwill	1,000

Answer to Interactive question 5

Recording investment in Eclipse plc
Shares to be issued 1 July 20X7

		£'000	£'000
DR	Investment in Eclipse plc (5m × 60p)	3,000	
CR	Cash (issue costs)		10
CR	Share capital (5m × 25p)		1,250
CR	Share premium (3,000 – 1,250 – 10 issue costs)		1,740

Cash

		£'000	£'000
DR	Investment in Eclipse plc	1,000	
CR	Cash		1,000

Shares to be issued 1 July 20X8

		£'000	£'000
DR	Investment in Eclipse plc (1m × 60p)	600	
CR	Shares not yet issued (heading under equity)		600

Goodwill on consolidation of Eclipse plc

	£'000	£'000
Consideration transferred		
Shares	3,000	
Cash	1,000	
Shares to be issued	600	
		4,600
Non-controlling interest at acquisition ((3,628 – 200) × 25%)		857
		5,457
Identifiable assets and liabilities		
Per books of Eclipse plc	3,628	
Contingent liability	(200)	
		(3,428)
Goodwill		2,029

Answer to Interactive question 6

Foot plc – Consolidated statement of financial position as at 31 December 20X8

Measurement of NCI at acquisition	*Proportionate basis* £	*Fair value* £
ASSETS		
Non-current assets		
Property, plant and equipment (150,000 + 500,000)	650,000	650,000
Intangibles (W3)	300,000	325,000
	950,000	975,000
Current assets (1,700,000 + 680,000)	2,380,000	2,380,000
Total assets	3,330,000	3,355,000
EQUITY AND LIABILITIES		
Attributable to owners of Foot plc		
Ordinary share capital (£1 shares)	500,000	500,000
Retained earnings (W5)	1,785,000	1,785,000
	2,285,000	2,285,000
Non-controlling interest (W4)	245,000	270,000
Equity	2,530,000	2,555,000
Current liabilities (600,000 + 200,000)	800,000	800,000
Total equity and liabilities	3,330,000	3,355,000

WORKINGS

(1) Group structure

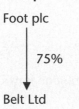

Foot plc

75%

Belt Ltd

(2) Net assets of Belt Ltd

	At period end £	*Acquisition date* £	*Post-acquisition* £
Share capital	100,000	100,000	–
Retained earnings	880,000	500,000	380,000
	980,000	600,000	380,000

(3) Goodwill

Measurement of NCI at acquisition	*Proportionate basis* £	*Fair value* £
Consideration transferred	750,000	750,000
NCI at the acquisition date – 25% × 600,000/at fair value	150,000	175,000
	900,000	925,000
Less net assets acquired	(600,000)	(600,000)
	300,000	325,000

(4) Non-controlling interest

Measurement of NCI at acquisition	*Proportionate basis* £	*Fair value* £
NCI at acquisition – 25% × 600,000 (W2)/fair value	150,000	175,000
Share of post-acquisition profits – 25% × 380,000 (W2)	95,000	95,000
	245,000	270,000

(5) Retained earnings

	£
Foot plc	1,500,000
Belt Ltd (75% × 380,000 (W2))	285,000
	1,785,000

1

	£'000
Vaynor plc	90
Weeton Ltd ((40 + 10) × 100%)	50
Yarlet Ltd ((70 – 30) × 80%)	32
Consolidated retained earnings	172

2

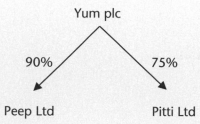

	£
Peep – consideration transferred	360,000
Non-controlling interest at acquisition (300,000 × 10%)	30,000
Net assets at acquisition	(300,000)
Goodwill	90,000
Pitti – consideration transferred	100,000
Non-controlling interest at acquisition (160,000 × 25%)	40,000
Net assets at acquisition	(160,000)
Gain on a bargain purchase	(20,000)*

* Recognised in consolidated profit or loss in the period in which the acquisition is made (ie on 31 December 20X6).

3

	£
Consideration transferred	77,000
Non-controlling interest at acquisition at fair value	32,000
	109,000
Net assets at acquisition (100,000 + 50,000)	(150,000)
Gain on a bargain purchase	(41,000)

4

	£'000
Fair value of consideration transferred	5,400
Non-controlling interest (4,250 × 20%)	850
Less fair value of net assets acquired (4,600 + 150 fair value adj – 500 goodwill)	(4,250)
Goodwill	2,000

5 Goodwill shown in the statement of financial position will be £7,600.

	£	£
Mabbutt Ltd		
Consideration transferred		35,000
Fair value of non-controlling interest at acquisition		13,000
Less net assets		
Share capital	15,000	
Retained earnings	21,000	
		(36,000)
Goodwill		12,000
Impairment to date		(4,400)
Balance c/f		7,600

Waddle Ltd

	£	£
Consideration transferred		20,000
Fair value of non-controlling interest at acquisition		10,000
Less net assets at acquisition		
Share capital	20,000	
Retained earnings	16,000	
		(36,000)
		(6,000) *

* Recognised as a gain in consolidated profit or loss in the year in which the acquisition was made.

6   (1) and (3)

Contingent liabilities should be recognised even though not provided for in the acquiree's books and the warranty provision should be recognised as it arises from past events.

Reorganisation plans are only put into effect once control is gained. No liability or contingent liability therefore exists at the time of acquisition.

7

	£	£
Consideration transferred		20,000
Fair value of non-controlling interest at acquisition		7,000
		27,000
Less: Net assets at acquisition		
Share capital	1,000	
Share premium	2,000	
Retained earnings – 1 October 20X1	12,000	
– Nine months ($^9/_{12} \times 21,000 - 12,000$)	6,750	
		(21,750)
Goodwill		5,250

8

	£m
Fair value of consideration	12
Less fair value of net assets acquired	(7)
Goodwill acquired	5

Acquirer's reorganisation plans and acquiree's or acquirer's future operating losses do not meet the recognition criteria for liabilities as the related liabilities did not exist at the acquisition date.

9

	£'000
Fair value of consideration	
Cash	1,000
Shares at fair value (300 × 3)	900
Non-controlling interest at FV	280
Less fair value of net assets acquired	(1,000)
Goodwill acquired	1,180

10   (4) The date on which control passes.

A business combination is accounted for from the acquisition date, which is the date on which control in the acquiree is obtained (IFRS 3 paragraph 8).

11   Tom plc has control of Sam Ltd and so should prepare consolidated financial statements.

Total number of votes:

		Votes
A shares 2,000 × 10	=	20,000
B shares 8,000 × 1	=	8,000
		28,000

$$\text{Tom plc controls } \frac{15,000}{28,000} = 54\% \text{ of the votes}$$

Note: We have to assume that 54% gives Tom control ie power, rights to variable returns and the ability to affect the level of returns.

12 ANDRESS LTD

Consolidated statement of profit or loss for the year ended 31 December 20X0

	£
Revenue (10,000 + 7,000)	17,000
Cost of sales (6,000 + 2,000)	(8,000)
Gross profit	9,000
Expenses and tax (3,000 + 2,000)	(5,000)
Profit	4,000
Profit attributable to	
Owners of Andress Ltd (ß)	3,400
Non-controlling interest (20% × 3,000)	600
	4,000

Consolidated statement of financial position as at 31 December 20X0

	£
ASSETS	
Non-current assets	
Property, plant and equipment (25,300 + 9,000)	34,300
Current assets (22,500 + 7,000)	29,500
Total assets	63,800
EQUITY AND LIABILITIES	
Equity attributable to owners of the parent	
Ordinary share capital	10,000
Share premium account	4,000
Retained earnings (2,000 + (80% × 7,000))	7,600
	21,600
Non-controlling interest (20% × 11,000)	2,200
Total equity	23,800
Non-current liabilities (10,000 + 2,000)	12,000
Current liabilities (25,000 + 3,000)	28,000
Total equity and liabilities	63,800

Point to note: Andress has owned the shares in Bacall since incorporation and the shares were acquired at nominal value (3,200 shares for £3,200). There is therefore no difference between the value of the consideration transferred by Andress and the value of the assets it acquired, so no goodwill was acquired.

13 CRAWFORD LTD PART 1

(a) **The objectives of producing group accounts**

Group accounts aim to reflect substance, ie if one company controls another, they effectively operate as a single economic entity.

Therefore, the parent, or controlling company, should provide information about the economic activities of the group by preparing consolidated accounts. These will show the economic resources controlled by the group, the obligations of the group and the results achieved with those resources. The overall aim is to present the results and state of affairs of the group as if they were those of a single entity.

(b) **Terms**

(i) **Single entity concept**

The single entity concept focuses on the existence of the group as an economic unit (as discussed above). This contrasts with legal form where each group company is actually a separate legal person.

(ii) **Control**

Control is defined as:

(i) Power

(ii) Exposure, or rights to variable returns from involvement with the investee

(iii) Ability to use power to affect the level of variable returns

In an individual company the assets are under the direct control of that company. However, where a company becomes a subsidiary, the assets are under indirect control of the parent via its control of the subsidiary.

Control can be achieved in a number of ways, the most obvious being a holding of over 50% of the ordinary, ie vote-carrying, shares.

(iii) **Equity**

Equity is defined in the IASB *Conceptual Framework* (Elements) as the residual amount found by deducting all of the entity's liabilities from all of its assets. In an individual company those net assets are owned by one ownership interest – the company's shareholders. However, in consolidated accounts the consolidated net assets will include 100% of the subsidiary even though some of those net assets may not be owned by the group. Therefore, the equity interest may be split between

- The parent company's shareholders
- The non-controlling shareholders in the subsidiary

(c) **Consolidated statement of financial position as at 30 June 20X0**

	£
ASSETS	
Non-current assets	
Property, plant and equipment (27,000 + 12,500)	39,500
Current assets (25,000 + 12,000)	37,000
Total assets	76,500
EQUITY AND LIABILITIES	
Equity attributable to owners of the parent	
Ordinary share capital	20,000
Share premium account	6,000
Retained earnings (9,000 + (2/3 × 14,000 – nil))	18,333
	44,333
Non-controlling interest (1/3 × 17,000)	5,667
Total equity	50,000
Non-current liabilities	12,000
Current liabilities (7,000 + 7,500)	14,500
Total equity and liabilities	76,500

Consolidated statement of profit or loss for the year ended 30 June 20X0

	£
Revenue (24,000 + 30,000)	54,000
Cost of sales (9,000 + 11,000)	(20,000)
Gross profit	34,000
Distribution costs (2,300 + 1,300)	(3,600)
Administrative expenses (1,500 + 2,700)	(4,200)
Profit from operations	26,200
Finance cost	(1,200)
Profit before tax	25,000
Income tax (3,000 + 5,000)	(8,000)
Profit for the year	17,000
Profit attributable to	
Owners of Crawford Ltd (ß)	13,667
Non-controlling interest (1/3 × 10,000)	3,333
	17,000

C
H
A
P
T
E
R

10

Consolidated statement of changes in equity for the year ended 30 June 20X0 (extracts)

	Attributable to owners of Crawford Ltd Retained earnings £	Non-controlling interest £
Balance brought forward (2,000 + (2/3 × 4,000)) (1/3 × (3,000 + 4,000))	4,666	2,334
Total comprehensive income for the period	13,667	3,333
Balance carried forward	18,333	5,667

Point to note: No goodwill arises on the acquisition of Dietrich Ltd as the shares were acquired at net asset value, ie their nominal value when retained earnings were £nil.

CHAPTER 11

Consolidated statement of financial position

Introduction

Learning objectives

Tick off

- Identify the financial effects of group accounting in the context of the IASB *Conceptual Framework* ☐

- Explain and demonstrate the concepts and principles surrounding the consolidation of financial statements including: ☐

    - The single entity concept
    - Substance over form
    - The distinction between control and ownership

- Calculate the amounts to be included in an entity's consolidated statement of financial position in respect of its new and continuing interests in subsidiaries in accordance with the international financial reporting framework ☐

- Prepare and present a consolidated statement of financial position (or extracts therefrom) including adjustments for intra-group transactions and balances, goodwill, non-controlling interests and fair values ☐

- Explain the application of IFRS to specified group scenarios ☐

Specific syllabus references for this chapter are: 1d,1h, 3d,3e, 3f, 3g.

Syllabus links

This chapter looks in detail at the preparation of the consolidated statement of financial position and is fundamental to the Financial Accounting and Reporting syllabus. It builds on the principles introduced in Chapter 10 and applies them to more complex situations. A detailed knowledge and understanding of this topic will also be assumed at the Advanced Stage.

Examination context

In a consolidated statement of financial position question the majority of marks are likely to be awarded for the preparation of the statement of financial position or extracts therefrom including a number of consolidation adjustments.

In the examination, candidates may be required to:

- Prepare a consolidated statement of financial position (or extracts therefrom) including the results of the parent entity and one or more subsidiaries from individual financial statements or draft consolidated financial statements and including adjustments for the following:

    - Acquisition of a subsidiary, including mid-year acquisitions
    - Goodwill
    - Intra-group items
    - Unrealised profits
    - Fair values
    - Other consolidation adjustments

- Explain the process of preparing a consolidated statement of financial position in the context of the single entity concept, substance over form and the distinction between control and ownership

- Explain the two methods of measuring the non-controlling interest at acquisition and prepare financial information by the two methods

- Explain and illustrate the difference between the relevant treatment under IFRS and UK GAAP

1 Context

Section overview

This chapter considers the preparation of the consolidated statement of financial position in more detail.

1.1 Consolidated statement of financial position

This chapter **builds on the basic principles** of group accounts (dealt with in Chapter 10) by applying them in more detail to the preparation of the consolidated statement of financial position. In particular it covers the following issues:

- **Standardised workings**
- **Intra-group balances**
- **Unrealised intra-group profit**
- **Fair value adjustments**

All of the above relate to the application of the single entity concept and reflect the distinction between control and ownership.

2 Consolidated statement of financial position workings

Section overview

A number of standard workings should be used when answering consolidation questions.

2.1 Question technique

As questions increase in complexity a formal pattern of workings is needed. Review the standard workings below, then attempt Interactive question 1 which puts these into practice.

(1) Establish **group structure**

P Ltd

80%

S Ltd

(2) Set out **net assets of S Ltd**

	At year end £	At acquisition £	Post acquisition £
Share capital	X	X	X
Retained earnings	X	X	X
	X	X	X

(3) Calculate **goodwill**

	£
Consideration transferred	X
Plus non-controlling interest at acquisition	X
	X
Less net assets at acquisition (W2)	(X)
	X
Impairment to date	(X)
Balance c/f	X

The double entry to consolidate the subsidiary will be:

		£	£
DR	Share of subsidiary's net assets	X	
DR	Goodwill	X	
CR	Investment in subsidiary		X

(4) Calculate **non-controlling interest** (NCI) at year end

	£
At acquisition ((NCI% × net assets (W2) or fair value)	X
Share of post-acquisition profits and other reserves (NCI% × post-acquisition (W2))	X
	X

(5) Calculate **retained earnings**

	£
P Ltd (100%)	X
S Ltd (share of post-acquisition retained earnings (W2)	X
Goodwill impairment to date (W3)	(X)
Group retained earnings	X

Point to note: You should use the proportionate basis for measuring the NCI at the acquisition date unless a question specifies the fair value basis.

Interactive question 1: Consolidated statement of financial position workings
[Difficulty level: Easy]

The following are the summarised statements of financial position of a group of companies as at 31 December 20X1.

	Rik Ltd £	Viv Ltd £	Neil Ltd £
Non-current assets			
Property, plant and equipment	100,000	40,000	10,000
Investments			
Shares in Viv Ltd (75%)	25,000		
Shares in Neil Ltd (2/3)	10,000		
Current assets	45,000	40,000	25,000
	180,000	80,000	35,000
Equity			
Share capital (£1 ordinary)	50,000	20,000	10,000
Retained earnings	100,000	40,000	15,000
Total equity	150,000	60,000	25,000
Liabilities	30,000	20,000	10,000
	180,000	80,000	35,000

Rik Ltd acquired its shares in Viv Ltd and Neil Ltd during the year, when their retained earnings were £4,000 and £1,000 respectively. At the end of 20X1 the goodwill impairment review revealed a loss of £3,000 in relation to the acquisition of Viv Ltd.

Requirement

Prepare the consolidated statement of financial position of Rik Ltd at 31 December 20X1.

Fill in the proforma below.

Rik Ltd: Consolidated statement of financial position as at 31 December 20X1

	£
Non-current assets	
Property, plant and equipment	
Intangibles (W3)	
Current assets	
Equity attributable to owners of the parent	
Share capital	
Retained earnings (W5)	
Non-controlling interest (W4)	
Total equity	
Liabilities	

WORKINGS

(1) **Group structure**

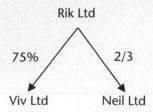

Rik Ltd

75%   2/3

Viv Ltd   Neil Ltd

(2) **Net assets**

	Year end £	Acquisition £	Post-acquisition £
Viv Ltd			
Share capital			
Retained earnings			

	Year end £	Acquisition £	Post-acquisition £
Neil Ltd			
Share capital			
Retained earnings			

(3) **Goodwill**

	Viv Ltd £	Neil Ltd £	Total £
Consideration transferred			
Plus non-controlling interest at acquisition			
Less net assets at acquisition			
Viv Ltd (W2)			
Neil Ltd (W2)			
Goodwill			
Impairment to date			
Balance c/f			

(4) **Non-controlling interest**

	£
Viv Ltd – Share of net assets at acquisition (W2)	
– Share of post-acquisition (W2)	
Neil Ltd – Share of net assets at acquisition (W2)	
– Share of post-acquisition (W2)	

(5) **Retained earnings**

	£
Rik Ltd	
Viv Ltd – Share of post-acquisition retained earnings (W2)	
Neil Ltd – Share of post-acquisition retained earnings (W2)	
Goodwill impairment to date (W3)	

See **Answer** at the end of this chapter.

3 Mid-year acquisitions

Section overview

- If a subsidiary is acquired mid-year, net assets at acquisition will need to be calculated.
- Unless told otherwise assume profits of the subsidiary accrue evenly over time.

3.1 Calculation

A parent entity might not acquire a subsidiary at the start or end of a year. If the subsidiary is acquired mid-year, it is necessary to calculate reserves, including retained earnings, at the date of acquisition.

This is necessary in order to:

- Calculate net assets at acquisition (which is required as part of the goodwill calculation)
- Calculate consolidated reserves, eg retained earnings

Point to note: It is usually assumed that a subsidiary's profits **accrue evenly over time**.

Interactive question 2: Mid-year acquisition   [Difficulty level: Easy]

P plc acquired 80% of S Ltd on 31 May 20X2 for £20,000. S Ltd's retained earnings had stood at £15,000 on 1 January 20X2.

S Ltd's equity at 31 December 20X2 was as follows.

	£
Share capital	1,000
Retained earnings	15,600
Equity	16,600

Requirements

(a) Produce the standard working for S Ltd's net assets (W2).
(b) Produce the standard working for goodwill on consolidation (W3).
(c) Calculate S Ltd's retained earnings which will be included in the consolidated retained earnings.

Fill in the proforma below.

(a) **Net assets (W2)**

	End of reporting period £	Acquisition £	Post acquisition £
Share capital			
Retained earnings	———	———	
	═══	═══	

(b) **Goodwill (W3)**

	£
Consideration transferred	
Plus non-controlling interest at acquisition (W2)	
Less net assets (W2)	———
	═══

(c) **Profit from S Ltd included in consolidated retained earnings**

	£
Share of post-acquisition retained earnings of S Ltd (W2)	———
	═══

See **Answer** at the end of the chapter.

4 Intra-group balances

Section overview

- Group accounts reflect transactions with third parties only.
- The effects of transactions between group members should be cancelled on consolidation.
- This is an application of the single entity concept.

4.1 The single entity concept

The objective of group accounts is to present the group **as a single entity**. Hence the effects of **transactions between group members** need to be **eliminated,** as the group has not transacted with any third party. These transactions could be between the parent company and a subsidiary or between two subsidiaries.

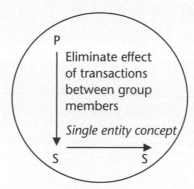

Reflecting the group as a single entity means that items which are assets in one group company and liabilities in another **need to be cancelled out**, otherwise group assets and liabilities will be overstated.

Intra-group balances result from, for example:

- One group company's loans, debentures or redeemable preference shares held by another group company.

- Intra-group trading.

4.2 Loans, debentures and redeemable preference shares

Cancel the **credit balance** in one company against the **debit balance** in the other before adding assets and liabilities line-by-line.

4.3 Intra-group trading

Outstanding amounts in respect of intra-group trading are usually recorded in the statement of financial position in current accounts (= receivable or payable account for a fellow group company).

Step 1
Check that current accounts **agree** before cancelling. They may not agree if goods or cash are in-transit at year end.

Step 2
Make balances agree by **adjusting for in-transit items** in the **receiving company's books**.

Step 3
Cancel intra-group balances.

Worked example: Intra-group trading

Extracts from the statement of financial position of Impala Ltd and its subsidiary Springbok Ltd at 31 March 20X4 are as follows.

	Impala Ltd £	Springbok Ltd £
Receivable from Springbok Ltd	25,000	–
Payable to Impala Ltd	–	(20,000)

Springbok Ltd sent a cheque for £5,000 to Impala Ltd on 28 March 20X4, which Impala Ltd did not receive until 2 April 20X4.

Solution

Steps 1 and 2

Assume that Impala Ltd had received the cash from Springbok Ltd.

	Impala Ltd £	Springbok Ltd £
Receivable from Springbok Ltd (25-5)	20,000	–
Cash and cash equivalents	5,000	–
Payable to Impala Ltd	–	(20,000)

Step 3

Cancel inter-company balances on consolidation, leaving just the cash in transit in the consolidated statement of financial position

	£
Cash and cash equivalents	5,000

5 Unrealised intra-group profit

Section overview

- The consolidated statement of financial position should show assets at their cost to the group.
- Any profit arising on intra-group transactions should be eliminated from the group accounts until it is realised, eg by a sale outside the group.

5.1 Introduction

One of the implications of the application of the single entity concept is that group accounts should only reflect profits generated from transactions which have been undertaken with **third parties**, ie entities outside the group.

Intra-group activities may give rise to profits that are **unrealised** as far as the group as a whole is concerned. These profits can result from:

- **Intra-group trading** when goods still held in inventory of buying company
- **Intra-group transfers of non-current assets**

Unrealised profits must be eliminated from the statement of financial position on consolidation to prevent the overstatement of group profits.

5.2 Inventories

As we have seen in Section 4.3 any receivable/payable balances outstanding between group companies, resulting from trading transactions, should be cancelled on consolidation. If these transactions have been undertaken at cost to the selling company no further problem arises.

However, each company in a group is a separate trading entity and may sell goods to another group member at a profit. **If these goods remain in inventories** at the end of the reporting period this profit is **unrealised** from the group's point of view.

In the consolidated statement of financial position, applying the **single entity concept**, inventories should be valued at the lower of cost and net realisable value **to the group**. Where goods transferred at a profit are still held at the year end the unrealised profit should be **eliminated on consolidation**. This is achieved by creating a **provision for unrealised profit (PURP)**.

The way in which this adjustment is made depends on whether the company making the sale is the parent or a subsidiary.

5.2.1 Parent sells goods to a subsidiary

The issues are best illustrated by an example.

Worked example: Intra-group profit (P→S)

Ant Ltd, a parent company, sells goods which cost £1,600 to Bee Ltd for £2,000. Ant Ltd owns 75% of the shares in Bee Ltd. Bee Ltd still hold the goods in inventories at the year end.

In the single entity accounts of Ant Ltd the profit of £400 should be recognised. In the single entity accounts of Bee Ltd the inventory should be valued at £2,000.

If we simply add together the figures for retained reserves and inventory as recorded in the individual statements of financial position of Ant Ltd and Bee Ltd the resulting figures for consolidated reserves and consolidated inventory will each be overstated by £400. A consolidation adjustment is therefore necessary as follows:

		£	£
DR	Seller's (Ant Ltd's) retained earnings (ie adjust in **retained earnings** working)	400	
CR	Inventories in consolidated statement of financial position		400

Point to note: In this example, as the **parent** was the seller the unrealised profit is **all 'owned' by the shareholders of Ant Ltd**. None is attributable to the **non-controlling interest**.

5.2.2 Subsidiary sells goods to parent or to another subsidiary

Where the subsidiary is the selling company the profit on the transfer will have been recorded in the subsidiary's books.

Worked example: Intra-group profit (S→P or S)

Using the worked example above, if we now assume that Bee Ltd sold the goods to Ant Ltd the adjustment would be as follows:

		£	£
DR	Seller's (Bee Ltd's) retained earnings (ie adjust in **net assets** working)	400	
CR	Inventories in consolidated statement of financial position		400

Points to note

1   The **net assets of the subsidiary making the sale at the end of the reporting period** will be reduced by the amount of the unrealised profit. Any **subsequent calculations** based on this net assets figure will therefore be affected as follows:

- The **group share** of the post-acquisition retained earnings of the subsidiary should be reduced, ie **the group will bear its share of the adjustment**.

- The **non-controlling interest** will be based on these revised net assets ie **the non-controlling interest will bear its share of the adjustment**.

2   Inventories in the consolidated statement of financial position should be reduced by the **full amount** of the unrealised profit **irrespective of whether the parent or a subsidiary is the selling company**.

3   If Bee Ltd had sold the goods to another subsidiary, rather than to the parent, the adjustment should be the same.

Interactive question 3: Unrealised profits   [Difficulty level: Intermediate]

P Ltd owns 80% of S Ltd, which it acquired when the retained earnings of S Ltd were £20,000. No goodwill was acquired. Statements of financial position at the end of the current accounting period are as follows.

	P Ltd £	S Ltd £
Assets	170,000	115,000
Share capital	30,000	10,000
Retained earnings	100,000	65,000
Equity	130,000	75,000
Liabilities	40,000	40,000
	170,000	115,000

During the current accounting period S Ltd sold goods to P Ltd for £18,000, which gave S Ltd a profit of £6,000. At the end of the reporting period half of these goods were included in P Ltd's inventories.

Requirement

Show how the adjustment to eliminate unrealised profits should appear in the consolidation workings for P Ltd.

Fill in the proforma below.

	£	£
DR		
CR		

WORKINGS

(1) **Group structure**

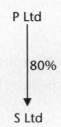

P Ltd

80%

S Ltd

(2) **S Ltd net assets**

	End of the reporting period £	£	Acquisition £	Post-acquisition £
Share capital				
Retained earnings				
Per question				
Less: PURP	_____			
		_____	_____	

(4) **Non-controlling interest**

	£
Share of net assets at acquisition (W2)	
Share of post-acquisition (W2)	_____
	======

(5) **Retained earnings**

	£
P Ltd	
Share of S Ltd	_____
	======

See **Answer** at the end of this chapter.

5.3 Non-current asset transfers

As well as trading with each other, group companies may wish to transfer non-current assets (NCA). If the asset is transferred at a price different from the transferor's carrying amount two issues arise:

- The selling company will have recorded **a profit or loss on sale**.

- The purchasing company will have **recorded the asset at the amount paid** to acquire it, and will use that amount as the basis for calculating **depreciation**.

On consolidation, the **single entity concept** applies. The consolidated statement of financial position should show assets at their **cost to the group**, and any **depreciation charged** should be based on **that cost**. In other words, the group accounts should reflect the non-current asset **as if the transfer had not been made**.

The adjustment in the consolidated statement of financial position should be calculated as follows:

	£
Carrying amount of NCA at year end in the transferee's financial statements	X
Less carrying amount of NCA at year end if transfer had not been made	(X)
Unrealised profit	X

The adjustment for unrealised profit should then be made as:

	£	£
DR Selling company retained earnings	X	
CR NCA carrying amount in consolidated statement of financial position		X

This treatment is consistent with that of inventories.

5.3.1 Parent sells non-current asset to subsidiary

As with inventories the impact of the adjustment will depend on whether the parent company or the subsidiary makes the sale.

Interactive question 4: Non-current asset transfers [Difficulty level: Easy]

P Ltd owns 80% of S Ltd. P Ltd transferred to S Ltd a non-current asset at a value of £15,000 on 1 January 20X7. The original cost to P Ltd was £20,000 and the accumulated depreciation at the date of transfer was £8,000. The asset had, and still has, a total useful life of five years.

Requirement

Calculate the consolidated statement of financial position adjustment at 31 December 20X7.

Fill in the proforma below.

Following the transfer the asset will be measured at

	£
Cost	
Less depreciation	_____
	≡≡≡

Had the transfer not been made, the asset would stand in the books at

	£
Cost	
Less: Accumulated depreciation at date of transfer	
Expense for current year	_____
	≡≡≡

Overall adjustment in CSFP

	£	£
DR Seller's (P Ltd's) retained earnings		
(ie adjust in **retained earnings** working)		
CR Non-current assets		

Point to note: In this question, as the **parent** is the selling company, **none of the adjustment is attributed to the non-controlling interest**.

See **Answer** at the end of this chapter.

5.3.2 Subsidiary sells non-current asset to parent

Again a consolidation adjustment should be made to reflect the situation that would have existed if the transfer had not been made.

The amount of the adjustment should be calculated as before (see above).

The adjustment is then made as follows:

	£	£
DR Seller's (S Ltd) retained earnings (adjust in net assets working)	X	
CR NCA carrying amount in consolidated statement of financial position		X

Points to note

1   As the subsidiary is the seller the **adjustment to retained earnings should be made in the net assets working**.

2   Any **subsequent calculations** based on this net assets figure will therefore be affected as follows:

- The **group share** of the post-acquisition retained earnings of the subsidiary will be reduced ie as for sale of inventories.

- The **non-controlling interest** will be based on these revised net assets, ie as for sale of inventories.

6   Fair value adjustments

Section overview

- In calculating the goodwill acquired in a business combination, the net assets of the subsidiary should be measured at their fair value.

- A consolidation adjustment will be required for any difference between the carrying amount and fair value of the net assets.

6.1   Calculation of goodwill

Where a subsidiary has not reflected fair values in its single entity financial statements, adjustments will need to be made as part of the consolidation process. Goodwill should be calculated by comparing the consideration transferred and the non-controlling interest in the subsidiary with the net assets acquired. The net assets brought into this calculation should be at **fair value**, which may be different to the carrying amount in the single entity financial statements.

6.2   Reflecting fair values

The **identifiable assets and liabilities** of a subsidiary should be brought into the consolidated financial statements at their **fair value**. Normally these fair values are **not reflected** in the **single entity financial statements**. Therefore the difference between fair values and carrying amounts should be treated as a **consolidation adjustment** made only for the purposes of the consolidated financial statements.

Fair value is defined as follows by IFRS 13 *Fair Value Measurement*: 'The price that would be received to sell an asset or paid to transfer a liability in an orderly transaction between market participants at the measurement date.'

Points to note

1   If all fair values have been recognised by the acquiree, then its financial statements are suitable for the consolidation process and no adjustment is necessary.

2   **Goodwill** in the subsidiary's individual statement of financial position is **not** part of the **identifiable** assets and liabilities acquired. If the subsidiary's own statement of financial position at acquisition includes goodwill, this **should not be consolidated**. In the **net asset working** retained earnings at acquisition and at the end of the reporting period should be reduced by the amount of the goodwill.

Adjustments should be made at acquisition and may also have to be taken up in subsequent periods:

- In the **consolidated statement of financial position** changes will often be necessary to the acquiree's carrying amounts for **non-current assets** and the **accumulated depreciation/ amortisation**.

- In the **consolidated statement of profit or loss** such changes will affect the **current period's depreciation/amortisation charges**.

Other adjustments may have to be made, depending on the circumstances. An adjustment will always be necessary for any **contingent liabilities** recognised at the acquisition date, to the extent they are only disclosed by way of note in the acquiree's financial statements.

Interactive question 5: Fair value adjustments [Difficulty level: Easy]

P Ltd acquires 60% of S Ltd on 31 December 20X4 for £80,000. The statement of financial position of S Ltd at this date is as follows.

	£
Freehold land (fair value £30,000)	20,000
Goodwill arising on the acquisition of a sole trader	5,000
Sundry assets (carrying amount = fair value)	130,000
	155,000
Share capital	20,000
Retained earnings	85,000
Equity	105,000
Liabilities	50,000
	155,000

Requirement

Calculate the goodwill acquired in the business combination with S Ltd. Fill in the proforma below.

(1) **Group structure**

P Ltd

60%

S Ltd

(2) **Net assets of S Ltd**

	Year end = Acquisition date	
	£	£
Share capital		
Revaluation surplus		
Retained earnings		
Add fair value uplift		
Less goodwill which is not an identifiable asset	_____	
	======	======

(3) **Goodwill**

	£
Consideration transferred	
Plus non-controlling interest at acquisition (W2)	
Less fair value of net assets at acquisition (W2)	
	_____
	======

Point to note: In the assets section of the **consolidated statement of financial position** the freehold land should be measured at £30,000. The goodwill in the subsidiary's **statement of financial position** of £5,000 should not be recognised as an intangible asset in the consolidated **statement of financial position**.

See **Answer** at the end of this chapter.

Interactive question 6: Fair value adjustments [Difficulty level: Exam standard]

Chris Ltd acquired 60% of Andy Ltd for £8m on 1 July 20X2 when Andy Ltd's statement of financial position showed net assets of £5m. The fair value of Andy Ltd's property, plant and equipment with a remaining useful life of 10 years was £1m higher than carrying amount, but this was not reflected in Andy Ltd's books. At 30 June 20X5 Andy Ltd's statement of financial position shows net assets of £10m. Andy Ltd's financial statements still disclose a contingent liability for a claim for damages against it. At the acquisition date its fair value was estimated at £100,000, which was its fair value until 30 June 20X5 when it was re-estimated at £80,000.

Requirement

Calculate as at 30 June 20X5 Chris Ltd's share of Andy Ltd's post-acquisition reserves, the goodwill arising on consolidation and the adjustment to be made to Andy Ltd's depreciation charge for the consolidated statement of profit or loss for the year ended 30 June 20X5.

Fill in the proforma below.

	£'000
Chris Ltd's share of Andy Ltd's post-acquisition reserves (W1)	_____
Goodwill arising on consolidation (W2)	_____
Adjustment to Andy Ltd's depreciation charge (W3)	_____

WORKINGS

(1) **Net assets and post-acquisition reserves**

	Year end £'000	At acquisition £'000	Post-acquisition £'000
Andy Ltd			
Net assets			
PPE fair value uplift			
Depreciation thereon			
Contingent liability	_____	_____	_____
	══════	══════	══════
Chris Ltd's share			══════

(2) **Goodwill**

	£'000
Consideration transferred	
Non-controlling interest at acquisition (W1)	
Net assets at acquisition (W1)	_____
	══════

(3) **Depreciation charge**

	£'000
Additional charge for year ended 30 June 20X5	══════

See **Answer** at the end of this chapter.

7 Other consolidation adjustments

Section overview

*   If a subsidiary has reserves other than retained earnings, the group share of post-acquisition reserves should be consolidated.

*   The balances of the subsidiary should be adjusted to reflect the accounting policies of the parent company prior to consolidation.

7.1 Other reserves in a subsidiary

A subsidiary may have other reserves apart from retained earnings in its statement of financial position, eg a revaluation surplus. If this is the case, such reserves should be treated in exactly the same way as retained earnings.

*   **Other reserves at acquisition** form part of the **net assets at acquisition**, ie they should be recorded in the net assets working at acquisition.

*   The **group share of any post acquisition** movement in other reserves should be **recognised** in the consolidated statement of financial position.

Points to note

1   A **separate working** should be used for **each reserve**; do not mix retained earnings with other reserves as the other reserves may include amounts which are not distributable by way of dividend.

2   If a subsidiary is **loss-making or has any other negative reserves** the group should consolidate its share of the **post-acquisition losses/negative reserves**.

7.2 Accounting policy alignments

On consolidation **uniform accounting policies should be applied for all amounts**. This is another consequence of the **single entity concept**.

If the parent company and subsidiary have different accounting policies the balances in **the subsidiary's financial statements** should be adjusted **to reflect the accounting policies of the parent company**.

Point to note: These adjustments are made in the **net assets working**.

Interactive question 7: Accounting policy alignments   [Difficulty level: Easy]

William Ltd has been 85% owned by Mary Ltd for some years. On 1 January 20X4 William Ltd acquired an item of plant for £40,000. William Ltd depreciates this item of plant at 15% on a reducing balance basis, while Mary Ltd's policy for this class of plant is 10% per annum on a straight-line basis.

Requirement

Set out the adjustment required in the preparation of the consolidated statement of financial position at 31 December 20X5.

Fill in the proforma below.

Following the transfer the asset will be included at:

	£	
Carrying amount of plant in CSFP		
Carrying amount in William Ltd's SFP		___
Increase in carrying amount		___
	£	£

DR   Non-current assets
CR   Consolidated retained earnings
CR   Non-controlling interest

See **Answer** at the end of this chapter.

8 UK GAAP comparison

Section overview

FRS 101 allows limited exemptions from the provisions of IFRS 3.

There are some differences between FRS 102 and IFRS.

8.1 Consolidated financial statements

FRS 102	IFRS
Non-controlling interest is always measured at its share of net assets.	IFRS 3 allows non-controlling interest to be measured at fair value or its share of net assets.
Acquisition-related costs are added to the cost of the investment in the subsidiary and affect goodwill.	Acquisition-related costs are recognised as an expense in profit or loss as incurred.
A reasonable estimate of the fair value of the amounts payable as contingent consideration (discounted where appropriate) is added to the cost of the investment at the acquisition date, **where it is probable that the amount will be paid and it can be measured reliably.** **All subsequent adjustments** to the amount of contingent consideration are **related back** to the acquisition date, increasing or decreasing goodwill.	At the acquisition date the fair value of contingent consideration (taking account of both discounting and the amount likely to be paid) is recognised as part of the consideration transferred. If subsequent adjustments to this fair value occur **within** the measurement period **and** are as a result of additional information about facts or circumstances at the acquisition date, those adjustments are related back to the acquisition date, increasing or decreasing goodwill. However, if subsequent adjustments to this fair value occur either: (i) **Within** the measurement period, but are **not** as a result of additional information about facts or circumstances at the acquisition date; or (ii) Are **outside** the measurement period, they are **not related back** to the acquisition date but are recognised as an expense in profit or loss. They do not increase or decrease goodwill.
Goodwill is **usually amortised over its estimated useful economic life.** There is a rebuttable presumption that this is not more than five years. Impairment reviews are required where evidence of impairment arises.	IFRS 3 **prohibits amortisation** and requires annual impairment reviews.
Negative goodwill is recognised as a separate item within goodwill. Negative goodwill up to the fair values of the non-monetary assets acquired should be recognised in the profit and loss account in the periods in which the non-monetary assets are recovered, whether through depreciation or sale.	IFRS 3 requires **immediate recognition as a gain in profit or loss**.

FRS 102	IFRS
A subsidiary should be excluded from consolidation if severe long-term restrictions prevent the parent exercising control.	No such exemption on this basis exists under IFRS 10 (although control may be lost as a result of the restrictions, such that the entity should no longer be classified as a subsidiary).

FRS 101 grants eligible entities exemption from the following disclosure requirements of IFRS 3:

- Reasons for acquisition and how control was obtained

- Description of factors making up goodwill

- Details of any contingent consideration

- Details of acquired receivables and contingent liabilities

- Details of goodwill (positive or negative) and non-controlling interests

- Details of any business combination for which the accounting is incomplete at the end of the period

For these exemptions to apply, equivalent disclosures must be included in the consolidated financial statements of the group in which the entity is consolidated.

Worked example: UK GAAP and IFRS

On 31 December 20X7 Magnate plc acquired 90% of the equity of Tycoon Ltd for a cash payment of £5 million. At that date the fair value of the 10% of the equity not acquired was £380,000.

Magnate plc incurred external professional fees in respect of this acquisition of £250,000 and estimated that the amount chargeable to the business combination in respect of the staff who worked on it was £200,000.

At 31 December 20X7 the carrying amount of the net assets recognised by Tycoon Ltd was £2.8 million, which approximated to their fair value. In addition Magnate plc identified the following:

- A trademark developed by Tycoon Ltd which at the acquisition date had a fair value of £400,000 and a useful life of four years.

Magnate plc adopts the following accounting policies:

- To measure the non-controlling interest at the acquisition date at fair value, where this is permitted.

- To amortise goodwill over five years, where amortisation is permitted.

Calculate under UK GAAP and IFRS the goodwill acquired in the business combination on 31 December 20X7.

Solution

The goodwill acquired in the business combination on 31 December 20X7

	UK GAAP £'000	IFRS £'000
Cost of investment/consideration transferred	5,000	5,000
External acquisition costs (Note 1)	250	–
Non-controlling interest at fair value	–	380
	5,250	5,380
Net assets recognised by Tycoon Ltd (UK = 90% × 2,800)	(2,520)	(2,800)
Trademark (Note 2) (UK = 90% × 400)	(360)	(400)
Goodwill (Note 3)	2,370	2,180

Notes

1   Both UK GAAP and IFRS require internal acquisition costs to be recognised as an expense as incurred.

   UK GAAP requires external costs to be added to the cost of the investment in the subsidiary, but IFRS require them to be recognised as an expense as incurred.

2   Both UK GAAP and IFRS require the recognition of the trademark as an acquired intangible, because it is separable.

3   UK GAAP requires the amortisation of goodwill, while IFRS prohibits it. Both require goodwill to be tested for impairment.

Summary and Self-test

Summary

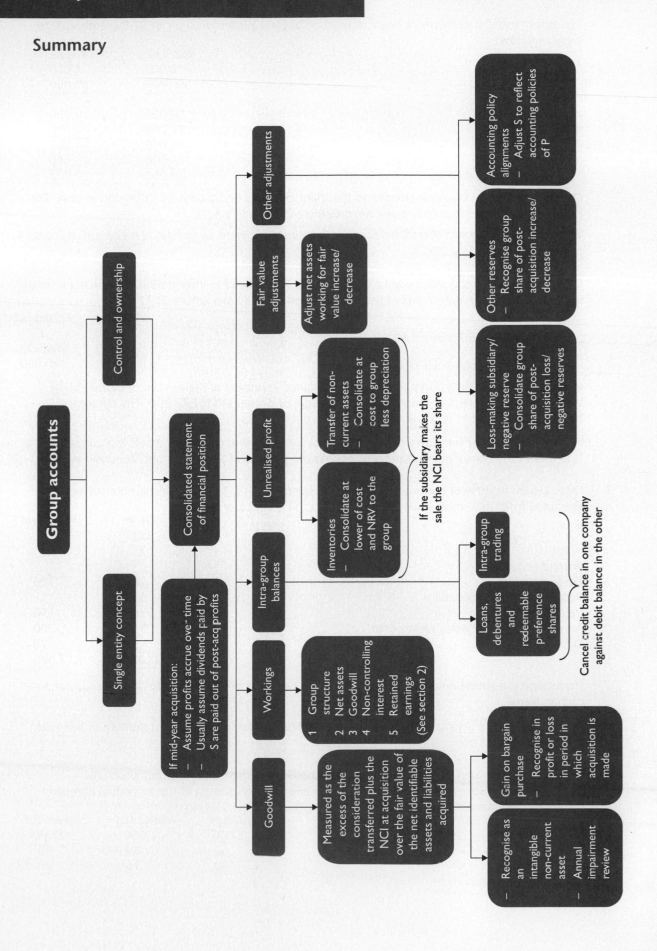

Group accounts

Control and ownership

Single entity concept

Consolidated statement of financial position

If mid-year acquisition:
- Assume profits accrue over time
- Usually assume dividends paid by S are paid out of post-acq profits

Other adjustments

Accounting policy alignments
- Adjust S to reflect accounting policies of P

Fair value adjustments

Adjust net assets working for fair value increase/decrease

Other reserves
- Recognise group share of post-acquisition increase/decrease

Unrealised profit

Transfer of non-current assets
- Consolidate at cost to group less depreciation

Inventories
- Consolidate at lower of cost and NRV to the group

Loss-making subsidiary/negative reserve
- Consolidate group share of post-acquisition loss/negative reserves

If the subsidiary makes the sale the NCI bears its share

Intra-group balances

Intra-group trading

Loans, debentures and redeemable preference shares

Cancel credit balance in one company against debit balance in the other

Workings

1 Group structure
2 Net assets
3 Goodwill
4 Non-controlling interest
5 Retained earnings
(See section 2)

Goodwill

Measured as the excess of the consideration transferred plus the NCI at acquisition over the fair value of the net identifiable assets and liabilities acquired

Gain on bargain purchase
- Recognise in profit or loss in period in which acquisition is made

- Recognise as an intangible non-current asset
- Annual impairment review

ICAEW

Self-test

Answer the following questions.

1 The summarised statements of financial position of Black plc and Red plc at 31 December 20X6 were as follows.

	Black plc £'000	Red plc £'000
Total assets	60,000	29,000
Share capital	20,000	10,000
Retained earnings	24,000	4,000
Equity	44,000	14,000
Current liabilities	16,000	15,000
Total equity and liabilities	60,000	29,000

On 1 January 20X7 Black plc bought all the share capital of Red plc for £17,000,000 in cash. The carrying amounts of Red plc's assets are considered to be fair values.

What will be the amount of retained earnings to be included in the consolidated statement of financial position as at 1 January 20X7?

2 Milton plc owns all the share capital of Keynes Ltd. The following information is extracted from the individual company statements of financial position as on 31 December 20X1.

	Milton plc £	Keynes Ltd £
Current assets	500,000	200,000
Current liabilities	220,000	90,000

Included in Milton plc's purchase ledger is a balance in respect of Keynes Ltd of £20,000. The balance on Milton plc's account in the sales ledger of Keynes Ltd is £22,000. The difference between those figures is accounted for by cash in transit.

If there are no other intra-group balances, what is the amount of current assets less current liabilities in the consolidated statement of financial position of Milton plc and its subsidiary?

3 Laker Ltd owns 80% of the ordinary shares of Hammond Ltd. The following amounts have been extracted from their draft financial statements at 31 December 20X0.

	Laker Ltd £	Hammond Ltd £
Current liabilities		
Trade payables	5,200	7,100
Amount owed to subsidiary	500	–
Income tax	100	150
Amounts owed to trade investments	150	200
Other payables	50	70
	6,000	7,520

Hammond Ltd shows an amount receivable from Laker Ltd of £620 and the difference is due to cash in transit.

What is the total carrying amount of current liabilities in the consolidated statement of financial position of Laker Ltd?

4 Austen plc has owned 100% of Kipling Ltd and 60% of Dickens Ltd for many years. At 31 December 20X5 the trade receivables and trade payables shown in the individual company statements of financial position were as follows.

	Austen plc £'000	Kipling Ltd £'000	Dickens Ltd £'000
Trade receivables	50	30	40
Trade payables	30	15	20

Trade payables are made up as follows.

Amounts owing to			
Austen	–	–	–
Kipling	2	–	4
Dickens	3	–	–
Other suppliers	25	15	16
	30	15	20

The intra-group accounts agreed after taking into account the following.

(1) An invoice for £3,000 posted by Kipling Ltd on 31 December 20X5 was not received by Austen plc until 2 January 20X6.

(2) A cheque for £2,000 posted by Austen plc on 30 December 20X5 was not received by Dickens Ltd until 4 January 20X6.

What amount should be shown as trade receivables in the consolidated statement of financial position of Austen plc?

5   The following is the draft statement of financial position information of Ho plc and Su Ltd, as on 30 September 20X2.

	Ho plc	Su Ltd
	£'000	£'000
Ordinary £1 shares	2,600	1,000
Retained earnings	750	700
Trade payables	350	900
Other payables	–	100
	3,700	2,700
Total assets	3,700	2,700

Ho plc acquired 60% of the share capital of Su Ltd several years ago when Su Ltd's retained earnings were £300,000. Su Ltd has not yet accounted for the estimated audit fee for the year ended 30 September 20X2 of £40,000.

What should the amount of consolidated retained earnings be on 30 September 20X2?

6   Oxford Ltd owns 100% of the issued share capital of Cambridge Ltd, and sells goods to its subsidiary at a profit margin of 20%. At the year end their statements of financial position showed inventories of

Oxford Ltd	£290,000
Cambridge Ltd	£160,000

The inventory of Cambridge Ltd included £40,000 of goods supplied by Oxford Ltd and there was inventory in transit from Oxford to Cambridge amounting to a further £20,000.

At what amount should inventory be carried in the consolidated statement of financial position?

7   Rugby Ltd has a 75% subsidiary, Stafford Ltd, and is preparing its consolidated statement of financial position as on 31 December 20X6. The carrying amount of property, plant and equipment in the two companies at that date is as follows.

Rugby Ltd	£260,000
Stafford Ltd	£80,000

On 1 January 20X6 Stafford Ltd had transferred some equipment to Rugby Ltd for £40,000. At the date of transfer the equipment, which had cost £42,000, had a carrying amount of £30,000 and a remaining useful life of five years. The group accounting policy is to depreciate equipment on a straight-line basis down to a nil residual value.

What figure should be disclosed as the carrying amount of property, plant and equipment in the consolidated statement of financial position of Rugby Ltd as on 31 December 20X6?

8   Lynton Ltd acquired 75% of the 200,000 £1 ordinary shares and 50% of the 100,000 £1 redeemable preference shares of Pinner Ltd when its retained earnings were £24,000. The retained earnings of Lynton Ltd and Pinner Ltd are now £500,000 and £60,000 respectively.

What figures for non-controlling interest and consolidated retained earnings should be included in the current consolidated statement of financial position?

9   Hill plc owns 60% of the ordinary share capital of Down plc and all of its 10% borrowings. The following transactions have been recorded by Down plc as at 31 December 20X3.

Half year's interest due	£15,000
Interim dividend paid	£50,000

Hill plc has not yet accounted for the interest receivable from Down plc.

In preparing the consolidated statement of financial position for Hill plc and its subsidiary at 31 December 20X3, what adjustments are required in respect of intra-group dividends and debenture interest?

10   Nasty Ltd and Horrid Ltd are wholly-owned subsidiaries of Ugly Ltd. Inventory in their individual statements of financial position at the year end is shown as follows.

Ugly Ltd	£30,000	Horrid Ltd	£10,000
Nasty Ltd	£20,000		

Sales by Horrid Ltd to Nasty Ltd during the year were invoiced at £15,000, which included a profit to Horrid Ltd of 25% on cost. Two thirds of these goods were in inventory at the year end.

At what amount should inventory appear in the consolidated statement of financial position?

11   Fallin Ltd acquired 100% of the share capital of Gaydon Ltd for £150,000 on 1 May 20X6. Equity at 30 April was as follows.

	Fallin Ltd	Gaydon Ltd	
	20X7	20X7	20X6
	£'000	£'000	£'000
Ordinary share capital	100	50	50
Revaluation surplus	–	25	15
Retained earnings	340	135	25
	440	210	90

An impairment review at 30 April 20X7 revealed that goodwill acquired in the business combination with Gaydon Ltd had become impaired by £6,000 in the year.

What should the consolidated equity of the Fallin Ltd group be on 30 April 20X7?

Data for questions 12 to 16

With reference to the information below, answer questions 12 to 16 with respect to the consolidated financial statements of VW plc.

Summarised statements of financial position as at 30 September 20X7

	VW plc	Polo Ltd	Golf Ltd
	£'000	£'000	£'000
ASSETS			
Property, plant and equipment	200	40	30
Investments			
100,000 shares in Polo Ltd	150	–	–
40,000 shares in Golf Ltd	70	–	–
Current assets			
Inventories	150	90	80
Trade receivables	250	40	20
Cash	50	20	10
	870	190	140

	VW plc £'000	Polo Ltd £'000	Golf Ltd £'000
EQUITY AND LIABILITIES			
Equity			
Ordinary shares of £1 each	500	100	50
Retained earnings	90	40	70
Total equity	590	140	120
Current liabilities	280	50	20
	870	190	140

Notes

(1) VW plc acquired its shares in Polo Ltd on 1 October 20X5 when Polo Ltd's retained earnings were £30,000.

(2) VW plc acquired its shares in Golf Ltd on 30 September 20X6. Golf Ltd's net profit for the year ended 30 September 20X7 was £30,000.

(3) It is the policy of the VW group to measure goodwill and the non-controlling interest using the proportionate basis.

(4) Included in Polo Ltd's inventory at 30 September 20X7 was £15,000 of goods purchased from VW plc during the year. VW plc invoiced Polo Ltd at cost plus 50%.

(5) During the year ended 30 September 20X7 Polo Ltd sold goods costing £50,000 to Golf Ltd for £70,000. Golf Ltd still had half of these goods in inventory at 30 September 20X7.

(6) The following intra-group balances are reflected in the above statement of financial position of VW plc at 30 September 20X7.

£20,000 receivable from Polo Ltd

£10,000 payable to Golf Ltd

12 What should the amount of non-controlling interest be?

13 What should the total of group inventories be?

14 What should the amount of trade receivables be?

15 What amount of goodwill should be included under intangible assets?

16 The consolidated retained earnings should be presented at what amount?

17 CRAWFORD LTD PART 2

Following on from the facts in Chapter 10 Self-test question 13 (Crawford Ltd part 1), assume that Crawford Ltd paid £2,500 (not £2,000) for the 2,000 shares in Dietrich Ltd and that Crawford Ltd's property, plant and equipment were £26,500 (not £27,000), all other information remaining the same. An impairment review at 30 June 20X0 revealed that goodwill in respect of Dietrich Ltd had fallen in value over the year by £40. By 1 July 20W9 goodwill had already been written down by £210.

Requirement

Prepare the consolidated statement of financial position of Crawford Ltd as at 30 June 20X0.

(7 marks)

18 DUBLIN LTD

The following are the summarised statements of financial position of a group of companies as at 31 December 20X9.

	Dublin Ltd £	Shannon Ltd £	Belfast Ltd £
ASSETS			
Non-current assets			
Property, plant and equipment	90,000	60,000	50,000
Investments: 40,000 £1 shares in Shannon	50,000	–	–
30,000 £1 shares in Belfast	45,000	–	–
	185,000	60,000	50,000
Current assets	215,000	50,000	30,000
Total assets	400,000	110,000	80,000
EQUITY AND LIABILITIES			
Equity			
Ordinary share capital	190,000	50,000	40,000
Revaluation surplus	–	10,000	–
Retained earnings	60,000	30,000	16,000
Total equity	250,000	90,000	56,000
Current liabilities	150,000	20,000	24,000
Total equity and liabilities	400,000	110,000	80,000

Dublin Ltd purchased its shares in Shannon Ltd five years ago when there were retained earnings of £20,000 and a balance on its revaluation surplus of £10,000.

Belfast Ltd had retained earnings of £16,000 when Dublin Ltd acquired its shares on 1 January 20X9.

At the end of 20X9 the goodwill impairment review revealed a loss of £300 in relation to the goodwill acquired in the business combination with Belfast Ltd.

During November 20X9, Shannon Ltd had sold goods to Belfast Ltd for £12,000 at a mark-up on cost of 20%. Half of these goods were still held by Belfast Ltd at 31 December 20X9.

Dublin Ltd prefers to measure goodwill and the non-controlling interest using the proportionate method wherever possible.

Requirement

Prepare the consolidated statement of financial position as at 31 December 20X9 of Dublin Ltd and its subsidiaries.

(12 marks)

19 EDINBURGH LTD

The following draft consolidated statement of financial position has been prepared for Edinburgh Ltd and its subsidiary Glasgow Ltd.

Draft consolidated statement of financial position as at 31 December 20X5

	£	£
ASSETS		
Non-current assets		
Property, plant and equipment		229,000
Intangible – goodwill		9,000
Investments		17,000
		255,000
Current assets		
Inventories	108,400	
Trade and other receivables	129,000	
Cash and cash equivalents	39,850	
		277,250
Total assets		532,250

EQUITY AND LIABILITIES
Equity attributable to owners of the parent

	£
Ordinary share capital	250,000
Revaluation surplus	12,000
Retained earnings	55,000
	317,000
Non-controlling interest	22,250
Total equity	339,250
Non-current liabilities	
6% loan notes	20,000
Current liabilities	
Trade and other payables	173,000
Total equity and liabilities	532,250

The following issues need to be accounted for in preparing the final financial statements.

(1) Edinburgh acquired its 80% interest in Glasgow Ltd on 1 January 20X5 and acquired £12,000 of Glasgow Ltd's 6% loan notes on the same date. Edinburgh's other investments amount to £5,000.

(2) In calculating goodwill, the fair value of the non-controlling interest in Glasgow Ltd was estimated at £15,500 but was erroneously included at £13,500.

(3) The post-acquisition retained earnings of Glasgow Ltd include £10,000 relating to a machine invoiced and delivered to a third-party customer on 1 July 20X5. This price includes a three-year support service which is usually sold for £400 per annum. The invoice has been paid in full.

(4) During the year Glasgow Ltd sold five machine tools for resale to Edinburgh Ltd priced at £2,400 each. Edinburgh had resold three of these at the year end. Glasgow Ltd applies a 20% mark-up on cost for all sales.

Requirement

Prepare the final consolidated statement of financial position for Edinburgh Ltd as at 31 December 20X5.   **(15 marks)**

20 CLOSE LTD

The summarised statements of financial position of Close Ltd and Steele Ltd as at 31 December 20X9 were as follows.

	Close Ltd		Steele Ltd	
	£	£	£	£
ASSETS				
Non-current assets				
Property, plant and equipment		80,000		58,200
Investments		84,000		–
		164,000		58,200
Current assets				
Inventories	18,000		12,000	
Trade and other receivables	62,700		21,100	
Investments	–		2,500	
Cash and cash equivalents	10,000		3,000	
Current account – Close Ltd	–		3,200	
		90,700		41,800
Total assets		254,700		100,000

	Close Ltd		Steele Ltd	
	£	£	£	£
EQUITY AND LIABILITIES				
Equity				
Ordinary share capital (£1 shares)		120,000		60,000
Share premium account		18,000		–
Revaluation surplus		23,000		16,000
Retained earnings		56,000		13,000
Total equity		217,000		89,000
Current liabilities				
Trade and other payables	35,000		11,000	
Current account – Steele Ltd	2,700		–	
		37,700		11,000
Total equity and liabilities		254,700		100,000

The following information is relevant.

(1) On 1 January 20X7 Close Ltd acquired 48,000 shares in Steele Ltd for £84,000 cash when the retained earnings of Steele Ltd were £8,000 and the balance on the revaluation surplus was £16,000.

(2) The inventories of Close Ltd include £4,000 of goods from Steele Ltd invoiced to Close Ltd at cost plus 25%.

(3) A cheque for £500 from Close Ltd to Steele Ltd, sent before 31 December 20X9, was not received by the latter company until January 20Y0.

(4) An impairment review at 31 December 20X9 revealed that an impairment loss of £500 in respect of goodwill on the acquisition of Steele Ltd needs to be recognised. By 1 January 20X9 this goodwill had already suffered impairments totalling £1,700.

(5) The non-controlling interest and goodwill arising on the acquisition of Steele Ltd were both calculated using the proportionate method.

Requirements

(a) Prepare the consolidated statement of financial position of Close Ltd and its subsidiary Steele Ltd as at 31 December 20X9. **(12 marks)**

(b) Explain the adjustments necessary in respect of intra-group sales when preparing the consolidated statement of financial position of the Close Ltd group. **(6 marks)**

(18 marks)

21 PAYNE PLC

The following draft statement of financial position has been prepared for Payne plc. Payne plc acquired its 80% subsidiary Glass plc on 30 September 20X4.

Payne plc – draft consolidated statement of financial position as at 31 March 20X5

	£000	£000
ASSETS		
Non-current assets		
Property, plant and equipment		3,690
Goodwill		145
Other intangibles		475
		4,310
Current assets		
Inventories	1,330	
Trade and other receivables	1,398	
Cash and cash equivalents	968	
		3,696
Total assets		8,006

EQUITY AND LIABILITIES
Equity attributable to owners of the parent

Ordinary share capital	2,400
Share premium account	640
Revaluation surplus	475
Retained earnings	1,859
	5,374
Non-controlling interest	320
Total equity	5,694
Non-current liabilities	
Provision for restructuring costs	78
Current liabilities	
Trade and other payables	2,234
Total equity and liabilities	8,006

A number of issues have not been taken into account in preparing the draft consolidated financial statements.

(1) Other intangibles includes £275,000 being goodwill in the books of Glass plc which arose on the acquisition of an unincorporated business some years ago. The carrying amount of this goodwill at the date when Payne plc acquired Glass plc was £300,000. It has since been amortised in the books of Glass plc.

(2) Freehold land held by Glass plc at the acquisition date had a carrying amount of £250,000. The market value of the land at that date was £683,000.

(3) At the acquisition date Glass plc disclosed a contingent liability as a potential £300,000, although its fair value was assessed at £58,000. A final decision on this matter is expected to be reached by the end of 20X5.

(4) At the acquisition date the directors of Payne plc intended to restructure and reorganise Glass plc and have provided for restructuring costs of £78,000.

(5) Glass plc sells part of its output to Payne plc. Included in the inventories of Payne plc are goods valued at £150,000 purchased from Glass plc since acquisition at cost to Glass plc plus 25%.

(6) Payne plc measures non-controlling interest at acquisition at fair value based on share price. NCI in the draft statement of financial position has been calculated as fair value at acquisition date plus 20% of the post-acquisition retained earnings of Glass plc. No adjustment has been made for (1) to (5) above.

Requirement

Prepare the final consolidated statement of financial position for Payne plc as at 31 March 20X5.

(13 marks)

Now, go back to the Learning objectives in the Introduction. If you are satisfied you have achieved these objectives, please tick them off.

For a comprehensive Technical reference section, covering all aspects of group accounts (except group statements of cash flows) see Chapter 10.

Answer to Interactive question 1

Rik Ltd: Consolidated statement of financial position as at 31 December 20X1

	£
Non-current assets	
Property, plant and equipment (100,000 + 40,000 + 10,000)	150,000
Intangibles (W3)	6,667
	156,667
Current assets (45,000 + 40,000 + 25,000)	110,000
	266,667
Equity attributable to owners of the parent	
Called up share capital	50,000
Retained earnings (W5)	133,334
	183,334
Non-controlling interest (W4)	23,333
Total equity	206,667
Liabilities (30,000 + 20,000 + 10,000)	60,000
	266,667

WORKINGS

(1) Group structure

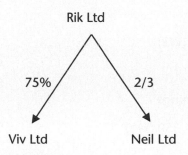

(2) Net assets

	Year end £	Acquisition £	Post-acquisition £
Viv Ltd			
Share capital	20,000	20,000	–
Retained earnings	40,000	4,000	36,000
	60,000	24,000	
Neil Ltd			
Share capital	10,000	10,000	–
Retained earnings	15,000	1,000	14,000
	25,000	11,000	

(3) Goodwill

	Viv Ltd £	Neil Ltd £	Total £
Consideration transferred	25,000	10,000	
Non-controlling interest at acquisition			
Viv Ltd (25% × 24,000 (W2))	6,000		
Neil Ltd (1/3 × 11,000 (W2))		3,667	
Net assets at acquisition	(24,000)	(11,000)	
Goodwill	7,000	2,667	9,667
Impairment to date	(3,000)	–	(3,000)
	4,000	2,667	6,667

(4) Non-controlling interest

	£	£
Viv Ltd – Share of net assets at acquisition (25% × 24,000 (W2))	6,000	
– Share of post-acquisition (25% × 36,000 (W2))	9,000	
		15,000
Neil Ltd – Share of net assets at year end (1/3 × 11,000 (W2))	3,667	
– Share of post-acquisition (1/3 × 14,000 (W2))	4,666	
		8,333
		23,333

(5) Retained earnings

	£
Rik Ltd	100,000
Viv Ltd – Share of post-acquisition retained earnings (75% × 36,000 (W2))	27,000
Neil Ltd – Share of post-acquisition retained earnings (2/3 × 14,000 (W2))	9,334
Goodwill impairment to date (W3)	(3,000)
	133,334

Answer to Interactive question 2

(a) Net assets (W2)

	Year end £	Acquisition £	Post-acquisition £
Share capital	1,000	1,000	–
Retained earnings (15,000 + (5/12 × (15,600 – 15,000)))	15,600	15,250	350
	16,600	16,250	

(b) Goodwill (W3)

	£
Consideration transferred	20,000
Plus non-controlling interest at acquisition (16,250 × 20% (W2))	3,250
Less net assets at acquisition (W2)	(16,250)
	7,000

(c) Profit from S Ltd included in consolidated retained earnings

	£
Share of post-acquisition retained earnings of S Ltd (80% × 350 (W2))	280

Answer to Interactive question 3

		£	£
DR	Seller's (S Ltd's) retained earnings (adjust in net assets working)	3,000	
CR	Inventories in CSFP (1/2 × 6,000)		3,000

WORKINGS

(1) Group structure

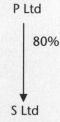

P Ltd
80%
S Ltd

(2) S Ltd net assets

	Year end £		Acquisition £	Post-acquisition £
	£	£	£	£
Share capital		10,000	10,000	
Retained earnings				
Per question	65,000			
Less PURP	(3,000)			
		62,000	20,000	42,000
		72,000	30,000	

(3) **Non-controlling interest**

		£
Share of net assets at acquisition	(20% × 30,000)	6,000
Share of post-acquisition (W2)	(20% × 42,000)	8,400
		14,400

(4) **Retained earnings**

	£
P Ltd	100,000
Share of S Ltd (80% × 42,000 (W2))	33,600
	133,600

Answer to Interactive question 4

Following the transfer the asset will be measured at

	£
Cost to S Ltd	15,000
Less depreciation – (15,000/3 remaining years (8,000 is 2/5 of cost))	(5,000)
	10,000

Had the transfer not been made, the asset would stand in the books at

	£
Cost	20,000
Less: Accumulated depreciation at date of 'transfer'	(8,000)
Charge for current year (£20,000/5)	(4,000)
	8,000

Overall adjustment in CSFP

	£	£
DR Seller's (P Ltd's) retained earnings	2,000	
CR Non-current assets		2,000

Answer to Interactive question 5

(1) **Group structure**

P Ltd

60%

S Ltd

(2) **Net assets of S Ltd**

		Year end = Acquisition date
	£	£
Share capital		20,000
Retained earnings	85,000	
Add fair value uplift (30,000 – 20,000)	10,000	
Less goodwill	(5,000)	
		90,000
		110,000

(3) **Goodwill**

	£
Consideration transferred	80,000
Non-controlling interest at acquisition (40% × 110,000 (W2))	44,000
Less FV of net assets at acquisition (W2)	(110,000)
Goodwill	14,000

Answer to Interactive question 6

	£'000
Chris Ltd's share of Andy Ltd's post-acquisition reserves (W1)	2,832
Goodwill arising on consolidation (W2)	4,460
Adjustment to Andy Ltd's depreciation charge (W3)	100

WORKINGS

(1) **Net assets and post-acquisition reserves**

	Year end £'000	At acquisition £'000	Post acquisition £'000
Andy Ltd			
Net assets	10,000	5,000	5,000
PPE fair value uplift	1,000	1,000	0
Depreciation thereon – 3 years = 30%	(300)	0	(300)
Contingent liability	(80)	(100)	20
	10,620	5,900	4,720
Chris Ltd's share – 60%			2,832

(2) **Goodwill**

	£'000
Consideration transferred	8,000
Non-controlling interest (40% × 5,900 (W1))	2,360
Net assets (W1)	(5,900)
Goodwill	4,460

(3) **Depreciation charge for year ended 30 June 20X5**

	£'000
Additional charge (10% × 1,000)	100

Point to note: If future events resulted in the contingent liability ceasing to exist (eg because it relates to a legal claim being defended and the court judgement is in favour of the defendant), it should be re-measured at £nil and the whole of the remaining £80,000 should be recognised in current period profit or loss. If future events result in the contingent liability crystallising into a liability (eg because the court judgement is in favour of the plaintiff), it should be re-measured at £nil but the carrying amount of the net assets would be after deducting the liability.

Answer to Interactive question 7

Following the transfer the asset will be included at

	£
Carrying amount of plant in CSFP (40,000 × 80%)	32,000
Carrying amount in William Ltd's SFP (40,000 × 85% × 85%)	28,900
Increase in carrying amount	3,100

		£	£
DR	Non-current assets	3,100	
CR	Consolidated retained earnings (85%)		2,635
CR	Non-controlling interest (15%)		465

1

	£'000
Retained earnings – Black plc only	24,000

No post-acquisition profits have yet arisen in Red plc.

2

	Milton £'000	Keynes £'000	Adjustment £'000	Consolidated £'000
Current assets	500	200	−22 + 2	680
Current liabilities	(220)	(90)	+20	(290)
	280	110		390

3

	£
Laker	6,000
Hammond	7,520
Less intra-group indebtedness	(500)
Total current liabilities	13,020

4

	£'000	£'000
Austen plc		50
Kipling Ltd		30
Dickens Ltd	40	
Less cash in transit	(2)	
		38
		118
Less intra-group receivables		
Owed to Kipling Ltd (2 + 3 + 4)	9	
Owed to Dickens Ltd	3	
		(12)
Group trade receivables		106

5

	£'000
Ho plc	750
Su Ltd – Ho plc's share of post-acquisition retained earnings (60% ((700 − 40) − 300))	216
Consolidated retained earnings	966

6

	£'000
Oxford Ltd	290
Cambridge Ltd	160
In transit to Cambridge Ltd	20
Less PURP ((40 + 20) × 20%)	(12)
Group inventory	458

7 The adjustment required following the intragroup transfer is £8,000.

	Is £	Should be £
Cost	40,000	42,000
Accumulated depreciation	(8,000)	(18,000)
Carrying amount	32,000	24,000

Adjustment required:

DR   Stafford Ltd retained earnings   £8,000
CR   Property, plant and equipment   £8,000.

PPE in consolidated statement of financial position = 260,000 + 80,000 − 8,000 = £332,000

8

	£
Non-controlling interest	
Ordinary shares (25% × (200,000 + 60,000))	65,000
Consolidated retained earnings	
Lynton Ltd	500,000
Pinner Ltd (75% × (60,000 − 24,000))	27,000
	527,000

Point to note: Redeemable preference shares should be classified as liabilities.

9

			£'000	£'000
(1)	DR	Current assets in Hill with interest receivable	15	
	CR	Retained earnings of Hill		15

To account for the interest receivable by Hill plc

			£'000	£'000
(2)	DR	Current liabilities in Down	15	
	CR	Current assets in Hill		15

To cancel intra-group balances for interest – there will be no o/s balances for the dividends as they have been paid and would not be included as payables even if unpaid.

		Summary:	£'000	£'000
	DR	Current liabilities	15	
	CR	Retained earnings of Hill		15

10

	£
Ugly Ltd	30,000
Nasty Ltd	20,000
Horrid Ltd	10,000
Less PURP (2/3 × 15,000 × $^{25}/_{125}$)	(2,000)
Group inventory	58,000

11

	£'000	£'000
Ordinary share capital		100
Revaluation surplus (25 − 15)		10
Retained earnings		
Fallin Ltd	340	
Gaydon Ltd (135 − 25)	110	
Goodwill impairment to date	(6)	
		444
Group equity		554

Questions 12 to 16

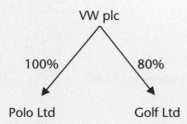

12   Non-controlling interest = 20% × (50,000 + 70,000) = £24,000

13

	£'000
VW plc	150
Polo Ltd	90
Golf Ltd	80
	320

Less PURP
  Note (3) (15,000 × $^{50}/_{150}$ in VW plc's retained earnings)   (5)
  Note (4) (1/2 × 70,000 – 50,000 in Polo Ltd's retained earnings)   (10)
Group inventories   305

14

	£'000
VW plc	250
Less intra-group receivable	(20)
Polo Ltd	40
Golf Ltd	20
Less intra-group receivable	(10)
Group trade receivables	280

15

	£	£
Polo – consideration transferred		150,000
Net assets		
Share capital	100,000	
Retained earnings at acquisition	30,000	
		(130,000)
Goodwill		20,000
Golf – consideration transferred		70,000
Non-controlling interest at acquisition (90,000 (below) × 20%)		18,000
		88,000
Net assets at acquisition		
Share capital	50,000	
Retained earnings (70 – 30)	40,000	
		(90,000)
Gain on a bargain purchase		(2,000)

– Recognised in consolidated statement of profit or loss in period
  of acquisition

16

	£
VW plc	90,000
Less PURP per 13 above	(5,000)
	85,000
Polo Ltd ((10,000 10,000 PURP per 13 above) – 30,000)	–
Golf Ltd (80% × 30,000)	24,000
Gain on bargain purchase of Golf Ltd	2,000
Consolidated retained earnings	111,000

17 CRAWFORD LTD PART 2

Consolidated statement of financial position as at 30 June 20X0

	£
ASSETS	
Non-current assets	
Property, plant and equipment (26,500 + 12,500)	39,000
Intangibles (W1)	250
	39,250
Current assets (25,000 + 12,000)	37,000
Total assets	76,250

EQUITY AND LIABILITIES
Equity attributable to owners of parent

		£
Ordinary share capital		20,000
Share premium account		6,000
Retained earnings (W3)		18,083
		44,083
Non-controlling interest (W2)		5,667
Total equity		49,750
Non-current liabilities		12,000
Current liabilities (7,000 + 7,500)		14,500
Total equity and liabilities		76,250

WORKINGS

(1) **Goodwill**

	£
Consideration transferred	2,500
Non-controlling interest at acquisition (3,000 × 1/3)	1,000
	3,500
Net assets at acquisition	(3,000)
	500
Impairment to date (210 + 40)	(250)
	250

(2) **Non-controlling interest at year end**

	£
1/3 × 17,000	5,667

(3) **Retained earnings**

	£
Crawford Ltd	9,000
Dietrich Ltd ($^2/_3$ × 14,000)	9,333
Less goodwill impairment to date (W1)	(250)
	18,083

18 DUBLIN LTD

Consolidated statement of financial position as at 31 December 20X9

	£
ASSETS	
Non-current assets	
Property, plant and equipment (90,000 + 60,000 + 50,000)	200,000
Intangibles (W3)	2,700
	202,700
Current assets (215,000 + 50,000 + 30,000 – 1,000 (W6))	294,000
Total assets	496,700

	£
EQUITY AND LIABILITIES	
Equity attributable to owners of the parent	
Ordinary share capital	190,000
Retained earnings (W5)	80,900
	270,900
Non-controlling interest (W4)	31,800
Total equity	302,700
Current liabilities (150,000 + 20,000 + 24,000)	194,000
Total equity and liabilities	496,700

WORKINGS

(1) Group structure

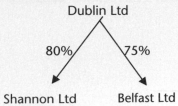

Dublin Ltd

80%   75%

Shannon Ltd   Belfast Ltd

(2) Net assets

	Year end £	Acquisition date £	Post-acquisition £
Shannon Ltd			
Share capital	50,000	50,000	–
Revaluation surplus	10,000	10,000	–
Retained earnings (30,000 – 1,000 (W6))	29,000	20,000	9,000
	89,000	80,000	
Belfast Ltd			
Share capital	40,000	40,000	–
Retained earnings	16,000	16,000	–
	56,000	56,000	

(3) Goodwill

	Shannon Ltd £	Belfast Ltd £
Consideration transferred	50,000	45,000
Non-controlling interest at acquisition		
((80,000 × 20% / 56,000 × 25%)	16,000	14,000
	66,000	59,000
Net assets at acquisition		
Shannon Ltd (W2)	(80,000)	
Belfast Ltd (W2)		(56,000)
(Gain on a bargain purchase)/goodwill	(14,000)	3,000
Recognised in profit or loss (impairment) to date	14,000	(300)
	–	2,700

(4) Non-controlling interest at year end

	£	£
Shannon Ltd		
NCI at acquisition (W3)	16,000	
Share of post-acquisition reserves ((W2) 9,000 × 20%)	1,800	
		17,800
Belfast Ltd		
NCI at acquisition (W3)	14,000	
Share of post-acquisition reserves ((W2) nil × 25%)	–	
		14,000
		31,800

(5) Retained earnings

	£
Dublin Ltd	60,000
Shannon Ltd (80% × 9,000 (W2))	7,200
Belfast Ltd (75% × nil (W2))	–
Less goodwill impairment to date (W3)	(300)
Add gain on a bargain purchase (W3)	14,000
	80,900

(6) PURP

£12,000 × 20/120 × 50% = £1,000

	£	£
DR Retained earnings (Shannon)	1,000	
CR Group inventory (current assets)		1,000

19 EDINBURGH LTD

Consolidated statement of financial position as at 31 December 20X5

	£	£
ASSETS		
Non-current assets		
Property, plant and equipment		229,000
Intangible – goodwill (W1)		11,000
Investments (17,000 – 12,000)		5,000
		245,000
Current assets		
Inventories (108,400 – 800 (W4))	107,600	
Trade and other receivables	129,000	
Cash and cash equivalents	39,850	
		276,450
Total assets		521,450
EQUITY AND LIABILITIES		
Equity attributable to owners of the parent		
Ordinary share capital		250,000
Revaluation surplus		12,000
Retained earnings (W2)		53,560
		315,560
Non-controlling interest (W3)		23,890
Total equity		339,450
Non-current liabilities		
6% loan notes (20,000 – 12,000)	8,000	
Deferred income (W5)	600	
		8,600
Current liabilities		
Trade and other payables	173,000	
Deferred income (W5)	400	
		173,400
Total equity and liabilities		521,450

WORKINGS

(1) Goodwill

	£
Per draft accounts	9,000
Additional NCI at acquisition date (15,500 – 13,500)	2,000
	11,000

(2) Retained earnings

	£
Per draft accounts	55,000
After-sales service (1,000 (W5) × 80%)	(800)
PURP (800 (W4) × 80%)	(640)
	53,560

(3) Non-controlling interest

	£
Per draft accounts	22,250
Additional fair value at acquisition date	2,000
After-sales service (1,000 (W5) × 20%)	(200)
PURP (800 (W4) × 20%)	(160)
	23,890

(4) PURP

	£
£12,000 × 20/120 × 2/5	800

(5) **Service support costs**

2.5 years @ £400 = £1,000

	£	£
DR Retained earnings (80%)	800	
DR NCI (20%)	200	
CR Deferred income – non-current		600
CR Deferred income – current		400

20 CLOSE LTD

(a) **Consolidated statement of financial position as at 31 December 20X9**

	£	£
ASSETS		
Non-current assets		
Property, plant and equipment (80,000 + 58,200)		138,200
Intangibles (W3)		14,600
		152,800
Current assets		
Inventories (18,000 + 12,000 – 800 PURP (W2))	29,200	
Trade and other receivables (62,700 + 21,100)	83,800	
Investments	2,500	
Cash and cash equivalents (10,000 + 3,000 + 500)	13,500	
		129,000
Total assets		281,800
EQUITY AND LIABILITIES		
Equity attributable to owners of the parent		
Ordinary share capital		120,000
Share premium account		18,000
Revaluation surplus		23,000
Retained earnings (W5)		57,160
		218,160
Non-controlling interest (W4)		17,640
Total equity		235,800
Current liabilities		
Trade and other payables (35,000 + 11,000)		46,000
Total equity and liabilities		281,800

(b) **Adjustments**

When group companies have been trading with each other two separate adjustments may be required in the consolidated statement of financial position.

(i) Elimination of unrealised profits

If one company holds inventories at the year end which have been acquired from another group company, this may include a profit element that is unrealised from a group perspective.

Here Steele Ltd has sold goods to Close Ltd at cost plus 25%. The mark-up of 25% will only become realised when the goods are sold to a third party. Therefore if any intra-group inventory is still held at the year end, the profit thereon should be eliminated from the consolidated accounts.

This will require an adjustment of £800 (4,000 × 25/125) which is always made against the selling company's retained earnings, ie

	DR £	CR £
Steele Ltd's retained earnings (W2)	800	
Consolidated inventory		800

As well as eliminating the unrealised profit, this reduces inventory back to its original cost to the group.

(ii) Eliminate intra-group balances

As group companies are effectively treated as one entity, any intra-group balances must be eliminated on consolidation. Here, intra-group current accounts have arisen as a result of the intra-group trading and these must be cancelled out. Before this can be done the current accounts must be brought into agreement by adjusting the accounts of the 'receiving' company (here Steele Ltd) for the cheque in-transit, ie

	DR £	CR £
Cash	500	
Current account		500

This will reduce the current account receivable to £2,700, which means that it now agrees with the payable balance shown in the accounts of Close Ltd.

	DR £	CR £
Current account in Close Ltd	2,700	
Current account in Steele Ltd		2,700

WORKINGS

(1) **Group structure**

Close Ltd

80%

Steele Ltd

(2) **Net assets of Steele Ltd**

	Year end £	Year end £	Acquisition date £	Post-acquisition £
Share capital		60,000	60,000	–
Revaluation surplus		16,000	16,000	–
Retained earnings				
Per question	13,000			
Less: PURP (4,000 × 25/125)	(800)			
		12,200	8,000	4,200
		88,200	84,000	

(3) **Goodwill**

	£
Consideration transferred	84,000
Non-controlling interest at acquisition (84,000 × 20% (W2))	16,800
	100,800
Less net assets at acquisition (W2)	(84,000)
	16,800
Impairment to date (500 + 1,700)	(2,200)
Balance c/f	14,600

(4) **Non-controlling interest at year end**

	£
Steele Ltd – NCI at acquisition (20% × 84,000 (W3))	16,800
Share of post-acquisition reserves (20% × 4,200 (W2))	840
	17,640

(5) **Retained earnings**

	£
Close Ltd	56,000
Steele Ltd (80% × 4,200 (W2))	3,360
Less goodwill impairment to date (W3)	(2,200)
	57,160

21 PAYNE PLC

Payne plc –consolidated statement of financial position as at 31 March 20X5

	£000	£000
ASSETS		
Non-current assets		
Property, plant and equipment (3,690 + (683 – 250))		4,123
Goodwill (W1)		70
Other intangibles (475 – 275)		200
		4,393
Current assets		
Inventories (1,330 – 30 (W4))	1,300	
Trade and other receivables	1,398	
Cash and cash equivalents	968	
		3,666
Total assets		8,059
EQUITY AND LIABILITIES		
Equity attributable to owners of the parent		
Ordinary share capital		2,400
Share premium account		640
Revaluation surplus		475
Retained earnings (W2)		1,933
		5,448
Non-controlling interest (W3)		319
Total equity		5,767
Current liabilities		
Trade and other payables		2,234
Acquired contingent liability		58
Total equity and liabilities		8,059

WORKINGS

(1) **Goodwill**

	£'000
Per draft	145
Goodwill in subsidiary (not recognised)	300
Fair value adjustment on land (683 – 250)	(433)
Contingent liability recognised (reduces net assets)	58
	70

(2) **Retained earnings**

	£'000
Per draft	1,859
Add back restructuring costs (not a liability at acquisition date)	78
Add back share of subsidiary's goodwill impairment ((300 – 275) × 80%)	20
Deduct share of PURP (30 (W4) × 80%)	(24)
	1,933

(3) **Non-controlling interest**

	£'000
Per draft	320
Add back share of subsidiary's goodwill impairment ((300 – 275) × 20%)	5
Deduct share of PURP (30 (W4) × 20%)	(6)
	319

(4) **PURP**

	%	£'000
Sale price	125	150
Cost	(100)	(120)
Gross profit	25	30

(5) **Non-amortisation of goodwill**

Current period profits have been reduced by the amortisation of the goodwill on acquisition of an unincorporated business, measured at £300,000 at acquisition less £275,000 carrying amount.

This goodwill is not identifiable, so it should not be recognised as an asset. Nor should any amortisation be recognised as an expense. Current period profits should be increased by £25,000.

CHAPTER 12

Consolidated statements of financial performance

Introduction

Learning objectives

- Identify the financial effects of group accounting in the context of the IASB *Conceptual Framework* ☐

- Explain and demonstrate the concepts and principles surrounding the consolidation of financial statements including:

    – The single entity concept ☐
    – Substance over form ☐
    – The distinction between control and ownership ☐

- Calculate the amounts to be included in an entity's consolidated statements of financial performance in respect of its new and continuing interests in subsidiaries in accordance with the international financial reporting framework ☐

- Prepare and present a consolidated statement of profit or loss (or extracts therefrom) including adjustments for intra-group transactions and balances, goodwill, non-controlling interests and fair values ☐

- Prepare and present a consolidated statement of changes in equity (or extracts therefrom) in accordance with the international financial reporting framework ☐

- Explain the application of IFRS to specified group scenarios ☐

Specific syllabus references for this chapter are: 1d, 1h, 3d ,3e, 3f, 3g.

Syllabus links

This chapter looks in detail at the preparation of the consolidated statement of profit or loss and is fundamental to the Financial Accounting and Reporting syllabus. It builds on the principles introduced in Chapter 10 and applies them to more complex situations. A detailed knowledge and understanding of this topic and of the consolidated statement of changes in equity will also be assumed at the Advanced Stage.

Examination context

The focus of questions on this topic will normally be on consolidation adjustments such as intra-group trading and unrealised profits. A mid-year acquisition is likely to be incorporated, so any dates given should be read carefully.

The consolidated statement of changes in equity could be examined in conjunction with the consolidated statement of profit or loss or could appear as part of another question.

In the examination, candidates may be required to:

- Prepare a consolidated statement of profit or loss (or extracts therefrom) including the results of the parent entity and one or more subsidiaries from individual financial statements or draft consolidated financial statements and including adjustments for the following:

    – Acquisition of a subsidiary, including a mid-year acquisition
    – Intra-group transactions
    – Unrealised profits
    – Interest and management charges

- Explain the preparation of a consolidated statement of profit or loss in the context of the single entity concept, substance over form and the distinction between control and ownership

- Prepare a consolidated statement of changes in equity (or extracts therefrom) including the effects of new and continuing interests in subsidiaries

1 Consolidated statement of profit or loss

Section overview

The preparation of the consolidated statement of profit or loss is consistent with the consolidated statement of financial position.

1.1 Basic principles

In Chapter 10 we introduced the basic principles and mechanics involved in the consolidation of the statement of profit or loss as follows:

Consolidated statement of profit or loss

	£
Revenue	X
(P + S (100%) – intra-group items)	
Profit after tax (PAT) (**Control**)	$\underline{\underline{X}}$
(**Ownership**)	
Attributable to:	
Owners of P (ß)	X
Non-controlling interest (NCI% × S's PAT)	$\underline{X}$
	$\underline{\underline{X}}$

The consolidated statement of profit or loss is prepared on a basis consistent with the consolidated statement of financial position. Therefore:

The consolidated statement of profit or loss shows income generated from the net assets under the parent company's **control**.	In the consolidated statement of profit or loss dividend income from the subsidiary is replaced with the subsidiary's income and expenses on a line-by-line basis as far as profit after tax (PAT).
The **single entity concept** is applied.	The effects of transactions between group members are eliminated on consolidation.
The **ownership** of profits is shared between the owners of the parent and any non-controlling interest.	Profit after tax is split between the profit attributable to the parent's shareholders (balancing figure) and the profit attributable to the non-controlling interest (calculated as the NCI's share of S's PAT).

In Sections 2–6 of this chapter we will consider a number of consolidation adjustments. We have already seen many of the issues raised in the context of the consolidated statement of financial position. In this chapter we will look at how the adjustments are made from the point of view of the consolidated statement of profit or loss.

2 Intra-group transactions and unrealised profit

Section overview

- The value of intra-group sales should be deducted as a consolidation adjustment from consolidated revenue and cost of sales.

- A provision for unrealised profit should be set against the selling company's profit.

- Profits or losses on non-current asset transfers should be eliminated against the selling company's profit.

- A depreciation adjustment may be required so that depreciation is based on the cost of the asset to the group.

2.1 Intra-group trading

When one company in a group sells goods to another group member an identical amount is added to the revenue of the first company and to the cost of sales of the second. Yet as far as the entity's dealings with third parties are concerned **no sale has taken place**.

The consolidated figures for sales revenue and cost of sales should represent **sales to**, and **purchases from third parties**. An adjustment is therefore necessary to reduce the sales revenue and cost of sales figures by the value of intra-group sales made during the year.

This adjustment is made as follows:

Step 1
Add across P and S revenue and P and S cost of sales.

Step 2
Deduct value of intra-group sales from revenue and cost of sales.

Points to note

This adjustment has **no effect on profit** and hence will have **no effect on the non-controlling interest** share of profit.

The intra-group trading could be between a parent and a subsidiary or between two subsidiaries.

2.2 Unrealised profits on trading

If any items sold by one group company to another are included in inventories (ie have **not been sold on outside the group** by the end of the reporting period), their value must be adjusted to the **lower of cost and NRV** to the group (as for CSFP), again applying the **single entity concept**.

Steps to set up the provision for unrealised profit (PURP) are:

Step 1
Calculate the amount of inventories remaining at the end of the reporting period.

Step 2
Calculate the intra-group profit included in it.

Step 3
Make a provision against the inventories to reduce them to cost to the group (or NRV if lower).

Points to note

1   In practical terms the provision is set up **by increasing cost of sales by the amount of the unrealised profit**. (If closing inventory is reduced, cost of sales is increased.)

2   This provision should always be set against the selling company's profit. As a result, where the seller is a **subsidiary that is not wholly owned**, the provision reduces the profit for the year for **NCI calculations**.

3   Where the purchasing company sold on to a third party some of the goods purchased from the selling company, any profit earned on those goods will have been realised as far as the group is concerned, so no adjustment is necessary.

Interactive question 1: Unrealised profits   [Difficulty level: Exam standard]

Whales Ltd owns 75% of Porpoise Ltd. The gross profit for each company for the year ended 31 March 20X7 is calculated as follows:

	Whales Ltd £	Porpoise Ltd £
Revenue	120,000	70,000
Cost of sales	(80,000)	(50,000)
Gross profit	40,000	20,000

During the year Porpoise Ltd made sales to Whales Ltd amounting to £30,000. £15,000 of these sales were in inventories at the year end. Profit made on the year end inventories items amounted to £2,000.

Requirement

Calculate group revenue, cost of sales and gross profit.

Fill in the proforma below.

	Whales Ltd £	Porpoise Ltd £	Adj £	Consol £
Revenue				
C of S – per Q				
– PURP	———	———	———	———
GP	═══	═══	═══	═══

See **Answer** at the end of this chapter.

2.3 Non-current asset transfers

The consolidated statement of profit or loss should include depreciation of non-current assets based on **cost to the group**, and should exclude any profit or loss on non-current asset transfers between group members. This is consistent with the treatment in the consolidated statement of financial position.

The adjustment is made as follows:

* Eliminate the **profit or loss on transfer** and adjust **depreciation in full** (control).

* The **profit or loss** is eliminated against the **seller**. This automatically affects the **non-controlling interest where S was the seller** (ownership).

* **Depreciation** is adjusted against the **seller** even though it is the purchaser who recorded it. This is because the depreciation adjustment reflects the realisation of the profit over time, ie over the asset's life (ownership).

Worked example: Non-current asset transfers

(Based on Interactive question 4 in Chapter 11)

P Ltd owns 80% of S Ltd. P Ltd transferred to S Ltd a non-current asset (NCA) at a value of £15,000 on 1 January 20X7. The original cost to P Ltd was £20,000 and the accumulated depreciation at the date of transfer was £8,000. The asset has a total useful life of five years, which is unchanged.

At 31 December 20X7 the adjustment in the **consolidated statement of financial position** (CSFP) was calculated by comparing

	£
Carrying amount of NCA with transfer (15,000 × 2/3)	10,000
Carrying amount of NCA without transfer	
((20,000 – 8,000) × 2/3)	(8,000)
	2,000

Adjustment made in CSFP was:

	£	£
DR Seller's retained earnings	2,000	
CR Non-current assets		2,000

In the **consolidated statement** of profit or loss **(CSPL)** for the year:

(a) **Eliminate the profit (or loss) on transfer** at 1 January 20X7 since it is unrealised

	£	£
DR Seller's profit or loss for year (heading where profit credited)		
(15,000 – 12,000)	3,000	
CR NCA carrying amount in CSFP		3,000

Point to note: For the non-current asset note to the consolidated statement of financial position, the credit to non-current asset carrying amounts should be split into a debit of £5,000 to the non-current asset cost account and a credit of £8,000 to the non-current asset accumulated depreciation account.

(b) **Increase/(decrease) the depreciation charge,** so that it is calculated on the asset's cost to the group. In this case, decrease the charge by

	£
Depreciation without transfer ((20,000 – 8,000)/3)	4,000
Depreciation with transfer (15,000/3)	(5,000)
	(1,000)

	£	£
DR NCA carrying amount in CSFP	1,000	
CR Selling company profit or loss for year (heading where depreciation charged)		1,000

Point to note: The non-current asset note to the consolidated statement of financial position should include this debit in accumulated depreciation. The overall effect is an adjustment of £2,000 in both the consolidated statement of profit or loss and consolidated statement of financial position.

 Interactive question 2: Non-current asset transfers   [Difficulty level: Exam standard]

P Ltd owns 80% of S Ltd. P Ltd transferred a non-current asset to S Ltd on 1 January 20X7 at a value of £15,000. The asset originally cost P Ltd £12,000 and depreciation to the date of transfer was £4,800. The profit on transfer has been credited to depreciation expense. The asset has a useful life of five years, which is unchanged. Total depreciation for 20X7 was £35,000 for P Ltd and £25,000 for S Ltd.

Requirement

Show the adjustments required for the above transaction in the consolidated statement of profit or loss for the year ended 31 December 20X7.

Fill in the proforma below.

	P Ltd £	S Ltd £	Adj £	Consol £
Depreciation – per Q				
NCA PURP				
Depreciation adjustment				

See **Answer** at the end of this chapter.

3   Consolidated statement of profit or loss workings

 Section overview

The key working for the preparation of the consolidated statement of profit or loss is the consolidation schedule.

3.1   Pro forma workings

As questions increase in complexity a formal pattern of workings is needed.

(1) Establish **group structure**

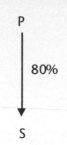

```
          P
          |
         80%
          |
          ↓
          S
```

(2) Prepare **consolidation schedule**

	P £	S £	Adj £	Consol £
Revenue	X	X	(X)	X
Cost of sales – Per Q	(X)	(X)	X	} (X)
– PURP (seller's books)	(X)	or (X)		
Expenses – Per Q	(X)	(X)		} (X)
– Goodwill impairment (if any)*	(X)	(X)		
Tax – Per Q	(X)	(X)		(X)
Profit		X̲		

May need workings for (eg)

- PURPs
- Goodwill impairment

(3) Calculate **non-controlling interest** (NCI)

				£
S PAT × NCI%	NCI% ×	X	=	X̲

* If the non-controlling interest is measured at fair value, then the NCI% of the impairment loss will be debited to the NCI. This is based upon the NCI shareholding. For instance, if the parent has acquired 75% of the subsidiary and the NCI is measured at fair value, then 25% of any goodwill impairment will be debited to NCI. See example Chapter 10 Section 8.

Interactive question 3: Statement of profit or loss workings   [Difficulty level: Easy]

Pathfinder Ltd owns 75% of Sultan Ltd. Statements of profit or loss for the two companies for the year ending 30 September 20X7 are as follows.

	Pathfinder Ltd £	Sultan Ltd £
Revenue	100,000	50,000
Cost of sales	(60,000)	(30,000)
Gross profit	40,000	20,000
Expenses	(20,000)	(10,000)
Investment income from Sultan Ltd	1,500	–
Profit before tax	21,500	10,000
Income tax expense	(6,000)	(3,000)
Profit for the year	15,500	7,000

During the year one group company sold goods to the other for £20,000 at a gross profit margin of 40%. Half of the goods remained in inventories at the year end.

Requirements

(a) Prepare extracts from Pathfinder Ltd's consolidated statement of profit or loss for the year ended 30 September 20X7 showing revenue, cost of sales, gross profit and non-controlling interest, assuming that the intra-group sales have been made by Pathfinder Ltd to Sultan Ltd.

(b) Prepare the whole of Pathfinder Ltd's consolidated statement of profit or loss for the year ended 30 September 20X7, assuming that the intra-group sales have been made by Sultan Ltd to Pathfinder Ltd.

Fill in the proforma below.

(a) **Consolidated statement of profit or loss (extracts) for the year ended 30 September 20X7**

	£
Revenue	
Cost of sales	_____
Gross profit	=====
Non-controlling interest (W3)	=====

WORKINGS

(1) **Group structure**

```
        P
        │
        │ 75%
        ▼
        S
```

(2) **Consolidation schedule**

	Pathfinder Ltd £	Sultan Ltd £	Adj £	Consol £
Revenue				
Cost of sales – per Q				
– PURP (W4)				
Expenses				
Income tax		_____		
Profit		=====		

(3) **Non-controlling interest**

	£
Sultan Ltd	_____

(4) **PURP**

	%	£	£
Selling price			
Cost			
Gross profit	_____	_____	_____
	=====	=====	=====

(b) **Consolidated statement of profit or loss for the year ended 30 September 20X7**

	£
Revenue	
Cost of sales	
Gross profit	_____
Expenses	
Profit before tax	_____
Income tax expense	
Profit for the year	=====
Profit attributable to:	
Owners of Pathfinder Ltd (β)	
Non-controlling interest (W3)	
	_____
	=====

WORKINGS

(1) **Group structure**

As part (a)

(2) **Consolidation schedule**

	Pathfinder Ltd £	Sultan Ltd £	Adj £	Consol £
Revenue				
Cost of sales – per Q				
– PURP (W4)				
Expenses				
Income tax				
Profit				

(3) **Non-controlling interest**

£

Sultan Ltd

(4) **PURP**

As part (a)

See **Answer** at the end of this chapter.

4 Mid-year acquisitions

Section overview

- The results of the subsidiary should be consolidated from the date of acquisition.
- The profit or loss amounts of the subsidiary should be time apportioned.

4.1 Method of apportionment

When we looked at the statement of financial position we saw that consolidated retained earnings included only the **post-acquisition profits** of the subsidiary. This principle also applies to the consolidated statement of profit or loss. If the subsidiary is **acquired during the accounting period**, the **entire statement of profit or loss of the subsidiary should be split** between pre-acquisition and post-acquisition proportions. Only the **post-acquisition** figures should be included in the consolidated statement of profit or loss.

Points to note

1 Assume revenue and expenses accrue evenly over the year unless the contrary is indicated – therefore time-apportion results of the subsidiary from the date of acquisition.

2 Time-apportion totals for revenue, cost of sales, expenses and tax first, then deduct post-acquisition intra-group items.

3 Recognise as an expense any goodwill impairment losses arising on the acquisition (calculation of goodwill was dealt with in Chapter 11). Note that if the NCI is held at **fair value, part of that impairment loss will be allocated to the NCI.**

Interactive question 4: Mid-year acquisition
[Difficulty level: Easy]

P Ltd acquired 75% of S Ltd on 1 April 20X7. Extracts from the companies' statements of profit or loss for the year ended 31 December 20X7 are as follows.

	P Ltd £	S Ltd £
Revenue	100,000	75,000
Cost of sales	(70,000)	(60,000)
Gross profit	30,000	15,000

Since acquisition P Ltd has made sales to S Ltd of £15,000. None of these goods remain in inventories at the year end.

Requirement

Calculate revenue, cost of sales and gross profit for the group for the year ending 31 December 20X7.

P Ltd Consolidated statement of profit or loss for the year ended 31 December 20X7

	P Ltd £	S Ltd £	Adj £	Consol £
Revenue				
Cost of sales				
Gross profit				

See **Answer** at the end of this chapter.

5 Dividends

Section overview

- Intra-group dividends should be cancelled on consolidation.
- The uncancelled amount should be disclosed in the consolidated statement of changes in equity.

5.1 Treatment

Dealing with intra-group dividends is made a bit more complicated by the fact that:

- Dividends received are shown as **income** in the statement of profit or loss; but
- Dividends paid are shown in the **statement of changes in equity**.

Nevertheless the **single entity concept** must be applied to dividends paid by the subsidiary, by:

- Cancelling P's dividend income from S in P's statement of profit or loss against S's dividends in S's statement of changes in equity.

- Leaving the uncancelled amount of S's dividends to be shown as the dividends to the non-controlling interest in the consolidated statement of changes in equity (see Section 7 below).

6 Other adjustments

Section overview

The effect of all other intra-group transactions should be cancelled on consolidation.

6.1 Redeemable (and some irredeemable) preference shares

Redeemable (and some irredeemable) preference shares are treated as a **financial liability** (under IAS 32 *Financial Instruments: Presentation*) rather than as part of equity. Consequently, distributions to shareholders are classed as **finance costs** rather than as dividends.

On consolidation **finance income received/receivable** in the parent's books is **cancelled** against the amount **paid/payable** in the subsidiary's books, leaving only the portion paid/payable to third parties as a finance cost.

6.2 Interest and management charges

Interest or management charges paid/payable in the statement of profit or loss of the subsidiary (expense) **should be cancelled** against the **interest or management charges received/receivable** in the statement of profit or loss of the parent company (income).

7 Consolidated statement of changes in equity

Section overview

- The consolidated statement of changes in equity (CSCE) shows the change in group equity reconciling the position at the start of the year with the position at the end of the year.

- There are separate analysis columns for each type of share capital and reserves in respect of the parent's equity holders.

- Changes in the non-controlling interest in share capital and reserves are presented in a single column.

7.1 Structure of CSCE

The CSCE is the **link** between the consolidated statement of profit or loss or consolidated statement of profit or loss and other comprehensive income and the figures for equity shown in the consolidated statement of financial position, in that it shows the movement between the retained earnings brought forward at the start of the year and those carried forward at the end of the year. As can be seen in the proforma layout in Chapter 2, the CSCE also shows movements on share capital, other reserves and on the non-controlling interest. Listed below are the main points.

- **Owners of the parent**: there are **separate analysis columns** for each type of **share capital** and **reserves**, together with a total column.

    - There will nearly always be entries for total comprehensive income for the year and dividends paid/payable. Total comprehensive income for the year will be the profit for the year plus any item of 'other comprehensive income'.

    - There will sometimes be entries for issues of share capital and revaluations of non-current assets (dealt with in Chapter 4). Revaluation gains or losses will be shown as part of total comprehensive income.

- **Non-controlling interest in subsidiaries**: there is only a **single column**, which is the equivalent of the total column for the owners of the parent.

  - There will nearly always be entries for the NCI's share of S's total comprehensive income for the year and dividends paid/payable.

  - There will sometimes be entries for S's revaluations of non-current assets (dealt with in Chapter 4).

  - In practice there will sometimes be entries for issues of share capital by S, but these fall outside the syllabus.

  - Transfers between reserves in S should never be shown, because they contra out against each other in this single column.

  - If a partly-owned subsidiary is acquired during the year there will be an entry for NCI added on the acquisition of a subsidiary (see Section 7.4).

Worked example: CSCE

The following are extracts from the financial statements for the year ended 30 June 20X8 of William plc and Rufus Ltd.

	William plc £	Rufus Ltd £
Profit from operations	196,000	95,000
Dividends from Rufus Ltd	24,000	–
Profit before tax	220,000	95,000
Income tax expense	(70,000)	(30,000)
Profit for the year	150,000	65,000
Dividends paid	20,000	30,000
Share capital (£1 shares)	200,000	50,000

William plc purchased 40,000 shares in Rufus Ltd some years ago. William plc's retained earnings at 1 July 20X7 were £270,000.

Prepare the consolidated statement of profit or loss and the consolidated statement of changes in equity for William plc for the year ended 30 June 20X8, as far as the information permits. You should assume that Rufus Ltd had no retained earnings at 1 July 20X7. NCI is measured on the proportionate basis.

Solution

Consolidated statement of profit or loss for the year ended 30 June 20X8

	£
Profit from operations (196 + 95)	291,000
Income tax expense (70 + 30)	(100,000)
Profit for the year	191,000
Profit attributable to:	
Owners of William plc (β)	178,000
Non-controlling interest (20% × 65)	13,000
	191,000

Point to note

The amount attributable to the owners of William plc can be separately calculated, omitting the intra-group dividend (as William plc's shareholders are given their share of Rufus Ltd's profits, they cannot also be given their share of a dividend paid out of those profits):

100% of (150,000 – 24,000) + 80% of £65,000 = £178,000.

Consolidated statement of changes in equity for the year ended 30 June 20X8

	Share capital £	Attributable to owners of William plc Retained earnings £	Total £	Non-controlling interest £	Total £
Balance at 1 July 20X7 (W)	200,000	270,000	470,000	10,000	480,000
Total comprehensive income for the year	–	178,000	178,000	13,000	191,000
Dividends (W)	–	(20,000)	(20,000)	(6,000)	(26,000)
Balance at 30 June 20X8	200,000	428,000	628,000	17,000	645,000

WORKING

NCI share of Rufus Ltd's: dividend   20% × 30,000 = £6,000
                             share capital   20% × 50,000 = £10,000

7.2 Transfers to reserves

Some companies transfer amounts from **retained earnings to named reserves**. Such transfers are made in the analysis columns in the CSCE and are therefore shown **net of NCI**.

In the analysis columns in the CSCE:

Group transfers between reserves	=	P's transfers between reserves	+	P% of S's transfers between reserves

This **matches** with the treatment of reserves attributable to the owners of P in the **consolidated statement of financial position**, ie they include P's reserves and P's share of S's post-acquisition reserves.

7.3 Retained earnings brought forward

To calculate each of the group reserves brought forward, simply do a working, as you would for the consolidated statement of financial position, **but at the start of the year**. Therefore each group opening reserve will be:

Group reserve b/f	=	P's reserve b/f	+	P% of S's post-acquisition reserve b/f	±	Goodwill impairment (to start of year) and any other adjustments to opening position

Point to note: The NCI amount brought forward will be the **NCI share of S's equity** (ie NCI's share of S's capital and reserves) brought forward or **fair value of NCI** plus NCI share of the subsidiary's post-acquisition reserves.

Interactive question 5: Retained earnings brought forward

[Difficulty level: Exam standard]

Continuing the facts from Worked example: CSCE above, you should now assume that Rufus Ltd's retained earnings at 1 July 20X7 were £120,000.

You have also now ascertained that when William plc purchased its 40,000 shares in Rufus Ltd, Rufus Ltd's retained earnings stood at £70,000. NCI is measured at fair value. The fair value of the NCI at the date of acquisition was £25,000.

Three years ago a goodwill impairment loss of £10,000 was recognised in William plc's consolidated financial statements.

Requirement

Prepare the consolidated statement of changes in equity for William plc for the year ended 30 June 20X8 taking account of the additional information.

Fill in the pro forma below.

Consolidated statement of changes in equity for the year ended 30 June 20X8

	Attributable to owners of William plc			Non-controlling interest £	Total £
	Share capital £	Retained earnings £	Total £		
Balance at 1 July 20X7 (W)					
Dividends					
Total comprehensive income for the year	___	___	___	___	___
Balance at 30 June 20X8	═══	═══	═══	═══	═══

WORKING

	£
Group retained earnings b/f	
William plc	
Rufus Ltd	
Goodwill impairment to date	___
	═══

	£
NCI b/f	
Fair value at acquisition	
Share of post-acquisition retained earnings	
Goodwill impairment	___
	═══

See **Answer** at the end of this chapter.

7.4 Acquisition during the year

Section 4 explained that the results for the new subsidiary should only be brought into the consolidated statement of profit or loss **from the date of acquisition**. Any non-controlling interest in the results of the newly-acquired subsidiary should similarly be **calculated from that date** and the amount included as profit for the year in the non-controlling interest column in the CSCE in the normal way.

But in the year end consolidated statement of financial position, the non-controlling interest in the new subsidiary will be calculated as their share of the **year end equity** in the new subsidiary. This should include not only the profit for the post-acquisition period but also their share of the newly-acquired subsidiary's:

- Share capital; plus
- Retained earnings brought forward at the start of the current year; plus
- Current year profits to the date of acquisition.

Their share of the total of these amounts should be brought into the CSCE as a single line described as **'Added on acquisition of subsidiary'**.

Interactive question 6: Acquisition during the year   [Difficulty level: Exam standard]

Joseph plc acquired an 80% interest in Mary plc on 1 October 20X8. The following figures relate to the year ended 31 March 20X9.

	Joseph plc £'000	Mary plc £'000
Statement of profit or loss		
Revenue	800	550
Costs	(400)	(350)
Profit before tax	400	200
Income tax expense	(140)	(50)
Profit for the year	260	150

	Retained earnings	
Statements of changes in equity (extracts)	£'000	£'000
Brought forward	400	300
Total comprehensive income for the year	260	150
Carried forward	660	450

	£'000	£'000
Additional information		
Share capital	500	100

NCI is measured on the proportionate basis

Requirement

Prepare the consolidated statement of profit or loss and the consolidated statement of changes in equity for the Joseph plc group for the year ended 31 March 20X9.

Fill in the pro forma below.

Consolidated statement of profit or loss for the year ended 31 March 20X9

	£'000
Revenue	
Costs	
Profit before tax	___
Income tax expense	
Profit for the year	___
Profit attributable to:	
Owners of Joseph plc	
Non-controlling interest (W1)	___
	___

Consolidated statement of changes in equity for the year ended 31 March 20X9

	Attributable to owners of Joseph plc			Non-controlling interest £'000	Total £'000
	Share capital £'000	Retained earnings £'000	Total £'000		
Brought forward					
Total comprehensive income for the year					
Added on acquisition of subsidiary (W2)					
	___	___	___	___	___
Carried forward	═══	═══	═══	═══	═══

WORKINGS

(1) **Non-controlling interest in profit for the year**

	£'000

(2) **Non-controlling interest added on acquisition**

	£'000	£'000
Share capital		
Retained earnings b/f		
Profit for first half of current year		
20% of		

See **Answer** at the end of this chapter.

Summary

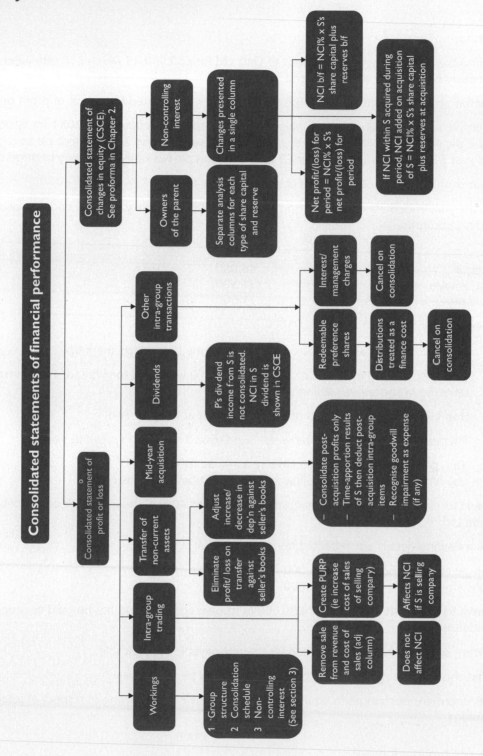

Consolidated statements of financial performance

- **Consolidated statement of changes in equity (CSCE). See proforma in Chapter 2.**
  - **Non-controlling interest**
    - **Changes presented in a single column**
      - **NCI b/f = NCI% × S's share capital plus reserves b/f**
      - **Net profit/(loss) for period = NCI% × S's net profit/(loss) for period**
        - **If NCI within S acquired during period, NCI added on acquisition of S = NCI% × S's share capital plus reserves at acquisition**
  - **Owners of the parent**
    - **Separate analysis columns for each type of share capital and reserve**

- **Consolidated statement of profit or loss**
  - **Other intra-group transactions**
    - **Interest/ management charges**
      - **Cancel on consolidation**
    - **Redeemable preference shares**
      - **Distributions treated as a finance cost**
        - **Cancel on consolidation**
  - **Dividends**
    - **P's dividend income from S is not consolidated. NCI in S dividend is shown in CSCE**
  - **Mid-year acquisition**
    - **– Consolidate post-acquisition profits only**
    - **– Time-apportion results of S then deduct post-acquisition intra-group items**
    - **– Recognise goodwill impairment as expense (if any)**
  - **Transfer of non-current assets**
    - **Adjust increase/ decrease in dep'n against seller's books**
    - **Eliminate profit/ loss on transfer against seller's books**
  - **Intra-group trading**
    - **Create PURP (ie increase cost of sales of selling company)**
      - **Affects NCI if S is selling company**
    - **Remove sale from revenue and cost of sales (adj column)**
      - **Does not affect NCI**
  - **Workings**
    - **1 Group structure**
    - **2 Consolidation schedule**
    - **3 Non-controlling interest (See section 3)**

Self-test

Answer the following questions

1   Barley Ltd has owned 100% of the issued share capital of Oats Ltd for many years. Barley Ltd sells goods to Oats Ltd at cost plus 20%. The following information is available for the year.

	Revenue £
Barley Ltd	460,000
Oats Ltd	120,000

During the year Barley Ltd sold goods to Oats Ltd for £60,000, of which £18,000 were still held in inventory by Oats Ltd at the year end.

At what amount should total revenue appear in the consolidated statement of profit or loss?

2   Ufton plc is the sole subsidiary of Walcot plc. The cost of sales figures for 20X1 for Walcot plc and Ufton plc were £11 million and £10 million respectively. During 20X1 Walcot plc sold goods which had cost £2 million to Ufton plc for £3 million. Ufton plc has not yet sold any of these goods.

What should the consolidated cost of sales figure be for 20X1?

3   For the year ended 30 April 20X6 Hop Ltd and its 90% subsidiary Skip Ltd had the following trading accounts.

	Hop Ltd £	Skip Ltd £
Revenue	100,000	46,000
Cost of sales	(70,000)	(34,500)
Gross profit	30,000	11,500

Notes

(1)   In each company all sales were made at the same percentage mark-up.

(2)   Goods purchased by Skip Ltd at a cost of £9,000 were sold to Hop Ltd. This transaction is reflected in the above trading accounts.

(3)   Hop Ltd had sold two-thirds of these purchases at the year end.

(4)   There had been no trading between Skip Ltd and Hop Ltd in previous years.

    (a)   What should the consolidated revenue be for the year?
    (b)   What should the consolidated gross profit be for the year?

4   Shaw Ltd owns 75% of the ordinary share capital and 40% of the £125,000 of 8% debt of Wilde Ltd.

The following details are extracted from the books of Wilde Ltd.

Income tax expense	£24,000
Profit after tax	£70,000

Shaw Ltd has profit before tax of £80,000 in its own accounts and has no paid or proposed dividends.

Neither company has yet accounted for interest payable or receivable.

What should the total consolidated profit before tax be for the year?

5   The statement of changes in equity of Suton Ltd shows the following in respect of retained earnings

	£'000
Balance brought forward	21
Total comprehensive income for the year	10
Interim dividend paid	(7)
Balance carried forward	24

80% of the share capital of Suton Ltd had been acquired by Teigh plc some years ago when Suton Ltd's retained earnings amounted to £5,000.

(a) How much of Suton Ltd's retained earnings should be included in closing consolidated retained earnings?

(b) How much of Suton Ltd's profit for the period should be included in the consolidated profit for the financial year attributable to the owners of Teigh plc?

(c) If the non-controlling shareholders' interest in Suton Ltd amounted to £5,200 at the start of the year, how much should it be at the end of the year?

6 Cherry plc owns 75% of Plum plc and 60% of Peach plc. For the year ended 31 December 20X1 Plum plc reported a net profit of £118,000 and Peach plc reported a net profit of £56,000. During 20X1 Plum plc sold goods to Peach plc for £36,000 at cost plus 50%. At the year end these goods are still held by Peach plc.

In the consolidated statement of profit or loss for the year ended 31 December 20X1 what should the profit attributable to the non-controlling interest be?

7 Chicken plc owns 80% of Egg plc. Egg plc sells goods to Chicken plc at cost plus 50%. The total sales invoiced to Chicken plc by Egg plc in the year ended 31 December 20X1 were £900,000 and, of these sales, goods which had been invoiced at £60,000 were held in inventory by Chicken plc at 31 December 20X1.

What should the reduction in aggregate group gross profit be?

8 Marlowe Ltd owns 60% of the ordinary share capital and 25% of the £200,000 5% loan stock of Southey Ltd. Neither company has yet accounted for interest payable or receivable.

The following details are extracted from the books of Southey Ltd.

Profit   £100,000
Dividend paid   £40,000

What amount should be shown as the profit attributable to the non-controlling interest in the consolidated statement of profit or loss of Marlowe Ltd?

9 Several years ago Horace Ltd acquired 75% of the ordinary share capital of Sylvia Ltd. The statement of profit or loss of Sylvia Ltd for the year ended 28 February 20X7 showed profit after tax of £4,000. During the year Horace Ltd sold goods to Sylvia Ltd at a mark up on cost of 50%. 75% of these goods had been sold to third parties by the year end.

What should the non-controlling interest be in the consolidated statement of profit or loss of Horace Ltd for the year ended 28 February 20X7?

10 Set out below are the summarised statements of profit or loss of Dennis plc and its 80% subsidiary Terry Ltd.

	Dennis plc £	Terry Ltd £
Profit from operations	89,000	45,000
Dividend from Terry Ltd	16,000	–
Profit before tax	105,000	45,000
Income tax expense	(42,000)	(15,000)
Profit for the year	63,000	30,000

What is the profit for the year attributable to the owners of Dennis plc to be disclosed in the consolidated statement of profit or loss?

11 HUMPHREY PLC

The following are the draft statements of profit or loss for the year ended 30 September 20X5 of Humphrey plc and its subsidiary Stanley plc.

	Humphrey plc £'000	Stanley plc £'000
Revenue	1,100	400
Cost of sales	(600)	(240)
Gross profit	500	160
Distribution costs	(60)	(50)
Administrative costs	(65)	(55)
Profit from operations	375	55
Finance cost	(25)	(6)
Investment income	20	5
Profit before tax	370	54
Income tax expense	(160)	(24)
Profit for the year	210	30

The following information is relevant

(1) Humphrey plc acquired 80% of Stanley plc many years ago, when the retained earnings of that company were £5,000. Both companies have only ordinary shares in issue. Non-controlling interest is measured at fair value. At the acquisition date the fair value of the NCI was estimated at £13,000.

(2) Total intra-group sales in the year amounted to £100,000, Humphrey plc selling to Stanley plc.

(3) At the year end the statement of financial position of Stanley plc included inventory purchased from Humphrey plc. Humphrey plc had recognised a profit of £2,000 on this inventory.

(4) The retained earnings of Humphrey plc and Stanley plc as at 30 September 20X4 were £90,000 and £40,000 respectively. Stanley plc's share capital is comprised of 50,000 £1 ordinary shares.

(5) Humphrey plc paid dividends of £100,000 in the year. Stanley plc paid a dividend of £20,000.

Requirement

Prepare a consolidated statement of profit or loss and extracts from the consolidated statement of changes in equity in respect of retained earnings and non-controlling interest for the year ended 30 September 20X5.   **(8 marks)**

12 HIGH PLC

High plc acquired its 80% interest in the ordinary shares and 25% interest in the redeemable preference shares of Tension plc for £9,000 and £1,000 respectively on 1 April 20X3 when Tension plc's retained earnings were £4,000. There were no other reserves at that date. The preference shares carry no votes.

The following are the draft statements of profit or loss of High plc and Tension plc for the year ended 31 March 20X9.

	High plc		Tension plc	
	£	£	£	£
Revenue		274,500		181,250
Dividends from Tension plc				
Ordinary		4,800		–
Preference		150		–
Bank deposit interest		250		100
		279,700		181,350
Less: Cost of sales	126,480		86,520	
Distribution costs	67,315		42,885	
Administrative costs	25,555		17,295	
Preference dividend paid	–		600	
		(219,350)		(147,300)
		60,350		34,050
Income tax expense		(29,000)		(15,100)
Profit for the year		31,350		18,950

The following information is also available.

(1) The inventory of High plc at 31 March 20X9 includes goods purchased from Tension plc at a profit to that company of £700. Total intra-group sales for the year amounted to £37,500.

(2) On 1 April 20X8 High plc sold plant costing £7,000 to Tension plc for £10,000. The profit on sale has been taken to cost of sales. Depreciation has been provided by Tension plc at 10% per annum on the cost of £10,000.

(3) Included in Tension plc's administrative costs is an amount for £3,500 in respect of management charges invoiced and included in revenue by High plc.

(4) Tension plc's issued share capital comprises 10,000 50p ordinary shares and 4,000 £1 15% redeemable preference shares.

(5) Four years ago a goodwill impairment loss was recognised in High plc's consolidated financial statements leaving goodwill in the consolidated statement of financial position at £1,200. A further £180 impairment loss needs to be recognised in the current year.

(6) Retained earnings at 1 April 20X8 were £576,000 for High plc and £72,600 for Tension plc.

(7) Non-controlling interest is measured on the proportionate basis.

Requirements

(a) Prepare the consolidated statement of profit or loss for the year ended 31 March 20X9 and calculate the retained earnings brought forward attributable to the owners of High plc and to the non-controlling interest. **(9 marks)**

(b) For each adjustment you have made in the consolidation schedule explain why you have made it (include in your answer the journal adjustment and the impact on consolidated profit). **(8 marks)**

(17 marks)

13 ETHOS PLC

The following draft statements of profit or loss and extracts from the statements of changes in equity were prepared for the year ended 31 March 20X9.

Statements of profit or loss	Ethos plc	Pathos Ltd
	£	£
Revenue	303,600	217,700
Cost of sales	(143,800)	(102,200)
Gross profit	159,800	115,500
Operating costs	(71,200)	(51,300)
Profit from operations	88,600	64,200
Investment income	2,800	1,200
Profit before tax	91,400	65,400
Income tax expense	(46,200)	(32,600)
Profit for the year	45,200	32,800

Statements of changes in equity (extracts)

	Ethos plc		Pathos Ltd	
	General reserve £	Retained earnings £	General reserve £	Retained earnings £
Balance brought forward	–	79,300	–	38,650
Total comprehensive income for the year	–	45,200	–	32,800
Transfer between reserves	15,000	(15,000)	5,000	(5,000)
Dividends paid on ordinary shares	–	(30,000)	–	–
Balance carried forward	15,000	79,500	5,000	66,450

On 30 November 20X8 Ethos plc acquired 75% of the issued ordinary capital of Pathos Ltd for £130,000. Pathos Ltd has in issue 100,000 £1 ordinary shares. Ethos plc has 500,000 £1 ordinary shares in issue.

Ethos plc measures non-controlling interest at fair value. The fair value of the non-controlling interest in Pathos Ltd at the date of acquisition was £42,000.

Profits of both companies accrue evenly over the year.

Requirements

(a) Prepare the consolidated statement of profit or loss and consolidated statement of changes in equity for the year ended 31 March 20X9. **(9 marks)**

(b) Explain why only four months of Pathos Ltd's profit or loss should be included in the consolidated statement of profit or loss. **(2 marks)**

(11 marks)

14 HIGG PLC

The draft consolidated statement of profit or loss of Higg plc for the year ended 30 June 20X5, incorporating the results of its two subsidiaries Flapp Ltd and Topp Ltd, is as follows:

	£
Revenue	1,265,900
Cost of sales	(806,400)
Gross profit	459,500
Operating costs	(213,800)
Profit from operations	245,700
Finance cost	(12,500)
Investment income	13,600
Profit before tax	246,800
Income tax expense	(115,000)
Profit for the year	131,800

	£
Profit attributable to:	
Owners of the parent	119,850
Non-controlling interest	11,950
	131,800

The following information is relevant:

(1) Higg plc has owned 90% of the £100,000 share capital of Flapp Ltd since its date of incorporation ten years ago.

(2) Higg plc acquired 70% of the £100,000 issued ordinary shares of Topp Ltd for £95,000 on 1 July 20X1 when the retained earnings of Topp Ltd were £13,200. On the same date Higg plc acquired 20% of the £100,000 8% loan stock of Topp Ltd.

(3) The revenue of Flapp Ltd includes sales to Topp Ltd of £36,000, all invoiced at cost plus 25%. On 30 June 20X5 the inventory of Topp Ltd included £9,000 in respect of such goods.

(4) Three years ago a goodwill impairment loss of £5,910 was recognised in Higg plc's consolidated financial statements. A further loss of £1,970 needs to be reflected in the current year financial statements.

(5) Higg plc paid ordinary dividends of £20,000 and dividends to irredeemable preference shareholders of £8,000. Topp Ltd paid ordinary dividends of £10,000.

(6) The retained earnings of Higg plc, Flapp Ltd and Topp Ltd as at 1 July 20X4 were £72,400, £46,900 and £29,600 respectively. The share capital of Higg plc comprises 500,000 £1 ordinary shares and 100,000 £1 irredeemable preference shares.

The draft statement of profit or loss has been prepared by simply adding together the line items for all three companies. Profit attributable to the non-controlling interest has been arrived at by adding together 10% of the profit after tax of Flapp Ltd and 30% of the profit after tax of Topp Ltd.

No adjustments have been made for any of the issues arising from (1) to (6) above.

Higg plc prefers to measure goodwill and the non-controlling interest using the proportionate method wherever possible.

Requirement

Prepare the final consolidated statement of profit or loss and statement of changes in equity for the year ended 30 June 20X5 for the Higg group. **(8 marks)**

Now, go back to the Learning objectives in the Introduction. If you are satisfied you have achieved these objectives, please tick them off.

Technical reference

For a comprehensive Technical reference section, covering all aspects of group accounts (except group statements of cash flows) see Chapter 10.

Answer to Interactive questions

Answer to Interactive question 1

	Whales Ltd £	Porpoise Ltd £	Adj £	Consol £
Revenue	120,000	70,000	(30,000)	160,000
C of S – per Q	(80,000)	(50,000)	30,000	
– PURP		(2,000)		(102,000)
GP	40,000	18,000	–	58,000

Points to note

1 The intra-group sale is eliminated in the **adjustments column**. It has no effect on the overall profit.

2 The unrealised profit is eliminated by increasing the cost of sales of the selling company. Where the selling company is the subsidiary this will reduce the profit figure on which the calculation of non-controlling interest is subsequently based.

Answer to Interactive question 2

	P Ltd £	S Ltd £	Adj £	Consol £
Depreciation – per Q	(35,000)	(25,000)		
NCA PURP (15,000 – (12,000 – 4,800))	(7,800)			
Depreciation adjustment				
((15,000/3) – ((12,000 – 4,800*)/3))	2,600			(65,200)

* 4,800 is 2/5 of cost

Answer to Interactive question 3

(a) **Consolidated statement of profit or loss (extracts) for the year ended 30 September 20X7**

	£
Revenue (W2)	130,000
Cost of sales (W2)	(74,000)
Gross profit	56,000
Non-controlling interest (W3)	1,750

WORKINGS

(1) **Group structure**

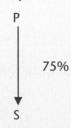

P

75%

S

(2) **Consolidation schedule**

	Pathfinder Ltd £	Sultan Ltd £	Adj £	Consol £
Revenue	100,000	50,000	(20,000)	130,000
C of S – per Q	(60,000)	(30,000)	20,000	
– PURP (W4)	(4,000)			(74,000)
Expenses		(10,000)		
Income tax		(3,000)		
Profit		7,000		

(3) Non-controlling interest

				£
Sultan Ltd	25% ×	7,000	(W2)	1,750

(4) PURP

	%	£		£
Selling price	100	20,000		
Cost	(60)	(12,000)		
Gross profit	40	8,000	× ½ =	4,000

(b) Consolidated statement of profit or loss for the year ended 30 September 20X7

	£
Revenue (W2)	130,000
Cost of sales (W2)	(74,000)
Gross profit	56,000
Expenses (W2)	(30,000)
Profit before tax	26,000
Income tax expense (W2)	(9,000)
Profit for the year	17,000
Profit attributable to:	
Owners of Pathfinder Ltd (β)	16,250
Non-controlling interest (W3)	750
	17,000

WORKINGS

(1) Group structure

As part (a)

(2) Consolidation schedule

	Pathfinder Ltd £	Sultan Ltd £	Adj £	Consol £
Revenue	100,000	50,000	(20,000)	130,000
C of S – per Q	(60,000)	(30,000)	20,000	
– PURP (W4)		(4,000)		(74,000)
Expenses	(20,000)	(10,000)		(30,000)
Income tax	(6,000)	(3,000)		(9,000)
Profit		3,000		

(3) Non-controlling interest

				£
Sultan Ltd	25% ×	3,000	(W2)	750

(4) PURP

As part (a)

Answer to Interactive question 4

P Ltd Consolidated statement of profit or loss for the year ended 31 December 20X7

	P Ltd £	$^{9}/_{12}$ S Ltd £	Adj £	Consol £
Revenue	100,000	56,250	(15,000)	141,250
C of S	(70,000)	(45,000)	15,000	(100,000)
Gross profit	30,000	11,250	–	41,250

Answer to Interactive question 5

Consolidated statement of changes in equity for the year ended 30 June 20X8

	Share capital £	Attributable to owners of William plc Retained earnings £	Total £	Non-controlling interest £	Total £
Brought forward (W)	200,000	302,000	502,000	33,000	535,000
Total comprehensive income for the year	–	178,000	178,000	13,000	191,000
Dividends	–	(20,000)	(20,000)	(6,000)	(26,000)
Carried forward	200,000	460,000	660,000	40,000	700,000

WORKING

	£
Group retained earnings b/f	
William plc	270,000
Rufus Ltd (80% × (120,000 – 70,000))	40,000
Goodwill impairment to date (10,000 × 80%)	(8,000)
	302,000

	£
NCI b/f	
Fair value at acquisition	25,000
Share of post-acquistion retained earnings ((120,000 – 70,000) × 20%)	10,000
Goodwill impairment (10,000 × 20%)	(2,000)
	33,000

Answer to Interactive question 6

Consolidated statement of profit or loss for the year ended 31 March 20X9

	£'000
Revenue (Joseph + half Mary)	1,075
Costs (Joseph + half Mary)	(575)
Profit before tax	500
Income tax (Joseph + half Mary)	(165)
Profit for the year	335

	£'000
Profit attributable to:	
Owners of Joseph plc (β)	320
Non-controlling interest (W1)	15
	335

Consolidated statement of changes in equity for the year ended 31 March 20X9

	Share capital £'000	Attributable to owners of Joseph plc Retained earnings £'000	Total £'000	Non-controlling interest £'000	Total £'000
Brought forward	500	400	900	–	900
Total comprehensive income for the year	–	320	320	15	335
Added on acquisition of subsidiary (W2)	–	–	–	95	95
Carried forward	500	720	1,220	110	1,330

WORKINGS

(1) **Non-controlling interest in profit for the year**

	£'000
20% of (150,000 × 50%)	15

(2) **Non-controlling interest added on acquisition**

	£'000	£'000
Share capital	100	
Retained earnings b/f	300	
Profit for first half of current year (150,000 × 50%)	75	
20% of	475	95

1. Revenue = 460,000 + 120,000 – 60,000 = £520,000

2. £19 million

	Walcot plc £m	Ufton plc £m	Adj £m	Consol £m
Cost of sales	(11)	(10)	3	(19)
PURP	(1)			

3. (a) £134,000

	£'000
Hop Ltd	100
Skip Ltd	46
Less intra-group sales (9 × 46/34.5)	(12)
	134

   (b) £40,500

	£'000
Hop Ltd	30.0
Skip Ltd	11.5
Less PURP ((12 – 9) × $\frac{1}{3}$)	(1.0)
	40.5

4. £168,000

	Shaw Ltd £	Wilde Ltd £	Adj £	Cons £
Interest receivable (40% × 10,000*)	4,000		(4,000)	–
Interest payable		(10,000)	4,000	(6,000)
PBT	80,000	94,000		174,000
				168,000

*125,000 × 8%

5. (a) Share of Suton's post-acquisition retained earnings = (24,000 – 5,000) × 80%
                                        = 19,000 × 80% = £15,200

   (b) Profit for the year = 10,000 × 80% = £8,000

   (c) NCI c/f will be £5,800

	£'000
B/f	5.2
Share of TCI for year (10 × 20%)	2.0
Less share of dividends (7 × 20%)	(1.4)
C/f	5.8

6. £48,900

	£
Share of Plum plc profit (25% × 118,000)	29,500
Share of Peach plc profit (40% × 56,000)	22,400
Less share of PURP (25% × 36,000 × 50/150)	(3,000)
	48,900

7. £20,000

	%	£
Sales price	150	60,000
Cost	(100)	(40,000)
Gross profit	50	20,000

8   £36,000

		£
Profit prior to finance cost		100,000
Finance cost (200,000 × 5%)		(10,000)
		90,000
	× 40%	36,000

9   £1,000

	£
Share of profit after tax (25% × 4,000)	1,000

Point to note: As the inventory was sold by Horace Ltd, the PURP adjustment would be against Horace Ltd's profits and would have no impact on the NCI.

10 £71,000

	£
Profit from operations – Dennis plc	89,000
Less income tax expense	(42,000)
	47,000
Group share of Terry Ltd (80% × 30,000)	24,000
	71,000

11 HUMPHREY PLC

Consolidated statement of profit or loss for the year ended 30 September 20X5

	£'000
Revenue (W2)	1,400
Cost of sales (W2)	(742)
Gross profit	658
Distribution costs (W2)	(110)
Administration expenses (W2)	(120)
Profit from operations	428
Finance cost (W2)	(31)
Investment income (W2)	9
Profit before tax	406
Income tax expense (W2)	(184)
Profit for the year	222

Profit attributable to

	£'000
Owners of Humphrey plc (β)	216
Non-controlling interest (W3)	6
	222

Consolidated statement of changes in equity for the year ended 30 September 20X5 (extracts)

	Retained earnings attributable to owners of Humphrey plc £'000	Non-controlling interest £'000	Total £'000
Balance brought forward (W4 and W6)	118	20	138
Total comprehensive income for the year	216	6	222
Dividends paid on ordinary shares (W5)	(100)	(4)	(104)
Balance carried forward	234	22	256

WORKINGS

(1) **Group structure**

Humphrey plc

↓ 80%

Stanley plc

(2) **Consolidation schedule**

	Humphrey plc	Stanley plc	Adj	Consol
	£'000	£'000	£'000	£'000
Revenue	1,100	400	(100)	1,400
C of S				
Per Q	(600)	(240)	100	
PURP	(2)	–	–	(742)
Distribution	(60)	(50)		(110)
Administrative	(65)	(55)		(120)
Finance cost	(25)	(6)		(31)
Inv income (20 – 16 (W5))	4	5		9
Income tax	(160)	(24)		(184)
PAT		30		

(3) **Non-controlling interest**

	£'000
20% × 30,000 (W2) or as PAT in question	6

(4) **Retained earnings b/f**

	£'000
Group	
Humphrey plc	90
Stanley plc (80% × (40 – 5))	28
	118

(5) **Intra-group dividend**

Check consistency between companies.

	£'000
Received by Humphrey plc (80% × 20)	16
Received by NCI (20% × 20)	4
Paid by Stanley plc	20

(6) **Non-controlling interest b/f**

	£'000
Fair value at acquisition	13
Share of post-acquisition retained earnings to 1 October 20X4	
(40,000 – 5,000) × 20%	7
	20

(a) **Consolidated statement of profit or loss for the year ended 31 March 20X9**

	£
Revenue (W2)	414,750
Cost of sales (W2)	(178,900)
Gross profit	235,850
Distribution costs (W2)	(110,200)
Administration expenses (W2)	(39,530)
Profit from operations	86,120
Finance cost (W2)	(450)
Investment income (W2)	350
Profit before tax	86,020
Income tax expense (W2)	(44,100)
Profit for the year	41,920
Attributable to	
Owners of High plc (β)	38,270
Non-controlling interest (W3)	3,650
	41,920
Retained earnings brought forward	
Attributable to owners of High plc (W5)	630,280
Non-controlling interest (W5)	14,520

(b) **Adjustments in consolidation schedule**

(i) **Intra-group sales of inventory**

As the consolidated accounts treat High plc and Tension plc as one entity, the total intra-group trading needs to be eliminated on consolidation. The total of £37,500 will be in both Tension plc's revenue and High plc's cost of sales. The adjustment required is

	DR	CR
	£	£
Revenue	37,500	
Cost of sales		37,500

This has no impact on net consolidated profit.

For the same reason, it is also necessary to eliminate the unrealised profit on the inventory held by High plc at the year end. This adjustment will also reduce inventory to original cost to the group.

The adjustment is

	DR	CR
	£	£
Cost of sales of Tension plc	700	
Inventory in the consolidated statement of financial position		700

This will reduce consolidated profit.

(ii) **Intra-group sale of plant**

For the same reasons as given for inventory above, it is necessary to eliminate the unrealised profit and reduce the plant to its original cost.

The adjustment is

	DR	CR
	£	£
Cost of sales of High plc	3,000	
Cost of plant in the consolidated statement of financial position		3,000

This will have a one-off impact on consolidated profit this year.

In current and future years (until the plant has been fully depreciated by Tension plc) it will also be necessary to adjust the depreciation charge by 10% of the PURP, to reflect the gradual realisation of the above profit through the annual depreciation charge. This will require the following.

	DR £	CR £
Accumulated depreciation in the consolidated statement of financial position	300	
Cost of sales of High plc		300

Therefore the net impact is to reduce current year consolidated profit by £2,700.

(iii) Management charges

As with intra-group trading, this charge must be contra'd out on consolidation to reflect the single entity concept.

The adjustment required is

	DR £	CR £
Revenue of High plc	3,500	
Administrative costs of Tension plc		3,500

This has no impact on consolidated profit.

(iv) Impairment of goodwill

Goodwill only exists in the consolidated accounts and therefore the individual statements of profit or loss include no impairment of goodwill. The impairment charge for the year is dealt with as follows.

	DR £	CR £
Administration costs	180	
Goodwill in the consolidated statement of financial position		180

This will reduce consolidated profit.

(v) Redeemable preference shares

These are in substance liabilities and the net 'dividend' payable outside the group should be included as part of the consolidated finance cost.

Effectively the 'dividends' paid by Tension plc are contra'd against the dividends received by High plc and the adjustment required is

	DR £	CR £
Dividends received	150	
Dividends paid (25% × £600)		150

This leaves £450 payable to third parties.

WORKINGS

(1) Group structure

High plc

80% ords (25% prefs)

Tension plc

(2) **Consolidation schedule**

	High plc £	Tension plc £	Adj £	Consol £
Revenue	274,500	181,250	(37,500)	414,750
			(3,500)	
C of S				
Per Q	(126,480)	(86,520)	37,500	
Inventory PURP		(700)		
NCA PURP	(3,000)			
Depreciation (10% × 3,000)	300			(178,900)
Distrib	(67,315)	(42,885)		(110,200)
Admin				
Per Q	(25,555)	(17,295)	3,500	
Impairment of goodwill	(180)			(39,530)
Preference dividends received	150		(150)	
Preference dividends paid		(600)	150	(450)
Inv income – interest	250	100		350
Income tax	(29,000)	(15,100)		(44,100)
PAT		18,250		

(3) **Non-controlling interest**

20% × £18,250 = £3,650

(4) **Goodwill**

	£
Consideration transferred	9,000
Non-controlling interest at acquisition (9,000 × 20%)	1,800
Less net assets at acquisition	
Ordinary shares	(5,000)
Retained earnings	(4,000)
On acquisition	1,800
Carrying amount at last impairment	(1,200)
Impairment loss previously recognised	600

(5) **Retained earnings b/f**

	£
Group:	
High plc	576,000
Tension plc ((72,600 – 4,000) × 80%)	54,880
Less impairment loss to date (W4)	(600)
	630,280
Non-controlling interest (72,600 × 20%)	14,520

Point to note

Alternative calculation for PAT of Tension plc (W2)

	£
PAT per question	18,950
Less inventory PURP	(700)
	18,250

(a) **Consolidated statement of profit or loss for the year ended 31 March 20X9**

	£
Revenue (W2)	376,167
Cost of sales (W2)	(177,867)
Gross profit	198,300
Operating costs (W2)	(88,300)
Profit from operations	110,000
Investment income (W2)	3,200
Profit before tax	113,200
Income tax expense (W2)	(57,067)
Profit for the year	56,133
Profit attributable to	
Owners of Ethos plc (β)	53,400
Non-controlling interest (W3)	2,733
	56,133

Consolidated statement of changes in equity for the year ended 31 March 20X9

	Attributable to owners of Ethos plc					
	Ordinary share capital £	General reserve £	Retained earnings £	Total £	Non-controlling interest £	Total £
Balance brought forward	500,000	–	79,300	579,300	–	579,300
Total comprehensive income for the year	–	–	53,400	53,400	2,733	56,133
Transfer between reserves (W4)	–	16,250	(16,250)	–	–	–
Added on acquisition of subsidiary	–	–	–	–	42,000	42,000
Dividend paid on ordinary shares	–	–	(30,000)	(30,000)	–	(30,000)
Balance carried forward	500,000	16,250	86,450	602,700	44,733	647,433

(b) **Time apportionment**

The results of a subsidiary are included in the consolidated accounts only from the date control is achieved.

Ethos plc acquired 75% of the issued ordinary capital of Pathos Ltd on 30 November 20X8. This is the date on which control passed and hence the date from which the results of Pathos Ltd should be reflected in the consolidated statement of profit or loss.

Therefore only profits earned by Pathos Ltd in the four months since that date are post-acquisition profits.

The remaining previous eight months profit from 1 April 20X8 to 30 November 20X8 are all pre-acquisition profits and should be included in the calculation of goodwill on consolidation.

WORKINGS

(1) **Group structure**

Ethos plc

75% (acq 30 November 20X8 ∴ 4/12 in)

Pathos Ltd

(2) **Consolidation schedule**

	Ethos plc £	4/12 Pathos Ltd £	Adj £	Consol £
Revenue	303,600	72,567	–	376,167
C of S	(143,800)	(34,067)	–	(177,867)
Op costs	(71,200)	(17,100)		(88,300)
Inv income	2,800	400		3,200
Income tax	(46,200)	(10,867)		(57,067)
PAT		10,933		

(3) **Non-controlling interest in profit for the year**

	£
25% × 10,933 (W2)	2,733

(4) **Transfer to general reserve**

	£
Ethos plc	15,000
Pathos Ltd (75% × 5,000 × 4/12)	1,250
	16,250

Points to note

1 The NCI in Pathos Ltd's reserve transfer does not appear because the two entries are cancelled out in the single NCI column

2 Alternative calculation for PAT of Pathos Ltd (W2)

	£
PAT per question 32,800 × 4/12	10,933

14 HIGG PLC

Consolidated statement of profit or loss for the year ended 30 June 20X5

	£
Revenue (1,265,900 – 36,000)	1,229,900
Cost of sales (806,400 – 36,000 + 1,800 (W1))	(772,200)
Gross profit	457,700
Operating costs (213,800 + 1,970 goodwill impairment)	(215,770)
Profit from operations	241,930
Finance cost (12,500 – 1,600)	(10,900)
Investment income (13,600 – 1,600 – 7,000 (W4))	5,000
Profit before tax	236,030
Income tax expense (W2)	(115,000)
Profit for the year	121,030
Profit attributable to	
Owners of Higg plc (β)	109,260
Non-controlling interest (W2)	11,770
	121,030

Consolidated statement of changes in equity for the year ended 30 June 20X5

	Ordinary share capital £	Preference share capital (irredeemable) £	Retained earnings £	Total £	Non-controlling interests £	Total £
		Attributable to owners of Higg plc				
Balance brought forward (W3, W5)	500,000	100,000	120,180	720,180	53,570	773,750
Total comprehensive income for the year	–	–	109,260	109,260	11,770	121,030
Dividend paid on ordinary shares (W4)	–	–	(20,000)	(20,000)	(3,000)	(23,000)
Total dividends on preference shares (irredeemable)	–	–	(8,000)	(8,000)	–	(8,000)
Balance carried forward	500,000	100,000	201,440	801,440	62,340	863,780

WORKINGS

(1) PURP (9,000 × 25/125)   £1,800

(2) **Non-controlling interest**

	£
Per draft statement of profit or loss	11,950
PURP in Flapp (1,800 (W1) × 10%)	(180)
	11,770

(3) **Retained earnings b/f**

	£
Group	
Higg plc	72,400
Flapp Ltd (90% × 46,900)	42,210
Topp Ltd (70% × (29,600 – 13,200 at acquisition))	11,480
Less goodwill impaired to 1 July 20X4	(5,910)
	120,180

(4) **Intra-group dividends and interest**

	£
Paid by Topp Ltd	
Dividends	10,000
Interest (8% × 100,000)	8,000
Received by Higg plc	
Dividends (70% × 10,000)	7,000
Interest (20% × 8,000)	1,600
Dividends received by NCI (30% × 10,000)	3,000

(5) **Non-controlling interest b/f**

Flapp Ltd

	£
Share capital	100,000
Retained earnings	46,900
	146,900
× 10%	14,690

Topp Ltd

	£
Share capital	100,000
Retained earnings	29,600
	129,600
× 30%	38,880
Total	53,570

CHAPTER 13

Associates and joint ventures

Introduction

Examination context

Topic List

Learning objectives

- Explain the relationship between a group and its associate or joint venture

- Explain the principles behind the treatment of the associate or joint venture

- Reflect an associate in group accounts by means of equity accounting

- Reflect a joint venture in group accounts by means of equity accounting

- Deal with transactions between a group and its associate or joint venture

Specific syllabus references for this chapter are: 3c, 3d, 3e 3f, 3g.

Syllabus links

More complex aspects of group financial statements will be examined at the Advanced stage. It is therefore important that you have a sound understanding of the accounting treatment of associates and joint ventures to carry forward.

Examination context

It is likely that associates and joint ventures will be examined in the context of the preparation of a consolidated statement of financial position or statement of profit or loss, within a group structure which includes at least one subsidiary. A written element of such a question could focus on an explanation of equity accounting by reference to the underlying principles. Alternatively, a 'mixed topic' question could require the preparation of extracts from the consolidated financial statements in relation to an associate or joint venture.

In the examination candidates could be required to:

- Explain the equity method and the principles behind it

- Incorporate the results of an associate in the consolidated financial statements using the equity method

- Incorporate the results of a joint venture in the consolidated financial statements using the equity method

- Explain and illustrate the difference between the relevant treatment under IFRS and UK GAAP

1 Investments in associates

1.1 Introduction

In the previous chapters we have seen that where a parent entity controls another entity (normally by holding over 50% of the ordinary share capital) it is said to have a subsidiary. The results of the parent and subsidiary are consolidated in group accounts as if they were a single entity.

However, investments can take a number of different forms. An investing entity may obtain sufficient shares such that it has **significant influence** over it, without achieving control. This type of investment is referred to as an **associate** and is dealt with by IAS 28 *Investments in Associates and Joint Ventures*.

In the first part of this chapter we will look at how to account for an associate.

1.2 Scope and definitions

IAS 27 *Separate Financial Statements* is to be applied in **accounting for investments in associates in the investor's own financial statements** as an individual company.

So **IAS 28** is to be applied in the **CFS only**. The definition of an associate is as follows:

Definitions

Associate: An entity, including an unincorporated entity such as a partnership, over which the investor has significant influence and that is neither a subsidiary nor an interest in a joint venture.

Significant influence: The power to participate in financial and operating policy decisions of the investee, but is not control or joint control over those policies.

Points to note

1 **A holding of 20% or more of the voting power** in an investee (but less than the 51% which would create a parent/subsidiary relationship) **is presumed to provide** the investor with that **significant influence**, while a holding of less than that is presumed not to do so. Both of these presumptions are rebuttable on the facts of the case.

2 It is the **mere holding of 20% which is sufficient**.

3 It is possible for an investee to be the **associate of one investor** and **the subsidiary of another**, because the former investor can still have significant influence when the latter has control. A holder of more than 75% can do most things in a company, such as passing a special resolution, without paying much attention to the other shareholders, so someone else holding 20% is unlikely to have significant influence. But it is always necessary to have regard to the facts of the case.

4 **Significant influence is evidenced in a number of ways**. It is presumed in the case of a 20% shareholding but IAS 28 also states that significant influence can be shown by one or more of the following:

- Representation on the board of directors
- Participation in policy making decisions

- Material transactions between the investor and investee
- Interchange of managerial personnel
- Provision of essential technical information

5   **Significant influence may be lost** in the same circumstances as a parent may lose control over what was a subsidiary.

1.3   Equity method

The equity method should be used in relation to **associates**, the rationale being that it reflects the **significant influence** the investor holds by making the investor answerable for the associate's overall performance, not just for the distributions received. So the investor's share of the associate should be included in the investor's financial statements.

Under the equity method, the investment in the associate is **initially recognised at cost**, but the carrying amount is then increased or decreased **by the investor's share in the post-acquisition change in the associate's net assets**.

Shares of post-acquisition profits/losses should be recognised in the investor's consolidated statement of profit or loss.

When an investment in an associate meets the 'held for sale' criteria of IFRS 5 *Non-current Assets Held For Sale and Discontinued Operations,* eg it is expected to be sold within 12 months of acquisition, it is still classified as an associate, but it is not subject to equity accounting; IFRS 5 is applied instead.

Once significant influence is lost, the investee is no longer an associate, so the investor's statements of profit or loss should subsequently include only distributions received.

The procedures used in consolidation are applied wherever possible to accounting for associates. So:

- **Profits and losses on transactions between the investor and the associate should be eliminated** to the extent of the investor's share.

- There are provisions as to **reporting dates**, adjustments for material transactions when the dates do not coincide and **uniform accounting policies** which are very similar to those for subsidiaries.

- Recognition of a share of an associate's losses should only result in the investor's interest being written down below nil (so as to become a liability) **if the investor has incurred obligations on behalf of the associate**.

The differences are that:

- **There is no cancellation of the investment against the share of the associate's net assets.** This is because there is no line-by-line addition to items in the statement of financial position of the investor's share of the associate's assets and liabilities. Such addition is appropriate under conditions of control, but not under those of significant influence.

- **There is no goodwill calculation** at the date the investment is made.

- Instead, the investor's interest in the associate is shown in the statement of financial position, **as a single line** under non-current assets.

- The **whole of that interest is subjected to an impairment review** if there is an indicator of impairment.

- That interest includes **items which are in substance a part of the investment**, such as long-term loans to the associate. But short-term receivables which will be settled in the ordinary course of business remain in current assets.

- The **investor's interest in the associate's post-tax profits less any impairment loss** is recognised in its consolidated statement of profit or loss.

1.4   Investor's separate financial statements

Under IAS 27, the investment in the associate is carried **at cost in the investor's statement of financial position**.

The knock-on effect is that the only income included in the investor's statement of profit or loss are the distributions received.

Point to note: For examination purposes you should assume that a holding of **20% or more** of the **ordinary share capital** constitutes **significant influence**.

1.5 Relationship with the group

An associate is **not part of the group** as a group comprises the parent and its subsidiaries only. In terms of the syllabus, the group investment in the associate is always held by the parent company, not a subsidiary. So:

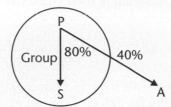

1.6 Treatment in consolidated financial statements: accounting principles

An investment in an **associate** should be accounted for in the consolidated financial statements using the **equity method** of accounting. This method reflects the **substance** of the relationship between the entities rather than their **legal form**. The **group's share** of the associate's **profits, assets and liabilities** should be included in the consolidated financial statements rather than the cost of the investment and dividend income received.

Point to note: The equity method is **only used in the group accounts** ie when the parent company holds investments in subsidiaries as well as associates. If the investor does not issue consolidated financial statements the investment will be shown in the investor's individual financial statements as described in Section 1.4 above.

2 Equity method: consolidated statement of financial position

Section overview

- The investment in the associate should be shown as a single line entry in the consolidated statement of financial position.

- If the carrying amount of the investment has suffered an impairment it should be written down to its recoverable amount.

2.1 Basic principle

An associate should be accounted for as follows:

- The interest in the associate should be presented as a **single line** under non-current assets described as '**Investments in Associates**'.

- It should initially be recognised at **cost** and is subsequently adjusted in each period for the **parent's share of the post-acquisition change in net assets (retained earnings)**.

- In group retained earnings the **group's share of the associate's post-acquisition retained earnings** should be included (as for a subsidiary).

Point to note: The assets and liabilities of the associate are **not** included on a line-by-line basis.

2.2 Calculation of carrying amount

The investment in the associate should be calculated as follows:

	£
Original cost (in P's books)	X
Share of post-acquisition change in net assets	X
	$\overline{\overline{X}}$
Less impairment losses to date	(X)
	$\overline{\overline{X}}$

Point to note: If the parent company has made any **long term loans** to the associate which are not expected to be repaid in the foreseeable future these should be **included as part of the investment in the associate**.

2.3 Initial cost of investment

At the date the investment in the associate is made it is recognised at **cost** (see Section 2.1). This represents the **investor's share of the fair value of the net assets acquired plus goodwill arising on acquisition**. This goodwill is **not separately calculated or disclosed** (the treatment with a subsidiary) but instead **is included as part of the carrying amount of the investment**. This presentation aims to avoid giving the misleading impression that the investor has acquired a goodwill asset through control over its share of the associate's individual assets and liabilities. It has only gained **significant influence** over the affairs of the associate so **no goodwill** is calculated at the date the investment is made.

If the fair value of the net assets of the associate did exceed their carrying amount, the original cost of the investment will effectively have included a fair value uplift. In this case, additional depreciation on the fair value uplift will subsequently be deducted from the investment in the associate in the statement of financial position.

2.4 Impairment losses

As a result of the above, **impairment tests** are performed in relation to the **investment as a whole**. If the investment has suffered an impairment it should be written down to its recoverable amount (see Section 2.2).

Point to note

If there is a **discount** on the purchase of the investment (ie the cost is less than the fair value of the net assets acquired) it should be recognised **in profit or loss** for the period in which the investment is made.

In practice this is unlikely to occur.

Worked example: Investment in associate

P Ltd acquired 30% of the ordinary share capital of A Ltd on 1 January 20X8 for £275,000. At that date A Ltd had retained earnings of £468,000. The fair value of its net assets was the same as the carrying value apart from a building with a fair value of £725,000 and a carrying value of £500,000. The building had 30 years of remaining useful life at 1 January 20X8. No fair value adjustment has been carried out in the books of A Ltd.

At 31 December 20X9 A Ltd had retained earnings of £521,000. This was substantially below expectations and P Ltd intends to recognise an impairment loss of £50,000 against the value of its investment in A Ltd.

What should be shown as 'investment in associate' in the financial statements of P Ltd at 31 December 20X9?

Solution

	£
Cost of investment	275,000
Share of post-acquisition increase in net assets ((521,000 – 468,000) x 30%)	15,900
Share of additional depreciation on FV uplift (((725,000 – 500,000) x 2/30) x 30%)	(4,500)
Impairment loss	(50,000)
Investment in associate	236,400

2.5 Application of the equity method in the consolidated statement of financial position

Remember that the equity method is only used in group accounts. This means that the parent has subsidiaries as well as an associate. In an examination question the practical implication of this is that you will need to produce the consolidation workings for the subsidiaries (see Chapter 11). These workings are adapted for the inclusion of the associate as follows:

Working 1: Group structure	• Include the associate in the group structure diagram
Working 6: Investment in associate	• Cost of investment • Plus share of post-acquisition retained earnings • Less any impairment losses to date
Working 5: Consolidated retained earnings (reserves)	• Include the group share of the associate's post-acquisition retained earnings • Include any impairment losses to date

The **calculation of the carrying amount of the investment in the associate** will usually be **Working 6**.

Interactive question 1: Equity method (CSFP)   [Difficulty level: Easy]

P Ltd owns 80% of S Ltd and 40% of A Ltd. Statements of financial position of the three companies at 31 December 20X8 are as follows.

	P £	S £	A £
Investment: shares in S	800	–	–
Investment: shares in A	600	–	–
Sundry assets	6,600	5,800	5,400
	8,000	5,800	5,400
Share capital – £1 ordinary shares	1,000	400	800
Retained earnings	4,000	3,400	3,600
Equity	5,000	3,800	4,400
Liabilities	3,000	2,000	1,000
	8,000	5,800	5,400

P acquired its shares in S when S's retained earnings were £520, and P acquired its shares in A when A's retained earnings were £400.

In 20X7 an impairment loss of £20 was recognised in relation to the investment in A.

Requirement

Prepare the consolidated statement of financial position at 31 December 20X8.

Fill in the proforma below.

P Ltd: Consolidated statement of financial position as at 31 December 20X8

	£
Intangibles (W3)	
Investments in associates (W6)	
Sundry assets	
	————
	════
Equity attributable to owners of the parent	
Share capital	
Retained earnings (W5)	
	————
Non-controlling interest (W4)	
Total equity	
Liabilities	
	————
	════

WORKINGS

(1) **Group structure**

(2) **Net assets**

	Year end £	Acquisition £	Post acquisition £
S Ltd			
Share capital			
Retained earnings			
	————	————	
	════	════	

(3) **Goodwill**

	£
S Ltd	
Consideration transferred	
Non-controlling interest	
Net assets	
Balance c/f	————
	════

(4) **Non-controlling interest**

	£
Share of net assets at acquisition (W2)	
Share of post-acquisition (W2)	————
	════

(5) **Retained earnings**

	£
P Ltd	
S Ltd	
A Ltd	
Impairment to date	————
	════

(6) **Investment in associate**

	£
Original cost	
Share of post-acquisition retained earnings	————
Impairment losses to date	————
	════

See **Answer** at the end of this chapter.

3 Equity method: consolidated statement of profit or loss

Section overview

Share of profit of associates should be recognised as a single line entry in the consolidated statement of profit or loss.

3.1 Basic principle

The associate should be accounted for as follows:

- The **group's share of the associate's profit after tax** should be recognised in the consolidated statement of profit or loss as a **single line entry**.

- This should be disclosed **immediately before the group profit before tax** as 'Share of profit of associates'.

- If the associate is acquired **mid-year** its results should be **time-apportioned**.

Points to note

1   It may seem odd to include an after tax amount in arriving at the profit before tax, but this is in line with the Guidance on Implementing IAS 1 *Presentation of Financial Statements*.

2   The revenues and expenses of the associate should **not** be consolidated on a line-by-line basis.

3.2 Impairment review

Where an impairment review in the current period has revealed an impairment loss to be **charged to profit or loss**, the loss should be **deducted from the parent's share of the profit after tax** of the associate (or added to the parent's share of a post-tax loss).

3.3 Application of the equity method in the consolidated statement of profit or loss

An **additional working** will be required to calculate the parent's share of the associate's profit after tax.

Point to note: The consolidation schedule (Working 2) will only include the parent and any subsidiaries as the associate is **not** consolidated.

Interactive question 2: Equity method   [Difficulty level: Easy]

P Ltd has owned 80% of S Ltd and 40% of A Ltd for several years. Statements of profit or loss for the year ended 31 December 20X8 are as follows.

	P Ltd £	S Ltd £	A Ltd £
Revenue	14,000	12,000	10,000
Cost of sales	(9,000)	(4,000)	(3,000)
Gross profit	5,000	8,000	7,000
Administrative expenses	(2,000)	(6,000)	(3,000)
Profit from operations	3,000	2,000	4,000
Investment income (not intra-group)	1,000	–	400
Profit before tax	4,000	2,000	4,400
Income tax expense	(1,000)	(1,200)	(2,000)
Profit for the year	3,000	800	2,400

An impairment loss of £120 is to be recognised in 20X8 in relation to the investment in A Ltd.

Requirement

Prepare the consolidated statement of profit or loss for the year ended 31 December 20X8.

Fill in the proforma below.

P Ltd: Consolidated statement of profit or loss for the year ending 31 December 20X8

	£
Revenue (W2)	
Cost of sales (W2)	_____
Gross profit	
Administrative expenses (W2)	_____
Profit from operations	
Investment income (W2)	
Share of profit of associates (W4)	_____
Profit before tax	
Income tax expense (W2)	_____
Profit for the year	======
Profit attributable to:	
Owners of P Ltd (β)	
Non-controlling interest (W3)	_____
	======

WORKINGS

(1) **Group structure**

(2) **Consolidation schedule**

	P Ltd £	S Ltd £	Adj £	Consol £
Revenue				
Cost of sales				
Admin expense				
Investment income				
Tax		_____		
		======		

(3) **Non-controlling interest**

	£
S Ltd	_____
	======

(4) **Share of profit of associates**

	£
A Ltd	_____
	======

See **Answer** at the end of this chapter.

4 Associate's losses

Section overview

Losses recognised in respect of the associate should be limited to the carrying amount of the associate.

4.1 Accounting treatment

Where an associate makes a loss the following treatment should be adopted:

Consolidated statement of financial position	The group's share of the loss should be recognised as a reduction in the carrying amount of the associate.
Consolidated statement of profit or loss	The group share of the post-tax loss should be recognised.

Point to note: Once the carrying amount of the investment in the associate has been **reduced to zero, no further losses should be recognised by the group**. The investor is only required to make a provision for any additional losses incurred by the associate to the extent that the investor has a legal or constructive obligation to make good these amounts.

Worked example: Associate's losses

At 31 December 20X6, the carrying amount of P Ltd's 40% interest in A Ltd is £600,000.

In the year ended 31 December 20X7 A Ltd makes a post-tax loss of £2,000,000.
The associate should be recognised in the consolidated financial statements at 31 December 20X7 as follows:

	Consolidated statement of profit or loss £	Consolidated statement of financial position £
40% × £2,000,000 = £800,000	(600,000)	Nil

The loss recognised should be limited to the carrying amount of the investment ie £600,000.

5 Transactions between a group and its associate

Section overview

- Transactions between the group and its associates should not be cancelled on consolidation.
- An adjustment is required for any unrealised profit.

5.1 Basic principle

As we said in section 1 the associate is **not** part of the group. This means that whilst the single entity concept applies to the parent and subsidiaries it does not apply to any associates. One of the consequences of this is that transactions between a group member and an associate should **not** be cancelled on consolidation.

5.2 Trading transactions

Trading transactions should **not be cancelled on consolidation**.

Consolidated statement of profit or loss	**No adjustment should be made** to revenue or cost of sales for transactions between the group and the associate.
Consolidated statement of financial position	**Receivables and payables balances** due from/to the associate in the individual statement of financial position of the parent or its subsidiaries should be carried across into the consolidated statement of financial position.

Point to note: In the consolidated statement of financial position balances relating to loans and trading balances between the group and the associate should be shown separately.

5.3 Dividends

Dividend income from the associate should **not be recorded in the consolidated statement of profit or loss**. This is because under the equity method the group's share of the associate's profit before dividends has been recognised. If the dividend income was also recognised the same profits would be **recognised twice**.

5.4 Unrealised profits

Whilst transactions between the group and the associate are not cancelled on consolidation any **unrealised profit on these transactions should be eliminated.** In this respect the principle applied is similar to that applied to a subsidiary (see Chapters 11 and 12).

But the key difference is that only the **investor's share** of the unrealised profit should be eliminated, because only this share of the associate's net assets and profit for the year is brought into the consolidated financial statements.

Unrealised profit could also arise on transactions between a subsidiary and an associate but the FAR exam will only test unrealised profit arising from transactions between the parent and an associate.

 Worked example: Unrealised profits

A sale is made by A Ltd to P Ltd. P Ltd has a 25% holding in A Ltd. All of the goods remain in inventory at the year-end.

75% of the profit made from the sale relates to interests held by other investors therefore only 25% of the profit (that part which belongs to the group) should be eliminated.

The adjustment is made in the **books of the seller**. The way that the adjustment is made depends on whether the selling company is the investor or the associate.

Points to note

1   Unrealised profit will only arise if the goods transferred **are still held by the investor or associate.** If the goods have been sold to a **third party** there is **no unrealised profit**.

2   Unrealised profit adjustments apply to the **transfer of non-current assets** as well as the transfer of goods.

5.4.1 Investor (parent) sells goods to the associate

Consolidated statement of financial position:

- Reduce P's **retained earnings by its share of the unrealised profit.**
- Reduce the **carrying amount of the investment in A** by P's share of the unrealised profit.

Point to note

The carrying amount of the associate is adjusted rather than inventory as the inventory of the associate is **not consolidated**.

Consolidated statement of profit or loss:

- Increase P's cost of sales **by its share of the unrealised profit**.

Point to note: This adjustment **reduces group profit by its share of the unrealised profit**.

Interactive question 3: Unrealised profits (P → A)   [Difficulty level: Exam standard]

P Ltd owns 35% of A Ltd. During the current financial year P Ltd sold goods to A Ltd for £300,000 on which its gross margin was 40%. A Ltd held £50,000 of these goods in its inventories at the year end.

Requirement

Show the journal entries necessary to adjust for the PURP in P Ltd's consolidated statement of financial position and set out the adjustment necessary to P Ltd's consolidated statement of profit or loss.

Fill in the proforma below.

Consolidated statement of financial position journal

	£	£
DR		
CR		

Consolidated statement of profit or loss

See **Answer** at the end of this chapter.

5.4.2 Associate sells goods to the investor (parent)

Consolidated statement of financial position

- **Reduce P's share of A's retained earnings** by its **share of the unrealised profit**.
- **Reduce P's inventory** on consolidation by its **share of the unrealised profit**.

Point to note

The effect on retained earnings is dealt with by **deducting the group share of the unrealised profit from the group retained earnings** and from **group inventory**.

Consolidated statement of profit or loss

- **Reduce P's share of A's profits after tax** by its **share of the unrealised profit**.

Interactive question 4: Unrealised profits (A → P)   [Difficulty level: Exam standard]

Assume the same facts as in Interactive Question 3 except that A Ltd is the seller and P Ltd holds the £50,000 goods in inventory.

Requirements

(a) Show the journal entries to adjust for the PURP in P Ltd's consolidated statement of financial position.

(b) If A Ltd has profit after tax of £75,000 calculate the share of profit of associates figure which should appear in the consolidated statement of profit or loss.

Fill in the proforma below.

(a) **Journal – consolidated statement of financial position**

	£	£

DR
CR

(b) **Share of profit of associates for consolidated statement of profit or loss**

	£

Associate's PAT
× group share
Less PURP

See **Answer** at the end of this chapter.

5.5 Disclosures

The minimum disclosures are:

- The **fair value** for an investment in any associate for which there are published price quotations (ie the associate's securities are dealt in on a public market).

- **Summarised financial statements** of the associate.

- **Reasons** why the investor thinks the 20% presumptions are overcome, if that is the case.

- The associate's **reporting date**, if different from that of the investor.

- **Restrictions** on funds transfers from the associate.

- **Losses in the associate**, both current period and cumulative, which have not been recognised in the investor's financial statements (because the investment has already been written down to nil).

- The **investment** to be shown as a non-current asset in the statement of financial position.

- The **investor's share** of the associate's:

  - **After-tax profits**, to be shown in the investor's statement of profit or loss

  - **Discontinued operations**

  - **Changes in equity** recognised directly in equity, to be shown in other comprehensive income in the investor's statement of profit or loss and other comprehensive income

  - **Contingent liabilities**

6 IFRS 11 *Joint Arrangements*

Section overview

- IFRS 11 classifies joint arrangements as either **joint operations** or **joint ventures**.
- There must be a **contractual arrangement** for a joint arrangement to exist

6.1 What is a joint arrangement?

Definition

A **joint arrangement** is a contractual arrangement whereby two or more parties undertake an economic activity that is subject to joint control.

The key characteristics of a joint arrangement are that:

- The parties have a contractual agreement between themselves
- The agreement results in them having **joint control** over the shared activities

Definitions

Joint control is the contractually agreed sharing of control over an arrangement, which exists only when the decisions about the relevant activities require the unanimous consent of the parties sharing control.

A **party to a joint arrangement** is an entity that participates in a joint arrangement, regardless of whether that entity has control of the arrangement.

6.2 Context

Entities often operate together as strategic alliances to overcome commercial barriers and share risks. These alliances are often contractually structured as joint arrangements. The objective of a joint arrangement may be to carry out a one-off project, to focus on one area of operations or to develop new products jointly for a new market. The joint arrangement focuses on the parties' complementary skills and resources. The creation of synergies amongst the parties creates value for each. Joint arrangements provide the opportunity for organisations to obtain a critical mass and more competitive pricing.

There are many factors critical to the success of joint arrangements, the most important being the relationship between the parties. It is essential that all contractual terms and arrangements are agreed in advance including the process for resolving disputes. An exit strategy should be developed and the terms for dissolution agreed between the parties at the outset. It is particularly important that the agreement identifies the party which will at dissolution retain any proprietary knowledge held within the joint arrangement.

The different joint arrangement structures available provide challenges for financial reporting. The unique risks of joint arrangements need to be readily apparent to users of financial statements, since their financial and operational risks may be substantially different from those of other members of the reporting group.

6.3 Forms of joint arrangement

IFRS 11 *Joint Arrangements* identifies, and deals with, two types of joint arrangement:

- Joint operations
- Joint ventures

Only joint ventures are included in the FAR syllabus

7 Joint operations

Section overview

- A joint operation is structured differently from a joint venture.

7.1 What is a joint operation?

This is a joint arrangement whereby the parties that have joint control (the joint operators) have rights to the assets and obligations for the liabilities of that joint arrangement.

A joint arrangement that is **not structured through a separate entity** is always a **joint operation**.

If the arrangement is structured through a separate entity it may be **either a joint operation or a joint venture.** Classification depends upon the rights and obligations of the parties to the arrangement

The **substance** of this type of joint arrangement is that each party is carrying on its own activities as a separate part of its own business and the accounting procedures reflect this.

A party to a joint operation will recognise its share of the assets, liabilities, revenue and expenses of the joint operation.

8 Joint ventures

Section overview

- Joint ventures are separate legal entities, so they should prepare their own financial statements.

- In the consolidated statements of the venturer the results and position of the joint venture should be included using the equity method of accounting.

- The equity method of accounting is the same as that used for accounting for associates in accordance with IAS 28 *Investments in Associates and Joint Ventures.*

8.1 What is a joint venture?

This is a joint arrangement whereby the parties that have joint control of the arrangement have **rights to the net assets** of the arrangement.

The key identifying factor for a joint venture is that in this type of arrangement a **separate legal entity** is set up, with the ownership of that entity being shared by the venturers.

This separate entity may be a:

- Company or
- Partnership

As a separate legal entity the joint venture can enter into contracts and raise finance in its own name. It will maintain its own accounting records and prepare its own financial statements.

The joint venture will own its own assets, incur its own liabilities, incur its own expenses and earn its own income.

Normally each joint venturer will be entitled to a pre-determined share of the profits made by the joint venture.

An **investor** in a joint venture is a party to a joint venture that does **not** have joint control over that joint venture. If the investor has significant influence, he should account for his investment in accordance with IAS 28. If he does not have significant influence he should account for it as a financial asset.

Worked example: Joint venturers and investors

An entity is established to build a sports stadium for a customer. Once the stadium is built, the entity will be wound up.

Eight contractors invest in the equity of the entity. Contractors 1 to 5 own 14% each and contractors 6 to 8 own 10% each. There is a contractual arrangement whereby all relevant decisions are taken unanimously by contractors 1, 2, 3 and 8.

Do these arrangements give rise to a joint venture? If so, who are the venturers and who are the investors?

Solution

The contractual agreement provides for joint control. The contractors who are parties to the contractual agreement are Contractors 1, 2, 3 and 8. Between them they own 52% ((3 × 14%) + 10%) of the entity and the contractual agreement provides that decisions are taken unanimously by them, so they have joint control over it. There is a joint venture as far as they are concerned and they are venturers.

The other contractors are not involved in the contractual arrangement and therefore are only investors in the joint venture.

A **contractual arrangement** will usually be in writing either as a formal document or in the form of minutes from a meeting. It will normally cover the purpose of the joint venture, its expected duration, any financial reporting requirements, appointments to the managing committee, voting rights, capital contributions, procedures for running the day to day operations and how expenses and income are to be shared.

8.2 Accounting for joint ventures

IFRS 11 requires each venturer in a joint venture to recognise in its **consolidated financial statements** its share of the venture using the **equity method of accounting**.

8.3 Equity method of accounting

You have used the equity method of accounting when accounting for associates under IAS 28.

Under the equity method:

- The investment in the joint venture is initially recorded at cost.

- There are adjustments each period for the venturer's share of the post-acquisition reserves of the joint venture, less any impairment losses. Profits are added to the investment and losses deducted.

- In the venturer's consolidated **statement of financial position** the investment in the joint venture is shown as a single line figure as part of non-current assets.

- In the venturer's consolidated **statement of profit or loss** there is a single line for the share of the joint venture's results.

- The group share of the joint venture's other comprehensive income will be included in the consolidated statement of profit or loss and other comprehensive income.

Worked example: Joint venture

AB controls a number of subsidiaries and therefore prepares consolidated financial statements.

AB is also a venturer in JV, a joint venture in which AB owns 25%. AB acquired its share of JV at a cost of £1 million on the creation of JV. At that time JV had net assets of £4 million.

A summarised draft statement of financial position of the AB Group (AB and its subsidiaries, but not its interest in JV), and JV is as follows:

	AB Group £m	JV £m
Non-current assets		
Property, plant and equipment	60	20
Intangibles	30	8
Investment in JV	1	0
Current assets		
Inventories	50	16
Other	80	24
Current liabilities	(90)	(36)
	131	32

Equity

	£m
The equity in AB Group plus JV can be calculated as:	
AB Group	131
JV post-acquisition ((32 – 4) × 25%)	7
	138

Requirement

Using the equity method prepare the AB Group consolidated statement of financial position including JV.

Solution

	£m
Non-current assets	
Property, plant and equipment	60
Intangibles	30
Investment in JV (cost £1m plus 25% x increase in retained reserves [£28m])	8
	98
Current assets	
Inventories	50
Other	80
	228
Equity and liabilities	
Equity	138
Current liabilities	90
	228

8.4 Transactions between a venturer and the joint venture

In joint ventures adjustments similar to those in respect of associates are required where there are sales or purchases between the venturer and the joint venture. An adjustment is required for any **profit** on the transaction that is internal to the entity.

If a venturer sells an asset to the joint venture at a profit and the asset is still held by the joint venture:

- The proportion of the asset that is consolidated includes an element of profit recorded by the venturer.

- This should be removed as it is unrealised profit.

- What remains is only the profit that relates to the share of the asset relating to the other venturers.

Where a venturer purchases assets from the joint venture the venturer's share of the profit made by the joint venture should not be recognised until the asset is sold to a third party.

Where a loss is made on a transaction between the venturer and joint venture, it should be recognised immediately if it represents a reduction in realisable value of current assets or an impairment loss.

8.5 Receivables and payables

If there are receivables or payables outstanding between a joint venture and the venturer the outstanding balances between the venturer and the joint venture should **not** be eliminated.

Interactive question 5: Joint venture
[Difficulty level: Intermediate]

Bodmas plc acquired 30% of the equity capital of a joint venture, Matrix Ltd, in 20X2 when the reserves of Matrix were £120 million. It is currently preparing its financial statements for the year ending 31 December 20X5.

The summary statements of financial position for Bodmas and Matrix at 31 December 20X5 were as follows.

	Bodmas plc £m	Matrix Ltd £m
Property, plant and equipment	820	320
Investment in Matrix	100	–
Current assets	240	160
Loan to Matrix	60	–
	1,220	480
Share capital (£1 shares)	780	100
Retained earnings	440	320
Loan from Bodmas	–	60
	1,220	480

Requirement

Prepare the summarised consolidated statement of financial position of Bodmas plc at 31 December 20X5 using the equity method in accordance with IAS 28 *Investments in Associates and Joint Ventures* .

Fill in the proforma below.

Consolidated statement of financial position

	£m
Non-current assets	
Property, plant and equipment	
Investment in JV	
Current assets	
Loan	
Other	
Equity	
Share capital	
Retained earnings	

See **Answer** at the end of this chapter.

9 IFRS 12 *Disclosure of Interests in Other Entities*

Section overview

IFRS 12 sets out the disclosure requirements for associates and joint ventures.

9.1 Significant judgments and assumptions

IFRS 12 sets out the sort of facts that would be made regarding significant judgements and assumptions (and changes to those judgements and assumptions) regarding an entity. The focus would be on how the entity concluded that it controlled another entity or how it determined that it had joint control and/or was a party to a joint arrangement, and what the nature of the joint arrangement was. For example, disclosures might discuss why or how an entity does not control another entity even though it holds more than half of the voting rights of the other entity, or how and why it does control another entity even though it holds less than half of the voting rights of the other entity.

9.2 Disclosures

The following disclosures are required in respect of associates and joint arrangements:

- Nature, extent and financial effects of an entity's interests in associates or joint arrangements, including name of the investee, principal place of business, the investor's interest in the investee, method of accounting for the investee and restrictions on the investee's ability to transfer funds to the investor.

- Risks associated with an interest in an associate or joint venture.

- Summarised financial information, with more detail required for joint ventures than for associates.

10 UK GAAP comparison

Section overview

There are some differences between FRS 102 and IFRS in accounting for associates and joint ventures.

FRS 101 does not provide any disclosure exemptions.

10.1 Associates and joint ventures

FRS 102	IFRS
Implicit goodwill is recognised on acquisition of an interest in an associate or joint venture, being the difference between the consideration transferred and the investor's share of the fair value of the net assets. This amount is then amortised.	No implicit goodwill is recognised or amortised.
FRS 102 does not require such detailed information about the investee or about risks associated with the investment.	IFRS 12 specifies disclosure requirements for interests in associates and joint ventures as per 9.2 above.

FRS 101 does not grant any disclosure exemptions in respect of IAS 28, IFRS 11 or IFRS 12.

Summary and Self-test

Summary

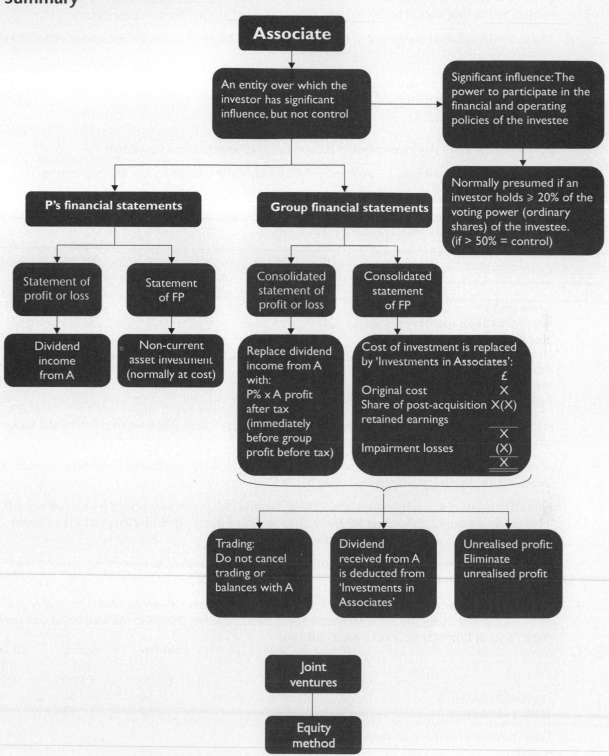

Associate

An entity over which the investor has significant influence, but not control

Significant influence: The power to participate in the financial and operating policies of the investee

Normally presumed if an investor holds ⩾ 20% of the voting power (ordinary shares) of the investee. (if > 50% = control)

P's financial statements

Group financial statements

Statement of profit or loss

Statement of FP

Consolidated statement of profit or loss

Consolidated statement of FP

Dividend income from A

Non-current asset investment (normally at cost)

Replace dividend income from A with:
P% x A profit after tax (immediately before group profit before tax)

Cost of investment is replaced by 'Investments in Associates':

	£
Original cost	X
Share of post-acquisition retained earnings	X(X)
	X
Impairment losses	(X)
	X

Trading:
Do not cancel trading or balances with A

Dividend received from A is deducted from 'Investments in Associates'

Unrealised profit:
Eliminate unrealised profit

Joint ventures

Equity method

ICAEW

Self-test

Answer the following questions

1   Durie plc has many subsidiary companies. On 1 January 20X6 Durie plc bought 30% of the share capital of Edberg Ltd for £6,660. The retained earnings of Edberg Ltd at that date were £13,000 and the fair value of its assets less liabilities was £20,000. The excess of fair value over carrying amount related to a plot of land which was still owned at 31 December 20X9; its fair value was unchanged at that date. The fair value was not reflected in the books of Edberg Ltd.

The summarised draft statement of financial position of Edberg Ltd on 31 December 20X9 includes the following.

	£
Share capital – £1 ordinary shares	5,000
Retained earnings	17,000
Total equity	22,000

By the end of 20X9 the investment in Edberg Ltd had been impaired by £264.

At what amount should the investment in Edberg Ltd be shown using the equity method on 31 December 20X9?

2   Extracts from the statements of profit or loss of Pik plc and its subsidiaries and Wik Ltd, its associate, for the year ended 31 March 20X6 are as follows.

	Pik plc (inc subsidiaries) £'000	Wik Ltd £'000
Gross profit	2,900	1,600
Administrative expenses	(750)	(170)
Distribution costs	(140)	(190)
Dividends from Wik Ltd	20	–
Profit before tax	2,030	1,240
Income tax expense	(810)	(440)
Profit for the year	1,220	800

Pik plc acquired 25% of the ordinary shares in Wik Ltd on 1 April 20X3 when the retained earnings of Wik Ltd were £80,000.

At what amount should the profit before tax be shown in the consolidated statement of profit or loss of Pik plc for the year ended 31 March 20X6?

3   Albert Ltd owns many subsidiaries and 25% of Victoria Ltd. In the year ended 31 December 20X5 Albert Ltd sold goods to Victoria for £400,000, earning a gross profit of 20%. Victoria Ltd held £120,000 of them in its inventories at the year end.

By what amount should Albert Ltd's cost of sales be increased when preparing its consolidated statement of profit or loss?

4   Austen plc has owned 100% of Kipling Ltd and 30% of Dickens Ltd, an associate, for many years. At 31 December 20X5 the trade receivables and trade payables shown in the individual company statements of financial position were as follows.

	Austen plc £'000	Kipling Ltd £'000	Dickens Ltd £'000
Trade receivables	50	30	40
Trade payables	30	15	20
Trade payables included amounts owing to:			
Austen plc	–	–	–
Kipling Ltd	2	–	4
Dickens Ltd	7	–	–
Other suppliers	21	15	16
	30	15	20

The inter-company accounts agreed after taking into account the following.

(1) A sales invoice for £3,000 posted by Kipling Ltd on 31 December 20X5 was not received by Austen plc until 2 January 20X6.

(2) A cheque for £6,000 posted by Austen plc on 30 December 20X5 was not received by Dickens Ltd until 4 January 20X6.

What amount should be shown as trade receivables in the consolidated statement of financial position of Austen plc?

5   H plc and its subsidiaries (S1 and S2) and associate (A) have the following inter-company balances at the year end.

	H £'000	S1 £'000	S2 £'000	A £'000
H with A	50 CR			50 DR
S2 with A			75 DR	
S1 with A		80 CR		80 DR

All the differences related to cash in transit and where this is the case adjustments are to be made in the books of the receiving company.

After making the necessary adjustments to reflect the above, what amounts due to or from associates should be recognised in the consolidated statement of financial position at the year end?

6   Helen plc, a company with several subsidiaries, acquired 35% of Troy Ltd on 1 January 20X6 for £90,000. At that date Troy Ltd had share capital of £70,000 and retained earnings of £96,000. It also owns a plot of land which had a fair value of £60,000 compared to a carrying amount of £42,000; this fair value has not been incorporated into the books of Troy Ltd and the fair value is unchanged at 31 December 20X9. Since the investment was made, Troy Ltd has made total profits after tax of £118,000 including £110,000 made in the current year. The investment in Troy Ltd has become impaired by £2,560 during the current year.

What is the net amount to be included in the consolidated statement of profit or loss for the year ended 31 December 20X9 in respect of Troy Ltd?

7   On 1 January 20X0 Adam Ltd purchased 30% of Eve Ltd for £55,000. At this date the retained earnings of Eve Ltd stood at £60,000 and the fair value of net assets, which was subsequently reflected in Eve Ltd's books, was £170,000. The excess of fair value over carrying amount related to a plot of land which was still owned at 31 December 20X4.

The statement of financial position of Eve Ltd on 31 December 20X4 showed the following.

	£
Share capital	100,000
Revaluation surplus	10,000
Retained earnings	200,000
Total equity	310,000

At what amount should Adam Ltd's investment in Eve Ltd be stated in its consolidated statement of financial position at 31 December 20X4?

8   Drought plc became a venturer in a joint venture by acquiring 40% of the ordinary shares of Deluge Ltd, on 1 January 20X7 for £250,000. At that date Deluge Ltd had retained earnings of £210,000 and a factory building with a fair value £60,000 in excess of its carrying amount and a remaining useful life of 20 years. No fair value adjustment has been carried out in the books of Deluge Ltd. At 31 December 20X9 Deluge Ltd had retained earnings of £420,000.

What amount should be shown as 'investment in joint venture' in the consolidated statement of financial position of Drought plc at 31 December 20X9?

9 HALEY PLC

The draft statements of financial position of three companies as at 31 December 20X9 are set out below.

	Haley plc £	Socrates Ltd £	Aristotle Ltd £
Property, plant and equipment	300,000	100,000	160,000
Investments at cost			
18,000 shares in Socrates Ltd	75,000	–	–
18,000 shares in Aristotle Ltd	30,000	–	–
Current assets	345,000	160,000	80,000
	750,000	260,000	240,000
Ordinary shares of £1 each	250,000	30,000	60,000
Retained earnings	400,000	180,000	100,000
Total equity	650,000	210,000	160,000
Current liabilities	100,000	50,000	80,000
	750,000	260,000	240,000

The retained earnings of Socrates Ltd and Aristotle Ltd when the investments were acquired eight years ago were £70,000 and £30,000 respectively.

Impairment reviews to date have resulted in the need for the following amounts to be written off Haley plc's investments.

	£
Socrates Ltd	12,000
Aristotle Ltd	2,400

Requirement

Prepare the consolidated statement of financial position as at 31 December 20X9.   **(10 marks)**

10 CORFU LTD

Corfu Ltd holds 80% of the ordinary share capital of Zante Ltd (acquired on 1 February 20X9) and 30% of the ordinary share capital of Paxos Ltd. Paxos Ltd is a joint venture set up by Corfu Ltd and two other venturers on 1 July 20X8. The contractual agreement provides for joint control of Paxos Ltd. Corfu Ltd uses the equity method of accounting wherever possible.

The draft statements of profit or loss for the year ended 30 June 20X9 are set out below.

	Corfu Ltd £'000	Zante Ltd £'000	Paxos Ltd £'000
Revenue	12,614	6,160	8,640
Cost of sales and expenses	(11,318)	(5,524)	(7,614)
Trading profit	1,296	636	1,026
Dividends received from Zante Ltd	171	–	–
Profit before tax	1,467	636	1,026
Income tax expense	(621)	(275)	(432)
Profit for the year	846	361	594

Included in the inventory of Paxos Ltd at 30 June 20X9 was £150,000 for goods purchased from Corfu Ltd in May 20X9, which the latter company had invoiced at cost plus 25%. These were the only goods Corfu Ltd sold to Paxos Ltd but it did make sales of £50,000 to Zante Ltd during the year. None of these goods remained in Zante Ltd's inventory at the year end.

Requirement

Prepare a consolidated statement of profit or loss for Corfu Ltd for the year ended 30 June 20X9.

(8 marks)

11   KING LTD

King Ltd acquired shares in two other companies as follows.

Company	Acquisition date	Shares acquired %	Goodwill on acquisition £	Retained earnings at acquisition £
Prawn Ltd	1 October 20X7	80	90,000	260,000
Madras Ltd	31 December 20X5	25	–	340,000

The results and changes in retained earnings of the three companies for the year ended 30 September 20X9 are as follows.

	King Ltd £'000	Prawn Ltd £'000	Madras Ltd £'000
Revenue	800	430	600
Dividend from Prawn Ltd	40	–	–
Dividend from Madras Ltd	10	–	–
Cost of sales and expenses	(550)	(255)	(440)
Profit before tax	300	175	160
Income tax expense	(80)	(45)	(60)
Profit for the year	220	130	100

	Retained earnings		
	King Ltd £'000	Prawn Ltd £'000	Madras Ltd £'000
Balance brought forward	600	320	540
Total comprehensive income for the year	220	130	100
Dividends paid	(110)	(50)	(40)
Balance carried forward	710	400	600

You are also given the following information.

(1) During the year King Ltd made sales of £80,000 to Prawn Ltd at a gross profit of 25%. At the year end Prawn Ltd still held £36,000 of these goods in inventory.

(2) Impairment reviews at the following dates revealed the following amounts to be written off in respect of King Ltd's investment in Prawn Ltd and Madras Ltd.

	Prawn Ltd £'000	Madras Ltd £'000
Review at		
30 September 20X8	9	17
30 September 20X9	9	6

Requirement

Prepare the consolidated statement of profit or loss and the retained earnings column in the consolidated statement of changes in equity of the King Ltd group for the year ended 30 September 20X9. Work to the nearest £'000.   **(13 marks)**

12   WATER LTD

The draft statements of financial position of three companies as at 30 September 20X5 are as follows.

	Water Ltd £	Hydrogen Ltd £	Oxygen Ltd £
Non-current assets			
Property, plant and equipment	697,210	648,010	349,400
Investments			
160,000 shares in Hydrogen Ltd	562,000	–	–
80,000 shares in Oxygen Ltd	184,000	–	–
	1,443,210	648,010	349,400
Current assets			
Inventories	495,165	388,619	286,925
Trade receivables	415,717	320,540	251,065
Cash	101,274	95,010	80,331
Total assets	2,455,366	1,452,179	967,721
Equity			
Ordinary share capital	600,000	200,000	200,000
Retained earnings	1,015,000	820,000	463,000
Total equity	1,615,000	1,020,000	663,000
Non-current liabilities	400,000	150,000	100,000
Current liabilities			
Trade payables	440,366	282,179	204,721
Total equity and liabilities	2,455,366	1,452,179	967,721

You are given the following additional information.

(1)   Water Ltd purchased the shares in Hydrogen Ltd on 1 October 20X0 when the retained earnings of Hydrogen Ltd were £500,000. The goodwill and non-controlling interest arising on the acquisition of Hydrogen Ltd should be measured using the proportionate method.

(2)   The shares in Oxygen Ltd were acquired on 1 October 20X2 when its retained earnings were £242,000.

(3)   Included in the inventory figure for Water Ltd is inventory valued at £20,000 which had been purchased from Hydrogen Ltd at cost plus 25%.

(4)   Included in the trade payables figure of Water Ltd is £18,000 payable to Oxygen Ltd, the amount receivable being recorded in the trade receivables figure of Oxygen Ltd.

(5)   Impairment reviews to date have revealed a total of £1,000 to be written off goodwill in respect of Hydrogen Ltd and £2,000 off in respect of Water Ltd's investment in Oxygen Ltd.

Requirements

(a)   Prepare the consolidated statement of financial position for Water Ltd as at 30 September 20X5.   **(13 marks)**

(b)   Identify the required accounting treatment for different levels of investment in undertakings for consolidated accounts purposes, explaining why these are appropriate.   **(4 marks)**

(c)   Set out a brief explanation in note form of how subsidiaries and associates are accounted for in the consolidated statement of financial position.   **(4 marks)**

(21 marks)

13 MINNIE PLC

Minnie plc has a number of wholly-owned subsidiaries and a 50% interest in Mouse Ltd, an entity set up and controlled jointly with a third party.

The statements of financial position of the two entities as at 31 December 20X5 are as follows:

	Minnie Group £'000	Mouse Ltd £'000
Non-current assets		
Property, plant and equipment	406	160
Investment in Mouse Ltd	10	
	416	160
Current assets		
Inventories	100	50
Others	200	110
	716	320
Equity		
Share capital	200	20
Retained earnings	366	180
	566	200
Current liabilities	150	120
	716	320

Their respective statements of profit or loss for the year ended 31 December 20X5 are as follows:

	Minnie Group £'000	Mouse Ltd £'000
Revenue	490	312
Cost of sales and expenses	(280)	(200)
Dividend from Mouse Ltd	20	–
Profit before tax	230	112
Income tax expense	(100)	(32)
Profit for the year	130	80

Dividends recognised in the statement of changes in equity during the period:	60	40

During December 20X5 Minnie plc transferred goods to Mouse Ltd for £50,000. Minnie plc sells goods at a mark-up of 25%. Mouse Ltd had not paid Minnie plc's invoice or sold any of the goods to third parties by the year end.

No dividends from Mouse Ltd are outstanding in Minnie plc's books.

Requirement

Prepare a consolidated statement of financial position and statement of profit or loss for Minnie plc and its joint venture as at 31 December 20X5 using equity accounting. **(8 marks)**

Now, go back to the Learning objectives in the Introduction. If you are satisfied you have achieved these objectives, please tick them off.

Point to note: The following sets out the examinability of the standards covered in this chapter.

IAS 28   All paragraphs are examinable.
IFRS 11   Only joint ventures are examinable in full. Only knowledge of the existence of other joint arrangements is required.

The paragraphs listed below are the key references you should be familiar with.

IAS 28 *Investments in Associates and Joint Ventures*

Definitions

• The investor has joint control or significant influence over an investee.	IAS 28 (2)
• Significant influence is the power to participate in financial and operating policy decisions of the investee, but is not control or joint control of those policies.	
• A joint venture is a joint arrangement whereby the parties that have joint control of the arrangement have rights to the net assets of the arrangement.	IAS 28 (3)
• Presumptions with regard to less than 20%, 20% or more for an associate.	IAS 28 (6)
• Can be an associate, even if the subsidiary of another investor.	
• No significant influence if 'associate' in legal reorganisation and so on.	IAS 28 (10)

Equity method

• In statement of financial position: joint venture or associate presented as non-current asset = cost plus share of post-acquisition profit or loss.	IAS 28 (10)
• In statement of profit or loss: share of joint venture or associate's post-tax profits less any impairment loss.	IAS 28 (10)
• In other comprehensive income: share of changes to investee's other comprehensive income.	IAS 28 (10)
• Use cost/under IAS 39 to account in investor's separate financial statements.	IAS 28 (44)
• An entity which is exempt from preparing CFS under the exemptions in IFRS 10 need not apply the equity method.	IAS 28 (17)
• Investment or portion of investment which is held for sale should be accounted for under IFRS 5.	IAS 28 (20)

IFRS 11 *Joint Arrangements*

• A joint arrangement is an arrangement in which two or more parties have joint control and are bound by a contractual arrangement.	IFRS 11 (5)
• A joint venture gives venturers joint control and rights to the net assets of the arrangement.	IFRS 11 (16)
• A joint venturer's interest in a joint venture is recognised as an investment and accounted for using the equity method in accordance with IAS 28.	IFRS 11 (24)
• A party that participates in a joint venture but has neither joint control nor significant influence should account for its interest in accordance with IFRS 9 (IAS 39).	IFRS 11
• In its separate financial statements a joint venture shall account for its interest in a joint venture at cost or in accordance with IFRS 9 (IAS 39).	IFRS 11 (26)

IFRS 12 *Disclosure of Interests in Other Entities*

- An entity should disclose information that enables users to evaluate:

    – The nature, extent and financial effects of its interests in joint arrangements   IFRS 12 (21)
      and associates.

    – The nature of, and changes in, the risks associated with its interests in joint   IFRS 12 (23)
      ventures and associates.

Answers to Interactive questions

Answer to Interactive question 1

P Ltd: Consolidated statement of financial position as at 31 December 20X8

	£
Intangibles (W3)	64
Investments in associates (W6)	1,860
Sundry assets (6,600 + 5,800)	12,400
	14,324
Equity attributable to owners of the parent	
Share capital	1,000
Retained earnings (W5)	7,564
	8,564
Non-controlling interest (W4)	760
Total equity	9,324
Liabilities (3,000 + 2,000)	5,000
	14,324

WORKINGS

(1) **Group structure**

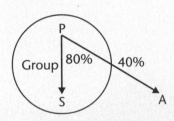

(2) **Net assets**

	Year end £	Acquisition £	Post-acquisition £
S Ltd			
Share capital	400	400	–
Retained earnings	3,400	520	2,880
	3,800	920	

(3) **Goodwill**

	£
S Ltd	
Consideration transferred	800
Non-controlling interest at acquisition (20% × 920 (W2))	184
Net assets at acquisition	(920)
Goodwill	64

(4) **Non-controlling interest at year end**

	£
Share of net assets at acquisition (20% × 920 (W2))	184
Share of post-acquisition (20% × 2,880 (W2))	576
	760

(5) **Retained earnings**

	£
P Ltd	4,000
S Ltd (80% × 2,880 (W2))	2,304
A Ltd (40% × (3,600 – 400))	1,280
Impairment to date	(20)
	7,564

(6) Investment in associate

	£
Original cost	600
Share of post-acquisition retained earnings (40% × (3,600 – 400))	1,280
	1,880
Impairment losses to date	(20)
	1,860

Answer to Interactive question 2

P Ltd: Consolidated statement of profit or loss for the year ending 31 December 20X8

	£
Revenue (W2)	26,000
Cost of sales (W2)	(13,000)
Gross profit	13,000
Administrative expenses (W2)	(8,000)
Profit from operations	5,000
Investment income (W2)	1,000
Share of profit of associates (W4)	840
Profit before tax	6,840
Income tax expense (W2)	(2,200)
Profit for the year	4,640

Profit attributable to:	
Owners of P Ltd (β)	4,480
Non-controlling interest (W3)	160
	4,640

WORKINGS

(1) Group structure

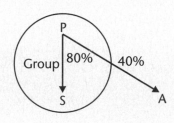

(2) Consolidation schedule

	P Ltd £	S Ltd £	Adj £	Consol £
Revenue	14,000	12,000		26,000
Cost of sales	(9,000)	(4,000)		(13,000)
Admin expenses	(2,000)	(6,000)		(8,000)
Inv. income	1,000	–		1,000
Tax	(1,000)	(1,200)		(2,200)
		800		

(3) Non-controlling interest

	£
S Ltd (20% × 800 (W2))	160

(4) Share of profit of associates

	£
A Ltd ((40% × 2,400) – 120)	840

Answer to Interactive question 3

Consolidated statement of financial position journal

	£	£
DR P's retained earnings (35% × (50,000 × 40%))	7,000	
CR Investment in A		7,000

Consolidated statement of profit or loss

In the consolidation schedule increase P's cost of sales by £7,000 (50,000 × 40% × 35%). This reduces P's profit by £7,000.

Answer to Interactive question 4

(a) Consolidated statement of financial position journal

	£	£
DR Group retained earnings (35% × (50,000 × 40%))	7,000	
CR Group inventories		7,000

(b) Share of profit of associates for consolidated statement of profit or loss

	£
Associate's PAT	75,000
Group share × 35%	26,250
Less: PURP	(7,000)
	19,250

Answer to Interactive question 5

Consolidated statement of financial position as at 31 December 20X5

	£m
Non-current assets	
Property, plant and equipment	820
Investment in JV (100 + ((320 – 120) × 30%))	160
	980
Current assets	
Loan	60
Other	240
	300
Total assets	1,280
Equity	
Share capital	780
Retained earnings (440 + ((320 – 120) × 30%))	500
Total equity	1,280

1 £7,596

	£
Cost of investment in Edberg Ltd	6,660
Share of post acquisition change in net assets	
(calculated as 30% × change in retained earnings (17,000 – 13,000))	1,200
	7,860
Impairment losses to date	(264)
	7,596

Tutorial note:

If

(a)   The amount of the fair value adjustment is the same at the end of the reporting period and the date the investment is made; and

(b)   It has not been reflected in the associate's books, then it can be omitted from the calculation of the post-acquisition change in the associate's net assets.

2 £2,210,000

	£'000
Pik plc (incl subsidiaries)	
Gross profit	2,900
Less: Administrative expenses	(750)
Distribution costs	(140)
Share of profit of associates (25% × 800)	200
	2,210

3 Albert Ltd's share of the profit it recognised in respect of the goods held in inventories should be eliminated, so 25% × £120,000 × 20% = £6,000.

4 £75,000

	£'000	£'000
Austen plc		50
Kipling Ltd	30	
Less Intra group (2 + 3)	(5)	
		25
		75

Do not cancel balances with Dickens Ltd as Dickens Ltd is an associate.

5 £130,000 due to associates

All balances with associates are retained on consolidation.

	£'000
H	50 CR
S1	80 CR
	130 CR

The £75,000 DR in S2 disappears once adjustment has been made for cash in transit.

6 £35,940

	£
Share of PAT (110,000 × 35%)	38,500
Less impairment	(2,560)
	35,940

CHAPTER

13

7 £97,000

	£
Cost of investment in Eve Ltd	55,000
Share of post acquisition change in net assets (30% × (310,000 – 170,000))	42,000
	97,000

As the excess of fair value over carrying amount at the date the investment was made was subsequently reflected in Eve Ltd's books, no fair value adjustment needs to be made at 31 December 20X4.

8 £330,400

	£
Cost of investment	250,000
Share of post acquisition increase in net assets ((420,000 – 210,000) × 40%)	84,000
Share of depreciation on FVA ((60,000 × 3/20) × 40%)	(3,600)
Investment in joint venture	330,400

9 HALEY PLC

Consolidated statement of financial position as at 31 December 20X9

	£
ASSETS	
Non-current assets	
Property, plant and equipment (300,000 + 100,000)	400,000
Intangibles (W3)	3,000
Investments in associates (W6)	48,600
	451,600
Current assets (345,000 + 160,000)	505,000
Total assets	956,600
EQUITY AND LIABILITIES	
Equity attributable to owners of parent	
Ordinary share capital	250,000
Retained earnings (W5)	472,600
	722,600
Non-controlling interest (W4)	84,000
Total equity	806,600
Current liabilities (100,000 + 50,000)	150,000
Total equity and liabilities	956,600

WORKINGS

(1) **Group structure**

(2) **Net assets**

Socrates Ltd

	Year end £	Acquisition £	Post acquisition £
Share capital	30,000	30,000	–
Retained earnings	180,000	70,000	110,000
	210,000	100,000	

(3) **Goodwill**

	Socrates Ltd £
Consideration transferred	75,000
Non-controlling interest at acquisition (40% × 100,000 (W2))	40,000
Net assets at acquisition (W2)	(100,000)
	15,000
Impairment to date	(12,000)
Balance c/f	3,000

(4) Non-controlling interest at year end

	£
Share of net assets at acquisition (40% × 100,000 (W2))	40,000
Share of post-acquisition reserves (40% × 110,000 (W2))	44,000
	84,000

(5) Retained earnings

	£
Haley plc	400,000
Socrates Ltd (60% × 110,000 (W2))	66,000
Aristotle Ltd (30% × (100,000 – 30,000))	21,000
Less Impairment to date (12,000 + 2,400)	(14,400)
	472,600

(6) Investment in associate

	£
Cost of investment in Aristotle Ltd	30,000
Share of post acquisition retained earnings (30% × (100,000 – 30,000))	21,000
	51,000
Impairment to date	(2,400)
	48,600

10 CORFU LTD

Consolidated statement of profit or loss for the year ended 30 June 20X9

	£'000
Revenue (W2)	15,131
Cost of sales and expenses (W2)	(13,579)
	1,552
Share of profit of joint venture (W4)	178
Profit before tax	1,730
Income tax expense (W2)	(736)
Profit for the year	994
Profit attributable to	
Owners of Corfu Ltd (β)	964
Non-controlling interest (W3)	30
	994

WORKINGS

(1) Group structure

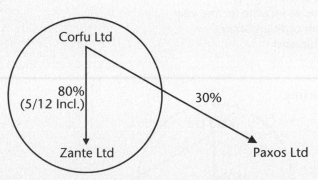

Corfu Ltd

80% (5/12 Incl.)

30%

Zante Ltd

Paxos Ltd

(2) Consolidation schedule

	Corfu Ltd £'000	Zante Ltd 5/12 £'000	Adj £'000	Consol £'000
Revenue	12,614	2,567	(50)	15,131
C of S				
Per Q	(11,318)	(2,302)	50	
PURP re Paxos (30% × (150,000 × 25/125))	(9)			(13,579)
Income tax	(621)	(115)		(736)
		150		

(3) Non-controlling interest

	£'000
Zante Ltd (20% × 150,000 (W2))	30

(4) Share of profit of joint venture

	£'000
Paxos Ltd (30% × 594)	178

11 KING LTD

Consolidated statement of profit or loss for the year ended 30 September 20X9

	£'000
Revenue (W2)	1,150
Cost of sales and expenses (W2)	(743)
	407
Share of profit of associates (W5)	19
Profit before tax	426
Income tax expense (W2)	(125)
Profit for the year	301
Profit attributable to:	
Owners of King Ltd (β)	275
Non-controlling interest (W3)	26
	301

Consolidated statement of changes in equity for the year ended 30 September 20X9 (extract)

	Retained earnings £'000
Balance brought forward (W4)	672
Total comprehensive income for the year	275
Dividends paid on ordinary shares	(110)
Balance carried forward	837

WORKINGS

(1) Group structure

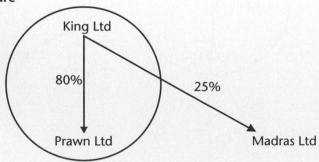

(2) **Consolidation schedule**

	King Ltd £'000	Prawn Ltd £'000	Adj £'000	Consol £'000
Revenue	800	430	(80)	1,150
C of S and expenses				
Per Q	(550)	(255)	80	
PURP (36 × 25%)	(9)			
Impairment of goodwill re Prawn Ltd	(9)			(743)
Income tax	(80)	(45)		(125)
PAT		130		

(3) **Non-controlling interest**

	£'000
Prawn Ltd (130,000 × 20%)	26

(4) **Retained earnings brought forward**

	£'000
King Ltd	600
Prawn Ltd (80% × (320 – 260))	48
Madras Ltd (25% × (540 – 340))	50
Less Impairment to date (9 + 17)	(26)
	672

(5) **Share of profit of associates**

	£000
Madras Ltd ((25% × 100) – 6)	19

12   WATER LTD

(a) **Consolidated statement of financial position as at 30 September 20X5**

	£	£
ASSETS		
Non-current assets		
Property, plant and equipment (697,210 + 648,010)		1,345,220
Intangibles (W3)		1,000
Investments in associates (W7)		270,400
		1,616,620
Current assets		
Inventories (495,165 + 388,619 – 4,000 (W6))	879,784	
Trade and other receivables (415,717 + 320,540)	736,257	
Cash and cash equivalents (101,274 + 95,010)	196,284	
		1,812,325
Total assets		3,428,945
EQUITY AND LIABILITIES		
Equity attributable to owners of the parent		
Ordinary share capital		600,000
Retained earnings (W5)		1,353,200
		1,953,200
Non-controlling interest (W4)		203,200
Total equity		2,156,400
Non-current liabilities		
Borrowings (400,000 + 150,000)		550,000
Current liabilities		
Trade payables (440,366 + 282,179)		722,545
Total equity and liabilities		3,428,945

(b) **Required accounting treatment for different levels of investment**

(i) **Control**

The investment will be treated as a subsidiary and consolidated in accordance with IFRS 10 *Consolidated Financial Statements*.

The ability to direct the decision making of the undertaking means that full consolidation is appropriate. The assets/liabilities and income/expenses under group control are shown as if they belonged to a single entity.

The non-controlling share is shown in order to indicate the proportion not owned by the group.

(ii) **Significant influence**

Many investments involve the influencing of decisions rather than outright control.

Such investments are treated as associates and equity accounted on consolidation in accordance with IAS 28 *Investments in Associates and Joint Ventures*.

This level of involvement is reflected by showing the underlying value of the investment in the statement of financial position and the share of profit in the statement of profit or loss.

(iii) **Simple investment**

Here the investor has no significant involvement in the investee undertaking.

Consequently only amounts paid/payable or received/receivable are reflected in the group accounts.

The cost of such investments is shown in the statement of financial position, whilst dividend income is reflected in the statement of profit or loss.

(c) **Explanation of accounting methods used**

(i) **Subsidiary – Impact on statement of financial position**

- 100% of the net assets of a subsidiary will be included on a line-by-line basis.

- Intra-group balances will be contra'd out.

- Unrealised profits on intra-group sales of inventory and property, plant and equipment will be removed.

- Goodwill is recognised if the consideration transferred plus the non-controlling interest at acquisition exceeds the fair value of the net assets acquired.

- Consolidated retained earnings will include

 – Parent company's percentage of subsidiary's post-acquisition profits
 – Cumulative goodwill impairments to date

- The non-controlling interest will show the value of the net assets included in the consolidated statement of financial position but owned by 'outside' interests.

(ii) **Associate – Impact on statement of financial position**

- The cost of the investment is increased by the share of the post-acquisition increase in the associate's net assets and decreased by any impairment losses.

- Consolidated retained earnings will include

 – The investor company's percentage of the associate's post-acquisition profits
 – Cumulative investment impairments to date

WORKINGS

(1) Group structure

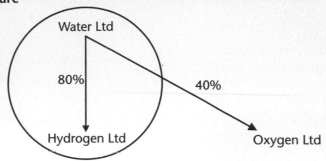

(2) Net assets

Hydrogen Ltd

	Year end date £	£	Acquisition £	Post-acquisition £
Share capital		200,000	200,000	–
Retained earnings				
Per question	820,000			
Less PURP (W6)	(4,000)			
		816,000	500,000	316,000
		1,016,000	700,000	

(3) Goodwill

Hydrogen Ltd

	£
Consideration transferred	562,000
Non-controlling interest at acquisition (20% × 700,000 (W2))	140,000
Net assets at acquisition	(700,000)
	2,000
Impairment to date	(1,000)
Balance c/f	1,000

(4) Non-controlling interest at year end

	£
Share of net assets at acquisition (20% × 700,000 (W2))	140,000
Share of post-acquisition (20% × 316,000 (W2))	63,200
	203,200

(5) Retained earnings

	£
Water Ltd	1,015,000
Hydrogen Ltd (80% × 316,000 (W2))	252,800
Oxygen Ltd (40% × (463,000 – 242,000))	88,400
Less Impairment to date (1,000 + 2,000)	(3,000)
	1,353,200

(6) PURP

	%	£
Selling price	125	20,000
Cost	(100)	(16,000)
GP	25	4,000

(7) Investments in associates

	£
Cost of investment in Oxygen Ltd	184,000
Share of post acquisition retained earnings (40% × (463,000 – 242,000))	88,400
	272,400
Impairment to date	(2,000)
	270,400

13 MINNIE PLC

Consolidated statement of financial position as at 31 December 20X5

	£'000
Non current assets	
Property, plant and equipment	406
Investment in joint venture (W4)	95
	501
Current assets	
Inventories	100
Others	200
Total assets	801
Equity attributable to owners of the parent	
Share capital	200
Retained earnings (W2)	451
	651
Current liabilities	150
Total equity and liabilities	801

Consolidated statement of profit or loss for the year ended 31 December 20X5

	£'000
Revenue	490
Cost of sales and expenses (280 + (W3) 5)	(285)
Share of profit of joint venture (80 × 50%)	40
Profit before tax	245
Income tax expense	(100)
Profit for the year	145
Profit attributable to:	
Owners of the parent	145
Non-controlling interests	0
	145

WORKINGS

(1) **Group structure**

Minnie

50%

Mouse   Pre acq'n ret'd earnings £0 (set up by Minnie plc)

(2) **Consolidated retained earnings**

	Minnie plc £'000	Mouse Ltd £'000
Per question	366	180
PURP (W3)	(5)	
Pre-acquisition retained earnings		(0)
		180
Group share of post-acquisition earnings		
Mouse Ltd (180 × 50%)	90	
	451	

(3) **Provision for unrealised profit on inventories**

Investor's share of unrealised profit in inventories:

£50,000 × (25%/125%) × 50% = £5,000

∴   DR Cost of sales & Retained earnings   £5,000

CR Investment in Mouse Ltd   £5,000

(4) **Investment in Mouse Ltd**

	£'000
Cost of joint venture	10
Add post-acquisition retained reserves (W2)	90
Less PURP (W3)*	(5)
	95

* Adjusted against the joint venture rather than group inventories because in this scenario it is the joint venture that holds the inventories. The credit adjustment is made wherever the inventories are held under equity accounting.

Financial Accounting and Reporting

CHAPTER 14

Group accounts: disposals

Introduction

Examination context

Topic List

Summary and Self-test

Technical reference

Answers to Interactive questions

Answers to Self-test

Introduction

Learning objectives

Tick off

- Account for the complete disposal of a subsidiary in the parent's books and in the group accounts

- Explain how the underlying principles of group accounts are applied in accounting for disposals

- Explain the application of IFRS to specified group scenarios

Specific syllabus references for this chapter are: 1g, 3d, 3e, 3f.

Syllabus links

This topic is introduced in Financial Accounting and Reporting at a basic level – only complete disposals are covered. More complex aspects are covered at the Advanced Stage.

Examination context

Preparation of consolidated financial statements represents 30% of the syllabus and disposals of subsidiaries forms part of this. Calculation of the group profit or loss on disposal could feature in a mixed topic question. Longer questions are more likely to focus on the impact of the disposal on the consolidated financial statements as a whole.

In the examination candidates may be required to:

- Prepare consolidated financial statements including the effects of a complete disposal of a subsidiary

- Prepare extracts from the consolidated financial statements including the calculation of the group profit or loss on complete disposal of a subsidiary

- Explain the principles behind the treatment of the complete disposal of a subsidiary

1 Introduction

Section overview

An entity may dispose of all or some of its shares in a subsidiary.

1.1 Disposal

When a group disposes of all or part of its interest in a subsidiary this needs to be reflected in the **parent's individual financial statements** and in the **group financial statements**.

The Financial Accounting and Reporting syllabus only examines **complete disposal** of subsidiaries.

2 Treatment of disposal in parent company's own financial statements

Section overview

A profit or loss will be calculated by comparing the sale proceeds with the carrying amount of the investment disposed of.

2.1 Recording the disposal

In the individual financial statements of the parent company the investment in the subsidiary will have been recorded as follows:

Statement of financial position

- **Non-current asset investment** (normally at cost)

Statement of profit or loss

- **Dividend income received** from the subsidiary

When the investment is sold this should be treated as a non-current asset disposal. This will usually give rise to a **profit or loss on disposal** in the parent's individual financial statements.
The disposal will be recorded as follows:

		£		£
DR	Cash/receivables (proceeds)	X		
CR	Investment in S (Carrying amount – usually cost)			X
DR or CR	Profit or loss (loss/profit on disposal)	X	or	X

3 Complete disposal of a subsidiary

Section overview

- The subsidiary disposed of should not be included in the subsequent consolidated statement of financial position.

- In the consolidated statement of profit or loss:

    - The results of the subsidiary should be time-apportioned and consolidated up to the date of disposal.

    - The non-controlling interest should be based on the subsidiary's results up to the date of disposal.

    - The group profit or loss on disposal should be recognised.

- In the consolidated statement of changes in equity the balance relating to the non-controlling interest in the subsidiary sold should be removed.

3.1 Consolidated statement of financial position

The consolidated statement of financial position shows the financial position **at a particular point** in time (ie the end of the reporting period). As a result, if a subsidiary has been disposed of during the year, that subsidiary **should not be reflected in the consolidated statement of financial position** at the end of the year. A consolidated statement of financial position will only need to be prepared if the parent has other subsidiaries and should be prepared as though the subsidiary disposed of **had never existed**.

3.2 Consolidated statement of profit or loss

When a subsidiary is disposed of, its resources cease to be controlled by the group at the date of disposal. Prior to that point, they are under the group's control and therefore the results of the subsidiary **up to the disposal date** should be included in the consolidated statement of profit or loss. So there will always be a consolidated statement of profit or loss in the year of disposal, even if the parent has no other subsidiaries. The consolidated statement of profit or loss should include:

- S's results **up to the date of disposal**.

- If there is a **non-controlling interest** in the subsidiary, **its share of S's results up to the date of disposal**.

- The profit or loss arising on the disposal.

3.3 Group profit/loss on disposal

The group profit or loss on disposal is the difference between the **sales proceeds and the parent's total investment in the subsidiary**, ie the amounts in respect of the subsidiary which would appear in a consolidated statement of financial position prepared immediately before the disposal. These amounts are the sum of:

- **P's share of S's net assets at the date of disposal**. These net assets will be the net assets at the start of the year in which the disposal takes place, plus/minus the net asset increase/decrease arising through S's profit/loss in the period up to the disposal and minus any dividends paid by S in that period; and

- The **goodwill** acquired in the business combination with S, to the extent that it has **not already been recognised as an expense** as a result of impairment reviews.

So the calculation is as follows:

		£	£
Sales proceeds			X
Less: Carrying amount of goodwill at date of disposal:			
	Consideration transferred	X	
	NCI at acquisition	X	
	Less net assets at acquisition	(X)	
	Goodwill at acquisition	X	
	Less impairment to date	(X)	
			(X)
Less: Carrying amount of net assets at date of disposal			
	Net assets b/f	X	
	Profit/(loss) for current period to disposal date	X/(X)	
	Dividends paid prior to disposal date	(X)	
			(X)
Add back NCI in net assets at date of disposal			X
Profit (loss) on disposal			X (X)

Points to note

1   The retained reserves/net assets at the date of disposal of the subsidiary should be calculated deducting only those dividends to which the parent is entitled ie **dividends paid up to the date of disposal**.

2   In examination questions you should assume that a subsidiary which is fully disposed of is a separately reportable business segment and meets the IFRS 5 *Non-current Assets Held for Sale and Discontinued Operations* definition of a **discontinued activity** (the presentation of discontinued operations was discussed in Chapter 3). As such the disposal should be disclosed in accordance with IFRS 5.

These learning materials adopt the approach illustrated in IFRS 5 IG example 11. This includes a one line entry in the statement of profit or loss which incorporates both the subsidiary's results up to the date of disposal and the group profit or loss arising on disposal. You should adopt this approach in the examination.

Interactive question 1: Profit/loss on disposal   [Difficulty level: Exam standard]

Champion plc has held a 70% investment in Hercules Ltd for many years. On 31 December it disposed of all of this investment. Further details are as follows:

	£
Consideration transferred on acquisition	2,000
Hercules Ltd's net assets at the date of acquisition	1,900
Sale proceeds	2,100
Hercules Ltd's net assets at the date of disposal	2,400

Requirement

Calculate the profit/loss on disposal:

(a)   In Champion plc's individual accounts

(b)   In the consolidated accounts assuming that in respect of goodwill

    (i)   There has been no impairment
    (ii)   There has been an impairment loss of £470

Fill in the proforma below.

(a)   **Champion plc's separate financial statements**

	£
Proceeds	
Cost	
Profit on disposal	

(b) Consolidated financial statements

	No impairment		Impairment £470	
	£	£	£	£
Sales proceeds				
Less carrying amount of goodwill at				
Date of disposal:				
Consideration transferred				
NCI at acquisition				
Less net assets at acquisition	_____		_____	
Goodwill at acquisition				
Less impairment to date	_____		_____	
Less carrying amount of net assets at date of disposal				
Add back NCI in net assets at date of disposal (net assets x NCI%)	_____		_____	
Profit (loss) on disposal	=======		=======	

See **Answer** at the end of this chapter.

3.4 Consolidated statement of changes in equity

There will almost always be a need for a consolidated statement of changes in equity (CSCE) in the year of disposal (the only exception would be if the parent had no other subsidiaries and there had been no non-controlling interest in the subsidiary now disposed of). In relation to the subsidiary disposed of, the CSCE will contain the following in the non-controlling interest column:

- S's total comprehensive income (to the date of disposal) attributable to the non-controlling interest. This reflects the **non-controlling interest** amount shown **in the consolidated statement of profit or loss**.

- The non-controlling interest in S's share capital and retained earnings brought forward, ie **the non-controlling interest as shown in the previous period's consolidated statement of financial position**.

- A **deduction for the total of the above amounts**. This deduction should be made because at the end of the current period there will be no non-controlling interest in relation to S, which has now been disposed of.

Point to note: There is no need to make a similar deduction in the CSCE for P's share of S's post-acquisition retained earnings brought forward plus P's share of S's current period profits. That deduction has in effect already been made in the profit or loss on disposal calculation.

Worked example: Complete disposal

Ben plc bought 80% of the share capital of Bill Ltd for £950,000 on 1 October 20X1. At that date Bill Ltd's retained earnings stood at £510,000.

Ben plc has several other subsidiaries, which are wholly owned.

The statements of financial position at 30 September 20X8 and the summarised statements of profit or loss to that date are given below:

Statement of financial position

	Ben plc Group £'000	Bill Ltd £'000
Property, plant and equipment	2,050	600
Investment in Bill Ltd	950	–
Current assets	2,700	1,300
	5,700	1,900
Share capital (£1 ordinary shares)	2,000	300
Retained earnings	2,500	1,100
	4,500	1,400
Current liabilities	1,200	500
	5,700	1,900

Statement of profit or loss

	£'000	£'000
Profit before interest and tax	1,400	180
Income tax expense	(400)	(50)
Profit for the year	1,000	130

Statement of changes in equity (extract)

	£'000	£'000
Retained earnings at 1 October 20X7	1,500	970
Total comprehensive income for the year	1,000	130
Retained earnings at 30 September 20X8	2,500	1,100

To date no impairment losses on goodwill have been recognised. The Ben plc group figures exclude any amounts for Bill Ltd. No entries have been made in the accounts for the disposal described below.

Requirement

Prepare the consolidated statement of financial position, consolidated statement of profit or loss and consolidated statement of changes in equity extracts for retained earnings and non-controlling interest at 30 September 20X8 on the basis that Ben plc sells its entire holding in Bill Ltd for £2,100,000 on 30 September 20X8.

You should assume that the disposal is a discontinued operation in accordance with IFRS 5 *Non-current Assets Held for Sale and Discontinued Operations*.

Solution

Ben and Bill

Consolidated statement of financial position as at 30 September 20X8

	£'000
Property, plant and equipment	2,050
Current assets (2,700 + 2,100 disposal proceeds)	4,800
	6,850
Share capital	2,000
Retained earnings (W4)	3,650
	5,650
Current liabilities	1,200
	6,850

ICAEW

Consolidated statement of profit or loss for the year ended 30 September 20X8

	£'000
Continuing operations	
Profit before tax	1,400
Income tax expense	(400)
Profit for the year from continuing operations	1,000
Discontinued operations	
Profit for the year from discontinued operations (678 (W2) + 130 (W1))	808
Profit for the year	1,808
Profit attributable to:	
Owners of Ben plc (β)	1,782
Non-controlling interest (20% × 130)	26
	1,808

Consolidated statement of changes in equity (extract)

	Ben plc Retained earnings £'000	Non-controlling interest (Bill Ltd) £'000
Balance at 1 October 20X7 (W3 + W5)	1,868	254
Total comprehensive income for the year	1,782	26
Eliminated on disposal of subsidiary (W2)	–	(280)
Balance at 30 September 20X8 (W4)	3,650	–

WORKINGS

(1) **Profit of Bill Ltd for year to disposal**

	£'000
PAT	130
× 12/12	130

(2) **Profit on disposal of Bill Ltd**

	£'000	£'000
Sales proceeds		2,100
Less: Carrying amount of goodwill at date of disposal		
Consideration transferred	950	
NCI at acquisition (20% × (300 + 510))	162	
Less net assets at acquisition	(810)	
		(302)
Less carrying amount of net assets at date of disposal		(1,400)
Add back NCI in net assets at date of disposal (20% × 1,400)		280
Profit on disposal		678

(3) **Retained earnings brought forward**

	£'000
Ben plc	1,500
Bill Ltd (80% × (970 – 510))	368
	1,868

(4) **Retained earnings carried forward**

	£'000
Ben plc	2,500
Profit on disposal (2,100 – 950 (see Point to note below))	1,150
	3,650

(5) **NCI b/f**

	£'000
Share capital	300
Retained earnings b/f	970
	1,270
× 20%	254

Point to note:

The profit on disposal figure in the retained earnings carried forward balance is the profit which would appear in Ben plc's own statement of profit or loss.

This adjustment is required as Ben plc's own financial statements do not reflect the disposal. (We are told that no entries have been made in respect of this transaction.)

Interactive question 2: Complete disposal   [Difficulty level: Exam standard]

Daring plc has a number of subsidiaries, one of which, Glory Ltd, was sold in the current year. The draft accounts for the Daring Group (being Daring plc and the subsidiaries it still owns) and Glory Ltd at 31 March 20X1 are as follows:

Statements of financial position

	Daring Group £m	Glory Ltd £m
Intangibles – goodwill	4,000	–
Investment in Glory Ltd at cost	3,440	–
Sundry assets	42,450	9,500
	49,890	9,500
Equity attributable to owners of parent		
Share capital (£1 ordinary shares)	8,000	3,000
Retained earnings	11,000	3,500
	19,000	6,500
Non-controlling interest	12,000	–
Total equity	31,000	6,500
Liabilities	10,000	3,000
Sales proceeds account	8,890	–
	49,890	9,500

Statements of profit or loss

	Daring Group £m	Glory Ltd £m
Profit before tax	12,950	3,800
Income tax expense	(5,400)	(2,150)
Profit for the year	7,550	1,650
Profit attributable to:		
Owners of Daring plc	5,050	
Non-controlling interest	2,500	
	7,550	

Statements of changes in equity

	Daring Group					Glory Ltd
	Attributable to owners of					
	Daring plc			Non-		
	Share capital £m	Retained earnings £m	Total £m	controlling interest £m	Total £m	Retained earnings £m
Balance b/f	8,000	5,950	13,950	9,500	23,450	1,850
Total comprehensive income for the year	–	5,050	5,050	2,500	7,550	1,650
Balance c/f	8,000	11,000	19,000	12,000	31,000	3,500

Daring plc acquired 90% of Glory Ltd when the retained earnings of Glory Ltd were £700m. In an earlier accounting period an impairment loss of £20m was recognised in relation to the goodwill acquired in the business combination with Glory Ltd.

On 31 December 20X0 Daring plc sold all its shares in Glory Ltd for £8,890m. Daring plc has debited cash and credited a sales proceeds account in the statement of financial position with this amount, as it is unsure what entries are needed.

Requirement

Prepare the Daring Group consolidated statement of financial position, consolidated statement of profit or loss and consolidated statement of changes in equity for the year ended 31 March 20X1.

You should assume that the disposal of Glory Ltd constitutes a discontinued operation in accordance with IFRS 5 *Non-current Assets Held for Sale and Discontinued Operations*.

Fill in the proforma below.

Daring Group

Consolidated statement of financial position at 31 March 20X1

	£m
Intangibles – goodwill	
Sundry assets	_____
	======
Equity attributable to owners of the parent	
Share capital (£1 ordinary shares)	
Retained earnings	_____
Non-controlling interest	_____
Total equity	
Liabilities	_____
	======

Consolidated statement of profit or loss for the year ended 31 March 20X1

	£m
Continuing operations	
Profit before tax (W2)	
Income tax expense (W2)	_____
Profit for the year from continuing operations	
Discontinued operations	
Profit for the year from discontinued operations (W4 and W5)	_____
Profit for the year	======
Profit attributable to:	
Owners of Daring plc (β)	
Non-controlling interest (W3)	_____
	======

Consolidated statement of changes in equity for the year ended 31 March 20X1

	Share capital £m	Attributable to owners of Daring plc Retained earnings £m	Total £m	Non-controlling interest £m	Total £m
Balance b/f (W7 and W8)					
Total comprehensive income for the year					
Eliminated on disposal of subsidiary (W5)	_____	_____	_____	_____	_____
Balance c/f	======	======	======	======	======

WORKINGS

(1) Group structure

(2) Consolidation schedule for CSPL

	Daring Group £m	Consol £m
Profit before tax		
Tax		

(3) Non-controlling interest in Glory Ltd for CSPL

	£m

(4) Profit of Glory Ltd for year to disposal

	£m

(5) Profit on disposal of Glory Ltd for CSPL

	£m	£m
Sales proceeds		
Less: Carrying amount of goodwill at date of disposal		
Consideration transferred		
NCI at acquisition		
Less net assets at acquisition	———	
Goodwill at acquisition		
Less impairment to date	———	
Less carrying amount of net assets at date of disposal (W6)		
Add back NCI in net assets at date of disposal		———
Profit on disposal		═══

(6) Net assets at disposal

	£m
Share capital	
Retained earnings b/f	
Profit for year to disposal (W4)	———
	═══

(7) Group retained earnings b/f for CSCE

	£m
Daring Group	
Glory Ltd	
Goodwill impairment to date	———
	═══

(8) Non-controlling interest b/f for CSCE

	£m
	═══

See **Answer** at the end of this chapter.

3.5 Non-controlling interests and disposals

If a subsidiary is disposed of and on acquisition some goodwill was attributed to the NCI as a result of it being measured at fair value, the calculation of the parent's profit or loss on disposal should allow for some of the carrying amount of goodwill at the disposal date being attributable to the NCI. This is automatically achieved by measuring the carrying amount of the NCI at the date of disposal per the adjusted standard consolidation working 4 provided the working measures the NCI at acquisition at fair value.

Interactive question 3: NCI and disposal [Difficulty level: Exam standard]

On 1 January 20X5 Foot plc acquired 75% of the equity shares in Cone Ltd for £800,000. At that date the fair value and carrying amount of Cone Ltd's net assets was £640,000. On the same date the fair value of the equity shares in Cone Ltd not acquired by Foot plc was estimated at £180,000. At 31 December 20X7 the fair value and carrying amount of the net assets recognised by Cone Ltd was £900,000 and Cone Ltd's profit for the year ended 31 December 20X8 was £400,000.

Foot plc disposed of its interest in Cone Ltd for £1.35 million on 30 September 20X8.

Requirement

Calculate the profit or loss on disposal to be recognised in Foot plc's consolidated profit or loss for the year ended 31 December 20X8 on the basis that at acquisition the non-controlling interest was measured at:

(a)   Its share of net assets
(b)   Fair value

See **Answer** at the end of this chapter.

Summary and Self-test

Summary

	CSFP	CSPL	CSCE
• Complete disposal of S	• Reflect year end position – no subsidiary	• Consolidate results to date of disposal • NCI based on S's results up to date of disposal • Recognise group profit or loss (combine with S's results to date of disposal)	• Remove balances relating to NCI in S sold

Self-test

Answer the following questions

1   On 1 January 20X1 Rainbow Ltd acquired all of Zippy Ltd's 1,000 £1 ordinary shares. The goodwill acquired in the business combination was £10,000 of which 40% had been written off as impaired by the end of 20X2.

On 1 January 20X3 Rainbow Ltd sold all the shares for £140,000 when Zippy Ltd's retained earnings amounted to £112,000.

What is the profit on disposal which should be included as part of the profit for the period from discontinued operations figure in the consolidated statement of profit or loss of Rainbow Ltd?

2   Yogi plc has held an 80% investment in Bear Ltd for many years. On 31 December 20X6 it disposed of all of its investment. Details for the acquisition and disposal are as follows.

	£'000
Consideration transferred on acquisition	7,380
Fair value of Bear Ltd's net assets at acquisition (reflected in Bear Ltd's books)	9,000
Sale proceeds on 31 December 20X6	9,940

Goodwill acquired in the business combination has been fully written off as a result of impairment reviews.

The summarised statement of financial position of Bear Ltd on 31 December 20X6 showed the following.

	£'000
Called up share capital	3,000
Retained earnings	7,350
Equity	10,350

What is the profit/(loss) on disposal of the shares in Bear Ltd that should be included as part of the profit for the period from discontinued operations figure in the consolidated statement of profit or loss of Yogi plc for the year ended 31 December 20X6?

3   The Gill Group disposed of the following mid way through the financial year.

Tracey Ltd (100% subsidiary) for	£150,000
Debbie Ltd (55% subsidiary) for	£70,000

Goodwill acquired in the business combinations has been fully written off as a result of impairment reviews. The retained earnings of the companies are as follows.

	At acquisition	At disposal
Tracey Ltd	£70,000	£100,000
Debbie Ltd	£25,000	£40,000

The consolidated retained earnings of the remaining Gill Group, including the profit/loss made on the disposal of the investments in the year, were £230,000 at 31 December 20X6.

What amount for consolidated retained earnings should be included in the consolidated statement of financial position for the Gill Group as at 31 December 20X6?

4   PARABLE PLC

Parable plc is a holding company with a number of subsidiaries. The consolidation for the year ended 31 December 20X8 has been carried out to include all subsidiaries except Story Ltd. Story Ltd has been 80% owned by Parable plc since 20X2, at which date Story Ltd's retained earnings amounted to £50,000, but on 30 June 20X8 Parable plc sold all of its shares in Story Ltd.

Details are as follows.

	£
Cost of original investment (80,000 out of 100,000 £1 ordinary shares)	150,000
Goodwill acquired in the business combination fully recognised as an expense as a result of impairment reviews	30,000
Sales proceeds	500,000

Because Parable plc is unsure how to deal with its investment in Story Ltd in the 20X8 consolidation, it has not yet consolidated Story Ltd into the group financial statements.

Statements of profit or loss for the year ended 31 December 20X8 are set out below.

	Parable plc group £	Story Ltd £
Profit from operations	875,500	325,600
Sales proceeds on disposal of Story Ltd	500,000	–
Profit before tax	1,375,500	325,600
Income tax expense	(405,000)	(102,500)
Profit for the year	970,500	223,100
Profit attributable to		
Owners of Parable plc	870,300	
Non-controlling interest	100,200	
	970,500	

The Parable plc group and Story Ltd had retained earnings brought forward of £1,926,300 and £326,400 respectively. Other non-controlling interests brought forward were £507,500.

Requirements

Prepare the consolidated statement of profit or loss and the retained earnings and non-controlling interest columns for the statement of changes in equity for the Parable plc group for the year ended 31 December 20X8 in so far as the information is available. **(8 marks)**

5   ARBITRARY PLC

Arbitrary plc holds 80% of the ordinary shares of Contrary Ltd which it purchased five years ago, on 1 July 20X0, for £175,000. On 1 July 20X5 Arbitrary plc sold all of these shares and used the proceeds (£212,000) to purchase 65% of the ordinary shares of Enthusiast Ltd on the same date. The share capitals of Contrary Ltd and Enthusiast Ltd have remained constant for many years at £100,000 and £200,000 respectively. Net assets of Contrary Ltd and Enthusiast Ltd were as follows.

	Contrary Ltd		Enthusiast Ltd
	At acquisition £	At 1 January 20X5 £	At 1 January 20X5 £
Net assets	187,000	150,000	280,000

Statements of profit or loss and extracts from the statements of changes in equity for all three companies for the year ended 31 December 20X5 were as follows.

Statements of profit or loss

	Arbitrary plc £	Contrary Ltd £	Enthusiast Ltd £
Revenue	1,926,500	521,600	792,400
Cost of sales	(1,207,200)	(386,200)	(405,900)
Gross profit	719,300	135,400	386,500
Distribution costs	(207,500)	(79,200)	(198,200)
Administrative expenses	(192,600)	(26,100)	(107,100)
Dividend received from Contrary Ltd	8,000	–	–
Profit before tax	327,200	30,100	81,200
Income tax expense	(110,000)	(9,500)	(27,500)
Profit for the year	217,200	20,600	53,700

Statements of changes in equity

	Arbitrary plc £	*Retained earnings* Contrary Ltd £	Enthusiast Ltd £
Balance brought forward	671,300	50,000	80,000
Total comprehensive income for the year	217,200	20,600	53,700
Dividends paid on ordinary shares	(50,000)	(10,000)	–
Balance carried forward	838,500	60,600	133,700

No entries have been made in Arbitrary plc's statement of profit or loss relating to the sale of Contrary Ltd.

Contrary Ltd's dividends were paid prior to disposal.

In an earlier accounting period an impairment loss of £12,700 was recognised in relation to the goodwill arising on the acquisition of Contrary Ltd.

Requirements

(a) Prepare the consolidated statement of profit or loss and the retained earnings and non-controlling interest columns for the consolidated statement of changes in equity for Arbitrary plc for the year ended 31 December 20X5 in so far as the information is available. **(15 marks)**

Note: You should assume that the disposal of Contrary Ltd constitutes a discontinued operation in accordance with IFRS 5 *Non-current Assets Held for Sale and Discontinued Operations.*

(b) Calculate the profit on disposal that would be shown in the individual accounts of Arbitrary plc and explain how and why this differs from group profit on disposal. **(4 marks)**

(c) Briefly discuss the concepts of control and ownership in the context of this disposal. **(4 marks)**

(23 marks)

Now, go back to the Learning objectives in the Introduction. If you are satisfied you have achieved these objectives, please tick them off.

Technical reference

For a comprehensive Technical reference section, covering all aspects of group accounts (except group statements of cash flows) see Chapter 10.

Answer to Interactive question 1

(a) Champion plc's individual accounts

	£
Proceeds	2,100
Cost	(2,000)
Profit on disposal	100

(b) Consolidated accounts

	No impairment		Impairment £470	
	£	£	£	£
Sales proceeds		2,100		2,100
Less carrying amount of goodwill at date of disposal:				
Consideration transferred	2,000		2,000	
NCI at acquisition (1,900 × 30%)	570		570	
Less net assets at acquisition	(1,900)		(1,900)	
Goodwill at acquisition	670		670	
Less impairment to date	–		(470)	
		(670)		(200)
Less carrying amount of net assets at date of disposal		(2,400)		(2,400)
Add back NCI in net assets at date of disposal (2,400 × 30%)		720		720
Profit (loss) on disposal		(250)		220

Answer to Interactive question 2

Daring Group

Consolidated statement of financial position at 31 March 20X1

	£m
Intangibles – goodwill	4,000
Sundry assets	42,450
	46,450
Equity attributable to owners of parent	
Share capital (£1 ordinary shares)	8,000
Retained earnings (from CSCE)	16,450
	24,450
Non-controlling interest (from CSCE)	12,000
Total equity	36,450
Liabilities	10,000
	46,450

Consolidated statement of profit or loss for the year ended 31 March 20X1

	£m
Continuing operations	
Profit before tax (W2)	12,950
Income tax expense (W2)	(5,400)
Profit for the year from continuing operations	7,550
Discontinued operations	
Profit for the year from discontinued operations (1,238 (W4) + 3,321(W5))	4,559
Profit for the year	12,109
Profit attributable to:	
Owners of Daring plc (β)	9,485
Non-controlling interest (2,500 other subsidiaries + 124 (W3))	2,624
	12,109

Consolidated statement of changes in equity for the year ended 31 March 20X1

	Share capital £m	Attributable to owners of Daring plc Retained earnings £m	Total £m	Non-controlling interest £m	Total £m
Balance b/f (W7 and W8)	8,000	6,965	14,965	9,985	24,950
Total comprehensive income for the year	–	9,485	9,485	2,624	12,109
Eliminated on disposal of subsidiary (W5)	–	–	–	(609)	(609)
Balance c/f	8,000	16,450	24,450	12,000	36,450

WORKINGS

(1) **Group structure**

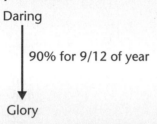

Daring

90% for 9/12 of year

Glory

(2) **Consolidation schedule for CSPL**

	Daring Group £m	Consol £m
Profit before tax	12,950	12,950
Tax	(5,400)	(5,400)

> **Tutorial note.** In this case the consolidation schedule only includes the results of the parent group as those of Glory Ltd are to be treated as discontinued (see Working 4). In an examination question it is likely that you will have to deal with another subsidiary still owned at the year end as well as the company disposed of so this working will be required.

(3) **Non-controlling interest in Glory Ltd for CSPL**

	£m
1,238 (W4) × 10%	124

(4) **Profit of Glory Ltd for year to disposal**

	£m
PAT	1,650
× 9/12	1,238

(5) **Profit on disposal of Glory Ltd for CSPL**

	£m	£m
Sales proceeds		8,890
Less: Carrying amount of goodwill at date of disposal:		
Consideration transferred	3,440	
Non-controlling interest at acquisition (3,700 × 10%)	370	
Less net assets at acquisition (3,000 + 700)	(3,700)	
Goodwill at acquisition	110	
Less impairment to date	(20)	
		(90)
Less carrying amount of net assets at disposal (W6)		(6,088)
Add back NCI in net assets at date of disposal (6,088 × 10%)		609
Profit on disposal		3,321

(6) **Net assets at disposal**

	£m
Share capital	3,000
Retained earnings b/f	1,850
Profit for year to disposal (W4)	1,238
	6,088

(7) **Group retained earnings b/f for CSCE**

	£m
Daring Group	5,950
Glory Ltd (90% × (1,850 – 700))	1,035
Goodwill impairment to date	(20)
	6,965

(8) **Non-controlling interest b/f for CSCE**

	£m
Glory Ltd ((3,000 + 1,850) × 10%) = 485 + other subsidiaries 9,500	9,985

Answer to Interactive question 3

	NCI at acquisition at share of net assets		NCI at acquisition at fair value	
	£'000	£'000	£'000	£'000
Sales proceeds		1,350		1,350
Less: Carrying amount of goodwill at date of disposal:				
Consideration transferred at acquisition date	800		800	
Non-controlling interest at acquisition date (25% × 640 and fair value)	160		180	
	960		980	
Net assets at acquisition date	(640)		(640)	
Goodwill at acquisition date		(320)		(340)
Carrying amount of net assets at date of disposal (W1)		(1,200)		(1,200)
Add back NCI in net assets at date of disposal (W2)		300		320
Profit/(loss) on disposal		130		130

WORKINGS

(1) **Net assets at date of disposal**

Net assets b/f	900	900
Profit for current period to date of disposal (400 × 9/12)	300	300
	1,200	1,200

(2) **Non-controlling interest at date of disposal**

(25% × 1,200 (W1)) and (180 fair value + (25% × (1,200 – 640 increase in net assets)))	300	320

Answers to Self-test

1 **£21,000**

	£	£
Sale proceeds		140,000
Goodwill at acquisition	10,000	
Less impairment	(4,000)	
Carrying amount of goodwill at date of disposal		(6,000)
Net assets at disposal (1,000 + 112,000)		(113,000)
Profit on disposal		21,000

2 **£1,660,000**

	£'000
Sales proceeds	9,940
Net assets at disposal	(10,350)
Add back NCI in net assets (10,350 × 20%)	2,070
Profit on disposal	1,660

3 **£230,000**

As the profit on disposal has been included within the remaining Gill Group retained earnings, no further adjustment is necessary.

4 PARABLE PLC

Consolidated statement of profit or loss for the year ended 31 December 20X8

	£
Continuing operations	
Profit before tax	875,500
Income tax expense	(405,000)
Profit for the year from continuing operations	470,500
Discontinued operations	
Profit for the year from discontinued operations (111,550 (W2) + 69,640 (W3))	181,190
Profit for the year	651,690
Profit attributable to	
Owners of Parable plc (β)	529,180
Non-controlling interest (W4)	122,510
	651,690

Consolidated statement of changes in equity for the year ended 31 December 20X8 (extracts)

	Owners of Parable plc Retained earnings £	Non-controlling interest £
Balance brought forward (W5 and W6)	2,117,420	592,780
Total comprehensive income for the period	529,180	122,510
Eliminated on disposal of subsidiary (W3)	–	(107,590)
Balance carried forward	2,646,600	607,700

WORKINGS

(1) **Group structure**

Parable plc group

80% (sold 30 June 20X8 ∴ 6/12m)

Story Ltd

(2) Profit for year to disposal

	£
PAT of S Ltd	223,100
× 6/12 =	111,550

(3) Profit on disposal of operations

	£	£
Sale proceeds		500,000
Less net assets at disposal:		
Net assets at 1 January 20X8 (100,000 + 326,400)	426,400	
Profit to 30 June 20X8 (W2)	111,550	
		(537,950)
Add back NCI in net assets (537,950 x 20%)		107,590
Profit on disposal		69,640

(4) Non-controlling interest for year

	£
Story Ltd (111,550 (W2) × 20%)	22,310
Other	100,200
	122,510

(5) Retained earnings b/f

	£
Parable plc group	1,926,300
Add Story Ltd (80% × (326,400 – 50,000))	221,120
Less goodwill impairment to date	(30,000)
	2,117,420

(6) Non-controlling interest b/f

	£
Story Ltd ((100,000 + 326,400) × 20%)	85,280
Other	507,500
	592,780

5 ARBITRARY PLC

(a) Consolidated statement of profit or loss for the year ended 31 December 20X5

	£
Continuing operations	
Revenue (W2)	2,322,700
Cost of sales (W2)	(1,410,150)
Gross profit	912,550
Distribution costs (W2)	(306,600)
Administrative expenses (W2)	(246,150)
Profit before tax	359,800
Income tax expense (W2)	(123,750)
Profit for the year from continuing operations	236,050
Discontinued operations	
Profit for the year from discontinued operations (10,300 (W3) + 79,060 (W4))	89,360
Profit for the year	325,410
Profit attributable to	
Owners of Arbitrary plc (β)	313,952
Non-controlling interest (W5)	11,458
	325,410

Consolidated statement of changes in equity for the year ended 31 December 20X5 (extracts)

	Attributable to owners of Arbitrary plc Retained earnings £	Non-controlling interest £
Balance brought forward (W6) + (W7)	629,000	30,000
Total comprehensive income for the year	313,952	11,458
Added on acquisition of subsidiary (W8)	–	107,397
Eliminated on disposal of subsidiary (W4)	–	(30,060)
Dividend paid on ordinary shares (20% × 10,000)	(50,000)	(2,000)
Balance carried forward	892,952	116,795

Non-controlling interest carried forward: proof

Enthusiast	£
Net assets at 1 January 20X5	280,000
Profit for year ended 31 December 20X5	53,700
	333,700
NCI 35%	116,795

(b) **Calculation of profit in individual accounts of Arbitrary plc**

	£
Sale proceeds	212,000
Less cost	(175,000)
Profit	37,000

The different calculations of profit on disposal reflect the different way in which the subsidiary (Contrary Ltd) is accounted for in the individual and consolidated accounts.

In the individual statement of financial position of Arbitrary plc Contrary Ltd is carried at cost of £175,000. The profit on disposal is therefore the sale proceeds less this cost.

In the consolidated financial statements the cost of Contrary Ltd is replaced with its underlying net assets and with goodwill acquired in the business combination. The profit on disposal is therefore based on sale proceeds less the percentage of net assets being sold (here 80%) less the unimpaired goodwill which is being sold in full (as it only ever related to the 80% share of net assets acquired).

(c) **Application of control and ownership ideas**

Control

Up to 1 July 20X5 Arbitrary plc owns 80% of Contrary Ltd and therefore controls it. So the consolidated statement of profit or loss should include 100% of Contrary Ltd's profits up to that date.

After 1 July 20X5 Arbitrary plc no longer controls Contrary Ltd. Its results should be excluded from the consolidated statement of profit or loss for the last six months of the year and also from the consolidated statement of financial position at the year end.

This treatment reflects the fact that once Contrary Ltd has been sold its resources are no longer under group control.

Ownership

For the first six months of the year 100% of Contrary Ltd's profits are included in the consolidated statement of profit or loss. However, 20% of its profits are owned by the non-controlling interest and this has to be deducted in arriving at the group's share of profit (£20,600 × 6/12 × 20%).

When the disposal occurs the group is selling its ownership interest in the net assets and the associated goodwill. Therefore the group profit on disposal is calculated from the point of view of ownership.

WORKINGS

(1) **Group structure**

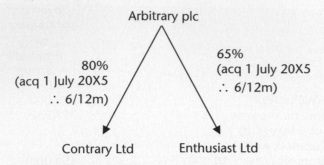

```
                    Arbitrary plc

        80%                      65%
    (acq 1 July 20X5        (acq 1 July 20X5
      ∴ 6/12m)                 ∴ 6/12m)


    Contrary Ltd         Enthusiast Ltd
```

(2) **Consolidation schedule**

	Arbitrary Plc £	Enthusiast Ltd 6/12 £	Consol £
Revenue	1,926,500	396,200	2,322,700
Cost of sales	(1,207,200)	(202,950)	(1,410,150)
Distribution cost	(207,500)	(99,100)	(306,600)
Admin exp	(192,600)	(53,550)	(246,150)
Tax	(110,000)	(13,750)	(123,750)
PAT		26,850	

(3) **Profit for year to disposal**

	£
PAT of C Ltd	20,600
× 6/12	10,300

(4) **Profit on disposal of Contrary Ltd**

	£	£
Sale proceeds		212,000
Less: Carrying amount of goodwill at date of disposal:		
Consideration transferred on acquisition	175,000	
NCI at acquisition (187,000 × 20%)	37,400	
Less net assets at acquisition	(187,000)	
Goodwill at acquisition	25,400	
Less impairment to date	(12,700)	
		(12,700)
Less: Carrying amount of net assets at disposal:		
Net assets at 1 January 20X5	150,000	
Profit to 1 July 20X5 (W3)	10,300	
Dividends paid	(10,000)	
		(150,300)
Add back NCI in net assets (150,300 × 20%)		30,060
Profit on disposal		79,060

(5) **Non-controlling interest in year**

	£
Contrary Ltd (20% × 10,300 (W3))	2,060
Enthusiast Ltd (35% × 26,850 (W2))	9,398
	11,458

(6) **Retained earnings b/f**

	£
Arbitrary plc	671,300
Contrary Ltd (80% × (50,000 − (187,000 − 100,000)))	(29,600)
Goodwill impairment to 31 December 20X4	(12,700)
	629,000

(7) **Non-controlling interest b/f**

	£
Contrary Ltd (150,000 × 20%)	<u>30,000</u>

(8) **Non-controlling interest added on acquisition of subsidiary**

	£
Enthusiast Ltd ((280,000 + 26,850 (W2)) × 35%)	<u>107,397</u>

CHAPTER 15

Group statement of cash flows

Introduction

Examination context

Topic List

Summary and Self-test

Technical reference

Answers to Interactive questions

Answers to Self-test

Learning objectives

Tick off

- Prepare a statement of cash flows for an individual entity including the effects of revaluations of property, plant and equipment and payments of instalments under finance leases

- Prepare a consolidated statement of cash flows including the effects of

    - Dividends paid to the non-controlling interest
    - Dividends received from associates and joint ventures
    - Acquisitions/disposals of subsidiaries and acquisitions of associates

Specific syllabus references for this chapter are: 2c, 2d,3e.

Syllabus links

This chapter develops many of the ideas which were introduced in Chapter 2. As you will see, the process involved in preparing a consolidated statement of cash flows is very similar to that used in the preparation of a statement of cash flows for an individual entity.

The preparation of individual and consolidated statements of cash flows is also highly relevant at the Advanced Stage, where the emphasis will change to the analysis and interpretation of these statements.

Examination context

In the examination candidates may be required to:

- Prepare and present a consolidated statement of cash flows for a group of companies including subsidiaries and associates

- Prepare extracts from a consolidated statement of cash flows

1 Individual company statement of cash flows

Section overview

- The statement of cash flows of an individual entity was covered in Chapter 2.

- An instalment paid under a finance lease must be split between interest and capital repaid and the two elements presented separately in the statement of cash flows.

1.1 Revision

As we saw in Chapter 2 the objective of a statement of cash flows is to provide information about the historical changes in **cash and cash equivalents** during the accounting period.

In accordance with IAS 7 *Statement of Cash Flows* cash flows are classified under the following headings:

- **Cash flows from operating activities**
- **Cash flows from investing activities**
- **Cash flows from financing activities**

Cash generated from operations is shown as part of cash flows from operating activities. A note to the statement of cash flows is then presented showing how the cash generated from operations has been calculated using:

- The **direct method**; or
- The **indirect method**.

Refer back to Chapter 2 if you need a reminder of the proforma for a statement of cash flows and its supporting note.

1.2 Finance leases

The payment of an instalment under a finance lease represents a **cash outflow** which must be reflected in the statement of cash flows. As we saw in Chapter 7, however, **an individual instalment may represent the repayment of interest accrued to date and a repayment of a proportion of the capital outstanding.** For the purposes of preparing the statement of cash flows these two elements must be **presented separately** as follows:

- The **repayment of interest** is presented within interest paid as part of **cash flows from operating activities**

- The **repayment of capital** is presented as a separate item under **cash flows from financing activities**.

Points to note

1   The acquisition of assets under a finance lease requires separate disclosure as a non-cash transaction.

2   For the purposes of the statement of cash flows additions to PPE should exclude the effects of any new assets acquired under finance leases as these have not been purchased for cash.

Interactive question 1: Finance lease   [Difficulty level: Easy]

Camel Ltd enters into a finance lease on 1 January 20X7. Lease payments comprise three annual payments of £10,000 commencing on 31 December 20X7. The asset would have cost £24,869 to buy outright. The implicit interest rate is 10%.

Requirement

Show the effect of the finance lease on the statement of cash flows on the basis that Camel Ltd uses the actuarial method to allocate interest to the periods of borrowing.

C
H
A
P
T
E
R

15

Complete the following proforma.

Statement of cash flows (extract) for the year ended 31 December 20X7   £

Cash flows from operating activities
Interest paid

Cash flows from financing activities
Payment of finance lease liabilities

WORKING

	Bal b/f 1.1.X7 £	Interest accrued at 10% £	Payment 31 December 20X7 £	Bal c/f 31.12.X7 £
Year ended 31 December 20X7				

See **Answer** at the end of this chapter.

1.3 Property, plant and equipment – revaluations

Any revaluation of property, plant and equipment during the period must be taken into account when calculating cash paid for purchases.

The T account will be as follows:

PROPERTY, PLANT AND EQUIPMENT

	£		£
Balance b/d	X	Disposals	X
Revaluation surplus	X		
Additions (balancing figure)	X	Balance c/d	X
	X		X

Worked example: Revaluation

A company's financial statements at 31 December 20X8 showed property, plant and equipment at cost or valuation of £9,300,000. During the year to 31 December 20X9 it disposed of vehicles that had cost £450,000 and revalued a freehold property upwards by £750,000. At 31 December 20X9 the company's property, plant and equipment at cost or valuation amounted to £11,235,000.

The T account will be as follows:

PROPERTY, PLANT AND EQUIPMENT

	£'000		£'000
Balance b/d	9,300	Disposals	450
Revaluation surplus	750		
Additions (balancing figure)	1,635	Balance c/d	11,235
	11,685		11,685

ICAEW

2 Group statement of cash flows

> **Section overview**
>
> - The consolidated statement of cash flows shows the cash flows of the group (ie parent and subsidiaries) with third parties.
>
> - The basis of preparation is essentially the same as for the individual statement of cash flows.
>
> - Dividends to the non-controlling interest are disclosed separately, classified as cash flows from financing activities.
>
> - Dividends received from associates and jointly controlled entities are disclosed separately, classified as cash flows from investing activities.
>
> - The net cash effect of the acquisition/disposal of a subsidiary should be disclosed separately and classified as cash flows from investing activities.
>
> - Cash payments to acquire an associate or joint venture should be classified as cash flows from investing activities.

2.1 Basic principle

In principle the preparation of the group statement of cash flows is the same as that for the individual entity in that statement of financial position and statement of profit or loss information is converted into cash flow information, the difference being that this source information is consolidated.

The **aim of the consolidated statement of cash flows is to show the cash flows of the group with third parties.** (This is consistent with the preparation of the consolidated statement of financial position and consolidated statement of profit or loss.) This is achieved 'automatically' as the information forming the basis of the preparation of the consolidated statement of cash flows (ie the consolidated statement of profit or loss and consolidated statement of financial position) has already been adjusted for intra-group transactions.

A number of additional issues do need to be considered however:

- **Cash flows to the non-controlling interest**
- **Cash received from associates and joint ventures**
- **Acquisitions/disposals of subsidiaries**
- **Acquisitions of associates and joint ventures**

We will consider each of these in the remainder of this chapter.

Note: For simplicity, the examples in this chapter all have non-controlling interest valued on the proportionate basis. The method used to value non-controlling interest does not affect cash flows, which is the focus of this chapter.

2.2 Cash flows to the non-controlling interest

The non-controlling interest represents a third party so **dividends paid to the non-controlling interest should be reflected as a cash outflow.** This payment should be presented separately and classified as **'Cash flows from financing activities'**.

As we saw in Chapter 2 many of the cash flows were calculated by using a T account working. This technique also applies to the consolidated statement of cash flows. Dividends paid to the non-controlling interest may be calculated using a T account as follows:

NON-CONTROLLING INTEREST

	£		£
NCI dividend paid (balancing figure)	X	b/f NCI (CSFP)	X
c/f NCI (CSFP)	X	NCI (CSPL)	X
	X		X

Interactive question 2: Non-controlling interest [Difficulty level: Exam standard]

Consolidated statement of profit or loss (extract) for the year ended 31 December 20X7

	£'000
Group profit before tax	60
Income tax expense	(20)
Profit for year	40
Profit attributable to:	
Owners of the parent	30
Non-controlling interest	10
	40

Consolidated statement of financial position (extract) as at 31 December

	20X7	20X6
	£'000	£'000
Non-controlling interest	204	200

Requirement

Calculate the dividend paid to the non-controlling interest during 20X7.

Complete the T account below.

NON-CONTROLLING INTEREST

	£'000		£'000

See **Answer** at the end of this chapter.

2.3 Associates and joint ventures

There are two issues to consider with regard to associates and joint ventures:

1   The aim of the statement of cash flows is to show the cash flows of the parent and any subsidiaries with third parties, therefore **any cash flows between the associate or joint ventures and third parties are irrelevant.** As a result, **the group share of profit of the associate or joint venture must be deducted as an adjustment in the reconciliation of profit before tax to cash generated from operations.** This is because group profit before tax includes the results of the associate and joint venture.

Worked example: Cash flows from operating activities

Consolidated statement of profit or loss (extract) for the year ended 31 December 20X7

	£'000
Group profit from operations	273
Share of profit of associates	60
Profit before tax	333
Income tax expense	(63)
Profit for the year	270

Consolidated statement of financial position (extracts) as at 31 December

	20X7	20X6
	£'000	£'000
Inventories	867	694
Receivables	1,329	1,218

Cash generated from operations would be calculated and shown as follows:

	£'000
Profit before tax	333
Adjustments for:	
Share of profit of associates	(60)
	273
Increase in trade receivables (1,329 – 1,218)	(111)
Increase in inventories (867 – 694)	(173)
Cash absorbed by operations	(11)

2   **Dividends received** from an associate or joint venture must be disclosed as a **separate cash flow** classified as '**Cash flows from investing activities**'. The cash receipt can be calculated as follows:

INVESTMENTS IN ASSOCIATES

	£		£
b/f Inv in A (CSFP)	X		
Share of profit of A (CSPL)	X	Dividend received (balancing figure)	X
		c/f Inv in A (CSFP)	X
	X		X

Interactive question 3: Dividends received from joint ventures

[Difficulty level: Exam standard]

Consolidated statement of profit or loss (extract) for the year ended 31 December 20X7

	£'000
Group profit from operations	100
Share of profit of joint venture	20
Profit before tax	120
Income tax expense	(50)
Profit for the year	70

Consolidated statement of financial position (extract) as at 31 December

	20X7	20X6
	£'000	£'000
Investments in joint ventures	184	176

Requirement

Calculate the dividend received from joint ventures during 20X7.

Complete the T account below.

INVESTMENTS IN JVs

£'000		£'000

See **Answer** at the end of this chapter.

2.4 Acquisitions and disposals of subsidiaries

If a subsidiary is acquired or disposed of during the accounting period **the net cash effect of the purchase or sale transaction should be shown separately under 'Cash flows from investing activities'**. The net cash effect will be the cash purchase price/cash disposal proceeds net of any cash or cash equivalents acquired or disposed of.

Worked example: Acquisition of a subsidiary

Warwick plc acquired 75% of Leamington Ltd by issuing 250,000 £1 shares at an agreed value of £2.50 and £200,000 in cash. At the date of acquisition the cash and cash equivalents in Leamington Ltd's statement of financial position amounted to £30,000.

In the statement of cash flows this would be shown as follows:

	£'000
Cash flows from investing activities	
Acquisition of subsidiary Leamington Ltd, net of cash acquired (200 – 30)	(170)

Disclosure is required in **the notes to the statement of cash flows** of the following in aggregate in respect of both acquisitions and disposals of subsidiaries during the period:

- **Total purchase price/disposal consideration**

- **Portion** of purchase price/disposal consideration **discharged by means of cash and cash equivalents**

- **Amount of cash and cash equivalents** in the subsidiary acquired or disposed of

- **Amount of assets and liabilities** other than cash and cash equivalents **in the subsidiary acquired or disposed of**, summarised by major category

Examples of these disclosures can be found in IAS 7 Appendix A.

Point to note

As the cash effect of the acquisition/disposal of the subsidiary is dealt with in a single line item as we saw above, **care must be taken not to double count the effects of the acquisition/disposal when looking at the movements in individual asset balances**.

Each of the individual assets and liabilities of a subsidiary acquired/disposed of during the period must be excluded when comparing group statements of financial position for cash flow calculations as follows:

Subsidiary acquired in the period	**Subtract** PPE, inventories, payables, receivables etc at the date of acquisition from the movement on these items.
Subsidiary disposed of in the period	**Add** PPE, inventories, payables, receivables etc at the date of disposal to the movements on these items.

This would also affect the calculation of the **dividend paid to the non-controlling interest**. The T account working introduced in Section 2.2 above would be modified as follows:

NON-CONTROLLING INTEREST

	£		£
NCI in S at disposal	X	b/f NCI (CSFP)	X
NCI dividend paid (balancing figure)	X	**NCI in S at acquisition**	X
c/f NCI (CSFP)	X	NCI (CSPL)	X
	X̲		X̲

Worked example: Calculating cash flows

Continuing from the worked example above (Acquisition of a subsidiary) you have the following additional information.

Consolidated statement of financial position (extract) of Warwick plc at 31 December

	20X7 £000	20X6 £000
Property, plant and equipment	500	400

At the date of acquisition Leamington Ltd's statement of financial position included property, plant and equipment at a carrying amount of £75,000.

There were no disposals of property, plant and equipment in the period. Depreciation of £25,000 was charged to the consolidated statement of profit or loss.

Calculate the amount to be disclosed as 'Purchase of property, plant and equipment' under 'Cash flows from investing activities'.

Solution

Normally, when preparing the statement of cash flows, a comparison of the opening and closing assets adjusted for depreciation would be made to determine the cost of additions. In this case if we make the comparison there are £125,000 of additional assets (500 + 25 – 400). However, £75,000 of these additional assets **are as a result of the acquisition of the subsidiary**. The cash outflow due to the purchase of the subsidiary as a whole is dealt with separately as we described above, therefore we are only concerned with any **other assets** purchased. Therefore the information would be presented as follows:

	£'000
Cash flows from investing activities	
Acquisition of subsidiary Leamington Ltd, net of cash acquired	(170)
Purchase of property, plant and equipment (500 + 25 – 400 – 75)	(50)

Alternatively the adjustment could be made in a T account working as follows:

PROPERTY, PLANT AND EQUIPMENT

	£'000		£'000
b/f	400	Depreciation	25
On acquisition	75		
Additions (balancing figure)	50	c/f	500
	525		525

Interactive question 4: Acquisition of a subsidiary   [Difficulty level: Exam standard]

On 1 October 20X8 P plc acquired 90% of S Ltd by issuing 100,000 shares at an agreed value of £2 per share and paying £100,000 in cash.

At that time the net assets of S Ltd were as follows:

	£'000
Property, plant and equipment	190
Inventories	70
Trade receivables	30
Cash and cash equivalents	10
Trade payables	(40)
	260

The consolidated statements of financial position of P plc as at 31 December were as follows:

	20X8 £'000	20X7 £'000
Non-current assets		
Property, plant and equipment	2,500	2,300
Goodwill	66	–
	2,566	2,300
Current assets		
Inventories	1,450	1,200
Trade receivables	1,370	1,100
Cash and cash equivalents	76	50
	2,896	2,350
	5,462	4,650
Equity attributable to owners of the parent		
Ordinary share capital (£1 shares)	1,150	1,000
Share premium account	650	500
Retained earnings	1,791	1,530
	3,591	3,030
Non-controlling interest	31	–
Total equity	3,622	3,030
Current liabilities		
Trade payables	1,690	1,520
Income tax payable	150	100
	1,840	1,620
	5,462	4,650

The consolidated statement of profit or loss for the year ended 31 December 20X8 was as follows:

	£'000
Revenue	10,000
Cost of sales	(7,500)
Gross profit	2,500
Administrative expenses	(2,080)
Profit before tax	420
Income tax expense	(150)
Profit for the year	270
Profit attributable to:	
Owners of P plc	261
Non-controlling interest	9
	270

The statement of changes in equity for the year ended 31 December 20X8 (extract) was as follows:

	Retained earnings £'000
Balance at 31 December 20X7	1,530
Total comprehensive income for the year	261
Balance at 31 December 20X8	1,791

You are also given the following information:

(1) All other subsidiaries are wholly owned.
(2) Depreciation charged to the consolidated statement of profit or loss amounted to £210,000.
(3) There were no disposals of property, plant and equipment during the year
(4) Goodwill is not impaired
(5) Non-controlling interest is valued on the proportionate basis

Requirement

Prepare a consolidated statement of cash flows for P plc for the year ended 31 December 20X8 under the indirect method in accordance with IAS 7 *Statement of Cash Flows*. The only notes required are those reconciling profit before tax to cash generated from operations and a note showing the effect of the subsidiary acquired in the period.

Complete the proforma below.

Consolidated statement of cash flows for the year ended 31 December 20X8

	£'000	£'000

Cash flows from operating activities
Cash generated from operations (Note 1)
Income taxes paid
Net cash from operating activities

Cash flows from investing activities
Acquisition of subsidiary S Ltd, net of cash acquired (Note 2)
Purchase of property, plant & equipment
Net cash used in investing activities

Cash flows from financing activities
Proceeds from issue of share capital
Dividend paid to non-controlling interest
Net cash from financing activities

Net increase in cash and cash equivalents
Cash and cash equivalents at the beginning of period
Cash and cash equivalents at the end of period

Notes to the statement of cash flows

(1)   **Reconciliation of profit before tax to cash generated from operations**

	£'000
Profit before taxation	
Adjustments for:	
Depreciation	
Increase in trade and other receivables	
Increase in inventories	
Increase in trade payables	
Cash generated from operations	

(2)   **Acquisition of subsidiary**

During the period the group acquired subsidiary S Ltd. The fair value of assets acquired and liabilities assumed were as follows:

	£'000
Cash and cash equivalents	
Inventories	
Receivables	
Property, plant and equipment	
Trade payables	
Non-controlling interest	
Goodwill	
Total purchase price	
Less: Cash of S Ltd	
Non-cash consideration	
Cash flow on acquisition net of cash acquired	

WORKINGS

(1)   PROPERTY, PLANT AND EQUIPMENT

	£'000		£'000

(2) GOODWILL

£'000	£'000

(3) NON-CONTROLLING INTEREST

£'000	£'000

(4) INCOME TAX PAYABLE

£'000	£'000

See **Answer** at the end of this chapter.

Interactive question 5: Disposal   [Difficulty level: Exam standard]

Below is the consolidated statement of financial position of the Othello Group as at 30 June 20X8 and the consolidated statement of profit or loss for the year ended on that date:

Consolidated statement of financial position as at 30 June

	20X8	20X7
	£'000	£'000
Non-current assets		
Property, plant and equipment	4,067	3,950
Current assets		
Inventories	736	535
Receivables	605	417
Cash and cash equivalents	294	238
	1,635	1,190
	5,702	5,140
Equity attributable to owners of the parent		
Share capital	1,000	1,000
Retained earnings	3,637	3,118
	4,637	4,118
Non-controlling interest	482	512
Total equity	5,119	4,630
Current liabilities		
Trade payables	380	408
Income tax payable	203	102
	583	510
	5,702	5,140

Consolidated statement of profit or loss for the year ended 30 June 20X8 (summarised)

	£'000
Continuing operations	
Profit before tax	862
Income tax expense	(290)
Profit for the year from continuing operations	572
Discontinued operations	
Profit for the year from discontinued operations	50
Profit for the year	622
Profit attributable to:	
Owners of Othello plc	519
Non-controlling interest	103
	622

You are given the following information:

(1) Othello plc sold its entire interest in Desdemona Ltd on 31 March 20X8 for cash of £400,000. Othello plc had acquired an 80% interest in Desdemona Ltd on incorporation several years ago. The net assets at the date of disposal were:

	£'000
Property, plant and equipment	390
Inventories	50
Receivables	39
Cash and cash equivalents	20
Trade payables	(42)
	457

(2) The profit for the period from discontinued operations figure is made up as follows:

	£'000
Profit before tax	20
Income tax expense	(4)
Profit on disposal	34
	50

(3) The depreciation charge for the year was £800,000.

There were no disposals of non-current assets other than on the disposal of the subsidiary.

Requirements

With regard to the consolidated statement of cash flows for the year ended 30 June 20X8:

(a) Show how the disposal will be reflected in the statement of cash flows.

(b) Calculate additions to property, plant and equipment as they will be reflected in the statement of cash flows.

(c) Calculate dividends paid to the non-controlling interest.

(d) Prepare the note to the statement of cash flows required for the disposal of the subsidiary.

(e) Prepare the reconciliation of profit before tax to cash generated from operations.

Work to the nearest £000

Complete the proforma below.

(a) **Cash flows from investing activities**

£'000

(b) **Cash flows from investing activities (W1)**

£'000

(c) **Cash flows from financing activities** (W2)

£'000

(d) **Note to the statement of cash flows**

During the period the group disposed of its subsidiary Desdemona Ltd. The carrying amount of assets and liabilities disposed of were as follows:

£'000

Cash and cash equivalents
Inventories
Receivables
Property, plant and equipment
Payables
Non-controlling interest (W2)

─────

Profit on disposal
Total sale proceeds
Less cash of Desdemona Ltd disposed of
Cash flow on disposal net of cash disposed of

─────
═════

(e) **Reconciliation of profit before tax to cash generated from operations**

£'000

Profit before tax
Adjustments for:
Depreciation

─────

Increase in receivables
Increase in inventories
Increase in payables
Cash generated from operations

─────
═════

WORKINGS

(1)   PROPERTY, PLANT AND EQUIPMENT – CARRYING AMOUNT

£'000		£'000

(2)   NON-CONTROLLING INTEREST

£'000		£'000

See **Answer** at the end of this chapter.

2.5 Acquisitions of associates and joint ventures

Payments of cash to acquire associates and joint ventures should be classified as '**Cash flows from investing activities.**'

Summary

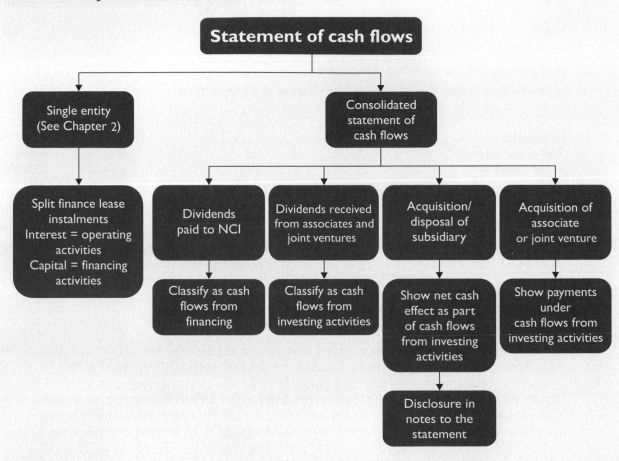

Self-test

Answer the following questions

1   In accordance with IAS 7 *Statement of Cash Flows* what is the net cash flow from financing activities given the information below?

Receipts	£	Payments	£
Share issue	5,000	Loan repayments (including £300 interest)	2,200
Loan	9,000	Expense of share issue	500

2   Sun plc provides the following information:

Consolidated statement of financial position as at 31 December

	20X8	20X7
	£	£
Inventories	550,000	475,000
Trade receivables	943,000	800,000
Trade payables	620,000	530,000

Consolidated statement of profit or loss for the year ended 31 December 20X8

	£
Profit before tax	775,000

During the year Sun plc acquired an 80% interest in the equity share capital of Shine Ltd. Extracts from Shine Ltd's statement of financial position at acquisition were as follows:

	£
Inventories	80,000
Trade receivables	110,000
Trade payables	70,000

In accordance with IAS 7 *Statement of Cash Flows* what is the cash generated from operations in the consolidated statement of cash flows of Sun plc for the year ended 31 December 20X8?

3   Spades plc, which has a number of subsidiaries, acquired an 80% interest in the share capital of Clubs Ltd on 1 May 20X6, when the net assets of Clubs Ltd were £600,000. Extracts from the consolidated statement of financial position of Spades plc as at 30 September 20X6 are as follows:

	20X6	20X5
	£	£
Non-controlling interest	750,000	720,000

Non-controlling interest in the profit for the year was £100,000.

What is the amount to be included in the consolidated statement of cash flows for the dividends paid to the non-controlling interest according to IAS 7 *Statement of Cash Flows*?

4   The following are extracts from the statement of financial position of Scratch Ltd as at 31 December:

	20X4	20X3
	£m	£m
Property, plant and equipment (Note 1)	192	175
Obligations under finance leases (Note 2)		
Within one year	20	10
After more than one year	51	45

Notes

1   During 20X4, Scratch Ltd disposed of property, plant and equipment with a carrying amount of £10 million and charged depreciation of £42 million.

2   Rentals paid under finance leases during 20X4 amounted to £18 million. Interest charged to the statement of profit or loss amounted to £6 million.

What amount should be included as purchase of property, plant and equipment in the statement of cash flows for the year ended 31 December 20X4 in accordance with IAS 7 *Statement of Cash Flows*?

5   The following extracts relate to Rain plc:

Consolidated statement of profit or loss for the year ended 31 December 20X5

	£
Group profit before tax	500,000
Income tax expense	(150,000)
Profit for the year	350,000
Profit attributable to:	
Owners of Rain plc	295,000
Non-controlling interest	55,000
	350,000

Consolidated statement of financial position as at 31 December

	20X5	20X4
	£	£
Non-controlling interest	550,000	525,000

During the year ended 31 December 20X5 Rain plc acquired a 75% interest in the equity shares of Puddle Ltd when the net assets of Puddle Ltd were £400,000.

In accordance with IAS 7 *Statement of Cash Flows* what was the amount of dividend paid to the non-controlling interest in the year ended 31 December 20X5?

6   Brink plc acquired a 75% interest in the share capital of Edge Ltd on 1 January 20X6. The balance on Edge Ltd's property, plant and equipment at that date was £500,000.

Extracts from the consolidated statement of financial position of Brink plc as at 31 December 20X6 are as follows:

	20X6	20X5
	£	£
Property, plant and equipment	4,100,000	3,700,000

Depreciation charged for the year ended 31 December 20X6 was £970,000.

What is the amount to be included in the consolidated statement of cash flows for purchase of property, plant and equipment in accordance with IAS 7 *Statement of Cash Flows*?

7   The consolidated financial statements of Brad plc show the following information:

Consolidated statement of profit or loss (extract) for the year ended 31 December 20X7

	£'000
Group profit from operations	220
Share of profit of associates	44
Profit before tax	264
Income tax expense	(110)
Profit for year	154

Consolidated statement of financial position (extract) as at 31 December 20X7

	20X7	20X6
	£'000	£'000
Investments in associates	405	387

In accordance with IAS 7 *Statement of Cash Flows* what is the dividend received from associates by the Brad group during the year ended 31 December 20X7?

8   Romeo plc had acquired 75% of Juliet Ltd for £750,000 a number of years ago. During the year ended 31 December 20X7 Romeo plc disposed of its entire interest in Juliet Ltd for £1,020,000 in cash. The net assets of Juliet Ltd at the date of disposal were:

	£'000
Property, plant and equipment	700
Inventories and receivables	150
Cash and cash equivalents	75
Trade payables	(47)
	878

In accordance with IAS 7 *Statement of Cash Flows* what amount would be disclosed as 'Disposal of subsidiary' under cash flows from investing activities?

9 CLOUDESDALE PLC

Cloudesdale plc has a number of subsidiaries and an investment in a joint venture. A junior accountant has prepared the following group statement of cash flows.

Consolidated statement of cash flows for the year ended 31 December 20X9

	£m	£m
Net cash from operating activities		354
Cash flows from investing activities		
Purchase of property, plant and equipment	(105)	
Net cash used in investing activities		(105)
Cash flows from financing activities		
Repayment of loan notes	(80)	
Net cash used in financing activities		(80)
Net increase in cash and cash equivalents		169

Note: Reconciliation of profit before tax to net cash from operating activities

	£m
Group profit before taxation	335
Depreciation	120
Interest expense	15
	470
Decrease in inventories	42
Increase in trade receivables	(16)
Decrease in trade payables	(57)
Cash generated from operations	439
Interest paid	(20)
Income tax paid	(65)
Net cash from operating activities	354

The increase in cash and cash equivalents shown above does not agree to the amounts of cash and cash equivalents shown in the consolidated statements of financial position at 31 December 20X8 (£124,000) and 31 December 20X9 (£235,000). This is because the following issues have not been taken into account:

(1) Cloudesdale plc acquired a 100% subsidiary during the year. The assets acquired and consideration transferred were as follows:

	£m
Property, plant and equipment	90
Inventories	20
Trade receivables	25
Cash and cash equivalents	15
Trade payables	(40)
Goodwill	30
Consideration transferred (all cash)	140

(2) Non-controlling interest brought forward at the beginning of the year was £70m. Profit attributable to the non-controlling interest for the year ended 31 December 20X9 was £35m. The consolidated statement of financial position at 31 December 20X9 showed non-controlling interest at £79m.

(3) The group profit before taxation includes £8m being group share of profit of a joint venture. During the year dividends of £6m were received from the joint venture.

Requirement

In accordance with IAS 7 *Statement of Cash Flows*, prepare an amended statement of cash flows and reconciliation of profit before tax to net cash from operating activities for Cloudesdale plc for the year ended 31 December 20X9, taking account of issues 1 to 3 above.

10   GREENFINGERS PLC

Greenfingers plc is a 40-year-old company producing wooden furniture. Twenty-two years ago it acquired a 100% interest in a timber import company, Arbre Ltd. In 20W9 it acquired a 40% interest in a competitor, Water Features Ltd and on 1 January 20X7 it acquired a 75% interest in Garden Furniture Designs Ltd. The draft consolidated accounts for the Greenfingers Group are as follows.

Draft consolidated statement of profit or loss for the year ended 31 December 20X7

	£'000
Profit from operations	4,455
Share of profit of associates	1,050
Dividends from long-term investments	465
Interest payable	(450)
Profit before taxation	5,520
Income tax expense	(1,485)
Profit for the year	4,035
Profit attributable to:	
Owners of Greenfingers plc	3,735
Non-controlling interest	300
	4,035

Draft consolidated statement of financial position as at 31 December

	20X7		20X6	
	£'000	£'000	£'000	£'000
ASSETS				
Non-current assets				
Property, plant and equipment				
Buildings at carrying amount		6,225		6,600
Machinery: Cost	9,000		4,200	
Accumulated depreciation	(3,600)		(3,300)	
Carrying amount		5,400		900
		11,625		7,500
Goodwill		300		–
Investments in associates		3,300		3,000
Available-for-sale financial assets		1,230		1,230
		16,455		11,730
Current assets				
Inventories	5,925		3,000	
Receivables	5,550		3,825	
Cash and cash equivalents	13,545		5,460	
		25,020		12,285
Total assets		41,475		24,015

	20X7		20X6	
	£'000	£'000	£'000	£'000
EQUITY AND LIABILITIES				
Equity attributable to owners of the parent				
Ordinary share capital (25p shares)	11,820		6,000	
Share premium account	8,649		6,285	
Retained earnings	10,335		7,500	
	30,804		19,785	
Non-controlling interest	345		–	
Total equity		31,149		19,785
Non-current liabilities				
Finance lease liabilities	2,130		510	
Loans	4,380		1,500	
		6,510		2,010
Current liabilities				
Trade payables	1,500		840	
Finance lease liabilities	720		600	
Income tax payable	1,476		690	
Accrued interest and finance charges	120		90	
		3,816		2,220
Total equity and liabilities		41,475		24,015

Additional information

(1) There have been no acquisitions or disposals of buildings during the year.

Machinery costing £1.5 million was sold for £1.5 million resulting in a profit of £300,000. New machinery was acquired in 20X7, including additions of £2.55 million acquired under finance leases.

(2) Information relating to the acquisition of Garden Furniture Designs Ltd is as follows:

	£'000
Property, plant and equipment	495
Inventories	96
Trade receivables	84
Cash	336
Trade payables	(204)
Income tax	(51)
	756
Non-controlling interest	(189)
	567
Goodwill	300
	867
2,640,000 ordinary shares issued as part consideration	825
Balance of consideration paid in cash	42
	867

Requirement

Prepare a consolidated statement of cash flows for the Greenfingers Group for the year ended 31 December 20X7 using the indirect method. The only note required is that reconciling profit before tax to cash generated from operations. **(17 marks)**

Technical reference

Point to note: All of IAS 7 is examinable with the exception of paragraphs 24–28, 38 and Appendix B. The paragraphs listed below are the key references you should be familiar with.

1 Statement of cash flows and finance leases

- Disclose the assets acquired via finance leases as a non-cash transaction · · · · · · · · · IAS 7 (43–44)

2 Group statements of cash flows

- Example of a consolidated statement of cash flows · · · · · · · · · IAS 7 Appendix A

- Cash flows arising from acquisitions/disposals of subsidiaries and acquisitions of associates should be · · · · · · · · · IAS 7 (39)

  - Presented separately

  - Classified as investing activities

- Additional information should be disclosed in respect of acquisitions and disposals · · · · · · · · · IAS 7 (40)

Also see **Chapter 2** Technical reference section.

Answer to Interactive question 1

Statement of cash flows (extract) for the year ended 31 December 20X7

	£
Cash flows from operating activities	
Interest paid	(2,487)
Cash flows from financing activities	
Payment of finance lease liabilities	(7,513)

WORKING

Year ended 31 December 20X7	Bal b/f 1.1.X7 £	Interest accrued at 10% £	Payment 31 December 20X7 £	Bal c/f 31.12.X7 £
	24,869	2,487	(10,000)	17,356

The payment of £10,000 therefore represents:

	£
Interest	2,487
Capital (10,000 – 2,487)	7,513
	10,000

Answer to Interactive question 2

NON-CONTROLLING INTEREST

	£'000		£'000
		b/f NCI (CSFP)	200
		NCI (CSPL)	10
NCI dividend paid (bal figure)	6		
c/f NCI (CSFP)	204		
	210		210

Answer to Interactive question 3

INVESTMENTS IN JVs

	£'000		£'000
b/f Inv in JV	176		
Share of profit of JV	20	**Dividend received** (balancing figure)	12
		c/f Inv in JV	184
	196		196

Answer to Interactive question 4

Consolidated statement of cash flows for the year ended 31 December 20X8

	£'000	£'000
Cash flows from operating activities		
Cash generated from operations (Note 1)	340	
Income taxes paid (W4)	(100)	
Net cash from operating activities		240
Cash flows from investing activities		
Acquisition of subsidiary S Ltd, net of cash acquired (Note 2)	(90)	
Purchase of property, plant and equipment (W1)	(220)	
Net cash used in investing activities		(310)
Cash flows from financing activities		
Proceeds from issue of share capital (1,150 + 650 − 1,000 − 500 − (100 × £2))	100	
Dividend paid to non-controlling interest (W3)	(4)	
Net cash from financing activities		96
Net increase in cash and cash equivalents		26
Cash and cash equivalents at the beginning of period		50
Cash and cash equivalents at the end of period		76

Notes to the statement of cash flows

(1) **Reconciliation of profit before tax to cash generated from operations**

	£'000
Profit before taxation	420
Adjustments for:	
Depreciation	210
	630
Increase in trade receivables (1,370 − 1,100 − 30)	(240)
Increase in inventories (1,450 − 1,200 − 70)	(180)
Increase in trade payables (1,690 − 1,520 − 40)	130
Cash generated from operations	340

(2) **Acquisition of subsidiary**

During the period the group acquired subsidiary S Ltd. The fair value of assets acquired and liabilities assumed were as follows:

	£'000
Cash and cash equivalents	10
Inventories	70
Receivables	30
Property, plant and equipment	190
Trade payables	(40)
Non-controlling interest	(26)
	234
Goodwill	66
Total purchase price	300
Less: Cash of S Ltd	(10)
Non-cash consideration	(200)
Cash flow on acquisition net of cash acquired	90

WORKINGS

(1) PROPERTY, PLANT AND EQUIPMENT

	£'000		£'000
b/f	2,300	Depreciation	210
On acquisition	190	c/f	2,500
Additions (balancing figure)	220		
	2,710		2,710

(2)

GOODWILL

	£'000		£'000
b/f	–		
Additions (300 – (90% × 260))	66	Impairment losses (balancing figure)	0
		c/f	66
	66		66

(3)

NON-CONTROLLING INTEREST

	£'000		£'000
Dividend (balancing figure)	4	b/f	–
c/f	31	On acquisition	26
		CSPL	9
	35		35

(4)

INCOME TAX PAYABLE

	£'000		£'000
		b/f	100
Cash paid (balancing figure)	100	CSPL	150
c/f	150		
	250		250

Answer to Interactive question 5

(a) **Cash flows from investing activities**

	£'000
Disposal of subsidiary Desdemona Ltd, net of cash disposed of (400 – 20)	380

(b) **Cash flows from investing activities**

	£'000
Purchase of property, plant and equipment (W1)	(1,307)

(c) **Cash flows from financing activities**

	£'000
Dividends paid to non-controlling interest (W2)	(42)

(d) **Note to the statement of cash flows**

During the period the group disposed of subsidiary Desdemona Ltd. The book value of assets and liabilities disposed of were as follows:

	£'000
Cash and cash equivalents	20
Inventories	50
Receivables	39
Property, plant and equipment	390
Payables	(42)
Non-controlling interest (W2)	(91)
	366
Profit on disposal	34
Total sale proceeds	400
Less cash of Desdemona Ltd disposed of	(20)
Cash flow on disposal net of cash disposed of	380

(e) **Reconciliation of profit before tax to cash generated from operations**

	£'000
Profit before tax (862 + 20)	882
Adjustments for:	
Depreciation	800
	1,682
Increase in receivables (605 – 417 + 39)	(227)
Increase in inventories (736 – 535 + 50)	(251)
Increase in payables (380 – 408 + 42)	14
Cash generated from operations	1,218

(1)

PROPERTY, PLANT AND EQUIPMENT – CARRYING AMOUNT

	£'000		£'000
b/f	3,950	c/f	4,067
Additions (balancing figure)	1,307	Disposal of sub	390
		Depreciation charge	800
	5,257		5,257

(2)

NON-CONTROLLING INTEREST

	£'000		£'000
c/f	482	b/f	512
Disposal of sub (457 × 20%)	91	CSPL	103
Dividends to NCI			
(balancing figure)	42		
	615		615

1   £11,600

		£
Inflows	Share issue	5,000
	Loan	9,000
		14,000
Outflows	Share expenses	(500)
	Loan repayments, less interest (2,200 – 300)	(1,900)
		11,600

2   £767,000

	£
Profit before tax	775,000
Decrease in inventory (550 – 475 – 80)	5,000
Increase in receivables (943 – 800 – 110)	(33,000)
Increase in payables (620 – 530 – 70)	20,000
	767,000

3   £190,000

NON-CONTROLLING INTEREST

	£'000		£'000
c/f	750	b/f	720
		Non-controlling interest in profit for the year	100
Dividend paid to non-controlling interest (β)	190	Acquisition of subsidiary (600 × 20%)	120
	940		940

4   £41 million

The additions in the statement of cash flows should only be additions for cash. The commencement of a finance lease is not a cash transaction and must therefore be excluded. The amount of assets acquired under finance leases is calculated by looking at the movement in the liability for finance leases. As this balance represents capital only, the payment which goes into the working must exclude the interest element.

NON-CURRENT ASSETS – CARRYING AMOUNT

	£m		£m
b/f	175	Depreciation	42
Total additions (β)	69	Disposals	10
		c/f	192
	244		244

OBLIGATIONS UNDER FINANCE LEASES

	£m		£m
Payment	12	b/f	55
		Additions (β)	28
c/f	71		
	83		83

Therefore additions for cash (69 – 28) = £41m

5 £130,000

NON-CONTROLLING INTEREST

	£		£
		b/f (CSFP)	525,000
NCI dividend paid (β)	130,000	NCI (CSPL)	55,000
		NCI in S acquired (400,000 × 25%)	100,000
c/f (CSFP)	550,000		
	680,000		680,000

6 £870,000

PPE – CARRYING AMOUNT

	£'000		£'000
b/f	3,700		
Acquired with Edge	500	Depreciation charge	970
Additions (β)	870	c/f	4,100
	5,070		5,070

7 £26,000

INVESTMENTS IN ASSOCIATES

	£'000		£'000
b/f (CSFP)	387		
Share of profit (CSPL)	44	Dividend received (β)	26
(tax already deducted)			
		c/f (CSFP)	405
	431		431

8 £945,000 (1,020,000 – 75,000)

9 CLOUDESDALE PLC

Statement of cash flows for the year ended 31 December 20X9

	£m	£m
Net cash from operating activities		351
Cash flows from investing activities		
Purchase of property, plant and equipment (105 – 90 re acq)	(15)	
Acquisition of subsidiary net of cash acquired (140 – 15)	(125)	
Dividend received from joint venture	6	
Net cash used in investing activities		(134)
Cash flows from financing activities		
Repayment of loan notes	(80)	
Dividend paid to non-controlling interest (70 + 35 – 79)	(26)	
Net cash used in financing activities		(106)
Net increase in cash and cash equivalents		111
Cash and cash equivalents at 31 December 20X8		124
Cash and cash equivalents at 31 December 20X9		235

Note: Reconciliation of profit before tax to net cash from operating activities

	£m
Group profit before taxation	335
Less share of profit of joint venture	(8)
Depreciation	120
Interest expense	15
	462
Decrease in inventories (42 + 20 re acq)	62
Decrease in trade receivables (16 – 25 re acq)	9
Decrease in trade payables (57 + 40 re acq)	(97)
Cash generated from operations	436
Interest paid	(20)
Income tax paid	(65)
Net cash from operating activities	351

CHAPTER

15

ICAEW

10 GREENFINGERS PLC

Consolidated statement of cash flows for the year ended 31 December 20X7

	£'000	£'000
Cash flows from operating activities		
Cash generated from operations (Note)	1,116	
Interest paid (W2)	(420)	
Income taxes paid (W3)	(750)	
Net cash used in operating activities		(54)
Cash flows from investing activities		
Acquisition of subsidiary Garden Furniture Designs Ltd, net of cash	294	
Purchase of property, plant and equipment (W5)	(3,255)	
Proceeds from sale of property, plant and equipment	1,500	
Dividends received from investments	465	
Dividends received from associates (W6)	750	
Net cash used in investing activities		(246)
Cash flows from financing activities		
Proceeds from issue of ordinary share capital (W7)	7,359	
Proceeds from issue of loan notes (W8)	2,880	
Payments under finance leases (W10)	(810)	
Dividends paid to shareholders of Greenfingers plc (3,735 + 7,500 – 10,335)	(900)	
Dividends paid to non-controlling interests (W9)	(144)	
Net cash from financing activities		8,385
Net increase in cash and cash equivalents		8,085
Cash and cash equivalents at beginning of year		5,460
Cash and cash equivalents at end of year		13,545

Note: Reconciliation of profit before tax to cash generated from operations

	£'000
Profit before tax	5,520
Adjustments for:	
Depreciation (W1)	975
Profit on sale of property, plant and equipment	(300)
Share of profits of associates	(1,050)
Investment income	(465)
Interest expense	450
	5,130
Increase in receivables (5,550 – 3,825 – 84)	(1,641)
Increase in inventories (5,925 – 3,000 – 96)	(2,829)
Increase in trade payables (1,500 – 840 – 204)	456
Cash generated from operations	1,116

WORKINGS

(1) ACCUMULATED DEPRECIATION – MACHINERY

	£'000		£'000
		b/f (Machinery)	3,300
Disposal	300		
		Depreciation charge (β)	600
c/f (Machinery)	3,600		
	3,900		3,900

Total depreciation:	£'000
Freehold buildings (6,600 – 6,225)	375
Machinery	600
	975

(2) INTEREST PAYABLE

	£'000		£'000
Cash paid (β)	420	b/f	90
c/f	120	CSPL	450
	540		540

TAXATION

	£'000		£'000
Cash paid (β)	750	b/f	690
c/f	1,476	CSPL	1,485
		On acquisition	51
	2,226		2,226

(4) Purchase of subsidiary

	£'000
Cash received on acquisition	336
Less cash consideration	(42)
Net cash inflow	294

(5)

MACHINERY – COST

	£'000		£'000
b/f	4,200	Disposal	1,500
On acquisition	495		
Leased	2,550		
Additions (β)	3,255	c/f	9,000
	10,500		10,500

(6)

INVESTMENTS IN ASSOCIATES

	£'000		£'000
b/f	3,000		
Share of profit (CSPL)	1,050	Dividends received (β)	750
		c/f	3,300
	4,050		4,050

(7)

SHARE CAPITAL AND PREMIUM

	£'000		£'000
		b/f (6,000 + 6,285)	12,285
		Non-cash consideration (660 + 165)	825
c/f (11,820 + 8,649)	20,469	Proceeds from issue (β)	7,359
	20,469		20,469

(8)

LOAN NOTES

	£'000		£'000
		b/f	1,500
		Proceeds from issue (β)	2,880
c/f	4,380		
	4,380		4,380

(9)

NON-CONTROLLING INTEREST

	£'000		£'000
		b/f	–
Dividends to NCI (β)	144	Share of profits (CSPL)	300
c/f	345	On acquisition	189
	489		489

(10)

OBLIGATIONS UNDER FINANCE LEASES

	£'000		£'000
		b/f Current	600
		Long-term	510
Capital repayment (β)	810	New lease commitment	2,550
c/f Current	720		
Long-term	2,130		
	3,660		3,660

CHAPTER

15

CHAPTER 16

UK GAAP – FRS 102

Introduction
Examination context
Topic List

Learning objectives

- Explain the standard-setting process used by UK and international bodies and the authority of UK and international standards, using appropriate examples as illustration ☐

- Describe the principal differences between IFRS and UK GAAP and prepare simple extracts from single entity financial statements in accordance with UK GAAP ☐

- Describe the principal differences between IFRS and UK GAAP and prepare simple extracts from consolidated financial statements in accordance with UK GAAP ☐

Specific syllabus references for this chapter are: 1a, 2e, 3g.

Examination context

Explain and illustrate the differences between the relevant treatment under IFRS and UK GAAP

1 Scope

Section overview

- FRS 102 is derived from the IFRS for SMEs. It is one of the new financial reporting standards replacing old UK GAAP. It can be used by UK unlisted groups and by listed and unlisted individual entities.

FRS 102 'is a single financial reporting standard that applies to the financial statements of entities that are not applying EU-adopted IFRS, FRS 101 or the FRSSE… [It] aims to provide entities with succinct financial reporting requirements. The requirements in the FRS are based on the IASB's IFRS for SMEs issued in 2009. The IFRS for SMEs is intended to apply to the general purpose financial statements of, and other financial reporting by, entities that in many countries are referred to by a variety of terms including 'small and medium-sized', 'private' and 'non-publicly accountable'.

'The IFRS for SMEs is a simplification of the principles in IFRS for recognising and measuring assets, liabilities, income and expenses; in most cases it includes only the simpler accounting treatment where IFRS permits accounting options, it contains fewer disclosures and is drafted more succinctly than IFRS. Whilst respondents to FRED 44 welcomed simplification, many did not support the removal of accounting options where those options were permitted in extant FRS. As a consequence, the ASB amended the IFRS for SMEs to include accounting options in current FRS and permitted by IFRS, but not included in the IFRS for SMEs'. (FRS 102 *Summary*)

Listed UK groups are required to prepare their consolidated financial statements in accordance with IFRS. FRS 102 may be applied by any other entity or group, including parent and subsidiary companies within a listed group. A company applying FRS 102 is reporting under the Companies Act. FRS 102 can also be used by entities that are not companies and therefore not subject to company law.

Qualifying entities may take advantage of certain disclosure exemptions within the standard. A qualifying entity for this purpose is a member of a group where the parent of that group prepares publicly available consolidated financial statements intended to give a true and fair view of the position and performance of the group and that member is included in the consolidation.

The key exemptions (not to be confused with the exemptions available under FRS 101) are:

- Preparation of a statement of cash flows
- Certain financial instrument disclosures
- Certain share-based payment disclosures
- Disclosure of key management personnel compensation
- Reconciliation of shares outstanding in the period

Entities that are required to disclose earnings per share or segment information in their financial statements should also apply IAS 33 *Earnings per Share* and/or IFRS 8 *Operating Segments*.

FRS 102 is effective for accounting periods beginning on or after 1 January 2015. It is also applicable to public benefit entities.

Point to note: This chapter covers FRS 102 in its entirety, so includes issues such as share-based payment which are not in the FAR syllabus. This is to give students a broad overview of the standard. Section 13 is a good summary of those topics which are examinable.

2 Concepts and pervasive principles

Section overview

- FRS 102 states that the objective of financial statements is to provide information about the financial position, performance and cash flows of an entity to aid users in decision-making.

2.1 Qualitative characteristics

The qualitative characteristics of financial information set out in FRS 102 include those characteristics recognised under IFRS in the *Conceptual Framework*, with a few additions.

2.1.1 Understandability

The information provided in financial statements should be presented in a way that makes it comprehensible by users who have a reasonable knowledge of business, economic activities and accounting and a willingness to study the information with reasonable diligence. However, the need for understandability does not allow relevant information to be omitted on the grounds that it may be too difficult for some users to understand.

2.1.2 Relevance

The information provided in financial statements must be relevant to the decision-making needs of users. Information has the quality of relevance when it is capable of influencing the economic decisions of users by helping them evaluate past, present or future events or confirming, or correcting, their past evaluations.

2.1.3 Materiality

Information is material – and therefore has relevance – if its omission or misstatement, individually or collectively, could influence the economic decisions of users taken on the basis of the financial statements. Materiality depends on the size and nature of the omission or misstatement judged in the surrounding circumstances. The size or nature of the item, or a combination of both, could be the determining factor.

2.1.4 Reliability

The information provided in financial statements must be reliable. Information is reliable when it is free from material error and bias and represents faithfully that which it either purports to represent or could reasonably be expected to represent. Financial statements are not free from bias (ie not neutral) if, by the selection or presentation of information, they are intended to influence the making of a decision or judgement in order to achieve a predetermined result or outcome.

2.1.5 Substance over form

Transactions and other events and conditions should be accounted for and presented in accordance with their substance and not merely their legal form. This enhances the reliability of financial statements.

2.1.6 Prudence

The uncertainties that inevitably surround many events and circumstances are acknowledged by the disclosure of their nature and extent and by the exercise of prudence in the preparation of the financial statements. Prudence is the inclusion of a degree of caution in the exercise of the judgements needed in making the estimates required under conditions of uncertainty, such that assets or income are not overstated and liabilities or expenses are not understated. However, the exercise of prudence does not allow the deliberate understatement of assets or income, or the deliberate overstatement of liabilities or expenses. In short, prudence does not permit bias.

2.1.7 Completeness

To be reliable, the information in financial statements must be complete within the bounds of materiality and cost. An omission can cause information to be false or misleading and thus unreliable and deficient in terms of its relevance.

2.1.8 Comparability

Users must be able to compare the financial statements of an entity through time to identify trends in its financial position and performance. Users must also be able to compare the financial statements of different entities to evaluate their relative financial position, performance and cash flows. Hence, the measurement and display of the financial effects of like transactions and other events and conditions must be carried out in a consistent way throughout an entity and over time for that entity, and in a consistent way across entities. In addition, users must be informed of the accounting policies employed in the preparation of the financial statements, and of any changes in those policies and the effects of such changes.

2.1.9 Timeliness

To be relevant, financial information must be able to influence the economic decisions of users. Timeliness involves providing the information within the decision time frame. If there is undue delay in the reporting of information it may lose its relevance. Management may need to balance the relative merits of timely reporting and the provision of reliable information. In achieving a balance between relevance and reliability, the overriding consideration is how best to satisfy the needs of users in making economic decisions.

2.1.10 Balance between benefit and cost

The benefits derived from information should not exceed the cost of providing it. The evaluation of benefits and costs is substantially a judgemental process. Also, the costs are not necessarily borne by those users who enjoy the benefits, often the benefits of the information are enjoyed by a broad range of external users.

Interactive question 1: Which concepts apply in these scenarios? [Difficulty level: Easy]

Question	Fill in your answer
(a) Oak plc is being sued for a large amount of money by a supplier. Legal opinion is that there is a high probability that Oak plc will lose the case. The managing director says he feels confident that this will not happen, so decides to spend the money on a dividend to keep the shareholders happy.	
(b) Elm plc is being sued for compensation by an ex-employee. Legal advice is that the ex-employee does not have a good case and the possibility of having to pay compensation is remote. However, the managing director says he always prefers to err on the side of caution and the financial statements are showing a large profit so he inserts a provision for the full amount.	
(c) Sycamore plc has always valued inventories using the FIFO basis. A new financial controller has pointed out that the weighted average basis is more appropriate for their industry, so for this year inventories will be valued using the weighted average method.	

See **Answer** at the end of this chapter.

2.2 Financial position

The financial position of an entity is the relationship of its assets, liabilities and equity as of a specific date as presented in the statement of financial position. These are defined as follows:

(a) An **asset** is a resource controlled by the entity as a result of past events and from which future economic benefits are expected to flow to the entity.

(b) A **liability** is a present obligation of the entity arising from past events, the settlement of which is expected to result in an outflow from the entity of resources embodying economic benefits.

(c) **Equity** is the residual interest in the assets of the entity after deducting all its liabilities.

2.3 Financial performance

Performance is the relationship of the income and expenses of an entity during a reporting period. FRS 102 permits entities to present performance in a single financial statement (a statement of comprehensive income) or in two financial statements (an income statement and a statement of comprehensive income).

Income and expenses are defined as follows:

(a) **Income** is increases in economic benefits during the reporting period in the form of inflows or enhancements of assets or decreases of liabilities that result in increases in equity, other than those relating to contributions from equity investors.

(b) **Expenses** are decreases in economic benefits during the reporting period in the form of outflows or depletions of assets or incurrences of liabilities that result in decreases in equity, other than those relating to distributions to equity investors.

The recognition of income and expenses results directly from the recognition and measurement of assets and liabilities.

2.4 Income

The definition of income encompasses both revenue and gains.

(a) Revenue is income that arises in the course of the ordinary activities of an entity and is referred to by a variety of names including sales, fees, interest, dividends, royalties and rent.

(b) Gains are other items that meet the definition of income but are not revenue.

2.5 Expenses

The definition of expenses encompasses losses as well as those expenses that arise in the course of the ordinary activities of the entity.

(a) Expenses that arise in the course of the ordinary activities of the entity include, for example, cost of sales, wages and depreciation. They usually take the form of an outflow or depletion of assets such as cash and cash equivalents, inventory, or property, plant and equipment.

(b) Losses are other items that meet the definition of expenses and may arise in the course of the ordinary activities of the entity.

2.6 Recognition

Recognition is the process of incorporating in the statement of financial position or statement of comprehensive income an item that meets the definition of an asset, liability, equity, income or expense and satisfies the following criteria:

(a) It is probable that any future economic benefit associated with the item will flow to or from the entity; and

(b) The item has a cost or value that can be measured reliably.

2.6.1 Assets

An entity should recognise an asset in the statement of financial position when it is probable that the future economic benefits will flow to the entity and the asset has a cost or value that can be measured reliably.

2.6.2 Liabilities

An entity should recognise a liability in the statement of financial position when:

(a) The entity has an obligation at the end of the reporting period as a result of a past event;

(b) It is probable that the entity will be required to transfer resources embodying economic benefits in settlement; and

(c) The settlement amount can be measured reliably.

2.6.3 Income

The recognition of income results directly from the recognition and measurement of assets and liabilities.

2.6.4 Expenses

The recognition of expenses results directly from the recognition and measurement of assets and liabilities.

2.7 Measurement

At initial recognition, an entity should measure assets and liabilities at **historical cost** unless FRS 102 requires initial measurement on another basis such as **fair value**.

2.8 Accrual basis

An entity should prepare its financial statements, except for cash flow information, using the **accrual basis** of accounting.

2.9 The statutory 'true and fair override'

The CA 2006 requires that where compliance with its accounting rules would not lead to a true and fair view, **those rules should be departed from** to the extent necessary to give a true and fair view.

Where the override of the statutory accounting requirements is invoked, eg to comply with an accounting standard, **the Act requires disclosure** of the particulars of the departure, the reason for it, and the financial effect.

The CA 2006 also states that where compliance with its disclosure requirements is insufficient to give a true and fair view, **additional information should be disclosed** such that a true and fair view is provided.

3 Financial statement presentation

Section overview

- Financial statements are used to make economic decisions by a wide range of users.

- Financial statements must present fairly the financial position, financial performance and cash flows of an entity.

3.1 Going concern

When preparing financial statements, the management of an entity using FRS 102 should make an assessment of the entity's ability to continue as a going concern.

When management is aware, in making its assessment, of material uncertainties related to events or conditions that cast significant doubt upon the entity's ability to continue as a going concern, the entity should disclose those uncertainties. When an entity does not prepare financial statements on a going concern basis, it should disclose that fact, together with the basis on which it prepared the financial statements and the reason why the entity is not regarded as a going concern.

3.2 Complete set of financial statements

A complete set of financial statements of an entity includes all of the following:

(a) A statement of financial position as at the reporting date;

(b) Either:

    (i) A single statement of comprehensive income for the reporting period showing all items of income and expense recognised during the period and items of other comprehensive income; or

    (ii) A separate income statement and a separate statement of comprehensive income.

    If an entity chooses to present both an income statement and a statement of comprehensive income, the statement of comprehensive income begins with profit or loss and then displays the items of other comprehensive income.

(c) A statement of changes in equity for the reporting period;

(d) A statement of cash flows for the reporting period; and

(e) Notes, comprising a summary of significant accounting policies and other explanatory information.

3.3 Statement of financial position

The statement of financial position (which is referred to as the balance sheet in the Act) presents an entity's assets, liabilities and equity as of a specific date – the end of the reporting period.

3.3.1 Debtors due after more than one year

In instances where the amount of debtors due after more than one year is so material in the context of the total net current assets that the absence of disclosure may lead readers to misinterpret the financial statements, the amount should be disclosed on the face of the statement of financial position within current assets.

3.3.2 Creditors: amounts falling due within one year

An entity should classify a creditor as due within one year when the entity does not have an unconditional right, at the end of the reporting period, to defer settlement of the creditor for at least 12 months after the reporting date.

3.4 Statement of comprehensive income and income statement

An entity should present its total comprehensive income for a period using either the single statement or two statement approach as identified above.

Note: A change from the single-statement approach to the two-statement approach, or vice versa, is a change in accounting policy.

3.4.1 Extraordinary items

Ordinary activities are any activities which are undertaken by a reporting entity as part of its business and such related activities in which the reporting entity engages in furtherance of, incidental to, or arising from, these activities.

Extraordinary items are material items possessing a high degree of abnormality which arise from events or transactions that fall outside the ordinary activities of the reporting entity and which are not expected to recur.

3.4.2 Discontinued operations

These are shown as a **separate column** in the income statement or statement of comprehensive income and restated for the prior year.

3.5 Statement of changes in equity and statement of income and retained earnings

3.5.1 Statement of income and retained earnings

If the only changes to equity during the periods for which financial statements are presented arise from profit or loss, payment of dividends, corrections of prior period errors and changes in accounting policy, an entity may present a single **statement of income and retained earnings** in place of the statement of comprehensive income and statement of changes in equity.

3.5.2 Information to be presented in the statement of changes in equity

An entity should present a statement of changes in equity showing in the statement:

(a) Total comprehensive income for the period, showing separately the total amounts attributable to owners of the parent and to non-controlling interests;

(b) For each component of equity, the effects of retrospective application or retrospective restatement recognised in accordance with Section 10 *Accounting Policies, Estimates and Errors*; and

(c) For each component of equity, a reconciliation between the carrying amount at the beginning and the end of the period, separately disclosing changes resulting from:

(i) Profit or loss;

(ii) Other comprehensive income; and

(iii) The amounts of investments by, and dividends and other distributions to, owners, showing separately issues of shares, purchase of own share transactions, dividends and other distributions to owners and changes in ownership interests in subsidiaries that do not result in a loss of control.

3.5.3 Information to be presented in the statement of income and retained earnings

An entity should present, in the statement of income and retained earnings, the following items in addition to the information required to be shown in the statement of comprehensive income and income statement:

(a) Retained earnings at the beginning of the reporting period;
(b) Dividends declared and paid or payable during the period;
(c) Restatements of retained earnings for corrections of prior period material errors;
(d) Restatements of retained earnings for changes in accounting policy; and
(e) Retained earnings at the end of the reporting period.

3.6 Statement of cash flows

The statement of cash flows provides information about the changes in cash and cash equivalents of an entity for a reporting period, showing separately changes from operating activities, investing activities and financing activities. This is the same as the IFRS format.

Cash equivalents are short-term, highly liquid investments that are readily convertible to known amounts of cash and that are subject to an insignificant risk of changes in value.

Cash flows from operating activities can be presented using either the direct or the indirect method.

4 Reporting financial performance

Section overview

- In this section we will be looking at:
    - Accounting policies
    - Discontinued operations
    - Related party disclosures
    - Foreign currency translation

4.1 Accounting policies, estimates and errors

4.1.1 Accounting policies

Accounting policies are the specific principles, bases, conventions, rules and practices applied by an entity in preparing and presenting financial statements.

Management should use its judgement in developing and applying an accounting policy that results in information that is:

(a) Relevant to the economic decision-making needs of users; and

(b) Reliable, in that the financial statements:

    (i) Represent faithfully the financial position, financial performance and cash flows of the entity;

    (ii) Reflect the economic substance of transactions, other events and conditions and not merely the legal form;

    (iii) Are neutral, ie free from bias;

    (iv) Are prudent; and

    (v) Are complete in all material respects.

An entity should change an accounting policy only if the change:

(a) Is required by an FRS or FRC Abstract; or

(b) Results in the financial statements providing reliable and more relevant information about the effects of transactions and events on the entity's financial position, financial performance or cash flows.

The following are **not** changes in accounting policies:

(a) The application of an accounting policy for transactions, other events or conditions that differ in substance from those previously occurring;

(b) The application of a new accounting policy for transactions, other events or conditions that did not occur previously or were not material; and

(c) A change to the cost model when a reliable measure of fair value is no longer available (or vice versa) for an asset that would otherwise be measured at fair value.

4.1.2 Changes in accounting estimates

A change in accounting estimate is an adjustment of the carrying amount of an asset or a liability, or the amount of the periodic consumption of an asset, that results from the assessment of the present status of, and expected future benefits and obligations associated with, assets and liabilities.

Changes in accounting estimates result from new information or new developments and, accordingly, are not corrections of errors. When it is difficult to distinguish a change in an accounting policy from a change in an accounting estimate, the change is treated as a change in an accounting estimate.

An entity should recognise the effect of a change in an accounting estimate prospectively by including it in profit or loss in:

(a) The period of the change, if the change affects that period only; or

(b) The period of the change and future periods, if the change affects both.

4.1.3 Correction of prior period errors

Prior period errors are omissions from, and misstatements in, an entity's financial statements for one or more prior periods arising from a failure to use, or misuse of, reliable information that:

(a) Was available when financial statements for those periods were authorised for issue; and

(b) Could reasonably be expected to have been obtained and taken into account in the preparation and presentation of those financial statements.

To the extent practicable, an entity should correct a material prior period error retrospectively in the first financial statements authorised for issue after its discovery by:

(a) Restating the comparative amounts for the prior period(s) presented in which the error occurred; or

(b) If the error occurred before the earliest prior period presented, restating the opening balances of assets, liabilities and equity for the earliest prior period presented.

4.2 Discontinued operations

An entity is required to disclose on the face of the income statement an amount comprising the total of:

(a) The post-tax profit or loss of discontinued operations; and

(b) The post-tax gain or loss attributable to the impairment or on the disposal of the assets or disposal groups constituting discontinued operations.

This is presented in a separate column headed 'Discontinued operations' and showing the amount for all income and expense lines attributable to discontinued operations. A total column showing both continuing and discontinued operations is also presented and comparatives are shown for all three columns, if applicable.

This is a fuller presentation than under IFRS, which only requires the total of (a) and (b) above as a single amount, analysed in the notes.

Assets of the discontinued operation **continue to be depreciated** up to the date of disposal.

4.3 Related party disclosures

FRS 102 requires disclosure in the financial statements to draw attention to the possibility that the financial position and profit or loss have been affected by the existence of related parties and transactions and outstanding balances with such parties.

Disclosures are **not** required of transactions entered into between two or more members of a group as long as any subsidiary which is a party to the transaction is **wholly owned** by the other party to the transaction.

Disclosure is required of:

(a) Relationships between a parent and its subsidiaries
(b) Key management personnel compensation
(c) Related party transactions

4.4 Foreign currency translation

On initial recognition, foreign currency transactions are recognised in the **functional currency** using the spot exchange rate at the date of the transaction. At the end of each reporting period the entity should:

(a) Translate foreign currency monetary items (such as debtors) using the **closing rate**

(b) Translate non-monetary items measured at historical cost using the exchange rate at the date of the transaction

(c) Translate non-monetary items measured at fair value using exchange rates at the date when fair value was determined

An entity should recognise, in profit or loss in the period in which they arise, exchange differences arising on the settlement of monetary items or on the translation of monetary items.

When a gain or loss on a non-monetary item is recognised in other comprehensive income, any associated exchange gain or loss should also be recognised in other comprehensive income.

When a gain or loss on a non-monetary item is recognised in profit or loss, any exchange component is also recognised in profit or loss.

5 Non-current assets

Section overview

The requirements of FRS 102 in respect of non-current assets are to a large degree the same as under IFRS. However, entities can choose whether or not to capitalise borrowing costs.

5.1 Property, plant and equipment

5.1.1 Eligibility for capitalisation

Property, plant and equipment are tangible assets that:

(a) Are held for use in the production or supply of goods or services, for rental to others, or for administrative purposes; and

(b) Are expected to be used during more than one period.

The cost of an item of property, plant and equipment should be recognised as an asset if, and only if:

(a) It is probable that future economic benefits associated with the item will flow to the entity; and
(b) The cost of the item can be measured reliably.

Similar provisions to IAS 16 in respect of complex assets and regular major inspections also form part of FRS 102. Spare parts and servicing equipment, if expected to be used over more than one period, are treated as items of property, plant and equipment. Replacement parts and regular major inspections are added to the carrying amount of the asset and depreciated over the period to the next replacement or inspection.

Property, plant and equipment can be carried under the **cost** or the **revaluation** model.

5.1.2 Cost model

Under the cost model, an item of property, plant and equipment is measured at cost less any accumulated depreciation and any accumulated impairment losses.

Cost includes:

(a) Purchase price, legal costs, import duties

(b) Any costs directly attributable to bringing the asset to the location and condition necessary for it to be capable of operating in the manner intended. This would include site preparation, installation etc

(c) Unavoidable costs of dismantling and removing the asset at the end of its useful life and restoring any site on which it is located

(d) Any capitalised borrowing costs

5.1.3 Revaluation model

Under the revaluation model, an item of property, plant and equipment whose fair value can be measured reliably is carried at a revalued amount, being its fair value at the date of revaluation less any subsequent accumulated depreciation and subsequent accumulated impairment losses. Revaluations should be made with sufficient regularity to ensure that the carrying amount does not differ materially from fair value at the end of the reporting period.

Revaluation gains are recognised in other comprehensive income. However the increase is recognised in profit or loss to the degree that it reverses a previous revaluation loss on the same asset which was recognised in profit or loss.

Revaluation losses are recognised in other comprehensive income to the extent of the amount held in revaluation surplus in respect of the asset. Revaluation losses in excess of this amount are recognised in profit or loss.

Interactive question 2: Measuring cost [Difficulty level: Easy]

A business incurs the following costs in relation to the construction of a new facility, which is completed on 31 December 20X0:

	£'000
Cost of land	500
Site preparation	300
Materials used	1,000
Labour costs	3,000
Initial safety inspection – next inspection due 31 December 20X4	200
Professional fees	250
Construction overheads	300
Apportioned general overheads	200
Maintenance agreement for first year	600
Estimated unavoidable cost of dismantling after ten years, discounted at 8%	350

Requirement

Calculate the total cost to be capitalised in respect of the facility in accordance with FRS 102 and the total amount which will be charged to profit or loss in respect of the facility for the year ended 31 December 20X1.

See **Answer** at the end of this chapter.

5.1.4 Derecognition

An item of property, plant and equipment is derecognised

(a) On disposal; or
(b) When no future economic benefits are expected from its use or disposal

FRS 102 has no 'held for sale' classification as in IFRS 5 and items of property, plant and equipment continue to be held as part of fixed assets and depreciated up to the point of derecognition.

5.2 Investment properties

Investment property is property (land or a building, or part of a building, or both) held by the owner or by the lessee under a finance lease to earn rentals or for capital appreciation or both, rather than for:

(a) Use in the production or supply of goods or services or for administrative purposes; or
(b) Sale in the ordinary course of business.

It does not include property held for the provision of social benefit, such as social housing.

5.2.1 Measurement at initial recognition

Investment property is measured at its **cost** upon initial recognition.

5.2.2 Subsequent measurement

Investment property whose fair value can be measured reliably without undue cost or effort should be measured at **fair value** at each reporting date with changes in fair value recognised in profit or loss. If a reliable measure of fair value is no longer available without undue cost or effort for an item of investment property at fair value, it should then be accounted for as property, plant and equipment.

5.3 Intangible assets other than goodwill

An intangible asset is an identifiable non-monetary asset without physical substance. Such an asset is identifiable when:

(a) It is separable, ie capable of being separated or divided from the entity and sold, transferred, licensed, rented or exchanged, either individually or together with a related contract, asset or liability; or

(b) It arises from contractual or other legal rights, regardless of whether those rights are transferable or separable from the entity or from other rights and obligations.

All intangible assets are considered to have a **finite useful life**. If no reliable estimate can be made of this, it should not exceed **five years**.

An intangible asset should be recognised as an asset if, and only if:

(a) It is probable that the expected future economic benefits that are attributable to the asset will flow to the entity; and

(b) The cost or value of the asset can be measured reliably.

Internally generated intangible assets **may** be recognised if they constitute **development costs**.

An entity may recognise an intangible asset arising from development (or from the development phase of an internal project) if, and only if, an entity can demonstrate all of the following:

(a) The technical feasibility of completing the intangible asset so that it will be available for use or sale.

(b) Its intention to complete the intangible asset and use or sell it.

(c) Its ability to use or sell the intangible asset.

(d) How the intangible asset will generate probable future economic benefits. Among other things, the entity can demonstrate the existence of a market for the output of the intangible asset or the intangible asset itself or, if it is to be used internally, the usefulness of the intangible asset.

(e) The availability of adequate technical, financial and other resources to complete the development and to use or sell the intangible asset.

(f) Its ability to measure reliably the expenditure attributable to the intangible asset during its development.

Note that this allows the option to write off development costs which are eligible for capitalisation.

5.4 Borrowing costs

An entity **may** (it has a choice) adopt a policy of capitalising borrowing costs that are directly attributable to the acquisition, construction or production of a qualifying asset as part of the cost of that asset. Where an entity adopts a policy of capitalisation of borrowing costs, it should be applied consistently to a class of qualifying assets.

The amount eligible for capitalisation is the actual borrowing costs incurred less any investment income on the temporary investment of those borrowings.

Where an entity **does not** adopt a policy of capitalising borrowing costs, all borrowing costs are recognised as an **expense in profit or loss** in the period in which they are incurred.

An entity should:

(a) Capitalise borrowing costs as part of the cost of a qualifying asset from the point when it first incurs both expenditure on the asset and borrowing costs, and undertakes activities necessary to prepare the asset for its intended use or sale

(b) Suspend capitalisation during extended periods where active development of the asset has paused

(c) Cease capitalisation when substantially all the activities necessary to prepare the qualifying asset for its intended use or sale are complete

5.5 Impairment of non-current assets

5.5.1 Impairment loss

An impairment loss occurs when the **carrying amount** of an asset exceeds its **recoverable amount**.

If the recoverable amount of an asset is less than its carrying amount, the carrying amount of the asset should be reduced to its recoverable amount. That reduction is an **impairment loss**.

If it is not possible to estimate the recoverable amount of the individual asset, an entity shall estimate the recoverable amount of the **cash-generating unit** to which the asset belongs.

In assessing whether there is any indication that an asset may be impaired, the following external and internal indications should be considered.

5.5.2 External sources of information

(a) During the period, an asset's market value has declined significantly more than would be expected as a result of the passage of time or normal use.

(b) Significant changes with an adverse effect on the entity have taken place during the period, or will take place in the near future, in the technological, market, economic or legal environment in which the entity operates or in the market to which an asset is dedicated.

(c) Market interest rates or other market rates of return on investments have increased during the period, and those increases are likely to affect materially the discount rate used in calculating an asset's value in use and decrease the asset's fair value less costs to sell.

(d) The carrying amount of the net assets of the entity is more than the estimated fair value of the entity as a whole.

5.5.3 Internal sources of information

(a) Evidence is available of obsolescence or physical damage of an asset.

(b) Significant changes with an adverse effect on the entity have taken place during the period, or are expected to take place in the near future, in the extent to which, or manner in which, an asset is used or is expected to be used. These changes include the asset becoming idle, plans to discontinue or restructure the operation to which an asset belongs, plans to dispose of an asset before the previously expected date, and reassessing the useful life of an asset as finite rather than indefinite.

(c) Evidence is available from internal reporting that indicates that the economic performance of an asset is, or will be, worse than expected.

5.5.4 Other issues

If there is an indication that an asset may be impaired, this may indicate that the entity should review the remaining useful life, the depreciation (amortisation) method or the residual value for the asset and adjust it in accordance with the section of FRS 102 applicable to the asset, even if no impairment loss is recognised for the asset.

5.5.5 Measuring recoverable amount

The **recoverable amount** of an asset or a cash-generating unit is the higher of its **fair value less costs to sell** and its **value in use**.

5.5.6 Fair value less costs to sell

Fair value less costs to sell is the amount obtainable from the sale of an asset in an arm's length transaction between knowledgeable, willing parties, less the costs of disposal.

5.5.7 Value in use

Value in use is the present value of the future cash flows expected to be derived from an asset. This present value calculation involves the following steps:

(a) Estimating the future cash inflows and outflows to be derived from continuing use of the asset and from its ultimate disposal

(b) Applying the appropriate discount rate to those future cash flows

6 Revenue and inventories

Section overview

- The provisions for recognition of revenue from sale of goods, rendering of services, construction contracts and grants are broadly the same as under IFRS.

- As in IFRS, measurement of inventories under LIFO is prohibited.

6.1 Measurement

Revenue should be measured at the fair value of the consideration received or receivable. The fair value of the consideration received or receivable takes into account the amount of any trade discounts, prompt settlement discounts and volume rebates allowed by the entity.

6.2 Sale of goods

Revenue from the sale of goods should be recognised when all the following conditions are satisfied:

(a) The entity has transferred to the buyer the significant risks and rewards of ownership of the goods;

(b) The entity retains neither continuing managerial involvement to the degree usually associated with ownership nor effective control over the goods sold;

(c) The amount of revenue can be measured reliably;

(d) It is probable that the economic benefits associated with the transaction will flow to the entity; and

(e) The costs incurred or to be incurred in respect of the transaction can be measured reliably.

6.3 Rendering of services

When the outcome of a transaction involving the rendering of services can be estimated reliably, revenue associated with the transaction should be recognised by reference to the stage of completion of the transaction at the end of the reporting period (the percentage of completion method). The outcome of a transaction can be estimated reliably when all the following conditions are satisfied:

(a) The amount of revenue can be measured reliably;

(b) It is probable that the economic benefits associated with the transaction will flow to the entity;

(c) The stage of completion of the transaction at the end of the reporting period can be measured reliably; and

(d) The costs incurred for the transaction and the costs to complete the transaction can be measured reliably.

When the outcome of the transaction involving the rendering of services cannot be estimated reliably, an entity should recognise revenue only to the extent of the expenses recognised that are recoverable.

6.4 Construction contracts

A construction contract is a contract specifically negotiated for the construction of an asset or a combination of assets. The contract activity takes place over more than one financial period.

When the outcome of a construction contract can be estimated reliably, contract revenue and contract costs associated with the construction contract should be recognised as revenue and expenses respectively by reference to the stage of completion of the contract activity at the end of the reporting period (the percentage of completion method).

The stage of completion of a transaction or contract should be determined using the method that measures most reliably the work performed. Possible methods include:

(a) The proportion that costs incurred for work performed to date bear to the estimated total costs. Costs incurred for work performed to date do not include costs relating to future activity, such as for materials or prepayments;

(b) Surveys of work performed; and

(c) Completion of a physical proportion of the contract work or the completion of a proportion of the service contract.

When the outcome of a construction contract cannot be estimated reliably:

(a) Revenue should be recognised only to the extent of contract costs incurred that it is probable will be recoverable; and

(b) Contract costs should be recognised as an expense in the period in which they are incurred.

When it is probable that total contract costs will exceed total contract revenue on a construction contract, the expected loss should be recognised as an expense immediately, with a corresponding provision for an **onerous contract**.

6.5 Government grants

Government grants, including non-monetary grants shall not be recognised until there is reasonable assurance that:

(a) The entity will comply with the conditions attaching to them; and
(b) The grants will be received.

Grants should be recognised based on either the **performance model** or the **accrual model**. This policy choice should be applied on a class-by-class basis.

6.5.1 Performance model

Under the performance model grants are recognised as follows:

(a) A grant that does not impose specified future performance-related conditions on the recipient is recognised in income when the grant proceeds are received or receivable.

(b) A grant that imposes specified future performance-related conditions on the recipient is recognised in income only when the performance-related conditions are met.

(c) Grants received before the revenue recognition criteria are satisfied are recognised as a liability.

6.5.2 Accrual model

Under the accrual model grants are classified as either a grant relating to revenue or a grant relating to assets.

Grants relating to revenue are recognised in income on a systematic basis over the periods in which the entity recognises the related costs for which the grant is intended to compensate.

A grant that becomes receivable as compensation for expenses or losses already incurred or for the purpose of giving immediate financial support to the entity with no future related costs is recognised in income in the period in which it becomes receivable.

Grants relating to assets are recognised in income on a systematic basis over the expected useful life of the asset.

Where part of a grant relating to an asset is deferred it is recognised as deferred income and **not** deducted from the carrying amount of the asset.

6.6 Inventories

Inventories are assets:

(a) Held for sale in the ordinary course of business;

(b) In the process of production for such sale; or

(c) In the form of materials or supplies to be consumed in the production process or in the rendering of services.

6.6.1 Measurement

Inventories are measured at the lower of cost and estimated selling price less costs to complete and sell.

Inventories held for distribution at **no or nominal consideration** should be measured at **cost**, adjusted for any loss of service potential.

The cost of inventories should include all costs of purchase, costs of conversion and other costs incurred in bringing the inventories to their present location and condition.

The costs of purchase of inventories comprise the purchase price, import duties and other taxes (other than those subsequently recoverable by the entity from the taxing authorities), and transport, handling and other costs directly attributable to the acquisition of finished goods, materials and services. Trade discounts, rebates and other similar items are deducted in determining the costs of purchase.

Costs of inventories are to be measured using the FIFO or weighted average methods. Use of LIFO is not permitted.

Inventories are to be **assessed for impairment** at the end of each reporting period. Impairment losses can be reversed if there are changes in economic circumstances or if the circumstances which led to the impairment no longer exist.

7 Leases

Section overview

- FRS 102 sets out the criteria for distinguishing between finance and operating leases and the accounting treatment of leases and sale and leaseback transactions.

7.1 Classification

A lease is classified as a finance lease if it transfers substantially all the risks and rewards incidental to ownership. A lease is classified as an operating lease if it does not transfer substantially all the risks and rewards incidental to ownership.

Whether a lease is a finance lease or an operating lease depends on the substance of the transaction rather than the form of the contract. Examples of situations that individually or in combination would normally lead to a lease being classified as a finance lease are:

(a) The lease transfers ownership of the asset to the lessee by the end of the lease term;

(b) The lessee has the option to purchase the asset at a price that is expected to be sufficiently lower than the fair value at the date the option becomes exercisable for it to be reasonably certain, at the inception of the lease, that the option will be exercised;

(c) The lease term is for the major part of the economic life of the asset even if title is not transferred;

(d) At the inception of the lease the present value of the minimum lease payments amounts to at least substantially all of the fair value of the leased asset; and

(e) The leased assets are of such a specialised nature that only the lessee can use them without major modifications.

7.2 Accounting treatment

At the commencement of the lease term, a lessee recognises its rights of use and obligations under **finance leases** as **assets and liabilities** in its statement of financial position at amounts equal to the fair value of the leased asset or, if lower, the present value of the minimum lease payments, determined at the inception of the lease.

During the period of the **finance lease,** minimum lease payments are to be apportioned between the finance charge and the reduction of the outstanding liability using the **effective interest rate**.

For **operating leases**, lease payments go straight to profit or loss with incentives spread over the life of the lease on a straight line basis.

7.3 Sale and leaseback

7.3.1 Sale and leaseback resulting in a finance lease

If a sale and leaseback transaction results in a finance lease, the seller-lessee should not recognise immediately, as income, any excess of sales proceeds over the carrying amount. Instead, the seller-lessee should defer such excess and amortise it over the lease term.

7.3.2 Sale and leaseback resulting in an operating lease

If a sale and leaseback transaction results in an operating lease, and it is clear that the transaction is established at fair value, the seller-lessee recognises any profit or loss immediately.

If the sale price is below fair value, the seller-lessee recognises any profit or loss immediately unless the loss is compensated for by future lease payments at below market price. In that case the seller-lessee should defer and amortise such loss in proportion to the lease payments over the period for which the asset is expected to be used.

If the sale price is above fair value, the seller-lessee should defer the excess over fair value and amortise it over the period for which the asset is expected to be used.

8 Financial instruments

Section overview

FRS 102 gives entities an accounting policy choice in relation to the treatment of financial instruments. They can choose to apply the provisions of FRS 102, or they can apply the recognition and measurement provisions of IAS 39 or the recognition and measurement provisions of IFRS 9. Under all of these options, the disclosure provisions of FRS 102 should be applied.

8.1 Basic financial instruments

Initial recognition of financial assets and liabilities

A financial asset or a financial liability should be recognised only when the entity becomes a party to the contractual provisions of the instrument.

Initial measurement

When a financial asset or financial liability is recognised initially, it should be measured at the transaction price (including transaction costs except in the initial measurement of financial assets and liabilities that are measured at fair value through profit or loss).

Subsequent measurement

Debt instruments should be measured at **amortised cost** using the **effective interest method.**

The amortised cost of a financial asset or financial liability at each reporting date is the net of the following amounts:

(a)   The amount at which the financial asset or financial liability is measured at initial recognition

(b)   Minus any repayments of the principal

(c)   Plus or minus the cumulative amortisation using the effective interest method of any difference between the amount at initial recognition and the maturity amount

(d)   Minus, in the case of a financial asset, any reduction for impairment or uncollectability

8.2 Liabilities and equity

A financial liability is any liability that is:

(a)   A contractual obligation:

    (i)   To deliver cash or another financial asset to another entity; or

    (ii)   To exchange financial assets or financial liabilities with another entity under conditions that are potentially unfavourable to the entity; or

(b)   A contract that will or may be settled in the entity's own equity instruments and:

    (i)   Under which the entity is or may be obliged to deliver a variable number of the entity's own equity instruments; or

    (ii)   Which will or may be settled other than by the exchange of a fixed amount of cash or another financial asset for a fixed number of the entity's own equity instruments.

A **preference share** that provides for **mandatory redemption** by the issuer for a fixed or determinable amount at a fixed or determinable future date, or gives the holder the right to require the issuer to **redeem the instrument** at or after a particular date for a fixed or determinable amount, is a **financial liability.**

Financial instruments are classified as **equity** where they represent the residual interest in the net assets of the entity.

8.3 Compound financial instruments

On issuing convertible debt or similar compound financial instruments that contain both a liability and an equity component, the proceeds should be allocated between the liability component and the equity component.

In making the allocation, an entity should first determine the amount of the liability component. This can be taken as the fair value of a similar liability that does not have a conversion feature or similar associated equity component. The residual amount is allocated as the equity component.

Transaction costs are allocated between the debt component and the equity component on the basis of their relative fair values.

8.4 Treasury shares

Treasury shares are the equity instruments of an entity that have been issued and subsequently reacquired by the entity. An entity should deduct from equity the fair value of the consideration given for the treasury shares. No gain or loss should be recognised in profit or loss on the purchase, sale, transfer or cancellation of treasury shares.

9 Provisions and contingencies

Section overview

* Section 21 applies to all provisions, contingent liabilities and contingent assets, except those covered by other sections of FRS 102.

9.1 Provisions

A provision should be recognised only when:

(a) The entity has an obligation at the reporting date as a result of a past event;

(b) It is probable (ie more likely than not) that the entity will be required to transfer economic benefits in settlement; and

(c) The amount of the obligation can be estimated reliably.

The obligation can be **legal** or **constructive**. Obligations arising from future actions do not give rise to provisions.

A provision should be measured at the best estimate of the amount required to settle the obligation at the reporting date. Where the obligation involves a large population of items, the weighted average method is used.

Provisions are recognised for onerous contracts but they are not recognised for future operating losses.

9.1.1 Subsequent measurement of provisions

An entity can charge against a provision only those expenditures for which the provision was originally recognised.

An entity should review provisions at each reporting date and adjust them to reflect the current best estimate of the amount that would be required to settle the obligation at that reporting date.

Any adjustments to the amount previously recognised should be recognised in profit or loss unless the provision was originally recognised as part of the cost of an asset (such as decommissioning costs).

When the provision has been measured at the present value of the amount expected to be required to settle the obligation, the unwinding of the discount should be recognised as a finance cost in profit or loss.

9.2 Contingent assets and liabilities

A contingent asset should **not** be recognised as an asset. Disclosure of a contingent asset is required when an inflow of economic benefits is probable. However, when the flow of future economic benefits to the entity is **virtually certain**, then the related asset is not a contingent asset, and its recognition is appropriate.

A contingent liability is either a possible but uncertain obligation or a present obligation that is not recognised because it fails to meet one or both of the conditions (b) and (c) above. A contingent liability should not generally be recognised as a liability. The exception to this is a provision for the contingent liabilities of an acquiree in a business combination. Disclosure of a contingent liability is required unless the possibility of an outflow of resources is remote.

9.3 Restructuring

A restructuring gives rise to a constructive obligation only when an entity:

(a) Has a detailed formal plan for the restructuring identifying at least:

   (i) The business or part of a business concerned;

   (ii) The principal locations affected;

   (iii) The location, function, and approximate number of employees who will be compensated for terminating their services;

   (iv) The expenditures that will be undertaken; and

   (v) When the plan will be implemented; and

(b) Has raised a valid expectation in those affected that it will carry out the restructuring by starting to implement that plan or announcing its main features to those affected by it.

10 Group accounts

Section overview

- Consolidated financial statements are only required where the entity is a parent at the year end.

- Goodwill should be recognised as an asset on the initial acquisition of a subsidiary and should be amortised over its useful life.

- Negative goodwill should be shown separately as a negative asset.

10.1 Requirement to present consolidated financial statements

Except as permitted below, a parent entity should present consolidated financial statements in which it consolidates all its investments in subsidiaries in accordance with FRS 102. A parent entity need only prepare consolidated accounts under the Act if it is a parent at the year end.

A parent is exempt **under the Companies Act** from the requirement to prepare consolidated financial statements on any one of the following grounds:

(a) The parent is a wholly-owned subsidiary and its immediate parent is established under the law of an EEA State. Exemption is conditional on compliance with certain further conditions set out in Section 400(2) of the Act.

(b) The parent is a majority-owned subsidiary and meets all the conditions for exemption as a wholly-owned subsidiary set out in Section 400(2) of the Act as well as the additional conditions set out in Section 400(1)(b) of the Act.

(c) The parent is a wholly-owned subsidiary of another entity and that parent is not established under the law of an EEA State. Exemption is conditional on compliance with certain further conditions set out in Section 401(2) of the Act.

(d) The parent is a majority-owned subsidiary and meets all of the conditions for exemption as a wholly-owned subsidiary set out in Section 401(2) of the Act as well as the additional conditions set out in Section 401(1)(b) of the Act.

(e) The parent, and group headed by it, qualify as small as set out in Section 383 of the Act and the group is not ineligible as set out in Section 384 of the Act.

(f) All of the parent's subsidiaries are required to be excluded from consolidation under the conditions set out in Section 10.3 below.

(g) For parents not reporting under the Act, if its statutory framework does not require the preparation of consolidated financial statements.

10.2 Control

A subsidiary is an entity that is controlled by the parent. Control is the power to govern the financial and operating policies of an entity so as to obtain benefits from its activities.

Control is presumed to exist when the parent owns, directly or indirectly through subsidiaries, more than half of the voting power of an entity. That presumption may be overcome in exceptional circumstances if it can be clearly demonstrated that such ownership does not constitute control. Control also exists when the parent owns half or less of the voting power of an entity but it has:

(a) Power over more than half of the voting rights by virtue of an agreement with other investors;

(b) Power to govern the financial and operating policies of the entity under a statute or an agreement;

(c) Power to appoint or remove the majority of the members of the board of directors or equivalent governing body and control of the entity is by that board or body; or

(d) Power to cast the majority of votes at meetings of the board of directors or equivalent governing body and control of the entity is by that board or body.

Control can also be achieved by having options or convertible instruments that are currently exercisable or by having an agent with the ability to direct the activities for the benefit of the controlling entity.

Control can also exist when the parent has the power to exercise, or actually exercises, dominant influence or control over the undertaking or it and the undertaking are managed on a unified basis.

10.3 Exclusion of a subsidiary from consolidation

A subsidiary should be excluded from consolidation where:

(a) Severe long-term restrictions substantially hinder the exercise of the rights of the parent over the assets or management of the subsidiary; or

(b) The interest in the subsidiary is held exclusively with a view to subsequent resale; and the subsidiary has not previously been consolidated in the consolidated financial statements prepared in accordance with FRS 102.

10.4 Consolidation procedures

The consolidated financial statements present financial information about the group as a single economic entity. In preparing consolidated financial statements, an entity should:

(a) Combine the financial statements of the parent and its subsidiaries line by line by adding together like items of assets, liabilities, equity, income and expenses;

(b) Eliminate the carrying amount of the parent's investment in each subsidiary and the parent's portion of equity of each subsidiary;

(c) Measure and present non-controlling interest in the profit or loss of consolidated subsidiaries for the reporting period separately from the interest of the owners of the parent;

(d) Measure and present non-controlling interest in the net assets of consolidated subsidiaries separately from the parent shareholders' equity in them. Non-controlling interest in net assets consists of:

(i) The amount of the non-controlling interest's share in the net amount of the identifiable assets, liabilities and contingent liabilities recognised and measured at the date of the original combination; and

(ii) The non-controlling interest's share of changes in equity since the date of the combination.

There is no option to measure non-controlling interest at **fair value**.

(e) Eliminate intragroup balances and transactions and profits and losses on intragroup transactions;

(f) Use financial statements of the parent and its subsidiaries prepared as of the same reporting date unless this is impracticable, in which case appropriate adjustments should be made; and

(g) Apply uniform accounting policies for like transactions and make appropriate adjustments where the financial statements of any group member are prepared using accounting policies that differ from those applied in the consolidated financial statements.

10.5 Goodwill

At the acquisition date the acquirer should:

(a) Recognise goodwill acquired in a business combination as an asset; and

(b) Initially measure that goodwill at its cost, being the excess of the cost of the business combination over the acquirer's interest in the net amount of the identifiable assets, liabilities and contingent liabilities.

The cost of the business combination includes **acquisition-related costs**.

After initial recognition, goodwill acquired in a business combination should be measured at cost less accumulated amortisation and accumulated impairment losses.

Goodwill is considered to have a **finite useful life**, and shall be amortised on a systematic basis over its life. If an entity is unable to make a reliable estimate of the useful life of goodwill, the life shall not exceed **five years**.

If **negative goodwill** arises:

(a) Reassess the identification and measurement of the acquiree's assets, liabilities and provisions for contingent liabilities and the measurement of the cost of the combination.

(b) Recognise and separately disclose the resulting excess on the **face of the statement of financial position** on the acquisition date, immediately below goodwill, and followed by a subtotal of the net amount of goodwill and the excess.

(c) Recognise subsequently the excess up to the fair value of non-monetary assets acquired in profit or loss in the periods in which the non-monetary assets are recovered. Any excess exceeding the fair value of non-monetary assets acquired should be recognised in profit or loss in the periods expected to be benefited.

10.6 Separate financial statements

Investments in subsidiaries, associates and joint ventures in the parent company's separate financial statements can be shown at:

(a) Cost less impairment;
(b) Fair value through other comprehensive income; or
(c) Fair value through profit or loss

11 Associates and joint ventures

Section overview

- Both associates and joint ventures are accounted for in consolidated financial statements using the **equity** method.

- Note that goodwill is recognised and amortised.

11.1 Investments in associates

An associate is an entity, including an unincorporated entity such as a partnership, over which the investor has **significant influence** and that is neither a subsidiary nor an interest in a joint venture.

Significant influence is the power to participate in the financial and operating policy decisions of the associate but is not control or joint control over those policies.

(a) If an investor holds, directly or indirectly (eg through subsidiaries), 20% or more of the voting power of the associate, it is presumed that the investor has significant influence, unless it can be clearly demonstrated that this is not the case.

(b) Conversely, if the investor holds, directly or indirectly (eg through subsidiaries), less than 20% of the voting power of the associate, it is presumed that the investor does not have significant influence, unless such influence can be clearly demonstrated.

(c) A substantial or majority ownership by another investor does not preclude an investor from having significant influence.

In the **consolidated** financial statements an investment in an associate is measured using the **equity method**.

In the **individual** financial statements of the investor an investment in an associate is measured using the **cost** or **fair value** models.

Equity method

Under the equity method of accounting, an equity investment is initially recognised at the transaction price (including transaction costs) and is subsequently adjusted to reflect the investor's share of the profit or loss, other comprehensive income and equity of the associate.

Implicit goodwill

On acquisition of the investment in an associate, an investor should account for any difference (whether positive or negative) between the cost of acquisition and the investor's share of the fair values of the net identifiable assets of the associate in accordance with the goodwill provisions of FRS 102, set out in Section 10 above.

Impairment

If there is an indication that an investment in an associate may be impaired, the entire carrying amount of the investment should be tested for impairment as a single asset. Any goodwill included as part of the carrying amount of the investment in the associate is not tested separately for impairment but, rather, as part of the test for impairment of the investment as a whole.

Investor's transactions with associates

Unrealised profits and losses resulting from upstream (associate to investor) and downstream (investor to associate) transactions should be eliminated to the extent of the investor's interest in the associate. Unrealised losses on such transactions may provide **evidence of an impairment** of the asset transferred.

11.2 Investments in joint ventures

A joint venture is a contractual arrangement whereby two or more parties undertake an economic activity that is subject to joint control. Joint ventures can take the form of jointly controlled operations, jointly controlled assets, or jointly controlled entities.

A venturer which is a parent should measure its investments in jointly controlled entities by the **equity method** in its consolidated financial statements. This is as described above for associates.

A venturer which is not a parent can measure its investments in joint ventures using the **cost** or **fair value** models. This also applies to the individual entity financial statements of a parent.

12 Other issues

Section overview

- In this section we will look briefly at the sections of FRS 102 not covered above.

12.1 Events after the end of the reporting period

Events after the end of the reporting period are those events, favourable and unfavourable, that occur between the end of the reporting period and the date when the financial statements are authorised for issue. There are two types of events:

(a) Those that provide evidence of conditions that existed at the end of the reporting period (**adjusting** events after the end of the reporting period); and

(b) Those that are indicative of conditions that arose after the end of the reporting period (**non-adjusting** events after the end of the reporting period).

An entity should adjust the amounts recognised in its financial statements to reflect adjusting events after the reporting period. Non-adjusting events should be disclosed.

Going concern

Financial statements should not be prepared on a going concern basis if management determines after the reporting period either that it intends to liquidate the entity or to cease trading, or that it has no realistic alternative but to do so.

Dividends

If an entity declares dividends to holders of its equity instruments after the end of the reporting period, those dividends should not be recognised as a liability at the end of the reporting period because no obligation exists at that time.

12.2 Share-based payment

Share-based payment transactions can be:

(a) Equity-settled share-based payment transactions, in which the entity:

    (i) Receives goods or services as consideration for its own equity instruments (including shares or share options); or

    (ii) Receives goods or services but has no obligation to settle the transaction with the supplier;

(b) Cash-settled share-based payment transactions, in which the entity acquires goods or services by incurring a liability to transfer cash or other assets to the supplier of those goods or services for amounts that are based on the price (or value) of the entity's shares or other equity instruments of the entity or another group entity; and

(c) Transactions in which the entity receives or acquires goods or services and the terms of the arrangement provide either the entity or the supplier of those goods or services with a choice of whether the entity settles the transaction in cash (or other assets) or by issuing equity instruments.

12.2.1 Recognition

An entity should recognise the goods or services received or acquired in a share-based payment transaction when it obtains the goods or as the services are received. It should recognise a corresponding increase in equity if the goods or services were received in an equity-settled share-based payment transaction, or a liability if the goods or services were acquired in a cash-settled share-based payment transaction.

When the goods or services received or acquired in a share-based payment transaction do not qualify for recognition as assets they should be recognised as expenses.

12.3 Employee benefits

Employee benefits are all forms of consideration given by an entity in exchange for service rendered by employees, including directors and management. Employee benefits will be one of the following four types:

(a) Short-term employee benefits, which are employee benefits (other than termination benefits) that are expected to be settled wholly before 12 months after the end of the reporting period in which the employees render the related service;

(b) Post-employment benefits, which are employee benefits (other than termination benefits and short-term employee benefits) that are payable after the completion of employment;

(c) Other long-term employee benefits, which are all employee benefits, other than short-term employee benefits, post-employment benefits and termination benefits; or

(d) Termination benefits, which are employee benefits provided in exchange for the termination of an employee's employment as a result of either:

    (i) An entity's decision to terminate an employee's employment before the normal retirement date; or

(ii)   An employee's decision to accept voluntary redundancy in exchange for those benefits.

12.3.1   Recognition

An entity should recognise the cost of all employee benefits to which its employees have become entitled as a result of service rendered during the reporting period:

(a)   As a liability, after deducting amounts that have been paid either directly to the employees or as a contribution to an employee benefit fund. If the amount paid exceeds the obligation arising from service before the reporting date, that excess can be recognised as an asset to the extent that the prepayment will lead to a reduction in future payments or a cash refund.

(b)   As an expense, unless another section of FRS 102 requires the cost to be recognised as part of the cost of an asset such as inventories or property, plant and equipment.

12.3.2   Post-retirement benefits

Post-employment benefit plans are classified as either **defined contribution plans** or **defined benefit plans**.

Defined contribution plans are post-employment benefit plans under which an entity pays fixed contributions into a separate entity (a fund) and has no legal or constructive obligation to pay further contributions or to make direct benefit payments to employees if the fund does not hold sufficient assets to pay all employee benefits relating to employee service in the current and prior periods.

Defined benefit plans are post-employment benefit plans other than defined contribution plans. Under defined benefit plans, the entity's obligation is to provide the agreed benefits to current and former employees, and actuarial risk (that benefits will cost more or less than expected) and investment risk (that returns on assets set aside to fund the benefits will differ from expectations) are borne, in substance, by the entity.

12.3.3   Defined contribution plans

In accounting for **defined contribution plans** an entity should recognise the contribution payable for a period:

(a)   As a liability, after deducting any amount already paid. If contribution payments exceed the contribution due for service before the reporting date, that excess can be recognised as an asset to the extent that the prepayment will lead to a reduction in future payments or a cash refund.

(b)   As an expense, unless another section of FRS 102 requires the cost to be recognised as part of the cost of an asset such as inventories or property, plant and equipment.

12.3.4   Defined benefit plans

In accounting for **defined benefit plans**, an entity should recognise:

(a)   A liability for its obligations under defined benefit plans net of plan assets – its '**net defined benefit liability**'; and

(b)   The net change in that liability during the period as the cost of its defined benefit plans during the period.

The **net defined benefit liability** for its obligations under defined benefit plans should be measured at the net total of the following amounts:

(a)   The present value of its obligations under defined benefit plans (its defined benefit obligation) at the reporting date; minus

(b)   The fair value at the reporting date of plan assets (if any) out of which the obligations are to be settled.

12.4   Income tax

12.4.1   Current tax

A current tax liability is recognised for tax payable on taxable profit for the current and past periods. If the amount of tax paid for the current and past periods exceeds the amount of tax payable for those periods, the excess is recognised as a current tax asset.

A current tax asset is recognised for the benefit of a tax loss that can be carried back to recover tax paid in a previous period.

A current tax liability/asset is measured at the amounts of tax the entity expects to pay/recover using the tax rates and laws that have been enacted or substantively enacted by the reporting date.

12.4.2   Deferred tax

FRS 102 recognises deferred tax on the basis of **timing differences**, not temporary differences.

Deferred tax should be recognised in respect of all timing differences at the reporting date, subject to the points below. Timing differences are differences between taxable profits and total comprehensive income as stated in the financial statements that arise from the inclusion of income and expenses in tax assessments in periods different from those in which they are recognised in financial statements.

Unrelieved tax losses and other deferred tax assets shall be recognised only to the extent that it is probable that they will be recovered against the reversal of deferred tax liabilities or other future taxable profits.

Deferred tax is recognised on timing differences between tax allowances and depreciation of fixed assets. If and when all conditions for retaining the tax allowances have been met, the deferred tax is reversed.

Deferred tax is not recognised on income and expenses from a subsidiary, associate, branch or joint venture when:

(a)   The reporting entity is able to control the reversal of the timing difference; and

(b)   It is probable that the timing difference will not reverse in the foreseeable future.

An example of this would be undistributed profits held in the other entity.

Deferred tax may arise when assets and liabilities in a business combination are recognised at fair value, which may be an amount different from the value at which they are assessed for tax.

12.5   Hyperinflation

12.5.1   Indicators

The hyperinflation section of FRS 102 only applies to an entity whose functional currency is the currency of a hyperinflationary economy. It requires such an entity to prepare financial statements that have been adjusted for the effects of hyperinflation.

The following are possible indicators of hyperinflation:

(a)   The general population prefers to keep its wealth in non-monetary assets or in a relatively stable foreign currency. Amounts of local currency held are immediately invested to maintain purchasing power.

(b)   The general population regards monetary amounts not in terms of the local currency but in terms of a relatively stable foreign currency. Prices may be quoted in that currency.

(c)   Sales and purchases on credit take place at prices that compensate for the expected loss of purchasing power during the credit period, even if the period is short.

(d)   Interest rates, wages and prices are linked to a price index.

(e)   The cumulative inflation rate over three years is approaching, or exceeds, 100%.

12.5.2 Measurement

All amounts in the financial statements of an entity whose functional currency is the currency of a hyperinflationary economy should be stated in terms of the **measuring unit current at the end of the reporting period**.

The restatement of financial statements in accordance with FRS 102 requires the use of a **general price index** that reflects changes in general purchasing power. In most economies there is a recognised general price index, normally produced by the government, that entities will follow.

Statement of financial position amounts not expressed in terms of the measuring unit current at the end of the reporting period are restated by applying a **general price index**.

All items in the **statement of comprehensive income** shall be expressed in terms of the measuring unit current at the end of the reporting period. Therefore, all amounts need to be restated by applying the change in the general price index from the dates when the items of income and expenses were initially recognised in the financial statements.

13 IFRS comparison

Section overview

- Although FRS 102 is based on the IFRS for SMEs, there are still a number of differences between FRS 102 and IFRS and we summarise here those differences that are examinable under the Financial Accounting and Reporting syllabus.

13.1 Concepts

FRS 102 identifies (among others) the qualitative characteristics of **materiality**, **substance over form** and **prudence**. These are not identified as separate qualitative characteristics in the IASB *Conceptual Framework*.

13.2 Format of financial statements

Under FRS 102 financial statements are prepared in accordance with the Companies Act formats, not the IAS 1 formats.

Companies reporting under FRS 102 can present a single statement of comprehensive income or a separate income statement and statement of comprehensive income. This is as per IFRS. However, FRS 102 also allows the option, in certain circumstances, to present a single 'statement of income and retained earnings' in place of the (separate) statement of comprehensive income and statement of changes in equity.

13.3 Discontinued operations

These are shown in a separate income statement column under FRS 102, in keeping with the Companies Act format. IFRS 5 requires the results of discontinued operations to be presented in a single amount on the face of the statement of profit or loss.

Under FRS 102 assets of a discontinued operation continue to be depreciated up to the date of disposal, whereas under IFRS 5 depreciation ceases when an asset is classified as 'held for sale'.

13.4 Borrowing costs

FRS 102 states that an entity can choose whether or not to capitalise borrowing costs. IAS 23 requires all eligible borrowing costs to be capitalised.

13.5 Property, plant and equipment

FRS 102 has no 'held for sale' category as in IFRS 5. Items of property, plant and equipment continue to be held as part of fixed assets and are depreciated up to the date of disposal.

13.6 Intangible assets

Under FRS 102 an entity can choose whether or not to capitalise development costs. IAS 38 requires all eligible development costs to be capitalised.

FRS 102 treats all intangible assets as having a finite useful life with a rebuttable presumption that this should not exceed five years. Under IFRS intangible assets can have an indefinite life.

13.7 Government grants

Under both FRS 102 and IAS 20 grants related to assets are recognised in income over the expected useful life of the asset.

IAS 20 allows this to be done either by recognising the grant as deferred income or by deducting the amount of the grant from the carrying amount of the asset.

FRS 102 specifies the deferral method. There is no option to deduct the amount of the grant from the carrying amount of the asset.

13.8 Financial instruments

Entities reporting under FRS 102 measure financial instruments initially at transaction price, unless they are measured at fair value through profit or loss. Under IAS 39 initial measurement is at fair value.

13.9 Goodwill

FRS 102 requires goodwill to be amortised over its useful life and there is a rebuttable presumption that this should not exceed five years. It is also subject to impairment review. Under IFRS 3 goodwill is not amortised but is subject to an annual impairment review.

FRS 102 allows the reversal of an impairment loss in respect of goodwill. This is not allowed under IFRS.

FRS 102 requires acquisition-related costs to be added to the cost of the combination. Under IFRS 3 these costs are expensed. The value of goodwill will therefore be higher under FRS 102.

Under FRS 102 negative goodwill is presented in the statement of financial position directly under positive goodwill, as a negative asset. Under IFRS 3 negative goodwill is recognised in profit or loss.

13.10 Non-controlling interest

FRS 102 states that a non-controlling interest should be measured using the **proportionate** method. The option to measure non-controlling interest at **fair value** is not available under FRS 102.

13.11 Exclusion of a subsidiary from consolidation

FRS 102 states that a subsidiary should be excluded from consolidation where severe long-term restrictions apply or where the interest in the subsidiary is held exclusively with a view to subsequent resale.

IFRS 10 does not allow any exclusions from consolidation.

13.12 Associates and joint ventures

FRS 102 recognises implicit goodwill on acquisition and requires it to be amortised. No separate goodwill is recognised under IFRS.

Appendix

FRS 102 Financial statement formats (comparatives not shown)

Group income statement

	Continuing operations £m	Discontinued operations £m	Total £m
Turnover	170	35	205
Cost of sales	(135)	(21)	(156)
Gross profit	35	14	49
Distribution costs	(9)	(4)	(13)
Administrative expenses:			
Before exceptional items	(11)	(5)	(16)
Fire damage	(4)	–	(4)
	(15)	(5)	(20)
	11	5	16
Other operating income	3	–	3
Group operating profit	14		19
Share of profit of associate	4	–	4
Amortisation of goodwill	(2)	–	(2)
Loss on sale of discontinued operations	–	(7)	(7)
Profit on ordinary activities before investment income, interest and taxation	16	(2)	14
Interest receivable	1	–	1
Interest payable	(2)	–	(2)
Profit on ordinary activities before tax	15	(2)	13
Tax on profit on ordinary activities	(4)	–	(4)
Profit for the financial year	11	(2)	9

Profit for the financial year attributable to:	
Non-controlling interests	2
Owners of the parent company	7
	9

Group statement of comprehensive income

	£m
Profit for the financial year	9
Gains on property revaluation	2
Share of other comprehensive income of associates	1
Remeasurement loss on defined benefit scheme	(2)
Total other comprehensive income	1
Total comprehensive income for the year	10
Total comprehensive income for the year attributable to:	
Non-controlling interests	2
Owners of the parent company	8
	10

Group statement of financial position (balance sheet)

	£m	£m
Fixed assets		
Intangible assets		15
Tangible assets		27
Investments:		
Investment in associate	6	
Other investments	2	
		8
		50
Current assets		
Stocks	7	
Debtors:		
Amounts falling due within one year	10	
Amounts falling due after one year	3	
	20	
Short term deposits	4	
Cash at bank and in hand	3	
	27	
Creditors: amounts falling due within one year	(5)	
Net current assets		22
Total assets less current liabilities		72
Creditors: amounts falling due after more than one year		(8)
Provisions for liabilities		(5)
Accruals and deferred income		
Deferred government grants		(7)
Net assets		52
Capital and reserves		
Called up share capital		20
Share premium account		6
Capital redemption reserve		8
Other reserves		1
Equity component of convertible preference shares		2
Profit and loss account		15
		52
Equity attributable to:		
Owners of the parent company		48
Non-controlling interests		4
		52

Group statement of changes in equity

	Share capital £m	Share premium £m	Capital redemption reserve £m	Other reserves £m	Equity component £m	Profit and loss account £m	Shareholders equity £m	Non-controlling interest £m	Total equity £m
At 1 January 2013	12	4	6		2	10	34	2	36
Profit and loss account						7	7	2	9
Other comp income				1			1		1
Total comp income				1		7	8	2	10
Equity dividends paid						(4)	(4)		(4)
New shares issued	10	3					13		13
Share issue costs		(1)					(1)		(1)
Share buy back	(2)		2			(4)	(4)		(4)
Share-based payment transactions						2	2		2
At 31 December 2013	20	6	8	1	2	11	48	4	52

Group statement of cash flows

The format for this is the same as the IFRS format which is shown in Chapter 2.

Answer the following questions

1   What are the requirements needed for information in financial statements to be considered **reliable**?

2   How are the results of discontinued operations presented under FRS 102?

3   FRS 102 allows some accounting policy choices which are not permitted under IFRS. What are they?

4   Explain the calculation and accounting treatment under FRS 102 of goodwill arising on a business combination. How does this differ from IFRS?

Now go back to the Learning objectives in the Introduction. If you are satisfied you have achieved these objectives, please tick them off.

Technical reference

1 Scope and application

- Scope of the standard
- Basis of preparation of financial statements   FRS 102 (Section 1)
- Reduced disclosures

2 Concepts and pervasive principles

- Qualitative characteristics   FRS 102 (Section 2.4)
- Financial position   FRS 102 (Section 2.15)
- Performance   FRS 102 (Section 2.23)
- Recognition of assets, liabilities, income and expenses   FRS 102 (Section 2.27)
- Measurement of assets, liabilities, income and expenses   FRS 102 (Section 2.33)
- Accrual basis   FRS 102 (Section 2.36)
- Recognition and measurement in financial statements   FRS 102 (Section 2.37)

3 Financial statement presentation

- Going concern   FRS 102 (Section 3)
- Statement of financial position   FRS 102 (Section 4)
- Statement of comprehensive income and income statement   FRS 102 (Section 5)
- Statement of changes in equity and statement of income and retained earnings   FRS 102 (Section 6)
- Statement of cash flows   FRS 102 (Section 7)

4 Reporting financial performance

- Accounting policies, estimates and errors   FRS 102 (Section 10)
- Discontinued operations   FRS 102 (Section 5.7)
- Related party disclosures   FRS 102 (Section 33)
- Foreign currency translation   FRS 102 (Section 30)

5 Non-current assets

- Property, plant and equipment   FRS 102 (Section 17)
- Investment properties   FRS 102 (Section 16)
- Intangible assets other than goodwill   FRS 102 (Section 18)
- Borrowing costs   FRS 102 (Section 25)
- Impairment of non-current assets   FRS 102 (Section 27)

6 Revenue and inventories

7 Leases

8 Financial instruments

9 Provisions and contingencies

10 Group accounts

11 Associates and joint ventures

12 Other issues

Answer to Interactive question 1

Question	Answer
(a) Oak plc is being sued for a large amount of money by a supplier. Legal opinion is that there is a high probability that Oak plc will lose the case. The managing director says he feels confident that this will not happen, so decides to spend the money on a dividend to keep the shareholders happy.	The relevant concept here is **prudence**, which requires 'a degree of caution' in the exercise of judgements. The degree of caution is missing here and failure to make this provision will cause liabilities to be understated. This is then compounded by the payment of a dividend which Oak plc probably cannot afford. By ignoring the legal opinion, the managing director is also introducing bias into the financial statements, thus undermining **reliability**.
(b) Elm plc is being sued for compensation by an ex-employee. Legal advice is that the ex-employee does not have a good case and the possibility of having to pay compensation is remote. However, the managing director says he always prefers to err on the side of caution and the financial statements are showing a large profit so he inserts a provision for the full amount.	This example also concerns **prudence**. In this case prudence has been used to justify making an unwarranted provision in what looks like an attempt at profit-smoothing. Prudence does not permit *bias* and the bias that has been inserted into these financial statements means that their **reliability** is also in doubt.
(c) Sycamore plc has always valued inventories using the FIFO basis. A new financial controller has pointed out that the weighted average basis is more appropriate for their industry, so for this year inventories will be valued using the weighted average method.	This is a change of accounting policy. The change of valuation method will affect the **comparability** of the financial statements from one year to the next, so Sycamore plc must restate the prior year financial statements to show inventories under the weighted average method.

Answer to Interactive question 2

The cost of the facility will be calculated as follows:

	£'000
Cost of land	500
Site preparation	300
Materials used	1,000
Labour costs	3,000
Initial safety inspection	200
Professional fees	250
Construction overheads	300
Estimated discounted cost of dismantling after 10 years	350
	5,900

The apportioned general overheads will have been charged as expenses during 20X0.

The cost of the safety inspection will be capitalised and spread over the period to the next inspection.

The discount on the dismantling costs will be unwound over 10 years and charged to finance costs.

The total charge to profit or loss for the year to 31 December 20X1 will be:

	£'000
Depreciation ((5,900 – 500 – 200)/10)	520
Safety inspection (200/4)	50
Unwinding of discount on dismantling costs (350 × 8%)	28
	598

1   Information in financial statements is *reliable* when it is free from material error and bias and represents faithfully that which it purports to represent.

2   FRS 102 requires the results of discontinued operations to be presented in the income statement in a separate column both for the current year and for comparatives. The column includes all income and expense lines with separate presentation of any profit or loss on disposal.

3   Under FRS 102 entities can choose whether or not to capitalise development costs and whether or not to capitalise borrowing costs. Under IFRS eligible development costs and eligible borrowing costs must be capitalised.

4   FRS 102 defines goodwill as the excess of the cost of the business combination over the acquirer's interest in the net amount of the identifiable assets, liabilities and contingent liabilities of the acquiree. This is the same as the proportionate method under IFRS. FRS 102 does not allow the option of measuring non-controlling interest at fair value.

The cost of the business combination under FRS 102 includes professional costs which would be written off to profit or loss under IFRS.

Goodwill is carried at cost less accumulated amortisation and accumulated impairment losses. It is considered to have a finite useful life. If this cannot be reliably estimated, it should not exceed five years. Under IFRS goodwill is not amortised but subjected to annual impairment reviews.

Negative goodwill, after reassessment and remeasurement of the net assets and the cost of the combination, is shown in the statement of financial position as a deduction from positive goodwill. Under IFRS negative goodwill is recognised as a gain in profit or loss.

APPENDIX

Model financial statements

Topic List

This appendix illustrates the layout and presentation of an **individual company's financial statements** in line with IAS 1 (Revised).

It is not a full-scale disclosure checklist and comparative figures have been omitted.

1 Statement of profit or loss and other comprehensive income

SPECIMEN PLC

Statement of profit or loss for the year ended 31 March 20X6

Notes		£'000
2	Revenue	X
	Cost of sales	(X)
	Gross profit	X
	Other income	X
	Distribution costs	(X)
	Administrative expenses	(X)
3	Profit/(loss) from operations	X/(X)
4	Finance costs	(X)
5	Investment income	X
	Profit/(loss) before tax	X/(X)
	Income tax expense	(X)
	Profit/(loss) for the year from continuing operations	X/(X)
	Discontinued operations	
20	Profit/(loss) for the year from discontinued operations	(X)
	Profit/(loss) for the year	X/(X)

SPECIMEN PLC

Statement of profit or loss and other comprehensive income for the year ended 31 March 20X6

	£'000
Profit/(loss) for the year	X/(X)
Other comprehensive income:	
Gains on property revaluation	X
Income tax relating to components	X
of other comprehensive income	(X)
Other comprehensive income for the year net of tax	X
Total comprehensive income for the year	X

Note: Revaluation gains and losses are the only items of other comprehensive income included in the syllabus and it is unlikely that you will be given tax amounts relating to these, so any statement of profit or loss and other comprehensive income in the exam will be relatively straightforward.

2 Statement of financial position

SPECIMEN PLC

Statement of financial position as at 31 March 20X6

Notes		£'000	£'000
	ASSETS		
	Non-current assets		
6	Property, plant and equipment		X
7	Intangibles		X
	Investments		X
			X
	Current assets		
8	Inventories	X	
	Trade and other receivables	X	
	Investments	X	
	Cash and cash equivalents	X	
		X	
20	Non-current assets held for sale	X	
			X
	Total assets		X
	EQUITY AND LIABILITIES		
	Equity		
9	Ordinary share capital		X
9	Share premium account		X
6	Revaluation surplus		X
	Treasury shares		(X)
	Shares to be issued		X
	Other reserves		X
10	Retained earnings		X
	Total equity		X
	Non-current liabilities		
11	Preference share capital (redeemable)	X	
12	Finance lease liabilities	X	
13	Borrowings	X	
			X
	Current liabilities		
	Trade and other payables	X	
	Dividends payable	X	
	Taxation	X	
20	Liabilities held for sale	X	
14	Provisions	X	
13	Borrowings	X	
12	Finance lease liabilities	X	
			X
	Total equity and liabilities		X

Date authorised by the Executive Board for issue.

3 Statement of cash flows

SPECIMEN PLC

Statement of cash flows for the year ended 31 March 20X6

Notes		£'000	£'000
	Cash flows from operating activities		
21	Cash generated from operations	X	
	Interest paid	(X)	
	Income taxes paid	(X)	
	Net cash from operating activities		X
	Cash flows from investing activities		
	Purchase of property, plant and equipment	(X)	
	Proceeds from sale of property, plant and equipment	X	
	Interest received	X	
	Dividends received	X	
	Net cash used in investing activities		(X)
	Cash flows from financing activities		
	Proceeds from issue of share capital	X	
	Proceeds from issue of long-term borrowings	X	
	Dividends paid	(X)	
	Net cash used in financing activities		(X)
	Net increase in cash and cash equivalents		X
	Cash and cash equivalents at beginning of period		X
22	*Cash and cash equivalents at end of period*		X

4 Statement of changes in equity

SPECIMEN PLC

Statement of changes in equity for the year ended 31 March 20X6

	Ordinary share capital £'000	Share premium £'000	Revaluation surplus £'000	Retained earnings £'000	Total £'000
At 1 April 20X5	X	X	X	X	X
Changes in equity					
Issue of share capital	X	X	–	–	X
Dividends	–	–	–	(X)	(X)
Total comprehensive income for the year	–	–	X	X	X
Transfer to retained earnings	–	–	(X)	X	–
At 31 March 20X6	X	X	X	X	X

5 Notes to the financial statements

(1) **Accounting policies**

(a) **Accounting convention**

The financial statements are prepared in accordance with International Financial Reporting Standards and under the historical cost convention, modified to include the revaluation of freehold and long leasehold land and buildings.

(b) **Intangibles**

Goodwill is the difference between the fair value of the consideration transferred plus the value of any non-controlling interest and the aggregate of the fair values of the identifiable assets and liabilities. It is subject to annual impairment reviews.

Development expenditure is recognised as an intangible asset to the extent it is expected to generate future economic benefits. It is amortised over its useful life, typically five years.

(c) **Property, plant and equipment**

Non-current asset properties are valued at least every three years, and in intervening years if there is an indication of a material change in value.

Surpluses on valuations of freehold and long leasehold non-current asset properties are recognised directly in equity in the revaluation surplus, and any deficits below original cost are recognised in profit or loss.

Plant and equipment is carried at cost.

Any plant and equipment expected to be sold within 12 months of the decision to dispose of it is reclassified as assets held for sale, presented separately in the statement of financial position. It is carried at the lower of its carrying amount at the date of the decision to sell and fair value less costs to sell. Any write-down is shown as an impairment loss.

(d) **Depreciation**

Depreciation is recognised in respect of property, plant and equipment other than freehold land and assets classified as held for sale, at rates calculated to write off the cost or valuation, less estimated residual value, of each asset evenly over its expected useful life, as follows:

(i) Freehold buildings – over 50 years
(ii) Leasehold land and buildings – over the lease term
(iii) Plant and equipment – over 5 to 15 years

The depreciation methods and the useful lives and residual values on which depreciation is based are reviewed annually.

(e) **Leased assets**

Assets held under finance leases are included in property, plant and equipment at their fair value and depreciated over their useful lives. Lease payments consist of capital and interest elements and the interest is recognised in profit or loss. The annual rentals in respect of operating leases are recognised in profit or loss.

(f) **Borrowings**

Borrowings are recognised at the proceeds received. Preference shares which are redeemable on a specific date are classified as long-term liabilities, while the dividends relating to them are recognised in the finance cost in profit or loss.

(g) **Provisions**

Provisions are recognised when the company has a present obligation which will result in an outflow of resources. Restructuring provisions mainly comprise lease termination penalties and employee termination payments.

(h) **Revenue**

Sales are recognised on delivery of the goods to customers and on the performance of services for customers. They are shown net of VAT and discounts.

(i) **Research costs**

Research costs are recognised in profit or loss as incurred. Some development costs are capitalised (see (b) above).

(j) **Inventories**

The cost of inventories comprises all costs of purchase and conversion and other costs incurred in bringing them to their present location and condition. The FIFO cost formula is applied.

(2) **Revenue**

	£'000
Sale of goods	X
Performance of services	X
	X

(3) **Profit/loss from operations**

Profit/loss from operations is shown after charging/crediting:

	£'000
Research and development costs	X
Depreciation of property, plant and equipment	X
Profit/loss on disposal of property, plant and equipment	(X)
Impairment of assets held for sale	X
Impairment of goodwill	X
Amortisation of development costs	X
Operating lease payments	X
Employee benefits	X
Cost of inventories sold, included in cost of sales	X

(4) **Finance costs**

	£'000
Interest on borrowings	X
Dividends on redeemable preference shares	X
Interest on finance lease liabilities	X
	X

(5) **Investment income**

	£'000
Interest	X
Dividends	X
	X

(6) **Property, plant and equipment**

	Free-hold £'000	Long leasehold £'000	Short leasehold £'000	Under construction £'000	Plant and equipment £'000	Total £'000
Cost or valuation						
At 1 April 20X5	X	X	X	X	X	X
Revaluation surplus	X	–	–	–	–	X
Additions	X	X	X	X	X	X
Acquired in business combination	–	–	X	–	–	X
Transfers	X	–	–	(X)	–	–
Classified as held for sale	–	–	(X)	–	(X)	(X)
Disposals	(X)	(X)	(X)	–	(X)	(X)
At 31 March 20X6	X	X	X	X	X	X
Depreciation						
At 1 April 20X5	(X)	(X)	(X)	–	(X)	(X)
Classified as held for sale	–	–	X	–	X	X
Disposals	X	X	X	–	X	X
Charge for year	(X)	(X)	(X)	–	(X)	(X)
At 31 March 20X6	(X)	(X)	(X)	–	(X)	(X)
Carrying amount						
At 31 March 20X6	X	X	X	X	X	X
At 31 March 20X5	X	X	X	X	X	X

The carrying amounts at 31 March 20X6 on the historical cost basis were £X for freehold properties and £X for long leasehold properties.

Non-current asset properties were revalued as follows.

Freehold properties were revalued on 1 April 20X5 by Messrs Tottitup, an independent firm of Chartered Surveyors, at £X, on the basis of existing use value. Open market value is not considered to be materially different to existing use value.

Long leases were revalued in 20X4 at £X by Messrs Tottitup, Chartered Surveyors, on the basis of open market value. In the directors' opinion, there has been no indication of a material change in value during the year.

The carrying amount of plant and equipment of £X includes an amount of £Y in respect of assets held under finance leases.

(7) Intangibles

	Goodwill £'000	Development costs £'000	Total £'000
Cost			
At 1 April 20X5	X	X	X
Additions during year	X	X	X
At 31 March 20X6	X	X	X
Amortisation/impairment			
At 1 April 20X5	X	X	X
Charge for the year	X	X	X
At 31 March 20X6	X	X	X
Carrying amount			
At 31 March 20X6	X	X	X
At 31 March 20X5	X	X	X

(8) Inventories

	£'000
Raw materials and consumables	X
Work in progress	X
Finished goods and goods for resale	X
	X

(9) Ordinary share capital

	Authorised		Issued and fully paid	
Ordinary shares of 50p each	Number	£'000	Number	£'000
At 1 April 20X5	X	X	X	X
Issued during the year	X	X	X	X
At 31 March 20X6	X	X	X	X

On 30 December 20X5 X ordinary shares were issued fully paid for cash at a premium of Xp per share.

As described in note 19, X ordinary shares were issued at a premium of Xp per share in the acquisition of the trade and assets of A Ltd.

(10) Retained earnings

The restatement of the balance brought forward is to correct an error arising out of the overvaluation of inventories at 31 March 20X4. The effect on the profit for the year ended 31 March 20X5 was £X. Comparative information has been adjusted accordingly.

(11) Preference share capital

The 10% preference shares of £1 carry no voting rights and are redeemable at par on 31 March 20Z5. Dividends are paid half-yearly and on a winding up these shares rank ahead of the ordinary shares.

(12) Finance lease liabilities

The minimum lease payments on finance leases are as follows:

	Minimum lease payments £'000	Present value £'000
Within one year	X	X
Two to five years	X	X
More than five years	$\underline{X}$	$\underline{X}$
	X	X
Future finance charges	(X)	–
Present value	$\underline{\underline{X}}$	$\underline{\underline{X}}$
Being:		
Current liabilities	X	
Non-current liabilities	$\underline{X}$	
	$\underline{\underline{X}}$	

(13) Borrowings

Borrowings comprise:

	£'000
Bank loans and overdrafts	X
Debentures	$\underline{X}$
	$\underline{\underline{X}}$
Being:	
Current liabilities	X
Non-current liabilities	$\underline{X}$
	$\underline{\underline{X}}$

The debentures have a coupon of 11% and are redeemable at par on 31 March 20Z5.

The bank loans are secured by a fixed charge on the freehold property and are repayable on 31 March 20Y5. The interest rate is variable, currently 6%.

(14) Provisions

	Warranty provision £'000	Returns provision £'000	Total £'000
At 1 April 20X5	X	X	X
Additions	X	X	X
Amounts used during year	(X)	(X)	(X)
At 31 March 20X6	$\underline{\underline{X}}$	$\underline{\underline{X}}$	$\underline{\underline{X}}$

The warranty provision relates to estimated claims on those products sold in the year ended 31 March 20X6 which come with a one year warranty. A weighted average method is used to provide a best estimate. It is expected that the expenditure will be incurred in the next year.

The returns provision relates to an open returns policy offered on all goods. Customers are given 28 days in which to return goods and obtain a full refund. The provision at the year end is based on a percentage, using past experience, of the number of sales made in March 20X6.

(15) Dividends

The dividends recognised in the statement of changes in equity comprise:

	Per share	£'000
Final dividend for 20X5	Xp	X
Interim dividend for 20X6	$\underline{Xp}$	$\underline{X}$
	$\underline{\underline{Xp}}$	$\underline{\underline{X}}$

A resolution proposing a final dividend for 20X6 of Xp per share, £X in total, will be put to the Annual General Meeting.

(16) Events after the reporting period

Following a decision of the board, a freehold property was classified as held for sale on 1 May 20X6. The sale was completed on 15 June 20X6, realising a gain of £X after tax of £X. The transaction will be reflected in the company's financial statements to 31 March 20X7.

(17) Contingent liabilities

The company is being sued in the USA for damages of $X million (approximately £X million) in respect of sale of faulty goods. The directors do not expect to lose the case and do not believe any provision needs to be made.

(18) Commitments

Capital commitments

Capital expenditure on property, plant and equipment contracted for at the end of the reporting period but not recognised in these financial statements amounted to £X.

Operating lease commitments

At the year end the company had commitments to make payments under non-cancellable operating leases, which fall due as follows:

	£'000
Within one year	X
Two to five years	X
More than five years	X
	X

(19) Goodwill arising during the year

X 50p ordinary shares were issued on 30 December 20X5 to acquire the assets and trade of A Ltd. Details of the consideration and assets acquired were as follows:

	£'000
Fair value of assets acquired:	
Short leasehold property	X
Inventories	X
	X
Goodwill	X
Fair value of consideration transferred	X

The statement of profit or loss includes revenue of £X and profit of £X in relation to this trade since the date of acquisition. If the acquisition had been made on 1 April 20X5, profit or loss would have included revenue of £X and profit of £X.

(20) Discontinued operations

Division A is being closed down and was classified as held for sale on 1 February 20X6. Completion of the closure and accompanying sale is expected by the end of September 20X6. The carrying amount of assets held for sale was £X on 31 March 20X6. The results of Division A for the year ended 31 March 20X6 were: revenue £X, expenses £X, pre-tax loss £X, tax in respect of the pre-tax loss £X, loss on the remeasurement of assets at fair value less costs to sell £X and tax in respect of that remeasurement loss £X.

(21) Reconciliation of profit/loss before tax to cash generated from operations for the year

	£'000
Profit/(loss) before tax	X/(X)
Finance cost	X
Investment income	(X)
Depreciation charge	X
Amortisation charge	X
Loss/(profit) on disposal of non-current assets	X/(X)
(Increase)/decrease in inventories	(X)/X
(Increase)/decrease in trade and other receivables	(X)/X
(Increase)/decrease in prepayments	(X)/X
Increase/(decrease) in trade and other payables	(X)/X
Increase/(decrease) in accruals	(X)/X
Increase/(decrease) in provisions	(X)/X
Cash generated from operations	X

(22) Cash and cash equivalents

Cash and cash equivalents consist of cash on hand and balances with banks, and investments in money market instruments. Cash and cash equivalents included in the statement of cash flows comprise the following amounts.

	£'000
Cash on hand and balances with banks	X
Short-term investments	X
Cash and cash equivalents	X

The company has undrawn borrowing facilities of £Xm of which only £Xm may be used for future expansion.

(23) Property, plant and equipment

During the period the company acquired property, plant and equipment with an aggregate cost of £X of which £X was acquired by finance lease. Cash payments of £X were made to purchase property, plant and equipment.

(24) Details of Specimen plc

The company is incorporated in England. In the opinion of the directors, the immediate and ultimate controlling party of the company is its parent company, XYZ Ltd, a company incorporated in the Isle of Man. No transactions took place between the company and XYZ Ltd during the year and there are no outstanding balances.

Index

Notes

Notes

REVIEW FORM – FINANCIAL ACCOUNTING AND REPORTING STUDY MANUAL

Your ratings, comments and suggestions would be appreciated on the following areas of this Study Manual.

	Very useful	Useful	Not useful
Chapter introductions	☐	☐	☐
Examination context	☐	☐	☐
Worked examples	☐	☐	☐
Interactive questions	☐	☐	☐
Quality of explanations	☐	☐	☐
Technical references (where relevant)	☐	☐	☐
Self-test questions	☐	☐	☐
Self-test answers	☐	☐	☐
Index	☐	☐	☐

	Excellent	Good	Adequate	Poor
Overall opinion of this Study Manual	☐	☐	☐	☐

Please add further comments below:

Please return completed form to:

The Learning Team
Learning and Professional Department
ICAEW
Metropolitan House
321 Avebury Boulevard
Milton Keynes
MK9 2FZ
E learning@icaew.com